W9-BSX-946

JAMES WOODRESS

Willa Cather

A Literary Life

University of Nebraska Press: Lincoln and London

Copyright 1987 by the University of Nebraska Press

Manufactured in the United States of America

First Bison Book printing: 1989
Most recent printing indicated by the first digit below:

2   3   4   5   6   7   8   9   10

Library of Congress Cataloging-in-Publication Data
Woodress, James Leslie.
Willa Cather : a literary life.
Bibliography: p.
Includes index.
1. Cather, Willa, 1873-1947   2. Novelists,
American – 20th century – Biography.   I. Title
PS3505.A87Z939   1987   813'.52 [B]   86-30894
ISBN 0-8032-4734-6
ISBN 0-8032-9708-4 (pbk.)

♾

This book is dedicated to the community of

Cather scholars, past and present.

CONTENTS

ILLUSTRATIONS

Edith Lewis

Cather's 1920 passport photo

Cather at Grand Manan in the thirties

Following page 498

Cather at Grand Manan, also in the thirties

Cather by photographer Edward Steichen in the twenties

Cather by photographer Nicholas Muray

Cather's portrait by Leon Bakst, Paris, 1923

Cather's portrait by Nikolai Fechin

Honorary degree recipients at Princeton, June, 1931

570 Park Avenue

Cather at Grant Manan in 1931

Cather on her sixty-third birthday

Cather and Yehudi Menuhin

Alfred Knopf, 1947

Cather's grave at Jaffrey, New Hampshire

Mount Monadnock, viewed from the cemetery

PREFACE

Although forty years have passed since the death of Willa Cather in 1947, she never has been the subject of a full-length biography. When she died, her reputation was firmly established as one of the most significant American novelists, and during the succeeding decades her stature has continued to grow. At the time of her death J. Donald Adams wrote in the *New York Times* that "no American novelist was more purely an artist," and George Whicher declared four years later that "no American writer . . . can be more certain than she to capture ultimately the admiration of posterity." The absence of a detailed biography is probably due to the traps, pitfalls, and barricades she placed in the biographer's path, and until now sufficient material has not been available to flesh out more than a medium-length life. While no biography ever can be definitive, this study contains a great deal more material than any previous one and goes considerably beyond my own earlier biography, as well as the efforts of others, in presenting a life-size portrait of this remarkable woman.

When E. K. Brown's biography of Cather appeared in 1953, Alfred Knopf wrote on the jacket: "Here is all the biographical information anyone is likely ever to gather about Willa Cather." Even though he was understandably interested in promoting the sale of Brown's book, he no doubt also thought Cather had been such a private person that biographical data actually was meager. He was wrong, of course, and since Cather died there has been a steady accumulation of material to fuel the ever-growing interest in her life and work. Hundreds of pages of Cather's journalistic writings have been dug from the dusty magazine and newspaper files where they first appeared and republished. All of her stories have been collected, including many she gladly would have expunged from the record if she could have. She left a trail of published interviews and speeches and public statements that surprises anyone who knows only her own pronouncements desiring privacy. Perhaps fifteen hundred of her letters by now have found their way into institutional collections from Maine to California, even though she and Edith Lewis destroyed as many of her letters as they could lay their hands on. Fortunately, correspondents who outlived her had the good sense to realize that Cather belongs to the world and her letters ought to be preserved. It is still impossible to publish or quote from her letters (her will forbids it), but they are available for consultation, and the information they contain is public property.

Knopf tried his best to preserve Cather's privacy, but it was difficult. He said himself at the time of the centennial celebration of her birth in 1973 that "anyone who abhors contact with members of the public is best advised not to produce work which has public interest." Cather resented the fact that she could not sit on a bench in Central Park without being recognized and accosted by strangers, but all her efforts to keep out of the limelight and control access to her life have been unsuccessful in keeping biographers off her trail. She certainly made the task of writing her life more difficult; yet she and other writers who have wanted to cover their tracks always have been doomed to failure. Still, one envies the chroniclers of those public figures who carefully saved for posterity the documentation of their lives.

The problems that the biographer of Cather has to face, however, are more complicated than merely locating the raw materials for the life. She threw up roadblocks, consciously and unconsciously, to frustrate pursuit. During her own lifetime she managed her image rather successfully by writing biographical sketches of herself and telling interviewers what she wanted printed about her. She changed her birth date; she altered details of her life; she exaggerated many events; she revised her opinions. She made no effort to be accurate in recalling facts, and it is hard sometimes to tell where the reality leaves off and the fiction begins. The biographer continually has to separate the fact from the fantasy, and he never can be sure he has succeeded completely. To make matters still more difficult, Lewis's memoir of her friend also tries to manage the image, and one has to use her data with caution.

If he can successfully negotiate the minefields, the biographer of Cather has a great deal of autobiographical fiction to help in his task. She turned her own life and experiences into literature to a degree uncommon among writers. I have used many passages from her fiction to document her life, keeping in mind constantly the need for caution. There are, fortunately,

enough letters and contemporary documents, such as interviews and reminiscences of friends, to corroborate many events in her life that have passed
through the crucible of her imagination to emerge in her stories and novels.
My notes make it clear when I am working from letters and when I am
drawing on her fiction.

Sir Isaac Newton in a letter to his rival scientist Robert Hooke wrote in
1676 that "if I have seen further, it is by standing on the shoulders of giants." I
feel somewhat the same in writing Cather's biography four decades after her
death. I have built on the work of many scholars, as my notes will indicate,
and without their pioneering this book could not have been written. Mildred
Bennett, the first of the Cather scholars, wrote an invaluable study of places
and people important in Cather's work in *The World of Willa Cather* (1951).
She was on the scene in Red Cloud and able to interview old friends and
relatives. Lewis's memoir, which was prepared for the use of E. K. Brown, is,
of course, of immense assistance, as it was the work of a friend of more than
forty years. Brown's biography is the pioneering life, and when he died
before completing his book, the very able Leon Edel finished it for him.
Bernice Slote at the University of Nebraska was indefatigable in recovering
and organizing Cather's fugitive essays, editing her poems and stories, and
writing about her. Virginia Faulkner and the University of Nebraska Press
carried out a large publishing venture in making Cather's early work available, and William Curtin, editor of *The World and the Parish*, two volumes of
Cather's journalistic writings, is the benefactor of all Cather scholars. Elizabeth Sergeant's memoir of her long friendship with Cather is another
important contribution to Cather studies, as are the reminiscences of Ferris
Greenslet, Alfred Knopf, and many others who knew her.

I came to my interest in Cather in 1967 or 1968 when I was invited to
contribute a brief critical biography to a series brought out by the now-
defunct publisher Pegasus. My book, *Willa Cather: Her Life and Art*, appeared
in 1970 and was based on much primary material that had not been available
to Brown. I was able to correct errors and add details, but my record was far
from complete, and it also contained its own errors. I never planned to write
another biography of Cather, but after the death in 1983 of Bernice Slote,
who had spent nearly a lifetime gathering material for the definitive biography, I decided to return to the project, and I have been able to use her papers.

My present view of Cather does not change in any basic way the image of
her contained in my earlier book. I have found no skeletons in the closet or
sensational data to titillate the reader. There are, however, hundreds of new
details, much fuller accounts of events in her life, new and expanded critical
examinations of her works, and details of her reception. I have tried hard to

get all the facts right. I have changed many of my opinions about her life and work over the past twenty years, and these are reflected in the portrait that emerges. I also have dealt with the issues of lesbianism and sexual orientation, which interest many contemporary readers, and taken into account recent feminist criticism. I have gone into her personality, beliefs, prejudices, aspirations, loves, and hates in considerable detail. In the past two decades a large and impressive body of criticism has grown up about Cather's fiction, and any biography that ignores this work cannot lay claim to much significance.

The person who moves through these pages is an extraordinarily gifted woman. From her Virginia childhood and Nebraska adolescence she made her way through the world with energy and dedication. She went from college journalism to professional journalism, then to magazine writing and editing, pushing steadily towards her artistic objective. Her progress was slow, however, and she did not publish her first novel until she was thirty-eight. The official face she presented to the public in her collected works was only the one-tenth of the iceberg that appears above the surface, for when she reached the top of her profession, she wanted the apprentice work forgotten. It is the task of the biographer, however, to search among the shards to discover the abandoned designs and the crudities later perfected. The themes and subjects that she treated so luminously in her mature work all appeared in her earliest efforts. She was a Romantic and a primitive from the start, but it was not until she was in her forties that she was able to utilize effectively her own experiences to weave the myths of the American past into the magical fabric of her best fiction. There was much trial and error in her apprenticeship, but the outlines were all present by the time she was twenty.

Although Cather wrote an old friend in 1945 that she never had been very ambitious, the truth was just the opposite. Her career down to the publication of *O Pioneers!*, her first important novel, reveals a very eager young woman from the provinces determined to make good. She did what she had to do to make a living and was not above writing potboilers and doing hackwork. Yet she had all the while a single-minded dedication to the pursuit of art. During the years of struggle, moreover, her attachment to family, old friends, and home remained strong, and after settling permanently in the East, she returned to Lincoln and Red Cloud frequently to renew her sources. Her feeling for Nebraska, however, was ambivalent until she had been away for about fifteen years; then the post-pioneer period of her childhood became the epic material of her romances and led her still deeper into the past. She went through a period in the twenties when she felt alienated from American life but produced her greatest novels in that era. In the thirties she lived a very private life and continued to write well but with diminishing vitality.

Her old age is not sad, like the blackness of Mark Twain's final pessimism, though her health began to break down in her last years. She hated many things about the world that rotated outside her self-imposed isolation in the forties, but she did not become embittered at the end. She had achieved most of the things she wanted from life and knew that her career had been a success. She did not have to write, as Howells did to James, that she had become a dead cult with her statues cut down and grass growing over them in the moonlight. Her literary reputation was secure, and that was what really mattered.

The critics usually have treated Cather very well, though she often thought otherwise. From H. L. Mencken's delighted discovery of her first novels to the latest international bibliography published by the Modern Language Association, she has been regarded as an important writer. And people have continued reading her work, despite her strenuous efforts to keep her books from being dramatized, anthologized, and reprinted in inexpensive editions. A writer of lesser stature might well have consigned herself to oblivion by such tactics. I know of no other American writer of this century who is more likely to go on being read than Cather. The statement she made in her preface to the stories of Sarah Orne Jewett in 1925 is prophetic: "If I were asked to name three American books which have the possibility of a long, long life, I would say at once: *The Scarlet Letter*, *Huckleberry Finn*, and *The Country of the Pointed Firs*. I can think of no others that confront time and change so serenely." And the last of the three, she added, fairly shines with "the reflection of its long, joyous future." Of the best of Willa Cather, one could say the same.

ACKNOWLEDGMENTS

During the writing of this book I have received help from a great many individuals, to whom I wish to express my gratitude: to Margaret Anne O'Connor, who read and edited my manuscript, loaned me her collection of Cather reviews, and performed many acts of friendship; to Susan Rosowski, who also gave my manuscript a meticulous reading, the benefit of her impressive knowledge of Cather, and encouragement throughout the writing; to Mildred Bennett, who answered many queries; to Helen Cather Southwick, who loaned me letters, pictures, answered questions, and arranged for me to visit Cather's summer cottage on Grand Manan Island; to Reg Flagg and Kathleen Buckley, who talked to me and showed me about Grand Manan; to Charles Cather, who allowed me to have copies of certain letters; to Elaine Walker Hall, director of the Frederick County Historical Society at Winchester, Virginia, who secured information for me regarding Cather genealogy; to Doris Grumbach, who answered questions; to Patricia Lee Yongue, who let me see correspondence from Cather to Stephen Tennant; to Leon Edel, who answered queries; to David Stouck, who supplied some research materials, to Brent Bohlke, who let me use the manuscript copy of his collection of Cather interviews and speeches; to Mary Weddle, who loaned me letters written by Cather to Aunt Franc; to Harry Finestone, who gave me materials he had used for his dissertation; to John Broderick of the Library of Congress, who searched the Manuscript Division for Cather letters; to Cathy Henderson, Research Librarian at the Harry Ransom Humanities Research Center, University of Texas, and Patience-Anne W. Lenk, Colby College Library, both of whom were helpful in my obtaining copies of letters.

I am also grateful to librarians and libraries at the following institutions which I visited in the course of collecting material for this book: Elizabeth Anne Falsey and the Houghton Library of Harvard University, Virginia Renner and the Huntington Library, Saundra Taylor and the Lilly Library at Indiana University, Barbara A. Paulson and the Morgan Library, Andrea I. Paul and the Nebraska State Historical Society Library, Joseph Svoboda and Elsie V. Thomas and the University of Nebraska Archives, Carolyn A. Sheehy and the Newberry Library, John A. Stinson and the New York Public Library, Connell Gallagher and the University of Vermont Library, Gregory Johnson and the Barrett Collection at the University of Virginia Library, Ann Billesbach and the Willa Cather Historical Center at Red Cloud, David E. Schoonover and the Beinecke Rare Book and Manuscript Library at Yale University.

Other libraries I want to thank for supplying me with photocopies of Cather letters: Allegheny College, Amherst College, the University of Arkansas, the American Antiquarian Society, the Boston Public Library, Brown University, Bryn Mawr College, the Buffalo and Erie County Public Library, the Chicago Historical Society Library, Colby College, Columbia University, Dartmouth College, Enoch Pratt Free Library (Baltimore), Georgetown University, the University of Kentucky, Holy Cross College, Loyola University (New Orleans), Middlebury College, the Newark Public Library, the State University of New York (Binghamton), the University of Notre Dame, the University of Pennsylvania, Pennsylvania State University, Phillips Exeter Academy, Princeton University, the University of Southern California, Stanford University, Sweet Briar College, the University of Texas, the Virginia Baptist Historical Society (Richmond), Wellesley College, the Western Reserve Historical Society (Cleveland), and the Wisconsin State Historical Society (Madison).

In addition, I wish to thank Alfred A. Knopf, Inc., and Houghton Mifflin for permission to quote from the Cather titles on which they hold copyright; William A. Koshland for supplying me with photos of Alfred Knopf and for permission to quote from Blanche Knopf's letters to Cather; the Lilly Library for permission to quote from S. S. McClure's letters to Cather; the Houghton Library of Harvard University for permission to quote from the letters of Ferris Greenslet to Cather.

My final debts are to the Research Committee of the University of California at Davis for grants that speeded and facilitated the preparation of this book; to Delfina Redfield for many kindnesses; to Diana Dulaney, who put the entire opus into the word processor, promptly, efficiently, enthusiastically; to Roberta Woodress, who has been a scholar's ideal companion for nearly half a century.

JAMES WOODRESS

WILLA CATHER

Pittsburgh passengers waiting to board a train for Chicago at the Union Station one day in early April 1912 might have noticed among their ranks a handsome woman, perhaps even beautiful, whose bearing and composure suggested a person of some importance. Though she was no longer young, she had a sturdy build and a clear complexion. Her skin was off-white, perhaps creamy, "rather like the outside of any well-washed plate." Her rosy cheeks indicated boisterous good health. Weighing 125 pounds and standing five feet six, she had eyes of a distinct blue, and when she looked at one, her glance was open and direct. Her hair, what one could see under a large hat, was straight and dark brown, combed back simply and parted slightly off-center. Her lashes were dark, her eyebrows strongly marked. Her other features were regular and pleasant to look at, her mouth was generous and good-humored, and her hands were broad and strong. She looked like a person used to getting things done, someone accustomed to giving orders; maybe she was, a rarity in those days, a successful business woman. The more observant passengers would have detected an air of keen anticipation in her manner as she stood with her luggage watching the train pull into the station.

This was Willa Cather, thirty-eight years old, recently managing editor of the spectacularly successful *McClure's Magazine*, on leave from her job, en route to Arizona to visit her brother, and at a critical juncture in her career. For nearly six years she had been editing, dealing with contributors, reading other people's manuscripts, curbing the half-baked impulses of her boss, Sam McClure. She had become one of the most important women editors in magazine journalism, but those six years had kept her marking time in her own literary career. A few months before, she finally had broken away from the grind of putting out a monthly magazine, taken a leave of absence, and gone to upstate New York for rest, recuperation, and writing. Now she was ready to strike out in a new direction, and as it turned out, she was never again to return to the office routine at *McClure's*. Although she had managed to write her first novel while she still worked for McClure, it was a novel she later wanted to disown. Although she also had published a few stories during those years, none did she ever think worth reprinting. The trip to the Southwest that began on a spring day in 1912 was to leave an indelible impression on her and to mark the turning point in her career. The successful magazine executive who left Pittsburgh that April morning returned the novelist that we know. The Pennsylvania, Burlington, and Santa Fe railroads, which carried her from Pennsylvania to Arizona, transported her from one life to another.

After changing trains in Chicago, she boarded the Burlington and headed west. As she crossed the Mississippi, she again experienced the tightness in her chest and a bit of the fright she had felt as a child when she was taken to Nebraska at the age of nine. The West always paralyzed her a little, she wrote, but when she was away from it, she remembered only the tang on the tongue. Though she had lived in the East a long time by 1912, she still had trouble letting herself go with the current when she reached the wide, rolling prairies of Nebraska. She felt like a person who could not swim when dropped into the water. There were just so many, many miles of the West. When she was a child growing up in Nebraska, she had been sure that she would never get away and that she would die in a cornfield. Now that she had escaped, she no longer had that fear, though she still got attacks of fright. But after a few days in Red Cloud visiting her parents and old friends, she was ready to push on farther west, and she boarded another Burlington train, this time for Denver.

Colorado and the Rocky Mountains were familiar territory for her, as her oldest brother, Roscoe, lived in Wyoming and she had visited him on a number of occasions. Once she left Colorado, however, she was seeing new and exciting country. From Trinidad to Albuquerque the land was utterly splendid, she wrote. The Valley of the Rhone was nothing to it. All the way from Trinidad, Colorado, to Las Vegas, New Mexico, she wrote her good friend Elsie Sergeant, there was a continuous purple mountain that tuned one up. Albuquerque delighted her, though she stayed only a few days before continuing on to Arizona. There was a strong pull about the place, something Spanish in the air that teased one. She had known Mexicans during her Red Cloud adolescence, but Albuquerque far exceeded her expectations. Such color! The Lord had set the stage splendidly there. It was the most beautiful country she had seen anywhere, even more brilliant than the French Riviera. She caught sight of some of the most wonderful Indian villages, each one built close about its church, and there were abandoned villages, too, she marveled, that had been Spanish missions during the time of Queen Elizabeth. She wanted to return later with her brother Douglass for a longer visit.

On April 19 she arrived in Winslow, a little desert town on the Santa Fe where Douglass, who worked for the railroad, made his headquarters. He immediately began showing her about the pueblo towns and taking her to see ancient cliff dwellings nearby. They planned to visit an Indian snake dance and projected a trip to Old Mexico. How splendid this part of the world is, she wrote McClure. But then there was a letdown.

Douglass had to go off with his construction crew for three days, leaving Willa alone in his little eggshell of a house with his roommate, a brakeman named Tooker. Staying alone with Tooker, she wrote, was quite in accord with the proprieties of Winslow, but even Tooker had been off on his run for the past two nights, and then she had no protector except the drunken London cockney whom Douglass had picked up to do his cooking and housekeeping. He was no protection at all. She did not mind being left alone, however, because Tooker was a great bore. He read Emerson *all the time*, looked just like a character in William Vaughn Moody's *The Great Divide*, and dressed the part. Life, she thought, was nothing but a poor imitation of art. Tooker was simply encrusted with information gleaned from millions of magazines, and though he was one of nature's noblemen with a square jaw and bold carriage, she did not know how long she could stand either his nobleness or his information. She was doing target practice with a pistol and might let drive at Tooker, she wrote. He never permitted himself an action in one syllable. He "arrived" and he "removed" his hat, and he "reflected" that when the wind blew it "retarded" his train. The cockney Englishman was great fun, but he was reeling drunk all the time and had to be sat upon and sent away. He once had worked in a stable in Paris and spoke a queer kind of fluent French, and when he was the drunkest, he always wept and began reciting the same sentimental verses.

When Cather looked about outside, she found that Winslow was an ugly little western town. It had been founded some thirty years before as a division point on the Santa Fe, and there was no one there but railroad people. The only excitement occurred when the trains stopped and passengers got off to eat at the Fred Harvey hotel, La Posada. Although the desert was very fine, one had to cross two miles of tin cans and old shoes to get to it. There were bright red sunsets, like brick dust, but the sandstorms were a terror and often stopped the trains. If she had arrived two months earlier, there would have been plenty of excitement, for on Valentine's Day 1912, President Taft in Washington had signed the proclamation admitting Arizona to the Union as the forty-eighth state. For the first time in history movie cameras had photographed a president signing a law, and when the news had been telegraphed to Arizona, there was wild celebrating everywhere. Whistles shrieked at mines, church bells rang, schools and businesses closed, and parades surged through the streets. Even William Jennings Bryan came west to make a two hour speech in the state capital at Phoenix.

Life was very quiet for the first two weeks. Then things began to happen so fast that she had no time to write letters. She did manage a postcard to Sergeant on May 12, reporting that she had caught step at last and was very happy. She had been on a trip with the local priest, Father Connolly, a friend of Douglass's, who had taken her to visit some of the missions. They had talked about the country and the people, and he had filled her full of Spanish and Indian legends. He was the first of many Catholic missionary priests she came to know in the Southwest, and like a sponge she soaked up the land, the people, and the culture for future use. Her letters from this trip west reveal an intoxicating sense of discovery. The Southwest became one of the passions of her life.

Even more exciting was the appearance one day of four Mexicans who came to serenade her: two section hands, a bartender who played divinely, and a boy of unearthly beauty who sang. The last reminded her of a statue she had seen in Naples of Antinous, who was loved and deified after his death by Emperor Hadrian. This boy was simply Antinous come to life. The Mexican trio returned night after night, and Cather was captivated by the singer, whose name turned out to be Julio (pronounced *Hulio*, she explained to Sergeant). Her letters for the next several months were filled with Julio. He was too beautiful to be true and utterly different from anyone she ever had met. He was from Vera Cruz, knew a great many Mexican and Spanish songs, and he was won-der-ful, she wrote Sergeant, as she enclosed the translation she had made of one of his songs. After singing to her nightly, Julio took her off to visit the Painted Desert, and it took her days to get over that expedition. Julio was without beginning and without end. He had a personal elegance, the like of which she had never known, and a grace of expression that simply caught one up. He wasn't soft and sunny like an Italian; he was indifferent and opaque. He had the long, strong upper lip seen in Aztec sculpture, somber eyes filled with lots of old trouble, and the pale yellow skin of very old gold and old races. Talking to him was like learning a new language because he spoke so directly. He would drive any number of miles to see flowers or running water, but she could not get him the least bit interested in the ancient cliff dwellers. Why, he said, raising his brows, was she interested in *los muertos?* We are living. It was fitting to say masses for the dead, but that was the end of it. Further attention was a waste of time. But he did tell her one memorable story of ancient times, the tale of an Aztec Cleopatra, "The Forty Lovers of the Queen." Cather wrote Sergeant that she must come to the Southwest, and if she did, she was sure to pick up a Mexican sweetheart, who would take as much time and strength as she would give him. Afterwards Sergeant remembered that when someone asked how Mabel Dodge could have married Tony Luhan, an Indian, Cather replied, "How could she help it?"

Cather never found occasion in her later career to put Julio into a novel, unless there is a bit of him in Spanish Johnny in *The Song of the Lark*, but she remembered the story of the Aztec Cleopatra. At the time she heard it, she said she was going to write it up when she visited the place where it happened, but she never got to Old Mexico. She also thought she remembered reading the tale in Prescott's *Conquest of Mexico*, but Julio's account was much more alive. He never had read anything but prayer books and had no stale ideas, in fact not many ideas at all. The story, a brutal tale of forty secret lovers, each killed after the queen tired of them, appears in Cather's 1920 story "Coming, Aphrodite!" and is told by Don Hedger to Eden Bower the night he becomes her lover.

Also in May Julio took Cather to a Mexican dance, where she was the only Anglo-Saxon present. This dance may well have been the source for the Mexican dance scene in *The Song of the Lark*, for it made a strong impression. Such dancing! she wrote. There was in particular a curious pantomime waltz in which a man danced with two women, the prettiest dance she ever had seen. Cather's feeling in the novel for the natural grace of the Mexicans, their love of music are very much of a piece with her letters from this trip to the Southwest: "The Mexican dance was soft and quiet. There was no calling, the conversation was very low, the rhythm of the music was smooth and engaging, the men were graceful and courteous." There were no constraints of any kind but a kind of natural harmony about their movements.

But Cather had other things to do with her life than idle away the days with a beautiful Mexican boy, no matter how captivating he was. She finally severed what she called Julio's strong Egyptian fetters, went to Albuquerque, and then back to Nebraska. He was wonderful but could not take the place of a whole civilization. However, after returning to Red Cloud she wrote that she might still go back for Julio. He would look lovely in Boston at Mrs. Fields's house, but then Mrs. Isabella Gardner would sweep him up and take him to Fenway Court, which he would like better than her apartment. Earlier she had thought that she must get him to New York, where he could make an easy living as an artist's model. Artists would fight for him. In August, after returning to Pittsburgh, she was still talking about Julio, but after that he disappears from her letters completely.

In between outings with Julio, Cather had plenty to occupy her time. On Douglass's next three days off they went out with Tooker on daily excursions to nearby canyons: Clear Creek, Chevelon, and Jack's, all gorges carved by tributaries of the Little Colorado River. Those were lovely days with all the advantages of a camping trip and none of the disadvantages. They started off each morning with a wagon and light camping gear, canteens, coffee, bacon, fruit, cream, and so forth; and each night they returned to town, where they had hot baths and beds to sleep in. Cather had canvas shoes with red rubber soles that she had bought in Boston, and with them, she said, she could walk up a forty-five-degree rock surface. One day they went down a cliff for 150 feet, using handholds to descend. The experience was exhilarating. Tooker, a great bore in town, turned out to be a splendid companion on the trail. All his miserable information fell away, Cather wrote Sergeant, like a boy dropping his clothes to go swimming. The real Tooker, who had worked in the sheep camps and the mines, was strong, active, and resourceful. He was full of interesting stories, she found, once one got through the sediment deposited by the magazine articles. Tooker later turns up very sympathetically portrayed as Ray Kennedy, the brakeman, in *The Song of the Lark*.

These expeditions were a prelude to the Grand Canyon, where Cather went on May 16. She was properly impressed with this "wonder," and agreed it was indeed wonderful, but she thought that not even this marvel, which had only a geologic history, could be interesting for more than a limited time. But besides the great spectacle of the canyon, there was wonderful walking and riding, and one day she accompanied some English visitors down to the Halfway House in the canyon. It was an awful pull, she wrote, but she was always a good walker, and her climbs around Winslow had been good conditioning. She was pleased to find that the canyon was still completely unspoiled, not one shop. A visitor couldn't even buy an orange, and there was not one civilized amusement. It was still seven years before the Grand Canyon would become a national park. There were two hotels, however, one magnificent and one excellent, set down in the immense pine forest, and there were modest lodgings at Bright Angel Camp. She stayed at the last, which was comfortable, simple, and only cost her three dollars a day. It was the only reasonable place she could find. Everything was very expensive, and all the places one wanted to see were off the railroad. To get to them it was necessary to hire a horse for two-fifty a day or a team and open wagon for five dollars. The scenery was worth it, however, and she urged Sergeant to come and see for herself.

As soon as she left the Grand Canyon, she retraced her steps to Flagstaff, where she met her brother. They were going to explore more cliff dwellings. Walnut Canyon, now a national monument, was only a few miles outside of Flagstaff, and there she could see a spectacular collection of some three hundred cliff dwellings about one thousand years old. These houses, which were built into the limestone walls of the canyon, had been abandoned probably because of a prolonged drought in the twelfth century. But they had remained largely intact, preserved by the dry desert air, as though in a time capsule, a silent, ghostly city. They are a smaller version of the cliff dwellings now protected within the boundaries of Mesa Verde National Park, which Cather visited three years later.

As she and Douglass drove by wagon out of Flagstaff, they could see the blue slopes and snowy summit of San Francisco Mountain to the north. They then entered the first great forest she had ever seen, magnificent stands of huge ponderosa pines spaced well apart. The wagon road dipped lower, falling away from the high plateau on which Flagstaff sat, and soon the forest closed behind them and the mountain disappeared. Then they left the forest, the sparse growth of piñon pine and scrub began, and the country broke into open, stony clearings. Finally they came to Walnut Canyon, called Panther Canyon in *The Song of the Lark*. It was "like a thousand others—one of those abrupt fissures with which the earth in the Southwest is riddled; so abrupt that you might walk over the edge of any one of them on a dark night and never know what had happened to you." The canyon walls for the first two hundred feet below the surface were perpendicular cliffs, striped with even-running strata of rock.

"From there on to the bottom the sides were less abrupt, were shelving, and lightly fringed with *piñons* and dwarf cedars. The effect was that of a gentler canon within a wilder one. The dead city lay at the point where the perpendicular outer wall ceased and the V-shaped inner gorge began. There a stratum of rock, softer than those above, had been hollowed out by the action of time until it was like a deep groove running along the sides of the cañon. In this hollow (like a great fold in the rock) the Ancient People had built their houses of yellowish stone and mortar. The overhanging cliff above made a roof two hundred feet thick. The hard stratum below was like an everlasting floor. The houses stood along in a row, like the buildings in a city block, or like a barracks."

Although Cather's surviving letters do not report the visit to Walnut Canyon, she was deeply moved by the experience. In her first fictional setting in the Southwest her memories of Walnut Canyon inform an important section of *The Song of the Lark*, written three years later. The canyon is the scene of a pivotal decision in the career of Thea Kronborg, its protagonist. Thea leaves Chicago for Arizona to rest, recuperate, and think. She has been ill during the previous winter and needs the dry desert air of the Southwest. But more important, she needs to get "out of the stream of meaningless activity and undirected effort." Ever since leaving home for Chicago to study music, she has always been a "little drudge" working to get on in the world and never having time to sort out her values or chart her future. But on the ranch she visits near Flagstaff "the personality of which she was so tired seemed to let go of her," and as she climbs into her big German feather bed the first night, she feels a complete sense of release from the struggles and anxieties of her former life. Day after day while she is at the ranch, which adjoins Panther Canyon, she takes her lunch basket and descends to one of the cliff houses, where she lies lazily in the sun high above the bottom of the canyon. All her life "she had been hurrying and sputtering, as if she had been born behind time and had been trying to catch up." Now it is as though she were waiting for something to catch up with her. At the end of her stay at Panther Canyon, Thea makes up her mind to go to Germany to continue her musical education. This is the turning point in her career. She finally knows what she wants out of life and goes on to become a great Wagnerian soprano.

The Song of the Lark is heavily autobiographical in its early books, as it details the life of the young singer-heroine. Cather herself was at a crossroads in her career when she went to the Southwest for the first time. She had been ill during the previous winter and needed the bracing air of Arizona and New Mexico. She too was tired and felt unfulfilled in her journalistic career. She too had been a little drudge hurrying from one task to another. Undecided about her future when she left the East, she was planning to return to *McClure's Magazine* as a staff writer, though she had resigned already as managing editor, but during her weeks in the Southwest she saw clearly that she had been frittering away her life in the editorial routine. It was time to get out completely. She gathered her courage and struck out in a new direction. This time of rest, recuperation, and thought gave her a clear vision of where she wanted to go in the future.

There is a difference, however, between Thea's decision, which is concentrated dramatically in the Panther Canyon episode, and Cather's, because life is often less dramatic than fiction. Cather's departure from the magazine was aided by a change in ownership and a shake-up in staff, but when she returned to New York, she felt obliged to give the magazine some of her time in the balance of 1912 and in 1913 before severing all connections. And she also had a good start on her rest and rehabilitation during the autumn of 1911 at Cherry Valley, New York, where she did some important writing. But the trip to the Southwest, nonetheless, was a watershed in her career.

After she visited Flagstaff, she returned to Winslow briefly; then she and her brother continued on to Albuquerque at the end of May. Ten days later she wrote McClure that she was just back from a long and delightful horseback trip into the desert. She was then at Lamy, the nearest town to Santa Fe on the main line of the railroad, and about to leave for Red Cloud. She went roundabout through El Paso, where she caught a Southern Pacific train that took her back into the Middle West. By June 12 she was home and writing to McClure about his problems. But she also summarized her stay in the Southwest. She had not written a line since leaving the East, but she had returned with such a head full of stories that she was dreaming about them at night. She had ridden and driven hundreds of miles in Arizona and New Mexico, and McClure would not recognize her, she was so dark-skinned and good-humored. She urged McClure to forget how cranky she used to be when she was tired. She could not bear to be remembered that way, and she resolved never to get fussy like that again. She was now happier than she had been since she was a youngster. Those weeks off in the desert with her big, handsome brother were weeks that she would never forget. They took all the kinks and crinkles out, and she felt as if her mind had been freshly washed and ironed and made ready for a new life. She felt somehow confident, as if she had gotten her second wind.

In describing her return to civilization to Sergeant she put it another way. The Southwest had been so big and so consuming that she was now glad to be back in the East, where she could slowly come to herself without that swift, yellow excitement to think of. Before she left, the real meaning came to her of a sentence she once had carelessly read in Balzac: "Dans le desert, voyez-vous, il y a tout et il n'y a rien; Dieu sans les hommes" ("In the desert, you see, there is everything and nothing; God without men"). That sentence really means a great deal, she wrote. She was sitting mournfully beside the Rio Grande one day, just outside a beautiful Indian village, Santo Domingo, when she looked up and saw that sentence written in the sand. It explained what was the matter with her. One could play with the desert, love it, and go hard night and day and be full of it and quite tipsy with it, and then there came a moment when one must kiss it goodby and go, go bleeding, but go.

CHAPTER I

Virginia

Back Creek Valley in Frederick County, Virginia, at the end of 1873 was a thinly settled district on the Northwest Turnpike linking Winchester and Romney, some thirty miles to the west. The farms in that part of the Shenandoah Valley, which lies some fifty miles west-northwest of the national capital, were mostly hilly, and their thin, rocky soil was not well suited to agriculture. The farmers would have been poor even if marauding soldiers had not destroyed their crops, driven off their stock, and burned their barns during the Civil War. Because the land was poor, field hands were not needed there as on the richer plantations farther east. No family had owned more than a few slaves before the war, and many settlers who did not believe in slavery owned none and worked their slatey acres with their own sweat. So much of the land was still wild forest that the lumber they had in abundance was of no value at all. The people along Back Creek were predominantly Protestant, a mixture of Calvinists from Northern Ireland and German Lutherans, many newly arrived in the United States, augmented by native Pennsylvanians or older immigrants who had moved down into Virginia. Some, like Willa Cather's parents, were fourth-generation Virginians.

Less than a decade after the Civil War ended, the South was still recovering from the wracking agonies of the terrible conflict. Although Virginia escaped much of the punishment inflicted on the Confederacy during Reconstruction and was readmitted to the Union by 1870, the state had lost thousands of its young men and had been a battleground during much of the war. The Shenandoah Valley in particular was a strategic highway connecting North and South. Winchester, the county seat, stood at the crossroads of major highways running north and south, east and west, the latter being the Northwest Turnpike. The area had been stubbornly fought over throughout the four-year struggle, and Winchester changed hands many times. One resident of the area remembered: "So rapidly did it change hands that the inhabitants found it necessary [each morning] to look to the surrounding forts to see which flag was floating over them." The register at the Taylor Hotel had many pages with names of officers of both sides under the same date: Union officers had eaten dinner; Confederate officers had spent the night.

"Stonewall" Jackson had humiliated the Union forces under General Nathaniel Banks in the Shenandoah Valley in May 1862. General Philip Sheridan had turned defeat into a victory with his famous ride from Winchester to Cedar Run in October 1864 and had finally defeated Confederate general Jubal A. Early there the following March, a few weeks before Lee surrendered to Grant at Appomattox Courthouse. Although the valley was largely Southern in its sympathies and did not, as West Virginia did, split away from the Confederacy, many pro-Northerners lived there, and the sectional differences that divided father and son, brother and brother, sister and sister, were nowhere more evident. Prominent among the Union supporters in the valley was William Cather, grandfather of Willa.

The Cather family originated in Wales. After Willa Cather had become a well-known novelist, she received a letter one day from a Cather in England asking if she were a descendant of the Jasper Cather who had emigrated to America from Northern Ireland. This distant English cousin explained that the original family home was the Cadder Idris, the highest mountain in Wales, from which the name apparently had come. An ancestor in the seventeenth century, the cousin also reported, had fought for Charles I, and in appreciation Charles II after the Restoration had given land in Ireland to Edmund and Bertram Cather, twin brothers, who then had settled in County Tyrone. There is a Cather coat of arms in British records of heraldry: a buck's head cabossed on a shield surmounted by a crest of a swan among reeds with the motto "Vigilans non cadet" ("He who is vigilant will not fall").

This Jasper Cather, who was the first Cather in America, was a red-haired schoolteacher who settled in Western Pennsylvania around the middle of the eighteenth century. He fought in the Revolution, but little is known about him until he turned up in Frederick County, Virginia, after independence and bought land on Flint Ridge, two miles southeast of Back Creek Valley. In 1786 he married Sarah Moore, who bore him seven children, one of whom was James Cather, the great-grandfather of Willa, born in 1795. James in 1819 married Ann Howard, whose parents had emigrated from Ireland in the last year of the eighteenth century, when she was an infant. She bore James eight children, one of whom was William, the grandfather of Willa.

James Cather, who was much admired by his grandson Charles, Willa's father, was a man of some distinction in the community. A local historian describes him as "above the average farmer in intellect. Possessed with rare physical strength and wonderful energy, these qualities gave him an advantage over weaker men. Always informed on the current topics of the day, his conversational abilities were admirable. Young men were always benefited by having him as a friend." James, who lived to be eighty, is much like Mr. Cartmell, the postmistress's father in *Sapphira and the Slave Girl*. As young Rachel Blake overhears him talking to his daughter, she thinks that his "talk had a flavour of old-fashioned courtesy." Mr. Cartmell also believes, as James Cather and his widowed daughter Sidney Gore did, that owning slaves is wrong.

James, however, sided with the South during the Civil War. Though he opposed both slavery and secession, he believed strongly in states' rights, and as a member of the legislature voted with the majority when Virginia left the Union. He made the same painful decision many southerners made that fateful spring. Robert E. Lee wrote his sister on April 10, 1861: "With all my devotion to the Union and the feeling of loyalty and duty of an American citizen, I have not been able to make up my mind to raise my hand against my relatives, my children, my home. I have therefore resigned my commission in the Army, and save in defense of my native State, with the sincere hope that my poor service may never be needed, I hope I may never be called on to draw my sword." The choice was easier, however, for James Cather, farmer, than for an army officer and West Point graduate.

William Cather, Willa's grandfather, grew up on the Flint Ridge farm and in 1846 married Emily Anne Caroline Smith. William and Caroline are important characters in *My Ántonia* (1918), though they are seen there as an elderly couple after they have joined the westward movement and resettled in Nebraska. Cather's narrator, Jim Burden, who goes to live with his grandparents after the death of his Virginia parents, describes his grandfather: "My grandfather said little. . . . I felt at once his deliberateness and personal dignity, and was a little in awe of him. The thing one immediately noticed about him was his beautiful, crinkly snow-white beard. . . . His bald crown only made it more impressive. Grandfather's eyes were not at all like those of an old man; they were bright blue, and had a fresh, frosty sparkle." In his photograph William looks like an Old Testament prophet, and in keeping with this appearance, he was deeply religious. In his youth his conscience had led him to drop his inherited Calvinism and become a Baptist.

Caroline Cather, whose father kept a popular tavern on the turnpike, was descended from Jeremiah Smith, who came to Virginia from England in 1730. He had been deeded land on Back Creek in 1762 by Lord Fairfax, who, one remembers, once had employed George Washington to survey his vast holdings. The deed to this small parcel of Fairfax's five million acres still remains in the possession of Cather descendants. To Jim Burden his grandmother appears "a spare, tall woman, a little stooped, and she was apt to carry her head thrust forward in an attitude of attention. . . . She was quick-footed and energetic in all her movements. Her voice was high and rather shrill, and she often spoke with an anxious inflection. . . . Her laugh, too, was high and perhaps a little strident, but there was a lively intelligence in it. She was then fifty-five years old, a strong woman, of unusual endurance."

In 1851 William and Caroline settled on a farm about a mile east of the village of Back Creek. William bought 130 acres and later more than doubled his property. He built a large, solid three-story brick house on the north side of the turnpike and named it Willow Shade. It still stands on the outskirts of what is now the town of Gore. Across the façade are five large single windows, each with twelve panes, and behind is a brick extension rising two stories. Each room once had a fireplace, and surrounding the house in the nineteenth century were great willow trees. A stream ran through the front yard, spanned by a rustic bridge, and a spring from the mountain behind provided cool water for refrigeration and household use. A flight of steps still leads to a porch supported by white columns and an entranceway into the second story. Across the turnpike is a steep hill that cuts off the view from the lower story.

As an adult, Cather remembered the kitchen on the ground floor as being the most pleasant room in the house, also the most interesting. The parlor was stiff and formal except when it was full of company, which was often, but the kitchen was comfortable. Besides the eight-hole range, there was a huge fireplace with a crane to lift heavy pots. There was always a roaring fire in the winter, which was kept up at night after the stove fires went out. There were three kitchen tables: one for making bread, another for pastry, and a third covered with zinc used for cutting up meat. There were also tall cupboards used for storing sugar and spices and groceries. The farm wagons brought supplies from Winchester in large quantities so that the Cathers did not have to make the trip often. There was a special cupboard that held jars of brandied fruit, ginger, and orange peel soaking in whiskey. Vegetables for winter were kept in a storeroom at the back cooled by the spring that supplied the house. This house and its surroundings are the center of all of Willa Cather's early memories.

Before she was born, however, the war split the Cathers and alienated neighbors. William and Caroline, as strong Union supporters, broke with William's father and brothers and sisters. Their two sons, Charles (Willa's father) and George, were too young for military duty at the beginning of the conflict, but before the end they were sent across the border less than five miles away to West Virginia to avoid conscription into the Confederate Army. As the war went on around them, the Cathers lived in fear of trouble. Both Confederate and Union troops were continually moving up and down the turnpike and demanding of local residents food and shelter. The Cathers were lucky, however, and survived the war with no great loss of property. On one occasion a neighbor who had remained friendly warned them that Confederate soldiers were about to raid the valley and take all the stock of Northern sympathizers. The Cathers took their animals to the neighbor's barn until the threat passed. Later they returned the favor when Union troops swept through the area. At still another point in the war when an epidemic of measles broke out among occupying Confederate troops, the Cathers turned Willow Shade into an emergency hospital.

The events of the war in Back Creek Valley are vividly recounted in the diary of William Cather's sister, Sidney Gore, a widow who lived in the village and kept a rooming and boarding house. She quartered and ministered to soldiers of both armies and could hear the cannon and rifle fire from the battles fought around Winchester. But no real battles were fought in Back Creek. The Gores' greatest problem was hiding food, money, and livestock from thieving bushwackers who straggled through the valley. Mrs. Gore's son remembered that they put their bread in pillowcases after each meal. They tied their money up with medicinal herbs that were hung from the rafters. They built secret closets in the attic, induced the hens to lay their eggs deep in the woods, fattened their hogs in pens hidden in large piles of firewood, and hid the family silver under a false bottom in the kitchen woodbox.

There were agonizing moments, however. Mrs. Gore was stunned when Union troops killed her neighbor in August 1863. The neighbor had been surprised when asleep by soldiers' appearing at the window and without reflecting had grabbed a gun and fired a shot. Whereupon fifty Union soldiers opened fire. On another occasion Willa Cather's Aunt Sidney opened the door to find a Union officer who asked for James Cather. When she said that she was his daughter, the enemy officer introduced himself as her cousin, but

1. Grandfather William Cather. Courtesy of Willa Cather Pioneer Memorial Collection, Nebraska State Historical Society (WCPMC-NSHS)

2. Grandmother Cather. Courtesy of WCPMC-NSHS

3. Grandmother Boak.

4. Cather's Aunt Franc (Mrs. George
Cather). Courtesy of WCPMC-NSHS

5. Jennie (Virginia) Cather, Willa's
mother. Courtesy of WCPMC-NSHS

6. Charles Cather, Willa's father.
Courtesy of WCPMC-NSHS

7. Roscoe Cather, Willa's oldest brother. Courtesy of WCPMC-NSHS

8. Douglass, Willa's brother. Courtesy of Helen Cather Southwick

9. Willa reading to Jack and Elsie Cather. Courtesy of WCPMC-NSHS

10. Cather with nieces: Virginia and twins, Margaret and Elizabeth. Courtesy of WCPMC–NSHS

11. Cather and niece Helen Louise. Courtesy of WCPMC–NSHS

12. Charles, Willa, Jennie (Virginia), and Douglass Cather. Courtesy of WCPMC–NSHS

family members on opposite sides during the Civil War was a commonplace in Back Creek.

The tragedies of fratricidal war are poignantly set down in Walt Whitman's memory of his experiences as a volunteer nurse in Washington hospitals: "I staid to-night a long time by the bedside of a new patient, a young Baltimorean, aged about 19 years . . . very feeble, right leg amputated, can't sleep . . . held on to my hand and put it by his face, not willing to let me leave. As I was lingering, soothing him in his pain, he says to me suddenly, 'I hardly think you know who I am . . . I am a rebel soldier.' I said I did not know that, but it made no difference. . . . In an adjoining ward I found his brother, an officer of rank, a Union soldier . . . wounded in one of the engagements at Petersburgh. . . . It was in the same battle both were hit. One was a strong Unionist, the other Secesh; both fought on their respective sides, both badly wounded, and both brought together here. . . . Each died for his cause."

After Lee's surrender the Back Creek boys came home to their farms and set about planting their neglected fields, which had been farmed in their absence by the women and children. Most of them had been Confederate soldiers. They still had their land, but there were few horses left to work the soil, most having been driven off or killed as the tide of battle surged back and forth. They also had to replenish their livestock. Cather writes in *Sapphira*: "The Rebel soldiers who came back were tired, discouraged, but not humiliated or embittered by failure. The country people accepted the defeat of the Confederacy with dignity, as they accepted death when it came to their families. Defeat was not new to these men. Almost every season brought defeat of some kind to the farming people. Their cornfields, planted by hand and cultivated with the hoe, were beaten down by hail, or the wheat was burned up by drought, or cholera broke out among the pigs. The soil was none too fertile, and the methods of farming were not very good.

"The Back Creek boys were glad to be at home again; to see the sun come up over one familiar hill and go down over another. Now they could mend the barn roof where it leaked, help the old woman with her garden, and keep the woodpile high. They had gone out to fight for their home State, had done their best, and now it was over. They still wore their army overcoats in winter, because they had no others, and they worked the fields in whatever rags were left of their uniforms. The day of Confederate reunions and veterans' dinners was then far distant."

William Cather, however, profited by his Union allegiance and after the war was appointed sheriff for Frederick County by the military government, a job that he performed with the aid of his sons as deputies. He also ended the

war more affluent than his neighbors, and after life returned to normal hired a
Baptist preacher to conduct a school at Willow Shade. All the people of the
neighborhood, Northern and Southern sympathizers alike, were invited to
send their children. In addition, he sent some of the older ones—including his
son Charles and a neighbor's daughter, Mary Virginia Boak, who had had
three brothers in the Confederate Army—to school in Baltimore. These acts
helped heal the wounds caused by the war, and the healing process was
abetted further when Charles Cather and Mary Virginia Boak fell in love.
They were married on December 5, 1872, in the home of the bride's mother,
Rachel Boak.

Rachel Boak, whose influence on her granddaughter was considerable, has
been portrayed indelibly as Old Mrs. Harris in Cather's story of that name
and as Rachel Blake in *Sapphira*. Her family history furnished the plot of that
novel: her father was the miller and her mother the title character. She was the
one who helped the slave Nancy escape via the underground railway to
Canada. In real life she had been born Rachel Elizabeth Seibert in 1816. She
married William Lee Boak at the age of fourteen and was widowed at thirty-
eight. Her husband, who was three times a member of the Virginia House of
Delegates, died in Washington as an official of the Department of the Interior.
When Rachel returned to Virginia with a family of five, her father bought her
a house in the village. There she raised her children and ministered to the sick,
as Rachel Blake does in the novel. She abhorred slavery, as the William
Cathers did, but when the war came, her three sons served the Confederacy.
Only two returned from the war. William Seibert Boak died at nineteen as the
result of wounds received at Manassas.

Cather in 1902 dedicated a poem to his memory, "The Namesake," and
after going to Pittsburgh adopted Seibert as her own middle name, though
she always spelled it Sibert. She also liked to pretend that she was named for
this uncle she never had met. She writes:

> Somewhere there among the stones,
> All alike, that mark their bones,
> Lies a lad beneath the pine
> Who once bore a name like mine,—
> Flung his splendid life away
> Long before I saw the day.

And the poem ends:

> And I'll be winner at the game
> Enough for two who bore the name.

Cather also wrote a story in 1907 with the same title as the poem, in which a sculptor explains to his colleagues that the inspiration for his statue *The Color Sergeant* came from his uncle who was killed in the war. Cather's mother always revered this brother and kept his sword and a Confederate flag with her when the family moved to Nebraska.

When Cather was editing the *Home Monthly* in Pittsburgh, she wrote an article on nursing as a profession for women. She used her grandmother as an example "of those unprofessional nurses who served without recompense, from the mere love of it. She had a host of little children of her own, poor woman, but when a child was burned, when some overworked woman was in her death agony, when a man had been crushed under falling timber, or when a boy had cut his leg by a slip of the knife in the sumach field, the man who went to town for the doctor always stopped for her on the way. Night or day, winter or summer, she went. . . . I have often heard the old folks tell how, during those dreadful diphtheria scourges that used to sweep over the country in the fifties, she would go into a house where eight or ten children were all down with the disease, nurse and cook for the living and 'lay out' the dead."

Grandmother Boak as Rachel Blake in *Sapphira* is a "short, stalwart woman in a sunbonnet, wearing a heavy shawl over her freshly ironed calico dress . . . a woman of thirty-six or -seven, though she looked older." The set of her head was "enduring yet determined," her face broad, "highly coloured," her "fleshy nose, anchored deeply at the nostrils," her eyes grave and dark, "set back under a broad forehead." As Grandma Harris, she is seen by her neighbor Mrs. Rosen: "There was the kind of nobility about her head that there is about an old lion's: an absence of self-consciousness, vanity, preoccupation—something absolute. Her grey hair was parted in the middle, wound in two little horns over her ears, and done in a little flat knot behind. Her mouth was large and composed, — resigned, the corners drooping."

Charles Cather, Willa's father, was an amiable young man, soft-spoken and tender-hearted. He was tall, fair-haired, gentle, and did not inherit the inflexible will and evangelical zeal of his Calvinist-turned-Baptist father. He was handsome in a boyish southern way and never hurt anybody's feelings. Willa Cather loved him dearly and was always much closer to him than to her mother. Before his marriage Charles had studied law for two years, and though he never practiced, he often was called on to help his neighbors untangle their affairs; when he gave up farming in Nebraska to open an insurance office in Red Cloud, his legal training was useful. He appears in a partial portrait in "Old Mrs. Harris" as Mr. Templeton, an easygoing businessman who hates to press his debtors: "His boyish, eager-to-please manner, his fair complexion and blue eyes and young face, made him seem very soft to some of the hard old money-grubbers on Main Street, and the fact that he always said 'Yes, sir,' and 'No, sir,' to men older than himself furnished a good deal of amusement to by-standers." But his appearance was deceiving. Charles Cather operated Willow Shade profitably, later made money farming in Nebraska, and as a businessman in Red Cloud supported a large family.

Mary Virginia Boak, Willa's mother, who had taught school in Back Creek Valley before her marriage, was a woman of energy and force. Handsome and domineering, she provided the power that drove the household, often producing sparks, and she more than made up for Charles's easygoing manner. She ruled her family tyrannically, exacted strict obedience to a domestic discipline, and punished disobedience with a rawhide whip. Her children, however, apparently never objected to her draconian measures for enforcing good behavior. She also had a great capacity for enjoying life and for caring about things—whether the coffee was hot, whether a neighbor's child was ill, whether the weather was right for a picnic. She had the good sense to let her children develop their own personalities. Willa Cather remembered in her old age that her mother kept her seven children clean but allowed them to be individuals from the time they could crawl. She cared for their bodies and kept her hands off their souls. They were all different, and she let them be different. As Victoria Templeton in "Old Mrs. Harris," she is seen through the eyes of the title character: "Victoria had a good heart, but she was terribly proud and could not bear the least criticism." Willa inherited her mother's temperament, and the two often clashed.

One of Mary Virginia's projects early in her marriage was to bring her divided families together again. She planned a large party at Christmastime in 1875 and drove about the valley issuing her invitations in person. Because of her charm and the fact the Boaks had been staunch supporters of the Confederacy, none of the pro-Southern relatives was able to decline. The war, of course, had been over for a decade, and it no doubt was time for reconciliation. Besides, as the William Cathers were such a prominent part of the family, it was very inconvenient to keep up the enmity. Everyone showed up, and the party was a great success. William's mother, Ann Howard Cather, then seventy-seven, attended the festivities and had the satisfaction of seeing her sons and daughters once again at peace with each other.

Charles and Mary Virginia (usually called Jennie) lost no time in starting a family. By March 1873 Jennie was pregnant. Caroline Cather, her mother-in-law, wrote to one of her daughters after Jennie began to have morning sickness that Charles's Jennie was sick and had called the doctor twice. "I went up to see her with your Aunt Sidney and I think we understand her case as well as the Dr. and think he was not needed as much now as he may be after while, but I did not tell her so for she is so easily insulted. I knew she would fly right up for she thinks she is awfully sick. Her mother and Charley [have] a happy time waiting on her." Less than eight months later, as the winter began mildly, Willa Cather was born in her grandmother's house in Back Creek Valley on December 7, 1873.

She was named Wilella after her father's youngest sister, who had died of diphtheria in childhood, but she was always called Willie by her family and oldest friends. Willa was her own invention and appears in her own hand in the family Bible, altered from the original Wilella. The weather turned cold in January, when the first report of the baby appears in the record. Charles wrote his brother George, who had gone west to Nebraska: "We have just been treated to a slice of cold weather; the first of the season—last week we had three of our coldest days so far. The thermometer stood at 10 above zero. . . . We filled our ice house during the freeze. . . . Jennie and I were at town today. Jennie went to have a tooth drawn, the first time she has been out. We left the baby at home with its grandma. She said it did not cry once while we were gone. She grows very fast, and is just as good as she is pretty." This description is perhaps a proud father's exaggeration, for the earliest photograph extant is not particularly attractive. It shows a rather square head, very prominent ears, and a large nose, but by the time Willa was a little girl her features had refined, and she begins to be recognizable as the adult Willa Cather.

In the fall of 1874 William and Caroline Cather left Virginia to visit their son George, who had married a New England girl and had taken up a homestead in Nebraska. They left Charles and Jennie in charge of the farm. The young Cathers and the baby moved into Willow Shade, where they lived until they too, in 1883, decided to go west. In mid-February Jennie wrote her sister- and brother-in-law in Nebraska that Willa was walking and beginning to talk. She was then fourteen months old. While Jennie minded the baby and looked after the house, Charles supported his wife and child by raising sheep. Not much of his father's land could be farmed profitably, but sheep found a ready market in Washington and Baltimore. He ran the farm efficiently and, according to his nature, tender-heartedly. When his favorite sheep dog cut its paws, he fashioned little leather shoes to protect its feet from the rocks, and, Willa Cather remembered, the dog would come begging for its shoes. Her most vivid memories of early childhood, however, were the times her father carried her with him when he went out at night to drive the sheep into the fold. Her poem "The Swedish Mother," published in *McClure's Magazine* in 1911, recalls this early experience. The mother is telling the child about her childhood:

> All time in spring, when evening come,
> We go bring sheep and li'l' lambs home.
> We go big field, 'way up on hill,
> Ten times high like our windmill.
> One time your grandpa leave me wait
> While he call sheep down. By de gate
> I sit still till night come dark;
> Rabbits run an' strange dogs bark,
> Old owl hoot, and your modder cry,
> She been so 'fraid big bear come by.
> Last, 'way off, she hear de sheep,
> Li'l' bells ring and li'l' lambs bleat.
>
> .   .   .   .
>
> Then come grandpa in his arms
> Li'l' sick lamb that somet'ing harm
> He so young then, big and strong,
> Pick li'l' girl up, take her 'long.

Early memories of childhood are like islands in an empty sea—isolated and unconnected to each other. As an adult, Cather's earliest memory was of a ride in a steamboat when she was still an infant. She could remember the terror she felt as she held tightly to her mother while being taken on board. She also recalled another occasion at about the age of three when her parents went ice-skating on Back Creek and took her with them. Skating was a sport they loved and one that she also enjoyed later in Nebraska. She was not content to sit and watch, however, but wanted attention. Her indulgent father cut a pine bough, set her on it, and pulled her across the ice. She remembered still another time when she was taken visiting up on Timber Ridge. She was supposed to walk home because it was all down hill, but as she was on her way a violent rainstorm came up, and she was wearing only a pair of light slippers. Providentially, Snowden Anderson, a man she hardly knew, came up from his house on the Hollow Road riding a gray horse and wearing an old gray Confederate Army overcoat. He stopped, picked her up, sat her on the old cavalry saddle in front of him, and took her home. She remembered feeling contented and safe. Children, she thought, knew when people were honest and good. They did not reason about it. They just knew.

At least that is the way she felt about her Virginia childhood some sixty years after.

Many of the incidents of her childhood, however, come from the recollections of her parents. Her mother was fond of showing her daughter's early linguistic proficiency by telling of the visit of a little cousin named Philip Frederic, who came to Willow Shade with his parents. The house was full of guests, as it often was, and Philip Frederic was put in Willa's crib while she slept with her grandmother. After the cousin left, however, Willa refused to go back to her bed: "No, no," she kept repeating, "my cradle is all Philip Frederic'd up." Her precocity was demonstrated other times after she had listened to her grandmother read to her from *Peter Parley's Universal History*, one of Samuel Goodrich's enormously popular children's books. She would make a chariot by putting one chair upside down on another, climbing on top, and driving the chariot. She would sit silently for long intervals riding while an invisible slave ran beside her repeating the words, "*Cato, thou art but man!*"

Her grandmother Boak, who had come to live with them, took charge of her preschool education, read to her from the Bible and *The Pilgrim's Progress*, as well as from Peter Parley. The Bible she absorbed so thoroughly that her writing throughout her life is loaded with biblical quotations and allusions. John Bunyan's allegory of the Christian life made a deep impression. It was a book, she wrote nearly half a century later, with "scenes of the most satisfying kind; where little is said but much is felt and communicated." At the end of her career, in *Sapphira,* she has her miller read Bunyan as he wrestles with the moral problem of slavery. Before she was old enough to go to school, her father took her to a private school nearby where older children were being taught, and she was allowed to sit quietly and listen. Her father would carry her over on his horse and leave her there for half a day. Later she attended a school kept by a Mr. Smith in Back Creek.

There is no record of serious illness during Cather's childhood, but she had the usual colds during the damp winters. When she was shut up in the house, she remembered many years later, her parents would send for Mary Ann Anderson (the mother of Snowden), who lived up on the ridge, to come down and help out. Cather used to watch out of the front windows, hoping to see Mrs. Anderson come down the road: she was such fun to talk to and very kind to a sick child. She became a great favorite and appears as Mrs. Ringer in *Sapphira*, the woman who "was born interested." Cather renewed her childhood friendship with Mrs. Anderson when she returned to Virginia in 1896 and heard from her all the stories of the lives of people she had known as a child. "She got a great deal of entertainment out of the weather and the behaviour of the moon. Any chance bit of gossip that came her way was a godsend. . . . Her spirits bubbled into the light like a spring and spread among the cresses."

Mrs. Anderson's simple-minded daughter Marjorie was one of Cather's companions, though much older, after she came to work at Willow Shade as nurse and housemaid. She and Willa roamed the woods and fields together and often walked up the double-S road, which Cather later thought the most beautiful piece of country road she had found anywhere in the world, to visit Margie's mother and listen to her tales of local folklore. Cather loved Margie, who served the family with single-minded devotion for the rest of her life. She and her brother accompanied the Cathers to Nebraska, and she was ultimately buried in the family plot in Red Cloud in 1928. Margie lived in Cather's imagination as Mahailey in *One of Ours*, Mandy in "Old Mrs. Harris," Sada in *Death Comes for the Archbishop*, and the title character in the poem "Poor Marty," written after Margie died. In *One of Ours* Cather writes: "She had never been sent to school, and could not read or write. Claude, when he was a little boy, tried to teach her to read, but what she learned one night she had forgotten by the next. She could count, and tell the time . . . and she was very proud of knowing the alphabet. . . . [However] Mahailey was shrewd in her estimate of people, and Claude thought her judgment sound in a good many things. He knew she sensed all the shades of personal feeling, the accords and antipathies in the household, as keenly as he did, and he would have hated to lose her good opinion." Cather understood this humble and defenseless woman, felt very protective of her, and when she visited Red Cloud in later years she often spent hours talking to Margie in the backyard or working with her in the kitchen. Both women shared a fondness for children. Margie loved to talk of old times in Virginia; and Cather's father, who subscribed to the weekly Winchester paper, always told her the news from home. After she died, Cather wrote in "Poor Marty":

> Little had she here to leave,
> Nought to will, none to grieve.
> Hire nor wages did she draw,
> But her keep and bed of straw.

Companions more Cather's own age included Mary Love, the daughter of the doctor who delivered her. Mary's grandfather had been minister to France in 1860–61, and Mary's mother liked to talk about her education in France and her experiences as a diplomat's daughter. Cather's lifelong love affair with France may well have begun with these accounts. Willa also had the companionship of her brother Roscoe, called Ross by the family, who was born in 1877. Douglass, who came along in 1880, did not become her close friend and confidant until they were growing up in Red Cloud years later. Jessica, the fourth and last child born in Virginia, was eight years younger, very different from Willa in temperament, and the two sisters had little to say to each other.

Young Willa Cather roamed the woods and the fields. She visited the mill house where her grandmother had grown up and the mill on Back Creek where her Great-grandfather Seibert had been the miller. There were plenty of rabbits in the woods, and she set traps that her father made for her. When she revisited Virginia thirteen years after the family moved away, she walked straight to her traps and found them still intact. A little to the west of Willow Shade was a suspension bridge over the creek. There she liked to walk to the middle and recite, "I stood on the bridge at midnight, / As the clocks were striking the hour."

Life at Willow Shade was orderly, comfortable, and continuously interesting. It was a stable world for a child to grow up in. The Cathers were better off than many of their neighbors, and there were always servants in the house to talk to and a few field hands, both black and white, on the farm to watch. There was a huge sheep barn, standing three stories and a loft above its ground-floor pens, where children could play. Spinning and quilting, butter-making, preserving, and candle-making went on regularly. Old women from the mountains came down to help during the busy seasons. Butchering, sheep-shearing, tanning of hides were done on the farm. During the winter evenings the black help sat around the kitchen fireplace, cracking nuts, telling stories, and cutting old clothes into strips, winding the strips into balls to send to Mrs. Kearns, a neighbor who made them into rag rugs. There was also a steady stream of guests at Willow Shade. The tin peddler and Uncle Billy Parks, the broom-maker, came often and were housed overnight in the two-story wing at the back of the house. Cather remembered once emptying her savings bank and giving the contents to Uncle Billy. More important guests, relatives from all over, friends from Winchester, sometimes even Washington, came to visit or stop over on their way somewhere else. It was open house most of the time.

The orderliness and continuity of Cather's first nine years in Virginia left their mark on her values and personality. Her old friend Dorothy Canfield Fisher, who knew her from the time she was sixteen, wrote that she spent this formative "period of life which most influences personality in a state which had the tradition of continuity and stability as far as they could exist in this country, and in a class which more than any other is always stubbornly devoted to the old ways of doing things." Cather always cherished tradition, and the older she grew, the more she felt the need to cling to the values she had grown up with. She watched with profound sorrow the ravages of World War I, then the Great Depression, and finally, late in her life, World War II and felt at the end that the world she knew had largely vanished.

By far the most memorable event of Cather's childhood occurred when she was five. This was the return of Nancy Till, the ex-slave her grandmother had helped escape. The event is recreated as the epilogue for *Sapphira*. On a clear, windy March day in 1879 Cather was in bed with a cold in her mother's bedroom on the third floor of Willow Shade. She had been put there so that she could watch the turnpike to see the stage when it appeared. Nancy was coming home from Montreal, where she had lived for twenty-five years following the midnight flight in which Rachel Boak had taken her across the Potomac River and delivered her to agents of the underground railroad. Suddenly her mother hurried into the room, wrapped her in a blanket, and carried her to the window as the stage stopped before the house. A woman in a black coat and turban descended. Then she was put back to bed. Old Till, who worked for the Cathers and was Nancy's mother, stayed in the room with the child so that the recognition scene could be enacted in her presence. There was talking on the stairs, and a minute later the door opened: "Till had already risen; when the stranger followed my mother into the room, she took a few uncertain steps forward. She fell meekly into the arms of a tall, gold-skinned woman, who drew the little old darky to her breast and held her there, bending her face down over the head scantily covered with grey wool. Neither spoke a word. There was something Scriptural in that meeting, like the pictures in our old Bible."

Sixty-four years later Cather still could remember the scene as though it had just happened. She wrote in 1943 that Nancy's dress in the novel is described in more detail than she could remember about a friend she had seen the week before. It all happened just as she told it, and it was the most exciting event of her life up to that time. Nancy already had become a legend in the community, and Mrs. Cather often had sung her daughter to sleep with,

> Down by de cane brake, close by de mill,
> Dar lived a yaller gal, her name was Nancy Till.

Another dramatic event occurred about the same time with five-year-old Willa as participant, but that experience was terrifying rather than exciting. She was playing by herself in an upstairs room at Willow Shade when a half-witted boy, the son of one of the servants, slipped into the room brandishing an open jackknife. He said he was going to cut off her hand. She was terrified. In recalling the experience, however, Cather remembered that she was scared, but she also knew that she must not show any sign of fear. She began talking to the boy to distract him and edging towards the window. Outside the room was a tall tree whose branches one could reach out and touch. She suggested to the boy that it would be fun to climb out the window and descend to the ground without having to go back down the stairs. The new idea drove out the old one. The boy forgot what he had planned to do, went out the window, and climbed down the tree.

Though the strategem worked, the experience left a deep trauma. Throughout her life Cather had a horror of mutilation, especially of the hands. Time and again in her fiction this horror appears—almost like an obsession. In an early story written while Cather was still in college, "The Clemency of the Court" (1893), Serge is tied by his arms in prison until "they were paralyzed from the shoulder down so that the guard had to feed him like a baby." In "The Profile" (1907) one of the characters speaks of the human body as sanctified by nature, "but lop away so much as a finger, and you have wounded the creature beyond reparation." In "The Bohemian Girl" (1912) Eric tears his hand on a cornsheller. In "The Namesake" (1907) Lyon's hand and forearm are torn away by exploding shrapnel. In "Behind the Singer Tower" (1912) an opera singer jumps from a burning hotel, flings his arm out, and his hand is "snapped off at the wrist as cleanly as if it had been taken off by a cutlass." In *One of Ours* (1922) Claude Wheeler and his company move into a captured trench, at the top of which the hand of a dead German reaches out "like the swollen roots of some noxious weed." In *Shadows on the Rock* (1931), when a missionary is feasting with a group of Huron Indians, "they pulled a human hand out of the kettle to show him that he had eaten of an Iroquois prisoner." When Aunt Jezebel, the old slave who was born in Africa, is dying in *Sapphira* and will not eat, she is told that she must eat to keep up her strength. She replies that nothing would tempt her "lessen maybe it was a li'l' pickaninny's hand." In Cather's unfinished novel laid in medieval Avignon, which she was writing when she died, one of the main characters was punished for thievery by being strung up by the thumbs so that his hands became useless.

In respect to this horror of mutilation Cather's life imitated her art. In 1934 she tore the big tendon in her left wrist and had to have her hand in splints for over a month, and four years later someone accidentally smashed one of her hands while she was shopping in a drugstore. In 1940, after signing five hundred copies of a de luxe edition of *Sapphira* for Knopf in three days, she had to have her right hand tied up in splints. The next year her hand was still in such bad shape that an orthopedic surgeon designed a special brace, which she wore for eight months in 1941 and off and on for the rest of her life.

13. Cather's birthplace, Back Creek,
Virginia. Courtesy of WCPMC-NSHS

14. Willow Shade. Courtesy of Margaret O'Connor

15. Cather as infant. Courtesy of
WCPMC–NSHS

16. Cather at the age of nine. Courtesy
of WCPMC-NSHS

17. The mill house once owned by
Cather's great-grandparents, the
Seiberts, who suggested the characters of Sapphira and Henry Colbert
in her last novel. Courtesy of Margaret O'Connor

18. The mill. Courtesy of WCPMC-
NSHS

If her quick wit saved her from the half-witted boy, on another occasion her wit must have embarrassed her elders. Among the guests who streamed through Willow Shade was an old judge to whom she apparently took an immediate dislike. The judge took the liberty of stroking her curls and addressing her with a string of platitudes that might have been acceptable to a child of less precocity. She stood it as long as she could, then blurted out: "I'se a dang'ous nigger, I is!" It is tempting to see in this episode the beginnings of Cather's adult distaste for the polite conventions and ritual blather of genteel southern society. Her friend Edith Lewis wrote in her memoir of Cather that "even as a little girl she felt something smothering in the polite, rigid social conventions of that Southern society—something factitious and unreal. If one fell in with those sentimental attitudes, those euphuisms that went with good manners, one lost all touch with reality, with truth of experience."

Cather always had ambivalent feelings about her southern background. When she revisited Virginia in 1913, she was eager to get away from the romantic southern attitude she found in both sexes, but the men in particular were all cowed and broken, good only for carrying wraps, dancing, and tipping their hats. She didn't go back to Virginia for a quarter of a century. In 1931 she did not want to be considered a southern writer and declined to serve on a committee of southern writers. During World War II when her niece and her doctor husband moved to Tennessee, she wrote an old friend that going south had to her a slight connotation of going backward. She told another old friend that southerners, herself included, scorn accurate knowledge and always think they can get by with "pretty near." She also never quite lost her southern accent, though she thought she had, and she was much surprised when she was vacationing incognito in New England in 1942 and someone recognized her, he said, by her southern accent.

On the other hand, she much admired her mother, despite clashes of personality, for her bearing as a southern lady and very much wanted to be one herself. When she was preparing to write her only novel about Virginia, she revisited the Shenandoah Valley in 1938 with Edith Lewis, and then memories refined and softened by time came flooding back. Lewis writes: "It was as memorable an experience, as intense and thrilling in its way, as those journeys in New Mexico, when she was writing the *Archbishop*. Every bud and leaf and flower seemed to speak to her with a peculiar poignancy, every slope of the land, every fence and wall, rock and stream. [But] I remember how she spoke of the limp, drooping acacia trees in bloom along all the roadsides—how they had the shiftless look that characterized so many Southern things, but how their wood was the toughest of all."

Her mixed emotions about Virginia may have kept her from making significant literary use of her childhood memories until she wrote *Sapphira* more than five decades after leaving the South. Lewis says she often was urged to write a Virginia novel, but for a long time some sort of inhibition deterred her. She sometimes spoke of incidents of her Virginia life that she might write about someday, but she never did. Several of her early stories, however, make use of Virginia memories: "The Elopement of Allen Poole" (1893), "A Night at Greenway Court" (1896), "The Sentimentality of William Tavener" (1900), and "The Namesake" (1907). While these stories are interesting chiefly as apprentice work, they do show that she began her career making use of the total range of her experience.

The first tale, "The Elopement of Allen Poole," published unsigned in *The Hesperian*, the University of Nebraska literary magazine of which Cather was literary editor, is an amateurish story that attempts to use the dialect of the Virginia mountain people. It is a melodrama of a moonshiner who is shot by the revenuers on the night of his elopement and dies in the arms of his beloved. The sense of place, however, is very strong. After having been away from Virginia for ten years, Cather, even as a sophomore in college, was able to evoke the region memorably, as she later did the Nebraska landscape after she had lived in Pittsburgh and New York for sixteen years. Her creative process required a long immersion of her experience in the deep well of her memory. The landscape she was able to call up in this scene is genuine. Before the fatal shooting in this story Allen throws himself down in the woods beside a laurel bush: "It was the kind of summer morning to encourage idleness. Behind him were the sleepy pine woods, the slatey ground beneath them strewn red with slippery needles. Around him the laurels were just blushing into bloom. Here and there rose tall chestnut trees with the red sumach growing under them. Down in the valley lay the fields of wheat and corn, and among them the creek wound between its willow-grown banks. Across it was the old black, creaking foot-bridge which had neither props nor piles, but was swung from the arms of a great sycamore tree. The reapers were at work in the wheat fields, the mowers swinging their cradles and the binders following close behind. Along the fences companies of barefooted children were picking berries. On the bridge a lank youth sat patiently fishing in the stream where no fish had been caught for years. Allen watched them all until a passing cloud made the valley dark, then his eyes wandered to where the Blue Ridge lay against the sky, faint and hazy as the mountains of Beulah Land."

The next two stories making early use of the Virginia material are less interesting. "A Night at Greenway Court" is a story that takes place in 1752 at the manor house of Lord Fairfax near Winchester, a place Cather certainly had visited as a child. In addition, that noble lord would have interested her because of the land grant he had made to her ancestor. But the story is historical melodrama that probably owes as much to Cather's early fondness for Anthony Hope Hawkins as to her Virginia childhood. It is significant, however, that here Cather makes an early use of a male narrator to tell her story of dueling over a woman's honor. "The Sentimentality of William Tavener" is laid in Nebraska, but the story turns on a reminiscence of Virginia in which a woman urges her farmer husband to let their boys attend the circus. The couple discover that when they were children they both had attended the same circus in their native Virginia. The memory of this experience softens the hardness that had grown up between them, and the boys are sent off to the circus. This is a rather skillful use of what must have been a family story, and it creates what is rare in Cather's fiction—a tender moment of conjugal affection. The feeling is genuine, though the story still is apprentice work.

"The Namesake," which makes the last direct use of Virginia until *Sapphira*, has intrinsic interest that goes beyond its use of early memories. The story conjures up the image of the uncle who was killed in the Civil War, though the sculptor-narrator who tells the story in Paris makes the uncle a Pennsylvanian. Yet the tale makes clear the powerful pull of family and old memories. Lyon Hartwell, the son of American parents, was born and raised abroad. He is somehow able to capture the spirit of America better in his sculpture than any of his co-artists then working in Paris who have had genuine American upbringings. Hartwell explains to his friends the inspiration for his statue *The Color Sergeant*, which is the figure of a young soldier running and clutching the folds of a flag, the staff of which has been shot away. Hartwell had gone to Pennsylvania to take care of an invalid aunt living in his grandfather's house on the banks of the Ohio River. During his two years in Pennsylvania he had one day found in the attic an old trunk containing his uncle's clothes, exercise books, letters written home from the army, first books, and even some toys. Inside the cover of a dog-eared *Aeneid* was inscribed "Lyon Hartwell, January 1862," the year before he had gone off to war at the age of fifteen. Inside the back cover was a crude drawing of the federal flag, and under it in a boyish hand were two lines of "The Star-Spangled Banner." "It was a stiff, wooden sketch, not unlike a detail from some Egyptian inscription," Hartwell narrates, "but, the moment I saw it, wind and color seemed to touch it."

This experience establishes contact between the sculptor and the uncle for whom he has been named. The experience of that night, he relates, almost rent him to pieces. "It was the same feeling that artists know when we, rarely, achieve truth in our work; the feeling of union with some great force, of purpose and security, of being glad that we have lived. For the first time I felt the pull of race and blood and kindred, and felt beating within me things that had not begun with me. It was as if the earth under my feet had grasped and rooted me, and were pouring its essence into me. I sat there until the dawn of morning, and all night long my life seemed to be pouring out of me and running into the ground." Cather's subsequent career was full of epiphanies like this, which inspired her novels, but when she wrote this story in 1907, the pull of family was strong, the tug of Virginia weak. She denied her uncle his allegiance to the Confederacy, for by that time she had not lived in Virginia for twenty-four years.

The Cathers' move to Nebraska was a decade in the making. First Willa's Uncle George and Aunt Franc went west in 1873, and the following year her Grandfather and Grandmother Cather left Back Creek Valley to visit Nebraska. They stayed a year, returned to Virginia, stayed only two years, then moved west for good. The Nebraska Cathers began urging Charles to join them, but he resisted for several years. In 1880 Charles went to Nebraska himself to see his father and brother and found them flourishing in their new prairie homes. But he still wasn't convinced. After he returned to Virginia, however, his four-story sheep barn mysteriously burned to the ground, and he took that as an omen. In February 1883, he auctioned off the farm and his equipment for six thousand dollars, and by April the family was in Nebraska. It was a formidable expedition: parents; four children ranging from nine to infancy; Margie Anderson, the hired girl, and her brother Enoch; Mrs. Cather's mother, Rachel Boak, and two of her grandchildren. Most of the furniture went into the auction, and the few things they moved, like dishes, were packed in barrels and shipped with them. Even Old Vic, the sheep dog, for whom Charles Cather had made shoes, was given to a neighbor. Willa remembered poignantly Old Vic on the day of departure. Just as the family was about to board the train at Back Creek, the old dog broke loose and came running across the fields dragging her chain. Young Willa felt that it was more than she could bear.

CHAPTER 2

On the Divide

Throughout the nineteenth century Americans from the eastern states and immigrants from the Old World were moving westward. The westering spirit was endemic in the restless population of the United States, and the aspirations of landless peasants drew Europeans toward America like a magnet. As soon as the Revolution ended and the Ohio Valley was safe for settlers, New Englanders, tired of scratching a living from their rocky fields, went west. They were joined by Virginians lured by the stories of rich land in Tennessee and Kentucky. Then the land east of the Mississippi began to fill up, and pioneers like Daniel Boone left Kentucky for the still-virgin land and wild forests of Missouri. By the middle of the century people from all over were digging for gold in California and later in Colorado and South Dakota. During the Civil War, in 1862, Congress passed the Homestead Act, which offered free land in the new territories to those who would live on it, and by 1869 the transcontinental railroad was completed, making it easy for settlers to reach the promised land.

Virginians in the Shenandoah Valley, exhausted by the Civil War, dispirited by Reconstruction, and eager for more fertile acres, also caught the westering fever. They talked of going west at corn-huskings, quilting bees, and church suppers. When the young men from Back Creek Valley rode into Winchester on Saturday nights, there was talk of it at the hitching post across from the courthouse. Out on the western prairies there were no trees to fell or stones to haul out of the fields. A man could plow a straight furrow as far as the horizon, and the rich top soil was said to be twelve feet deep. Promotional literature circulated widely among the discontented farmers of Virginia, for the railroads needed passengers and buyers for the large tracts of land given them by Congress. One brochure that reached Back Creek Valley asserted that "you can plant a walnut tree and in five years cut the tree for lumber." No one mentioned the grasshopper plagues that periodically stripped the fields of every bit of living vegetation or the lack of water in many places. Nor did they say that speculators were already busy buying up the choicest land and driving up prices.

George and Frances Cather, who were among the first of many Virginians to go west from the Shenandoah Valley, reached Iowa, where they first planned to settle, in September 1873. But there they found that the free government land was gone and that land on the market was already too expensive. They decided to go further west, either to Kansas or Nebraska. By December they had chosen Nebraska, but the free government land around Red Cloud was gone, and they had to go a dozen miles farther north. George bought 360 acres from the Burlington Railroad and hoped to get more. He also staked a claim for a homestead, onto which they moved the following year. Their first winter was mild, and they sent optimistic reports home. By the following June they wrote that settlers were coming in rapidly, that George was about to dig a well to avoid having to haul water. He already had planted seven apple trees and was writing home for more seeds. They were joined that year by George's parents, Willa's grandparents, who settled on the land George first had acquired about two miles away. Both parents and children at first lived primitively in dugouts they cut into the prairie and roofed over with sod. Despite the grasshoppers the next year and occasional prairie fires, they prospered. George wrote in 1876 that he had beans a foot long and corn eleven feet tall with ears measuring fifteen inches. By this time there were enough settlers in their area to petition Washington for a post office, but after their suggestions of "Grand Prairie" and "Bloomington" were turned down, George, the leader in the effort, said he was going to name the town after himself. He did, and the post office became Catherton.

The Cathers had a far stronger motivation for moving west than rich, cheap land: the fear of disease. Tuberculosis was a killer in the Shenandoah Valley, and the Cathers seemed especially susceptible to the bacillus. All four of William Cather's brothers already had died of the disease, and two of his daughters, who had contracted tuberculosis, left Virginia too late. One died soon after moving to Nebraska; the other died later. It is no wonder the climate of Frederick County, Virginia, was generally regarded as unhealthy. Soon after settling in Nebraska, George Cather's wife, Aunt Franc, reported that the dry winters on the prairie were just the thing for people with tuberculosis. Everybody she had heard of who had come with lung trouble had been cured. She was too optimistic, of course, but the air of the high plains was much drier than that of the Shenandoah Valley, and the farther west one went, the better it was for weak lungs.

The state of Nebraska, which Willa Cather first saw in April 1883, at the age of nine, is part of the great plain that stretches west from the Missouri River, gradually rising until it reaches the Rocky Mountains. It is a rolling alluvial plain that grows gradually more sandy toward the west until it breaks into the white sand hills of western Nebraska and eastern Colorado. From east to west this plain measures about six hundred miles, and it is watered by slow-flowing, muddy rivers that run full in the spring, often cutting into farm lands along their banks. By midsummer, however, the streams lie low and shrunken, their current split by glistening white sandbars half overgrown with scrub willows.

The climate is capricious. There are sharp variations in temperature, typical of a large inland land mass that lacks the moderating influence of the sea, but there are compensations. Cather wrote in 1923: "We have short, bitter winters; windy, flower-laden springs; long, hot summers; triumphant autumns that last until Christmas—a season of perpetual sunlight, blazing blue skies, and frosty nights. In this newest part of the New World autumn is the season of beauty and sentiment, as spring is in the Old World."

The earliest settlements in Nebraska were along the Missouri River— Bellevue, Omaha, Brownville, Nebraska City—as the river was the natural pathway into the region. But before 1860 civilization did no more than nibble at the eastern edges of the state along the river bluffs. The whole of the great plain to the west was still a sunny wilderness where the tall red grass, the buffalo, and the Indians still possessed the land relatively undisturbed. Frémont, Kit Carson, and the Mormons crossed the state in the early days, and the fortune-seekers followed by the thousands in their Conestoga wagons after the gold rush began in California. It was at Brownville that the first telegraph line was brought across the river into Nebraska. Cather further remembered: "When I was a child I heard Ex-governor Furness relate how he stood with other pioneers in the log cabin where the Morse instrument had been installed, and how, when it began to click, the men took off their hats as if they were in church. The first message flashed across the river into Nebraska was not a market report, but a line of poetry: 'Westward the course of empire takes its way.'"

The Overland Stage, as Mark Twain describes it memorably in *Roughing It*, jolted regularly across the prairie in the sixties, following the meandering course of the Platte River and the Oregon Trail. When gold and silver were discovered in Colorado, large freight companies were organized to carry supplies across the plains to the mining camps. The wagons, pulled by teams of oxen, toiled over the long stretch of trackless grass from early spring until winter closed down the traffic. The oxen made from ten to twenty miles a day. "I have heard the old freighters say," continued Cather, "that after embarking on their six-hundred-mile trail, they lost count of the days of the week and the days of the month." The buffalo trails still ran north and south—deep, dusty paths the bison wore when, single file, they came north in the spring for summer grass and went south again in the fall. Along the trails were buffalo wallows, where rain collected, and the early settlers found water for their homesteads. The wagon drivers could recognize these water holes by their clouds of golden coreopsis growing out of the water. The grass was full of quail and prairie chickens in those days, and ducks swam on the lagoons.

In the same year that the Union Pacific and the Central Pacific met at Promontory, Utah, linking the Atlantic and Pacific oceans by rail for the first time, promoters of the Burlington and Missouri Railroad began building another rail line to link the Midwest with Denver. By 1882 their trains were running between Chicago, Kansas City, and the Colorado capital and passing through the Republican River Valley just north of the Kansas line. The town of Red Cloud, about one hundred and fifty miles west of the Missouri River, became a division point for the new railroad. It was also the county seat of Webster County, which had been organized in 1871, the year the town was settled. By 1880 there were over seven thousand people in the county, but one-third lived in town and the rest were spread thin, about nine per square mile. The pioneering period was coming to an end, even though it had lasted scarcely a decade. Still, much of the land had not yet been broken by the plow, and there was an abundance left of the sea of grass that had covered the prairie states since time immemorial from the Missouri River to the Rocky Mountains.

When the Cather entourage descended from a Burlington coach in April 1883, they were met at the Red Cloud depot by farm wagons from Catherton. Their destination was Grandfather Cather's farm, some twelve miles northwest of the town. Charles Cather loaded his wife, children, mother-in-law, nephew, and niece, the two Andersons, and all their baggage into the wagons for the final leg of their journey. They drove off on a fine spring day, but the road they traveled was no more than wagon tracks over the still untamed land. The terrain they crossed lay between the Republican River and the Little Blue, an area known locally as "the Divide," which was to be the setting for some of Cather's most memorable fiction. The jolting ride across the open, treeless country made an indelible impression on young Willa. She had come to Nebraska, she wrote later, from "an old and conservative society; from the Valley of Virginia, where the original land grants made in the reigns of George II and George III had been going down from father to son ever since, where life was ordered and settled." Now she was in a brand-new country lost in a sea of grass devoid of human habitation. The familiar mountains that she had seen every day of her life back home had been obliterated. She told an interviewer in 1913: "We drove out from Red Cloud to my grandfather's homestead one day in April. I was sitting on the hay in the bottom of a Studebaker wagon, holding on to the side of the wagon box to steady myself—the roads were mostly faint trails over the bunch grass in those days. The land was open range and there was almost no fencing. As we drove further and further out into the country, I felt a good deal as if we had come to the end of everything—it was a kind of erasure of personality. . . . I had heard my father say you had to show grit in a new country, and I would have got on pretty well during that ride if it had not been for the larks. Every now and then one flew up and sang a few splendid notes and dropped down into the grass again. That reminded me of something—I don't know what, but my one purpose in life just then was not to cry, and every time they did it, I thought I would go under."

She did not go under, and in her adult years she wore her allegiance to Nebraska like a badge. For the first week, however, she "had that kind of contraction of the stomach which comes from homesickness." She did not like the canned food they had to eat and made a pact with herself that she would not eat much until she could get back to Virginia and get some fresh mutton. The land seemed to her "as bare as a piece of sheet iron" or, as she put it another time, as "naked as the back of your hand." She also told an interviewer in 1921: "I was little and homesick and lonely and my mother was homesick and nobody paid any attention to us. So the country and I had it out together and by the end of the first autumn the shaggy grass country had gripped me with a passion that I have never been able to shake. It has been the happiness and the curse of my life."

In *My Ántonia* ten-year-old Jim Burden, Cather's narrator, reacts similarly to his abrupt translation from his native Virginia to Nebraska. Jim's parents have died, and he is being sent to live with his grandparents on the Divide. To heighten the dramatic effect, Cather places the action at night: "Cautiously I slipped from under the buffalo hide, got up on my knees and peered over the side of the wagon. There seemed to be nothing to see; no fences, no creeks or trees, no hills or fields. If there was a road, I could not make it out in the faint starlight. There was nothing but land. . . . I had the feeling that the world was left behind, that we had got over the edge of it, and were outside man's jurisdiction. I had never before looked up at the sky when there was not a familiar mountain ridge against it. But this was the complete dome of heaven, all there was of it."

Though Cather traveled with her parents, brothers, and sister, she felt Jim's sense of loneliness and loss keenly and never really got over it. Among the several dichotomies in her life, this is one. Throughout her life she was drawn back to the hills and mountains despite her acquired affection for the prairie. When she discovered Jaffrey, New Hampshire, in 1916, she immediately fell in love with the area and returned year after year for a month or more; and when she died, she was not buried in the family plot at Red Cloud with her parents, but on a hillside at Jaffrey, where one could look up and see "a familiar mountain" (Monadnock) against the sky.

When the Cathers got off the Burlington at Red Cloud, they probably were not the only new settlers arriving that day. Nearly every train brought immigrants from Europe. There were Swedes, Danes, Norwegians, Bohemians, Germans, and a few Russians mixed together in the polyglot population of Webster County, and there was a French Canadian settlement a little to the north. Jim Burden's train also brings immigrants, Ántonia's Bohemian family, to Nebraska. Before he is met by his grandfather's hired man, he sees these new arrivals "huddled together on the platform, encumbered by bundles and boxes. . . . The woman wore a fringed shawl tied over her head, and she carried a little tin trunk in her arms, hugging it as if it were a baby. There was an old man, tall and stooped. Two half-grown boys and a girl stood holding oilcloth bundles, and a little girl clung to her mother's skirts. Presently a man with a lantern approached them and began to talk, shouting and exclaiming. I pricked up my ears, for it was positively the first time I had ever heard a foreign tongue."

Coming from the long-settled Shenandoah Valley, Cather also at the age of nine probably never before had heard anything but English. In a biographical sketch she wrote for her publisher many years later to help promote her novels, writing in the third person, she recalls "getting acquainted with the neighbors, whose foreign speech and customs she found intensely interesting. Had she been born in that community, she doubtless would have taken these things for granted. . . . An imaginative child, taken out of the definitely arranged background, and dropped down among struggling immigrants from all over the world, naturally found something to think about." She goes on to say that no child with a spark of generosity could have kept from throwing herself heart and soul into the fight these people were making to master the language, to subdue the soil, to hold their land, and to get on in the world.

The foreign-born population of Nebraska greatly outnumbered the

American-born settlers during Cather's childhood and adolescence. The 1910 census reported a foreign population of 900,000 to 300,000 of native stock. Cather remembered: "On Sunday we could drive to a Norwegian church and listen to a sermon in that language, or to a Danish or a Swedish church. We could go to the French Catholic settlement in the next county and hear a sermon in French, or into the Bohemian township and hear one in Czech, or we could go to church with the German Lutherans. There were, of course, American congregations also." She remembered, too, once walking about the streets of Wilbur, only about thirty miles from Lincoln, for a whole day without hearing a word of English spoken.

As an adult, Cather was very critical of the indifference of native-born Americans to the immigrants. This attitude was especially prevalent among Virginians, who back home looked down on foreigners unless they were English or had titles. On the prairie they were seldom open-minded enough to understand the Europeans or to profit by their older traditions. The New England settlers in Nebraska also kept themselves insulated as much as possible from foreign influence and with the Virginians and other southerners were provincial and utterly without curiosity. "If the daughter of a shiftless West Virginia mountaineer," she declared, "married the nephew of a professor at the University of Upsala, the native family felt disgraced by such an alliance."

Cather perhaps exaggerates these feelings, but there is no doubt her mind was being stretched during the months she lived on her grandfather's farm. Her interest in the foreign-born farm families lasted all her life, and when she returned as an adult to visit her parents in Red Cloud, she usually managed to get out into the country to see old friends. She corresponded with them, sent them Christmas boxes, and during the Great Depression and years of drought in the thirties she sent them money and clothes to keep them afloat. She elaborated on the subject of the farm women in her 1913 interview: "We had very few American neighbors. They were mostly Swedes and Danes, Norwegians and Bohemians. I liked them from the first and they made up for what I missed in the country. I particularly liked the old women; they understood my homesickness and were kind to me. . . . these old women on the farms were the first people who ever gave me the real feeling of an older world across the sea. Even when they spoke very little English, the old women somehow managed to tell me a great many stories about the old country. They talk more freely to a child than to grown people. . . . I have never found any intellectual excitement any more intense than I used to feel when I spent a morning with one of these old women at her baking or butter-making. I used to ride home in the most unreasonable state of excitement; I always felt . . . as if I had actually got inside another person's skin."

When the old farm women began dying off, she wrote an old friend that there formerly had been fourteen of them on her Christmas list. Even when she was working in Pittsburgh and not making much money, she was never too poor to send these old friends some little gift. They loved her, she added, but she had loved them first. Cather romanticizes the old farm women in "The Bohemian Girl," her first important story to use Nebraska memories. In that story Nils Ericson, who has returned to his boyhood farm home after twelve years' absence, attends a barn-raising. All the neighbors for miles around come, especially the old women, who bring their pies, cakes, hams, and fried chicken. Nils's views are Cather's: "They were a fine company of old women, and a Dutch painter would have loved to find them there together, where the sun made bright patches on the floor and sent long, quivering shafts of gold through the dusky shade up among the rafters. There were fat, rosy old women who looked hot in their best black dresses; spare, alert old women with brown, dark-veined hands; and several of almost heroic frame, not less massive than old Mrs. Ericson herself." Then he reflects on the Herculean labors those fifteen pairs of hands had performed: "of the cows they had milked, the butter they had made, the gardens they had planted, the children and grandchildren they had tended, the brooms they had worn out, the mountains of food they had cooked. It made him dizzy."

When Cather told her interviewer that she felt as if she had gotten into another person's skin, she was using a simile that describes accurately her creative process. Her creative imagination required total absorption in her fictional world. She used this figure more than once in letters and interviews, and when she had finished writing novels that created strong central characters like Ántonia Shimerda, Thea Kronborg, and her archbishop, Father Latour, she always felt a sense of loss in parting with her protagonists. The images she was photographing on the brain during her months on the farm provided her first important literary material. A friend once had told her that great writers like Shakespeare or Balzac got thousands and thousands more distinct mental impressions every day of their lives than most men in a lifetime. Her mind worked the same way. Once the image was recorded on her brain, it never left her. But it was not available for immediate use. Her ability to remember mannerisms, turns of phrase, idioms, and all sorts of verbal nuances was like her ability to record visual images. Taking notes for her fiction, she told an interviewer, would kill the material. It was the memory that was important for her, and that went with the vocation. "When

I sit down to write, turns of phrase I've forgotten for years come back like white ink before fire." As she told Sergeant, "Life began for me when I ceased to admire and began to remember." She also believed that most of the basic material a writer works with is acquired before the age of fifteen. That's the important period, she said. Those years determine whether one's work will be poor and thin or rich and fine. On another occasion she narrowed this time span to the period between the ages of eight and fifteen, thus excluding from her scheme the years she had lived in Virginia.

Although Cather was soaking up impressions that she would use later, there survives from contemporary records only one anecdote of her life on the Divide. This is the memory of friends who saw her one day in 1883 when she was brought into Red Cloud to get new shoes. She was dressed in a leopard-skin fabric coat and hat, which made a lasting visual impression, but what they remembered most vividly was her precocity. As her father encouraged her to show off, she sat in the Miner Brothers' general store and discoursed on Shakespeare, English history, and life in Virginia. This episode in Cather's childhood may have informed the opening scene of O Pioneers! in which little Marie Tovesky, wearing an exotic outfit, is the center of attention in the Hanover (Red Cloud) general store.

The lack of contemporary detail from Cather's months on the farm is compensated for by Jim Burden's memories in My Ántonia. His description of his grandfather's house is very probably based on the home William Cather had built. In real life William returned to Virginia for a visit, leaving the house and farm to Charles, while Caroline, Willa's grandmother, went to live with her other son, George. In the novel the boy Jim wakes up the first morning on the farm and finds himself in a small bedroom on the first floor of the story-and-a-half house built on two levels. His grandmother takes him downstairs to the basement, which opens out onto a draw. In the basement, to the left of the stairs, is the kitchen. To the right is the dining room. Both rooms are plastered and whitewashed—the plaster laid directly upon the earth, as it was in sod-roofed dugouts. The floor is hard cement, and up under the ceiling are little half-windows with white curtains and pots of geraniums. Out behind the house is the farmyard, with a windmill close by the kitchen door. Beyond that are the corncribs, and at the bottom of a shallow draw is a muddy little pond. Farther off, behind the barn, one can see a large cornfield, a sorghum patch, and then nothing but rough, shaggy red grass, most of it as tall as Jim.

A grimmer picture of the view from the farmhouse appears in Cather's early story "A Wagner Matinee." Her memory in 1904 was that outside that door "lay the black pond with the cattle-tracked bluffs . . . the crook-backed ash seedlings where the dish-cloths hung to dry; the gaunt, moulting turkeys

19. Aunt Franc and Uncle George's
farmhouse. Courtesy of WCPMC-
NSHS

20. Site of William Cather's farm.
Courtesy of Bernice Slote

21. Webster Street, Red Cloud, 1889, during rally for William Jennings Bryan. Courtesy of Webster County Historical Museum

22. The Cather house at Third and Cedar, Red Cloud. Courtesy of WCPMC–NSHS

picking up refuse about the kitchen door." And the house itself was "tall, unpainted . . . with weather-curled boards; naked as a tower." Cather is indulging in artistic license when she writes that Jim learned that his grandfather's house was the only wooden building west of Black Hawk, a detail which serves to place the story back in the pioneering era. The pioneers were still there, of course, but most of them long since had built frame houses and abandoned the dugouts that first had served them. Those dugouts still in use when Cather reached Nebraska most likely sheltered animals or were used for storage.

One of the first stories that Cather heard after going to live at Catherton was the account of the suicide of Francis Sadilek, a Bohemian farmer. Readers of *My Ántonia* will recognize this event as the germ of an early episode in which Mr. Shimerda smashes his fiddle and then shoots himself. The story made a strong impression and furnished the plot for Cather's first published tale, "Peter," written during her freshman year in college. She rewrote it once and republished it twice before using it a fourth time in her novel. Some of the other material in *My Ántonia*, as well as material in *O Pioneers!*, "The Bohemian Girl," and early stories that take place on the Divide certainly derive from this time in Cather's life.

Jim Burden's memories of his first months on the Divide are Cather's memories: "All the years that have passed have not dimmed my memory of that first glorious autumn. The new country lay open before me: there were no fences in those days, and I could choose my own way over the grass uplands, trusting the pony to get me home again." As Jim did, she rode along the sunflower-bordered wagon tracks to get the mail at the Catherton post office, which was located in the Cowley farmhouse two or three miles away. She also went on errands and visited the neighbors, the nearest of whom were the German Lambrechts, whose children became her first Nebraska playmates. German settlers are next-farm neighbors both in *My Ántonia* and in *O Pioneers!* Lydia Lambrecht and her mother became lifelong friends, as did Annie Sadilek, the prototype of Ántonia. There is no evidence, however, that Cather met Annie until after she moved into town. Jim Burden remembers: "Sometimes I went south to visit our German neighbors and to admire their catalpa grove, or to see the big elm tree that grew up out of a deep crack in the earth and had a hawk's nest in the branches. Trees were so rare in that country . . . that we used to feel anxious about them, and visit them as if they were persons." There were other times that he rode to visit a huge prairie-dog town, but he had to be on guard against the rattlesnakes that preyed on the prairie dogs. Rattlesnakes were always a menace, and one of the first things Cather noticed after arriving at Catherton was the steel-tipped cane her grandmother carried to kill snakes with when she worked in her garden. One of the memorable episodes of *My Ántonia* is the scene in which Jim kills a huge snake before the fascinated gaze of Ántonia.

The biographer of a writer like Cather, whose memories and experiences are woven into the fabric of her fiction, has to separate the reality from the invention. Cather presents a special problem because she often treats her own life as though it were fiction. In the biographical sketch she provided her publisher she writes: "Willa Cather did not go to school. She had a pony and spent her time riding about the country." This is part of the myth Cather created out of her past, the image of the young girl running wild across the prairie, but the reality is more prosaic. She certainly had a pony, as Jim Burden does, but she also went to school, as he does in the novel. The school district at Catherton had been organized as early as 1876, and by 1883 classes were being held in the township's one-room schoolhouse. Records show that she was enrolled during the winter of 1883–84. She is probably drawing on real experience when Jim Burden says: "After I began to go to the country school, I saw less of the Bohemians. We were sixteen pupils at the sod school-house, and we all came on horseback and brought our dinner." The rural school at Catherton, however, was a frame building that doubled as a church, but it had only a three-month term, so that Cather is no doubt half accurate when she writes: "All the while that she was racing about over the country by day, Willa Cather was reading at night." She had begun her education at home with her grandmother Boak in Virginia, and she certainly continued this program in Nebraska. In addition, she also must have attended the Sunday school in which her Grandmother Cather taught the primary class every week nine months of the year.

Jim Burden's memories, like Cather's, are set down many years after the fact. By then the ugliness of the prairie had been filtered out, leaving only a retouched mythic landscape. When Cather suggests that she and the country had it out together by the end of the first autumn, she is foreshortening considerably. There is ample evidence, especially in her early stories, to show that the glow that lights the country in *O Pioneers!* and *My Ántonia* was a good while in coming. Soon after her first collection of stories, *The Troll Garden*, was published in 1905, she wrote Witter Bynner to explain the bleak tone of her western tales. She guessed then that her early experiences had clung to her, for she had been pretty much depressed as a child by all the ugliness around her. The contrast with Virginia had been stark. One simply could not imagine anything so bleak and desolate as a Nebraska farm in the 1880s, and she remembered coming as close to dying of homesickness as any healthy child could. About eighteen miles from their farm there was one miserable little sluggish stream, which in the spring was about ten feet wide and in the late summer no more than a series of black mudholes. Along its banks grew a few cottonwoods and dwarf elms. She and her little brothers would do almost anything to get to that creek. The country, moreover, was so treeless that when they went to town for supplies, they could hardly wait to reach a halfway point where a row of Lombardy poplars had been planted as a windbreak. And their first Christmas was never to be forgotten. She and her brothers were taken to a Christmas celebration at the Norwegian church. The Christmas tree was a naked little box elder wrapped in green tissue paper cut in fringes to simulate pine needles. In *My Ántonia* the Burdens's hired man, Jake, brings home a real Christmas tree, a five-foot cedar, on which they hang gingerbread animals, strings of popcorn, and brilliantly colored paper figures. Both this fictional Christmas described in 1918 and the letter written in 1905 are probably exaggerations. Certainly the Republican River that flows just south of Red Cloud is a good-sized river, and the Little Blue, which is only five miles away, is not "a miserable little sluggish stream."

Life on the farm came to an end in September 1884, less than eighteen months after it began. Charles Cather moved his family into Red Cloud and opened an office to sell real estate, insurance, and to make farm loans. Just why this move took place cannot be documented, but Jennie Cather, who always played the role of a Virginia lady, could hardly have been happy on an isolated Nebraska farm. During the first summer, when she was pregnant for the fifth time, she felt ill, took to her bed, and subsequently lost her baby. Also, on an occasion when she was lying ill in the kitchen, she looked up and saw smoke curling around the chimney. She screamed for help, and Margie Anderson, the hired girl from Virginia, rushed in and carried her out. The fire did not amount to much, but it scared her. It is also likely that Charles Cather did not find raising corn and hogs, fattening cattle, and breaking virgin prairie in Nebraska as congenial an occupation as raising sheep in Virginia. Furthermore, Willa was going on eleven, and she certainly needed better schooling than she could get in the farming community. Whatever the reasons, Charles Cather advertised a second public sale of his stock and farm equipment on September 11, 1884, and soon thereafter the family settled in Red Cloud, the county seat of Webster County.

CHAPTER 3

Red Cloud

There are three famous towns in America that belong both to fact and to fiction: William Faulkner's Oxford, Mississippi; Mark Twain's Hannibal, Missouri; and Willa Cather's Red Cloud, Nebraska. Time and change have altered the first two, but Willa Cather today could return to the town of her adolescence and feel at home. The house she grew up in is a National Landmark fully restored; the Miners's store on Third and Webster remains intact; the Burlington depot has been preserved; Silas Garber's bank building is the Willa Cather Pioneer Memorial Museum. Houses that once were owned by the prototypes of her fictional characters still shelter Red Cloud residents and attract the attention of a steady stream of year-round visitors. An annual spring conference draws scholars, teachers, business people, and professional men and women to Red Cloud for a day devoted to Cather's works. The town actually has shrunk from its maximum population of 1,839 in the 1890 census, when it was a division point on the Burlington Railroad, and now the road sign at the city limits reports 1,200 inhabitants.

Red Cloud (altitude 1,690 feet) was in 1884 about the size it is today, but it was growing vigorously. It had a roundhouse and railroad shops and was the center of a rapidly expanding farming community. Eight passenger trains a day passed through the town, going and coming between Kansas City, Chicago, and Denver. Because the dining car had not yet been introduced, the trains stopped in Red Cloud, and the passengers got off to eat. The Burlington tracks were laid along the Republican River a mile south of the business block, and the hotel and railroad installations were connected to the town by horsecar. The town, which had been founded before the railroad came, did not grow towards the depot but remained where it was. It consisted of one main business street running north and south with several blocks of stores and offices, and at its widest point from east to west there were perhaps a dozen streets. The State Bank Building, made of native brick, which had been built the year before the Cathers moved into town, dominated the business district. The opera house, which was to be one of the centers of Cather's interest, would be erected over a hardware store just to the north the following year.

Red Cloud was barely into its second decade when the Cathers arrived. The first homestead claims were filed in July 1870 by Silas Garber and others, who built a stockade as a protection from hostile Indians. But there was no need for a stockade, as the Indian wars already had moved farther west. The following year the first businesses were built on the town site—a store, a hotel, an eating house—and the stockade was turned into a school house. The next year, 1872, the town was surveyed and its streets laid out. They named it for Chief Red Cloud of the Oglala tribe, who had become a celebrity in 1870 when he made his first trip to Washington to negotiate with the government on behalf of the Sioux.

Although there were no Indian attacks, the town was beyond the line of established communities, and Indian hunting parties frequently passed through the region in search of buffalo, deer, and elk, then still plentiful. The Fourth of July celebration in 1872 was interrupted by a buffalo stampede, but the supply of game disappeared rapidly as the country filled up with farmers. The next year the first newspaper was started, the *Red Cloud Chief*, and the town prospered despite the early vicissitudes of an Easter blizzard, high winds, and a grasshopper plague that drove out some of the less intrepid pioneers.

Silas Garber, the founder of Red Cloud and a former Union Army officer, went on to greater things—from a sod dugout to the governor's mansion in four years. He became governor in 1874 but returned after serving two terms and built a spacious house on the outskirts of town, where he lived with his young wife until his death. He is an important character in the dramatis personae of Willa Cather's life, for he is the real-life model for Captain Forrester in *A Lost Lady*; and picnics in Garber's Grove, such as the one that opens the novel, were indelible memories. Cather once said that to work well she had to be carefree as if she were thirteen and going for a picnic in Garber's Grove. The Garber house, which burned down in the twenties, "stood on a low hill, nearly a mile east of town; a white house with a wing, and sharp-sloping roofs to shed the snow. It was encircled by porches, too narrow for modern notions of comfort, supported by the fussy, fragile pillars of that time, when every honest stick of timber was tortured by the turning-lathe into something hideous. Stripped of its vines and denuded of its shrubbery, the house would probably have been ugly enough. It stood close into a fine cottonwood grove that threw sheltering arms to left and right and grew all down the hillside behind it. Thus placed on the hill, against its bristling grove, it was the first thing one saw on coming into Sweet Water by rail, and the last thing one saw on departing."

This is the description of the house written by Cather at the age of forty-nine, but to the thirteen-year-old girl in 1886 it was a place of infinite charm and elegance. It was the center of a more expansive life-style than anything else she knew in Red Cloud. When Burlington executives traveled back and forth along their railroad, they often stopped off to visit the Garbers. The Garbers entertained graciously, and the captain became in Cather's mind the archetypal pioneer.

Once Cather began her literary career, Red Cloud entered the fictional landscape of America. Again and again the setting of her novels and stories is Red Cloud. It is the Sweet Water of *A Lost Lady*, the Frankfort of *One of Ours*, the Haverford of *Lucy Gayheart*, the Black Hawk of *My Ántonia*, and the Hanover of *O Pioneers!* In *The Song of the Lark* she places Moonstone in Colorado, but the topography of the town is still that of Red Cloud. It is also the locale of two of the stories in *Obscure Destinies* and of a good many of her early tales written during her apprentice period. Local residents will show you where Doctor Archie lived, where Wick Cutter planned to rape Ántonia, where the Harling family once resided and a descendant still lives.

As Cather describes Moonstone in *The Song of the Lark*: "The main business street ran, of course, through the center of the town. To the west of this street lived all the people who were, as Tillie Kronborg said, 'in society.' Sylvester Street, the third parallel with Main Street on the west, was the longest in town, and the best dwellings were built along it. Far out at the north end, nearly a mile from the court-house and its cottonwood grove, was Dr. Archie's house. . . . The Methodist Church was in the centre of town, facing the courthouse square. The Kronborgs lived half a mile south of the church, on the long street that stretched out like an arm to the depot settlement. This was the first street west of Main, and was built up only on one side. . . . The sidewalk which ran in front of the Kronborgs' house was the one continuous sidewalk to the depot, and all the train men and round-house employees passed the front gate every time they came uptown. . . . In the part of Moonstone that lay east of Main Street, toward the deep ravine which, farther south, wound by Mexican town, lived all the humbler citizens, the people who voted but did not run for office. The houses . . .

nestled modestly behind their cottonwoods and Virginia creeper; their occupants had no social pretensions to keep up."

Housing was scarce when the Cathers moved into Red Cloud, and they had to make do with a house that was too cramped for four children, parents, grandmother, servant girl, and a cousin. It was a great contrast to the spacious Willow Shade in Virginia. But the house, as it stands on the southwest corner of Third and Cedar, just a block away from the business section, is an attractive frame building surrounded by an ample, well-shaded corner lot. In *The Song of the Lark*, as Dr. Archie and the Rev. Mr. Kronborg approached the house, "they turned into another street and saw before them lighted windows; a low story-and-a-half house, with a wing built on at the right and a kitchen addition at the back, everything a little on the slant—roofs, windows, and doors."

Downstairs, besides a sitting room, dining room, and kitchen, there are bedrooms that served the parents and small children. Grandma Boak's room, described in "Old Mrs. Harris," had to serve as a passageway between dining room and kitchen. Up a narrow stairway from the kitchen one climbs to the large unfinished attic, where all the older children lived in a kind of dormitory. In "The Best Years" this attic is the private world of the children "where there were no older people poking about to spoil things." It runs the whole length of the house, and its charm for the children was that it was unlined. "No plaster, no beaver-board lining; just the roof shingles, supported by long, unplaned, splintery rafters that sloped from the sharp roofpeak down to the floor of the attic. Bracing these long roof rafters were cross rafters on which one could hang things." Up the center of this attic passed two brick chimneys "going up in neat little stairsteps from the plank floor to the shingle roof—and out of it to the stars." The beds stood in a row as in a hospital ward, and sometimes during a driving winter snowstorm frozen flakes drifted in through the cracks and sprinkled the beds.

When Cather grew too old to share the dormitory with her brothers, an ell-shaped gable wing of the main attic was partitioned off to give her a private room. This is the room that Thea Kronborg occupies in *The Song of the Lark* when she begins to make her own money by giving piano lessons. This room, also unplastered, was "snugly lined with soft pine. The ceiling was so low that a grown person could reach it with the palm of the hand, and it sloped down on either side. There was only one window, but it was a double one and went to the floor." Cather worked in Cook's drugstore to earn the wallpaper, given to her in lieu of wages, that she put on the wall of this room. This paper, red and brown roses on a yellowish background, still lines the walls, though it is faded by time and weather. In this room she kept her books and could escape from the rest of the family.

It was probably about the time the family moved to town that Cather produced her first piece of writing that has survived. This is an essay praising dogs and denigrating cats and seems to have been part of a debate judged by her grandfather. The misspellings are Cather's: "The dog is a very intelligent animal. . . . The nature of most dogs is kind, noble and generous. O! how different from the snarling, spitting crul cat. . . . Newfoundland dogs are also famous for their way of saving the lives of people when drowning. And the St. Brenards are often trained in Switzerland to find travelers in the snow and carry them to a place of safety. . . . Lord Byron, one of our greatest poets wrote a beautiful elegy on a dog, who ever wrote anything on a *Cat*? Did you ever see a tall massive dog with curly hair bright eyes and a knowing air? Did you ever see a poor thin scraggy cat, with dirty hair dull green eyes and a drooping tail. If so I leave it to your common sense to awnser for I know you will say the noble majestic dog." At the bottom of the page of this essay, in Grandfather Cather's hand and above his signature, is the word "defeated." Although Mozart was composing symphonies at the same age, Cather was still years away from discovering her vocation, and even then her development was very slow. But she was an omnivorous reader from the beginning, and hundreds of books of all kinds stoked the fires of her young mind. The Cathers had brought their books from Virginia, the nearby Wieners had a big collection, and Willa soon began to put together her own library.

Cather's serious schooling also began when the family moved into town. During her first year in Red Cloud she was put into Gertrude Scherer's class, a year that left little impression; but the next year she drew Miss King (later Mrs. Eva J. Case), the principal of the school, "a stalwart young woman with a great deal of mirth in her eyes and a very sympathetic, kind voice," Cather remembered in 1909. "I was a pupil in her A. grade. I am very sure that Miss King was the first person whom I ever cared a great deal for outside of my own family. I had been in her class only a few weeks when I wanted more than anything else in the world to please her. During the rest of that year, when I succeeded in pleasing her I was quite happy; when I failed to please her there was only one thing I cared about and that was to try again and make her forget my mistakes. I have always looked back on that year as one of the happiest I have ever spent. . . . As I went through the high school she always helped and advised me; she even tried very hard to teach me Algebra at night, but not even Miss King—who could do almost anything—could do that." At the end of her life, when Cather wrote "The Best Years," she drew an affectionate portrait of Miss King as Evangeline Knightly. "Miss Knightly was a charm-

ing person to meet—and an unusual type in a new country: oval face, small
head delicately set (the oval chin tilting inward instead of the square chin
thrust out), hazel eyes, a little blue, a little green, tiny dots of brown. . . .
Somehow these splashes of colour made light—and warmth. When she
laughed, her eyes positively glowed with humour, and in each oval cheek a
roguish dimple came magically to the surface."

Two other teachers who left their mark on Cather were the A. K. Goudys.
Mrs. Goudy was the principal of the high school and became a particular
friend and correspondent for forty years. Mr. Goudy was county superintendent of schools and taught Latin. Later when he became state superintendent
of schools, the Goudys moved to Lincoln while Cather was a student at the
University of Nebraska. When Cather visited Italy for the first time in 1908,
she wrote Mrs. Goudy that she had seen in the Naples museum the wonderful
head of Caesar that had illustrated the high school text of Caesar's commen-
taries she had studied under Mr. Goudy. Edith Lewis writes in her memoir:
"Both the Goudys became deeply attached to this new pupil, so unlike the
run of Red Cloud boys and girls; with her astonishing familiarity with
classical English literature, and her inability to spell correctly; her actual love
of Latin, and the great gaps in her knowledge of ordinary things every grade
school child knew; above all, with a personality so striking in its originality,
daring, vital force, that no one could possibly ignore her; she awakened either
strong liking or hostility and disapproval."

Cather's extracurricular reading during her adolescent years was more
important than her formal education. Red Cloud may have been an instant
prairie town, but it contained a fair share of cultivated people. Among them
were Mr. and Mrs. Charles Wiener, educated European Jews who had
immigrated to the United States and settled in Nebraska. The Wieners, who
owned a store in Red Cloud, lived around the corner from the Cathers on
Seward Street. They both spoke French and German, and when they discovered their neighbors' daughter had insatiable appetite for books, they
introduced her to French and German literature in translation and gave her
the run of their large library. The relationship between the Wieners and
Cather appears rather accurately drawn in "Old Mrs. Harris." Although the
title character is Grandma Boak, the story contains an engaging portrait of
the Wieners and the artist as adolescent. As Vickie Templeton sits in the
Rosens' library one hot summer afternoon, Mrs. Rosen observes her: "She
wasn't pretty, yet Mrs. Rosen found her attractive. She liked her sturdy
build, and the steady vitality that glowed in her rosy skin and dark blue eyes,
— even gave a springy quality to her curly reddish-brown hair, which she
still wore in a single braid down her back. Mrs. Rosen liked to have Vickie

about because she was never listless or dreamy or apathetic. A half-smile nearly always played about her lips and eyes, and it was there because she was pleased with something, not because she wanted to be agreeable. Even a half-smile made her cheeks dimple. She had what her mother called 'a happy disposition.'"

Vickie, for her part, loved the Rosens' cool, darkened library, where she could slip in and read or take a sofa pillow and lie on the floor looking up at the pictures and feeling a happy, pleasant excitement from the heat and glare outside and the deep shadow and quiet within. There was no other house the least like the Rosens': "It was the nearest thing to an art gallery and a museum that the Templetons had ever seen. All the rooms were carpeted alike. . . . The deep chairs were upholstered in dark blue velvet. The walls were hung with engravings. . . . There were a number of water-colour sketches, made in Italy by Mr. Rosen himself when he was a boy." And there was the library: it had a complete set of Waverly novels in German, "thick, dumpy little volumes bound in tooled leather[,] . . . many French books, and some of the German classics done in English such as Coleridge's translation of Schiller's *Wallenstein*." Cather was lucky in having the Wieners next door, and apparently they realized her extraordinary talent and encouraged her to go to college, as the Rosens do Vickie Templeton.

The Wiener library was one resource; the family bookcase was another. If the constant commotion in the little Cather house was not conducive to reading, Cather had her own room in the attic to withdraw to. There she read constantly and indiscriminately, good books, trashy books, whatever came her way. "Ray Kennedy [Thea Kronborg's brakeman friend] on his way from the depot to his boarding house, often looked up and saw Thea's light burning when the rest of the house was dark." The evidence in Cather's early writing during her years of journalism is that she had ranged widely in her reading—so widely that no brief summary can do justice to her huge, eclectic consumption of books. Like Vickie Templeton, she had not been taught to respect what the world called masterpieces; she cared about a book only if it took hold of her.

Many of the Cather family books have survived, and one can assume that she read everything in the collection. Among these books are complete editions of the standard nineteenth-century classics: Dickens, Scott, Thackeray, Poe, Hawthorne, Ruskin, Emerson, and Carlyle. There also are volumes of Shakespeare and Bunyan, anthologies of poetry, the works of Thomas Campbell and Thomas Moore, some translations of Latin and Greek classics, religious books, books on the Civil War, bound volumes of the *Century* and ladies' magazines; and although now lost, there once were copies

of Ben Jonson's plays and Byron's poems. Finally, there were popular romances, such as the novels of Ouida, which Mrs. Cather liked.

Fairly recent novels such as *Anna Karenina*, one of Cather's favorites,
probably came from the drugstore where she worked and took her pay in
merchandise. She was fourteen, she remembered, when paperbound copies
of Tolstoy, rendered into indifferent English, fell into her hands: *Anna
Karenina*, *The Cossacks*, "The Death of Ivan Ilych," and "The Kreutzer Sonata." For three years, she said later with characteristic exaggeration, she read
Tolstoy all the time, backward and forward. What she wanted at that age was
vitality. She wanted to read about life, about characters who were in the midst
of struggle. She did not pay any attention to style or form. She wanted color;
she wanted to be thrilled; she wanted excitement.

Some of the books that she collected into her own library also have
survived. They are all carefully labeled "Private Library" and numbered. The
earliest dated volume in the group is a battered copy of the *Iliad* in Pope's
translation with the year 1888 inside the cover and the number 70. Other titles
of the same period are Jacob Abbot's *Histories of Cyrus the Great and Alexander
the Great*, George Eliot's *The Spanish Gypsy*, Carlyle's *Sartor Resartus*, Alexander Winchell's *Sketches of Creation*, a paperback edition of *Antony and
Cleopatra*, and *Pilgrim's Progress*, the book she first encountered when
Grandma Boak had read it to her in Virginia. She later told Edith Lewis that
she had read it eight times during one of her first winters in Nebraska. She
also must have had a copy of *The Adventures of Huckleberry Finn*, which came
out the year the Cathers moved to Red Cloud. In the thirties she reported
rereading that novel for what she thought was the twentieth time.

She certainly was drawing on her own memories of childhood reading
when she wrote a book column in Pittsburgh in 1897. Then she recommended "that dear old book" *The Count of Monte Cristo* and another favorite,
Dinah Mulock's *John Halifax, Gentleman*. She also included, with *Pilgrim's
Progress*, a second book "essential to a child's library," *The Swiss Family
Robinson*. "Any child who has not read these has missed a part of his or her
childhood." And she added to the list the works of Howard Pyle, especially
Otto of the Silver Hand, from which a child could get a "very fair idea [of] what
that phrase 'the Middle Ages' meant." Pyle remained one of her heroes, and
even before she met him later as a co-worker on *McClure's Magazine*, she sent
him a copy of *The Troll Garden*, inscribed as follows: "Will Mr. Howard Pyle
accept through me the love of seven big and little children to whom he taught
the beauty of language and of line, and to whom, in a desert place, he sent the
precious message of Romance."

Outside of her formal education and her leisure reading a number of Red

Cloud people contributed to the growth of her mind. Her fondness for visiting the immigrant farm women on the Divide already has been noted, and she sought out interesting adults wherever she could find them. Like Thea Kronborg in *The Song of the Lark*, she had many adult friends. Dr. McKeeby, the family physician, was a particular one. He pulled her through a childhood illness that may have been polio (though if it was, she was left with no paralysis), much as Dr. Archie ministers to young Thea in the novel. Dr. McKeeby looked after the entire family for many years and was no doubt partly responsible for Cather's early ambition to study medicine. In pursuit of this interest she often went on calls with Dr. McKeeby and later put him into *The Song of the Lark* as the childhood friend and subsequent sponsor of the heroine's artistic career. Cather also made calls with another Red Cloud physician, Dr. Robert Damerell, and on one occasion she administered choloroform while the doctor amputated a boy's leg. Cather told an interviewer years later: "How I loved the long rambling buggy rides we used to take. . . . We went over the same roads this summer [1921]. I could tell who lived at every place and all about the ailments of his family. The old country doctor and I used to talk over his cases. I was determined then to be a surgeon."

Her interest in adults is well illustrated in "Two Friends," one of the stories in *Obscure Destinies*. Based on a childhood memory, the tale is narrated by a young girl who hangs about the general store to hear Mr. Dillon and Mr. Trueman talk. She liked to listen to those two because their talk was the only interesting conversation in the town. The older men always talked about politics and business—nothing else—and the young men's talk was empty-headed and supposed to be funny, but she found it utterly boring and banal. It was scarcely speech, she remembered, but noises, snorts, giggles, yawns, and sneezes, with a few abbreviated words and slang expressions. Mr. Dillon, the banker and proprietor of the general store, and Mr. Trueman, a cattleman, sat out each night in spring and summer on the boardwalk that ran along the long brick wall of Dillon's store and carried on their conversations.

She also liked the store and the brick wall and the sidewalk because they were solid and well built, and admired Dillon and Trueman for the same reason. They were secure and established, and they talked about everything—crops and the farmers they dealt with, trips they had taken, plays they had seen. Their talk was a window on a larger world. She found many pretexts for lingering near them, and they never seemed to mind her hanging about. She would sit on the edge of the sidewalk with her feet hanging down playing jacks. In the story the two friends finally split over the issue of William Jennings Bryan and free silver, something that could not have happened until after Cather had left Nebraska, but in real-life they were Mr. Richardson and Mr. Miner, the latter a neighbor of the Cathers and owner of the general store where young Willa did indeed hang about a great deal. Whether there is any basis in fact for the story, other than the conversations and the friendship, the record does not say.

Another of the girl's adult friends was William Ducker, an educated Englishman who was perhaps the most important influence of all her "friends of childhood." Ducker came to Red Cloud the year after the Cathers and clerked in his brother's store. He was generally regarded by his family as a failure, but that did not seem to bother him. He had a passionate interest in Latin, Greek, and science, and soon after he arrived Cather sought him out and began reading the classics with him. She was already studying Latin and probably began the study of Greek at this time. Under his guidance she read Virgil, Ovid, the *Iliad*, and the Odes of Anacreon; and after she went to the university, where she continued her Latin and Greek, she read with him during the summers. They also had long talks together about good and evil, life and death, and all the big questions. Ducker understood and valued his pupil and left an indelible memory. He also fueled her interest in science by inviting her to help him conduct experiments in a laboratory he built in his house. But the relationship ended abruptly during her second summer home from the university. One afternoon she was walking home with him from his brother's store when he said, "It is just as though the light were going out, Willie." A few minutes after she had left him, one of his children came running after her to call her back. She returned to find him dead on the couch of his living room with a copy of the *Iliad* open on the floor beside him. This death was the first great loss of her life.

Her lifelong devotion to the classics, which began during her Red Cloud adolescence, was paralleled by an absorbing interest in music. The person most responsible for this interest was Mrs. Julia Miner, whose husband was the Mr. Dillon of "Two Friends." Mrs. Miner had been born in Christiana (now Oslo), the daughter of the oboe soloist in Ole Bull's Royal Norwegian Orchestra. As a child she had gone to rehearsals and concerts and studied music, and when the vicissitudes of life made her the wife of a Nebraska merchant, she installed a new Chickering piano in her Red Cloud parlor and continued her music. When Mrs. Miner played for her own children, she gave Willa her first experience of serious music. Young Cather loved to listen to her play and to hear about her musical childhood in Norway.

The importance of Mrs. Miner in Cather's life is clearly discernible in *My Ántonia*, where she appears as Jim Burden's neighbor Mrs. Harling: "Mrs. Harling was short and square and sturdy-looking, like her house. . . . Her face was rosy and solid, with bright, twinkling eyes and a stubborn little chin. She was quick to anger, quick to laughter, and jolly from the depths of her soul." Jim liked to cross the street to the Harlings' house because it always was a gay, noisy place except when Mr. Harling was home. Someone was always at the piano. Julia practiced regularly every day. Frances played when she came home from her job in her father's store. Sally played after she got home from school, and even Nina, the youngest, played. Jim recalls: "Mrs. Harling had studied the piano under a good teacher, and somehow she managed to practise every day. I soon learned that if I were sent over on an errand and found Mrs. Harling at the piano, I must sit down and wait quietly until she turned to me." He remembered her vividly as she played—a short, square person planted firmly on the stool, her little fat hands moving quickly and neatly over the keys while her eyes were fixed on the music with intelligent concentration. Mrs. Miner died while *My Ántonia* was being written, and when Cather wrote Carrie Miner Sherwood a letter of condolence, she said she had tried hard to recall certain tricks of voice and gesture in creating Mrs. Harling. Her character, she said, was a clear little snapshot of Mrs. Miner as she first remembered her, and she added that there had been a little of Mrs. Miner in almost every mother she ever had done.

The Miner daughters, who were Cather's childhood companions, became lifelong friends. Mary, who appears in *My Ántonia* as Julia, "the musical one," and Carrie, the older one who worked in the store, remained in Red Cloud, and Cather visited them during her many trips back to Nebraska in later years. Irene, little Nina in the book, married and moved to Chicago. Her home became a stopping point for Cather between New York and Red Cloud. She corresponded regularly with both Carrie and Irene, and the dedication of *My Ántonia* is to "Carrie and Irene Miner / In memory of affections old and true." The Miner household was also of singular importance in another respect, for there Cather met Annie Sadilek, who came in from the farm to work as a hired girl for the Miners and remained her friend for life. Thirty years later she sat for the portrait of Ántonia Shimerda in what many think is Cather's best novel.

Despite the fact that Cather developed a passion for music, she had no formal music education and did not even try to learn to play the piano. Jennie Cather hired an itinerant German music teacher named Schindelmeisser to give her daughter lessons, but the effort was a failure. Harmony, counterpoint, the technical mastery of an instrument, held no attraction for her. Music to her was an emotional release, not an intellectual exercise. She nearly drove her teacher mad when he tried to give her lessons, and when Schindelmeisser told Mrs. Cather that she was wasting her money, she told him to keep coming. Her daughter, she said, was getting a lot out of listening to him play and talking to him about his musical life in the old country.

This alcoholic, derelict musician made a lasting impression, for he became Professor Wunsch in *The Song of the Lark*, the teacher who gives Thea Kronborg her first music lessons and bequeaths to her his cherished score of *Orfeo* and the desire to become an artist. "Wunsch was short and stocky, with something rough and bearlike about his shoulders. His face was a dark, bricky red, deeply creased rather than wrinkled, and the skin was like loose leather over his neckband—he wore a brass collar button but no collar. His hair was cropped close; iron-gray bristled on a bullet-like head. His eyes were always suffused and bloodshot. He had a coarse, scornful mouth, and irregular, yellow teeth, much worn at the edges. His hands were square and red, seldom clean, but always alive, impatient, even sympathetic." The actual Schindelmeisser had wandered into Red Cloud "from God knew where," and Mrs. Miner, who recognized in him a first-rate musician, had engaged him to teach her daughters. If he could not get young Cather to practice her scales, he, like the fictional Wunsch, must nevertheless have left something important in his talks with his pupil. In her later career as music critic and creator of fictional musicians Cather relied on instinct, intuition, and feeling to get her through.

Cather's adult friends certainly knew that she was a remarkable girl, but the average Red Cloud resident probably thought of her as that "show-off" tomboy Cather youngster. She was not disposed to conceal her talents during her Red Cloud years, and she must have been rather conspicuous in that small community. Half a century later she would go to any length to avoid publicity, but as an adolescent she was gregarious and fond of people. She was conspicuous not only because of her natural gifts, but also because she developed a wide streak of nonconformity. The long hair that Vickie Templeton wears in "Old Mrs. Harris" was not Willa Cather's hairstyle. Before she was thirteen she had cut her hair shorter than most boys and was signing her name William Cather, Jr., or Wm. Cather, M.D. She expressed a vast contempt for skirts and dresses, wore boys' clothes, a derby, and carried a cane. She wrote in a friend's album that slicing toads was her hobby, doing fancy work a real misery, and amputating limbs perfect happiness. Such a child must have taken her knocks from the local busybodies.

For several years, until after Cather left Red Cloud to attend the University of Nebraska, she defied Victorian norms of behavior for adolescent girls. Her goal in life was to become a surgeon, but that option was not open to girls, or so she must have thought, living in a little prairie town. As a result, she refused to be a girl, adopted male values and attitudes, and continued the tomboy life she had led in her prepubescent years in Virginia and on the farm at Catherton. Her father was always indulgent, and her mother, who no doubt deplored the male masquerade, nevertheless let her develop in her own way. What effect this denial of her sex had on her psychological development, her sexual orientation, and her life as an artist is a matter of considerable interest. Contemporary readers, especially feminist critics, have speculated at length on these matters. Did this pattern of adolescent behavior foreshadow, as some critics think, a latent or covert lesbianism? Did it make inevitable her remaining single, her selection of women as her closest friends, her creation of strong, resourceful heroines? Did it produce the large number of unhappy marriages in her fiction? Did it engender a fear of sex? Available data give no objective answers.

Cather's contempt for the role an adolescent girl was expected to play— learning to cook and sew, keep house, and care for children—may be seen in the way she contrasts the immigrant farm girls with the town girls in *My Ántonia*. The farm girls, who worked in the fields like men, were strong, vigorous, alive; and when they came to town to live, they developed a "positive carriage and freedom of movement" that "made them conspicuous among Black Hawk women. . . . physical exercise was thought rather inelegant for the daughters of well-to-do families. . . . they stayed indoors in winter because of the cold, and in summer because of the heat. When one danced with them, their bodies never moved inside their clothes." Their muscles seemed to ask only not to be disturbed.

Cather's youthful identification with male norms is further illustrated in an autobiographical story published the year after she graduated from college. Here she creates a very masculine young woman as protagonist in "Tommy, the Unsentimental" and places her tale in a town like Red Cloud. Tommy, who has a head for business and saves a run on a bank with a twenty-five-mile whirlwind bike ride, is a crony of her father's business friends. "She was just one of them; she played whist and billiards with them, and made their cocktails for them, not scorning to take one herself occasionally." She also is described as having "a peculiarly unfeminine mind that could not escape meeting and acknowledging a logical conclusion." In contrast with the masculine Tommy is Jessica, Tommy's girlfriend and rival, "a dainty, white, languid bit of a thing, who used violet perfumes and carried a sunshade." In the story's denouement Tommy tells her effete, ineffectual boyfriend Jay to marry Jessica: "We have been playing a nice little game, and now it's time to quit. . . . She's your kind."

When Cather was thirteen, a political skirmish took place in Red Cloud involving her father and some of her adult friends. Dr. McKeeby had been

23. Cather as Hiawatha. Courtesy of
    WCPMC-NSHS

24. Cather with boy's haircut, about
    age 13. Courtesy of WCPMC-NSHS

25. Cather in Confederate Army cap.
    Courtesy of WCPMC-NSHS

26. Cather's attic bedroom. Courtesy of Lucia Woods, photographer

27. Julia Erickson Miner, the model for Mrs. Harling in *My Ántonia*. Courtesy of Jennie Miner Reiher and WCPMC–NSHS

28. Irene Miner and her dog, Bert. Courtesy of WCPMC-NSHS

29. Dr. McKeeby, who is Dr. Archie in *The Song of the Lark*. Courtesy of WCPMC-NSHS

30. Carrie Miner. Courtesy of WCPMC-NSHS

31. The cast for *Beauty and the Beast* with Cather in top hat. Courtesy of WCPMC-NSHS

elected mayor and Charles Cather alderman. When the county treasurer was accused of misappropriating public funds, Willa's father was put on a committee to investigate. Dr. McKeeby, Charles Wiener, James Miner, and Silas Garber, all backing Charles Cather, carried on a running battle in the local press with supporters of the treasurer. This spectacle of grass-roots politicking, which young Cather observed firsthand, may have inspired the children in the neighborhood to enact a juvenile version of local government.

The result was the construction of a play town called "Sandy Point," built of packing boxes from the Miners' store along the south fence of the Cather yard under cottonwood and wild plum trees. Charles Cather ordered several loads of sand, which Willa's brothers shoveled out to make a main street, and each child set up shop in one of the boxes. Willa was elected mayor. Margie Miner was an alderman; Jessica Cather was postmistress; Mary Miner kept a candy shop; another child ran a hotel in a piano box. They carried on transactions with Confederate money the Cathers had brought from Virginia. This childhood playtime is commemorated in one of Cather's early stories, "The Way of the World" (1896), in which an all-boys town of packing boxes is invaded by Mary Eliza Jenkins. Mary Eliza—who pesters the boys to be admitted to their community until they give in, against their better judgment—takes over the town, sows dissension in the ranks, and then decamps. The story no doubt owes something to *Tom Sawyer*, but it anticipates interestingly the child's world of Crane's *Whilomville Stories* and Tarkington's *Penrod*. The ironic tone of the narrative never gets serious, but the comparison of Mary Eliza's machinations to Eve's role in man's fall suggests Cather's continuing distrust of her sex.

For any child of energy, imagination, and intelligence, drama offers a natural outlet. As soon as the family moved into town, young Cather began to take part in amateur theatricals. The *Red Cloud Argus* reported on May 14, 1885, that the Sunday school concert at the Baptist church had featured Miss Willie Cather, who "electrified the audience with elocutionary powers." And the following month there was a similar item. The performance perhaps was her rendition of *Hiawatha*, which she was in the habit of giving in a costume complete with bow and arrow. By the time she was thirteen, she was making up and staging her own plays in the upstairs attic and in the Miners' parlor. When she was fourteen, she and the Miner girls put on a play in the new opera house for the benefit of the victims of the blizzard of '88. They presented *Beauty and the Beast*, with Margie Miner as the beauty, Mary Miner as the beast, and Willie Cather, dressed in suit, hat, and waxed mustache, as the merchant-father. The *Red Cloud Chief* was much impressed with her performance. It was characteristic that she should have played a male role, which she did again when she dressed in black velvet knee pants and appeared as the old alchemist in the Merchants' Carnival. She represented Cook's drugstore, where she sometimes worked.

The opera house was perhaps the one place in town that held the most attraction for Cather. There she was introduced to the world of the theater, and though the quality of the road shows that visited Red Cloud must have been mediocre, the memory of plays and light operas there was golden. She wrote in 1929 that "half a dozen times during each winter . . . a traveling stock company settled down at the local hotel and thrilled and entertained us for a week." It was a wonderful week for the children. The excitement began when the advance man posted the bills on the lumberyard fence and the windows of the drug and grocery stores. Cather and her friends used to stand for hours studying every word on the posters and trying to decide whether they could get their parents to let them go every other night or just on opening and closing nights. No child ever got to go every night unless his father owned stock in the opera house. If the company arrived at night, she continued, "My chums and I always walked a good half mile to the depot . . . to see that train come in. . . . We found it delightful to watch a theatrical company alight, pace the platform while their baggage was being sorted, and then drive off—the men in the hotel bus, the women in the 'hack.' If by any chance one of the show ladies carried a little dog with a blanket on, that simply doubled our pleasure." Then the children invented pretexts to visit the hotel to see the actors lounging about.

One particular production that she recalled was Frank Lindon's performance in *The Count of Monte Cristo*: "When old Frank Lindon in a frilled shirt and a velvet coat blazing with diamonds, stood in the drawing room of Mme. Danglars' and revealed his identity to Mme. de Morcery, his faithless Mercedes, when she cowered and made excuses, and he took out a jeweled snuff box with a much powdered hand, raised his eyebrows, permitted his lip to curl, and said softly and bitterly, 'a fidelity of six months!' then we children were not in the opera house in Red Cloud; we were in Mme. Danglars' salon in Paris in the middle of lives so very different from our own. Living people were making us feel things, and it is through the feelings, not at all through the eyes, that one's imagination is fired. . . . It did us good to weep at 'East Lynne,' even if the actress was fairly bad and the play absurd. Children have about a hundred years of unlived life wound up in them, and they want to be living some of it."

Cather lived intensively during her high school years. When she wasn't doing her homework, reading the classics with Will Ducker, staging plays in the attic, or making calls with Drs. McKeeby and Damerell, she was writing up high school news for the *Argus*. She used her father's office while he was at the courthouse making title abstracts or out of town on business. She had her own desk where she wrote and studied. People of the community who came in to do business with her father often stayed to talk to her. They would tell her of "personal affairs in the way that grown-ups will disclose to a child matters which they would not discuss with a mature person." All these experiences, plus her incessant reading, prepared her mind for her future vocation.

She also was accumulating memories and experiences in the countryside surrounding Red Cloud. There were picnics in the fine cottonwood grove adjacent to Governor Garber's house; there were visits to Uncle George's farm at Catherton; there were outings at the Miners' ranch southwest of town, which still had a well-preserved sod house on the property. The most exciting place of all was the Republican River, just outside of town, and in particular one spot in the river known as Far Island. "Far Island is an oval sand bar, half a mile in length and perhaps a hundred yards wide, which lies about two miles up from Empire City in a turbid little Nebraska river." Such is the opening sentence of a story, "The Treasure of Far Island," published in 1902. The children, especially Willa and her brothers Roscoe and Douglass, loved that island, and there they played Long John Silver and Jim Hawkins, for *Treasure Island*, one of their favorite books, had appeared in 1883. They camped on the island and built their fires on the dazzling, white, ripple-marked sandy beach. The center of the island was thick with thousands of yellow-green willows and cottonwood seedlings, brilliantly green even in the hottest summer weather. The island was no-man's-land, but every summer a new chief claimed it, and Cather's memory also kept a tight hold on it. The island appears not only in "The Treasure of Far Island," but also in one of her most successful early stories, "The Enchanted Bluff" (1909). In the latter the boys of the town camp on the island during the last night of summer vacation. They are about to scatter for good, and the male narrator soon will leave to begin teaching school. As they lie on the sand looking up at the stars, they plan someday to climb the Enchanted Bluff somewhere down in New Mexico. The narrator of the tale wakes early the next morning, and as he looks at the other sleeping boys, he thinks of their aspirations. "It was still dark, but the sky was blue with the last wonderful azure of night. The stars glistened like crystal globes and trembled as if they shone through a depth of clear water. Even as I watched, they began to pale and the sky brightened. Day came suddenly, almost instantaneously. I turned for another look at the blue night, and it was gone." So were youth and the young days on Far Island. In her first book, *April Twilights* (1903), the dedicatory poem, addressed to her brothers Roscoe and Douglass, recalls

> the three who lay and planned at moonrise,
> On an island in a western river,
> Of the conquest of the world together.

Those golden days ended for Cather in June 1890, when she graduated from high school and prepared to enter the university at Lincoln. Her childhood was over, though she was only sixteen and a half. The bright Medusa was drawing her from the anonymity of the prairie town to a larger world of striving and achievement. Her parting message to Red Cloud, which both attracted and repelled her, was her graduation speech, "Superstition *versus* Investigation." She was one of three graduates that year, the second class to finish Red Cloud High School. Her remarks followed those of John Tulleys, who discoursed on "Self-Advertising," and Alex Bently, who asserted that "New Times Demand New Measures and New Men." Young Tulleys believed "a man should blow his own trumpet and the louder and longer he can blow the deeper impression he will make. . . . Taking *by any means* as a motto, a shrewd man will succeed in any business"—and on and on he went, sounding like a preview of Cather's money-grubbing Bayless Wheeler in *One of Ours* or the opportunistic Ivy Peters in *A Lost Lady*. The reporter for the *Red Cloud Chief* thought that John would "make his way to fame" and that Alex also would go far; but he was silent about the prospects of Willa Cather.

Her oration, however, is a remarkable performance for a youngster of her time and place. Although the *Chief* did not predict a bright future, it did publish her speech, which was obviously an answer to the small-town critics who had criticized her interests in biology, medicine, and vivisection. It is a ringing defense of scientific inquiry and ranges from the dawn of history to the present moment. As Jim Burden says of his high school graduation oration in *My Ántonia*, "It stated with fervor a great many things I had lately discovered." This essay, which never before has been reprinted in full, is her first extant piece of serious writing. It antedates by nearly a year the well-known Carlyle essay that bowled over her English teacher in Lincoln:

All human history is a record of an emigration, an exodus from barbarism to civilization. From the very outset of this pilgrimage of humanity, superstition and investigation have been contending for the mastery. Since investigation first led man forth on that great search for truth which has prompted all his progress, superstition, the stern Pharoah of his former bondage, has followed him retarding every step of advancement.

Then began a contest which will end only with time, for it is the warfare between radicalism and conservatism, truth and error, which underlies every man's life and happiness. The ancient orientals were highly civilized people but were dreamers and theorists who delved into the mystical and metaphysical, leaving the more practical questions unanswered, and were subject to the evils of tyranny and priestcraft. Those sacred books of the east we today regard as half-divine. We are not apt to think as we read those magnificent flights of metaphor that the masses of the people who read and believed them knew nothing of figures. It is the confounding of the literal and the figurative that has made atheists and fanatics throughout the ages.

All races have worshipped nature, the ruder as the cause, the more enlightened as the effect of one grand cause. Worship as defined by Carlyle is unmeasured wonder, but there are two kinds of wonder, that born of fear and that of admiration, slavish fear is never reverence.

The Greeks, lacking the intense religious fervor of the Orient, entertained broader views. Their standard of manhood was one of practical worth. They allowed no superstition, religious, political or social, to stand between them and the truth and suffered exile, imprisonment and death for the right of opinion and investigation.

Perhaps the strongest conflict ever known between the superstitious and investigative forces of the world raged in the dark ages. Earth seemed to return to its original chaotic state and there was no one to cry "fiat lux." The old classic creeds fell crashing into the boundless past and the new church was a scene of discord. All the great minds were crushed, for men were still ruled by the iron scepter of fear and it was essential that they should remain ignorant. Superstition has ever been the curse of the church, and until she can acknowledge that since her principles are true, no scientific truth can contradict them, she will never realize her full strength. There is another book of God than that of scriptural revelation, a book written in chapters of creation upon the pages of the universe bound by mystery. When we are mortal [morbid?] enough to say that the world degenerates with the age, we forget that the heroes and sages of history were the exceptions and not the rule. What age since the world's foundation can leave such a record across the paper [pages?] of time as the 19th century? What is it that characterizes our age and gives the present the superiority; not skill in handicraft, for the great masters of art lie sleeping among the founders of Attica and Italy; not in clearness of depth of thought, for our literary or philosophical lights are gleams from the fires of the past. In the Elizabethan age, a book was written asserting that nature is the only teacher, that no man's mind is broad enough to invent a theory to hold nature, for she is the universe. With the publication of the *Novum Organum* came a revolution in thought; scientists ceased theorizing and began experimenting. Thus we went painfully back to nature, weary and disgusted with our artificial knowledge, hungering for that which is meat, thirsting for that which is drink, longing for the things that are. She has given us the universe in answer.

It is the most sacred right of man to investigate; we paid dearly for it in Eden; we have been shedding our heart's blood for it ever since. It is ours; we have bought it with a price.

Scientific investigation is the hope of our age, as it must precede all progress; and yet upon every hand we hear the objections to its pursuit. The boy who spends his time among the stones and flowers is a trifler, and if he tries with bungling attempt to pierce the mystery of animal life, he is cruel. Of course if he becomes a great anatomist or a brilliant naturalist, his cruelties are forgotten or forgiven him; the world is very cautious, but it is generally safe to admire a man who has succeeded. We do not withhold from a few great scientists the right of the hospital, the post mortem or experimenting with animal life, but we are prone to think the right of experimenting with life too sacred a thing to be placed in hands of inexperienced persons. Nevertheless, if we bar our novices from advancement, whence shall come our experts?

But to test the question by comparison, would all the life destroyed in experimenting from the beginning of the world until today be as an atom to the life saved by that one grand discovery for which Harvey sacrificed his practice and his reputation, the circulation of the blood? There is no selfishness in this. It came from a higher motive than the desire for personal gain, for it too often brings destitution instead. Of this we have a grand example in the broken-down care-worn old man who has just returned from the heart of the Dark Continent. But perhaps you still say that I evade the question; has anyone a right to destroy life for scientific purposes? Ah, why does life live upon death throughout the universe?

Investigators have styled fanatics those who seek to probe into the mysteries of the unknowable. This is unreasonable. The most aspiring philosopher never hoped to do more than state the problem; he never dreamed of solving it. Newton did not say how or why every particle of matter in the universe attracted every other particle of matter in the universe. He simply said it was so. We can only judge these abstract forces by their effect. Our intellectual swords may cut away a thousand petty spiderwebs woven by superstition across the mind of man, but before the veil of the "Sanctum Sanctorum" we stand confounded; our blades glance and turn and shatter upon the eternal adamant. Microscopic eyes have followed matter to the molecule and fallen blinded. Imagination has gone a step farther and grasped the atom. There, with a towering height above and yawning death below even this grows sick at soul. For over six thousand years we have shaken fact and fancy in the dice box together and breathlessly awaited the result. But the dice of God are always loaded, and there are two sides which never fall upward, the alpha and omega. Perhaps when we make our final cast with dark old death, we may shape them better.

From June to September Cather was getting ready to go to college. Finding money to finance her education was difficult, as it is for Vickie Templeton in "Old Mrs. Harris." Charles Cather, who was land poor and now had six children to support, had to borrow money from a business associate, but both parents knew that their daughter wanted above all else to get an education. In the story the money is loaned by Mr. Rosen, the neighbor/merchant, who sends Vickie off to college with a quotation from the French historian Michelet written "on a sheet of purple paper, in his delicately shaded foreign script: '*Le but n'est rien; le chemin, c'est tout.*' " That means, he tells her, "The end is nothing; the road is all. Let me write it down for you and give you your first French lesson." This observation became a precept that she carried through life. She often quoted it, and when she reached the striving novelist's goal of fame and affluence, Michelet's truth haunted her.

CHAPTER 4

University Days

Lincoln, the state capital, was not a large city by any absolute standard when Cather got off the train at the Burlington depot in September 1890. But it was eighteen times the size of Red Cloud and by comparison a metropolis. She never had lived in a city, and the prospect was exciting. Although she was later to evoke the soil of Webster County in unforgettable prose, she took to the city life avidly, and later when the chance came to move on to Pittsburgh, she did not hesitate. Still later she moved on to New York with the same alacrity and made her home there for the rest of her life. Lincoln, however, was her first encounter with urban life.

The Nebraska capital then had a population of thirty-five thousand sprawled over several square miles of flat, open prairie in the typical mid-western pattern of city planning: perfectly rectangular blocks laid out by theodolite and surveyors' chains in a north-south, east-west grid. Lettered streets ran east and west, numbered streets north and south. The capitol building stood at the center, and a mile north, at the top of Eleventh Street, were the buildings of the university. By the time Cather arrived, eight miles of streets had been paved with red cedar blocks and brick; the inhabitants had ridden in horse cars for seven years, had possessed a waterworks for five, gas streetlights for four; and the telephone company had 615 subscribers. The first skyscraper, the six-story Burr Block, was finished the year before Cather came; there were five major hotels, about as many saloons as churches, five private schools, a public library, and an electric-light plant. Shade trees had had a quarter of a century to establish themselves, but the city still had a raw look about it. Outside of town there were people still living in dugouts, and some years when the grasshopper plague hit the neighboring farms, the insects stripped the young trees of the city. The smell of burning prairie grass often drifted over the city before it was replaced by progress and industrial fumes as the city grew.

The founders of the city "were the pioneers not of land but of commerce and the professions: judges, lawyers, merchants, publishers, railroad builders, professors. There were also the exploiters, the boomers of paper towns and promoters of wildcat banks. But good or bad, they did not come to Nebraska to build a different world; they wanted the kind of society they had always considered desirable—but they wanted it here, where success (so they thought) was quick as a grasshopper and sure as the wind." Many were disappointed, however, and when depression hit the state in the mid-nineties, they wished they were back where they came from.

Life in Lincoln was not primitive. The settlers from the East had not been in contact with the frontier long enough to be influenced by the wild land. They built the same square brick piles they had formerly lived in or constructed the frame houses ornamented with turrets, bulbous pillars, and other Victorian gimcracks. They brought their eastern culture and artifacts with them, and while they were digging up the buffalo grass to plant their lawns and flowerbeds, they were unpacking their Limoges china, Landseer lithographs, and Ticknor and Fields books. Lincoln was an instant city built like a movie set. It had been empty prairie in 1867 when Nebraska became a state, and it was a thriving city twenty-three years later, nearly tripling in size between 1880 amd 1890. It quickly became a railroad center, as it was on the direct route between Chicago and Denver, and by the end of the century nineteen different rail lines led into it. This fact is important for Cather's career, because it made Lincoln a convenient stop for first-rate theatrical and musical companies on their way to Denver and San Francisco. When Cather became drama critic for the *Nebraska State Journal*, she was able to review plays and musical events of major importance.

Lincoln at this time had two thriving theaters, the Lansing and the Funke, both large and well appointed. Together they could accommodate three thousand spectators, and when both were open sometimes one hundred traveling companies passed through Lincoln in one year. Often there were five or six plays a week, and one could see Julia Marlowe, Helena Modjeska, Margaret Mather, Richard Mansfield, the Drews, Otis Skinner, and many others. Symphony orchestras and opera companies with internationally acclaimed singers also passed through the city. Discouraged Bohemian farmers like Mr. Shimerda may have been blowing their brains out on the bleak, lonely prairie of Webster County, but in Lancaster County there were people in top hats and tails eating oysters shipped in from the East in blocks of ice and sipping French champagne at their after-theater parties.

The University of Nebraska was about the same age as Lincoln. Its buildings were laid out on four city blocks, neatly planted in grass and new trees and surrounded by a high iron fence. The largest building was University Hall, an ornate red-brick structure dominating the campus. "There before me," wrote Alvin Johnson, one of Cather's contemporaries, "was University Hall, as it was pictured in the university catalogue. I walked up to the gate, where I was almost trodden down by students scurrying from the classrooms. The building before me seemed huge and majestic. It had four strata of windows, some of them lighted, under a mansard roof. The building was topped with a square tower. To the right were three other buildings of varying architecture, all handsome to my country eyes." The library was housed in two crowded rooms, and although a separate library building was begun in 1893, it remained an empty, unfinished shell until the legislature appropriated money to complete it after Cather graduated.

The student population then was three or four hundred (with another one hundred in the prep school), but by the time Cather left, three times that many were straining the capacity of the physical plant. Jim Burden remembered the student body: "In those days there were many serious young men among the students who had come up to the university from the farms and the little towns scattered over the thinly settled state. Some of those boys came straight from the cornfields with only a summer's wages in their pockets, hung on through the four years, shabby and underfed, and completed the course by really heroic self-sacrifice."

The university already had attracted some prominent scholars and had begun giving graduate work in some disciplines. Cather is not very accurate when she has Jim Burden recall: "Our instructors were oddly assorted; wandering pioneer school-teachers, stranded ministers of the Gospel, a few enthusiastic young men just out of graduate schools." But Jim's following statement is correct enough: "There was an atmosphere of endeavor, of expectancy and bright hopefulness about the young college that had lifted its head from the prairie only a few years before."

Johnson remembers that it was the "chief mission of the university, as we saw it, to train young men and women and send them out to man the grade schools and eventually the high schools. . . . The older members of the faculty conceived of teaching Nebraskans as their essential function in life. Many of them had been students at the university in its early years and had risen through instructorships to the professorial ranks. Others had been drawn from neighboring institutions of the prairie states."

In addition to the homegrown talent, however, was imported scholarship and learning, like the city's imported oysters and champagne from the East and Europe. Bernice Slote says: "The University of Nebraska in the early 1890's was itself a little Renaissance world." There was A. H. Edgren from Sweden, translator of Sanskrit, former rector of the University of Gothenberg; James T. Lees, who taught Greek, a great scholar, British-born but educated at Johns Hopkins under the famous classicist Basil Gildersleeve; Herbert Bates, young poet and fiction writer who had studied under Barrett Wendell at Harvard. Roscoe Pound, who later became dean of the Harvard Law School, was both lawyer and a graduate teaching assistant in botany; John J. Pershing, later commander-in-chief of the American Expeditionary Forces in World War I, was a teacher of math and military science. The chancellor was James Canfield, later president of Ohio State University and librarian of Columbia University.

This community of scholars produced some distinguished graduates, besides Willa Cather, during the nineties. Louise Pound, the sister of Roscoe, became a famous scholar and folklorist and the first woman president of the Modern Language Association. Alvin Johnson went on to found the New School for Social Research in New York. D. N. Lehmer became a well-known composer and mathematician; Hartley Burr Alexander became an important philosopher, educator, and writer, and an associate editor of *Webster's New International Dictionary*. William Linn Westermann had a distinguished career as an ancient historian. There also was Dorothy Canfield, daughter of the chancellor, who, though still in high school in Cather's day, was destined to be a Pulitzer-Prize-winning novelist.

The girl who left Red Cloud to begin the next great adventure must have been much like Thea Kronborg in *The Song of the Lark*. As Thea sat in her Pullman car watching the cornfields flash by en route to Chicago to study music, it was herself and her own adventure that mattered. "If youth did not matter so much to itself, it would never have the heart to go on. Thea was surprised that she did not feel a deeper sense of loss at leaving her old life behind her." It seemed, on the contrary, as she looked out the train window, "that she had left very little. Everything that was essential seemed to be right there in the car with her." Cather had the same self-sufficiency, the same resolute determination to confront her destiny. She did not yet know what her destiny was to be, but there was no hanging back. She had wanted to go to college, and getting there had not been easy. She was going to make the most of it.

Although her father was forced to borrow money to send her, the expenses actually were modest. The three hundred dollars that Mr. Rosen lends Vickie Templeton in "Old Mrs. Harris" probably was enough to see a frugal student through two years of college. One could get room and board for three dollars a week, and the university fees consisted of a ten-dollar registration fee and a ten-dollar (refundable) chemistry breakage fee. Books and incidentals also were proportionately cheap. Once she got to Lincoln, Cather did not have to skimp. She boarded at the best eating place in town and was able to go to Omaha to the theater on occasion. She did have to tend her own stove in the rooming house, something she never had done before, but her later memories of her poverty-stricken college days are a good bit exaggerated. In 1940 she believed that no student ever had gone through college on a smaller allowance than she had. She went without some things in order to have other things she wanted, and for some of the books in her library she felt a particular affection because they were bought at the cost of considerable sacrifice during her student days.

Her memory of being poor in college applies more to her last two years than to the first two. In 1893 the nation was hit by a severe depression, and times were particularly hard in Nebraska. For several summers there were successive crop failures, and in 1893 a hot wind burned up the entire corn crop in three days. Banks failed; eastern investors withdrew their money; farm mortgages were foreclosed. The Farmers' and Merchants' Bank of Red Cloud failed, and while Charles Cather lost no money, many men who owed him money did. He owned a large amount of farm land that was heavily mortgaged and for a time was hard put to support his family. Cather's brother Roscoe did not go to college but began teaching country school at the age of sixteen to help support the family. Willa at this time became a professional journalist and for the last two years of her university career was probably self-supporting. Whether she earned enough to contribute to the family income, the record does not say; but she recognized family obligations, and later, when she was working in Pittsburgh, she sent money home. She continued to do this in New York when she worked for *McClure's Magazine*, and after she became a free-lance novelist, she helped put her younger brother Jack and sister Elsie through college.

Living arrangements for students in the 1890s were unorganized. Jim Burden remembers: "There were no college dormitories; we lived where we could and as we could." Cather first rented a room at 1019 H Street in the home of "Aunt Kate" Hastings, a friend of the family on the edge of town near open country, and later she lived with D. Neil Johnson, a real estate broker, and his family at 1029 L Street. While she was looking for a place to live, she and her mother, who accompanied her to Lincoln, stayed with the family of R. E. Moore, head of the Security Investment Company that employed Charles Cather as its southeastern Nebraska representative. If Jim Burden's memory of his room is an accurate description of Cather's first living quarters, she got two rooms for the price of one because the house was inconveniently located for students. Her bedroom, originally a linen closet, was unheated and just big enough for a cot, and her other room she fixed up as her study. "I worked at a commodious green-topped table placed directly in front of the west window which looked out over the prairie." In the corner at her right she put her books on shelves she made and painted herself, and on the blank wall to the left she tacked up a large, newly purchased map of ancient Rome. Rome was the one place in all the world, she had written in her friend's album two years before, that she most wanted to visit. Over the bookcase she hung a photograph of the Tragic Theater at Pompeii.

It is appropriate that Cather's alter ego narrator Jim in *My Ántonia* is male, for Cather was still refusing to act and dress like a girl. She continued to cut her hair short for at least her first year at the university and wore starched shirts like a man instead of feminine shirtwaists; she did put on skirts, though she wore them shorter than most women, daringly short, some of her classmates thought. She also continued taking male roles in dramatic productions and signing her name William Cather. This last went on, Louise Pound remembered, until her friends made her stop it. It was Mrs. Charles Gere, mother of one of her closest college friends and wife of the publisher of the *Journal*, who persuaded her to let her hair grow. Years later when Mrs. Gere died, Cather wrote Mariel Gere that her mother had done so much for a clumsy country girl. She had done it simply by being her lovely and gracious self; her charm and vivacity were something entirely new. No one but Mrs. Gere, she said, could have persuaded her to let her hair grow or to learn to spell. William Westermann recalled her first appearance in the elementary Greek class that he was enrolled in. While the students were awaiting the instructor, the door opened, and a head with short hair and a straw hat appeared. A masculine voice inquired if this were the beginning Greek class, and when someone said it was, the body attached to the head and hat opened the door wider and came in. The masculine head and voice were attached to a girl's body and skirts. The entire class laughed, but Cather, apparently unperturbed, took her seat and joined the waiting students.

Cather's fellow students remembered her well. When some of them were asked for their recollections soon after she died, they recalled her mannish attire, short hair, and independent manner. One remembered that she wore high, stiff collars, string or four-in-hand ties, and mannish white cuffs that stuck out of her jacket sleeves. "I never remember her wearing a dress at any time—always dark, man-tailored suits." But another recalled that she always dressed in middy blouses with full skirts that freed her from the restraints of clothes worn by most of the women of that day. This fashion, which she probably adopted in the latter part of her college years, was a style she liked throughout her later years. A third contemporary said Cather was the first woman she ever saw wearing suspenders, and a fourth remembered that the boys who dated her were scared off after one date. She modified her behavior during her college years, however, and by the time she was a junior she was doing her hair up, no doubt to the relief of her mother; her graduation picture shows her wearing a very feminine full-length dress with puff sleeves and long gloves.

Cather was a controversial figure in college, as she had been in high school, and her classmates either were fond of her or detested her. There seems to have been little middle ground. Her own memory of herself in college was not a pleasant one. Edith Lewis reports that in one of her letters to Mrs. Goudy there was a touching note of self-questioning, "touching because of its absolute candour; humble, and at the same time fearless. She believed in the power she felt in herself, but she had no soaring illusions about it." When one of her old schoolmates, Ned Abbott, proposed writing a biographical piece on her in 1921, she told him she hated biography because no biographical sketch is thought interesting unless the subject is presented as a freak. The external queerness of a person is seldom his or her reality, she wrote. But she told Abbott to go see Mrs. Goudy, who had known her intimately during her university days and who could tell him more about her than she could. Cather told Abbott she had assumed various poses in college. There are just a few rare, charming young people who are simple and natural in college, undistorted by any affectations, and she was not one of them. She often felt lonely and was very unhappy when people cut her. Underneath her sturdy independence and uncompromising nonconformity was a desire to be liked, a desire for society. When she later went to Pittsburgh to work, she went to parties, teas, and out-of-town excursions, dated, and loved the life. "Gad! how we like to be liked," she wrote Mariel Gere, quoting Charles Lamb.

When Cather arrived in Lincoln, she did not become a member of the freshman class. Despite the fact that the university was small, new, and served a state full of unassimilated foreign-born, its standards were high; and rather than admit those not sufficiently prepared, the university ran a two-year preparatory Latin school in conjunction with its baccalaureate and graduate offerings. Red Cloud High School graduates did not meet all the

32. The University of Nebraska campus in about 1892 when Cather was a student. Courtesy of the Nebraska State Historical Society

33. Louise Pound and Willa Cather in student days. Courtesy of WCPMC-NSHS

34. Cather as Electra. Courtesy of WCPMC-NSHS

35. Miss Day and Cather dressed for a male theatrical role. Courtesy of WCPMC-NSHS

36. Cather about 1893. Courtesy of the Nebraska State Historical Society

37. Cather on the university campus about 1894. Courtesy of WCPMC-NSHS

8. Cather working in the *Nebraska State Journal* office. Courtesy of WCPMC-NSHS

9. Cather ready for her trip to Chicago to hear grand opera, 1895. Courtesy of WCPMC-NSHS

40. Will Owen Jones. Courtesy of WCPMC-NSHS

41. Cather and friends: Front row (left to right) Frances and Ellen Gere, Jessica Cather, Margie Miner, Douglass Cather. Back row—Irene Miner, Elsie, Willa, and Roscoe Cather. Courtesy of WCPMC-NSHS

entrance requirements, and Cather was put in the "second prep" class. This meant that she had to take an additional year of work before she could enroll as a freshman. Thus she had five years of education in Lincoln before she graduated in June 1895.

She threw herself into her schoolwork with characteristic energy and concentration. There was nothing in her personality of the easygoing ways of her southern family. While her parents liked to sit about in leisurely discussion, never in any rush to face the problems of the day, she attacked her assignments with vigor. Professor Wunsch's feelings about Thea Kronborg in *The Song of the Lark* apply equally to Cather: "It was his pupil's power of application, her rugged will, that interested him." Viola Roseboro', later her colleague on *McClure's Magazine*, told Edith Lewis: "If Willa Cather had been a scrub-woman, she would have scrubbed much harder than other scrub-women." No grades were kept among the registrar's records at the University of Nebraska, but Lewis reports that Cather once stood first in her Latin class of fifty-three and used to get up at five o'clock to study. Dorothy Canfield later remembered Cather as the most brilliant student the university had, while Alvin Johnson remembered Cather and Louise Pound as the two most original students during his years in Lincoln.

Cather went to the university intending to study medicine and become a doctor, but she soon switched to the humanities. There is no record of the courses she had to take during her preparatory year except that she was allowed to take freshman chemistry and received advance credit for the course. She also took an English course from Professor Ebenezer Hunt, for whom she wrote the Carlyle essay that she thought later had turned her into a writer. Hunt used to say to her, as she was fond of quoting, "Life is one damn grind, Cather." Her interest in science continued at least into the summer after her prep year, for she wrote Mrs. Goudy then that she was chiefly interested in astronomy, botany, and chemistry, and she wrote Mariel Gere one day in July that she had spent the morning dissecting frogs to study their circulatory system. But she also said that she had been studying French history and reading George Eliot.

When she did matriculate as a regular degree candidate in the fall of 1891, she took freshman math, Greek, Latin, rhetoric and was allowed to enroll in the junior-level Shakespeare course. All of these were full year courses. Math nearly proved her undoing. She could not pass the course in her freshman year, and it was not until the second semester of her senior year that she completed freshman math and was able to graduate. She continued Latin and Greek in her sophomore year, and in her junior year took three semesters of Greek, including a course in lyric poetry. In her other Greek courses she read

Pindar, Herodotus, Homer, and the dramatists. She took a lot of English literature—fifteen semesters—during her entire undergraduate program: four semesters of Shakespeare, a semester of other Elizabethan dramatists, a year of Browning, a year of other writers (Tennyson, Emerson, Ruskin, Hawthorne), a course called dramatization, and Anglo-Saxon literature. In her last two years she studied French and German, carrying four semesters of the former, in which she read Daudet, Gautier, Balzac, Racine, Taine, and two semesters of the latter. In addition she took American and European history and philosophy. Her superior ability is shown on her transcript by the notation that she was allowed to substitute advanced classes in English literature for the introductory ones. For the first two years she studied hard, but by her third year she was working nearly full-time as a journalist and getting her education outside of the classroom. She remembered that she did very little work on her courses during her last two years and passed her examinations largely on inspiration.

The major event of her first year at Lincoln occurred in March 1891, when Professor Hunt assigned a theme topic: "The Personal Characteristics of Thomas Carlyle." He originally had called for themes on Thomas Paine, but was talked out of it by timid colleagues who thought Paine too dangerous a topic to give to impressionable "second prep" students. Cather already had a passionate interest in Carlyle, owned a copy of *Sartor Resartus,* and the assignment sent her up like a balloon. Professor Hunt must have been astounded when he read her essay. Any English teacher who has corrected the witless humor and semiliterate prose of countless college freshmen dreams of such a moment. When Hunt handed back the papers, he wrote on the board one of the final sentences of her essay: "Like the lone survivor of some extinct species, the last of the mammoths, tortured and harassed beyond all endurance by the smaller, though perhaps more perfectly organized offspring of the world's maturer years, this great Titan, son of her passionate youth, a youth of volcanoes, and earthquakes, and great, unsystematized forces, rushed off into the desert to suffer alone."

On a Sunday morning soon afterwards Cather opened the *Journal* and found her essay in print. Without her knowledge Professor Hunt had given the piece to the *Journal,* and somehow the undergraduate publication, the *Hesperian,* also got a copy. Both published it on the same day. A note on the editorial page of the *Journal,* no doubt written by Charles Gere, the editor, called attention to the essay, the work of "a young girl sixteen [actually seventeen] years of age who comes from Webster County." He went on to say that a careful reading would "convince any student of literature that it is a remarkable production, reflecting not a little credit on the author and the university."

Thirty-six years later Cather remembered: "Up to that time I had planned to specialize in science; I thought I would like to study medicine. But what youthful vanity can be unaffected by the sight of itself in print! It has a kind of hypnotic effect. I still remember that essay, and it was a splendid example of the kind of writing I most dislike; very florid and full of high-flown figures of speech." She further recalled that it did not deal at all with the personal characteristics of Carlyle but "poured out, as best I could, the feelings that a fervid reading of 'The French Revolution' and 'Sartor Resartus' had stirred up in me." Yet she had to admit that the essay was honest: "Florid as it was, it didn't over color the pleasure and delightful bitterness that Carlyle can arouse in a very young person. It makes one feel so grown up to be bitter."

The mouth-filling period that Professor Hunt picked out to write on the board is perhaps the most baroque sentence in the entire essay. Although the whole composition is highly charged with the author's emotional response to Carlyle, there are many short, pithy sentences and plenty of vigorous declarative ones. What is most interesting about the piece, however, is not the rhetoric but the image of young Willa Cather projected against the figure of Thomas Carlyle. Shot through the essay are sentences more revealing of the author's dreams about herself than of her subject. The personal characteristics of Carlyle are mostly those of Willa Cather, and they are characteristics that endured a lifetime.

Consider some of her observations: "He was a recluse, not that he had any aversion for men, but that he loved his books and loved Nature better." "His love and sympathy for humanity were boundless, and he understood great minds and earnest souls as no other man ever has. In this lay his power as a biographer and as a historian." "Carlyle posed but poorly as a political economist." "He went far out into one of the most desolate spots of Scotland, and made his home there. There among the wild heaths . . . he did his best work. He drew his strength from those wild landscapes." "Like Scott, he lived much in the open air." "The wife of an artist, if he continues to be an artist, must always be a secondary consideration with him." "He never strove to please a pampered public." "Nothing has so degraded modern literature as the desperate efforts of modern writers to captivate the public." "He was proud to the extreme, but his love was predominant even over his pride." "For his brother's sake he wrote for money. It seemed to him like selling his own soul. He wrote article after article for reviews, and cut up his great thoughts to fit the pages of a magazine. No wonder he hated it; it was like hacking his own flesh, bit by bit, to feed those he loved."

These quotations read like program notes for Cather's life: things she would be and do, things she was, things she would avoid. Written when she was seventeen, they show that her life patterns were drawn early. Finally, there is the most important statement of all, one that posits a lifelong conviction and a lifelong action. It comes immediately after her declaration that an artist's wife (and she meant husband too) must play a supporting role to his career. "Art of every kind is an exacting master, more so than even Jehovah. He says only, 'Thou shalt have no other gods before me.' Art, science, and letters cry, 'Thou shalt have no other gods at all.' They accept only human sacrifices."

It is clear from a review of Cather's entire career that this creed, embraced fervently at the age of seventeen, guided her throughout her life. From the moment she decided to become a writer she devoted all her energy and intelligence to this end. Fanny Butcher, who was editor of the *Chicago Tribune* book section and knew Cather for thirty-five years, said she never had known anyone else who had so successfully managed to get exactly what she wanted out of life. It wasn't fame, fortune, adulation. Material possessions meant to her only what they could do to make her life unencumbered, free to write, the only thing she really wanted to do. Butcher wrote in her memoirs: "I never knew anyone who seemed to be more wrapped around by her work, to be almost encircled in it like Laocoön in the coils of the sea serpent. Once she said to me that nothing mattered to her but writing books, and living the kind of life that makes it possible to write them." Cather wrote Mariel Gere soon after beginning her new job in Pittsburgh in 1896 that there was no god but one god and art is his revealer; that was her creed and she would follow it to the end, to a hotter place than Pittsburgh if need be.

The Carlyle essay was followed six months later by another remarkable performance, a long, two-part discussion entitled "Shakespeare and *Hamlet*," which the *Journal* also published. By then Cather was regularly enrolled as a freshman and taking the junior-level Shakespeare course. She also had read and pondered Shakespeare in Red Cloud, and again the essay is as much about the author and her aspirations as it is about Shakespeare and the prince of Denmark. The essay includes an inquiry into the nature of art and an analysis of what it takes to be an artist. Shakespeare as the supreme practitioner provides the inspiration for this discussion. It is as though she had made him her model. The great secret of Shakespeare's power, she wrote, was the supreme love, rather than the supreme intellect. Some writers are mere men of letters, presidents of literary clubs, and editors of magazines, but the real writers are those who have suffered the agonies of creation, "the agony in which all the forces of body, brain and soul are drawn to one vital center in the effort of one life to give individuality to a greater life, the agony of the Doric women who bore the sons of the gods." And what must an artist do to be saved? The answer she cast in the form of Christ's answer to the rich man (Luke 18:22): "Sell all that thou hast . . . and come, follow me." The mere man of letters, she wrote, like the rich man, will turn sorrowfully away. He will not give up the world to follow art.

This equating of art and religion is very characteristic of Cather. Three years later when she reviewed a superb performance by Richard Mansfield on Shakespeare's birthday, she wrote: "One felt that he was worthy to act on that night, the immortal twenty-third of April, the night on which three hundred and thirty years ago . . . God a second time turned his face in love toward man." In *The Professor's House* (1925) Cather has Professor St. Peter say in a lecture to his students: "Art and religion (they are the same thing in the end, of course) have given man the only happiness he has ever had." It seems clear that from 1891 on, art was to be her religion, and this single-minded pursuit of art helps to explain her subsequent life as a single artist.

By the time the Shakespeare essay appeared in print, Cather was busily engaged in extracurricular activities. A new campus magazine, the *Lasso*, appeared anonymously in October and November, but in December it identified James McDonald as editor and proprietor, and Willa Cather and Louise Pound as associate editors. The magazine lasted only one year, but by the beginning of her sophomore year Cather was on the staff of the oldest campus literary publication, the *Hesperian*. This was a combination magazine-newspaper of sixteen pages that appeared semimonthly and was published by the literary societies. Cather, who belonged to the Union Literary Society, was elected an associate editor with responsibility for the literary contents. She threw herself into this venture with characteristic energy and published four of her own stories and a short play during the first semester. Another play appeared in the winter, another story in the spring, and a sixth story the following fall.

During her junior year she became managing editor, and while she only used one of her own stories that year, she devoted a great deal of time to the magazine. One of her colleagues remembered later that "the truth is the *Hesperian* was Willa practically. . . . the rest of us looked wise and did nothing." The magazine had a sprightliness that year unmatched by volumes of the publication in years before and after. The first issue with "W. Cather— Managing Editor" on the masthead stated the editor's aims for the year: the *Hesperian* would be written "in plain, unornamented language which anyone can interpret without the aid of a handbook of mythology or a dictionary of similes." And she continued: "If there is any fighting to be done, we will be down in the line fighting on one side or the other, striking out from the shoulder. If we err, we will err through bad judgment, not through lack of enthusiasm." She also claimed the right to "pummel . . . as much as we please" any man who "says that the earth is flat, . . . slanders a great book or writes an absurd one." Finally, she promised that the paper would be decently proofread. Her greatest accomplishment of the year was in putting out a special, thirty-two-page Charter Day issue, commemorating the twenty-fifth anniversary of the university's founding.

The *Hesperian* was not her only extracurricular activity during her college years. She was literary editor of the 1894 *Sombrero*, the yearbook of her class of 1895, and apparently took part in campus debating clubs, but the record contains only secondhand references to this activity. She continued her high school interest in drama and appeared in at least two undergraduate productions. In her sophomore year she finally played a female role, appearing as Lady Macbeth in *Shakespeare up to Date*, a farce in which Shakespeare's characters accuse him of falsifying their true natures. During the same year she returned to her male roles as Diamond Witherspoon in a takeoff on university life thought to be written by Louise Pound. In this production Cather's recitation of "Curfew Must Not Ring Tonight" brought down the house.

Cather's career as a creative writer began during her freshman year, when she wrote a story that greatly impressed her English instructor, Professor Bates. That she was seriously studying the writing process at this time is documented by Alvin Johnson's memory of her as a paper-grader when he was in the Latin school prepping for college: "I had to produce 'themes.' . . . My themes were passed on by a rather mannish young woman . . . Willa Cather. She did me the great honor of calling me to her office. 'You write not badly,' she said, 'but you don't *see*. Learn French, a little French and read Flaubert or even Maupassant. They *see*. *Madame Bovary*: the book is worth committing to memory.' " From the beginning Flaubert was one of her masters and favorite authors. It was his painstaking attention to style and language, *le mot juste*, rather than his subject, that interested Cather. As her life turned out, she had a great deal in common with Flaubert: dedication to art, distrust of science, loyalty to friends, lack of interest in politics, and a desire for privacy. Neither writer ever married or thought the novel had any social purpose.

The story that delighted Herbert Bates, as the Carlyle essay had charmed Professor Hunt, was "Peter," the tale of the Bohemian immigrant who commits suicide on his Nebraska farm. Bates was so impressed that he sent the story off to a Boston magazine, *The Mahogany Tree*, which published it in May 1892. Cather then reprinted it with revisions in the *Hesperian* in November. Readers will recognize the story as an early version of the episode of Mr. Shimerda's death in *My Ántonia*. The Bohemian musician, who has emigrated from the Old World with his wife and children, is old, feeble, dispirited, and hardly able to play his violin any longer. His practical son wants to sell the fiddle, but the old man, defeated by the hard life in the alien land and unable to part with his instrument, cannot bear to go on living: "He took Anton's shotgun down from its peg, and loaded it by the moonlight which streamed in through the door. He sat down on the dirt floor, and leaned back against the dirt wall. He heard the wolves howling in the distance, and the night wind screaming as it swept over the snow. Near him he heard the regular breathing of the horses in the dark. He put his crucifix above his heart, and folding his hands said brokenly all the Latin he had ever known, '*Pater noster, qui in coelum est.*' . . . He held his fiddle under his chin a moment, where it had lain so often, then put it across his knee and broke it through the middle. He pulled off his old boot, held the gun between his knees with the muzzle against his forehead, and pressed the trigger with his toe."

This is a piece of narrative that any college freshman could be proud of. Cather liked it well enough to rewrite it and republish it for a third time, in Pittsburgh eight years later. This time she dropped the *thee*'s and *thou*'s that she had used to suggest the familiar second-person singular of the Czech language, sharpened the conflict between father and son, and expanded the beginning. The bulk of the tale remained the same, however, until she reworked it into a far more intricate design in the evocative prose of *My Ántonia*. In this early story and the next one she wrote, she had not yet learned how to use the Nebraska setting for more than a backdrop for the action. Eventually she worked out the way to involve the land as antagonist in her prairie fiction, but here the conflict is merely between father and son.

This conflict, which is over values, is interesting, however, because it announces at the outset of her career a theme that runs significantly through her mature fiction. The tale ends with this paragraph: "In the morning Antone found him stiff, frozen fast in a pool of blood. They could not straighten him out enough to fit a coffin, so they buried him in a pine box. Before the funeral Antone carried to town the fiddlebow which Peter had forgotten to break. Antone was very thrifty, and a better man than his father had been." Here already is the hard-headed, practical businessman farmer, a preview of Nat Wheeler in *One of Ours* (1922) or the shyster lawyer Ivy Peters in *A Lost Lady* (1923). The story also foreshadows the conflict between materialism and spirituality that looms large in *The Professor's House* (1925). The irony shown here seems remarkably sophisticated for a first story written at the age of eighteen.

Before Cather reprinted "Peter" in November, she already had used her second story, "Lou, the Prophet," in the *Hesperian* in October. This tale, which is just as precocious as the first one, also makes use of Nebraska material; and it too is a somber concoction of death and despair in the wild land of the Divide. Lou is a homesick Dane who has been trying to scratch a living from the recalcitrant prairie for seven years. He is rewarded for his herculean efforts by drought and crop failure, and becomes at the end a crazy religious fanatic who believes God is punishing the world for its sins. In setting this tale Cather writes: "His bill of fare never changed the year round; bread, coffee, beans and sorghum molasses, sometimes a little salt pork. After breakfast he worked until dinner time, ate, and then worked again. He always went to bed soon after the sunset, for he was always tired, and it saved oil. Sometimes, on Sundays, he would go over home after he had done his washing and house cleaning, and sometimes he hunted. His life was as sane and as uneventful as the life of his plow horses, and it was as hard and thankless." The opportunity is here to make the land the antagonist, but the story trails off into an account of Lou's religious visions and ends with his mysterious disappearance when the police come to lock him up as a dangerous lunatic.

The alchemy of time had not yet mellowed Cather's memory of the bleakness of Nebraska farm life. Her early stories of Nebraska farmers are all tales of hardship, failure, deprivation. But there is a paradox here, for her stories and her letters of this period are not of a piece. During her first summer back in Red Cloud from Lincoln she wrote of taking endless rides over the prairie, and the annual harvest was a spectacle she always loved. Another summer she wrote the Gere sisters that she wanted them to come down from Lincoln to see the country while it was looking like a garden— green and beautiful beyond words, with cornfields like forests everywhere. The tone and content of these grim early stories remind one of the tales that Hamlin Garland was writing about the same time. His bleak stories of Midwestern farm life, published as *Main-Travelled Roads*, had appeared in 1891. It is tempting to speculate that Cather as a college freshman thought the proper tone for a story of farmers on the prairie should be Garland's. She later repudiated these stories completely, regarded them as false pictures of the Nebraska reality, and wanted to forget them.

When Edward Wagenknecht wrote her in 1938 about her early stories, sending her a list of the ones he had uncovered, she assumed that he wanted to

reprint them. She wrote him a testy letter telling him that under no circumstances could he do anything with these stories. She regarded them as quite
worthless, unfit to be reprinted, and said that whenever possible she had
renewed her copyrights to prevent anyone from resurrecting them. Suppose
some apple grower were to pack only sound apples for market, she wrote,
and suppose someone came along while he was asleep and put the bad ones
left on the ground in the boxes; would that be a friendly act? Everyone has the
right of supervision over their handiwork, she added. The carpenter, the
dressmaker, the cabinet maker can put their flimsy work in the cellar and
forget it. The copyright laws give the writer the same privilege. She was
sorry her apprentice pieces still existed in the musty files of old periodicals
and would have liked to destroy them all.

Four more early stories appeared in the *Hesperian* during 1892 and 1893.
One was "The Elopement of Allen Poole," her Virginia story; two others
were exercises in exoticism that led nowhere. "A Son of the Celestial" is a tale
of a wise old Chinese scholar who dies in a San Francisco opium den. The
anonymous narrator attacks the pretension and dusty scholarship of American professors, a covert attack on some of Cather's own teachers, no doubt,
but the story is of no real importance. "A Tale of the White Pyramid" is laid in
ancient Egypt, concerns a marvelous feat of strength by an unknown youth
who saves from disaster the burial ceremony of the dead Pharaoh, but the
only thing of interest about this story is Cather's initial use of a first-person
narrator.

The last of these stories, however, is another matter. It is even grimmer
and more terrifying than "Peter" and "Lou, the Prophet." It is a grisly tale of
man's inhumanity to man, in which a poor, simple-minded Russian farm
worker is victimized by the society he has not asked to be part of. The
character, Serge Povolitchky, is the bastard child of a Russian immigrant girl
and a railroad contractor. As a farm worker on the ranch of a man with the
good English name of David, Serge befriends a mongrel dog, the first thing
in his life he ever has had a chance to love. The farmer in a fit of anger one day
kills the dog, and Serge instantly reacts by splitting the farmer's head with an
ax. In jail, Serge is too stupid to make barrel hoops and is punished by solitary
confinement, tortured, and killed. "The Clemency of the Court" is the ironic
title of this pathetic tale.

By the time Cather became a junior, she was no longer a docile student,
and her impatience with the quality and nature of her instruction grew.
Before she graduated, she quoted approvingly in her newspaper column a
remark Beerbohm Tree had made in an address at Harvard. While he thought
that a university education was of inestimable importance to chemists, engi-

neers, tradesmen, and bookkeepers, Tree doubted its beneficial effect on artists. Cather was like Jim Burden, who says: "I knew that I should never be a scholar. I could never lose myself for long among impersonal things." She had no sympathy with precise scholarship and said as early as the Shakespeare essay that the emotional plane of life is "infinitely higher than the intellectual," that this level was not reached by "mastering the pages of a Latin grammar." Her own criticism, which is highly emotional and impressionistic, owes its quality to her passionate commitment to the text rather than to literary analysis.

This passionate commitment was a quality that Dorothy Canfield Fisher later remembered vividly: "She amazed and sometimes abashed some of her professors by caring much more fiercely about their subjects than they did. Especially French. There seemed to be a natural affinity between her mind and French forms of art. During her undergraduate years she made it a loving duty to read every French literary masterpiece she could lay her hands on." In her French classes, though she was no doubt better read than the instructor, she had to be threatened with failing before she could be made to learn the grammar.

This antipathy for precise scholarship collided with the literary methods of the chairman of the English Department, Lucius Sherman. Though she took a number of courses from him and no doubt learned a great deal, she hated the kind of detailed literary analysis that he specialized in. He made exhaustive studies of sounds as expressions of emotions, and devised elaborate diagrams for the analysis of words. His *Elements of Literature and Composition* was about the dullest book Cather ever had encountered, and his *Analytics of Literature* she regarded as arid pedantry. Often his supposed scientific method of examining literature "came down to mere word-counting; judging by published examples, he and his students had counted words of nearly a hundred thousand sentences in works of seventy authors from Spenser to Henry James." Half of his *Analytics* is devoted to analysis of sentence length, comparative predication, and ratios of force, with charts, diagrams, formulae, and equations.

Cather never lost a chance to attack Sherman's scholarship, opinions, pedagogy. She wrote a number of satires on his *Analytics*, especially the word-counting exercises. One unsigned verse of this sort appeared in the *Hesperian* in December 1893:

> I am dying, Egypt, dying,
>   Ebbs the crimson life-tide fast;
> And the dark Plutonian shadows

Gather on the evening blast;
Ah I counted, Queen, and counted,
And rows of figures massed
Till e'en my days are numbered,
And I'm counted out at last.

She also crossed swords with Sherman in her book column in the *Journal*. When he attacked Du Maurier's *Trilby* as immoral in his book column in the *Lincoln Evening News*, she wrote a spirited defense of the novel. Sherman's pedagogical method on exams, which involved asking multiple, minute, nit-picking questions, also irritated Cather. Olivia Pound remembered that one day after an interminable number of these queries, Sherman asked, apropos of the mother of Coriolanus, "What did the noble matron Volumnia say then?" Cather's answer: "The noble matron Volumnia then said 'Bow-wow.' " Sherman apparently settled scores with her later when she applied, unsuccessfully, to fill a vacancy that occurred in the English Department the year after she graduated.

Even before Sherman had become her bête noire, she was attacking pedantry. In the freshman Shakespeare essay she wrote that the literary analysts never find life in what they analyze: "They never feel the hot blood riot in the pulses, nor hear the great heartbeat. That is the one great job which belongs exclusively to those of us who are unlearned, unlettered." She was disappointed not to find in Lincoln speculative, wide-ranging teachers like Will Ducker, the passionate amateur with whom she had read the classics in Red Cloud. "In the classical courses at Nebraska, as at most universities, there was altogether too much gerund-grinding. . . . The great initiation promised for the truly elect was into the mysterious classification of Sanskrit verbs."

There was one professor, however, who was different: Herbert Bates, with whom she developed a close relationship. He gave her the kind of stimulation and encouragement she needed. As a writer himself, he understood and befriended her. He sits for the portrait of Jim Burden's admired Gaston Cleric in *My Ántonia*: "I have sometimes thought that his bursts of imaginative talk were fatal to his poetic gift. He squandered too much in the heat of personal communication. How often I have seen him draw his dark brows together, fix his eyes upon some object on the wall or a figure in the carpet, and then flash into the lamplight the very image that was in his brain. He could bring the drama of antique life before one out of the shadows— white figures against blue backgrounds." It was his talk that she valued, as well as his knowledge. In the novel Jim recalls vivid memories of the evenings he spent with Cleric, who could recite Dante, canto after canto; and sometimes he stayed far into the night talking about Latin and English poetry and Italy.

Cather was highly selective in the friends she made in college, choosing the people she wanted and ignoring the rest, and the friendships she made were lifetime relationships. Her friends recognized her qualities and were devoted to her. In retrospect it seems that the people she chose were among the most cultivated and interesting people in Lincoln. Among them were the Westermanns, a German family that owned the *Evening News*; the Canfield family—James the chancellor, his wife Flavia, a painter, and Dorothy, who was in the eighth grade when Cather went to Lincoln; the Gere family— father and mother, daughters Mariel, Frances, and Ellen, Cather's fellow students; Will Owen Jones, managing editor of Charles Gere's *Journal*; Dr. Julius Tyndale, brother of Mrs. Westermann and fellow drama critic; and Louise Pound, the brilliant daughter of a prominent judge. All of these people are important dramatis personae in Cather's life.

The Westermanns, some of whom later moved to New York, where Cather saw them, appear briefly in *One of Ours* (1922) as the Erlich family. The protagonist of that novel, Claude Wheeler, visits the Erlichs during his college years in Lincoln, as Cather did the Westermanns. Julius Erlich takes Claude home to meet his mother and brothers: "Julius turned in at a rambling wooden house with an unfenced, terraced lawn. He led Claude around to the wing, and through a glass door into a big room that was all windows on three sides, above the wainscoting. The room was full of boys and young men, seated on long divans or perched on the arms of easy chairs, and they were all talking at once." Five of the young men were Julius's brothers. "Claude never before had seen brothers who were so outspoken and frank with one another." When their mother came in, she "seemed to him very young to be the head of such a family. Her hair was still brown, and she wore it drawn over her ears and twisted in two little horns, like the ladies in old daguerreotypes." Mrs. Westermann, who in real life also had six boys, was a gracious hostess who charmed Cather, as Mrs. Erlich does Claude. The house, which formerly had been occupied by the chancellor, stood on S Street, adjacent to the campus. William Westermann remembered that Cather's "depiction of the dinners which 'Claude' attended at the Erlich house contains memories of the many meals, on Sunday particularly, which Miss Cather took at our house." The Westermann family gave her the contact with a cultivated German family that she had had in Red Cloud with the Wieners.

The Canfields, at the head of the university hierarchy, were important people in Lincoln. James, according to Alvin Johnson, was adored by the students, who "regarded him not only as a shining representative of the world of culture, but as a true democrat, who used all his influence to abate the snobbishness of the students from the families that composed the rising middle class. He was constantly urging the more prosperous fathers to hold allowances to their sons and daughters to a minimum." Mrs. Canfield was mad about art, chiefly painting, which she did herself, but also literature and music. She was an irresponsible and outspoken woman, energetically involved in women's activities, a club woman almost to the point of caricature. Cather took an ironic view of this side of her nature but was genuinely interested in her French experiences. She had taken Dorothy to France with her for a year while she studied painting. Dorothy, the member of the family that Cather was genuinely attracted to, played the violin, fenced with skill, spoke fluent French, and captivated everyone. Johnson said the students idolized Dorothy, "a little girl . . . with lustrous brown eyes and abundant brown curls and the winning ways of a little fairy out of the storybooks." She went to college at Ohio State University after her father became president there, then took a Ph.D. in French at Columbia; but she did not make a career as a teacher. She on her part idolized Cather as a sort of talented older sister, and in later years, when both became novelists, they maintained their friendship and carried on an extensive correspondence.

The earliest fruit of Cather's friendship with Dorothy Canfield was a short story, " 'The Fear that Walks by Noonday,' " which Cather published in the *Sombrero* the year she was literary editor. Dorothy remembered: "At a football game where we happened to be on the same grandstand, I gave her the idea of a football story—of all things! A fancy that had just occurred to me. She wrote the story, and very generously, I thought, put my name with hers as if I had helped write her story although I would have been perfectly incapable of that at that age. The story got a prize, $10.00—all of that! She gave me half of it. I thought it was generosity itself and still do." The tale is noteworthy because it is the first example of the Gothicism that runs through Cather's work, becoming a major element in her final novels. The story is not very good: a very conventional ghost tale in which a football team is defeated by an invisible twelfth member of the opposing team, the ghostly extra player being the recently deceased star of the winning team. The story is full of terror and melodrama as eerie events take place on the field, but Cather had not yet learned how to introduce successfully supernatural events into the normal world. Susan Rosowski writes: "Yet because it *is* crude it is also clear and therefore useful in pointing to something important in Cather's writing: her acknowledgement that human experience contains dark mysteries, inexplicable by ordinary rules of logic but nonetheless there."

The Geres, Will Owen Jones, and Dr. Tyndale were friends of Cather's career in journalism. Charles Gere, editor and publisher of the *Journal*, was her employer during the last three years she lived in Lincoln. His daughters all were close friends, especially Mariel, with whom Cather corresponded long after she left Nebraska. On the *Journal*'s sixtieth anniversary Cather wrote a graceful tribute to Mr. Gere, whose patience with her early writing seemed to her monumental. "I was paid one dollar a column, which was certainly all my high-stepping rhetoric was worth. Those out-pourings were pretty dreadful, but . . . he let me step as high as I wished. It was rather hard on his readers, perhaps, but it was good for me, because it enabled me to riot in fine writing until I got to hate it, and began slowly to recover." She added that sometimes there would be a twinkle in his eye that made her distrustful of her rhetorical magnificence, but he never corrected her. Will Owen Jones, the young managing editor of the *Journal*, taught journalism part-time at the university. Her close relationship with him began during her junior year, when she took a course from him that led to her regular employment on the paper.

Dr. Tyndale, an uncle of the Westermann boys, had come to Lincoln in 1893 for his health and to practice medicine. He wrote drama criticism as a hobby. He had come from the East, knew a lot about the theater, and wrote cocky, humorous notices. He also was "a severe iconoclast, took especial interest in Willa Cather, and in revolutionizing some of her ideas." Before she began writing drama reviews, the *Courier* had complained that theater reviewing in Lincoln, except for the columns of Dr. Tyndale in the *News*, was "a dreary waste of undiluted mediocrity." Cather's friendship with this fifty-year-old single doctor, a rather debonair character, caused a lot of talk among self-appointed guardians of the public morals. But Cather paid no attention and cultivated this important friendship. Dr. Tyndale, Lewis believes, is the one who arranged for her to spend a week in Chicago seeing opera during her senior year, and there is a bit of him in the character of Dr. Englehardt in a late story, "Double Birthday." He also had a hand in persuading Cather to dress like a young woman. On one occasion, when she went to a party in boys' clothes, he told her "that was the last straw . . . she would have to be less conspicuous." She also went to him for counsel when she felt downhearted and discouraged.

Her relationship with Louise Pound was unlike any other friendship she made in college. When Cather arrived in Lincoln as a second prep, Pound was already a junior, though only a year and a half older. As a member of one of the pioneer first families of the city, she had social standing as well as brains. Cather's masculine nonconformity contrasted sharply with Pound's demeanor. Louise was beautiful, dressed fashionably, let her hair grow, and promoted the cause of women by becoming an athlete, pianist, and campus leader. Though she played tennis, golf, won prizes as a cyclist, managed the women's basketball team, helped organize a women's military company that drilled with Springfield rifles, she was very feminine in appearance. She also was a scholar and after college took a Ph.D. at Heidelberg. The two women were thrown together in Cather's freshman year when they both were associate editors of the *Lasso* and later when they took part in dramatic productions.

Cather fell in love, apparently for the first time in her life. Whether this love should be considered a serious affair or a short-lived freshman's "crush" on a senior is arguable. To call this a lesbian relationship, as some critics have done, is to give it undue importance. Pound did not return the affection with anything like the fervor with which it was given. She had many admirers of both sexes, was not inclined to focus her attention on any one individual, and this relationship came to an abrupt end after about two and a half years.

There is no doubt, however, that Cather went through a tempestuous psychological experience during this period. She confessed to Dorothy Canfield Fisher years later that during her youth she was mixed up, tormented; those were years of frenzy, she said. The earliest documentation of this frenzied period comes from an indiscreet letter Cather wrote Louise from her rooming house a few blocks from the Pound home. It was mid-June 1892 at the time of Louise's graduation. Willa was packing to go home to Red Cloud for the summer. She was very unhappy that she had been unable to bid Louise a proper good-bye the night before, that she had not told Louise how handsome she looked in her new Worth gown. The house had been full of people, all admirers of Louise. Cather was especially jealous of one young man in a dress coat who seemed to be enamoured of Louise. She was also unhappy that she would not see Pound for a long time, that her going away probably would not make much difference to Louise. The letter is highly charged with the emotions of unrequited love. It also states rather remorsefully Cather's view of close female relationships: it is manifestly unfair that feminine friendship should be regarded as unnatural, she told Pound. She felt much put upon by this social attitude and seemed willing to flout convention, as she had on other matters when she was in high school in Red Cloud. Pound apparently wanted only an ordinary friendship and continually held Cather at arm's length.

This infatuation continued during the following year, when Cather was a sophomore, and after she went home for the summer in 1893, she wrote Louise begging her to come to Red Cloud for a visit. She wrote that she was feeling blue and disconsolate. She was in a state of internal revolution. She implored her friend to come down and save her soul. But before she finished writing, she received a card from Pound announcing that she was not coming. Cather finished her letter reproachfully, saying that their friendship had been too one-sided, that she did not want to go on this way. Louise reconsidered and in July traveled down to Red Cloud.

Cather prepared for the visit like a general planning a campaign. Because Louise was not used to children, Willa bribed her seven-year-old brother James with two nickels and a bottle of pop to go out into the country to visit, but she forgot to tell him how long to stay away. The next day he hitchhiked home with a farmer driving into town and began lavishing his affections on the visitor. They got on much better than she expected, Cather wrote Mariel Gere, but it was a nuisance having the child underfoot all the time. For Cather the visit was all too short, just enough to make her feel the need for her friend. She drove Louise all over the country, driving with one hand, she said, and sometimes with no hands at all. She was eager to get back to Lincoln for school and to see Louise again. She was delighted to find out that one of her rivals for Pound's affections, a girl named DePue, was soon to be married. That meant victory for her. She would have won the ground from under her rival, and that marriage would be her coronation. She would be number one. Heaven help the Greek and Latin during the coming year, she wrote. She ended by urging Mariel not to let her younger sisters, Ellen and Frances, see the last page of her letter. She did not want to corrupt them with her "spooniness." Louise had broken her of writing letters like this, but every once in a while she could not help it, she added.

Eight months later Cather demolished her relationship with the entire Pound family. No one knew why she did it, and it is possible she did not even realize what she was doing. The cause of the rupture was a lampoon of Roscoe Pound that she published in the *Hesperian* in the form of a Theophrastean "character": the University Graduate. She had written other "characters" that were either innocuous or based on unidentifiable real people, but the piece on Louise Pound's brother was unmistakable and certainly unflattering. In it Roscoe Pound is pompous, stuffy, conceited, and impressed with his own importance. He stands "around the halls buttonholing old acquaintances and showing the University to them." He exhibits the buildings and faculty "with an air of proprietorship and pleased condescension." He belongs to the botany seminar and "calls everything by its longest and most Latin name." "In his earliest youth he was a notorious bully, and little boys of the neighborhood used to be afraid to go past his house." Now he bullies people verbally and loves to "browbeat them, argue them down, Latin them into a corner, and botany them into a shapeless mass." And he likes to hang around the university "in order that people may ask who he is and be told what fine marks he used to get in his classes."

There is no documentation other than this "character" to reconstruct the relationship between Cather and Louise's brother. There obviously was a sharp clash in personalities, and Willa and Roscoe no doubt often took adversarial positions. He was a lawyer-botanist whose scientific mind was preoccupied with the precise details of taxonomy. He also was the soul of propriety and convention, and Cather's aggressive nonconformity must have irritated him considerably. Her "crush" on his sister perhaps sharpened the antipathy, but it is pure speculation to suggest, as Phyllis Robinson does in her biography of Cather, that Roscoe had charged Willa with being a lesbian. There is a good bit of truth in the "character" she wrote, and she may not have given any thought to how easily identifiable her subject would be. The Pound family was furious and declared Cather *persona non grata* in their house, where she had been entertained many times. Louise Pound told an interviewer in 1937 that Cather had used material gained while a guest of the Pounds. "The breach of etiquette Mother Pound and Sister Oliva found unforgivable."

As the "character" of Roscoe Pound suggests, Cather was a long time learning tact and discretion. In her college years she expressed her distaste for Professor Sherman openly and made enemies among her classmates by her outspoken opinions. Just a decade later she raised a storm of protest from her family and Will Owen Jones when she put her beloved Aunt Franc into "A Wagner Matinee." She had no idea that the home folks would object to the story. About the time she published *The Troll Garden* she did something that greatly disturbed the Canfields. What it was can only be conjectured, but the ridiculous figure of Flavia Hamilton in the story "Flavia and Her Artists" is altogether too much like Flavia Canfield not to be noticed. In 1916 H. L. Mencken turned down her story "The Diamond Mine" for *The Smart Set*. He was afraid that the story, which is based on the career of Lillian Nordica, American soprano, would open him to a libel suit.

Throughout her life Cather put real people into her fiction, but in later years she was somewhat more circumspect. Though Thea Kronborg as an adult singer is based on the life of Olive Fremstad, the portrait is flattering, and Fremstad was pleased. So were Annie Pavelka and the Miner sisters when *My Ántonia* appeared. The character of Claude Wheeler, protagonist of *One of Ours* (1922), was drawn from her cousin who had been killed in World War I, but this too is a sympathetic portrayal. His widow, Enid in the novel, however, is drawn as a despicable character, and she must have been upset by the book; but there is no record of her reaction. There is a record, however, of an angry response from a minister in Lincoln who delivered a sermon defending a preacher friend named Welden against what he regarded as slander in Cather's creation of a bigoted, narrow-minded clergyman in the novel named Weldon. When Cather wrote *A Lost Lady*, both Garbers were dead and left no direct descendants who might object to the adultery in the plot. The unflattering portrait of Myra Henshawe in *My Mortal Enemy* is based on a real person who has not yet been positively identified. Cather was much upset by the anger she caused with her "character" of Roscoe Pound and still remembered it painfully two years later when she wrote Mariel Gere from Red Cloud. Mariel had been a bracer to her, she said, ever since she was a shaved-headed prep, and she never would have got through the Pound scrape without her. Her father, mother, other friends, and the Lord deserted her, but Mariel took her up. When would she ever be done making a fool of herself, she added. The break with Louise was not irrevocable, however, though they never were close again, and three years later Cather was writing her from Pittsburgh to describe in great detail her new job on the *Pittsburgh Leader*.

CHAPTER 5

Turning Professional

When readers of the *Nebraska State Journal* opened their Sunday papers on November 5, 1893, they found a new column, "One Way of Putting It," written, though unsigned, by Willa Cather. She was then in the first semester of her junior year and still a month short of being twenty. This was the debut of her professional career in journalism, which lasted until 1912 and took her from Lincoln to Pittsburgh and finally to New York. During this time she probably turned out more copy than appears in all of her collected works of the following thirty-five years. When she died in 1947 her public was virtually unaware of this long foreground as a newspaper and magazine writer. She did not talk about it and regarded it as a closed part of her life, but it is the long apprenticeship that leads to her mature artistry. The sheer bulk of her writing in her years as a journalist is astonishing, and even after a generation of scholarly digging into the archives, all of it has not yet been identified.

During the fall and early winter of 1893 she still was managing editor of the *Hesperian*, and until she got out the special Charter Day issue in mid-February, she had to divide her time. Even so, she appeared in the *Journal* more than once a week until February and for the rest of the year doubled her contributions. She stopped writing stories for the *Hesperian* and began turning out sketches and vignettes of real life written in a fictional form. None of these early columns is very remarkable, but her facility with words, her ability to turn a phrase, her eye for detail are already very competent. What she remembered as her "high-stepping rhetoric" more than thirty years later is actually a felicitous prose style. She had not yet learned to distinguish sentiment from sentimentality, and her striving for effect is unsubtle, but she already was the equal of the older professionals who wrote for the Lincoln papers.

Her beginning was modest enough. As her columns were unsigned, only her friends and the newspaper staff knew who had written "One Way of Putting It." At one dollar per column she had to work like the devil to earn enough to pay her board and room. It took about one thousand words to fill a column, so that she was being paid sweatshop wages of one-tenth of a cent per word. After a few weeks, however, the paper began giving her line drawings to illustrate her columns, and then they gave her a two-column box heading. But she did not get a real by-line until the twenty-seventh of May, when she wrote a feature story on the circus. She produced about sixty-five thousand words during her first year on the *Journal* and earned about sixty-five dollars, enough to pay her board and room for five months.

The opening column began with the description of a church service in a fashionable church: "The church was crowded; hundreds of men and women were sitting in front of the minister who stood under the twisted brass-chandeliers and spoke of the brotherhood of man. He looked over the well-dressed, well-educated audience and his interest quickened under the pleasant knowledge that he was being appreciated. His white face flushed and his thin lips trembled with enthusiasm, enthusiasm over the beauty of the women in the audience, the grandeur of the voluntary by Haydn that died from the great moaning pipes of the organ, and over his own eloquence and conscious power." This vignette then is followed by an account of a prison chaplain preaching to three hundred convicts "in a bare, barn-like room with a low ceiling and grated windows." He too speaks of the brotherhood of man. The third of these Sunday morning sketches takes place in a Salvation Army tent where a collection of human derelicts is singing "Washed in the Blood of the Lamb." Contrasts such as these supply the method in these early columns: a poor girl at Christmastime looking wistfully through a shop window at a beautiful doll; a drunken bum reciting Shelley and Browning; an unfeeling and bored son attending his mother's funeral; a whore in a theater balcony looking down on a happily married couple and their child in a box below. One little tale is like an O. Henry story with a surprise ending: an old, partly paralyzed man in the theater gallery turns out to be the former leading man of the actress performing on stage. Every once in a while something jumps off the page to arrest one's attention, a remark that is characteristic of Cather's whole attitude toward life and art or an idea that will inform her later work. After the Salvation Army scene, she writes: "By what is man ever saved other than by enthusiasm. . . . A genius is just another way of defining a great enthusiast." In another sketch she describes a businessman with a manuscript novel in his desk, the narrative device she later used in *My Ántonia*.

The theater setting of some of her columns is not surprising because she was also beginning to review plays. Her first play notice, unsigned in the "Amusements" column, was a review of Walker Whiteside's *Richelieu* on November 22, and four days later she reviewed Clara Morris's *Camille*, her first major piece of theater criticism. It was a memorable night at the theater, and she was thrilled by the performance of what she later called "the one great drama of the century." "To commend, even to speak of the great work done on the Lansing stage last night," she rhapsodized, "seems almost presumption. Better work has never been done by any actress in any country. Nothing can be more natural than nature, more lifelike than life. There are heights beyond which even art cannot rise. Comments upon the wonderful power of Clara Morris's voice, upon the technical perfection of her acting are utterly unnecessary." She continued: "*Camille* is an awful play. Clara Morris plays only awful plays. Her realism is terrible and relentless. It is her art and mission to see all that is terrible and painful and unexplained in life. It is a dark and gloomy work." Such a powerful impression did Dumas's play make on her that she recreated this performance twenty-five years later in *My Ántonia* when Jim Burden takes Lena Lingard to the theater during his student days in Lincoln.

Both of these early reviews were unsigned, but by the following month Cather was beginning to initial her theater notices. The extravagant praise she heaped on *Camille* was not typical of her drama criticism. The first signed notice, a review of Edwin Royle's *Friends*, praised the actors but panned the play, a "drama on one man's loving another better than himself. It is a beautiful idea, perhaps, but it does not exist outside of girls' boarding schools." Cather did not hesitate to call a play phony when she thought it was, even though the audience loved it. She was also blunt in her criticism of bad acting; and a few days later, after watching some particularly inept performances at the Funk Theater, she suggested, apropos of the large portrait of Shakespeare painted on the drop curtain, that "someone ought to have common decency enough to paint that great face out, and profane his name no more." When she had to review Robert Downing, she concluded that his forte was his neck. "Mr. Downing is a conscientious actor and he believes in giving the public their money's worth, and as he has very little else to give them, he gives with royal bounty the beauty of his physique. No actress, however aspiring, has ever dared to be quite so liberal with her neck as Mr. Downing. He makes it the chief attraction." And she went on to note that the reason he never played anything but classic roles was obvious: they allowed a man to wear "decolleté robes."

By the second semester of her junior year, Cather had become the regular drama critic for the *Journal*. She very soon acquired a reputation as the liveliest and least inhibited reviewer in the Midwest. The lack of tact that often caused her trouble in her personal relationships made her reviews lively reading for the paper's subscribers. She was the chief reason the *Des Moines Record* noted that "the best theatrical critics of the west are said to be connected with the Lincoln, Neb., press." Gustav Frohman, who was involved in sending out road companies to all parts of the country, visited Lincoln and declared: "Lincoln newspapers are noted for their honesty . . . in dramatic matters, and it is the best advertisement of intelligence and refinement that a town can have. I have heard of it from professionals and non-professionals all along the road, and poor companies begin to tremble long before they get here. That kind of respect is worth something." He too was generalizing on the basis of Cather's reviewing. Will Owen Jones remembered: "Many an actor of national reputation wondered on coming to Lincoln what would appear next morning from the pen of that meatax young girl of whom all of them had heard. Miss Cather did not stand in awe of the greatest actors, but set each one in his place with all the authority of a veteran metropolitan critic."

Cather also was willing to take on other drama critics. When an article by a pseudonymous "Jane Archer" appeared in the *Journal* attacking Cather's exuberant review of Clara Morris, she defended her views with spirit: "It is a score of years too late to say that Clara Morris is not a great actress. Time and the world have decided otherwise. That she is past her prime no one denies, but she has done her work and she will go down in stage traditions as one of the greatest actors of all time. . . . Clara Morris is undoubtedly a loud actress; she uses freely both noise and intensity; but she plays only loud and stormy roles. She never has offended public taste by shouting the lines of Juliet." Then she went on to say that "the curse of every school and phase of modern art is the guild of drawing-room critics; critics who sneer at the great and powerful, and adore the clever and the dainty. They refuse to read anything more stimulating than Howells' parlor farces, and to hear any play more moving than *The Rivals*. This race of critics has declared Ruskin and Wagner and Turner and Modjeska blasé. . . . They take books that look well on their tables; the music that is not too loud for their parlors; the pictures that hang well on their walls."

Cather expected writers, singers, actors, to give all to their art, and she had meant it when she wrote that the god of art accepts only human sacrifices. Artists also were a law unto themselves, she believed. When "Jane Archer" extolled Julia Marlowe over Clara Morris as someone she would be delighted and honored to know, Cather replied with disgust: "This is a final test of womanhood, perhaps, but not of art. Very few of the world's great artists have been desirable acquaintances. I would ask no greater boon of heaven than to sit and watch Sarah Bernhardt night after night, but heaven preserve me from any very intimate relations with her." Cather was herself a difficult person and became increasingly prickly as she grew older, a person of strong loves and equally strong hates.

On another occasion she scoffed at the efforts of the Society for the Prevention of Cruelty to Children to stop thirteen-year-old Elsie Graham from acting. "The Society claim that it is cruel for a child to be put to the strain of acting every night when she ought to be home in bed. Of course it is cruel, most art is cruel, and very few artists have time to sleep much in this world. . . . It is very kind of society to try to lighten the burden of genius, but it can't be done. Genius means relentless labor and passionate excitement from the hour one is born until the hour one dies." Later she observed that "the artist, poor fellow, has but one care, one purpose, one hope—his work. That is all God gave him; in place of love, of happiness, of popularity, only that. He is not made to live like other men; his soul is strung differently. . . . The fewer friends he has the better; every friend means one more manager." Cather too lived for her work, and the older she grew, the smaller her circle became. She clung to old friends and was reluctant to make new ones.

Cather praised and damned with great abandon during her first season as a drama critic. Julia Marlowe also was one of her favorites, and when she came to town in March, playing in Sheridan Knowles's *The Love Chase*, Cather wrote that "Julia Marlowe has come and gone again, leaving with us a sort of warm, rich delight that will hover about us for days." She was the "embodiment of beauty and good taste and good spirits." However, on stage she "lives too beautifully to live very hard, dies too gracefully to die very effectively. This is all very winning and beautiful, but it is not the highest kind of art." Marlowe, nevertheless, made a deep impression, and in one of Cather's last stories, "The Best Years," her character Miss Knightly is caught by a snowstorm in Lincoln because she stayed over to see Julia Marlowe in *The Love Chase*. When Richard Mansfield, another favorite, came to the Lansing Theater the next month, she thought his performance in Clyde Fitch's *Beau Brummell* "the most finished performance that Lincoln has seen for a long time. . . . Mr. Mansfield is perfectly self-contained and self-sufficient. He depends very little upon the applause or appreciation of his audience. . . . More than any other actor he acts for the play and for himself." His intelligence, his subtlety, his finesse, she found totally satisfying. When

James O'Neill came to Lincoln in his famous role as the Count of Monte Cristo, however, his leading lady drew Cather's scorn. "Mademoiselle Celeste is a dream of beauty. There are few handsomer women to be found in either the higher or lower walks of the profession, but her acting is weak, insipid and pointless. She is innocent of all art or even of a clever imitation of it, and her voice was a continual and painful surprise. It rather startles one to hear the tones of a cavalry officer issue from such very bewitching lips." Lillian Lewis also was impaled on Cather's pen, and when it was announced that she was going to play *Cymbeline* the following season, 1894–95, Cather hoped that "they dug Shakespeare's grave very deep." The possibility that Maggie Mitchell might return to Nebraska that year brought the comment: "It has been a hard year, theatrically and otherwise, and we have had most of the seven plagues of Egypt poured on us, but we have hoped the Lord would spare us Maggie Mitchell." When Louis James and Frederick Warde, who played together, were announced, she observed that "Mr. Warde has no talent at all; Mr. James has very little" and "would that we could forget" the *Othello* they put on last year. Lily Langtry particularly drew her ire as an actress who could neither act nor even read her lines properly.

Cather was sensitive to the charge that she used a meat-ax in her criticism, and after she had been reviewing plays for a year began to keep a box score. In November of her senior year she reported that so far that season she had praised fourteen companies and damned fifteen. "No critic," she wrote, "enjoys perpetually 'roasting' performances. It grows desperately monotonous after a time. There is a limit to the harsh adjectives in the English language. . . . But any newspaper that bestows the same exorbitant praise upon a No. 13 *Jane* [a popular play] company that it humbly tenders Richard Mansfield puts itself in a very ridiculous position." The *Beatrice* (Nebr.) *Express* commented that Cather "is rather given to indiscriminate roasting, but she does it so well that everything is forgiven," and the *Hesperian*'s rival, the *Nebraskan*, saluted her with:

> This is for "Billy" of journalist fame,
> Who writes her roasts in words of flame
> And gives it to everyone just the same.

The lines were accompanied by a sketch of a smoking pen. Cather's successor on the *Journal*, Keene Abbott, tried to write the same kind of scathing reviews but was called into the managing editor's office and told to desist. He said his reviews were "no worse than those Willa Cather did." "Well," Will Owen Jones replied, "but that was Miss Cather!" And it was. She was *sui generis*.

Her reviews were not only concerned with value judgments. She was interested in the whole world of art and ranged widely in her notices. Her work showed a maturity and poise not to be expected in so young a critic, and her knowledge of drama and literature, Continental and classic as well as English, was extensive. Thus her reviews were informed and informative and demonstrated a competence that lent authority to the value judgments. She was inclined to be impressionistic and to make frequent use of biographical anecdotes; she was interested in her own responses and very confident of her ability to evaluate. Some of her notions of the reviewer's task she summarized a year after she had begun her drama criticism: "A critic's first instincts are the best because they are the truest. . . . He must take his impression as he gets it and rush it upon paper. . . . That is the great object; to have a notice alive, to have the glare of the footlights and the echo of the orchestra in it. . . . to reproduce to some extent the atmosphere of the play, to laugh if it was funny, to weep a little if it was sad, to say plainly and frankly if it was bad." The journalistic principle involved here is the exact opposite of her mature literary method, which, in brief, is emotion recollected in tranquility. She never confused her journalism with her art and always made a clear distinction between what she did to make a living and what she did for literature.

As long as she stuck to play-reviewing, she was convincing and knowledgeable, but on occasion when she strayed to other sorts of reviews, her brashness got her into trouble. During her senior year she reviewed a concert devoted to the music of Mendelssohn in which she attacked the composer: "One never realizes how tiresome Mendelssohn is until he hears him for an hour and a half together. A Mendelssohn program is always a little monotonous and disappointing, just as a Mendelssohn composition is. There is always the exaggerated elaboration of an insufficient theme, always the same promise of something really great and the same recoil from the doing of it. Either a forced excitement which results in a series of technical tricks, or a simplicity which betrays a poverty of imagination. He always substitutes excitement for fervor and nervous agitation for passion." This wrong-headed review brought a sharp response from Professor August Hagenow of the university's School of Music, who had put on the concert. He wrote the editor of the *Journal* to voice "the general sentiment of all intelligent musicians in denouncing the article . . . as false and misleading." Mendelssohn's reputation had been secure for half a century, he pointed out, but along comes this "upstart critic who now at this late date adventures openly to confront the whole musical world . . . armed with the asserted criterion of his own personal 'feeling' and with opposed depreciations and detractions!" Cather— who also had asserted in the same review that "perhaps there were only two masters of music who were really great," Beethoven and Chopin—had the good sense not to attempt a rebuttal of Hagenow's letter. It did not stop her from writing music criticism, however, but as time went on, her knowledge, taste, and ability to discriminate improved measureably.

Her skill as a newspaper writer matured so rapidly that she was invited to help teach a course in journalism during the summer of 1894. For the annual Nebraska Chautauqua Assembly in July, Will Owen Jones organized a class in practical journalism with Cather as one of his two assistants. The assembly took place just west of Crete in southeastern Nebraska, where the Chautauqua grounds occupied 109 acres along the Big Blue River in a blue-green setting of woods and water. People by the thousands came by train from everywhere in the state to live for ten days in tents or cabins and attend classes, go to lectures, listen to concerts. Summer Chautauqua programs, which had begun in New York State, had spread through the country and reached Nebraska in 1882. They were an important movement in popular culture and education, and at Crete uneducated farmers from the plains mingled with people of some sophistication from Lincoln and Omaha. Cather not only taught in the journalism course, but she also was hired by Louis Westermann's paper, the *Evening News*, to cover the assembly.

Cather sent back to Lincoln nine well-written, informative, light-hearted reports of the annual Chautauqua. On opening day, July 3, when it rained, she described the activity of tent dwellers stretching damp canvas and cottage dwellers settling in. The next day was fair, and hammocks appeared everywhere, tennis players came out, and "sylvan wanderings" took place. Then she reported the serious business of the assembly, the lectures and concerts given by imported scholars and musicians. She was particularly impressed by the sculptor Loredo Taft, of the Chicago Art Institute, who lectured on French, Dutch, and German painting with stereopticon slides to illustrate his talks. Thirty-six years after covering his lectures she wrote him a fan letter to thank him for his fountain, which she enjoyed every time she passed through Chicago.

She also reported a lecture by Dr. Bayard Holmes, one of the promoters of Hull House and a social reformer; another by Charles Kent, professor of biblical literature from the University of Chicago. She was especially interested in Rev. Joseph Duryea, who gave a lecture course on Roman history, a subject that long had occupied her attention. Song recitals by two Chicago singers, Electa Gifford, soprano, and Katherine Fisk, contralto, drew enthusiastic comments, but she reserved her highest praise for Mrs. Will Owen Jones, whose playing of Chopin stirred the soul of an unshaven farmer sitting next to her. At the end of the Chautauqua season Cather's final report described the grounds "literally strewn with cots and camp chairs," everything "desolate and lonely," and a few lone souls wandering "about the graveyard reading epitaphs."

Another significant event that summer occurred later in July when Cather, her brother Roscoe, Mariel Gere, and another friend visited the decaying river community of Brownville on the fortieth anniversary of its founding. This visit resulted in her first long feature story, more than three thousand words, which the *Journal* published the next month. "It is almost unheard of to find a town in Nebraska that has a past," she began, " . . . though all of them have, or think they have, a future." The town, which had been the first settlement in the Nebraska Territory, had lost its future when the Missouri River silted up, the Union Pacific was routed through Omaha, and the founding fathers built a brand-new city at Lincoln for the state capital.

As the visitors walked through the town, they saw "handsome residences gone to [w]rack and ruin, terraces plowed up in cornfields and sloping lawns grown up in wheat and sunflowers." The main street was "lined with empty brick buildings and gaping cellar holes where the buildings have fallen down or been torn away." The white stone pavements and gutters were growing with pale, lifeless-looking grass. The rotting board sidewalks which ran over the hills clattered and creaked when one stepped on them, like rickety ladders. "Even the Lone Tree saloon [was] falling to pieces, and that, in a western town, is the sure sign that everything is gone." The article went on to recreate Brownville during its zenith before the crash, after which all the bigwigs left for Omaha. Here and there between the tumbled-down buildings were vacant lots "that fifteen or twenty years ago sold for six thousand dollars [but] would not bring six today. Lots are never sold in Brownville nowadays except cemetery lots."

The trip to Brownville made a lasting impression, and twice more she returned to the subject during her literary apprenticeship. Three years later in Pittsburgh she wrote a story, "A Resurrection," laid in Brownville and using some of the same descriptive detail. It is a sentimental tale of a widower who marries his former sweetheart years after he has been enticed into marriage by another woman. The tale is not memorable and probably was written to fill up the *Home Monthly*, the family magazine Cather edited after she left Lincoln; but the Brownville setting is memorable. What else was unforgettable about the town besides its decay and dilapidation was its heat. "The Hottest Day I Ever Spent" is the title of the second version of the visit, which she wrote and published in 1900. While the first account emphasized the town's fall from grandeur, the second featured the blazing inferno "when the government thermometer registered 115 degrees in the shade and 135 degrees in the sun. . . . That one day ruined the wheat and corn crops of two of the greatest agricultural states in the Union, Kansas and Nebraska." This rewriting used much of the original detail, but it added fiction to the account in the creation of Japanese and Swedish newspapermen who accompany the narrator. The Japanese, who has been to Arizona, never has seen such heat; the Swede lies "on the edge of his bed, panting like a dog," and the entire party gets sick.

Cather's last year at the university was a steady grind of newspaper work and little extracurricular activity. Carrying a full course load and reviewing theatrical events for the *Journal* really were two jobs. Between September and the time she graduated in June, she contributed ninety-five pieces to the paper, an average of four-plus per week. She also gave her column a new title, "As You Like It," and turned it out every week for the Sunday edition. While she spent her days going to classes, she spent her evenings at the theater. After the final curtain she had to go to the *Journal* office to write her review and frequently did not get home until two in the morning. When she went back to Red Cloud after graduation, she wrote Mrs. Goudy that she was dead tired, body and brain. It was one of these late nights after the theater that Stephen Crane, who was on assignment from the Bachellor Syndicate to report drought conditions in Nebraska, "was fascinated by the sight of a young girl . . . standing *fast asleep*. He said it was the only time he had ever seen anyone asleep on their feet like that."

This was early February 1895. The searing wind that Cather remembered in "The Hottest Day I Ever Spent" had turned Nebraska into a disaster area, and after two years of drought and crop failure, the plight of the plains states had aroused considerable interest and sympathy in the East. Crane visited Lincoln both at the beginning and the end of his two week stay in Nebraska, and Cather must have talked to him on both occasions. Cather, already interested in Crane, who was only two years older, had read *The Red Badge of Courage* when it was serialized in the *Journal* just two months earlier.

She did not write anything about this meeting at the time it took place, but she followed Crane's career, reviewed his books, and when he died wrote a piece entitled "When I Knew Stephen Crane." Writing in Pittsburgh under one of her several pseudonyms, Henry Nickelman, she created a semifictional account of this visit to Nebraska. Her male narrator is a naive college student writing for the *Journal* in his spare time and fresh off the range. The time is spring; the night is "oppressively warm; one of those dry winds that are the curse of the country was blowing up from Kansas." She describes Crane as thin to the point of emaciation, unshaven, slovenly dressed, and having a dark mustache and black hair. He carried with him a volume of Poe, which he was continually reading. "Crane was moody most of the time, his health was bad and he seemed profoundly discouraged." There was a "profound melancholy always lurking deep" in his eyes, that "seemed to be burning themselves out." He curses his trade and tells his male interviewer that he will be fortunate if he does not become a writer.

What is interesting about this account is the image it creates of Willa Cather in her senior year of college. It was Cather who was reading Poe about this time and finding him the archetypal unappreciated genius. The dark, brooding figure she draws of Crane more nearly fits the author of "The Fall of the House of Usher" than it does Stephen Crane. John Berryman says that "Crane's western journey in the first half of 1895 was the happiest time perhaps he was to know—an idyl . . . [and] his health would never be so good again." He loved the West and realized one of his desires—to be in a blizzard on the plains—an experience that resulted in one of his great stories, "The Blue Hotel." And what is more, Crane had fair hair and a light complexion. In her conclusion Cather remarks that Crane "had the precocity of those doomed to die in youth. . . . He drank life to the lees, but at the banquet table where other men took their ease and jested over their wine, he stood a dark and silent figure, somber as Poe himself."

Perhaps the most interesting detail in this sketch of Crane is even more pure Cather. She quotes him as saying that "after he got a notion for a story, months passed before he could get any sort of personal contact with it, or feel any potency to handle it. 'The detail of a thing has to filter through my blood, and then it comes out like a native product, but it takes forever.' " This remark, she adds, "rather took a hold of me," and well it might, for it is precisely the creative process that she employed in her mature fiction. But it hardly describes the method of Crane, whose collected works fill twelve volumes and were produced between *Maggie* (1892) and his death at the age of twenty-nine in 1900. The interview sounds authentic, however, when Cather quotes Crane as saying that "he led a double literary life; writing in the first place, the matter that pleased himself, and doing it very slowly; in the second place, any sort of stuff that would sell." She also was grinding out newspaper copy to keep the pot boiling, but her art, unlike Crane's, was painfully slow in coming to fruition.

This problem of the double life occupied her a good deal as she approached graduation. She wanted a literary career but had to make a living. Her reading of Poe focused her attention on the dilemma, and she put her thoughts into words in an essay on Poe she wrote that spring. After summarizing Poe's great accomplishment ("Poe found short story writing a bungling makeshift. He left it a perfect art"), and flinging barbs at Longfellow's popularity and the littleness of Poe's New York associates like Rufus Griswold and N. P. Willis, she addressed the central issue: "I have wondered so often how he did it. How he kept his purpose always clean and his taste always perfect. How it was that hard labor never wearied nor jaded him, never limited his imagination, that the jarring clamor about him never drowned the fine harmonies of his fancy. His discrimination remained always delicate, and from the constant strain of toil his fancy always rose strong and unfettered." This was a real question for an aspiring writer who had to hack out a living in journalism. Could one serve the gods of art and the marketplace without being corrupted? She intended to try, but she knew it would not be easy.

As she watched Crane through his brief career, she sometimes thought he had sold out. Her review of one of his poorest books, *Active Service* (1899), attacked the novel sharply as a work not concerned "with large, universal interests or principles, but with a yellow journalist grinding yellow copy" in a wooden fashion. "In spite of the fact that Mr. Crane has written some of the most artistic short stories in the English language, I begin to wonder whether, blinded by his youth and audacity . . . we have not taken him too seriously." But years after he died she wrote a favorable estimate of his work when she introduced *Wounds in the Rain*, one of the volumes of his collected works that Alfred Knopf published in 1926: "When you examine the mere writing in this unorganized material, you see at once that Crane was one of the first post-impressionists; that he began it before the French painters began it, or at least as early as the first of them. He simply knew from the beginning how to handle detail. He estimated it at its true worth—made it serve his purpose and felt no further responsibility about it. I doubt whether he ever spent a laborious half-hour in doing his duty by detail—in enumerating, like an honest, grubby auctioneer. If he saw one thing in a landscape that thrilled him, he put it on paper, but he never tried to make a faithful report of everything else within his field of vision, as if he were a conscientious salesman making out his expense account." Cather too had learned to do this. Her final view of Crane a decade later was just this: "He died young, but he had done something real. One can read him today."

Cather's meeting with Crane was not her only encounter during her college years with a figure of national visibility. William Jennings Bryan was rising to national prominence as a champion of western democracy, and Cather watched his progress with interest. The political and economic issues that produced the Populist party in the nineties interested her very little, but the personality of Bryan was fascinating. She stored her memories, and at the same time she wrote of her meeting with Crane, she turned out an essay entitled "The Personal Side of William Jennings Bryan." The occasion was

Bryan's second nomination for president by the Democratic National Convention in July 1900. This account of "the great commoner" sounds much more authentic than the memory of Crane, even though it too was written under the pseudonym of Henry Nickelman.

She met Bryan on a streetcar in Lincoln when she was a "second prep." He was stumping the first congressional district in his first campaign for public office, which he won by a resounding margin. He had just made a speech and was carrying an ugly floral tribute given him by his supporters. A talkative old lady sitting near him inquired sympathetically:

"Is it for a funeral?"

Mr. Bryan looked quizzically at the flowers and replied politely:

"Well, I hope not, madam."

After this encounter Cather saw him occasionally. He lived in Lincoln and was always at home to students in his library in the evenings, and he occasionally wrote for the *Hesperian* when she was editor. She must have visited his library a number of times, for she describes it in detail. It fascinated her because it was so different—except for the classics—from any library she would have collected: lives of American statesmen, marked and annotated schoolboy-fashion; works on political economy, mostly by quacks; much poetry of a didactic or declamatory nature; little fiction more recent than Thackeray. "Mr. Bryan used always to be urging us to read *Les Misérables* if we hadn't, and to re-read it if we had. He declared that it was the greatest novel written, yet I think he had never considered its merits or demerits as a novel at all. It was Hugo's vague hyperbolic generalizations on sociological questions that he marked and quoted." That was one of Cather's favorite novels too, but for entirely different reasons.

When Bryan was in good form, Cather remembered, his conversation was "absolutely overwhelming in its richness and novelty and power, in the force and aptness of his illustrations. Yet one always felt that it was meant for the many, not the few, that it was addressed to humanity, and that there should be a stenographer present to take it down." Sometimes what he said was strikingly original; sometimes it was trite. "He chipped his eggs to the accompaniment of maxims. . . . He buttered his toast with an epigram." She also heard him speak publicly in Red Cloud at the funeral of a friend who had been a member of Congress, but she could not have heard the famous "Cross of Gold" speech that stampeded the Democratic Convention in Chicago in July 1896 and brought him his first nomination for president. Henry Nickelman says he heard it, but Willa Cather was already in Pittsburgh.

For Cather, Bryan symbolized "the entire Middle West; all its newness and vigor, its magnitude and monotony, its richness and lack of variety, its inflammability and volubility, its strength and its crudeness, its high serious-ness and self-confidence, its egotism and its nobility." He never made a Democrat out of her or aroused any interest in politics, but the campaign of 1896 did give her the denouement for "Two Friends." Bryan is the only political figure she ever profiled. Like Carlyle, whom she characterized as a bad political economist, she was also inept and indifferent in the political realm. It was only the kingdom of art that she cared about.

Meeting Crane may have been stimulating, but the high spot of Cather's last semester in college was a trip to Chicago to hear grand opera. Less than a month after Crane left Lincoln, Cather and her friend Mary Jones, acting librarian of the university, boarded an eastbound Burlington train. She had not been out of Nebraska since her family migrated from Virginia. The New York Metropolitan Opera was bringing five operas to Chicago for a three-weeks' engagement. The only grand opera Cather ever had heard had been an indifferent performance of *Il Trovatore* by a traveling company that visited Lincoln the previous December and a concert version of *Cavalleria Rusticana* the year before. She had heard light opera, which she liked very much, since she was a child growing up in Red Cloud, and she had reviewed light opera for the *Journal*, but the real thing was still to be experienced. Her passion for opera dates from this week that she spent in Chicago hearing three Verdi operas (*Falstaff, Otello,* and *Aida*), Meyerbeer's *Les Huguenots*, and Gounod's *Romeo et Juliette.*

She was carried away by *Falstaff*, Verdi's final masterpiece, and felt priv-ileged to have heard only the fourth American performance of that new work. She wrote about it glowingly in the *Journal* after her return. The French baritone Victor Maurel, who had created the role in the French, British, and American premières, could both sing and act. His performance was not only a great operatic triumph but was also a faithful tribute to Shakespeare. In addition, she had an instinctive appreciation of the unique-ness of Verdi's final work and knew that she was hearing "an absolutely new creation." Except for one paragraph about *Otello* and the "fiery passion" of Francesco Tomagno in the title role, she wrote nothing more about this wonderful week, even though she also had heard Nellie Melba, Lillian Nordica, and Jean de Reszke; but she never forgot it. It turns up forty years later in her penultimate novel, *Lucy Gayheart.*

She had to pay for the trip, however, with a serious illness, the only recorded illness of her college years. Charles Cather, who was then working in Lincoln for the Security Investment Company, wrote his aunt Sidney Gore at the end of April that Willa was better but had not yet regained her strength. She had come back from Chicago sick and was in bed for a couple of weeks with what was then called typhoid-pneumonia. Her mother had come up from Red Cloud for a visit and stayed on to nurse her. She had been so exhausted from overwork that the week in Chicago was too much. She fell asleep during the final performance, *Les Huguenots*, but fortunately it was Meyerbeer, not Verdi, who concluded her week. She left for Chicago after writing her column for March 10 and was unable to write for the paper again until the thirty-first. But she appeared in the *Journal* nineteen more times before her graduation day, June 12.

The week before commencement she took part in a program held in the chapel by the three undergraduate literary societies. Cather, representing Union, read her Poe essay, while Hugh Walker, who was a Palladian, delivered an oration called "The Fate of the Greeks." The latter performance turned out to be a savage attack on the Greek-letter fraternities, rivals of the literary clubs, all of whose members were considered "barbarians" by the Greeks. Cather held no brief for the fraternities, or sororities, and never had been tempted to join one, but Walker's diatribe made her mad. She got up and tore into Walker in an extemporaneous denunciation of his immaturity and lack of humanity before turning to her own manuscript. The *Journal* reported laconically that she "pretty vigorously contested some of Mr. Walker's statements"; her friend Ned Abbott, who had arranged the program, reported that she "waded into Walker with an improvised roast." However, he thought the evening a glorious success, though he said the "partisans of both [Walker and Cather] lammed me for letting them be on the program."

Willa Cather, bachelor of arts, class of 1895, had her diploma but no regular job. The *Journal* was willing to continue paying her space-rates for her reviews and columns but did not have the wit to offer her a full-time, permanent position. She spent part of the summer in Red Cloud but continued to write regularly for the *Journal*. At the end of July she began a new column, "The Passing Show," which replaced "As You Like It." Then at the beginning of August the *Courier*, a weekly paper devoted to the arts and society and partly owned by her friend Sarah Harris, announced that "Miss Willa Cather [,] who for the past two years has been the dramatic critic and theatrical writer for the *Journal*, will become a member of the *Courier* staff. Miss Cather's reputation extends beyond Nebraska. She is thoroughly original and always entertaining." Subsequently her name began to appear on the masthead as associate editor, but it only remained there until the end of November. For two months "The Passing Show" appeared in the *Courier*, but she continued to review plays for the *Journal*. In December the *Journal* announced that beginning on the fifteenth, her column would again appear regularly in its Sunday issue. What was going on backstage during this period is unknown, but the *Journal* had her exclusive services for the balance of the year. She wrote very few pieces other than her weekly column, however.

She lived in Lincoln during the fall while she was on the *Courier*'s staff and at home in Red Cloud after Christmas, probably to save on board and room. She made frequent trips back to Lincoln and when she was there reviewed plays for her column. Red Cloud was less than 150 miles away, and the newspaper could get her passes on the Burlington whenever she wanted them. Her reputation continued to grow, and the *Nebraska Editor* described her as "a young woman with a genius for literary expression." The article went on to say that her work had made the *Courier* the brightest paper in Nebraska. "Her criticisms, both literary and dramatic, are clever and full of 'ginger.' . . . She keeps in touch with whatever is newest in literary work the world over, and writes her opinions freely. . . . If there is a woman in Nebraska newspaper work who is destined to win a reputation for herself, that woman is Willa Cather." When the Nebraska State Press Association met in Lincoln in January, Cather was invited to speak on "how to make a newspaper interesting." She argued for personal journalism, papers that took stands on issues, papers that allowed their writers to ride their hobbies. After the meeting the *Beatrice Weekly Express* called her "a young woman who is rapidly achieving a western reputation, and who will soon have a national reputation." Her column seems to have been regarded as a valuable asset; her colleague on the *Journal*, Walt Mason, said flatly that she is "unquestionably destined to be among the foremost of American literary women." Male chauvinism in that statement: she already was better than all of the male journalists in Nebraska.

Her growing reputation, her competence, and the lack of a real job depressed her during the winter and spring in Red Cloud. When she wrote Mariel Gere on January 2, she headed her letter "Siberia." Not only was it cold, but she felt she had been banished from Lincoln. She made the best of it by taking part in local social activities and reported that she had accompanied Douglass, then sixteen, to a New Year's dance. All the elite and *bon ton* of Red Cloud were there, she said, but the boys were rowdy, the seats were planks laid on chairs, and the refreshments were sandwiches served from bushel baskets. Douglass was the most civilized boy in the crowd. One of the charms of the provinces, she wrote, was that one gets indifferent to everything; but she was eager to know all the news from Lincoln. On March 12 she wrote again to complain of her bitter exile and her friend's silence. She had nothing to write about, as it was then Lent, and the mad festivities of the province had ceased. She was picking up the mail, reading the papers, eating, and sleeping. Occasionally to vary the monotony she tried cooking, and when the weather permitted she rode her bicycle. The high point of February was the marriage of her cousin Retta Ayres to her neighbor Hugh Miner. She took charge of the wedding breakfast, stayed up all night arranging it, and went to the extravagance of ordering strawberries, fresh tomatoes, and watercress from Chicago. Later her parents went to Hastings, leaving her in charge of the younger children: Jim, ten; Elsie, six; and Jack, four. Jack swallowed two pennies, Jim cut his lip, and she was acting as hospital matron as well as entertainer. She was sick of *Alice in Wonderland* after reading it to Jim sixteen times and had switched to *The Arabian Nights*.

Two days after writing Mariel Gere, she wrote Mariel's father imploring his aid in helping her get a teaching position. Her friend and former teacher Herbert Bates was resigning to return east, and she desperately wanted to be his replacement. She realized her age and sex were against her, but she knew she could do it, and she was willing to work for five hundred dollars a year, which would be less than they would have to pay the man they were planning to get. Bates, she said, would recommend her to any extent. She was naive in the ways of academic appointments and politics, however, and apparently never considered the fact that she had made an enemy out of Lucius Sherman, the head of the English Department. She did not get the job and continued to languish in Red Cloud.

When she wrote Mariel again on May 2, she was both depressed and broke. She felt she could not borrow any more money from her family, and the actresses she had loaned money to in Lincoln still owed her. They can't do without their paste diamonds and champagne, she remarked ruefully. To make matters worse, she felt she was growing away from her family, their way of looking at things, and they were no longer much comfort. They expected unusual things from her, she added, and she was getting nowhere. However, she was still going to dances with Douglass, and in Blue Hill the day before she had met Fred Sund, formerly one of her editors on the *Hesperian*, who was now a banker. He devoted the entire evening to her, and she had danced all thirty-five dances. She also had met a Miss Gayhardt, a teacher, who spoke French and German and could talk about books and theater. She was so glad to meet someone from civilization that she stayed up most of the night talking. She remembered and used Miss Gayhardt's name in 1935 when she created the heroine of her next-to-last novel.

During this period of exile in Red Cloud she turned again to writing fiction. She told Mariel Gere that she was working on various manuscripts, but she gave no details. One manuscript probably was "A Night at Greenway Court," her tale laid in eighteenth-century Virginia, which she placed in the *Nebraska Literary Magazine* in June. In none of her letters of the winter or spring of 1896, however, does she mention an event that should have given her satisfaction. The January issue of the *Overland Monthly* had carried one of her stories, "On the Divide," and for the first time she had appeared in a magazine of national prominence. This was the magazine Bret Harte originally had edited and written for, and though it had died and been reborn to lesser glory, publication there still was an advancement for her.

"On the Divide" was her best story to date, even though she later disowned it and thought it one of the bad apples best left on the ground. It is a grim story reminiscent of those she already had published in the *Hesperian*. It opens: "Near Rattlesnake Creek, on the side of a little draw, stood Canute's shanty. North, east, south stretched the level Nebraska plain of long rust-red grass that undulated constantly in the wind." To the west the ground was broken and rough, and there was a turbid little stream "that had scarcely ambition enough to crawl over its black bottom." The land is inhospitable: deceitfully lovely in the early summer, bitterly barren in autumn. Canute "had seen it smitten by all the plagues of Egypt. . . . parched by drought, and sogged by rain, beaten by hail, and swept by fire, and in the grasshopper years he had seen it eaten as bare and clean as bones that the vultures have left." For ten years Canute has lived alone fighting for possession of this intractable land and often contemplating suicide, but instead of killing himself, he has taken to drink to dull his senses and make life tolerable. Cather was still writing in her Hamlin Garland manner, and it would be many years before the "rust-red grass" became the "colour of wine-stains" in *My Ántonia*. She had not yet learned how to infuse the prairie with myth and symbol suggestive of Homer and the "wine-dark sea."

Yet there is something more in this story than the immigrant's defeat in the effort to tame the wild land. Canute, the blond Norwegian giant, has a soul, and he is not destroyed by the struggle. As the story develops, he falls in love with Lena Yensen and in the denouement carries her off bodily to his cabin, forces the preacher to marry them. Lena in the final paragraph succumbs to Canute's caveman tactics and submits happily, an ending that Jack London might well have written. This story not only reveals Cather's identification with male values, but it also shows a movement, however crude, toward the use of myth and symbol. As Canute carries off Lena, Cather writes: "So it was that Canute took her to his home, even as his bearded barbarian ancestors took the fair frivolous women of the South in their hairy arms and bore them down to their war ships."

This story would be even more interesting as an example of Cather's effort to move towards "the immigrant's spiritual confrontation with the plains" if one could be sure that all of the ideas in it were hers. Late in her life she said she had written the story in an English course and that her professor had touched it up and sent it off to the *Overland Monthly*. What he added, she said, was Canute's fantastic carvings that adorned his windowsills. Crudely done, the carvings showed men plowing with little horned imps on their shoulders, men praying with a skull hanging over their heads, men fighting with serpents, and skeletons dancing together. "It was a veritable Dance of Death by one who had felt its sting." This detail, whether or not it was Cather's invention, moves the fiction in the direction she was going: the creation of characters who have the power to make a world of their imagination.

During the year following her graduation Cather wrote a good deal about books and literature. Earlier, when she was busy reviewing plays, her columns were mostly filled with drama criticism and theatrical news. She continued to read omnivorously, and her observations in this period codify her principles and chart her future literary practice. Her love of romance; her distaste for realism; her search for artistic integrity; her devotion to style; her nostalgia, for a grander past—even at twenty-two—her passion for French literature; her distrust of women writers—all these subjects are documented in the columns she contributed to the *Courier* and the *Journal*.

When a play was made out of Anthony Hope's *The Prisoner of Zenda*, one of her favorite novels, she took the occasion to praise romance, Hope, Kipling, and above all her master Stevenson. "We are growing too analytical ourselves, and we need young men like Rudyard Kipling and Anthony Hope." They were carrying on in a small way the work of Stevenson, who had just died the previous winter. "We owe him much, that great master of pure romance. . . . Romance is the highest form of fiction, and it will never desert us." She added: "Ibsens and Zolas are great, but they are temporary. Children, the sea, the sun, God himself are all romanticists. Clouds cover the sun sometimes, and there is darkness upon the face of the deep, and God hides his face from us. But they come again, and with them Romance, as fair and beautiful and still as young as when it came with the troubadours to the springlit fields outside Verona where the Dukes held their Court of Love."

She seldom had anything good to say about the work of William Dean Howells, who led the battle for realism against the romancers of the 1890s. When he published *My Literary Passions* in 1895, Cather thought him something of a pompous ass: "Doesn't Mr. Howells know that at one time or another everyone raves over *Don Quixote*, imitates Heine, worships Turgenev and calls Tolstoy a prophet? Does Mr. Howells think that no one but he ever had youth and enthusiasm and aspirations? . . . He might as well write a detailed account of how he had the measles and the whooping cough." Her disparagement of Howells was partly due to her distaste for the new *Ladies'*

Home Journal in which his literary reminiscences appeared. He had been sandwiched between "those thrilling articles about how Henry Ward Beecher tied his necktie and what kind of coffee Mrs. Hall Caine likes."

She was quick to denounce the meretricious in art, and the appearance of a new novel by the romancer F. Marion Crawford gave her such an opportunity. She had hoped that his latest, *Casa Braccio*, would be one story written for his own personal pleasure, that he was rich and famous enough to do this, but it was not such a book. "I suppose the curse of having sold one's self is that one . . . can never escape from the habits of vice." What she could not forgive Crawford for was his view of the novel as a marketable commodity, his desire to please his readers at the expense of his artistic integrity. When Oscar Wilde was sent to prison for sodomy, she wrote a column attacking not his sins of the body (though she agreed that he deserved to be in prison) but his sins against literature. "To every man who has really great talent there are two ways open, the narrow one and the wide, to be great and suffer, or to be clever and comfortable." Wilde took the easy way. He lacked sincerity, reverence for his own gift, and now all one could see was "the chaos and confusion of wasted life."

The elegiac tone that permeates some of Cather's best novels is already detectable in these columns written at twenty-two. Current writers simply did not have the stature of the masters of the past. "I picked up an old American periodical last week. Among the contributors were Dickens, Thackeray, Emerson, Lowell, Longfellow, and Hawthorne. Heavens, what names to stir the hearts of men!" Nowadays essays are nothing but "pleasant little chats," and there has not been a "volume of verse worth reading twice put out by a native of these states for ten years or more." "In all the literature of the last ten years I have not found one burning conviction, one new and really confident truth wrested from the concealing elements." In one sweeping paragraph she disposed of some very good Howells, Twain, and Dickinson, not to mention the work of lesser folk like Garland, Bellamy, Bierce, Chopin, and her acquaintance Crane. She concluded these magnificent generalizations by observing: "Now that Stevenson is dead I can think of but one English-speaking author who is really keeping his self-respect and sticking for perfection. Of course I refer to that mighty master of language and keen student of human actions and motives, Henry James."

James always was one of her masters, but she never seems to have thought of him as a realist. Perhaps at the highest levels of art realism and romance begin to merge. Cather agreed perfectly with Hawthorne's view that a romance "sins unpardonably so far as it may swerve aside from the truth of the human heart." James never did, whether his works were called realism or romance. She added that anyone who reads his most recent collections of stories, *The Lesson of the Master* and *Terminations,* "may find out something of what it means to be really an artist. The framework is perfect and the polish is absolutely without flaw." She was fond of quoting from James's story "The Middle Years": "We work in the dark—we do what we can—we give what we have. Our doubt is our passion and our passion is our task. The rest is the madness of art." She owed a great deal to James in some of her apprentice stories and in her first novel, and so strong was his influence that it took her a while to slip out from under his shadow.

From the time she was carrying Flaubert with her as a freshman she was a student of style. James as stylist interested her as much as James the consummate creator of character. In the same essay she declared: "One could read him forever for the beauty of his sentences. He never lets his phrases run away with him. They are never dull and never too brilliant. He subjects them to the general tone of his sentence and has his whole paragraph partake of the same predominating color. You are never startled, never surprised, never thrilled or never enraptured; always delighted by that masterly prose that is as correct, as classical, as calm and as subtle as the music of Mozart."

She also admired the style of Ruskin, "the greatest living master of pure English prose" and the author of "some twelve or fifteen volumes of the most perfect prose of our generation." She devoted an entire column to Ruskin, one of the last she wrote before leaving Lincoln, on hearing news (premature, as it turned out) that he was dying. Outstripping his master Carlyle, he had taken "the wild and stirring strains of the peasant philosopher and set them to delicious harmony," and over the "rugged wisdom of the sage he has diffused the effulgent glory of a poet." She thought that his death would send people back to "the enchanted pages of *The Stones of Venice*" to "wonder at their melody." Ruskin had more than style for Cather; he was perhaps "the last of the great worshippers of beauty, perhaps the last man for many years to come who will ever kneel at the altar of Artemis, who will ever hear the oracle of Apollo." And, finally, he was "the last head on which the failing light of the Renaissance has lingered." His creed was, to express it roughly, that "beauty alone is truth and truth is only beauty; that art is supreme; that it is the highest, the only expression of whatever divinity there may be in man." Ruskin and Carlyle, whom she called her little tin gods, brought out her "high-stepping rhetoric."

The death of Verlaine in 1896 gave her a chance to demonstrate her devotion to French literature and defend the reputation of a favorite poet. She admitted that he was a "dirty old man," also "a profligate, a vagabond, a criminal." But he was a great poet, and that was all that mattered. She never gave a thought to a writer's morals if his work could stir her emotions. "Compared to the greatness of his work the weakness of his life is of small moment. Until we can write his verses and be respectable citizens at the same time we have small right to enter protests." These were bold words to write for the *Nebraska State Journal* in 1896, but she always said what she thought. "He was a practicer of every excess known to man, yet if ever inspiration and spiritual rapture came from a human pen it is in his verses on the Christ. This is all disease you say; certainly it is, but we all gather the pearls fast enough in this world and nobody troubles himself much about the disease of the oyster which produced it."

Readers of "The Passing Show" who did not know must at times have wondered if Willa Cather really were a woman. So completely had she embraced masculine values that when she wrote about women writers, she sounded like a patronizing man. One day when she saw an elevator boy reading Ouida's (Marie Louise de la Ramée's) *Under Two Flags* (1867), which she had read with enthusiasm as a child, she declared: "Sometimes I wonder why God ever trusted talent in the hands of women, they usually make such an infernal mess of it." *Under Two Flags* contained a good plot and the rudiments of a great style, but it also contained "some of the most drivelling nonsense and mawkish sentimentality and contemptible feminine weakness to be found anywhere." "Adjectives and sentimentality ran away with her, as they do with most women's pens. . . . And the worst of it is that the woman really had great talent." In all her books there "is not one sane, normal, possible man or woman. . . . They are one rank morass of misguided genius and wasted power."

Then Cather began to generalize: "I have not much faith in women in fiction. They have a sort of sex consciousness that is abominable. They are so limited to one string and they lie so about that. They are so few, the ones who really did anything worth while; there were the great Georges, George Eliot and George Sand, and they were anything but women, and there was Miss Brontë, who kept her sentimentality under control, and there was Jane Austen who certainly had more common sense than any of them and was in some respects the greatest of them all. Women are so horribly subjective and they have such scorn for the healthy commonplace." These were all the significant women fiction writers she could think of. She had not yet discovered Sarah Orne Jewett, who was to become her friend and mentor.

Cather also was not very charitable towards women poets. When Christina Rossetti died in 1894, she wrote an essay on three women poets: Rossetti, Elizabeth Barrett Browning, and Sappho. Rossetti, she thought, had written one perfect poem in "The Goblin Market," but "it is a very grave question whether women have any place in poetry at all. Certainly they have only been successful in poetry of the most highly subjective nature. If a woman writes any poetry at all worth reading it must be emotional in the extreme, self-centered, self-absorbed, centrifugal." Rossetti possessed a consciousness of her limits and confined herself to the simplist lyrics. Barrett Browning before her "tried to be versatile and to go beyond the artistic limitations of her sex" but achieved merit without greatness. She wrote but one great poem, "her little volume of *Sonnets from the Portuguese.*" Cather concluded this essay: "There is one woman poet whom all the world calls great"—Sappho. "All great poets have wondered at her verses; all inferior poets have imitated them. Twenty centuries have not cooled the passion in them." But even Sappho wrote of only one subject—love. "Save for her knowledge of human love she was unlearned, save for her perception of beauty she was blind, save for the fullness of her passions she was empty-handed."

Cather's great break came sometime late in the spring when she was offered a job on a new magazine in Pittsburgh. Axtell, Orr, and Company, publishers of the *Home Monthly*, needed an editor, and Cather jumped at the chance. Just how a Pittsburgh publisher happened to hire a twenty-two-year-old woman from Nebraska to edit his magazine is not known. There are a few clues, but no facts. George Gerwig, a Lincoln insurance man with an M.A. in English, had moved to Allegheny, Pennsylvania (now part of Pittsburgh), in 1892. He had written drama criticism for the *Journal* before Cather took over and was one of her early friends in Lincoln. He returned to Nebraska for a visit in March when Cather was trying unsuccessfully to get a teaching job. It is a reasonable guess to suppose that he knew of the opening and suggested her. Cather already had a reputation that extended beyond Nebraska, though perhaps not so far as Pennsylvania, and she certainly was well qualified. Further, James Axtell, one of the publishers, was a friend of Charles Gere, who certainly would have recommended his star columnist. Regardless of how she got the job, she was more than ready to leave Lincoln for a larger theater of operations. She lost no time in packing and departed for Pittsburgh in late June to begin the next phase of her career.

CHAPTER 6

Early Days in Pittsburgh

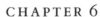

Still only twenty-two in June 1896, Cather travelled east towards Pennsylvania in a state of increasing excitement. She paused briefly in Chicago, where she took in a special exhibit of Paul Gustave Doré's paintings. There were great splurges of color, theatrical effects, enormous canvasses, but the whole show was a good bit like the billboards advertising *The Last Days of Pompeii*. Only one painting, *The Neophyte*, seemed to her real honest work; the rest either had a flat chromo look or were done by a trick. She continued on to Pittsburgh on the Baltimore and Ohio Railroad, and as the train rolled across Ohio, her spirits soared. When she saw hills, clear streams, and trees the Lord had planted, her delight was so transparent that the conductor asked if she were getting back home. In a sense she was, for Pittsburgh was only about one hundred miles from her birthplace in Back Creek Valley, Virginia, and her great-great-grandfather, Jasper Cather, had begun his life in America in western Pennsylvania. Three months after reaching Pittsburgh she was able to take time off from her job to make a bicycle trip through the Shenandoah Valley. Among the several polarities that pulled at Cather all her life was the attraction of the eastern mountains against the tug of the prairie of her adopted state.

When the train reached Pittsburgh, Cather's new boss, James Axtell, was at the station to meet her. She first gave him a withering look when he approached her, as he didn't look like a publisher, but he was very cordial and took her home with him to East Liberty to stay until she could find a boarding house. In the Axtell establishment she found herself in the midst of rock-ribbed, conservative Presbyterian Pittsburgh. Though the house was delightful, set in a beautiful hilly residential area and surrounded by large ivy-covered homes—a sharp contrast to the flatness and newness of Nebraska— her heart sank when she entered the parlor. It was furnished with pieces covered grimly with hair cloth, over which presided one forbidding picture—a crayon portrait of grandpa, a preacher, the sternest Presbyterian of them all. She was glad he was off visiting somewhere, as she feared the argus-eyed old patriarch, so accustomed to detecting the follies and foibles of this world, would penetrate her thin disguise and denounce her as the devotee of French fiction and the consort of musicians and strolling players. Further, she was put in the room of the Axtells' daughter, also off visiting, whose library consisted of six Bibles and many well-worn volumes of the trashy religious novels of E. P. Roe. She could stand the Bibles, she wrote Mariel Gere, but not E. P. Roe.

The conservative, Calvinist tone of the Pittsburghers, half of whom were Presbyterians, bothered her considerably at first. Her early letters from Pittsburgh and columns sent back to the *Journal* are full of impatient astonishment and irony. The Axtells were very nice to her, but their personalities were as chilly as a wine cellar, the result, she guessed, of believing in infant damnation. She wrote Ellen Gere, Mariel's younger sister, that Mr. Axtell meant to be a jolly man and really was awfully nice, but fun did not come naturally to him. The entire social life of the family centered on their church, and when they had parties, they invited their Sunday school class. To avoid getting entangled in Presbyterianism, Cather told the Axtells that her folks were Baptists. Alas, she added, the Baptist minister lived next door, and in ten minutes they had him over and upon her.

Before Cather moved into her own quarters, one of the Axtells' five thousand and seven hundred cousins, a young woman preparing to enter Vassar, came to dinner. When she talked about the courses she was going to take in the fall, Cather explained how many hours of coursework she had carried at the University of Nebraska. The girl looked up in sweet surprise and asked innocently how in the world Cather had managed to attend classes, write for the newspaper, and keep up her church work. Every girl here, Cather explained, has her church work, just as other girls have fans or powder boxes. Before she could get away from the Axtells, she had to go to church with them and listen to a sermon on the text "Whosoever will, let him drink of the water of life freely." Later, in her correspondence with the *Journal* she reported satirically on the rumpus raised in Pittsburgh when Anna Held sang "O Won't You Come and Play with Me" at a supper party given at the Duquesne Club by Henry Clay Frick, a prominent Presbyterian; and she made merry over the efforts of the Pittsburgh clergy to suppress Frederick Archer's free Sunday organ recitals at Carnegie Hall.

Cather herself lost no time in going to one of these concerts. She loved music and was much impressed by the grandeur of the auditorium. Carnegie Hall had just been completed the year before and was housed in a huge building containing also the Carnegie Library and Art Gallery. The library in particular impressed her—marble from end to end—and the colors and frescoes were just one artistic harmony. She had thought the new University of Nebraska Library was nice, but this greatly surpassed it. What was even better, the library was close to her office, and it had, she thought, all the books in the world. She planned to spend a lot of time there. She also had discovered right away that the Carnegie Theater was very close and that her old friend Pauline Hall would be playing there all the next week. While the Presbyterians were doing their church work, she was going to slip across to the theater to look on Pauline's glorious anatomy once again.

These satiric reports of her first impressions of Pittsburgh and her plans to haunt the library and theater make Cather sound like a bohemian intent on hedonism. When Mariel Gere accused her of this, she replied that she had taken the veil and retired to convent life. By this she meant that she was hard at work putting out the magazine. By the middle of July she was living in a boarding house in the east end of the city, six blocks from her office. The Axtells had gone west on a trip, leaving her in sole charge of the magazine, though she only had been hired to be assistant editor. She wrote Mrs. Gere that she saw no one except the old maid who ran her boarding house and her stenographer. She was proud of having her own stenographer—especially one who could spell—but she was so busy her only excitement was in racing the electric cars on her bicycle. She had had to write half of the first issue of the magazine herself. Because her printer was inexperienced in layout, she had been down in the composing room the night before until one o'clock sweating over the forms and making up the pages. She kept her irony and satire for her friends back home; and when three Misses Rush called on her—three tall, plain, stiff, prim Presbyterians—Cather was very demure, she told Mrs. Gere, and discussed flower gardening and church music.

The *Home Monthly* was not much of a magazine. It had been started two years before as the *Ladies' Journal*, an obvious effort to capitalize on the spectacular success of the *Ladies' Home Journal*. Cather was hired when Axtell, Orr, and Company bought the magazine and changed the name. It was aimed at half a million firesides within one hundred miles of Pittsburgh, and an editorial in the August issue, Cather's first, stated what she called its namby-pamby policies: "These pages will be kept clean and pure in tone, and . . . all plans for the *Home Monthly* center in the aim to entertain, to educate, to elevate." And the contents, she thought, were great rot—home and fireside stuff, all about babies and mince pies.

The opening editorial also declared that "every phase of home needs will receive attention" and that the best story writers of the country would "furnish entertainment for the idle hour." The former goal was easy enough to achieve, though Cather said she found it hard to turn out copy about raising children and keeping house; but the latter aim never was realized. She found that she had to write a good bit of the fiction herself, and though she sometimes solicited contributions from her friends, she had no budget to buy stories from writers of national visibility. After she had edited the magazine for nine months, she concluded that it was the worst trash in the world, but it was trash her employers wanted, trash they paid for, and trash they would get.

Even from the beginning she did not plan to stay with the enterprise very long. She wrote Mrs. Gere, however, that she was determined to show everyone that she could take up a thing and stick to it, even if it did not suit her. She was working very hard and liking the challenge of the job, grind though it was. Despite the depressing nature of the publication, the financial outlook was good. She was glad to have a steady income and a full-time job. Though her salary was perhaps only one hundred dollars a month, it seemed a princely figure to someone who previously had worked for a dollar a column on the *Nebraska State Journal*.

There were other compensations too. The city and the rivers, she said, would make up for almost anything, and she was meeting many different kinds of people. She had met a number of New York drama critics and recently had held a forty-six-minute talk with one of her favorites, Rudyard Kipling, when he passed through Pittsburgh. She also saw the city as a more promising place than Nebraska for the promotion of her own literary fortunes. She had met a travelling editor of *Cosmopolitan*, to whom she had shown her story "The Count of Crow's Nest," and he had offered her one hundred dollars for it. She turned down the proposal reluctantly because she needed the story to fill up the *Home Monthly*, but the fact that she could publish in an important national magazine excited her. She felt that her own work was improving, that she was not wasting her time. After a month on the job her employers were willing to give her a day off whenever she felt the urge to write.

From the start Cather loved Pittsburgh, though she did not hesitate to criticize it. She saved her strictures, however, for letters home and the columns she sent back to the *Journal*. She called Pittsburgh the "city of dreadful dirt" in her first letter and later referred to it as "dirty, prosaic Pittsburgh that doesn't care for anything but coal and iron mills and big houses on Fifth Avenue and Holy St. Andrew Carnegie." On the occasion of a trip to Homestead, where Carnegie's mills were located, she was appalled by the sight. It's like Hades when you get there, she said—all smoke and flames. She also commented on the dampness of the climate, which contrasted sharply with the bracing air of Nebraska.

The Pittsburgh that Cather saw in 1896 seemed a real metropolis, a city of over 400,000, including neighboring Allegheny, some twelve times the size of Lincoln. Built where the Allegheny and Monongahela rivers join to form the Ohio, the city always had occupied a strategic position, from colonial times when the French built Fort Duquesne there to the era of rapid industrial growth after the Civil War. Scenically the heart of the city, the "Golden Triangle," where the two rivers came together, was a spectacular location, and the surrounding hills were green and wooded. Because it was close to sources of coal and possessed excellent water and rail communications, it became a major manufacturing city by the end of the century. When Cather arrived, it already was a great steel-producing center, and it was becoming a city of great wealth. The business of Pittsburgh was business, dominated by men like Frick, Carnegie, Andrew Mellon, and George Westinghouse.

Representative of the Pittsburgh business community is Cather's character Marshall McKann in "A Gold Slipper." "He was born a Presbyterian, just as he was born a McKann. He sat in his pew in the First Church every Sunday, and he never missed a presbytery meeting when he was in town. His religion was not very spiritual, certainly, but it was substantial and concrete, made up of good, hard convictions and opinions. It had something to do with citizenship, with whom one ought to marry, with the coal business (in which his own name was powerful), with the Republican party, and with all majorities and established precedents. He was hostile to fads, enthusiasms, to individualism, to all changes except in mining machinery and in methods of transportation." His wife drags him to a concert, but he has no interest in or knowledge of music and regards artists as "fluffy-ruffles people."

Yet the wealth amassed in Pittsburgh by the nineteenth-century robber barons was already being recycled to make the city a cultural center. Carnegie, after applying Darwin's views on natural selection and the survival of the fittest to the ruthless creation of an industrial empire and smashing the union in the bloody Homestead Steel Strike in 1892, had turned to good works in funding libraries and concert halls. Pittsburgh profited handsomely by his notion, expressed in his essay "The Gospel of Wealth," that it was a

42. Pittsburgh Union Station with Central High School in upper right.
Courtesy of The Carnegie Library
of Pittsburgh

43. The McClung House, Pittsburgh.
Courtesy of Philip Southwick

44. Ethelbert Nevin. Courtesy of The Carnegie Library of Pittsburgh

45. Isabelle McClung. Courtesy of Helen Cather Southwick

46. Cather about 1902 in her first Paris gown. Courtesy of WCPMC-NSHS

47. Cather during her teaching years in
Pittsburgh. Courtesy of wcpmc-
nshs

48. Allegheny High School, Pittsburgh.
Courtesy of The Carnegie Library
of Pittsburgh

49. Cather on a handcar in Wyoming.
Courtesy of WCPMC-NSHS

disgrace for a man to die rich. Besides the Carnegie Library and Music Hall, Pittsburgh also had just acquired a symphony orchestra. All these cultural resources were much vaster than those of Lincoln, and Cather took advantage of them. She put a little of herself into the title character in "Paul's Case," whose spirits were released by the first strains of the symphony orchestra when he ushered at Carnegie Hall: "He felt a sudden zest of life; the lights danced before his eyes and the concert hall blazed into unimaginable splendour." Pittsburgh also had more theaters and plays than Lincoln; it was a first-run city, whereas Lincoln had been second-run. She did not wait long after beginning her job on the *Home Monthly* to get a part-time position as drama and music critic for the *Pittsburgh Leader* and to involve herself in the artistic life of the city.

Her involvement in the social life of Pittsburgh also began as soon as she finished putting out the August issue of the magazine. It was a remarkable change from her life the previous year, when she was moping in Red Cloud, like Hawthorne brooding in Salem or Leopardi pining away in Recanati. Five weeks after she got off the Baltimore and Ohio to begin her new life, she needed eight large sheets of paper to tell Mariel Gere what she had been doing. The week before she had gone on a picnic with the Press Club to Erie. The previous Sunday she went on an excursion to Rock Point, up in the mountains. The best outing of all had been a steam launch party of twenty that went thirty miles up the river. They had a catered dinner on board and two blacks who played the banjo and sang in the moonlight all the way back. The launch passed big green hills rising three hundred feet from the river and fleeced here and there with big patches of white river mist. All along the shore the iron furnaces glowed like calcium lights, and gas wells shot out long plumes of flame. Then the hills of the city loomed up with a thousand lights of a thousand colors. Her escort on this excursion was George Gerwig, her old friend from Lincoln, who was, she wrote Mariel Gere, her devoted slave. He and his wife both took the trouble to see that she got acquainted.

Her most astonishing experience occurred at a tea given for the federated women's clubs by the editor of the *Pittsburgh Dispatch*. Mrs. Gerwig took her to this function. The city was run by women's clubs, Cather explained, and all the women in the social register were club women. Their program that day was on Carlyle, and the chairwoman politely invited Cather to say something about Carlyle, if she wanted to. She told Mariel Gere that she had the nerve to get up and spiel off her old "second prep" essay that she had written for Professor Hunt. She delivered the piece, she said, with all the fire and fervor of the tragic muse. It all came back to her, and she just soared. The club women fell all over themselves to shake her hand afterwards. They thought it was impromptu. Cather did not think much of their brains, especially their liking that sophomoric performance.

The result of her oratorical flight was a procession of women calling on her until she was almost distracted. She had fifteen calls to return, she wrote, and did not know how she was going to get her work done. She guessed she would just have to shut it off, this social life, and apparently that is what she did. The Axtells were miffed by Cather's sudden popularity, as they were not in society at all, never saw anyone but relatives, and did not much like Cather's gadding about. The novelty of this social activity, however, which was totally uncharacteristic, soon wore off, but Cather made a good many friends in her first year in Pittsburgh, many of whom remained friends for life. She continued to write satirically of women's clubs and of the feminine pursuit of culture in weekly packaged doses. When Mrs. Canfield visited Pittsburgh later and asked to be introduced to some club women, Cather could hardly get over the reversal of roles that made her the club woman and Flavia Canfield the supplicant. She said it did her wicked, un-Christian heart good to get even, to pay off the old scores and make people take back the bitter things they once had said. She was remembering that Mrs. Canfield had disapproved of her life-style when she was an undergraduate in Lincoln and had written a sharp reply to an attack she had made on women's clubs in the *Journal*. She was now, she reported to Mariel Gere, a member of the "swell" woman's club of the town.

Except for George Gerwig, the only friend of her Pittsburgh years who carried over from Nebraska was Dorothy Canfield. Dorothy was a sophomore at Ohio State University, where her father was president. She visited Pittsburgh on occasion, and Cather sometimes went to Columbus. After Dorothy spent her spring vacation in Pittsburgh in 1897, Cather wrote Mariel Gere to tell her what a charming girl Dorothy was growing to be. Her visit had been a joy and comfort; Cather's friends had risen nobly to the occasion; they had had a downright jolly time. There were theater parties, excursions, drives in the park, until they were exhausted. Dorothy said it was the first time she had ever been treated like a young lady. It was lonesome for Cather to return from the office now and not find her cuddled up on the divan. In 1907 Dorothy married, settled in Vermont, and the two friends drifted apart, but after they resumed their friendship by correspondence in 1913, Cather wrote that there were long years when she loved her very, very dearly. Canfield wrote in 1947: "My occasional brief stopovers in Pittsburgh were golden days for me. When people talk about Pittsburgh as a dirty, dark, noisy, grimy city, I can't imagine what they are talking about. Over it hangs, for me, a shining cloud of young memories."

The Carnegie Library, which was a magnet from the first, also produced lasting friendships. The director, Edwin Anderson, and his wife, Frances, became friends and often invited Cather to dinner, and later when Anderson became head of the New York Public Library, she kept up the relationship. May Willard, who directed the reference department, became Cather's earliest Pittsburgh friend. She always saw May when she went back to the city in later years and in 1915, with May and others, joined a folk-dancing group taught by a visiting Englishman, Cecil Sharp. Another close friend was Ethel Litchfield, who was a fine pianist. She had studied in Vienna to become a concert artist but had given up her career to marry a Pittsburgh doctor. She kept up her music, often played in Pittsburgh concerts, and her home was a stopping place for visiting musicians. Cather used to pause by her house on her way home from work before they knew each other and "stand listening to the music that streamed from it at all hours of the day and night." After Dr. Litchfield's death Ethel moved to New York, where Cather saw her often.

Early in her editorial tenure at the *Home Monthly* a young journalist named George Seibel offered to write an article on Richard Wagner's wild pranks. She invited him to visit the office, accepted his proposal, and asked him for more contributions. This meeting led to a warm relationship between Cather and both George and Helen Seibel, who were recently married and only a little older. Cather visited their second-floor apartment on Seventeenth Street once or twice a week during her first years in Pittsburgh and usually stayed for supper. Although George was part of the German-American community, he and Cather shared a passion for French literature. She went there to read French with him, and during her visits she and Helen would follow a text while George translated. If either woman disagreed with his reading, they would stop and discuss the translation. In this manner they went through Daudet's *Les Femmes d'artistes*, de Musset's *Poésies nouvelles*, novels by Pierre Loti, Anatole France, Paul Bourget, and Georges Huysmans. They also read Victor Hugo's drama *Hernani* and poems by Théophile Gautier, Verlaine, and Baudelaire. Their taste was for the Romantics, and though they read the realistic *Madame Bovary*, which Cather had loved in college, her taste at this time was more for Flaubert's romantic *Salammbô*.

After the readings there would be a German supper: noodle soup, potato salad, cucumbers, and cookies. On Christmas Eves Cather usually helped trim the tree, and on one occasion she took Dorothy Canfield with her. Dorothy remembered clearly half a century later the cosmopolitan atmosphere, stimulating talk, and George standing against a background of Christmas greens reciting a Christmas poem by Heine:

> Der Stern blieb stehn über Josephs Haus.
> Da sind sie hineingegangen;
> Das Oechslein brullte, das Kindlein schrie,
> Die heil'gen drei Koenige sangen.

"It sounded wonderfully fine as he rolled it out in his rich German. Willa was enchanted by it, got the book out from the shelves back of us, copied off the poem, and before I had gone on from Pittsburgh to Vermont, had made an admirable rhymed translation."

> The star now stops above Joseph's roof,
>   And they enter the cottage lowly;
> The oxen bellowed, the infant cried,
>   While sang the three kings holy.

Many years later Canfield wrote Cather asking her if she remembered translating that poem. She replied that she did not, but it was just like her, she thought, to be translating from a language in which she could not have conjugated a single verb.

Seibel recalled Cather at this period as looking about eighteen: "She was plump and dimpled, with dreamy eyes and an eager mind." "More than books, Willa was interested in the study of human nature. She was avid of the world, always wondering, always questing, always digging." She and Seibel got on very well except when they disagreed over Henry James's novels, but they both admired his critical essays on French writers. It was also at this period that Cather discovered Sarah Orne Jewett and gave Seibel as a Christmas gift one year *The Country of the Pointed Firs*, then a new book. After Cather left Pittsburgh for New York, she corresponded with the Seibels and occasionally saw them on return visits to Pennsylvania or when they visited New York.

Subscribers to the *Home Monthly* were treated to a large dose of Cather's apprentice fiction during her editorship. In the thirteen months following her appointment she used eight of her own stories, one a two-part serial, two signed with pseudonyms. In addition, she let the magazine have another tale that appeared the year after she resigned her position. Most of these stories are unremarkable and would not detain anyone if they had not been written by young Willa Cather. The first to appear was "Tommy, the Unsentimental," her tomboy story, which is one of the more significant of her early fictions. It illustrates the ambivalence she always felt towards the East and the West, and curiously enough, this first published fiction in Pittsburgh contains praise for the flatlands of Nebraska. Tommy goes off to school in the East, but she can't wait to get back to her hometown on the prairie. When she returns she says: "It's all very fine down East there, and the hills are great, but one gets mighty homesick for this sky. . . . Down there the skies are all pale and smoky. . . . And this wind . . . I used to get hungry for this wind! I couldn't sleep in that lifeless stillness down there."

The two-part serial was "The Count of Crow's Nest," the story she could have sold to *Cosmopolitan*. It was the longest piece of fiction she yet had written and shows developing skill in narrative technique. Her passion for Henry James perhaps is shown in a plot that makes one think of "The Aspern Papers." Her setting, however, is a boarding house in Chicago rather than the exotic canals and palazzi of Venice, but the effort to obtain a bundle of letters is common to both stories. Cather, however, departs from the Jamesian model by making the unscrupulous letter-seeker a woman. The tale makes rudimentary use of a minor-character consciousness as it recounts the experiences of a young male college graduate who lives temporarily in a boarding house of failed people while he tries to decide on a career. One of the inmates, the main character, is an elderly count, Paul de Koch, born in the Winter Palace at St. Petersburg but now impoverished, the last of his line, exiled to darkest Chicago.

Young Harold Buchanan and the count are drawn together through a mutual interest in French literature, and as the plot unfolds Harold meets the count's no-good daughter, a third-rate singer who is venal, grasping, and dishonorable. The count has in his possession letters which if published would blast the reputations of unspecified titled Europeans. The daughter thinks there would be a fortune in publishing them. The father stoutly refuses. The daughter steals the letters, and in the denouement Harold accompanies the old man to his daughter's lodging in the middle of the night, and they force the daughter to give up the papers. The story is entertaining, a good yarn, and doubtless as good as much of the fiction the *Cosmopolitan* was publishing.

Two of the nine stories Cather published in the *Home Monthly* are fairy tales for children, the sort of tale she used to make up in Red Cloud to tell her younger brothers and sister. "The Princess Baladina—Her Adventure" is not much of a yarn and Cather signed it "Charles Douglass." "The Strategy of the Were-Wolf Dog" is a Santa Claus Christmas story something on the order of "Rudolph, the Red-Nose Reindeer." Appearing in the December 1896 issue of the magazine, it was well enough done that the author signed her own name. A third story of this period, "A Resurrection," is the Brownville tale;

and the one that appeared after she left the magazine was "The Way of the World," the story of the play town "Sandy Point."

A second story that appeared in the Christmas issue of the *Home Monthly*, also published pseudonymously, is "The Burglar's Christmas," a very amateurish and sentimental reworking of the prodigal son theme. But this tale, in the view of Sharon O'Brien, "is a crucial story in the Cather canon because its psychological themes connect both to her life and to her later fiction." A destitute and derelict young man named William breaks into a Chicago mansion on Christmas Eve and while robbing the boudoir of the owner finds the silver drinking cup he used as a child. He is robbing the home of his own parents. At that moment his mother comes into the room, recognizes him, and cries out: "Willie, Willie! Is it you?" In the recognition scene that follows the mother forgives her contrite son, and the tale ends with the young man sitting passively by the fire happily stuffed with a good dinner. O'Brien says, "He has returned to the oral stage, the period in human development symbolized by the baby's silver drinking mug." This critic sees the story as reflecting Cather's sexual identity problem, her "unconscious desires and fears," William as a mask for Willa, and the "young author unaware of what she is concealing or revealing." This psychoanalysis of Cather on the basis of a very minor and amateurish story may seem reductive, but there is no doubt that Cather's relationship with her mother was unsatisfactory in some respects and caused tensions and anxieties. She comments on occasion that her younger sister Jessica, who dressed and acted like a lady, was more her mother's idea of a proper daughter than she was. Fortunately the psychic problem, such as it was, had no crippling effect on her adult artistic career.

Two other *Home Monthly* stories are only worth brief comment. "The Prodigies" is her first story laid presumably in Pittsburgh and the first making the performing arts her subject. The story, which concerns the exploitation of two gifted child musicians by their ambitious mother, foreshadows the intense interest Cather took many years later in the Menuhin children. The tale is viewed from the point of view of a pianist like Cather's friend Ethel Litchfield, who gave up a career to marry a physician. Also, in the relationship between the ambitious mother and her husband Cather depicts the first of many unhappy marriages in her fiction. "Nanette: An Aside," Cather's first fictional creation of an opera singer, is a slight tale, mostly a dialogue between the singer and her maid, who has fallen in love with a headwaiter. The singer is a battle-scarred veteran, unhappily married, and the maid Nanette is full of romantic yearnings.

During her first year in Pittsburgh Cather was a bundle of energy. Not only did she edit the magazine almost single-handedly, write stories and nonfiction articles for it, carry on an active social life, but she also wrote and edited a page called "Our Young Folks" in the *National Stockman and Farmer*, another publication owned by Axtell, Orr, and Company. As if this were not enough, she began writing music and drama criticism for the *Pittsburgh Leader*, and before she went home for the summer had published twenty-six reviews. She also resumed writing "The Passing Show" for the *Nebraska State Journal*, producing seventeen columns between December and May. There was, of course, some overlap in what she published in both Lincoln and Pittsburgh.

A glance at the contents of the *Home Monthly* reveals Cather's industry, versatility, ingenuity, and literary enthusiasms at that period. She barely had arrived in Pittsburgh before she was writing Mrs. Gere for information about Mrs. William Jennings Bryan. Her Pittsburgh landlady was going to supply her with information on Mrs. William McKinley, whom she had known in her youth, and she was going to write an article on the wives of the two presidential candidates. After she finished that one, she wrote others on the Burns centenary, singers' salaries, the death of George Du Maurier, Queen Victoria's Diamond Jubilee, and nursing as a profession for women. She also turned out editorials and wrote a monthly book column that continued even after she resigned from the magazine.

Entitled "Old Books and New," the book column ranged widely over old favorites and new discoveries. She enthusiastically endorsed historical romance, recommending the novels of Stanley Weyman and Alexandre Dumas; *The Prisoner of Zenda*, which she never tired of; S. Weir Mitchell's *Hugh Wynn*; and the "greatest of all English novels," *Henry Esmond*. She thought that Thackeray and Shakespeare were "the two imperial Williams, joint kings of English letters." She also praised *David Copperfield* and *A Tale of Two Cities* (of all of Dickens's great characters she liked Sidney Carton best); she predicted that *Treasure Island* "was one of the boys' books destined to immortality," and she raved about William Allen White's Boyville stories when they came out. They were worthy successors to *Tom Sawyer*, for "I know of no one who writes of a boy's heart as understandingly." He seemed "not to have forgotten how it feels to be a boy." She added: "I read the 'Martyrdom of "Mealy" Jones' aloud to a western boy and a boy from New Hampshire and the effect was the same."

Another new book that enchanted her was A. E. Housman's *A Shropshire Lad*, and her reprinting of one of the poems was Housman's first appearance in an American magazine. "Who Mr. Housman may be I know not," she wrote, "save that he is an Englishman and that he has written some of the most musical lyrics that have been done in England for many a long day."

How she found out who Housman was is a story to be told in due course. Finally, no book column Cather was likely to write ever would be silent for long on French literature, and she needed no topical event to trigger a discussion of Hugo's *Les Misérables*. She opened one column simply by saying: "I never feel the spring come back . . . that I don't go back and read *Les Misérables* over again. It's a perennial passion with me, and comes every spring in violet time." On another occasion she urged her readers to try Daudet's *Kings in Exile* and Anatole France's *The Crime of Sylvester Bonnard*.

After ten months in Pittsburgh Cather's social life had become more pleasant than it ever had been or than she ever thought it could be. Her letter to Mariel Gere just after Dorothy Canfield's visit exudes euphoria. She was living a conventional life and enjoying it. No longer was she flouting social norms by wearing her hair short, going about with her middle-aged bachelor friend Dr. Tyndale, consorting with theater people, and getting criticized. Now there was nothing to "queer" her, she wrote. It was like the beginning of a new life in broad daylight away from the old mistakes. It was a rather novel experience for her, and it had quite gone to her head.

Her social life in Pittsburgh involved friends of both sexes. Since there were few women journalists, she worked mostly with men, and she inevitably saw a good bit of her co-workers after hours. Her editorship of the magazine and her reviewing for the *Leader* also brought her into contact with a large number of people, some of them eligible males her own age who found her both interesting and desirable. Similar friendships seem not to have developed in Lincoln in the two years after Cather's breakup with Louise Pound. There is scant evidence that she had any romantic male friendships before she went to Pittsburgh, though there was a relationship with one young man in Lincoln. He was Charles Moore, the nephew of the man who headed the company that employed Charles Cather. Young Moore gave Cather a gold snake ring that she wore all her life. They apparently carried on an extensive correspondence, but no letters have survived.

Some of the euphoria evident in Cather's letter to Mariel Gere resulted from a proposal of marriage she had just received from a young doctor. She had not yet decided if she would accept him. She thought it would be a very good match in every way, but she was not in love. She supposed, however, that one did not have to be in love to get married. She had introduced Dorothy Canfield to the young man, and Dorothy had approved of him. She was especially pleased with the way her suitor had treated the younger girl. But in the end Cather turned down the proposal and continued her unencumbered life.

Eight months later there was another applicant for matrimony: Preston

Farrar, who taught English at Allegheny High School. She dated him in the fall, and by January the affair had gotten serious. She wrote Mariel Gere that she was seeing him only in plaster these days because he had broken his leg playing football several months before. It was rather fun visiting him in his cast now that he wasn't suffering any more. Unfortunately, she added, she did not seem able to feel very deeply about him. His friendship was so warm and comfortable that she did not want to change it for the other article in which the personal equation would be sure to make trouble. She avoided matrimony again but was able to remain friends with Farrar, and in 1903 after he resigned his teaching position, she succeeded him. He later married, and Cather visited him and his wife in New York.

Cather at this time apparently came to a clear decision to remain single. She explained to Mariel Gere that she had grown fond of liberty. To be wholly free, to really be of some use somewhere, to do with her money what she wanted, to help those who had helped her, to pay the debts of her loves and her hates—those were the things she wanted to do with her life. She was at that moment sending money home to her brother Roscoe, who had been seriously ill and whom she loved more than any other man except her father. She had no need to get married for companionship, for she already had a large circle of friends and was kept very busy with her work and her social life. In the same letter she described her activities of recent days: first she had heard Melba at the opera; the next night there was a supper party given by her actress friend Lizzie Collier; the following day she had attended a dinner for Ethelbert Nevin, the composer; and a few hours before beginning her letter she had been out to dinner with a crowd at the Bishops'. She recently had got to know Anthony Hope Hawkins, who had lectured and spent several days in Pittsburgh, and had met F. Marion Crawford, who was a detestable snob. Her days and nights were more than full, and she was suffering from a lack of sleep.

To state the matter simply, Cather was married to her art and sublimated her sexual impulses in her work. Throughout her life she gave art her highest priority, preferring her work to society, to family, to friends. Few people, of course, could follow such a program rigorously, and Cather recognized her obligations to others. Nevertheless, her statements on this subject are unequivocal. On many occasions, beginning with her "second prep" essay on Carlyle, she declared that art was a merciless taskmaster, that an artist could not be successful without pouring all his energy and emotion into his art. In her *Hamlet* essay she had said: "If an artist does any good work he must do it alone. No number of encouraging or admiring friends can assist him. . . . He must go off alone with his own soul and they too must labor and suffer together." Twenty-four years later she had her Wagnerian soprano Thea Kronborg explain her work *was* her personal life; there was no way to separate her private self from her public self. The two were fused into one seamless whole. The heroine of *Lucy Gayheart* (1935) comes to a tragic end because she does not have this "art necessity."

Cather was convinced that marriage and art did not mix. Although she loved children and lavished her affections on her younger brothers and sister and later on her nephews and nieces, she had no desire to have children of her own. When actress Mary Anderson retired from the stage to get married, Cather reflected on the demands of career and matrimony. Mary Anderson was not a great artist, and for her perhaps the happiness of married life was the better choice. On another occasion, when Helena von Doenhoff retired from the operatic state to get married, Cather wrote a sort of obituary. The artist, she declared, must love his art above all things and must say to it, as Ruth said amidst the alien corn: "Where thou goest, I will go, and where thou lodgest I will lodge . . . thy people shall be my people, and thy God, my God." To this she added, "Married nightingales seldom sing." When actress Marie Burroughs's divorce was announced in the papers, Cather wrote in her column that Marie wanted to be free for her work and free from the obligation of matrimony. The fact that her husband had been her teacher and coach made her ungrateful, but then all actresses are ungrateful. "If they are actresses worthy of the name, they always have a *premier amour* to whom they return, their work." Another sentence she was fond of quoting: "He travels the swiftest who rides alone."

Cather knew, of course, that some artists combined marriage and careers successfully, and occasionally she admitted it. When she wrote a profile of Louise Homer, the Pittsburgh-born contralto, she reported that Homer was a good mother who managed "her own house, her own nursery, and her five children." She certainly knew that two of the women writers she most honored, George Eliot and George Sand, combined careers with heterosexual relationships, but they, along with Sappho, were women who had the "art instinct, the art necessity." "They had it genuinely; they tried other things and none could satisfy them." Few women, she thought, were able to commit themselves wholly to art, especially women writers. For that reason she wrote: "I have not a great deal of faith in women in literature. . . . the great masters of letters are men, and I prefer to take no chances when I read."

Cather generalized her views on matrimony to embrace marital relations between people of all types, not just artists. Late in her life when the husband of her old Red Cloud friend Mary Miner Creighton died, she wrote a letter of condolence, saying that she had known very few marriages as happy as

Mary's. Happy marriages in her fiction are rare. Her artist characters some-times avoid marriage, as does the singer Kitty Ayrshire in "A Gold Slipper," or suffer from bad marriages like Cressida Garnet, the protagonist of "The Diamond Mine." Myra Henshawe in *My Mortal Enemy* marries for love and lives to regret it. Marian Forrester in *A Lost Lady* satisfies her passion in extramarital relations. Sometimes Cather's characters, like Thea Kronborg and Alexandra Bergson, are allowed to marry late in their lives after the passions of youth are spent. On one occasion, in the story "Uncle Valentine," she turns a happy artistic marriage in real life into a disastrous one. Her conviction that artists ran inordinate risks in getting married was reinforced for her by one of her favorite authors, Alphonse Daudet, who argues the point in *Les Femmes d'artistes.*

Cather's views on marriage had their source in her own physiological and psychological makeup. They were motivated by her strongest impulse—the desire to preserve the inviolability of the self. Throughout her work there is a fear of sex, as character after character is destroyed by it or survives by escaping it. All the evidence suggests that Cather too avoided sex in her private life. As an adult she clung to the image of childhood as the autono-mous, sexless, happy period in life and tried to hang on to her own childhood through dress and memory. In all probability she lived the life of a celibate artist, for that life was the only one she could follow to achieve her artistic goals.

When Cather reported on her life in Pittsburgh, she said that the only activity she had in common with her years in Lincoln was theater-going. It was her passion for the stage no doubt that sent her to the *Leader* in search of a part-time job as music and drama critic. Pittsburgh had seven theaters and was often the first stop when New York companies took to the road. She began her reviewing in September 1896 with an unsigned notice of Roland Reed in *The Wrong Mr. Wright*, reviewed again in October, and covered Joseph Jefferson in *Rip Van Winkle* in November. By December she was writing for the *Leader* every week and signing her columns "Sibert," the middle name she was about to adopt permanently. During this first theatrical season in Pittsburgh she saw many of the great stars of the day: James Herne in his own play *Shore Acres*, Otis Skinner in *A Soldier of Fortune*, Fanny Davenport in Sardou's *Gismonda*, Olga Nethersole in *Carmen*, Julia Marlowe in *Romeo and Juliet*, Margaret Mather in *Cymbeline*, Nat Goodwin in *An American Citizen*, Maude Adams and John Drew in *Rosemary*, and Richard Mansfield in *The Merchant of Venice.*

Cather had matured as a reviewer by this time and no longer was she the "meat-ax girl" who had written for the *Journal.* This is not to say that she was no longer critical, but her judgments were more balanced and the tone pitched lower. "*Rip Van Winkle*," she wrote, "has been before the public now for five-and-thirty years; yet it has lost none of its matchless charm." And about Joseph Jefferson, she added, "one of the wonderful things . . . is that he never loses his freshness of touch." Concerning Sardou, she said: "The matronly Fanny Davenport has been giving him to us all week and he is just as great as ever—in spite of Fanny." However, she gave Fanny credit for some memorable scenes, though "it takes a great deal of steam to work Miss Davenport up to any intensity at all." About the "beauteous Julia Marlow" she wrote: "Her Juliet is beautiful, graceful, winsome; it is so surprisingly good that you can not understand why it is not better. . . . She invests the part with rare poetic charm, but of that warmer, tenser element which is peculiar to Juliet and to Italy there is never a trace." Margaret Mather's $40,000 production of *Cymbeline* was a marvel as a production but a disappointment as art. The problem, she thought, was partly Shakespeare's for "such a rambling, stringing together of impossible incidents," but Mather had "simply no intellectual conception at all of her part." Cather noted, however, that Mather had the grippe that night and her voice, "once her chiefest charm" was gone. When John Drew and Maude Adams came to town in *Rosemary*, Cather said she knew that New York had been raving about the play, but she thought it "just as nearly no play at all as anything I ever saw." Mr. Drew, however, played a poor part very well, but Miss Adams was greatly overrated. "Oh, she is so abominably sweet; such a china kitten, you want to drop her to see if she will break." When *The Merchant of Venice* came to Pittsburgh, Mansfield's Shylock, she wrote, was not one of his greatest parts, but "as an actor he is just the same great Richard." Everything he did commanded respect and admiration.

    Her review of James Herne's *Shore Acres* is particularly interesting in view of her general attitude towards realism. This play, generally regarded as the best realistic play written in America in the nineteenth century, pleased Cather. "It comes nearer than any other play to doing for New England life on the stage what Howells has done for it in fiction. . . . In this wicked and perverse generation that is so ridden by Ibsenism and Zolaism on the stage and off, it is a good thing to see plays like *Shore Acres* and players like James A. Herne. They are like health to a sick man and remind one that realism is not absolutely a synonym for evil." This oblique compliment to Howells is one of the few bouquets she ever threw him. She thought his best-known novel, *The Rise of Silas Lapham*, was a very dull book, and while she admitted Howells could create character, his people were always "very common little men in sack coats." She probably was generalizing from Howells when she wrote that the fault of most American writers is one of magnitude: "They are not large enough; they travel in small orbits; they play on muted strings. They sing neither of the combats of Atridae nor the labors of Cadmus, but of the tea table and the Odyssey of the Rialto."

While Cather was writing drama reviews for the *Leader*, she was sending back columns of music criticism for the *Journal*. For the first time in her life she was able to hear a great deal of music. Pittsburgh had a rich musical life. There was plenty of opera, symphony concerts, and a great deal of chamber and choral music. Her first column, sent back to Nebraska in December, reviewed *Eve*, an oratorio by Massenet, which delighted her. As she had no technical vocabulary or expertise to write about music, she resorted to the kind of impressionism she had used before. The music "comes in long, clear waves of sound like the glittering waves that break shoreward." The music is as "light as the mists on the hilltops." When the creation of Eve takes place "she is the mother of all things-to-be opening her eyes upon her world; it is Aphrodite rising from the sea foam; it is faultless beauty made of the sunshine and foam and the scent of roses blown seaward." Nice similes and imagery, but they hardly tell one much about the music.

When she reviewed instrumentalists, Cather showed her great interest in the personalities of the artists as well as her feelings about the music. The piano virtuoso Teresa Carreño from Venezuela made a strong impression. "She bursts upon you like a vision from the south. Dressed in flaming yellow, her magnificent head set like Athena's own upon her firm white shoulders, her blue-black hair touched slightly with gray about the temples, and her eyes—ah, they are Spanish nights!" Then the music leaped on one with a fiery passion. The massive chords and octaves pursued each other up and down the keyboard "as if the pianist were trying to compass all sound at once, to fathom and exhaust all the possibilities of sound." Carreño was playing Anton Rubinstein's Concerto in D Minor, about which Cather with her usual self-assurance declared, "There is nothing in modern romantic music that can touch it for grandeur and color."

Cather had her first chance to hear a Wagner opera during the spring of 1897 when Walter Damrosch took his opera company to Pittsburgh. Her interest in Wagner, which subsequently became a passion, began with what must have been a dismal week that included badly cast and poorly sung performances of *Lohengrin*, *Götterdämmerung*, and *Tannhäuser*. Cather sent back breezy descriptions of these disasters for the home folks in Lincoln. All the singers had colds, "which beset every singer who ventures into this foggy river atmosphere." Herr Kraus, who sang Lohengrin, had to stop in the middle of an aria for a coughing seizure, and "poor Frau Venus on her couch coughed until Tannhäuser's head which rested on her knee shook as if he had the palsy." The Elsa in *Lohengrin* was so fat that it was a wonder that any Lohengrin would "descend from the gleaming heights of Mt. Monsalvat to get her out of her scrape." And Cather reported that in order for Damrosch to afford Lilli Lehmann, who got a thousand dollars a night, he had to hire cheap singers for the other parts, and the chorus was abominable. Despite all these shortcomings the music was wonderful, "so beautiful . . . that one wishes the singers would not come on and spoil it."

Late in June Cather finished her year on the *Home Monthly* and went back to Nebraska for the summer, stopping off in Columbus to visit the Canfields, and was in Lincoln by the twenty-ninth. She spent the summer in Red Cloud, except for a week in the "wild west" in August. Writing Helen Seibel in July that the *Home Monthly* had been sold, she reported severing her connection with it. She would return to Pittsburgh in September to look for a newspaper job. Even though she was temporarily without employment, she seems not to have considered staying in Nebraska. She told the secretary of her class of 1895 the next year: "After spending the summer months of 1897 at home in Nebraska, I returned to Pittsburgh, leaving the *Home Monthly* at the expiration of my contract, to accept the more remunerative position of telegraph editor of the Pittsburgh *Daily Leader*, the largest evening paper in Pennsylvania."

On September 7, 1897, the *Pittsburgh Leader* telegraphed offering her a job at seventy-five dollars a month. She wrote Will Owen Jones asking him to get her transportation from Red Cloud to Lincoln and then on to Chicago. She said she had been writing stories that summer and getting on with them better than ever before, but she did not want to let the chance slip by to work full-time for the *Leader*. She did think she could write better in Red Cloud than anywhere, because in Pittsburgh she did the society act too much. Because Pittsburghers did not often take in strangers and she was as vain as the rest of her sex, she could not be a hermit there. But there were many summers ahead for writing, and in Pittsburgh there would be Calvé and Bernhardt and all the rest of the great. She was at the age of twenty-three far from ready to retire to a quiet corner to write. Besides, she was flattered to be offered this job when Pittsburgh was full of unemployed reporters. As far as journalism was concerned, she definitely had arrived.

A month after returning to Pittsburgh she wrote Louise Pound that she had expected to be the *Leader*'s drama critic, but a few days after her arrival the day telegraph editor had left for New York. Cather was asked to help do this work until they could get a man to take his place. She liked the work and had the wild idea of asking for the job herself. The management objected to her gender and inexperience, but she hung on and they said she could try. The work, she said, wasn't as thrilling as writing drama criticism, but the job was more responsible and remunerative. Her task was to edit and expand foreign cables. Foreign correspondents in those days did not file complete stories. She explained that a brief cable would come announcing the birth of a prospective duke of Marlborough and she would then have to supply a short history of the house. She also had to winnow the wheat from the chaff out of the vast amount of news that crossed her desk. The chief requisites were discretion, some general knowledge of foreign affairs and history, and the trick of writing headlines. She had trouble with the last. Then there were a dozen telegraph boys under foot all the time, and her copy was absolutely irrevocable once it went up the pneumatic tube to the linotype operators. She admitted that she was by nature slouchy and uncertain, and she thought Louise would appreciate how she had been on the race track since taking over the telegraph desk. Her efforts paid off, however, for the directors of the paper had met four days before and voted to give her the job permanently. She was now just one of the fellows and related with obvious satisfaction that the boys had given her a dinner to celebrate and another paper had run a story on her.

Thus the second year in Pittsburgh started off with a great burst of activity. Her hours on the telegraph desk were from eight until two, and she had the afternoons and evenings to herself to go to the theater and concerts and to write. Her six-hour stint, however, was strenuous. At one moment she had to hold the forms from going to press because some big news involving the king of Belgium was expected momentarily. Then she would be driven almost wild when some actress shot herself in Paris, and it was too late to get the story on the drama page where it belonged. The news would have to go with general coverage right next to a W.C.T.U. convention in Ohio. Then she had to think up different headlines for twelve suicides all at once. People, she said, showed such poverty of imagination in the way they killed themselves. But the political news was the toughest to handle. What was a person to do when one cable from Berlin reported that the kaiser had said thus and so and another from Vienna said just the opposite? The following summer she was still editing news on the telegraph desk, and because the Spanish-American War was going on, she had to postpone going home until August. She wrote in June that she had to stay in Pittsburgh grilling in the heat and writing headlines all about Cervera's being bottled up in Santiago Harbor. She thought the horrors of war were a good bit worse in newspaper offices than in the field.

The main event of 1898, however, was meeting Ethelbert Nevin. She may have met him through Mrs. John Slack, who lived lavishly in suburban Sewickley and gave musical parties to which Cather was sometimes invited. Her house and music room, which appear as part of the setting in "Uncle Valentine" (1925), were next door to Vineacre, the Nevin family estate. Or she could have met him through his brothers, who owned the *Leader*. In any event, the meeting took place in the winter after Nevin had returned from living in Europe to settle down at his boyhood home. Cather was charmed by him. He was her first real artist friend and in every way fitted her image of the artist. He had begun composing songs as a child, before he ever had studied music. His practical father had given him a musical education but then forced him to go into business. Escaping from this bondage, Nevin had become a restless world traveller, but wherever he went—Venice, Algiers, Boston— he wrote incessantly, turning out hundreds of musical compositions, often working at night, suffering from poor health most of the time. In an article Cather wrote on him for the *Ladies' Home Journal*, she said: "Temperamentally Mr. Nevin is much the same blending of the blithe and the *triste* that gives his music its peculiar quality, now exultantly gay, now sunk in melancholy, as whimsical and capricious as April weather."

Nevin found Cather attractive and turned on his charm. She wrote Mariel Gere twice about him, describing him in such glowing terms that she admitted she sounded like a girl infatuated with a matinee idol. She said she had been spending a good bit of her leisure time with him, and he was about the most lovable man she ever had met. She was prouder of this friendship than she ever was of anything. He had a nobleness of soul that helped every life he touched. In her next letter she listed Nevin as the prince and king of all her Pittsburgh friends. That afternoon he had gone shopping with her, carried her bundles, and then bought her (in January) a bunch of violets as big as a moon. Think of it, she wrote, the greatest of American composers and a fellow of thirty with the face of a boy and the laugh of a girl. He actually was thirty-five, but to her he represented youth, vivacity, golden talent. When she returned from Red Cloud in the fall of 1898, Nevin telephoned to welcome her back to Pittsburgh and sent her a copy of Shakespeare's sonnets.

The shopping scene appears in "Uncle Valentine," and when Nevin died three years later his death was a bitter blow. She also put him into an earlier story, " 'A Death in the Desert,' " as the fabulous Adriance Hillgarde, who shapes the tale but never appears on stage. The rather nasty portrait of Janet Oglethorpe, Uncle Valentine's ex-wife, has suggested to some observers that there may have been a rivalry between Cather and Anne Nevin, the composer's wife. The character of Janet is rather too much like Anne to be accidental. It is reasonable to conclude that Anne Nevin, who supplied the practical business sense her composer husband lacked, and Cather were opposites in temperament, as Cather and Roscoe Pound had been. Anne Nevin—who had a solid social position in Pittsburgh, two children, and a strong command of the situation—could not have felt threatened, but she may have felt that Cather came around too often. Nevin was dependent on his wife for her business acumen and for inspiration. He wrote his wife: "I am dependent on you. Miss Cather was right. My melody is you: my harmony is you." Cather realized this and said as much in a feature article in the *Courier*. Nevin thought enough of Cather to dedicate a love song to her, "The Silver Moon," and Cather wrote three poems in his memory, one of them, "Sleep, Minstrel, Sleep," beginning:

> Sleep, minstrel, sleep; the winter wind's awake,
> And yellow April's buried deep and cold.
> The wood is black, and songful things forsake
> The haunted forest when the year is old.

Also after Nevin died in 1901, Cather wrote the editor of the *Ladies' Home Journal* asking him to return to her the photographs of Nevin she had supplied for her article.

Cather's second year in Pittsburgh was as busy as the first. She continued to review plays and concerts, for which the paper paid her extra, and she covered special events. She also kept sending back columns to Nebraska, but this year she switched "The Passing Show" from the *Journal* to the *Courier*. She also conserved her energies by using the same material for both her *Leader* reviews and her *Courier* column. In October she wrote enthusiastically of John Philip Sousa's week of concerts at the Exposition Hall. Every newsboy was whistling music from his operetta *El Capitan*, and Cather "was inclined to think that [Sousa was] the only man who has written music that is characteristically American." She was equally delighted with the Pittsburgh Symphony's playing of Dvořák's *New World Symphony*. Its use of folk music, she thought, was splendid. Dvořák had composed it in Iowa in 1893, and Cather first had heard it in Lincoln the following year. It made a great impression on her then, and she recreated this response in Thea Kronborg, who hears it at her first symphony concert when she is studying music in Chicago. When Nellie Melba appeared in *The Barber of Seville*, Cather was on hand to report the event. She was in rapture after the famous aria "Una Voce Poco Fa," which she described as "flawless perfection." "And it was sung as just one voice in all this world can sing it. One upon another they came, each sweeter than the last, those round, full unclouded tones, those notes of silver, shaken from her throat as lightly as the water drops from a sea gull's wing when it flies sunward in the golden dawn."

Cather's interest in the stage remained undiminished. When Minnie Maddern Fiske appeared in the dramatization of Thomas Hardy's *Tess of the D'Urbervilles*, she thought it one of the "few really great plays" of the last quarter century. She even put it in the same class with the younger Dumas's *La Dame aux Camélias*. Mrs. Fiske's performance was worthy of the play: "Her triumph is one of absolute intelligence—of art." Her power was in "the naked truth and passionate sincerity of her work. . . . She appeals only to those who love the drama seriously as an art, not as a diversion." When Richard Mansfield introduced Shaw to America, Cather reviewed *The Devil's Disciple*, but she did not know exactly how to take Shaw. She found it impossible to judge him by ordinary laws of dramatic art because he violated all the rules, but she had to admit that "by its biting satire, its brilliant, whimsical intellectuality, [the play] achieves a distinct and startling originality which many a law-abiding drama woefully lacks. One thing is certain; from the Shaw and Mansfield combination nothing commonplace can ever come."

Cather also did general reporting from time to time. When President McKinley visited Pittsburgh, there was a great parade which Cather watched from the balcony of the *Leader* office on Fifth Avenue. She covered the event with her usual exuberance and noted that the crowds that greeted the chief executive's carriage seemed to love their president. As he passed through the streets, a cry went up "that will always echo in one's ears. It was so gigantic, this elephantine glee of the multitude, this transcendent passion of patriotism before which everything else is dwarfed and pale. It was like a mighty Wagnerian chorus." This demonstration took place just before the war with Spain, which the public was demanding, the "splendid little war," as John Hay, secretary of state, called it; and the president's popularity was running high. On another occasion Cather reported a lecture given by the Norwegian Arctic explorer Nansen and followed with an account of a banquet given in his honor. Although he had failed in his effort to reach the North Pole, he had come closer than anyone yet, and Cather thought him an authentic hero: "He went [for the Pole] because he was possessed of an old unrest, the Odysseus fever; because there sang in his blood that siren voice that is forever wooing us away from the life of hotels and theatres and electric lights, whispering to us of a larger liberty, of meeting Nature once more breast to breast, coping with her hand to hand."

Even though Cather was very busy with her new job and her reviewing, she was not chained to the telegraph desk all the time. She spent Thanksgiving with Dorothy Canfield, her brother Jim, and his fiancée in Columbus. Mr. and Mrs. Canfield were away, and the young people had a very social time with dinners, teas, and theater parties. At Christmas Dorothy and her mother came to Pittsburgh to visit. In February Cather made her first trip to New York when Franklin Fyles, the drama critic for the *New York Sun*, was ill and the paper invited her to be guest reviewer. Although she was only there a week, she thought she must have met every thespian in New York, but she did not much care for them. The high spot of the trip was lunch with Helena Modjeska, a delightful person whom Cather thought both a gentlewoman and a scholar. She had been interested in Modjeska ever since she had seen her in *As You Like It* in Lincoln six years before. She went to see her in New York in Schiller's *Mary Stuart*, which she reviewed for the *Sun*. Despite age and illness the great Polish actress's carriage was "beautifully graceful and dignified . . . queenly." "Nobody who sees Mme. Modjeska today . . . can fail to be impressed by the naturalness and simplicity of her method and its freedom from exaggeration." Younger actresses could learn a great deal from her. Many years later Mme. Modjeska appears at a New Year's Eve party in *My Mortal Enemy* much as Cather remembered her in 1898. Cather was offered a job on the *Sun*, but she found out it would be all night work, and besides, she wrote, she could not bear to leave her friends in Pittsburgh. She did not go to New York to stay for another eight years.

During the first two weeks of May she visited Washington for the first time, staying with her cousin Howard Gore, who was professor of mathematics at Columbian College (now George Washington University). This visit was more dazzling than she could have expected, for her cousin was getting ready to join the Wellman Polar Expedition and was busy saying good-bye to all his friends, many of whom were members of the diplomatic corps. Cather was thus on hand for a round of dinners and parties and wrote Frances Gere afterwards that she had met no end of interesting people. One dinner was with the Norwegian ambassador and diplomats from the German embassy, and on another occasion Cather went out to dinner with the chargé d'affaires of the Turkish embassy. She also was enchanted by her cousin's wife, the daughter of a former ambassador from Norway and a cousin of the king of Sweden, who was full of stories of court life in Scandinavia, sang Grieg's songs beautifully, and read from Ibsen like the tragic muse. Cather even talked of plans to visit Norway with her sometime. The busy round of social activities did not keep Cather from making the most of her opportunities and writing up the forthcoming polar expedition for the Associated Press.

Cather returned to Nebraska for two months' vacation in August. When she wrote a family friend at her mother's request, because she was a pencil-pusher by profession, she described activities in the Cather menage in Red Cloud. Jessica was playing waltzes on the piano, while she and Douglass danced. She and Roscoe were planning to leave for the Big Horn Mountains in Wyoming for ten days of shooting. Roscoe was going to be principal of South Ward School next winter, and Douglass had just gotten a job in the Cheyenne office of the Burlington Railroad. She told another friend that she had learned to mix cocktails. When she went back to Pittsburgh in September, she was about to meet the most important friend of her life. She was still not yet twenty-five.

CHAPTER 7

Isabelle McClung
and a New Career

Although the year 1898–99 was momentous for Cather, it began dismally. She no sooner returned from her summer travels than she came down with the grippe and for six weeks fought the virus without much success. Finally her doctor ordered her to go south to recuperate, but instead she decided she wanted the loving companionship of an old friend and went to Columbus. Dorothy Canfield, then a senior at Ohio State, was delighted to have her, pampered her, and after six days Cather was feeling like herself again. "She is a very different looking person from the parchment colored invalid who stepped off the train with such a cough," Dorothy wrote Mariel Gere in a letter that contains alternate pages written by both women. Cather reported that she had gone to Columbus hating the world and everyone in it. The next day after writing this joint letter she returned to Pittsburgh, and her first contribution to the *Leader* appeared on October 25. But she did not resume her column for the *Courier* until Christmas.

From the end of October until the end of July, when she returned home again, she contributed much less than usual to her papers in Pittsburgh and Lincoln. Whether her vitality was low or she was being paid better and did not have to write so much, the record does not say. In any event she wrote a book column about twice a month for the *Leader* and only occasionally reviewed plays. When she resumed her columns for the *Courier*, they also appeared about every other week. Meanwhile, there were no new stories appearing anywhere, nor would she place any fiction at all for another year and a half. This is a surprisingly barren period for one who had been writing so easily and with such demonic energy.

She apparently had one literary project in the works, however, an idea for a book that had resulted from her experiences as a theater and music critic. She decided to write a series of open letters to various stage personalities, letters that were assessments of the subjects' strengths and weaknesses. She put together such a volume and sent it off to a publisher, but nothing happened. The manuscript was considered by several publishers, but no one wanted to bring it out. Her cousin Howard Gore had encouraged her to produce the manuscript, but he was a mathematician, not a drama critic. She then sent it to Arthur Stedman, one of the minor New York literati, hoping that he could find her a publisher, but, as she wrote a year later to another New York friend, Leonard Van Noppen, writer and translator: "Stedman did nothing with the manuscripts except get them dirty and cause me a considerable loss of time. . . . [They] are now with R. H. Russell & Co. of New York. Do you happen to know any of his people? If you do I'd be mightily obliged if you could speak a word for them and ask him what he thinks of them. Rupert Hughes, of the *Criterion*, says they will surely go somewhere."

They did not, and it was perhaps just as well. The letters were all addressed to very active personalities who would not have been flattered by some of her remarks. Some of the things she had to say have survived because she published three of the letters in her "Passing Show" column. In the one addressed to Nat Goodwin, for example, she told him that he was a charming fellow but with a limited range—in short, an intellectual lightweight. She hoped he never would be tempted by his admirers to do Shakespeare's comedies; he wasn't up to them. Then she concluded: "At any rate we like you for what you are, not for what you might be; something of a scapegrace, a good deal of a vagabond, and just enough of an artist to redeem your qualities. You are incorrigible, sir, and I for one like you the more for it." Cather gave a copy of her manuscript to Dorothy Canfield, who found it among her papers twenty-five years later and asked what she should do with the letters. Burn them, Cather wrote back. If anyone ever got hold of them, she thought, they would be a prime source for blackmail.

One stage personality for whom Cather had only praise was Lizzie Hudson Collier, an actress she had first seen perform in Lincoln. She was the leading lady of the New Grand Opera Stock Company when Cather arrived in Pittsburgh, and the two women became good friends. Collier was enormously popular and was universally admired as an exemplary human being as well as a first-rate actress. To illustrate Collier's generous nature, Cather told her readers of an episode that had occurred when Collier was playing a role requiring a live baby. The woman who produced the child was a slum dweller who took her infant home to her tenement each night after the performance. On one particular night when the temperature dropped below zero Collier refused to let the mother take the ill-clad child home in such weather. She bundled the baby up in her furs and took it to her own hotel suite for the night. "When she arrived at 11:30, all dressed in black and carrying this unaccustomed burden through the snowy winter night," Cather wrote, "she looked for all the world like the betrayed and deserted heroine of a Bijou melodrama who returns to receive the paternal curse."

On another occasion, when Cather dropped into Collier's dressing room feverish with a severe bronchial cold, the actress insisted on taking her back in a cab to the Schenley Hotel and putting her to bed in her own room. Then she nursed her for several days, even though she was playing every night. Cather wrote of Collier after her first year in Pittsburgh: "I never come out of the theatre with her after a matinee that there is not a string of carriages lined up in front of the stage entrance full of worshipful girls, who wave and smile at her and gaze at me with green-eyed jealousy and deep-seated loathing . . . for here I am walking coolly with this 'popular idol' with my sordid, mundane little spirit fixed on nothing loftier than where we will go for dinner."

One day backstage in Collier's dressing room Cather met one of those worshipful girls. It was a meeting that changed her life, for the other Collier fan was Isabelle McClung, the tall, handsome daughter of a socially prominent and affluent Pittsburgh family. The two women were immediately drawn to one another, and the friendship that began that day grew into a great love that lasted a lifetime. They were inseparable companions during Cather's remaining years in Pittsburgh and spent a great deal of time together during the decade after Cather moved to New York. Two years after meeting her, Cather moved into the McClungs' large new house at 1180 Murray Hill Avenue, in the fashionable Squirrel Hill section of Pittsburgh. She lived there for the rest of the years she remained in Pennsylvania, and later often returned there for extended visits. She had a former sewing room on the third floor as her study and spent many profitable hours writing there. The relationship between the two women changed inevitably after McClung got married in 1916, but their mutual love never diminished. Though they saw each other rarely in later years, they corresponded frequently. When McClung died in 1938, Cather did not think she could go on living, but after she recovered from her grief and reflected on the long years of friendship, she believed that McClung had been the one person for whom all her books had been written.

McClung was not an artist herself, but she had a passionate interest in the arts, and promoting Cather's career became one of the major interests of her life. Her background was stern Pittsburgh Presbyterianism, such as Cather had satirized, but she was not at all like her dour, conservative father, a tough judge of Scottish descent. While the McClungs lived expansively and expected their children to conduct themselves as well-behaved young socialites, Isabelle cultivated actresses, musicians, and writers. Judge McClung ran his family with a heavy hand, but apparently he found Cather, despite her frivolous vocation, acceptable as his daughter's friend.

There has been considerable speculation over the circumstances surrounding Cather's moving into the McClung house as a permanent resident. Did the family oppose this move? Did Isabelle threaten to leave home if she could not have her friend live with them? Did Cather's presence create friction among members of the family? The answer to all these questions is probably no. Edith Lewis thought that Isabelle "apparently had no difficulty in persuading her father and mother to invite Willa Cather to become a member of the McClung household," and although Lewis was not an unbiased witness, she was in as good a position as anyone to know. It hardly seems likely that Cather would have thrust herself into a domestic imbroglio. It was an unusual arrangement, to be sure, but there is no reliable evidence that it did not work out reasonably well. As time went on, Cather became close to the entire family. She was present in Pittsburgh for the wedding of Edith McClung and later corresponded with her. She also let Isabelle's brother manage some of her investments. The McClungs visited her in New York, and she was on hand and deeply concerned when Mrs. McClung had a near-fatal stroke in 1912.

The McClung house was large, elegant, solid, comfortable. Operated by a staff of servants, it provided a sharp contrast to the boardinghouses Cather had lived in in Lincoln and Pittsburgh or the cramped little house in Red Cloud overflowing with siblings. She had her own room on the third floor, where there was a bathroom, and her study was nearby. From the study she could look down to the garden and trees. The house sat high on a hill overlooking the roofs of other elegant homes, the tops of trees, flowerbeds, and shrubbery. No longer did she have to stand in line to use the bathroom or live in a house where cooking odors permeated the bedrooms. This was luxury that Cather enjoyed. She never had extravagant tastes, but she liked comfort and above all privacy. Dorothy Canfield Fisher remembered: "There was a good deal of stately entertaining carried on in the McClung house too, the many-coursed dinners of the most formal kind, which seemed picturesque (and they really were) to Willa." Her friends in Nebraska who feared she was living a Bohemian life need not have worried. Her career as a novelist was actually delayed by her desire not to cut loose and live in a garret while she learned the craft of fiction. But she did write the first stories that she thought worth preserving in her study on Murray Hill Avenue.

Details of the Cather-McClung relationship come from secondhand sources or from occasional comments in letters Cather wrote other friends. All of the hundreds of letters that passed between the two women were destroyed, except for three letters written from Europe by Isabelle late in her life. These three letters are warm and affectionate, demonstrating that the love between the two remained constant; but the recent suggestion that Cather retrieved her letters after Isabelle's death and destroyed them to remove incriminating evidence of a sexual relationship is probably without merit. Cather as she grew older became increasingly obsessed with privacy and determined if possible to confront posterity with only the works that she had prepared for publication. She destroyed all the letters she could retrieve from any friend who predeceased her. She would have destroyed her early stories and her newspaper writing if she could have.

Cather's love for Isabelle McClung has created considerable speculation about her sexual orientation. Contemporary frankness in discussing sexual matters inevitably raises the question of lesbianism. Was this friendship a physical lesbian relationship? Some critics believe it was, but there is no external evidence to support it. Indeed, there is not one reference to sexual relations in all the hundreds of her letters that have survived. If one defines a lesbian as a woman who has sexual relations with another woman, Cather cannot be called a lesbian on the basis of available records. On the other hand, if a lesbian is a woman whose primary emotional attachments are to other women, regardless of sexual relations, the definition adopted by some feminists, then Cather was most certainly a lesbian. There is no disputing that her closest friends were women—Louise Pound first, then Isabelle McClung, later Edith Lewis, Zoë Akins, and Elizabeth Sergeant. After deciding not to marry Preston Farrar in 1898, Cather never had any close relationships with men whose friendships could or were likely to lead to matrimony. She was very close to her brothers and her father; to S. S. McClure, who was married and much older; and to Alfred Knopf, who also was married and young enough to be her nephew. It is impossible to say whether Cather's emotional ties to women resulted from inherent tendencies or from the fact that relations with women avoided involvement with male egos and the possibility of children. Critics are stating inference, not fact, when they say that "Cather was a lesbian who could not or did not, acknowledge her homosexuality and who, in her fiction, transformed her emotional life and experiences into acceptable forms and guises." Or who say she felt the need to be reticent about love between women in her fiction because "she bore a burden of guilt for what came to be labeled perversion." She knew, of course, that society regarded sexual relations between women as unnatural, as her early letter to Louise Pound implies, but this did not keep her from having close friendships with women or from living for nearly forty years with Edith Lewis. As Cather grew older, her high regard for traditional values, her strong sense of decorum, and her close ties to family would have been strong deterrents to anything she regarded as deviant behavior.

Cather's book notices during her third year in Pittsburgh show continuing interests and some new enthusiasms. When one of James's later long stories, *In the Cage*, came out, she reviewed it perceptively, called it a "remarkable story," and praised James's "sympathetic handling of his subject," the story of "a young lady telegraphist shut up for eight hours a day in a cage of a telegraph office . . . in a suburban district of London." She devoted two columns in the *Courier*, one in the *Leader*, and an article for the *Home Monthly* to Richard Realf, poet, soldier, and workman who had spent six of the "happiest years of his disordered life in Pittsburgh" and whose poems recently had been collected. He was a romantic, Byronic type who had committed suicide in San Francisco after a wasted life, and some of his poems she found powerful and poignant. The bitter, ironic poetry of Stephen Crane, however, she cared for not at all. When she reviewed *War Is Kind*, she wrote, "Either Mr. Crane is insulting the public or insulting himself, or he has developed a case of atavism and is chattering the primeval nonsense of the apes."

Of considerably more interest are her reviews of Frank Norris's *McTeague* and Kate Chopin's *The Awakening*. One might expect Cather to dislike Norris's naturalistic novel of a San Francisco dentist destroyed by his inability to cope with life. But she began her review, "A new and a great book has been written," and went on to praise the minute descriptions of Polk Street as "convincing proof of power, imagination and literary skill" and the invention as "vigorous and bold." On the other hand, Chopin's novel was a great disappointment. She wondered why Chopin devoted so "exquisite and sensitive, well-governed a style to so trite and sordid a theme." There was no need for a second *Madame Bovary*, as she termed the novel, and she had no patience with the heroine, Edna Pontellier, who demanded "more romance out of life than God put into it." Women of the Bovary type, she wrote, "really expect the passion of love to fill and gratify every need of life, whereas nature only intended that it should meet one of many demands." This response to the novel shows no sympathy at all for nineteenth-century women trapped in matrimony in a male-dominated society. It also reveals Cather's own belief in romantic love as a destructive force and helps to explain her own avoidance of entangling emotional relationships.

Two other novelists that Cather might have been expected to disparage but did not were Zola and Harold Frederic. Cather thought that Zola was perhaps the "greatest mind in France today," and she admired his courage in taking on the French establishment in the then-current Dreyfus affair. But "his greatness as a man," she wrote, "has not always been to his advantage as an artist." She had read Zola extensively and never had cared for the naturalism of the Rougon-Macquart novels; yet in *Germinal*, which had just appeared, she thought the artist and theorist were in perfect balance and the result was "the greatest of labor novels." Frederic, who had died relatively young in 1898, was a realist whose novels Cather liked, despite her usual aversion towards realism. She reviewed his posthumously published *The Market Place* as a book worth reading and deplored the untimely death of a promising talent. In summing up Frederic's career, she recalled that his best novel, *The Damnation of Theron Ware* (1896), which is about a Methodist minister's loss of faith, was for the first two hundred pages "as good as anything in American fiction."

Cather's occasional reviews of plays and musical events also gave her additional chances to extol the merits of her favorite actors and singers. She went to see Minnie Maddern Fiske, Julia Marlowe, Richard Mansfield, and Olga Nethersole on the stage. She reveled in Fiske's "penetrating intellect," thought Marlowe's Rosalind in *As You Like It* a marvel, enjoyed Mansfield's *Cyrano de Bergerac*, and found Nethersole's performance "interesting and artistic" in *The Second Mrs. Tanqueray*, "the greatest play written in the English tongue for many a long day." This year Cather also had a chance finally to hear Wagner well performed when the New York Metropolitan Opera Company brought *Lohengrin* and *Die Walküre* to Pittsburgh with Nordica, Schumann-Heink, and the two de Reszkes in the casts. These performances were "something long to be remembered."

When Cather went home for the summer in 1899, she treated herself to a leisurely boat trip through the Great Lakes, about one thousand miles by water, with a day's stopover at Mackinac Island. She wrote Mariel Gere that she would be in Nebraska by August 6, but her mother, who was then living in Lincoln, was sick and she expected to have to spend all her time with her and probably would not get to visit with Lincoln friends. She was not alarmed about her mother but worried and felt her filial duty strongly. Whatever else she did during that summer is unrecorded, but she certainly did some writing. She tried a one-act farce, "The Westbound Train," that she gave to Sarah Harris for the *Courier* in September, and she perhaps wrote an important story, "Eric Hermannson's Soul," that she sold to the *Cosmopolitan* for publication the following April.

Although she had been a drama critic for six years, she had not tried writing drama since she was literary editor of the *Hesperian*. Reprinted in her *Collected Short Fiction*, "The Westbound Train" is a unique item in that gathering. She never tried writing a play again. It resembles nothing so much as one of Howells's little farces that she earlier had been rather contemptuous of. Taking place in the Union Pacific depot at Cheyenne, the farce consists mostly of a monologue by a woman en route to San Francisco to meet her husband. It involves mistaken identity, another woman, a misdirected telegram, and, of course, a happy resolution of the muddle. The little piece is an entertaining trifle; but humor is relatively rare in Cather's work.

She returned to Pittsburgh early in October 1899 to begin her fourth year in the East. She stopped off in Chicago en route to Pennsylvania to see Elia Peattie and to have dinner with Peter Finley Dunne (Mr. Dooley). Her first surviving letter to Dorothy Canfield was written on the twelfth from the McClung home on Murray Hill Avenue. Cather must have gone there to stay for a while after returning from Nebraska before finding herself another boardinghouse. Canfield by this time had gone to Paris with her mother and was beginning her graduate work in Romance languages. Isabelle McClung, two years older than Dorothy but four years Cather's junior, was taking Dorothy's place as the adoring younger friend. Cather reported to Dorothy that Isabelle had met her at the Union Station and they had been tramping about in the hills and listening to Walter Damrosch's orchestra.

By the fall of 1899 it is clear that Cather was getting tired of daily journalism. She had been writing for the papers since her junior year in college and was ready for a change. Her old friend Elia Peattie, whom she had known as a columnist for the *Omaha World-Herald*, was then in Chicago and was urging her to come too. Peattie, who had become a nationally published fiction writer, thought that there was no woman journalist in Chicago who could touch Cather. At that moment Cather rather thought she would go to Chicago, but nothing came of this project. It is likely that by spring Isabelle was reason enough for Cather to stay on in Pittsburgh. She remained and the following summer for the first time did not go home to Nebraska. After deciding to stay, she also made the decision to quit the *Leader*, and her last contribution to the paper appeared on April 19, 1900.

The appearance of "Eric Hermannson's Soul" in a large national magazine may have given her the courage to leave the paper. The story, a long and subtle one, is a very competent piece of fiction and marks a clear advance in her narrative skill. Returning to the world of Nebraska and the material of "On the Divide," it creates another blond giant as a protagonist but a much more complex character than Canute Canuteson. Eric is a young Siegfried who has emigrated to Nebraska at eighteen, worked in the fields, played his fiddle at all the dances, hugged the girls, and visited Lena Henson, a woman of dubious reputation. When a passionate exhorter from the fundamentalist Free Gospellers captures Eric's soul, he puts away his violin and becomes another one of the dull clods from the Old World "sobered by toil and saddened by exile." At this juncture beautiful Margaret Elliot comes out of the East to visit on the Divide. She meets Eric, is attracted to him, rides with him, and plays the organ for him, "probably the first good music he had ever heard." The hold of the Free Gospellers loosens. Eric falls in love with the accomplished Margaret. He agrees, at her urging, to play his fiddle again and to attend a dance she is giving before her departure for home. In doing so, he barters his soul, as he believes, for one evening of pleasure. The story ends with Margaret getting on the train and Eric, in possession of his soul, deaf to the reproaches of the Free Gospellers' preacher.

A bare plot summary does injustice to this tale. It is the way the material is handled and the careful management of detail that make the story significant. One notices first of all that Cather is beginning to possess her material and to handle it with a measure of aesthetic distance that makes one both see and feel the world of immigrant farmers on the Divide. The prairie, the grass, the fields of wheat and rye, the western sky—all are evoked, not simply described. In one particularly effective scene Eric and Margaret climb the windmill, as Willa and her brother Roscoe had done in the summer of 1893 when they visited Uncle George's farm, to view the clear night sky stretching away to the distant horizon, "which seemed to reach around the world." As they watch, the weary wind carries the heavy odor of the cornfields to them and the music of the dance sounds faintly from below. Before they descend there is one passionate kiss, which frightens Margaret and makes her draw back from the love she sees in Eric's eyes. There is tension in this scene and a skillful development of the conflict between East and West. The author's sympathies lie with the West, but she understands the pull of culture and civilization. Also, her developing technique is nowhere better shown than in a scene depicting powerful sexual emotion without exceeding the limits permissible in magazine fiction of that day. In a ride across the prairie one afternoon Eric and Margaret meet a pack of wild horses, and Margaret's pony nearly stampedes. Eric jumps off his horse, grabs the bit of Margaret's rearing pony, and while it is biting and kicking viciously, subdues it. The scene, which has an orgastic intensity, is followed immediately by Eric's declaration of love. The entire story is well conceived and well executed and avoids the sentimental ending of the standard Western, which Owen Wister's *The Virginian* (1902) would inaugurate, in which boy gets girl and the happy couple ride off into the sunset together.

Even before her last by-line appeared in the *Leader*, Cather had made a change. She joined the staff of a short-lived, five-cent weekly paper called the *Library*. Charles Clark, a young man with literary ambitions, inherited twenty thousand dollars and launched the publication with great expectations and small realizations. The venture only lasted six months, until the money ran out, but during its brief life Cather contributed weekly stories and articles and was decently paid for her work. She wrote five stories, seven poems, and sixteen articles and essays, using her own name and five different pseudonyms. She also revised the early story "Peter" for its third appearance and reprinted "A Night at Greenway Court." The essays show a growing maturity and more leisurely composition, while the stories demonstrate that she was still trying out various subjects and themes. The essays include the article on Crane, the Brownville piece ("The Hottest Day I Ever Spent"), and the profile of Bryan. But she also wrote on opera personalities, pictures at the Carnegie Gallery, and "The Men Who Make the Pittsburgh Papers."

The five stories that appeared in the *Library* are not very important. "The Sentimentality of William Tavener" is the story with a Virginia memory already mentioned. "A Singer's Romance" is a reworking of the material in "Nanette, An Aside," an opera-singer story, but this time told from the point of view of the singer rather than her maid. The singer foreshadows the fictional portrait of Nordica, which appeared sixteen years later in "The Diamond Mine." "The Conversion of Sum Loo" is another Chinese story set in San Francisco, where Cather never had been, and invites comparison with the earlier tale, "The Son of the Celestial." This time the protagonist is a Chinese businessman whose infant son dies after he allows his wife to have the baby baptized at a Christian mission. The pathos is feeble, and the story is certainly one of Cather's bad apples. "The Dance at Chevalier's" is also a poor story that Cather signed with a pseudonym. Dealing with the rivalry of a Mexican and an Irishman for the affections of the beautiful Severina Chevalier, it ends with the Mexican poisoning the Irishman. This story's only interest lies in its use of the French Canadian settlement north of Red Cloud that Cather later evoked memorably in *O Pioneers!* "The Affair at Grover Station" is a ghost story far more skillfully done than the early football story that Dorothy Canfield supplied the plot for in 1893. Again Cather explored the dark underside of romanticism, the world of the grotesque, which would become an important aspect of her late novels. As the narrator says, "It's a grewsome tale, and someway we don't like to be reminded that there are more things in heaven and earth than our systems of philosophy can grapple with." The story has a deep-dyed villain of Oriental origin who murders the debonair station agent after quarreling with him over the beautiful daughter of a former Wyoming senator. The ghost of the dead man appears to the narrator and writes on a blackboard the clue to finding the body. When the body is found in a locked boxcar many miles away, it has chalk on its fingers. The story is a good yarn, set neatly in a framing device, and it no doubt owes its authentic command of technical railroading to Douglass Cather, who worked for the Burlington in Cheyenne.

After staying through the summer in Pittsburgh, Cather was ready by fall for a change of scenery. Writing Will Owen Jones from Pittsburgh on September 29, when she thought she soon would have to return to Nebraska, she said she had taken the position on the *Library* only temporarily. Though it was a good job, the problem was that her mother was sick again, and her family wanted to move to Lincoln. Her mother was too ill to load the cookstove, she reported, and she would have to do it. She expected to be in Nebraska by November to stay for the winter. Could Jones use her on the *Journal*? She would not be too haughty to work for her old paper, and besides, she had lost the art of loafing and couldn't write verse and fiction all the time: about three or four days a week were enough. After that her head got muddy. Her letter concludes by saying that she had had a wonderful year, the happiest of her life so far. There were a lot of her things coming out in the fall, both in prose and verse, and the world was a good place to live in. She was exaggerating a good deal in the first half of her statement, as she published only the piece on Nevin in November and two poems in December, but she may already have sold "Jack-a-Boy" to the *Saturday Evening Post*, which printed it in March. Undoubtedly her growing love for Isabelle McClung added greatly to the sum of happiness of that year.

Instead of returning to Nebraska, however, Cather went to Washington. She stayed with her cousin Howard Gore and found a job translating letters and documents for the United States Commission to the Paris Exposition of 1900. Tom Outland's impressions of the national capital in *The Professor's House* no doubt mirror her memories of working in a government building at this time: "How it did use to depress me to see all the hundreds of clerks come pouring out of that big building [the War Department] at sunset! Their lives seemed to me so petty, so slavish. . . . Thousands of them, all more or less like the couple I lived with. They seemed to me like people in slavery." But Tom also remembered from his walks about the White House grounds in late afternoon "those beautiful, hazy, sad sunsets, white columns and green shrubbery, and the [Washington] monument shaft still pink while the stars were coming out." Cather remained in Washington until about the middle of March, though she made a trip back to Pittsburgh for Nevin's funeral in February. As the writing habit was inveterate, she also became a Washington correspondent for the *Journal* and the *Index of Pittsburgh Life*, which had absorbed the defunct *Library*. Her Washington correspondence ran from December to March, after which she returned to Pittsburgh, moved into the McClungs' house, and became a high school teacher.

Her thirteen columns for the *Journal* and twelve for the *Index* reviewed plays and concerts, interviewed public personalities, covered art exhibitions, and described in general life in the capital. Her first column reported on the opening session of the Senate and another performance by Teresa Carreño. Because Washington did not have a proper auditorium, Señora Carreño had to play in a church where the Ten Commandments were frescoed in red and yellow above her head. At one point she was studying them so intently that she almost missed a cue. But the concert was a success: it "came in like a lamb and went out like a lion," beginning with Mozart and ending with Liszt.

Although Cather went back to Pittsburgh to spend her usual Christmas with the Seibels, she was in Washington for most of the holiday season, which supplied material for her column. The weather was so mild that people went about without wraps, but "the street corners were gay with flower stands" and there was a "forest of Christmas trees and holly bushes about the old market place." The avalanche of Christmas presents that descended on President McKinley from admirers throughout the country interested her. "During the W.C.T.U. convention here I heard one lady complain that an oil painting executed by herself, which she had sent the President last Christmas, was nowhere to be found in the White House reception rooms."

The theater, as usual, occupied a great deal of Cather's attention. She went to see a production of *Hedda Gabler* just after Christmas, and in January she had the unusual opportunity to see Maude Adams and Sarah Bernhardt perform in the same play, Rostand's *L'Aiglon*. Ibsen was never one of her favorites, and she thought the tragedy in *Hedda Gabler* was unconvincing; but she reported that the young actress, Blanche Bates, who played the title role had an enviable intellectual grasp of the role and was "one of the most intelligent faces among the actresses of the younger generation." After seeing Adams on Saturday night and Bernhardt on the following Monday, she wrote: "A complete analysis of the two renderings would be futile and would be little less than brutal to the young actress." But she made the analysis anyway, though she noted after panning Adams that her schooling had been "of the most superficial nature" and that her head had been "early turned by the indiscriminating adulation of a fatuous and fickle public." Bernhardt, on the other hand, after thirty-eight years on the stage still had the marvelous voice that French poets thirty years before used to write about: some of her lines "once heard cannot soon be forgotten." As for acting, in the duke's death scene Bernhardt "rose to absolute sublimity," while Adams failed utterly, getting from it only "cheap pathos."

For her last contribution to the *Index* Cather went to Georgetown to visit "one of the quaint 'literary landmarks' of Washington . . . the little red cottage . . . where for nearly fifty years Mrs. [E.D.E.N.] Southworth planned adventures for self-sacrificing chambermaids and noble, though affectionate factory girls." She confessed to her readers that she made the trip "in the spirit of jest," for the endless procession of novels produced by Mrs. Southworth belonged with the trashy fiction of Ouida and Marie Corelli that Cather never could stand. But she was rather humbled by the experience, as she reflected on the appalling amount of "physical labor the poor woman accomplished, sitting in the little library facing the river, writing thousands upon thousands of pages." Cather ended up marveling at the "passion for creative experiments" that drove Mrs. Southworth, and that artistically ended "just where it had begun." She doubted if Henry James himself was "more sincere, or whether his literary conscience [was] more exacting than was hers." Cather was no longer quite the brash, self-assured young critic she had been when she began her journalistic career.

About the time Cather was switching from journalism to teaching, two more of her stories appeared—"Jack-a-Boy" in the *Saturday Evening Post* (a magazine she later disparaged) and "Eldorado: A Kansas Recessional" in the *New England Magazine*. Neither story reflects much credit on her, but the former is interesting as a tribute to her youngest brother Jack, then eight years old. She always had special affection for this little brother, missed him when she was away from Red Cloud, and when he was ready for college, sent him to Carnegie Tech. The story is the sentimental tale of a little boy who moves into an urban apartment house and charms an elderly professor of classics, the Woman Nobody Called On, and the narrator, a female music teacher. After giving these characters a new lease on life with his winning ways, the little boy dies of scarlet fever. *Post* readers in 1900 probably found the pathos touching, but Cather had not yet learned how to inject sentiment without becoming sentimental. She was still under the deleterious influence of Nevin, who had told her that as a child he had been taught never to be afraid of sentiment. The other story, "A Kansas Recessional," also is hardly memorable. It concerns a scam in which a Virginia colonel, a former Confederate officer, is sold land in western Kansas. The story is told with heavy irony, with an O. Henry surprise ending in which the colonel gets his money back, but not much can be said for it. New England readers, however, may have been comforted to read about the horrors of life in Kansas and the misfortunes of gullible investors in western real estate.

Cather began her career as teacher at Central High School in March. Just how she got the job is not known, but she was a mid-semester replacement for a teacher who resigned because of ill health. Judge McClung may have heard of the opening and recommended her, as he and a senior member of the English Department were fellow alumni of Washington and Jefferson College. Also some of the members of the Pittsburgh School Board lived not far from the McClungs, and the judge may have suggested her to one of them. Or Charles Gerwig, then secretary of the Board of Education of Allegheny, across the river, may have been responsible. At any rate, the *High School Journal* reported in its Easter issue that "Miss Cather, another new teacher, has now taken Miss Heard's place in Room 19 as teacher of Latin, Algebra, and Composition." From March until the end of the school year in June Cather had to work harder than she ever had before to keep up with her classes. Teaching composition was a breeze, and Latin she knew well, though grammar never had received much of her attention; but algebra must have been an ordeal. She had taken four years to work off the freshman math requirement at the University of Nebraska, and having to teach algebra could only have cost her great effort. She really must have been weary of journalism to let herself in for this demanding schedule. When she returned to Red Cloud for the summer, she was worn out and had lost twenty pounds. She wrote the Seibels that she had not been able to see them before leaving because of the horrors of the high school final exams.

She was not too exhausted, however, to accept an invitation to be guest editor for the August numbers of Sarah Harris's *Courier*. This she did in July before leaving to spend several weeks in the Rocky Mountains. In the columns she wrote she discussed a wide variety of topics, including western railroads; the writer Ernest Seton-Thompson, whom she had met in Washington; the composers Edward MacDowell and Victor Herbert; the Chicago Art Institute; Eden Phillpott's new novel; small-town life; Homestead, Pennsylvania; D'Annunzio's novel *Il Fuoco*; and Eleanora Duse. She wrote enthusiastically about MacDowell's music, but to ask Herbert for inspired composition, she said, was like "asking for champagne at a mutton shop." Yet, Herbert, as conductor of the Pittsburgh Symphony, had proved a good business manager, was popular with his musicians, and had pulled the orchestra out of debt. The Chicago Art Institute, Cather thought, was a wonderful museum performing a valuable service in public education. "There are thousands of people all over the prairies who have seen their first and only good pictures there." Her taste in art at this point ran more to Jules Breton's *Song of the Lark* and the peasant folk of Millet than to the ballet dancers of Degas.

Eden Phillpott was one of Cather's literary enthusiasms, and she greeted his *Sons of the Morning* as "a remarkable new book." She liked his sympathetic portrayal of the British yeoman and thought he was one of the few younger writers who could step into the shoes of Hardy, Meredith, or George Moore. She wished that there were some American writer who "could write of the American common people, the people on whom the burden of labor rested, who plant the corn and cut the wheat and drive the drays and mine the coal and forge the iron and move the world." American writers who did write about the people, she declared, "all write of trusts and strikes and corporations and man-devouring railroads, of the mere conditions of labor and not of men at all." She was calling for a writer of her own description, for she herself would in a dozen years begin writing of the people who "plant the corn and cut the wheat."

Cather was always interested in story-telling for children and had done a great deal of it herself for her younger brothers and sister, but she took a dim view of the story-telling hours then becoming popular among children's librarians. "They tell the story of the Trojan War, omitting the story of Helen's elopement; the story of Faust expurgated for the youthful mind; the story of Napoleon's energy, maintaining a careful silence as to his ambition." These enthusiastic librarians were trying to abolish evil from literature for the benefit of young minds. She thought it did a child no service to keep him from "the knowledge that the world is a hard place to live in, and that he will have to do many difficult and distasteful things before he gets through with it."

Her account of Homestead, Pennsylvania, must have been eye-opening for Lincoln readers. She described in vivid detail the conditions in Potterville, the stockade within which lived the immigrant laborers who worked in the Carnegie steel plant. The stockade had been built by Superintendent John Potter during the strike of 1892 to house scab labor—Germans, Slavs, Italians, Russians, blacks—while the union was being crushed. They still lived there in a state of barbarism, seventy inmates in a six-room house, for example. When one worker got out of bed, another took his place, and on Saturday nights "the whiskey drunk in Homestead . . . would float an ocean steamer." She commented sardonically that the splendid library Carnegie had built at Homestead was used only by "the bosses and draughtsmen and office forces." The mill hands, who toiled twelve hours a day, six days a week, had no leisure to enjoy Carnegie's bounty.

When Cather returned to Pittsburgh in the fall of 1901, she resumed her duties at Central High School as a full-time English teacher. Perhaps she had been willing to put up with teaching Latin, algebra, and composition during the preceding spring because she knew there would be a resignation in the English Department in the fall. She remained at Central High for two more years, then moved across the river to Allegheny High School to replace her friend Preston Farrar, and taught there until 1906, when Sam McClure carried her off to New York to be one of his editors. Cather might have remained a high school teacher indefinitely if this had not happened. She wrote an old friend in 1940 that she liked to teach and could have stuck it out forever if McClure had not happened to see some of her stories. Apparently her plan was to use her spare time, especially her summer vacations, to write until she felt able to drop teaching and become a full-time writer. Her sale of stories to the *Cosmopolitan* and the *Saturday Evening Post* must have encouraged her to think she could do this. She also wanted to write a novel. Her salary was only $650 a year, certainly less than she had made at the *Leader*, but free room and board at the McClungs' more than made up the difference.

Central High School was a dismal, grimy structure on a bluff overlooking the Union Station. There were four stories of gray stone topped by two ugly towers. It seemed to Emerson Graves, the title character in "The Professor's Commencement," a story Cather published the year after she began teaching, like "a fortress set upon the dominant acclivity of that great manufacturing city, a stronghold of knowledge in the heart of Mammon's kingdom." In the fall and winter, fog from the river and smoke from the soft coal burned by Pittsburgh industries made the city dark and dirty. Sometimes street lights had to be turned on in mid-day. The trains passing below added their share to the noise and filth. "Often, when some lad was reading aloud in the classroom, the puffing of the engines in the switch yard at the foot of the hill would drown the verse and the young voice entirely." The inside of the building was old and decrepit—floors worn down, walls defaced, and one had to climb three dingy flights of stairs to get to Cather's room on the top floor.

Although "The Professor's Commencement" concerns the reflections of a high school English teacher on the eve of retirement, his attitude towards his work and his students is Cather's. "Nominally he was a professor of English Literature, but his real work had been to try to secure for youth the rights of youth; the right to be generous, to dream, to enjoy; to feel a little the seduction of the old Romance, and to yield a little." Many of Cather's students no doubt were like the professor's students, "boys and girls from the factories and offices, destined to return thither, and hypnotized by the glitter of yellow metal. They were practical, provident, unimaginative, and mercenary at sixteen." But not all.

One of her most famous students, Norman Foerster, who became a well-known critic and professor of American literature, remembered her as a teacher whose manner seemed natural and human, but without contagious sparks. "Her voice was deeper than is usual; she spoke without excitement; her manner was quiet, reposeful, suggesting reserves of energy and richness of personality." Another student recalled that Cather was "one of the very few young teachers in a faculty of gray-haired veterans." Still another remembered that her manner towards students was very forthright. She called the boys by their last names, which was unusual, and demanded their attention with a no-nonsense approach.

When her students walked into her classroom at the beginning of the school year, they found a rather masculine young woman sitting on her desk. She told them her name was not pronounced "Kyther" or "Kayther," but it rhymed with "Rather." Her voice was deep. She wore the starched shirtwaists that her journalistic colleagues were familiar with, sometimes Buster Brown collars with red or black ties knotted four-in-hand or Windsor style, and a skirt short enough to show her ankles. One day they saw blue stockings with white polka dots, another time spats. She walked about her classroom with a manly stride, wore shoes with rubber heels, and talked to her students with thumbs in belt or pockets. She had already begun to comb her hair back in pompadour fashion, and when she finished a discussion, she smiled. Her students remembered "beautiful, even white teeth."

As a composition teacher, Cather knew that the only way to learn to write was to write. "She set us to writing themes, one every class day, usually in the first ten minutes of the period." The subjects were simple: "My First Party," "An Italian Fruit Stand," "My Favorite Play." She red-penciled "fine writing" of the kind she had indulged in as an undergraduate in college. She probably was thinking of her former pupils when she wrote her well-known essay "The Novel Démeublé" twenty years later and referred to "that drudge, the theme-writing high school student." Her method was "designed to teach us first to observe carefully, then to describe and narrate clearly." She was hard to please and graded themes severely. She seldom gave a grade of more than 85 and that rarely. "Mostly we got 70s and occasionally achieved an 80 on our themes which were all carefully corrected and returned to us."

When she received an outstanding theme, however, she did not stint her praise. One student named George Hughey recalled an occasion when Cather asked him to stay after class. She wanted to know if he had attended the transportation exhibition that he had been assigned to write about for a contest. He said he had. She wanted to know why then he had not produced the required essay: "If you don't hand in an essay, you won't pass my course." Hughey wrote the piece and won a twenty-dollar gold piece, which was presented to him by Andrew Carnegie himself in a public ceremony. "When Hughey went to class the next day, Cather came down from her desk in front of the classroom, threw her arms about him, and kissed him."

Cather gave her students a lot of reading, both poetry and prose. She required them to memorize poetry, drilled them on prosody, insisted that they identify similes and metaphors as they read. Her classes were never dull, and often she digressed to tell them anecdotes of stage or literary personalities she had known. Her knowledge of Latin was always evident, as she frequently pointed out Latin origins of English words. Once when her class was reading the *Idyls of the King* and came across a line in "Lancelot and Elaine" that read, "There is many a youth now crescent," she pointed out that "crescent" comes from *cresco*, "I grow." She also made her students look up references to classic mythology and at the end of the semester gave her students summer reading lists.

Cather was not a success with all her students. She never concealed her likes and dislikes, was outspoken in condemning sloppy work, and had little patience with the duller students. She played favorites, often inviting the students she liked to Sunday tea at the McClungs. "She was greatly admired by some of her students, and just as heartily disliked by others." This apparently did not bother her and was indeed characteristic of the way she had made friends and enemies in Red Cloud and in college, and had spared no one's feelings in her years as drama critic in Lincoln and Pittsburgh. One former student thought that she demanded too much of her pupils, and another believed she was too much of a perfectionist. She also did not mind humiliating students whose ineptitude irritated her by reading their compositions aloud in class.

It is not surprising that Cather was not universally popular among her colleagues. Her natural talents no doubt caused resentment and jealousy, as did her inability to abide fools. One teacher who followed Cather some years after she had resigned recalled that bitter feelings still existed among faculty members. She attributed this to Cather's "devotion to the brilliant students and her intolerance of those who did not learn quickly." But it was equally true that she did not mix socially with her colleagues, and they never had a chance to get to know her. She went home when classes were over and spent her evenings grading papers, reading with Isabelle, and writing stories.

That her teaching at Central High School was successful is proven by her move in 1903 to a more desirable position at Allegheny High School. A great contrast with Central, Allegheny High was relatively new, located in a much more attractive area, and the salary was better. She began with a stipend of $750 a year and ended up making $1,300. She was by then a master teacher with two young recent college graduates as assistants. The only drawback to the new position was a longer distance to commute by streetcar, clear across the river to Allegheny from the Squirrel Hill section of Pittsburgh. As she began what was to be her last year of teaching, she wrote Mariel Gere, also a teacher, that she liked her work more every year and thought that she was doing it better all the time.

During Cather's first semester as a teacher at Central, she had no time to write, but during the next year as a full-time English teacher, she resumed writing for the newspapers. She wrote fifteen columns for the *Pittsburgh Gazette* during 1901–2, using her pseudonym Henry Nickelmann for all but four. She placed her work in the *Gazette* because her friend George Seibel had become Sunday editor and invited her to contribute. Again she wrote about what happened to interest her at the moment: two essays on viewers and pictures at the Carnegie Institute Art Gallery, "Pittsburgh's Mulberry Street," a tenement district, "Stage Celebrities Who Call Pittsburgh Home," "Pittsburgh's Richest Chinaman," and "Richard Mansfield as Actor." She also wrote an essay about children who lived in hotels and one called "Poets of Our Younger Generation."

She wrote relatively little fiction in this period, publishing only two stories in 1902, neither of which is very important. "The Professor's Commencement" is interesting chiefly as it reflects Cather's teaching experience, but the protagonist is an improbable scholar who has chosen to bury himself for thirty years in "a city high school where failures in every trade drift to teach the business they cannot make a living by." Although he has been writing a history of modern painting, he knows that he will never finish it. As he awaits his final commencement, which coincides with his retirement, he feels "like the ruin of some extinct civilisation," or as he switched the figure, all his students, "those hundreds of thirsty young lives had drunk him dry." Perhaps Cather was speculating on her fate if she were to spend thirty years in the Pittsburgh high schools. The most arresting thing about the story is the professor's memory of the one truly gifted student he had taught in his entire career, who had "died wretchedly at three-and-twenty in his master's arms."

Here in 1902 is the germ of Professor St. Peter's Tom Outland in *The Professor's House.*

The other story of this year is "The Treasure of Far Island," the autobiographical western tale previously mentioned. It concerns the return to his hometown of a successful playwright, Douglas Burnham, who was Speckle Burnham, mayor of the play town in "The Way of the World." He comes back to Empire City, which is Red Cloud again, twelve years after leaving home for college, the same interval that separated Cather from the writing of this story and her arrival in Lincoln in 1890. Although the story makes use of early memories, particularly the island in the Republican River, it is mawkish and uncontrolled. At the end Douglas and Margie, the tomboy he remembered from childhood, revisit Far Island, relive the old days, and find that they are destined for one another. In telling this story, Cather sprinkled over it a good two dozen allusions to myth, history, and literature. Seven years later, however, Far Island became the setting for an unforgettable story, "The Enchanted Bluff."

After nearly a year and a half of teaching, living economically with the McClungs, and saving her money, Cather planned her first trip to Europe. For any educated American with European antecedents the periodic need to visit Europe to water his or her cultural roots is a compelling imperative. For Cather the urge was especially intense. The European immigrants she had met on the Divide, the German-French culture of the Wieners in Red Cloud, her early love of the classics, her deep immersion in French literature starting in college, her reviewing of books and plays by European authors and playwrights, her wide reading of British writers—all these factors drew her inevitably to the Old World. As soon as school was out in June 1902, she and Isabelle McClung sailed from Philadelphia for Liverpool, embarking on the *Noorland* on the fourteenth and reaching England on the twenty-sixth. They planned a three-months' tour of England and France that would not bring them back until late September. To supplement her savings, Cather arranged to send back travel letters to the *Journal*, fourteen of which appeared between July and October. These letters gave her Nebraska friends a good account of her responses to Europe. They are charged with excitement and enthusiasm, the thrill of seeing for the first time places and things she had read about since she was a child. They have a freshness and charm that still attracts, and the picture that emerges of Europe nearly eight decades ago, before two world wars ravaged and changed the Old World unalterably, has intrinsic historic interest.

The two young women had the good luck to land in the grimy English Midlands on a radiant June day when the city of Liverpool was gaily decorated for the coronation of Edward VII. From their hotel they could see St. George's Hall across a square in which countless Union Jacks were fluttering in the breeze. At the foot of the Duke of Wellington's statue a blind man played a concertina, while in the square were throngs of bobbies, red-coated soldiers, and people in holiday spirit. From the hotel window it was all lively and picturesque, a tourist poster, but when they went into the street they were shocked by the shabby, tasteless dress of the working class, the stoop-shouldered, unhealthy physical appearance of the people, which they thought stood in marked contrast to the American reality. "I have been in England a week now," Cather wrote, "and I have not seen one English girl or woman of the middle class who is not stoop-shouldered to a painful degree. . . . Even in the little, little girls one sees the beginning of it. . . . It amounts to a national disfigurement." And she added: "Girls with [the] skin of a rose and well featured enough have the figures of riddled old dames." If the appearance of the working class depressed her, however, she was enchanted by the sound of British English and wrote that after "hearing only English voices for a few days, the first American voice you hear . . . is very apt to suggest something of the nature of burrs or sandpaper."

They did not stay in Liverpool long but departed soon for Chester, where Cather wrote delightedly on July 1 of the quaint red-brick houses, the majority very old, with diamond windowpanes and high-walled gardens behind. The walls were beautifully toned and colored by age and overgrown with ivy and Virginia creeper. Hedges of holly or alder trees rose above the walls, and underfoot was the matchless English green of the sod. They promenaded along the top of the old wall of the city and peered into tidy walled gardens below. Chester was an authentic bit of the Old World they had come to find. When they went out to Hawarden Castle, they spent nearly half a day of utter solitude at the foot of the splendid ruined Norman tower originally built in 1075. The rains and winds of nearly a thousand years had given the masonry of the tower a clean-washed look. She wrote: "One can understand, lying a morning through at the foot of the Norman tower, why there are Maurice Hewletts in England." It seemed to her an overwhelming temptation to try reconstructing old ruins in historical fiction. Ultimately she couldn't resist this urge and turned to historical fiction in *Death Comes for the Archbishop* (1927), *Shadows on the Rock* (1931), and *Sapphira and the Slave Girl* (1940). When she died, she was at work on a novel laid in medieval Avignon.

While the two women were in Chester, Cather's attention was drawn to what she called "The Strangest Tribe of Darkest England," the people who lived and worked on the canal boats. She devoted one whole letter to the *Journal* and later an article in the *Gazette* to the barge men and women, whom she found utterly picturesque. They had their own culture, a caste system, distinctive dress, and a life-style that set them apart from the rest of the English. They lived and died on their boats, ferrying goods back and forth between Liverpool and London. One particular boat woman that Cather observed "had been born in the cabin of a flat [boat], had been a baby and had had all her childish ailments and grown to maidenhood shut in a box [cabin] 5 x 6, with half a dozen brothers and sisters. She had been courted and married somewhere between the tiller and the tow-path . . . and borne her children in the cabin where she herself was born."

Cather's highest priority on her trip to England was to visit Shropshire and to meet A. E. Housman, whose poetry she admired extravagantly. She described herself as Housman's bond slave ever since *A Shropshire Lad* had appeared, and she wanted to see the places he wrote about. Her letter to the *Journal* of July 11 is datelined "Ludlow" and describes both Ludlow and Shrewesbury, the latter surrounded by a loop of the Severn River, "which is nowhere more green and cool and clear, and nowhere more indolent and inaudible in its flowing. The broad meadows across the stream from the town are those on which Housman says that boys played football in the days of his boyhood." As the literary pilgrims looked across the stream towards the meadows, a group of youngsters trooped out with a ball and began to play. It was a perfect experience: Housman's poems come to life. Later in Ludlow, twenty miles to the south, Cather found the real heart of Housman country. She and McClung drove to their hotel through noiseless streets of a town of thirty-five hundred, somewhat smaller than in Queen Elizabeth's time. "High green hills rise to the north and west, all marked off into tiny pocket handkerchief fields bordered by green hedge rows and looking like the beds of a large hillside garden. To the south lies the valley of the Teme, with low, round hills on either side, none of them wood covered."

But there was no trace of Housman in Ludlow or Shrewesbury. Cather told her *Journal* readers that she had gone to the library in Shrewesbury and seen "old files of the little country paper where many of his lyrics first appeared as free contributions signed 'A Shropshire Lad.'" This was sheer invention, as the poems never had been published in such a manner. She also told her readers that no one there knew anything in particular about Housman and that people "were greatly astonished to hear that the book [*A Shropshire Lad*] had been selling in America for six years." She wrote a friend the following year that no one in Shrewesbury she had talked to had ever heard of Housman. The public library, she said, had a copy of his book with uncut pages. When she got to London, she added, she battered the doors of his publisher until they gave her his address. Then she, Isabelle, and Dorothy

Canfield, who had joined them in London, all went to call on Housman. Dorothy wrote Cather many years later: "As we went out together, I remember your saying how odd it was that nobody knew a thing about him personally. . . . 'We may find that he is a blacksmith, for all we know.'"

Cather did not describe her visit to Housman in her *Journal* letters, but she told people about it later, and garbled versions got into print and vexed her the rest of her life. One of them by Ford Maddox Ford, whom she called the prince of prevaricators, said she went to Housman as the representative of the Pittsburgh Shropshire Lad Club and gave him a solid-gold laurel wreath. The three women did take a bus out to his lodgings in Highgate and found him living in a horrible boardinghouse in a miserable suburb. Cather wrote that he was the most gaunt and gray and embittered individual she knew, and the poor man's shoes and cuffs and the state of the carpet in his little hole of a study gave her a fit of dark depression. When they arrived, Housman, a bachelor, was expecting some Canadian cousins and came racing down the stairs to greet them. After the mistaken identity was discovered, "he was courteous, said with a neutral British pleasantness that he would be glad to have us go upstairs to his study." It was a plain, threadbare room with cheap furniture badly needing some wax and rubbing. Cather sat on a couch with broken springs and tried to talk to him about his poetry. He was manifestly uneasy talking about his verse and said that writing poetry was not his real business, that he took much more interest in his Latin texts and classical philology. He was then a teacher of Latin at University College, London, and a great classical scholar.

Fortunately Canfield saved the day by mentioning that she was working at the British Museum on a doctoral dissertation dealing with Corneille and Racine in England. Scholarly research was a topic Housman could talk about, and for the rest of the visit he and Canfield carried on a dialogue. Meantime, Cather sat brooding over the astonishing contrast between the man before her and the magical lyrics that had so moved her. He was, she thought, making just about the only English verse of the decade that would last, poetry remarkable technically as it was unique in the truth of its sentiment. Before they left Housman gave her the manuscript of an unpublished poem. When the three young women finally got out of Housman's boardinghouse and onto a bus headed back to London, they all burst into tears. It was probably her great disappointment that kept her from sending an account of the visit to the *Journal*. In her old age she always intended to write about the experience someday in order to set the record straight, but she never got around to it. One of the last letters she ever wrote was to Dorothy Canfield Fisher asking for memories of the visit.

The last three weeks of July were spent in London, and besides visiting Housman the travelers saw a great deal of the British capital. They put up at a hotel "almost under the dome of St. Paul's, and on the same street up which Lady Jane Grey daily went to meet her judges at the Guildhall. The lord mayor still goes up to the Guildhall by the same street, and he drives by our windows daily in scarlet and gold." But the picturesqueness and historical scenes were offset by the street life, which she thought nowhere "more gloomy, more ugly, more grimy, more cruel than in London." There were shabby people, bars filled with men "red-faced and wet-eyed, pouring can after can of liquor down their throats," "alley-nursed, street-bred" girls, sometimes sober, oftener not. The first charms of English speech also were tempered by the cockney flower vendor: "Her voice is harder than her gin-sodden face, it cuts you like a whiplash as she shouts: 'Rowses! rowses! penny a bunch.'"

Cather and McClung explored London's East End, which looked like Hogarth's "The Harlot's Progress," watched an Italian religious procession, visited galleries, parks, and the usual tourist attractions. They were especially interested in painters' studios, visiting several, and one entire letter to the *Journal* describes the studio of the Pre-Raphaelite painter Edward Burne-Jones, material Cather made use of later in "The Marriage of Phaedra," a story in *The Troll Garden*. Shortly before crossing the Channel to France, they saw Beerbohm Tree's production of *The Merry Wives of Windsor*, in which Tree played Falstaff. Cather thought the production pretty bad, as Tree had pruned all the bawdy lines so as not to offend his Victorian audience, and as a result presented a Falstaff "whose resemblance to Shakespeare [went] little further than the paunch." The performance was redeemed in part, however, by the appearance of two feuding leading ladies in the same cast, Madge Kendal and Ellen Terry, who played two of the merry wives, Mistress Ford and Mistress Page.

Cather had been a Francophile since early childhood. The stories in Virginia of Mrs. Love's French childhood, the *joie de vivre* of the French Canadian settlement north of Red Cloud, Mrs. Wiener's memories of France, Cather's saturation in French literature—all these made her eager to get to France. She empathized completely with the homesick, homeward-bound passengers on the Channel steamer as they approached Dieppe early one morning at the end of July. "Above the roar of the wind and thrash of the water I heard a babble of voices, in which I could only distinguish the word 'France' uttered over and over again with a fire and fervor that was in itself a panegyric. . . . All the prone, dispirited figures we left [on deck] two hours before were erect and animated, rhetorical and jubilant. They were French people from all over the world. . . . Above all the ardent murmurings and the exclamations of felicity, there continually rose the voice of a little boy who had been born on a foreign soil and who had never been home. He sat on his father's shoulder, with his arms locked tight about his neck and kept crying with small convulsions of excitement, 'Is it France? Is it France?' "

Then the dawn began to come. The sky was black in the direction of England, and the coast of France began to grow gray ahead of them. Soon the high chalk cliffs of Normandy were a pale purple in the half light, and fishing boats began to pass the ship. When they touched the dock, the sky, the gravel beach, and the white town were all wrapped in a pale mist, and the narrow streets were canals of purple shadows. Everyone was speaking French, "clear voices that phrased the beautiful tongue they spoke almost as music is phrased." In a sense she too was coming home with the French passengers.

The next six weeks in France were a deeply moving artistic and literary pilgrimage. Before getting to Paris they stopped to sightsee in Rouen, where Flaubert had been born and worked. They paid their respects to a monument to the master, then turned to a nearby statue of de Maupassant, friend and pupil of Flaubert and another of Cather's mentors. Cather saw her first French cathedral, the magnificent twelfth-century Notre Dame, which dominates the old city of beautiful half-timbered houses. She was even more impressed, however, with nearby St. Ouen, one of the jewels of French Gothic architecture. She remembered her emotional response to St. Ouen nearly twenty years later when she created Claude Wheeler, her Nebraska farm boy in One of Ours who visits Rouen as a member of the American Expeditionary Force in World War I: "When he reached the choir he turned, and saw, far behind him, the rose window, with its purple heart. As he stood staring, hat in hand, as still as the stone figures in the chapels, a great bell, up aloft, began to strike the hour in its deep, melodious throat; eleven beats, measured and far apart, as rich as the colours in the window, then silence . . . only in his memory the throbbing of an undreamed-of quality of sound." Although Claude is reminded of Joan of Arc when he visits Rouen, Cather nowhere mentions her in the newspaper letters for the Journal. She did note, however, that the heart of Richard Coeur-de-Lion was buried behind the choir of St. Ouen.

Although she read French fluently, she never had learned to speak the language, and Willa and Isabelle were glad to have Dorothy Canfield as their guide for the first few weeks in France. The three women reached Paris in early August and put up at a pension at 11 Rue de Cluny on the Left Bank. Canfield stayed with them a while, then left to join her parents in Scotland. Before she left, they all visited Barbizon near Fontainebleau in the environs of

Paris to see where Millet, Rousseau, and other painters of that school had worked. As they walked in the forest, Cather remembered that this was where Stevenson had fallen in love with the woman he later married in California. The village of Barbizon wasn't much, but the surrounding fields reminded her of the rolling Nebraska prairie on the Divide. "To complete the resemblance," she wrote in the *Journal*, "there stood a reaper of a well-known American make, very like the one on which I have acted as super-cargo many a time. There was a comfortable little place where a child might sit happily enough between its father's feet, and perhaps if I had waited long enough, I might have seen a little French girl sitting in that happy, sheltered place, the delights of which I have known so well." She admitted that those fields in harvest time made her a little homesick.

Back in Paris the pilgrims visited all the tourist sights, toured the Louvre, explored the city. Cather was especially interested in visiting cemeteries and devoted a letter to two of them, the Cemetery of Montmartre, near the white wedding-cake church of Sacré Coeur and overlooking the city, and the most famous burial ground of all, Père-Lachaise. She walked the streets of Montmartre, which Baudelaire and Verlaine had haunted, then inspected the grave of Dumas *fils*, who was buried hard by the grave of Alphonsine du Plessis, the original of *La Dame aux Camélias*. She also visited the grave of Heine, which was covered with flowers, "probably from some young German sojourning in Paris." At Père-Lachaise she looked up the tomb of Alfred de Musset and quoted from his verses. She was pleased that the grave was kept up and that Parisians cared enough to keep fresh flowers on it. Balzac's grave seemed ugly and deserted by contrast, but that did not matter, for Balzac "lives in every street and quarter; one sees his people everywhere."

At the end of August the two women took a train to the south of France to spend their last two weeks in Provence and on the Mediterranean coast. They traveled second class to Lyon and had an entire compartment to themselves, then to economize went on to Avignon third class. That was a great mistake for two fastidious American women addicted to bathing regularly. There were eight women and an infant jammed into their compartment, most of whom were women of the soil who "are all very well in pictures by Millet . . . but they are not the most desirable traveling companions in a little compartment on a burning August day." Then there was a German girl who "looked very much like a fat, pink pig . . . and had not bathed these many years." Once they got to Avignon, however, and put up at a good hotel, one that Henry James had written of affectionately, they were entranced by the old city with its wonderful papal palace and gardens overlooking the Rhone. From the gardens they could see the old Roman bridge still reaching partway out into the river, and in another direction the snowy peaks of the Alps shimmered in the smog-free air of 1902. They paid only two dollars a day for full pension at their hotel, which served them a gourmet ten-course dinner, "each better than the last, with wines that made us sad because we knew we would never taste their like again."

From Avignon Cather and McClung went on to Marseilles in the rain, but when they arrived on the coast the sun came out, and as they looked out to sea, "the sunlight played on the white cliffs of the little island . . . with the name of the Château d'If." This view took her back to her childhood, "when one lived and suffered and triumphed with Edmund Dantès" in *The Count of Monte Cristo*. Later at Le Seyne, a small port farther east, a squall came up while they were eating dinner. "Blue lightning and wild gusts of rain, and metallic thunder that rattled rather than roared, with a great dashing and splashing of water." She was perplexed for a moment. Where had she seen such a storm? Then she remembered: "It was on the stage of the Funke Theatre, when Mr. James O'Neill used to be sewn up in a sack and flung by the supers from the Chateau d'If into the Mediterranean." It was like a stage storm, ended abruptly, and two hours later the travelers left by train for Hyères, a health resort further down the coast. "Below Hyères, the scented pines slope down to the sea," and the sea was as "still and motionless as a plaque of blue porcelain, with a sky of enamel above it. In the distance the hills are a pale violet." After Hyères they visited Le Lavandou, where the coast for a hundred miles on either side was as wild as when the Saracens held it. Then they went on to Nice and Monte Carlo, which Cather did not like at all after the simplicity and peace of the coastal villages. There was nothing real about Monte Carlo, with its "oppressive splendour": "the sea was too blue to be wet, the casino too white to be anything but pasteboard." The final stop on their itinerary, however, was Arles, which was real and wonderful. She was greatly interested in the remains of Roman civilization, marveled at the well-preserved Roman arena, and was moved by the ruins of the Roman theater. But best of all, the area around Arles recalled Daudet at every turn. Cather's final letter from Europe, dated Arles, September 16, is entitled "In the Country of Daudet." He was the French writer of all French writers she then loved the most.

After leaving Arles, Cather and McClung retraced their steps to the north and sailed for home. Cather was late in getting back to her classroom, but her students must have profited from her travels, as she brought to life for them scenes she had visited and places they were reading about. She also was ready to begin assembling her first book.

CHAPTER 8

April Twilights and
The Troll Garden

Cather's first book was not a collection of stories, as one might expect, but a slim volume of poems, *April Twilights*. She had loved poetry since childhood, had delighted in the poems of Campbell, Moore, Longfellow, Keats, Arnold, Poe, and Byron that she found in the family bookcase, and probably began writing verse as soon as she began writing anything. When she entered the university, where publications existed for student writing, she promptly turned out thirty-five lines of blank verse in praise of Shakespeare for the June 1, 1892, issue of the *Hesperian*. Subtitled "A Freshman Theme," these lines are of a piece with the precocious essay on the great god Shakespeare published in the *Journal* the previous November. In these verses she sings of "The dwarfed children of earth's sterile age" who "Turn to thee once again, O sun born bard." She followed up this poetic flight with more blank verse in praise of Columbus, which the *Hesperian* obligingly printed the following fall. Then she did several translations from Horace and Anacreon.

"I do not take myself seriously as a poet," Cather said in 1925, but during her Pittsburgh years she wrote verse rather steadily. She apparently found no inconsistency in her versifying and her belief that women probably should not write poetry at all because their only theme was love and their good poetry "emotional in the extreme." But then she never thought of herself as a woman writer—only as a writer, *period*. After moving to Pittsburgh, she published seven of her own poems in the *Home Monthly*, sent a few more to the *Courier*, and contributed additional ones to the *Library*. By 1900 she was able to place her poems in national magazines, and before her *April Twilights* came out in 1903, she had sold eight poems to the *Critic, Lippincott's, Harper's Weekly,* and the *Youth's Companion.* She very much wanted to bring out a book to prove to the friends and relatives who were expecting great things from her that she was an author. "The Player Letters" had come to nothing, and she had not yet been able to write a novel. It must have seemed that she was not getting on very fast. She already was older than Keats, and as old as Shelley and Crane when they died, that is, going on thirty. Suddenly a volume of verse became a possibility.

By the end of 1902 Cather had enough visibility as a poet to attract the attention of Richard Badger of Boston, who operated a vanity press that specialized in publishing aspiring poets—often women. Referred to by one reviewer as "the befriender of the yet uncommissioned troubadour," Badger sent out seductive letters to prospective clients, praising their poems and offering to bring out their verses in handsome little volumes. He also indicated very delicately that the author would be allowed to share in the expense of publication. Either Cather was too naive to realize that the Badger imprint would be a signal to reviewers of an unpublishable poetaster or she was desperately eager for an audience.

In any event, she wrote Will Owen Jones in early January 1903 that she was publishing a book of poems in the spring. Badger, she said, had made her a good offer, and if the book sold well she would make a tidy little sum. To impress Jones, she added that Badger was bringing out a lot of new verse by such poets as Clinton Scollard, Edith M. Thomas, and Harriet Prescott Spafford. She thought she would be in good company and wanted Jones to lend her a Lincoln directory so that she could circularize her friends. Under such publication arrangements it is a wonder that *April Twilights* attracted any attention at all. But Badger's net sometimes caught a big fish, as it did when he landed E. A. Robinson's first book, and Cather's poems were good enough to receive over a dozen reviews, some of them thoughtful and intelligent. But it is doubtful if she made any money from this edition.

She later regretted publishing the volume and in 1908 bought up all the remaining copies and destroyed them. When Elizabeth Sergeant turned up a copy in a secondhand shop in 1912, Cather wrote that she had hoped her friend would never run across that book of bum verse. She said she had bought up and sunk in a tarn all the copies she could get. She did not want Sergeant reading her verses because they belonged to a period when she was young and had never been anywhere. This, of course, was not true, but by 1912 she had turned her entire attention to fiction and had lost interest in writing verse. She did not write much more poetry after the 1903 volume came out and published only sixteen more poems during the rest of her life.

She did allow Alfred Knopf to reprint the book in 1923 with thirteen of the original thirty-seven poems omitted and twelve new ones added. In her collected works she reprinted it once more but dropped two more poems and added one.

Cather's poetry is a minor part of her canon, but it is worth examining because it bears an integral relationship to her entire career. Nothing she wrote is unrelated to the entire body of her writing. Just as the early stories explore themes and motifs that later appear in her mature fiction, so do the poems. Her opinions, her interests, her enthusiasms, her influences, appear neatly encapsulated in the short lyrics she was fond of writing. That the poetry is bookish and literary is to be expected, but occasionally there is an inspired line or image or figure of speech. The poetry that readers hear in her later fiction has its foreground in her youthful verse.

Cather's taste in poetry, as in literature, was largely classical and romantic. When she reviewed William Archer's anthology of British and American poets, *Poets of Our Younger Generation*, which appeared while she was putting her own book together, she summarized her views on American verse. She recognized that Emerson was the great seminal influence on American poetry, but there were not many contemporary poets she admired. She never mentioned Dickinson or Robinson, who were new poets in the nineties, but she praised, with reservations, the work of Bliss Carman and gave her highest accolade to Louise Imogen Guiney, whose "achievement of excellence in expression and the mastery of meter none of our younger poets have equaled."

She did believe, however, that poets in the past thirty or forty years had naturalized American verse, in contrast to the Europeanized work of Longfellow, Bryant, Holmes, and Lowell. The dominant characteristics of new American poetry, she thought, were perfection of form and intensity of spiritual experience. Also it was moving toward shorter forms, chiefly the lyric, developing along the same lines as French poetry. Some of the masterpieces of American verse she listed as Thomas Bailey Aldrich's "Memory," Emerson's "April," Poe's "To Helen," and Sidney Lanier's "The Ballad of the Trees and the Master." It is not surprising that her own verse followed what she thought were the national trends.

"In *April Twilights*," writes Bernice Slote, "one moves in a mythic landscape. Figures of gods and god-men perform the rituals of legend in pastoral Arcadia, the world of Roman glory, or scenes from medieval balladry and romance. But the Virgilian shepherds and minstrels blend into the equally indefinite 'lads' of Housman, who had his own elegiac tone; Arcadia is also Shropshire and Provence, with life shown in allegory. The classical-pastoral scene is overlaid with a glitter of plumes and swords and roses from the mythical kingdom of Ruritania—a glow that might be called 'Zenda-romantic.' For there is in Willa Cather a good deal of her much-read, much-loved *Prisoner of Zenda*, with its far-away, heroic action and its bittersweet ending of unfulfilled love. The poems also have something of the neo-Greek or medieval tone of Rossetti, Swinburne, and Wilde, and more than a touch of Wagnerian story and song."

Relatively few of the poems (20%) are rooted in personal experience. The opening one, "Grandmither, Think Not I Forget," is a love poem that invokes the memory of Grandma Boak, who had died while Cather was in college. "The Namesake" commemorates her uncle who was killed in the Civil War, and the dedicatory poem to her brothers Roscoe and Douglass recalls memories of the Republican River, Red Cloud, and the dreams of childhood. "The Night Express" derives from a summer in Nebraska when the body of a Red Cloud boy who died away from home was brought back in a Burlington baggage car. The scene at the station parallels the opening of her story "The Sculptor's Funeral." "Poppies on Ludlow Castle," "The Mills of Montmartre," "Provençal Legend," "London Roses," and "Paris" were direct products of her trip to Europe. The last is a good imagistic poem evoking the French capital at evening:

> Behind the arch of glory sets the day;
> The river lies in curves of silver light,
> The Fields Elysian glitter in a spray
> Of golden dust; the gilded dome is bright,
> The towers of Notre Dame cut clean and gray
> The evening sky, and pale from left to right
> A hundred bridges leap from either quay.

Cather was deeply involved with the Arcadian theme: the lament for the lost glories of a grander past. She got this from her reading of the classics, but it suited her temperament. This motif appears in "Arcadian Winter," "Winter at Delphi," "Lament for Marsyas," and "I Sought the Wood in Winter." Apollo, Pan, minstrels, shepherds are all there, along with huntsmen, runners of races, laurels, and daffodils. The settings, of course, are the Old World, which fueled Cather's imagination through her reading; but the Arcadian theme persists in her best fiction, as in *My Ántonia*, where she succeeds in transplanting Arcadia from the Old to the New World, and therein lies one secret of her power as a novelist: the ability to naturalize ancient myth in an American setting.

The themes of loss and nostalgia, which are closely related to the Arcadian motif, also come from other classic and Renaissance sources. The poem "Eurydice" is built on the myth of Orpheus and Eurydice, which tells of the singer's loss of his beloved as he tries to lead her back to Arcadia from Hades. Cather made good use of this myth as a dominant theme when she came to write *The Song of the Lark* a decade later. The elegiac note of François Villon's "Où sont les neiges d'antan?" ("Where are the snows of yesteryear?"), which is prominent in her later fiction, is clearly sounded in "Aftermath," which celebrates the vanished past:

> Can'st thou conjure a vanished morn of spring,
> Or bid the ashes of the sunset glow
> Again to redness? Are we strong to wring
> From trodden grapes the juice drunk long ago?
> Can leafy longings stir in Autumn's blood,
> Or can I wear a pearl dissolved in wine,
> Or go a-Maying in a winter wood,
> Or paint with youth thy wasted cheek, or mine?

The answer, of course, is no: "I might as well / Covet the gold of Helen's vanished head, / Or kiss back Cleopatra from the dead!"

Cather's literary and artistic enthusiasms were both a help and a hindrance to her poetic composition. Being a "bond slave" to Housman inspired an attractive poem in "In Media Vita," but the verses sound entirely too much like an imitation of Housman:

> Lads and their sweethearts lying
> In the cleft of the windy hill;
> Hearts that hushed of their sighing,
> Lips that are tender and still.
> Stars in the purple gloaming,
> Flowers that suffuse and fall,
> Twitter of bird-mates homing,
> And the dead, under all!

Cather recognized her limitations in her verse, and when she wrote Sergeant disparaging her poems, she quoted as a horrible example the opening line of "White Birch in Wyoming." One might expect this to be an effective nature poem recreating memories of visits to her brother in the Rockies. "Stark as a Burne-Jones vision of despair," the poem begins, then goes on to describe the tree; not only does she require of the reader familiarity with Pre-Raphaelite painting, but also she ends the poem with Wagnerian metaphors of Valkyries and Brunhilda.

In one poem, however, she did make good use of western memories. This is "Prairie Dawn," a unique item in her volume, the only poem in blank verse and the only one without literary antecedents. With sharp visual imagery, plain language, the evocation of more than one sense perception, this poem probably strikes a contemporary reader as the best in the volume:

> A crimson fire that vanquishes the stars;
> A pungent odor from the dusty sage;
> A sudden stirring of the huddled herds;
> A breaking of the distant table-lands
> Through purple mists ascending, and the flare
> Of water ditches silver in the light;
> A swift, bright lance hurled low across the world;
> A sudden sickness for the hills of home.

Good as this poem is, Cather still had not discovered Nebraska as a subject for verse, though she sometimes laid her stories there. The landscape in this poem is probably Colorado or Wyoming, not the corn and wheat fields of the Divide, and the "sudden sickness for the hills of home" is no doubt a reference to her native Virginia. Emotionally, the Pittsburgh high school teacher who spent her days teaching English literature to Pennsylvanians was yet a long way from her prairie childhood.

The love poems in *April Twilights* illustrate further Cather's limitations. She seems to have felt that poets, especially women, were expected to write love poems, and she produced a number of them. But despite felicitous language and skillful metrics, they are strangely disembodied. There is no sense in them of the presence of the beloved. "Evening Song" begins:

> Dear love, what thing of all the things that be
> Is ever worth one thought from you or me,
>   Save only Love,
>   Save only Love?

Or in "The Hawthorne Tree," the one who climbs to the poet's "white bower" seems more an abstraction than a flesh-and-blood lover.

Cather's taste in prosody was conventional nineteenth-century rhymed verse and closed forms. Seven of the poems are sonnets, and most of the rest use regular stanzas and conventional rhyme schemes. Her metrics are skillful, and there is genuine melody in her verses, but she uses the *thee* and *thou* and second-person singular *-eth* verb endings of old-fashioned poetic diction. The use of refrain and incremental repetition is good, and there is a lot of variety in the verse forms. Although she admired the primitive elemental force and the joy of life in Whitman, she thought he had no sense of form and did not experiment with free verse.

Reviewers treated her book very well when it came out in April. Her friend George Seibel led off with a glowing notice in the *Pittsburgh Gazette*, calling the volume "a book of genuine poetry in unpretentious guise . . . singing its way straight to the heart of every one who looks within its covers." One would have anticipated praise from Seibel, but other reviewers were equally complimentary. The *New York Times* thought Cather's poetic gift was genuine and that the book gave "promise of an unfolding to be looked for with eagerness." She got a full page in *Poet Lore*, complete with picture and biographical data; but that magazine was published by the Gorham Press, which also printed Badger's books, and was somewhat suspect. Jeannette Gilder, who had bought two of Cather's poems as editor of the *Critic*, reviewed the book for the *Chicago Tribune* as the "work of a real poet." An English magazine that published a roundup review of a number of volumes of American verse thought Cather's work was better than most. It had "some tenderness, some music, and some originality. Nowhere does the verse reach a high level, but it is seldom bathetic and never silly."

When the book was reissued with deletions and additions in 1923, it was reviewed by the poet Eunice Tietjens, who stated judiciously the case for and against Cather as poet: "This is a book of poems by a great literary personality, who well deserves the Pulitzer Prize—but not by a great poet. . . . Her stories are unforgettable. They etch themselves into your consciousness. . . . Much of herself comes through. The same humanity, the same sense of drama, the same directness of vision. . . . Eighteen or twenty years ago I read several of these poems . . . and as I read them now they are as familiar as old friends. Yet now, examining them in the cold light of later knowledge, I see that I have loved and remembered them because of the humanity, and not because of the poetry."

While Cather was basking in the glow of being a published poet, a momentous chain of events was taking place. H. H. McClure, head of the McClure Syndicate, passed through Lincoln scouting for talent, and Will Owen Jones urged him to look at the work of his former columnist. H. H. McClure told his cousin, S. S. McClure, the magazine editor and publisher, and that volatile genius wrote Cather inviting her to submit her stories for possible magazine and book publication. She mailed them to him in April but without much confidence that anything significant would happen. She already had submitted some of her stories to *McClure's Magazine*, and they had come back with rejection slips. A week after the parcel left Pittsburgh, however, she received a telegram from McClure summoning her to his office immediately. As soon as she could get away from her school, she took the train to New York and presented herself to McClure on the morning of May 1, 1903. Life was never the same for her after that interview. She walked into the offices of *McClure's* on East Twenty-third Street at ten o'clock that morning not worrying much, she wrote Jones afterwards, about streetcar accidents and such; at one o'clock she left stepping carefully. She had become a valuable property and worth saving. McClure with characteristic enthusiasm for his discoveries had offered her the world. He would publish her stories in book form. He would use them first in his magazine, and those he could not use, he would place in other journals for her. He wanted to publish everything she wrote from that point on. When she told him that some of the stories already had been rejected by *McClure's*, he said he never had seen them and called in his manuscript readers and asked them in her presence to give an accounting of their stewardship. She wrote Jones: "I sat and held my chin high and thought my hour had struck." A moment like that turned back the clock for her and made her feel as important as when she was editor of the *Hesperian*. There were even more plans in the wind, she said, but if she wrote of them she would be writing until midnight. She thanked him for getting her launched at last, and with a light heart signed herself faithfully always.

There was more to come after the interview in the magazine office. McClure took her out to his home at Ardsley in Westchester County to meet his wife and children and Mrs. Robert Louis Stevenson, who was visiting the McClures. Mrs. Stevenson already had read the stories, and they talked them over together. McClure accepted the tales without any revisions and wanted to know all about his new discovery, who she was, where she came from, what she had done up to then. There was no circumstance of her life that he did not inquire into, and he began to plan her future for her. She said that if he had been a religious leader he would have had people going to the stake for him. What a genius he had for proselyting! He took a hold of one in such a personal way that business ceased to be a feature of one's relationship with him.

McClure urged her to stay with them until she had to return to Pittsburgh, but Cather could remain only a day because she had promised to visit the Canfields, who then lived in New York. When she left McClure, she was in a state of delirious excitement, his captive for life. Three years later she went to work for him, eleven years later wrote his autobiography, and in his old age, when she was rich and he was old and poor, contributed to his support. Next to her father and brothers he was the most important man in her life. Her devotion to McClure, however, was a hindrance to her career, for he kept her editing his magazine long after she should have been channeling all her creative energies into writing fiction.

Meantime, her future seemed assured, and her first volume of fiction would be published the following year. She was out in the current and moving swiftly at last, ten years after her debut as a newspaper columnist and drama critic. Though she still had a lot to learn about writing, she never again would have trouble placing her work. But she still had to return to Pittsburgh and her classroom. As it turned out, she would remain on the faculty of Allegheny High School for two more years. McClure was longer on promises than on performance and did not bring out her book until 1905. He also used only two of her stories in his magazine and did not find other magazines to take three more that had not been published previously. She never commented on his failure; she was happy enough to have a contract that assured publication.

Seven stories made up the collection that McClure, Phillips, and Company agreed to bring out. One, " 'A Death in the Desert,' " already had appeared in *Scribner's* the previous January; another, "A Wagner Matinee," was published by *Everybody's Magazine* the following February and may have been placed there by McClure. Two more, "The Sculptor's Funeral" and "Paul's Case," generally regarded as the two best tales in the group, came out in *McClure's* in 1905, the latter appearing actually a few weeks after the book. Given the title *The Troll Garden*, the collection was published in April. It carried on its title page a quotation from Charles Kingsley: "A fairy palace, with a fairy garden; . . . Inside the Trolls dwell, . . . Working at their magic forges, making and making always things rare and strange." Across from the title page was another epigraph from Christina Rossetti's "The Goblin Market": "We must not look at Goblin men, / We must not buy their fruits; / Who knows upon what soil they fed / Their hungry thirsty roots?" And the book was dedicated to Isabelle McClung.

All of the stories in *The Troll Garden* deal with art and artists. Readers of Cather's newspaper columns might have been surprised at these stories if they had remembered her writing in 1901, "The world is weary unto death of stories about artists and scholars and aesthetic freaks, and of studies of the 'artistic temperament.' " Nevertheless she was interested in the lives of artists and musicians and continued writing stories about them for the next two decades. The East still had most of her attention, for five of the tales take place in Pittsburgh and New York, Boston and London. The Boston story is about the West, but only two are laid in Western towns.

There is overall design and meaning in the collection and a careful arrangement of stories to support the themes woven into the fabric of the text. The two epigraphs provide a clue to Cather's meaning. The quotation from Kingsley comes from *The Roman and the Teuton* and is part of a parable he tells to introduce a discussion of the invasion of Rome by the barbarians. The forest people, who represent the barbarians, are attracted to the troll garden (Rome), covet it, and finally overrun it, only to discover afterwards that they have destroyed the marvels they sought.

In Rossetti's poem two sisters, Laura and Lizzie, live innocently together in a fairy-tale cottage. Every morning and evening animal-like goblin men emerge from a sinister glen nearby hawking their luscious fruit. The girls know these are forbidden fruits, but Laura cannot resist the temptation and buys the fruit, paying with a golden curl. The dire consequences of this act are that Laura can no longer hear the seductive cries of the goblin men and goes into a physical decline. As she becomes prematurely old and haggard, Lizzie, who still can hear the tempting offers, sets about to save her sister. She confronts the goblin men with an offer to buy, but she will not taste. A dreadful fracas results, and the men smear the fruit over her. She rushes home, invites Laura to "eat me, drink me." Laura kisses Lizzie hungrily but finds that the juices of the fruit are now bitter, repulsive. The outcome of this encounter, however, is the restoration to health and youth of the wayward sister.

In a column Cather wrote for the *Journal* in 1895 she quoted and summarized the poem, concluding, "Never has the purchase of pleasure, its loss in its own taking, the loathsomeness of our own folly in those we love, been put more quaintly and directly." For her story collection she equated the fruits of the goblin men to the magical things rare and strange made by the trolls in their garden. In either case the possession was fraught with danger: things desired are not only delightful and marvelous but also dangerous and capable of corrupting. There is no evidence that Cather was aware of the sexual allegory here that contemporary feminist critics have read as the cry of a Victorian woman against the sexual politics of the nineteenth century.

In the arrangement of the stories, the first and the last, "Flavia and Her Artists" and "Paul's Case," depict characters seduced by art. Flavia Hamilton, who operates a "hotel, habited by freaks," as the ironical actress-commentator Miss Broadwood puts it, is pursuing false gods in her worship of art. Cather must have observed archetypal Flavias in her years as a music and drama critic in Pittsburgh when she attended soirées given by Pennsylvania matrons, wives of steel and coal moguls, who devoted themselves to lion-hunting. Flavia Canfield was enough like the title character to cause a temporary estrangement between Cather and Dorothy Canfield. That Flavia cannot distinguish between the true and the false is overt enough in the talk, but her myopia is further accentuated by Cather's abundant use of Roman allusions, always ironically. Her house is a "temple to the gods of Victory, a sort of triumphal arch"; her relationship to her children is described as like that of Cornelia, the mother of the Gracchi; and the story ends with Arthur Hamilton, her husband, compared to Gaius Marius among the ruins of Carthage.

The Jamesian flavor of this story is obvious, for Cather was still in her Henry James phase, and the reason she never reprinted the story may well have been that it seemed later too much influenced by the master. But her attention to James's craftsmanship was important to her in developing narrative skill. The story is well told through the perspective of Imogen Willard, daughter of one of Flavia's old friends, who is invited to Flavia's menagerie because she has the odd distinction of being a woman who has earned a doctorate in philology. Imogen (perhaps suggested by Dorothy Canfield), because of her childhood friendship with Flavia's husband, can observe the relationship between the couple as Arthur's partisan. The invention of Miss Broadwood (much like the real actress Johnston Bennett), who doesn't take herself seriously, provides the running commentary on the "freaks" by one who is a real artist, not a stuffed shirt.

What Flavia does not know when she fills her house with artists is that her guests hold her in contempt. The story turns on the vicious profile of her that M. Roux, a famous French novelist, gives an interviewer after he leaves the house party. Flavia's indulgent, patient husband withholds knowledge of the interview from her and deliberately insults the guests in order to empty the house. The tale ends with her thinking that her husband is a barbarian incapable of appreciating art.

"Paul's Case," perhaps Cather's best-known story, depicts a forest child destroyed by the forbidden fruit. Paul is a Pittsburgh schoolboy who cares nothing about Latin or math but lives for Carnegie Hall, where he has a job ushering, and for the theater, where he has friends among the local stock company. He hates his life in a prosaic, conventional, middle-class neighborhood. Paul's principal and his father decide that he must leave school, go to work, and stop hanging around the theater and Carnegie Hall. But Paul cannot stand life in a business office and steals a thousand dollars from his employer. He goes to New York, buys himself elegant clothes, rents a suite at the Waldorf, and lives for a while his dream life as a rich patron of the arts; then when his money is gone and his father is about to come after him, he goes to Newark and quietly drops under the wheels of an oncoming locomotive.

The story has been justly admired for its narrative skill and its psychological portraiture. It is the only important use Cather ever made of her experience as a Pittsburgh high school teacher and the only story she would allow to be anthologized towards the end of her life. It captures the tone of Pittsburgh in 1905 and was compounded, she remembered in 1943, of two elements: the first was a boy she once had in her Latin class, a nervous youth who was always trying to make himself interesting and to prove that he knew members of the local stock company; the other was herself, particularly the feelings she had about New York and the old Waldorf-Astoria Hotel when she was teaching and occasionally visiting the city. Another ingredient that she never mentioned was the theft of an employer's money by two Pittsburgh boys who ran off to Chicago. They were found broke in a Chicago hotel a week later and brought back home, but not prosecuted because the families reimbursed the employer. The Pittsburgh papers were full of the story, reported the *Bookman* in a brief profile of Cather at the time *The Troll Garden* was published. Cather also had sat on disciplinary committees, such as the one Paul appears before at the outset of the story. Norman Foerster remembered being disciplined by a committee on which Cather sat for carrying a crib-sheet into an examination.

" 'A Death in the Desert,' " the first story to be published in a magazine, is the centerpiece of the book. Its chief character, Adriance Hilgarde, inspired by Nevin, the composer, never appears in the story but is the dominant influence on the other characters. Cather must have written the tale soon after Nevin's death, but she later would not admit that she had put him into the story. She did concede that if people saw him in it, something of his personality must have been there. He was the first artist she had ever known, she said, and made a deep impression on her. She remembered him as a figure full of charm and grace and was glad if the story recalled him to friends who had known and loved him.

The story takes place on a ranch near Cheyenne, where one can see from the ranch house "a blinding stretch of yellow, flat as the sea in dead calm, splotched here and there with deep purple shadows; and, beyond, the ragged blue outline of the mountains." Katherine Gaylord, singer, is dying of tuberculosis on her brother's ranch. Onto the scene comes Everett Hilgarde, younger brother of the great composer Adriance, who stops in Cheyenne en route to the West Coast. He accidentally discovers that Katherine is there dying and stays with her several weeks until the end. Years before when she had been on her way to stardom and one of his brother's students, he had loved her with a schoolboy's passion.

Not much happens in the story. Everett and Katherine talk, mostly about Adriance, and in their talk the lives of all three are revealed. Adriance sends the score of his latest sonata, the greatest composition he has yet written. As Everett plays it for her, she dissolves: "This is my tragedy, as I lie here spent by the race-course, listening to the feet of the runners as they pass me." Adriance, youthful, charming, and exuberantly creative, still leads the race. While Katherine is dying Everett reflects on his own life. If her life is tragedy, his is pathos. He had the bad luck to resemble his brother, to aspire to an artistic career, but to be endowed with mediocre talent. He has accepted his fate, however, and resolved "to beat no more at doors he would never enter."

Cather placed this story in the middle of the collection because it presents three different artists and three different careers. Katherine is a forest child who has entered the garden only to be destroyed there. Everett, who is always being mistaken for his brilliant brother, is one who is denied entrance. Adriance enters and survives. But Katherine and Adriance are really two sides of the same coin: Nevin in his prime and Nevin who died at the age of thirty-eight. The story gains irony from its setting in the stark landscape of eastern Wyoming and from the title, which comes from a poem by Browning, a dramatic monologue delivered by the Apostle John as he dies in a Middle Eastern cave attended only by a few faithful friends.

The second and sixth stories in *The Troll Garden* are an appropriate pair, because they both deal with western characters whose lives end in defeat. "The Sculptor's Funeral" is one of Cather's best-known stories because for many years she allowed anthologists to reprint it. Then late in her life she decided it presented a false picture of prairie towns and withdrew permission to use it. The tale is set in a little town like Red Cloud, though she moved it to Kansas, doubtless to avoid the charge of satirizing the homefolks. It falls into the category of revolt-from-the-village literature and invites comparison with the earlier work of E. W. Howe or Hamlin Garland and, later, the fiction of Sinclair Lewis and the poems of Edgar Lee Masters' *Spoon River Anthology*. The opening scene comes from the memory that inspired the poem "The Night Express," and the plot was suggested by the funeral of a Pittsburgh artist, Stanley Reinhart. Cather wrote in a newspaper column at the time that Reinhart's family had not appreciated him, that no one in Pittsburgh knew anything about him, or cared, and that it passed all understanding how he could have come out of that commercial city.

The story begins with the arrival in Sand City of the body of Harvey Merrick, world-famous sculptor, who is regarded by his fellow townsmen as one local boy who did not amount to much. As the various characters sit about the mean and tasteless Merrick house during the wake, Banker Phelps expresses the general sentiment: "What Harve needed, of all people, was a course in some first-class Kansas City business college." Then he might have amounted to something and helped run the family farm; instead, his father had indulged him and sent him off East and to France to study art. One man in town, however, knew, loved, and appreciated the sculptor, and voices scathing denunciation of the mean-spirited and ignorant villagers. He is Jim Laird, the local lawyer, who never managed to get away from Philistia, and by the time the sculptor's body is brought home, has become an alcoholic. The contrasts are further heightened by the creation of Henry Steavens, student and follower of the sculptor, who accompanies the body and provides a sympathetic audience for Laird.

"A Wagner Matinee" reverses the situation in "The Sculptor's Funeral" by taking a Nebraska farm wife to Boston. The story fits into the overall design of *The Troll Garden* because the narrator's Aunt Georgiana is a former musician who has been denied for more than thirty years any possibility of entering the garden. She has been exiled to the barbarous environment of a bleak prairie farm, where she has toiled like a slave helping her husband wrest a living from the inhospitable land. Cather paints a grim picture of Nebraska farm life in the pioneering days through her description of Georgiana with her "ill-fitting false teeth, and her skin . . . as yellow as a Mongolian's from constant exposure to a pitiless wind and to the alkaline water" and her hands that once had played the piano at the Boston Conservatory now "stretched and twisted into mere tentacles to hold and lift and knead with." When the aunt has to visit Boston to collect a legacy left her by a bachelor uncle, she stays with her nephew, a Nebraska farm boy who, like Hamlin Garland, has managed to shake the mud off his boots and get to Boston. The pathos of the tale is overwhelming as the narrator, with misguided kindness, takes his aunt to a symphony concert and reawakens in her the memory of the lost garden. This is an excellent story, lean and compact, narrated with skill from a young man's point of view, the same perspective Cather used later in *My Ántonia* and other works.

"A Wagner Matinee" caused Cather a great deal of embarrassment when it came out in *Everybody's* in 1904. Will Owen Jones took her to task in the *Journal*: "The stranger to this state will associate Nebraska with the aunt's wretched figure, her ill-fitting false teeth, her skin yellowed by the weather. . . . If the writers of fiction who use western Nebraska as material would look up now and then and not keep their eyes and noses in the cattle yards, they might be more agreeable company." Cather wrote Jones defending herself, denying that she had any intention of disparaging the state. She had placed the story back in pioneer times, she said, and thought that everyone admitted those were desolate days. She had thought she was paying tribute to those uncomplaining women, who weathered those times. Farm life was bad enough when she knew it, and what must it have been like before that? She had to admit, however, that she had used the farmhouse where she and her family had lived before they moved into Red Cloud and some of her recollections.

She also had to admit that her family felt insulted by the tale. Everyone assumed that her Aunt Franc had sat for the portrait of Aunt Georgiana, because Aunt Franc had graduated from Mt. Holyoke Female Seminary and had studied music before marrying George Cather in 1873 and moving to pioneer Nebraska. The family told her it was not nice to write about such things as she put into the description of Aunt Georgiana. Cather wrote a friend that the whole affair had been the nearest she ever had come to personal disgrace. She seemed to have done something horrid without realizing it, but someday she supposed it would seem funny. That she could not have intended cruelty to her aunt is perfectly clear from the warm, affectionate tone of all her letters to Aunt Franc. After visiting her aunt on the farm when she was in college, Cather wrote Mariel Gere that Aunt Franc had organized a literary society among the farm families at Catherton and she surely did her share of distributing manna in the wilderness.

The third and fifth stories in the collection are "The Garden Lodge" and "The Marriage of Phaedra," one dealing with a musician and the other a painter. These are the poorest tales in the volume, stories that were not placed in magazines before book publication, and stories that Cather never reprinted. "The Garden Lodge" concerns Caroline Noble, who deliberately gives up a career as a concert pianist (as Cather's friend Ethel Litchfield had done) to marry a Wall Street tycoon. Caroline had grown up in an artistic household where there had been intense devotion to art but never enough money to pay the bills. "Caroline had served her apprenticeship to idealism and to all the embarrassing inconsistencies which it sometimes entails, and she decided to deny herself this diffuse, ineffectual answer to the sharp questions of life."

After six years of marriage this practical, sensible woman is surrounded by children, wealth, and an indulgent, loving husband. One day she invites the great Wagnerian tenor Raymond d'Esquerré to stay with them, and they spend hours together in the garden lodge. He feels the need to get out of Klingsor's Garden occasionally and to work in a quiet place, and he knows Caroline Noble is no lion hunter but a serious, gifted nonprofessional artist. After he leaves, she goes to the garden lodge alone, plays the first act of *Die Walküre*, the last of his roles they had practiced together, and the memory of his presence overwhelms her. "It was not enough; this happy, useful, well-ordered life was not enough." A storm breaks and rain beats in, as Caroline passes the night in a dark agony of the soul. The next morning, however, she awakes, despises herself for her self-indulgence, creeps back to the house from the garden lodge, and resumes her life.

"The Marriage of Phaedra" is about the sale of an unfinished masterpiece by the widow of a recently deceased artist. The barbarian in this story is the widow, who sells the painting against the deathbed wishes of the painter to a Jewish art dealer from Australia. This, in the mind of the point-of-view character, a young artist-admirer who wishes to write a biography of the master, is the equivalent of destroying the great painting. The tale was obviously suggested by Cather's visit to Burne-Jones's studio in London during her European trip. The valet James, who presides over the empty studio and was invented for Cather's travel letter to the *Journal*, is appropriately named, for this story is very Henry Jamesian in its narrative technique. The story develops as the artist-biographer researches his subject by striking up an acquaintance with the valet and interviewing the dead artist's sister-in-law and wife. The tale owes a further debt to James in its use of the painting, "The Marriage of Phaedra," to give meaning. The marital difficulties of the painter of the story and his wife are suggested by the tangled affairs of the Greek myth in which Phaedra marries Theseus and then falls in love with her stepson Hippolytus.

McClure's enthusiasm for Cather's fiction notwithstanding, reviewers of *The Troll Garden* were not overwhelmed. The only long signed review in a national magazine appeared in the *Bookman*, but this reviewer, Bessie du Bois, was not enchanted. She called the book a "collection of freak stories that are either lurid, hysterical or unwholesome, and that remind one of nothing so much as the coloured supplement to the Sunday papers." Except for Jim Laird in "The Sculptor's Funeral" and Paul in "Paul's Case," she thought the characters all "mere dummies, with fancy names, on which to hang epigrams." And the subject matter dealt with "the ash-heap of the human mind—the thoughts and feelings that come to all of us when the pressure of the will is low, the refuse and sweepings of the mental life."

Other national reviewers treated the book among their brief notices. These were anonymous paragraphs that in general saw promise in Cather's work but were restrained. The *New York Times* thought the stories showed "deep feeling and ability," but many were too ambitious and seemed "to be more the work of promise than fulfillment." This reviewer probably had not read beyond the first story, for he called "Flavia and Her Artists" the best of the collection. The *Independent* reviewer would recommend the stories "strongly but not widely" among his friends, but he did select "The Sculptor's Funeral" and "Paul's Case" as the best. He rapped Cather on the knuckles for seeing only the ugly side of pioneer life. The *Dial* reviewer also seemed not to have read the entire book; the *Critic* found "real promise"; and the *Reader Magazine* described the tales as "singularly vivid, strong, true, original."

When book buyers did not rush out to get *The Troll Garden*, McClure, Phillips, and Company did not reprint it, and there were still copies left in stock when the company sold its book business to Doubleday, Page and Company the next year. Cather took the book's lack of success philosophically and went on teaching high school. Witter Bynner, however, who then was fresh out of Harvard and McClure's office boy, had great faith in the book and tried to interest Henry James in it. He sent James a copy and followed it up with a letter. James replied that he had received the book but had had no intention of reading it until getting Bynner's letter. "Being now almost in my 100th year, and with a long and weary experience of such matters [receiving complimentary works of fiction] behind me, promiscuous fiction has become abhorrent to me, and I find it the hardest thing in the world to read almost *any* new novel. Any is hard enough, but the hardest from the innocent hands of young females, young American females perhaps above all." But he added that in spite of these feelings he would do his best for Miss Cather. Bynner sent Cather a copy of the letter, to which she replied that it had given her a keen satisfaction. James's attitude was exactly the one she would have wished him to have, and she would have been very much hurt if he did not have the opinion he expressed about "promiscuous fiction." She felt exactly the same as James about fiction by young females. His letter, she thought, was a kind of moral stimulant, and she promised Bynner she would stand up with good grace to whatever punishment James might mete out. There was, however, no further communication from James.

In 1911 Elizabeth Sergeant bought a secondhand copy of the book and read it for the first time. She found "The Sculptor's Funeral," "A Wagner Matinee," and "Paul's Case" all exciting stories, full of passion and superbly executed and wrote Cather of her "joy and critical estimate." Cather replied that she was pleased Sergeant had found something to enjoy, but the stories had been written so long ago "that they now hardly seemed to belong to her. She herself had outgrown the harsh mood that had inspired the Western ones. The starvation of a girl avid for a richer environment seemed to stick out, to deform, to make the picture one-sided." When Cather was chiding Edward Wagenknecht for wanting to resuscitate her early fiction in 1936, she said that if he wanted evidence against her, wasn't " 'A Death in the Desert' " poor enough? There was a certain honest feeling in it, she thought, of a very young kind, but it was really flimsy enough to bring up as a reproach to any writer.

By the time she wrote that letter she had completely abandoned " 'A Death in the Desert' " and was omitting it from her collected works. She had cut a third of the story when she reprinted it in 1920 in *Youth and the Bright Medusa* and improved it substantially, so much so that Dorothy Canfield Fisher in reviewing the later version commented on the changes. She suggested that anyone who wanted to see how a real artist could "smooth away crudeness without rooting out the life" of a story should study the revisions. Cather, however, was never satisfied with the tale and apparently decided it would be impossible to rework it further. The story contains more obtrusive literary allusions and quotations than any of her other stories, and it is likely that a young artist's death in the desert no longer had the power to move her at the age of sixty-five that it had when she was twenty-nine.

The three stories that Sergeant liked particularly survived in the collected works. Cather touched up "The Sculptor's Funeral" and "Paul's Case" for the 1920 and 1937 reprintings but made no substantial changes. "A Wagner Matinee," however, underwent a successive softening of the harsh portrait of Aunt Georgiana, as Cather revised the tale in 1920 and again in 1937. One should read the story in *The Troll Garden* version, for the author performed so much plastic surgery on her character that she transformed Aunt Georgiana from a cruelly used, worn-out farm wife from a harsh, isolated prairie farm into a quaint little old lady from the boondocks.

After the book came out and the 1905 school year ended, Cather and Isabelle McClung traveled west to spend two months in Nebraska, Wyoming, and the Black Hills of South Dakota. They spent a week with Douglass in Cheyenne and a week camping in the Black Hills with Roscoe. After that they returned to Red Cloud for a month and helped Cather's father fix up a new house he had bought. She wrote Mariel Gere that her sister Jessica had a dear little home of her own and was pregnant and happy and that she had seen a good deal of Mrs. Garber, who was as charming as ever but greatly aged and saddened by the death of her husband. Her younger siblings Jack and Elsie were now big children, though they still seemed little to her. She thoroughly enjoyed her visit and thought the West was where she wanted to live. She said she was planning to get home to Red Cloud for a year before very long. After they left Red Cloud, McClung returned to Pittsburgh, and Cather went on to New York to visit Edith Lewis, whom she had met in Lincoln in the summer of 1903 and had visited in New York the summer before.

While Cather was awaiting publication of her book, she apparently tried to write a novel. If McClure wanted to publish everything she wrote, she would take him at his word. Little is known about this attempt, but several notes appeared in the *Journal* during the summer of 1905 when Cather was visiting Nebraska. The paper reported that she had finished a novel that would be published in the fall. It was said to be "in an entirely different vein from any of her previous work. It is her first long story . . . but will not make a very heavy book as it was cut down one-third with the intention of adding to its strength. The scene is laid in Pittsburgh." By the following February the enterprise was dead, the manuscript returned from McClure. Cather wrote Bynner, who had asked what she was doing with the novel, that she had not taken it out of the wrapper he had mailed it in until a few weeks before when she needed a piece of string. She had done absolutely nothing with it. It seemed not quite bad enough to throw away and not quite good enough to wrestle with again. Therefore it was reposing in her old hat box. Thus it was back to teaching for another year.

Even if McClure had decided her manuscript was unpublishable, he did not forget that she was one of his authors. He must have sent her an invitation to Mark Twain's seventieth birthday dinner held in the Red Room at Delmonico's in New York on December 5. She was one of 170 literary and quasi-literary notables who attended the banquet arranged by Colonel George Harvey, head of Harper and Brothers. Cather also was one of the 50 guests who got to meet Twain before the dinner. Twain and Howells were the celebrities on this occasion, but there were many lesser notables that Cather must have been excited to meet or at least to see: Mary E. Wilkins Freeman, Alice Brown, George Ade, Julian Hawthorne, and Owen Wister. Charles Major and Rex Beach were there too, but Cather disliked their writing. George Washington Cable and John Burroughs were present; so were Andrew Carnegie and Emily Post. Somehow Dorothy Canfield, who had not yet begun her literary career, managed an invitation. Viewed in retrospect, the only important writer at the dinner besides Twain and Howells was Cather. No one had thought E. A. Robinson, Edith Wharton, or Theodore Dreiser worth inviting. It was a glittering evening nonetheless, and Cather enjoyed it seated at a table between two editors, Edward Martin of the humor magazine *Life* and Frederick Duneka of *Harpers*. Cather had a high opinion of Twain's Mississippi River books, thought *Huck Finn* one of the three most enduring American classics, and later when she was living in Greenwich Village followed up her acquaintance.

By the time the second semester began during the winter of 1905–6, Cather's years in Pittsburgh were rapidly drawing to a close. Sometime in the early spring McClure made a quick trip to Pittsburgh, went to see Cather at the McClungs' house, stayed for dinner, and enchanted everyone with his talk. His magazine was in a state of crisis; he needed new editors immediately. When he returned to New York, he had persuaded Cather to join his staff even before the school year ended. The high school paper reported in March: "When we return from our April vacation, we shall fail to see Miss Cather; but . . . we feel relieved in knowing that next September she will again be able to take her classes." The canny McClure must have lured Cather to New York on a temporary basis, then after she arrived persuaded her to stay. The finality of her departure was made clear when the June issue of the paper printed her farewell letter, dated June 2:

Dear Boys and Girls:

Now that I find that I shall not return to the High School next fall, I have a word to say to you. A number of my pupils in various classes, and especially in my Reporting Class, asked me, when I came away, whether I should be with you next year. At that time I fully expected to be. The changes in my plans which will prevent my doing so have been sudden and unforeseen. I should hate to have you think that I had not answered you squarely when you were good enough to ask whether I should return, or to have you think that I put you off with an excuse.

I had made many plans for your Senior work next year and had hoped that we should enjoy that work together. I must now leave you to enjoy it alone. One always has to choose between good things it seems. So I turn to a work I love with very real regret that I must leave behind, for the time at least, a work I had come to love almost as well. But I much more regret having to take leave of so many students whom I feel are good friends of mine. As long as I stay in New York, I shall always be glad to see any of my students when they come to the city.

I wish you every success in your coming examinations and in your senior work next year.

Faithfully yours,
Willa S. Cather

McClure's Magazine

At the beginning of 1906 *McClure's Magazine* was a fabulously successful enterprise under the editorial direction of an erratic genius, Samuel S. Mc-Clure. As the journalist Mark Sullivan wrote in his autobiography, McClure "was the pre-eminent magazine genius, easily first, in a period in which magazines flowered as never before." For the previous three years his magazine had led the muckraking movement in exposing graft, corruption, dishonesty, and venality in big business, in government at all levels, and even in the labor unions. In January 1903, S. S. McClure had written an editorial announcing the movement, as he simultaneously published the third in Ida Tarbell's sensational series on the Standard Oil Company, Lincoln Steffens's exposure of municipal corruption in Minneapolis, and Ray Stannard Baker's article on lawlessness in the mineworkers' union.

Tarbell, Steffens, and Baker, all working for McClure at the same time, gave the magazine a brilliance perhaps unsurpassed in American magazine history. McClure had a genius for discovering talent and directing it. He had a passion for accuracy and facts and an old-fashioned missionary zeal to cure the ills in the body politic. As an impoverished Irish immigrant who had come to America with his widowed mother at the age of nine, he was Horatio Alger in real life. He worked his way through Knox College in Illinois, married a professor's daughter, talked his way into the editorship of a bicycle magazine in Boston, organized the first important newspaper syndicate, and founded his magazine in the midst of the Panic of 1893. Remarkably, his journal survived and in three years reached a circulation of three hundred thousand. The December 1896 issue, McClure wrote modestly, had "more pages of paid advertising than any other magazine at any time in the history of the world."

McClure's biographer believes the magazine "was the most exciting, the liveliest, the best illustrated, the most handsomely dressed, the most interesting, and the most profitable of an abundance of superior magazines. Indeed, for the fifteen years from 1895 to 1910 *McClure's* was probably the best general magazine ever to be published anywhere. Judged from the standpoint of impact on its times, of the daring and vision of its editorial formula, of the sustained excellence of its editorial matter, *McClure's* has never had a peer." The biographer, who is McClure's grandson, may exaggerate a little, but not much. *McClure's* was a supernova in the journalistic firmament. Besides a talent for picking writers, McClure could talk almost anyone into working for him, and when he did, he gave them a free hand. He plowed his profits back into the magazine and thought nothing of spending thousands of dollars on one story.

After Baker joined *McClure's*, he found everything different from the haste and superficiality of the newspaper world. When he was assigned to write a piece on General Leonard Wood, he visited Cuba, Massachusetts, and Washington and spent five or six weeks gathering material, all the while on salary and expense account. Ida Tarbell recalled in her autobiography: "I spent the greater part of five years on 'The History of the Standard Oil Company,' . . . I know of no other editor and no other publisher who has so fully recognized the necessity of generous pay and ample time." This openhandedness was unprecedented in that day; editors of most magazines sat in their offices and waited for contributions to come in the mail bag.

McClure not only hired brilliant investigative reporters; he also had a nose for sniffing out good fiction and paid generously for it. Much of Kipling's best work appeared in *McClure's*, and Stevenson was one of McClure's great enthusiasms. He published Thomas Hardy, Arnold Bennett, Stephen Crane, O. Henry, Jack London, Mark Twain, and Conan Doyle. He thought that he had probably lost more money publishing Joseph Conrad than anyone else. He also published Anthony Hope Hawkins, J. M. Barrie, William Allen White, Bret Harte, Booth Tarkington, Hamlin Garland, Howells, Joel Chandler Harris, and Sarah Orne Jewett. Then he bought memoirs of prominent people like Carl Schurz and Ellen Terry, commissioned interviews with Edison and Alexander Graham Bell, and gave his readers the first magazine accounts of the Wright brothers' flight and Marconi's wireless transmissions. When McClure read in the paper about Roentgen rays, he sent a reporter all the way to Germany to get a story on this new marvel.

As a genius, however, McClure was a hard man to work for. At the time he summoned Cather to New York in 1903 and bewitched her with his ebullient personality and undeniable charm, he was philandering with a third-rate woman poet, bounding back and forth across the country and to Europe looking for talent, throwing off editorial ideas like a Fourth of July pinwheel, and spending the company's money as though it were inexhaustible. The hard work of getting out the magazine was left for Ida Tarbell and others, and the business affairs fell to John Phillips, his former college classmate, who had been with him for many years. Finally the strain of living and working with McClure, of trying to keep his indiscretions from causing scandal, of thwarting his schemes for bankrupting the company, proved too much for Tarbell and Phillips. When McClure insisted on planning a new magazine, starting a People's University, a textbook publishing company, a People's Life Insurance Company, and a People's Bank, his associates had had all they could stand.

In late March 1906, when McClure returned from one of his many trips to Europe, they confronted him with an ultimatum. Either he would sell out his interest in the magazine to Tarbell and Phillips, or they would sell out to him. They could no longer work with him unless they could control the company's affairs. Both sides thrashed about during April. McClure wrote Phillips that he could not give up his magazine: "Kings who have come to the end of their tether, as a rule suffer death rather than give up part of their power." He felt the same way. The outcome was that McClure made arrangements to buy out his partners. His former associates then left him for good, taking with them Steffens, Baker, and a good many other members of the staff. McClure was left only with writer Burton Hendricks, his chief manuscript reader Viola Roseboro', and the office boy Witter Bynner. On May 10 the rebels cleaned out their desks and departed. Late that afternoon Bynner found McClure sitting alone in the editorial department. "Bynner," he asked, "are you leaving me too?" Bynner could not speak. McClure broke into sobs.

McClure had been hedging his bets, however, as he saw the blowup coming. His quick trip to Pittsburgh to hire Cather had taken place two months before, and on May 10 she was already at work. There wasn't even time to find a boardinghouse or apartment. She came to New York accompanied by her librarian friend May Willard, and the two women put up at the Hotel Griffon on West Ninth Street. She must have begun her new job in April and worked steadily through the spring. By the end of June she had to take a week off to rest. Events had moved so fast that she hardly had time to reflect that the girl from Red Cloud, Nebraska, had made it to the publishing capital of the United States and the staff of a great national magazine. She had

50. Washington Square taken in
December 1905, by George Balgue.
Courtesy of U.S. History, Local
History & Genealogy Division, The
New York Public Library; Astor,
Lenox, and Tilden Foundations

51. Cather as managing editor of *Mc-
Clure's*. The necklace was a gift
from Sarah Orne Jewett. Courtesy
of WCPMC–NSHS

52. S. S. McClure. Courtesy of The Lilly Library, Indiana University, Bloomington, Indiana

53. Portrait of Elizabeth Sergeant by Auguste Chabaud. Courtesy of WCPMC–NSHS

54. Zoë Akins. This item is reproduced
by permission of *The Huntington Library, San Marino, California*

55. Sarah Orne Jewett. Courtesy of Colby College, Waterville, Maine

56. Annie Fields. By permission of the Houghton Library, Cambridge, Massachusetts

In vain would my spirit be glad
If Love hath forgotten his way;
Or if slow he linger and sad,
In vain is the gladness of day.

Annie Fields.

fought her way to the top in a man's world, and in two more years she would be managing editor of *McClure's*.

There was plenty of action during the first few months that Cather worked for the magazine. In rapid succession McClure hired Perceval Gibbon, George Kibbe Turner, Henry Kitchell Webster, Will Irwin, Ellery Sedgwick, George Kennan, and Cameron Mackenzie. Bynner, who was only four years out of Harvard, found himself managing editor for five days until Irwin was lured away from the *New York Sun* to take the job. Gibbon, a Welsh journalist whom McClure hoped would be another Kipling, stayed only a few weeks, though he became a popular contributor; and Webster, a novelist, remained only a couple of months. Ellery Sedgwick, an experienced editor, lasted a year before moving on to the *Atlantic Monthly*. Kennan, uncle of the diplomat and also a Russian expert, was dispatched to San Francisco to carry on Lincoln Steffens's muckraking investigations of city government, and Turner, a veteran reporter, was sent off to Galveston to report on the creation of the commission form of city government. Of all the new employees only Cather and Mackenzie survived the vicissitudes of the magazine for the next six years. The faithful Viola Roseboro' inaugurated the new regime by discovering a writer, Damon Runyon.

Ellery Sedgwick in his autobiography reported that a week at *McClure's* "was the precise reversal of the six busy days described in the first chapter of Genesis. It seemed to end in a world without form and void. From Order came forth Chaos." The staff worked under some natural law of desperation. The chief was continually interrupting, cutting, and revising, and the staff made periodic efforts to circumvent him by hiding out in nearby hotel rooms in order to finish articles and to meet deadlines. "Yet with all his pokings and proddings the fires he kindled were brighter than any flames his staff could produce without him. . . . The intensity of McClure's enthusiasm would bring any project to a white heat." William Allen White used to say that "Sam had three hundred ideas a minute," and Edith Lewis, a proofreader on the magazine, remembered that he wanted all his ideas acted on immediately. "Some of his ideas were journalistic inspirations, some, of course, were very impractical; he did not bother to sort them out, he expected his staff to do that." Lewis also recalled that working on *McClure's* was like working in a high wind. Yet in spite of the fireworks McClure never lost his temper, treating everyone courteously, office boys and managing editors alike, and when Tarbel and Phillips defected, he wrote: "They leave me retaining my deepest love and affection and esteem and confidence. I think I may say it is the greatest tragedy thus far of my life to lose them."

This was the man whose life was inextricably entwined with Cather's for the next six years and to a lesser extent beyond that. That she was devoted to him is without question, but she could see him objectively; and a half a dozen years after they were both out of the magazine, she wrote a story "Ardessa," laid in a magazine office like *McClure's*. The editor, who is named O'Mally, has come out of the West like McClure and has built a great muckraking magazine in six incredible years. On his staff are five famous men, every one of whom he has made ("it amused him to manufacture celebrities"); but no amount of recognition can make a stuffed shirt out of O'Mally. He is a born gambler and a soldier of fortune: "O'Mally went in for everything; and got tired of everything; that was why he made a good editor." It is restful, however, when O'Mally is back visiting in Nevada, his home state. Then the great men of the staff are left alone, "as contemplative as Buddhas in their private offices, each meditating upon the particular trust or form of vice confided to his care." The story concerns the boss's secretary, Ardessa, who has grown lazy during O'Mally's many absences, and O'Mally's devious efforts to get rid of her. He has a soft heart like McClure, and when he asks the business manager to take his secretary off his hands, he says: "I can't do anything. She's got the upper hand of me. . . . I can't discipline people."

Cather must have wondered sometimes about the fate that had landed her on the staff of a muckraking magazine. She had little interest in McClure's crusading zeal, found social reformers very dull people, and took the dimmest possible view of literature that had a social message. She did not despise the expert investigative reporting that *McClure's* published and thought it had its place, but her eye was always on art. "Economics and art are strangers," she wrote later. Fortunately Cather usually could concentrate on buying fiction and poetry for the magazine and leave the social issues for her colleagues to contend with. She and Viola Roseboro' read the manuscripts that flooded in from hopeful fiction writers and poets, nearly all of which were uniformly bad and unpublishable. She did have to spend some of her time whipping into publishable form articles by semiliterate writers who knew all about copper mines in the West but could not get their material down on paper.

One of the first writers Cather dealt with as a member of *McClure's* staff was Harrison Dwight, who had been born in Constantinople, had been a diplomat and foreign correspondent, and was then curator of the Author's Club in New York. He was a friend of May Willard, who introduced him to Cather soon after she arrived in New York. She slipped easily into the role of fiction editor, just as she had assumed without any experience the role of drama and music critic. She liked a story he submitted, "The Valley of the Mills," which had an exotic Turkish setting. She suggested changes and cuts, and after he tinkered with the tale, she bought it for a future issue. She must have been rather blunt in her criticism, however, for when Dwight commented on her candor, she replied that there was no use talking about such things unless one were candid. She admitted that when she read stories she had violent feelings one way or the other. She always wanted to hang garlands on people or to put them to torture, according to the way they managed or mismanaged a possibility. She liked Dwight's story enough to persuade McClure to spend five hundred dollars commissioning Frank Brangwyn, a British artist whom she thought the best painter of oriental subjects alive, to illustrate it.

Meetings and discussions of this story led to a friendship and Cather's requests to see more of Dwight's work. She liked another story, but Dwight apparently couldn't revise it to her satisfaction, and she never bought anything more from him. They must have disagreed on a number of things, and in a letter after he had gone back to Europe, Cather wanted to know why he so scorned Pierre Loti. She had seen a resemblance to Loti in some of his work, but he had not been flattered. She said that she would swoon with joy if anyone saw traces of Loti in her work. She said she could not figure out why he was afraid to touch the poetic aspect of things and concluded that his problem was that he was afraid of being sentimental. She envied him his travels while she was grinding away at the office and hoped he would find some more exotic tales for them. As long as she was at *McClure's,* his work would have an ardent advocate. She loved his outlandish and picturesque settings, but what he had to do was to make the story run a little hotter and swifter through his atmosphere. She also told him on another occasion that she always held out in argument that a feeling could be a story just as much as an incident.

It was hot in New York that summer, and Cather did not get back to Red Cloud that year. Life in New York, however, was exciting, and she was thrilled to be a part of the metropolis. She had been to New York perhaps eight times during her Pittsburgh years, and in Edith Lewis she had a friend who already was working there. After making her way by stages from the Divide, to Red Cloud, to Lincoln, to Pittsburgh, and finally to New York, she never left the city to live elsewhere. She made many trips to the West in subsequent years and later spent the summers on Grand Manan Island in the Bay of Fundy and autumns in New Hampshire, but she remained a resident of New York. She often complained about the noise and dirt and the ever-increasing vulgarity, but she died in Manhattan forty-one years later. Even before she had been in New York a year, she was writing Dwight that the city was big and raw and relentless and grinds one up into little bits every day. The

New York Philharmonic, the Metropolitan Opera, and all the amenities of life available in the metropolis kept her there.

In October Cather went back to Pittsburgh for three weeks to visit Isabelle, and when she returned she moved into a studio apartment at 60 South Washington Square, in the same building with Lewis, and commuted to the magazine office on East Twenty-third Street. Greenwich Village at that time was a pleasant place to live. Few automobiles yet marred the urban scene, and on the north side of Washington Square the long row of mellow brick houses gave the area an aristocratic look. On the south side of the square were less pretentious buildings occupied by writers and artists. The studio apartments that painter Don Hedger and singer Eden Bower occupy in the story "Coming, Aphrodite!" are drawn from Cather's memory of her early years in New York. These characters live on the top floor of an old house and share a grubby bathroom at the end of the hall. Hedger's single room with a cheerless northern exposure looks out on a court and the roofs and walls of other buildings. He has a sink, a table, and two gas burners in one corner. Eden Bower's apartment is somewhat pleasanter—two rooms facing west on the square.

But down below, the square was lovely that summer. The fountain had been turned on for the season and was "throwing up a mist of rainbow water which now and then blew south and sprayed a bunch of Italian babies that were being supported on the outer rim by older, very little older brothers and sisters. Plump robins were hopping about on the soil; the grass was newly cut and blindingly green. Looking up the Avenue through the Arch, one could see the young poplars with their bright, sticky leaves, and the Brevoort [Hotel] glistening in its spring coat of paint, and shining horses and carriages, —occasionally an automobile." Farther uptown were the theaters and the opera house, and still beyond them was Central Park.

Cather's ambition to make a successful career in a man's world was realized brilliantly at *McClure's*, but her other goal, to become an artist, was derailed during her years on the magazine. She wrote Dwight nine months after going to New York that she wondered if she ever would write another line of anything she cared about. It seemed improbable at that point, and she thought that people seldom got out of this sort of coil once they were in it. Her mind was so full of things other than her own writing that ideas had simply stopped coming. She was feeling no impulse to do anything except grind and edit. As a result, she wrote very little to please herself during her years at *McClure's*. She published four stories in 1907, but these no doubt had been written before leaving Pittsburgh. In 1908 and 1909 she wrote just one story each year, and the following year is a total blank. During 1911, the last year in which she gave the magazine her full attention, she published one tale and managed to write a short novel, her first.

All four of the stories Cather published in 1907 are very competently written, very professional, and very Jamesian. They also are rather bloodless. She still was playing the sedulous ape to Henry James in matters of style and technique, character, subject matter, and theme. Three of the four tales deal with artists, and three are testimony to her lifelong love affair with France, with settings in Paris and Normandy. She placed three in *McClure's*, and sold the fourth to the *Century*. "The Namesake," which appeared first, is the story that owes its inspiration to the uncle who had died in the Civil War. The others are "The Profile," "The Willing Muse," and "Eleanor's House."

"The Profile" also has a literary antecedent in Hawthorne and is so reminiscent of "The Birthmark" that Witter Bynner in his old age remembered it by that title. He recalled that *McClure's* staff tried to talk her out of publishing the tale on grounds that it would hurt the friend on whose physical disfigurement it was based. The story appeared in the magazine, however, and nothing happened; but it is another case of Cather's insensitivity to the use of real people as suggestions for her fictional characters.

The story deals with a portrait painter who is commissioned to paint the daughter of a rich California rancher. The girl is painted in profile because she has a dreadful scar from a burn sustained in childhood, but she acts totally unconscious of the mark, as though she never had seen herself in the mirror. The artist falls in love with the girl, marries her, and as the years pass becomes obsessed with the necessity of making his wife acknowledge just once her disfigurement. Meantime, a young cousin comes to Paris to study and stays with the painter and his wife. The painter falls in love with the cousin, the wife reproaches him, and in a moment of anger he speaks to her of the scar. The wife reacts violently and takes the next train for Nice; and the next morning the cousin's face is badly burned when her study lamp explodes. After the wife sues for divorce, the painter marries the cousin, his second wife with a facial disfigurement. The story is interesting as an experiment in the use of symbol, but it lacks the subtlety that Cather achieves in her later fiction.

"The Willing Muse" is a story about two writers who marry: Kenneth Gray, who writes rather anemic scholarly novels that cost him a great deal of time and effort, and Bertha Torrance, who turns out two best-sellers every year. Friends hope the marriage will inspire Kenneth to reach his full potential, but his reaction to Bertha's astounding fecundity is a complete inability to write. He is reduced to answering his wife's fan mail until one day he simply can't take it any longer and disappears. Cather again makes use of a male narrator and a very Jamesian minor-character point of view. Bertha Gray may remind readers of Jane Highmore in James's "The Next Time" and Kenneth Gray of Paul Overt in "The Lesson of the Master" or Ray Limbert in "The Next Time."

The last of these four stories, "Eleanor's House," is the most Jamesian of all. It is about a man who is so devoted to the memory of his first wife, Eleanor, that he cannot bear to take his second wife, Ethel, to visit the home created by Eleanor. The main character, Harold Forscythe, is thirty-eight when the story opens. Eleanor has died after ten years of a very happy marriage, and now Harold has remarried; but Ethel has lived for two years in the shadow of Eleanor. She comes to the point where she has to do something and while her husband is away goes to visit Eleanor's house. She finds Harold there stretched out on the bed in Eleanor's boudoir. Ethel's appearance on the scene, however, has the effect of exorcising the dead Eleanor's hold on Harold. The story ends with the couple sailing to America and a new life, leaving the Norman countryside and selling the house to Eleanor's best friend. The story, which is pretty good psychological drama, is told from the point of view of this best friend.

Cather never reprinted any of these stories, regarding them all as bad apples and apprenticework. When F. L. Pattee wanted to anthologize "The Willing Muse" in 1926, she rejected the proposal out of hand. The story, she wrote, was so tepid and bloodless that she would not consider under any circumstances letting it be reprinted. Yet these stories are better than she remembered, and as they appear in her *Collected Short Fiction*, one can see a steady development in narrative technique and character portrayal. She no doubt did not want to be reminded of her Henry James phase, and of course, she had not yet found her authentic voice.

After Cather had been reading and editing manuscripts for eight months, McClure gave her an important assignment. He had in his files a manuscript he had bought some time before from Georgine Milmine on the life of Mary Baker Eddy, the founder of Christian Science. Milmine had collected an enormous amount of interesting—even sensational—material, all meticulously researched, but she was incapable of writing a publishable biography. Because Mrs. Eddy had led a rather bizarre life and was the founder of a religion, the material was potentially explosive. McClure, with his passion for accuracy, had put several of his staff members to work on it. He sent Mark Sullivan to New England to check facts; then he asked Burton Hendricks to rewrite the biography. Hendricks produced the first installment, which *McClure's* published in January 1907, but McClure wasn't satisfied with it. At that point he turned to Cather and told her to take over. She was to continue checking facts where Sullivan had left off and to finish rewriting the manuscript. To do this she went to Boston, moved into the Parker House until she found an apartment on Chestnut Street, traveled about rural New England, and spent most of 1907 and part of 1908 on this assignment.

Leaders of the Church of Christ, Scientist were upset when they learned of *McClure's* plans to publish this series. Spokesmen for the church visited McClure's office one day and insisted that the articles be suppressed. They were assured that the facts all had been checked carefully, that the series would be perfectly straightforward. When the visitors wanted to see the material in advance of publication, McClure flatly refused. Then they threatened him with a loss in advertising revenue, but McClure went ahead with the publication, and nothing came of the threat. The series was a great success, circulation figures increased, and McClure was delighted with Cather's work. *Mary Baker G. Eddy: The Story of Her Life and the History of Christian Science* ran in fourteen installments over the next eighteen months.

McClure had not lost his touch. While the Christian Science series was being prepared, *McClure's* was publishing a serial by Kipling, Carl Schurz's memoirs, and Hendrick's exposé of the life insurance industry. While the series was running, the magazine ran fiction by Conrad and began Ellen Terry's memoirs. McClure could find new writers to replace the stars who had left him, but it turned out that he could not get along without John Phillips to manage the business end of the magazine. He had to mortgage his property to buy out his partners and was in financial trouble from then on. Even with a circulation of over half a million the magazine never made a profit after 1906.

For Cather the Christian Science assignment brought her both grief and the managing editorship. She wrote her father in December that she would not be able to come home for Christmas because she had to work on the Christian Science articles. She was bitter about giving up the trip she had planned, but she couldn't desert McClure. He apparently had convinced her that the magazine faced a crisis and persuaded her to work through the holidays getting the March installment ready for publication on time. Otherwise people would think the church had scared him off. The articles, she reported, were under such a glare of publicity and fire of criticism. The following month she wrote Dwight, who was off in Italy, that she was the fourth person to undertake to rewrite Milmine's manuscript and was about to spend the next five months grubbing among newspaper files and court records. This was the most laborious and sordid work she had ever done, and it was taking every bit of her time and as much vitality as she could put into it. It was sapping her brain and wringing it dry. She was jumping about like a squirrel in a cage and wondering how she ever got into it. She never in her life had wanted to do this sort of thing, but there she was hammering away at it. McClure, however, had promised her six months in Europe after she finished the series.

Following publication of the *Life* in the magazine, Doubleday, Page, and Company brought it out in book form as *The Life of Mary Baker G. Eddy and the History of Christian Science*. Although Georgine Milmine's name was on the title page both in serial and book form, Cather was the real author of all but the first installment. But the work was so foreign to what she really wanted to write that for the rest of her life, with one exception, she stoutly maintained that all she had done was edit the manuscript. In 1922, however, she felt the need to tell someone the true story and put it in a letter to her old friend Edwin Anderson. But she swore him to silence, and the secret was not divulged until Cather's letter eventually turned up in the archives of the New York Public Library. She ended her letter by saying that Milmine was in the awkward position of having her name on a book of which she did not write a word.

Cather regarded this book as part of her apprenticeship and wanted to forget it, as she did her early stories and her journalism. She said she wrote it as a sort of discipline, an exercise. It was her first long piece of work, however, and marked another milestone on her way to becoming a novelist. In her essay "The Novel Démeublé" she writes that "the novelist must learn to write, and then he must unlearn it; just as the modern painter learns to draw, and then learns when utterly to disregard his accomplishment, when to subordinate it to a higher and truer effect." Cather's experience with the life of Mary Baker Eddy was an analogous lesson.

Cather thought that McClure picked her to write the series because she was unprejudiced. She hadn't a bone to pick with Christian Science, she told Anderson. The subject was sensitive, however, as the church in its thirty-year history had grown powerful and Mrs. Eddy's book, *Science and Health*, was, next to the Bible, the most important book to her followers. In June 1906, Christian Scientists from all over the world had met in Boston to dedicate "the most costly church building in New England and one of the most pretentious in the United States." By that time there were already six hundred other Christian Science churches and many thousands of adherents. Hot arguments raged, nonetheless, over the sources of Mrs. Eddy's system of healing disease by the mind, whether it was from divine inspiration, as she claimed, or borrowed from Phineas P. Quimby of Portland, Maine, who had treated her in the 1860s.

The book that Cather wrote reads like a legal brief. She presented the materials dispassionately, documenting Mrs. Eddy's life every step of the way with hard evidence—letters, court records, sworn affidavits. There is none of the emotional coloring and figurative language that characterizes all of Cather's previous journalism. She not only worked with the data in Milmine's manuscript, but she also collected new material, for a number of the documents are sworn statements dated February 1907, after she went to Boston. Also, because Mrs. Eddy was still living, she added several more years to Milmine's biographical material. The series as a whole is an astonishing performance. McClure's erstwhile star Ida Tarbell could not have done it better, and Cather, had she wanted, could have been as good as any of the magazine's investigative reporters in uncovering political corruption and corporate venality. The *New York Times* commented editorially after the series began that *McClure's* was performing a large public service.

If the work of writing the Christian Science series was distasteful and uncongenial, the assignment to Boston was a marvelous stroke of good luck. She was excited about seeing for the first time the literary and historic landmarks of Boston she had read about all her life and traveling through the mountains and towns of rural New England. While Nebraska had only a geologic past, Massachusetts had as much history behind it as her native Virginia. She also discovered the White Mountains of New Hampshire, which drew her back year after year and eventually became her final resting place. The stay in Boston was richly productive of friendships: Ferris Greenslet of Houghton Mifflin, who became her publisher; Margaret Deland, writer, and Louise Imogen Guiney, poet; Louis Brandeis, future Supreme Court justice, his wife, and her sister Pauline Goldmark, social worker; Laura Hills, painter.

Her most important friendships began, however, one day in February 1908, when she set out to pay a call on Mrs. Brandeis in Otis Place. When she arrived, her hostess said she wanted to take her to visit a very charming old lady, Mrs. James T. Fields, widow of the former Boston publisher, who lived in nearby Charles Street. Together they began what for Cather was to be a moving journey into the past. The famous firm of Ticknor and Fields was a part of literary history, the imprint on some of the books she had read as a child in Red Cloud. That Mrs. Fields could still be living in Boston in 1908 seemed incredible. Her husband had been the friend and publisher of Hawthorne, Emerson, Lowell, Holmes, and Longfellow, an early editor of the *Atlantic Monthly*, and a key figure in New England's golden literary age. Annie Fields was in fact living at 148 Charles Street in the same house where

Dickens, Thackeray, Arnold, and a host of other notables had been entertained. She had married young, when Fields was a middle-aged widower,
and already had survived her husband by twenty-seven years.

Although Mrs. Fields was over seventy, she did not seem old when Cather
was conducted into her drawing room. "Frail, diminished in force, yes; but,
emphatically, *not* old." She was still a cheerful, vital spirit, a woman with a
merry, musical laugh, a hostess of consummate skill and grace. In her
presence Cather relived literary history. Mrs. Fields had talked to Leigh Hunt
about Shelley; she had known Joseph Severn, who had given her a lock of
Keats's hair. The house was full of treasures: rare editions, manuscripts of
great authors, association copies of books written by her guests. If one did
not "go at" her, she would talk of her famous visitors just as though they were
people who had dropped in for tea last week. For the first time in her life,
Cather later wrote, she felt that Americans had a past of their own, and she
went away with an exultant feeling. "It was at tea-time, I used to think, that
the great shades were most likely to appear; sometimes they seemed to come
up the deeply carpeted stairs, along with living friends. At that hour the long
room was dimly lighted, the fire bright, and through the wide windows the
sunset was flaming, or softly brooding, upon the Charles River and the
Cambridge shore beyond. The ugliness of the world, all possibility of
wrenches and jars and wounding contacts, seemed securely shut out."

Cather loved going to that house on Charles Street, and she loved its
occupant, though she never quite got over her sense of awe. She also visited
Mrs. Fields at her Massachusetts summer place at Manchester and wrote her
frequently, but in her letters she was always afraid of touching on one of Mrs.
Fields's prejudices and letting the noisy modern world in on her. When
DeWolfe Howe disposed of Mrs. Fields's correspondence after her death,
Cather insisted that her own letters be destroyed. They were too artificial and
unrepresentative, she said. When she was with Mrs. Fields, however, she did
not feel constraint, and their relations were natural. She delighted in the sharp
contrasts between her world of *McClure's Magazine* and the surviving bit of
the Victorian era on Charles Street. It was delicious to have Mrs. Fields look
up from the paper and ask gravely who Rex Beach was and did he have
anything to do with letters? Mrs. Fields was the soloist, and she was the
accompanist, Cather wrote Howe, and she did not mind learning from her
hostess. One day Mrs. Fields quoted a line of poetry: "A bracelet of bright
hair about the bone."

"That's very nice," said I, "but I don't recognize it."

"Surely," she said, "that would be Dr. Donne."

"I never pretended to Mrs. Fields," Cather continued, and so she asked brazenly, "And who . . . was Dr. Donne?" Mrs. Fields was patient with her ignorance and sent her up to bed with two thick volumes of Donne to read. Despite her omnivorous reading, Cather had many gaps in her knowledge of English literature, and there are no references at all in her years of journalism to the seventeenth-century metaphysical poets.

She learned a great deal from Mrs. Fields, not just the anecdotes of literary history or who John Donne was. It was her manner, her complete faith in the great tradition, her life-style, to use the contemporary term, that instructed Cather. She was an exemplary figure, a role model, even though Cather regarded herself as a liberated woman, modern and progressive. When she reviewed Howe's edition of Mrs. Fields's diaries, *Memories of a Hostess*, in 1922, she quoted a sentence from Aristotle that Mrs. Fields had copied in her diary as a young woman: "Virtue is concerned with action; art with production." The problem of life, she added, was to harmonize the two. In a long life, wrote Cather, "she went far toward working out this problem. . . . In the patriot, the philanthropist, the statesman, she could forgive abominable taste. In the artist . . . she could forgive vanity, sensitiveness, selfishness, indecision, and vacillation of will." Cather too pondered this maxim and tried to reconcile these dichotomies.

When Cather first climbed the stairs to Mrs. Fields's drawing room that memorable day in February 1908, there were two women having tea together, Mrs. Fields and her old friend and sometime companion Sarah Orne Jewett. It was a wonderful surprise to meet Jewett, "who looked very like the youthful picture of herself in the game of 'Authors' I had played as a child, except that she was fuller in figure and a little grey." The friendship with Jewett that began over tea that afternoon lasted only sixteen months, but it was one of Cather's most cherished relationships. Jewett died unexpectedly at the age of sixty; yet in those sixteen months she became one of the most prepotent forces in Cather's literary development. She was, moreover, the first important woman writer Cather knew.

Cather saw her on other occasions at Mrs. Fields's that winter and spring, again when she visited Mrs. Fields in the summer at Manchester, and in the fall at Jewett's home in South Berwick, Maine. She tried to get Jewett to write a story for *McClure's*, and she promised she would, but her health was precarious and she never managed to do it. Jewett was strongly attracted to Cather and wrote her in August: "I wish that I could see you and that something might bring you to Boston and for a night to Manchester. For more than a night, or as long as you could stay." After Cather's visit to Maine in November, Jewett wrote: "I was sorry to miss the drive to the station and a last talk about the story and other things; but I was too tired. . . . And I knew

that I was disappointing you, besides disappointing and robbing myself."
After Jewett's death Cather visited Sarah's sister Mary in South Berwick, and
for her Jewett's room and desk became a sort of shrine. Jewett served Cather
as an important role model as she struggled to find her authentic voice.

Cather had not begun to appreciate the stories of Sarah Orne Jewett,
however, until she was an adult. At the age of nineteen, she wrote Alexander
Woollcott in 1942, she was not the least interested in Jewett. She found
nothing in her stories that she wanted in a book. She was blind alike to their
elegance and truthfulness. She was then reading Balzac furiously and everything of Tolstoy. Young people, she said, don't care how a thing is done;
refinement simply goes over their heads, and form means nothing. By the
time *The Country of the Pointed Firs* came out in 1896 Cather had developed a
passion for Jewett's work, and when she edited a collection of Jewett's best
stories in the twenties, she ranked *The Pointed Firs* along with *The Scarlet
Letter* and *Huck Finn* as one of the three most enduring American classics.

The six months in Europe that McClure promised Cather when she began
work on the Christian Science series shrank to four months and was belated.
She was able to make a trip back to Red Cloud in the summer of 1907, but the
life of Mrs. Eddy took longer to complete than anyone anticipated. In April
1908, however, Cather and McClung again sailed for Europe, this time going
directly to Italy. They spent a week in Tuscany and visited Rome, Naples,
Pompeii, and the Amalfi coast on the Gulf of Salerno. Cather responded to
this first trip to Italy with intense delight. Her letters are rhapsodies to the
beauty of the land and the grandeur of the antiquities.

After reaching Naples, she wrote Mrs. Goudy, her old teacher, about her
first couple of weeks in Italy. She and McClung had tramped about the
Apennines visiting old monasteries. In one lonely sanctuary high on a mountaintop they found a single monk living amid the ruins, who showed them
wonderful Latin manuscripts in his crumbling library. On another day they
found an original code of the Lombard League in a Benedictine abbey that
had been founded in the eleventh century. Then the two women moved on to
Naples and Pompeii, which were more wonderful than anyone could imagine. They spent two days amid the ruins of that buried city before returning
to Naples to look at the art treasures in the museums there. Naples itself was a
marvel, and their hotel overlooked the bay, which Cather thought the most
beautiful body of water in the world. She was sitting on her balcony every
afternoon and watching Mt. Vesuvius change from violet to lilac to purple.
She could almost throw a stone to the tiny island of Megaris where Lucullus
once had his garden and where Brutus met Cicero after the murder of Caesar.

Street singers sang under her window every night, and every morning she went to the flower market to buy roses and camellias.

She was captivated by the Roman sculpture in the Royal Museum. It was full of royal Roman families in youth and in age, and she felt as if she had known them all personally. She was brushing up on her Latin and reading Tacitus and Suetonius. They also had been going about in the country looking at vineyards and fields in bloom. The vines were in new leaf; oranges and lemons were ripe; peach and cherry trees were blooming. The olive trees above the Mediterranean were soft and gray, and all the country folk were out digging in their fields, just as Virgil described it in the *Georgics*. Such a ravishing world, she concluded, and such a short life to see it in!

One week later she was writing Jewett from the Hotel and Pension Palumbo in Ravello overlooking the Mediterranean high above Amalfi. The camellias were in bloom in the Rufolo Garden, and the hotel was covered with yellow roses. She had a room facing the sea. Apparently Jewett had once stayed in the same hotel, for Cather refreshed her memory of the breathtaking view. The land dropping down to the sea looked like hot green porcelain whose flow had been checked by the jagged cliffs along which ran the Salerno road. It was surely a sea of legend, a sea that glimmered centuries away with the opaque blue water that Puvis de Chavannes painted. The day before there had been a religious festival in Amalfi, and she had started out gaily in the company of Italians along the footpath leading down to the town. Just as the path came out on an open place along the carriage road, a group of Nebraskans she had not seen for years came into sight. There was nothing she could do but go back to Ravello with them and leave her Italian companions and the fiesta.

The Italian interlude ended all too soon, and Cather was back at her desk by August 6. She later told people that she had become managing editor about this time, but she never listed herself as more than an associate editor in her *Who's Who* entries. McClure's biographer believes she shared the duties of managing editor with George Turner, but he was off on roving assignments much of the time, while Cather remained in the office doing the work. In actual fact McClure was his own managing editor as well as editor-in-chief, and the person or persons who sat on the editorial desk were merely expected to handle routine editorial correspondence, dispose of would-be contributors who insisted on calling in person, recognize any new talent that swam into view, and keep McClure informed of what was going on. But McClure himself also spent much of his time traveling so that whoever was in the office did the work of putting out the magazine.

Cather also was able to get along with McClure better than anyone else. They had their common Western background as a bond, also their mutual interest in romance and writers like Kipling and Stevenson. Sergeant, who saw them both in action in 1910, reported: "Clearly the two of them were partners in an alliance that had tang and motion. Their Midwest voices harmonized, their seething inner forces supplemented each other. There was an inspirational quality about the dynamic unspoiled assistant that kept the older editor afloat on his sea of discovery."

Every editor who worked for McClure had the unofficial job of trying to keep the chief from going off half-cocked. Cather said later that she spent a lot of her energy helping the magazine wriggle out of commitments McClure had made to writers and their agents. She didn't have enough help in this duty, however, and was unable to prevent McClure's ultimate downfall. When he had Tarbell, Phillips, and Steffens with him, the three of them could hold him down, but they had been with him for a long time and knew how to do it. The newer employees like Cather didn't have the experience. Will Irwin, who was managing editor for a year after the blow-up, remembered: "As a curb on genius, I was not a success."

Cather made a significant change in her living arrangements after her return home from Europe. She and Edith Lewis took an apartment together at 82 Washington Place and began a relationship that lasted until Cather died thirty-nine years later. The two women had met in 1903 when Lewis was visiting her family in Lincoln after graduating from Smith. She then had gone to New York to seek her fortune in the publishing business, and Cather had visited her there several times. When Cather went to work for *McClure's*, she helped Lewis get a job as proofreader on the magazine. They had lived as neighbors at 60 South Washington Square, and when Cather was working on the Christian Science articles, the magazine had sent Lewis to Boston with proof. Now they were to be permanent apartment-mates. The relationship was a close, loving friendship that survived the vicissitudes of nearly four decades.

The close bond between Cather and Lewis has been described as a marriage, but that term is misleading and suggests more than the evidence warrants. Isabelle McClung always remained number one in Cather's affections, even after she married in 1916. Lewis, however, was devoted to Cather and spent her life smoothing the way and protecting the privacy of her more gifted friend. Sergeant wrote of the relationship: "A captain, as Will White of Emporia said . . . must have a first officer, who does a lot the captain never knows about to steer the boat through rocks and reefs." Lewis was the one who bought the railroad tickets, made the hotel reservations (usually in her own name to avoid publicity), acted as traveling companion when she could get away from her job, and in general was Cather's "stand in." The arrangement worked out very well, and the two women lived together harmoniously and comfortably. Lewis, however, had her own career, first as copy reader for *McClure's*, later a magazine editor, and then an advertising writer for J. Walter Thompson.

The only story that Cather was able to publish in 1908 was "On the Gull's Road," which *McClure's* uséd in its December issue. It owes its setting to the transatlantic crossing she and McClung had just made in July, and the story might well have been suggested by people encountered during the voyage. There is little action in the story, simply a developing relationship between two characters who spend their days in deck chairs talking as their ship travels from Genoa to New York. Mrs. Ebbling, the Scandinavian wife of the ship's chief engineer, and a young diplomat-artist gradually fall in love. As the young man's love grows, he becomes aware that Mrs. Ebbling is intensely unhappy in her marriage and proposes an elopement. She, however, is suffering from an incurable heart disease and refuses to encumber his life. The admirer is left with bittersweet memories, as he tells the story twenty years later.

A plot summary does not convey the skill of the narration or the subtlety of the character development. Though the influence of James still seems apparent, the story has originality and sentiment without becoming sentimental. There are some good moments in the tale, as Mrs. Ebbling's entrapment in an unhappy marriage and the narrator's growing love are gradually revealed. Cather suggests sexual passion by associating Mrs. Ebbling continually with the sea, as though she were Venus emerging on her scallop, describing her with metaphors of water. To reenforce this image Cather leaves the narrator with a memento from Mrs. Ebbling—a coil of her hair that curls and clings about his sleeve like a living thing and two pink sea shells, both enclosed in a little box.

Cather had doubts about this story when she read proof and sent a copy to Jewett. She was afraid the scent of the tube-rose was still clinging to it and it rather screamed, but her fears that her friend would not like it were unfounded. Jewett read the story with "deep happiness," and it made her feel very near to the writer's "young and loving heart." Mrs. Ebbling was drawn with "unerring touches and wonderful tenderness for her." She added: "It makes me the more sure that you are far on your road toward a fine and long story of a very high class." She had one stricture, however; she thought the lover should have been a woman, or the story should have been told in the third person. "The lover is as well done as he could be when a woman writes in the man's character—it must always, I believe, be something of a masquerade. I think it safer to write about him as you did about the others, and not try to be he! And you could almost have done it as yourself—a woman could love her in the same protecting way—a woman could even care enough to wish to take her away from such a life. But oh, how close—how tender—how true the feeling is! the sea air blows through the very letters on the page."

Jewett was responding to what she saw as a technical problem in the narration, but feminist critics see the use of a male narrator here and elsewhere in Cather's fiction as a masquerade, because no magazine would have published a story in 1908 of a love between two women. The gender of the narrator, however, is almost undetectible, and if the subtitle, "The Ambassador's Story" were dropped and one clause ("I threw my cigar away") cut, no one could identify the sex of the anonymous first-person narrator. In fact, one sentence reads: "I returned to the deck and joined a group of my countrywomen." But Cather certainly intended the narrator to be male and never paid any attention to critics who thought she should write more like a woman. She had been writing from a male point of view from the beginning and had begun her adolescence in the role of William Cather, M.D. If anyone had charged her with a deliberate masquerade, she would have denied it indignantly and defended her male point of view on aesthetic grounds.

Jewett was not satisfied with the letter she had written about "On the Gull's Road." She thought about the story and her young friend for the next two weeks and then wrote a long second letter which really said what was on her mind. She saw enough potential in Cather that she felt obliged to level with her. "I cannot help saying what I think," she began, "about your writing and its being hindered by such incessant, important, responsible work as you have in your hands now." She thought it impossible for her to be a magazine editor and at the same time have her writing talent mature properly. Although *The Troll Garden* contained some good work, especially "The Sculptor's Funeral," "you are older now than that book . . . but if you don't keep and guard and mature your force, and above all, have time and quiet to perfect your work, you will be writing things not much better than you did five years ago."

Then she went on to review Cather's background and career to date. "You have your Nebraska life,—a child's Virginia, and now an intimate knowledge of what we are pleased to call 'the Bohemia' of newspaper and magazine office life. These are uncommon equipment, but . . . you stand right in the middle of each of them when you write, without having the standpoint of the looker-on who takes them each in their relations to letters, to the world." Cather also had had a good education, which was essential and important to her, but at this point in her career (age thirty-five) she needed a quiet place to write. "Your vivid, exciting companionship in the office must not be your audience, you must find your own quiet centre of life, and write from that to the world . . . in short, you must write to the human heart, the great consciousness that all humanity goes to make up." Otherwise, she added, what might be strength in a writer is only crudeness, what might be insight is only observation, and what might be sentiment is only sentimentality. "You can write about life, but never write life itself. And to write and work on this level, we must live on it."

This remarkable letter from an old writer to a young one touched Cather deeply. She responded with an eight-page reply a day or two after receiving it. In her answer she analyzed herself, her prospects, her ambitions, her talents, more profoundly perhaps than ever before. The letter is very revealing of her state of mind thirty-three months after joining McClure's staff. She admitted that she was deeply perplexed about her life. She was not made to have to do with what McClure called "men and measures." In order to get on with that kind of work, she had to go at it with the sort of energy most people had to exert only on rare occasions. Consequently, she was living from day to day much like a trapeze performer on the bar. It was catch the right bar at the right time or onto the net you go. Her mind was off doing trapeze work all day and only came back to her at night dog tired and wanting to sleep.

Then the reading of so many poorly written manuscripts had a deadening effect. She knew that some people could do it, but it gave her a kind of dread of everything made out of words. She felt diluted and weakened by it all the time as though she were in a tepid bath and could no longer stand heat or cold. She often thought of trying to get three or four months a year of free time to write, but then the planning of articles for the magazine was pretty much in her head, and it was difficult to hand the details over to anyone else. Her mind had become a sort of card catalogue of notes meaningless except to her. What McClure wanted to do was to make her into as good an imitation of Ida Tarbell as he could. He wanted her to write articles on popular science and other things for half of each week and attend to the office work in the other half. That combination would be perfectly possible, she feared, but quite deadening. He wanted above all things good, clear-cut journalism. She did not despise such writing, but she got no satisfaction out of it.

It seems clear from this letter that McClure was engaged in brainwashing.

She said he kept telling her that she would never be able to do much in writing stories, but she could be a good magazine executive and had better let it go at that. She often thought that he probably was right. If she had been making any progress during the past five years, it was progress of the head and not of the hand. At her age she ought to have some sureness in her pen and some facility in turning out a story. In other matters—things about the office—she could usually do what she set out to do, and she could learn by experience; but when it came to writing she was a new-born baby every time. She always came into it naked and shivering and without any bones. She never seemed to learn anything about it at all.

She thought one had a right to live and reflect and feel a little. When she was teaching she did. She learned more or less all the time, but now she had the feeling of standing still except for a certain kind of facility in getting the sort of material McClure wanted. This was stiff mental exercise, but it was about as much food to live by as elaborate mental arithmetic. Of course, there were interesting people and interesting things in the day's work, but it was all like going around the world in a train and never getting off to see anything close up. She did not have a reportorial mind, couldn't get things in fleeting glimpses, and the excitement did not stimulate her; it only wore her out. It did to her brain exactly what she had seen alcohol do to men's. It spread out their brain cells so that they didn't touch, and everything leaked out, as power did in a broken circuit.

Whether or not McClure was right in thinking she would never be a writer, she thought perhaps she ought to consider her immortal soul. He thrived on the perpetual debauch of editorial work, but five years more would make her fat, sour, ill-tempered and—worst of all—fussy. She added that she was still sending money home now and then, but if she stopped working the following summer, she would have savings enough to live very simply for three or four years, which would give her time to pull herself together. Since she was fifteen she had never had six months free in a stretch. It was foolish to lose one's real pleasures for the supposed pleasures of the chase or the stock exchange.

When Jewett warned Cather that she needed a quiet center for her life or her writing would not improve, she obviously touched a raw nerve. One wonders why Cather did not take this advice and get out of McClure's office. The answer must lie in the hypnotic influence McClure had on her, the attractions of New York, the things a very good salary could buy, the satisfaction of having fought her way to the top, and the genuine self-doubts that this letter reveals. She concluded her letter by observing that she must have something like a split personality.

The work of managing editor took its toll physically as well as mentally. She quoted Jewett a couplet from Goldsmith:

> And as an hare whom horns and hounds pursue,
> Pants for the place from which at first she flew.

She felt like such a rabbit most of the time, even though she was called an executive at the office. By the following March she was seriously ill and had to be hospitalized. Whether it was exhaustion, flu, or something else, the record does not say, but she was being looked after by Isabelle McClung, and McClure wrote in mid-March: "I am anxious about . . . your health; but I hope that you will soon recover your vigor. . . . I want you to rest as long as Miss McClung feels that it is necessary." McClure also told her that she had worked a remarkable change in the way the magazine was being run. "I have a sense of things being in a competent condition that I have not had . . . for a long time." He confessed to a sense of loneliness "not only personal but professional, when you are not around." He later told his wife: "The best magazine executive I know is Miss Cather."

She was much too severe, however, in her self-analysis. In her previous letter to Jewett enclosing a copy of "On the Gull's Road" she said she had finished a western story her friend might like better. McClure had sniffed at it, said it was all introduction, and apparently did not want to publish it, but she had made use of her Nebraska memories and felt the tale had merit. It did indeed: It was "The Enchanted Bluff," the tale that evokes her memories of her brothers and camping on Far Island. It is as good as anything she had done up to that time, and *Harper's* liked it and published it the next April. A rich evocation of her adolescence in Red Cloud, it foreshadows very directly her mainstream fiction. It uses the same setting as "The Treasure of Far Island," making use of memories of camping on an island in the Republican River, but this time Cather realized she did not need any formal plot structure. The story merely brings together six boys who talk around a campfire on an island the night before the narrator leaves home to begin teaching school on the Divide. It introduces the legend of Coronado and the Spaniards on the Great Plains, which recurs in *My Ántonia*; the symbol of the rock, which appears in *Death Comes for the Archbishop* and *Shadows on the Rock*; and the Southwest, which fired Cather's imagination long before she ever visited the area.

As in "On the Gull's Road," she created a male narrator, and again the story is told twenty years after the fact. As the boys sit about their fire, one of them tells the legend of the Enchanted Bluff in far-off New Mexico, the story of a lost Indian village on top of an inaccessible rock in the midst of the desert. All the boys resolve someday to climb that rock. When morning comes, the boys disperse and in the years between the time of the story and the telling of it, they all go off into prosaic adult occupations. The narrator ends the tale reminiscing about their youthful dreams and aspirations. The prose in the story is vintage Cather, as it opens: "We had our swim before sundown, and while we were cooking our supper the oblique rays of light made a dazzling glare on the white sand about us. The translucent red ball itself sank behind the brown stretches of corn field as we sat down to eat, and the warm layer of air that had rested over the water and our clean sand bar grew fresher and smelled of the ironweed and sunflowers growing on the flatter shore. The river was brown and sluggish, like any other of the half-dozen streams that water the Nebraska corn lands. On one shore was an irregular line of bald clay bluffs where a few scrub oaks with thick trunks and flat, twisted tops threw light shadows on the long grass. The Western shore was low and level, with corn fields that stretched to the skyline, and all along the water's edge were little sandy coves and beaches where slim cottonwoods and willow saplings flickered."

There is no doubt that McClure appreciated Cather's work and rewarded her generously. "I have been greatly pleased with your letters and your work," and "I am awfully proud of your splendid work," he would write when she was out of town on magazine business. He had another way of holding on to her, perhaps even more effective than praise. He sent her to Europe in May 1909 on a trip to hunt for writers and manuscripts. He believed in frequent trips to Europe and elsewhere and thought a roving editor was more likely to discover talent than a sedentary one. When he hired Lincoln Steffens, he told him he had to learn to be an editor.

"How can I learn?" Steffens asked him. "He laid his hand on my knee. 'Not here,' he said. 'You can't learn to edit a magazine here in this office.'

"Where then can I learn? Where shall I go to learn to be an editor?

"He sprang up and waved his hand around a wide circle.

'Anywhere,' he said. 'Anywhere else. Get out of here, travel, go—someplace.' " Steffens took a train for Chicago and began his distinguished career as magazine writer and editor.

Cather was in England for two months on this scouting trip. She went to hear Vera Figner, a Russian political prisoner who had been released after twenty-two years of mostly solitary confinement in the dread Schlusselburg Prison on an island in the Neva River near St. Petersburg. From this lecture came a series of articles by David Soskice, *The Secrets of the Schlusselburg*, for which she wrote the introduction. She also met interesting theatrical and literary people, one of whom was William Archer, drama critic, writer, and contributor to *McClure's*. He took her to the funeral of George Meredith and to the first London performance of the Abbey Theater. They sat with Lady Gregory in Yeats' box and saw Synge's *The Playboy of the Western World*. One Irish actress became the model later for a character in her first novel, *Alexander's Bridge*. She also met H. G. Wells, Ford Maddox Ford (then Ford Maddox Hueffer), Edmund Gosse, and Katherine Tynan, Irish poet and novelist.

This trip made a lasting impression, especially the association with Archer, whom she saw on subsequent occasions when he visited New York. She recalled another performance of the Abbey Theater that she also saw with Archer in a letter to her biographer E. K. Brown. This was a second play by Synge, the one-act *Rising of the Moon*, which puzzled the audience a good deal, including Cather. At supper after the performance Archer asked her what she thought of the play. She replied that it was interesting but not very dramatic. He responded gently that anything interesting in theater belongs there and is dramatic. Recalling this incident, she thought she had learned something important from Archer. All at once he had struck out a foolish platitude she had previously respected devotedly. Archer's idea became a principle she applied to her own best work.

While she was in London, she received the devastating news that Sarah Orne Jewett had died. She heard the news on Saturday, June 26, and immediately wrote Mrs. Fields a letter of sympathy and an expression of her own grief. She was overcome by the fact, and as she went about feeling numb and inert she realized that everything she had been doing in London was in hopes of interesting Jewett. She was even having clothes made that she hoped her friend would like. Now all the wheels were standing still and the ways of life seemed dark and purposeless. The day after she wrote a letter came from Mrs. Fields in an effort to soften the blow. Cather was deeply touched by her kindness, as she wrote Mrs. Fields from her ship the day she reached New York, July 13.

There was no time to grieve. As soon as the *Kaiser Wilhelm der Grosse* docked, she had to get back to the office. For the next twenty months she was chained to her editorial desk most of the time. She did manage six weeks in Nebraska in September and October, but McClure spent a great deal of time in Europe leaving her to run the magazine alone. The year before, he had gone abroad the day after she landed from Italy; he simply could not sit still. By Christmas she was so tired that she went to bed for the holidays. Fortunately she had Isabelle McClung with her for November and December, she wrote Aunt Franc, and that was a comfort, especially at Christmas, which always was a homesick time for her. McClung also had been shopping for her and had trained a new maid. Meantime, Cather still was doing her trapeze act at the office. She had commissioned an article on the Cherry Mine disaster and was keeping an eye on a grand jury investigation resulting from a *McClure's* article on Tammany Hall and white slavery. Later in the spring she went up to Boston to talk to Hugo Munsterberg, a Harvard psychologist, about a series of articles he would write during a forthcoming trip to Germany.

McClure's did well under Cather's stewardship. During the first year of her managing editorship the circulation rose by sixty thousand, and in the second the figures were even better. In June 1910, a special announcement stated that three issues had gone out of print in the past year and the current number was the largest in the magazine's history. McClure was still so much in debt, however, that the company was not making a profit. The articles and stories that *McClure's* published in this period are pretty much of a piece with the material used in previous years. Mrs. Humphrey Ward, then very popular, was the serialized novelist, and Cather bought fiction from Arnold Bennett, O. Henry, Theodore Dreiser, and Jack London. She also accepted stories from Rex Beach, whose work she usually disparaged, and three tales from Kathleen Norris in six months. Nonfiction articles included muckraking pieces by Turner, a series on Grover Cleveland, and work by Jane Addams. William Archer wrote on the theater, and there were more reminiscences by Ellen Terry. One day she bought an article on the sweated workers in the garment industry from a brisk young woman from Boston and Bryn Mawr.

This was Elizabeth Sergeant, who walked into *McClure's* offices with her manuscript and a letter of introduction from Pauline Goldmark. Cather was not much interested in sweatshops, but she liked her visitor immediately and found Sergeant really was more concerned with literature, France, and general culture than with social issues. A friendship developed that was very close for the next two decades. It was never broken off, though the two women did not see each other often after the twenties. Cather's friendships— and her hates—usually were formed on the basis of instant, intuitive reactions; she knew right away if she wanted to bother with a person, and Sergeant met the test. Cather also did not drop old friends, even when they displeased her; and when Sergeant became an ardent New Dealer in the thirties while Cather remained a staunch Republican, they steered clear of politics.

The editor that Sergeant met in *McClure's* offices in January, 1910, was a buoyant, rather square woman with no trace of the reforming feminist about her. She shook hands in a direct, almost brusque manner and led her visitor through the jostle of the noisy anterooms to her private office. Her boyish, enthusiastic manner was disarming. Her voice had a western resonance about it that contrasted sharply with Sergeant's Boston accent, and her clothes were informal, as if she rebelled against urban conformities. She wore a bright striped blouse and a loud Irish-tweed skirt that cut her sturdy legs in half. During the interview that followed Cather read Sergeant's article, found it sufficiently objective and factual for *McClure's* and after some cuts and condensation agreed to accept it. Then she changed the subject:

"Tell me . . . why you joined the reforming pamphleteers? This all has its place—it's good—but aren't short stories more in your line? I don't mean tenement stories—you look like a Jamesian—am I right?" Sergeant argued vigorously that society had to protect the exploited immigrant families crowded into lower Manhattan, but before long she was telling Cather about her recent trip to Greece and how she met Anatole France in the Athens museum. This led to Flaubert, Balzac, Tolstoy, Henry James, Edith Wharton, and Jewett; and when Sergeant said she had given a copy of *The Country of the Pointed Firs* to a French writer who compared it to Turgenev's *A Sportsman's Sketches*, there was no doubt this was going to be a close friendship.

Another lifelong friendship began at *McClure's* when the future playwright Zoë Akins submitted verse to the magazine. Cather rejected the verse but found the poet a delightful young woman of twenty-three who had come to New York from St. Louis to be a writer. When she sent back the verse, Cather told Akins she ought to try playwriting. She did, and after achieving success with *Déclassée* in 1919 went on to write one successful play after another until she won a Pulitzer Prize in 1935. Cather and Akins carried on a lifelong correspondence, writing each other warm and affectionate letters several times a year. Although Akins settled in California in the thirties, she came to New York on theater business every year and the two friends always got together. Cather had no hesitation in telling Akins when her plays were bad, but Akins always took the criticism good naturedly. She also had a genius for sending gifts that pleased Cather, such as a blooming apple tree at Christmas, a green jacket to work in, a Chinese nightingale. The only time Cather ever addressed sharp words to this friend was when Akins sent her a dramatized version of *A Lost Lady* that some young Hollywood writer had made. She wrote in 1936 that Akins was one of her comforts and one of the few people she trusted. On another occasion she wrote that she envied Akins's natural ability to enjoy life and her courage to take chances. When Akins got married for the first time at the age of forty-six, Cather wrote a warm letter of congratulations, wished she were going to California that year so that she could hear all about it. She thought that Akins, if anyone, could make matrimony go. Always for Cather there was a golden glow about this friend.

Besides Sergeant and Akins, there was a widening circle of friends in New York. She no longer found her friends among theater folk, except for George Arliss and his wife, who lived near Washington Place and were frequent guests. She thought his characterization of Disraeli was one of the great performances of the era, and she enjoyed frequent after-theater parties at his apartment. She developed a close friendship with Viola Roseboro', her colleague at *McClure's*, and came to know and admire Ida Tarbell, even though the latter had left McClure in the celebrated break. Another friend and neighbor was Mrs. Clara Potter Davidge, who had built E. A. Robinson a studio behind her house at 121 Washington Place. Cather met Robinson there but never bought any of his poems for *McClure's*.

Cather also got to know Mark Twain during his last years when he lived at 21 Fifth Avenue not far from Washington Square. He spent a good deal of time in bed in those years and entertained three or four young people at a time, including Cather on occasion, in his bedroom. Cather recalled these sessions when she wrote William Lyon Phelps in 1936 to praise an article he had written on Twain for the *Yale Review*. She was glad he did not accept Van Wyck Brooks's thesis that Twain was a blighted genius. If he had been the imaginary character Brooks created in *The Ordeal of Mark Twain*, she said, he never would have written *Huck Finn*; and if Brooks had ever seen that old lion in bed telling stories, he never could have written his book. Twain, for his part, was much taken with Cather's poem, "The Palatine," when it appeared in *McClure's* in June 1909, and read it to his secretary, young Albert Bigelow Paine.

For most of 1910 she drudged away on Twenty-third Street while Mc-Clure remained away. In July she wrote her former pupil Norman Foerster, then a recent Harvard graduate, that she was editing the magazine all alone and did not expect a vacation until October. She managed to get away at the end of September for two months but was too worn out to go home and only went to New England. McClure returned long enough for her to get her energy back and return to the office, but then he left for Europe once more. Christmas, 1910, however, was a happy occasion. Her younger sister Elsie, whom she was sending to Smith, came to visit, and McClung also was there for a month. The black maid Isabelle had trained the year before was Cather's chief treasure, and the little apartment ran like clockwork. She wrote Aunt Franc on February 22 that her health had been much better than the previous winter.

She spoke too soon, however, for almost immediately she woke up in the night with an agonizing earache. After pacing the floor in increasing pain, she and Lewis got dressed and went to see the only doctor they knew, whose home and office were uptown. There were no cabs available; so they took a streetcar. At the doctor's home they stood a long time on the doorstep ringing the bell before lights appeared in an upper window. The doctor diagnosed the case as acute mastoiditis and sent Cather to the hospital where she was operated on and remained for several weeks. Before she was fully recovered, Lewis remembered, Cather went back to London on magazine business. Although she wrote Aunt Franc that she might have to go to London in April, there are no contemporary records documenting this trip. If she did make the journey, she could not have been gone much more than a month, for she was back in the office in early May.

At the end of the month she went to Boston on business and spent a very pleasant week with Mrs. Fields, one of her best visits. She was in good spirits when she described the visit to Louise Guiney. Mrs. Fields, then seventy-six, had come down to the South Station to meet her, the first time in years she had been there. The charm of the house at 148 Charles Street was never so potent. That other rare spirit, Jewett, seemed not far away, and the house was full of her things. A lift had been installed for Mrs. Fields, and Cather wrote that she had become an expert elevator boy. If she failed as managing editor, she told Guiney, she always could get a job as an elevator operator.

The euphoria revealed in this letter lasted into the summer. She had fully recovered from the mastoid infection of the winter, and though she did not yet know it, her years of editing *McClure's Magazine* were about to end. Several weeks after returning to New York from Boston, she went back to New England to visit Mary Jewett at South Berwick. She wrote Sergeant that she was saluting her from Sarah Orne Jewett's desk where it all happened. There she could rest perfectly and forget the facts that confront one— Rex Beach, the white slave trade, and all the overwhelming vulgarity in which we all live. Never was a home so pervaded by a presence, she concluded. The visit must have inspired her, for by this time she was at work on her first novel, a three-part serial that she finished by the end of the summer. She also was writing a Nebraska story, "The Joy of Nelly Dean." *McClure's* would publish the novel early the next year, and the *Century* would take the story.

Her last three months of editing the magazine were a grind. The summer was hot and she had to stay in the city. When she wrote Harrison Dwight turning down a poem that was too long for *McClure's*, she reported that she would be leaving on September 28 for a six month vacation. As it turned out, these six months stretched into fifteen months, and she never again was in the office for more than brief periods. About the time her extended vacation was to begin, the magazine reached another moment of crisis, and this time Cather was one of those who departed—not for another editorial job but for a career as a free lance.

The new life was precipitated by a financial reorganization of the McClure Company. The "chief" finally had gotten himself into such a financial tangle that his son-in-law Cameron Mackenzie had to raise outside capital. The outcome was a reorganization in which McClure lost control of his empire. He signed a contract for the lease of his magazine with an option to buy. The contract provided that he was to be retained as editor-in-chief, at least outwardly, but as Curtis Brady, the business manager, later said: "What was going to happen . . . was so clear a blind man could have felt it with his cane." At this juncture both Brady and Cather resigned their positions, and Mackenzie, who moved over from the business office, and Frederick Collins, editor of the *Woman's Home Companion* and one of the reorganizers, took over the real editorial reins. The next year McClure was ousted from his position by the new owners—unhorsed after twenty years as founder, editor, and guiding genius. Thus one reorganization whisked Cather from Pittsburgh to New York, and another shake-up pried her loose from the magazine. She did not sever her connection, however, but took a leave of absence and planned to come back as a staff writer rather than as an editor.

CHAPTER 10

Alexander's Bridge

The escape from organized chaos at *McClure's* came just in time. The euphoria of June soon vanished, and Cather barely avoided turning into the sour, ill-tempered, fussy woman she feared she was becoming. She not only got out of the magazine office but also left the city. She and Isabelle McClung went to upstate New York where they rented a house in Cherry Valley near Cooperstown and Lake Otsego, about forty miles west of Schenectady. There they settled down for three months of quiet and seclusion. Mrs. McClung had grown up in Cherry Valley, and Isabelle, who loved the place, selected their retreat. After three weeks of rest Cather was able to sleep nine hours a night without turning over. There had been four straight days of unrelenting rain, she wrote McClure, but she liked it and had been hiking about in the wet woods no matter what the weather. In fact, the weather was about the only thing that happened in Cherry Valley, but when one was resting, that was quite enough. She wasn't really resting, however; she was writing very industriously and enjoying it immensely. She needed exactly this kind of life, she said, and had not felt so well or been so happy for several years.

At the end of October McClure stopped off in Cherry Valley en route to Michigan on one of his periodic trips to the Battle Creek Sanitarium. He had become greatly attached to Cather after six years of close association and was worried about her state of mind and health. She was feeling guilty over leaving McClure naked unto his enemies. He tried to relieve her feelings before his visit: "You must dismiss the magazine from your mind entirely; forget it exists; and when you come back I hope you will not let yourself be tied up in office machinery." When he got to Cherry Valley, however, he found Cather doing so well that he could not resist talking business. He must have showered her with ideas for articles she could write and urged her to come back to the magazine soon. But outside of the office and New York City she was able to withstand his blandishments, and after he left she wrote that she wasn't even going to think about magazine work for a while. Anyway, McClure was about to leave for Europe again and she would wait until he got back to see what his needs were. She had plenty of her own writing to keep her busy and planned to stay until after Christmas. Nevertheless, his visit had done her a lot of good. His talk had straightened her out more than anything else could have done, and she had never been more delighted to see anyone. When McClure sent her his picture, which arrived on McClung's birthday, she received it with pleasure, and the two women had a grand dinner together and wished for McClure's presence.

About the time Cather left New York for Cherry Valley the *Century* published a story she had managed to write in 1910 despite her heavy editorial duties, "The Joy of Nelly Deane," another western tale. It is less successful than "The Enchanted Bluff" in evoking her Nebraska memories, but it creates a well-drawn, believable character in Nelly, the "prettiest girl in Riverbend," a prairie town. The story has another first-person narrator, a woman this time, and at first glance one might think Cather was taking Jewett's advice. Peggy, who tells the tale, and Nelly are seniors in high school, members of the Baptist choir, and best friends. The logic of the story, however, requires a female narrator who can receive Nelly's confidences as they sleep together in her bedroom, and Cather could not have told this tale using her preferred male point of view.

"The Joy of Nelly Deane" recounts the brief life and death of a beautiful woman, one of the favorite themes of Cather's early enthusiasm, Edgar Allan Poe. Nelly is seen at two different times, the year she and Peggy graduate from high school, and four years later when Peggy comes back during her senior year in college. Nelly at the outset is not only beautiful, but she also is the happiest, best-natured girl in town. When she isn't singing, she is laughing. She is full of high spirits, but she's also careless and irresponsible. She broke her arm in a foolhardy coasting escapade, got suspended from school for playing hooky to go buggy-riding with her boy friend, and fell through the ice twice because she didn't look where she was skating. Her good looks and gaiety make her the darling of all the older women.

When Peggy returns to Riverbend, Nelly, who has been jilted by the traveling salesman she was engaged to, has become a discontented school teacher. She finally has accepted the proposal of "grim and saturnine" Scott Spinny, owner of the local hardware store. After Peggy goes away again,

Nelly settles down, unhappy and rebellious, to the dull routine of village life. In the final scene Peggy comes back ten years later after learning that Nelly has died in childbirth, leaving an eight-year-old daughter and her baby. Peggy sees in young Margaret the reincarnation of Nelly's once-buoyant spirit, and when she picks up the baby, "he had the flush of new beginnings, of the new morning. . . . It was as if I held her youth and all her young joy."

This affirmation of life after death and sorrow looks ahead to some of Cather's memorable later fiction. After the tragedy in *O Pioneers!* the novel ends with affirmation; life batters the heroine in *My Ántonia*, but the book concludes positively; the title character in "Old Mrs. Harris" dies but life goes on in the younger members of the family; Archbishop Latour's death at the end of *Death Comes for the Archbishop* concludes a life of rich fulfillment. Cather felt the poignancy of the foreshortened life of Nelly Deane and before the story was published wrote the editor of the *Century* suggesting a change in title. She wanted to call it "The Flower in the Grass" because that was the real idea of the tale: a beautiful girl hidden away in the prairie country where nobody ever saw her. There must have been such girls in Red Cloud, whom she saw when she, like her narrator, returned from the outside world. She might have quoted Gray's "Elegy":

> Full many a flow'r is born to blush unseen,
> And waste its sweetness on the desert air.

Cather still had another eastern story to get off her chest before she could turn all her attention to fictional Nebraska. From Cherry Valley she wrote the editor of the *Century* that she was about to send him a story she thought rather "yellow" [sensational] but dealing with an aspect of New York not often written about. This tale must have been "Behind the Singer Tower," an uncharacteristic and mediocre story that the *Century* turned down. *Collier's* bought it, however, and published it in May, by which time Cather was two thousand miles physically and spiritually away from New York.

"Behind the Singer Tower" returns to the use of a male narrator and the frame story. Six friends are cruising New York Bay in a motor launch the day after the great Mont Blanc Hotel has burned down with a large loss of life. An engineer recounts an experience he had many years before as a young man working on the construction of the hotel. He describes his friendship with one of the Italian laborers in his gang, who had been killed by falling machinery. The accident was caused by the stinginess of the chief engineer, who repeatedly refused to replace worn cables. The narrator had sued and won damages from his boss on behalf of the Italian's family. Though the story deals with the exploitation of immigrant labor, Cather's chief animus is with man's inhumanity to man and the indifference of the chief engineer to the cost in human lives in building skyscrapers. The tale belongs in the category of social-protest fiction, but she allows the narrator to undercut her theme. He reflects that the hordes of immigrants who come to America only to be ground up in the great industrial machine are attracted "like iron dust to the magnet" because in building the great city "there must be something wonderful coming."

The story is muddled, the subject uncongenial to Cather's interests, and the pitiful death of the little Italian laborer scarcely arouses pathos. The Singer Tower in the title, which stands near the burned-out hotel, is intended to symbolize the garish vitality of the metropolis: it watches "over the city and harbor like a presiding Genius." The hotel represents the destructive forces of the city. But the symbols are not very effective, and the description of the Singer Tower as a "Jewy-looking thing . . . when it's lit up" is one of several surprisingly anti-Semitic remarks—usually directed at a Jewish doctor who is one of the listeners. This story perhaps was suggested by the infamous Triangle factory fire in Manhattan in 1911, and it was written while *McClure's* was running a series of articles on the appalling lack of fire escapes in New York's high-rise buildings. She certainly was thinking about engineers when she wrote this story, as she then was revising *Alexander's Bridge* for publication in *McClure's* the next year. It is, finally, the only fictional evidence in her canon that the social policies and contents of the magazine had filtered into her blood.

One of Cather's first chores at Cherry Valley was the revision of the initial installment of *Alexander's Bridge*, which was scheduled to appear in the February, March, and April issues of *McClure's* under the title *Alexander's Masquerade*. It is hard to see how she found time in the previous nine months to write even a short novel between her serious illness, trip to London, visits to Boston and Maine, and her editorial duties through the summer while McClure was in Europe. But she remembered writing it in 1911, and it must have been accepted for publication by September. After making her revisions, she sent another copy of her manuscript to Houghton Mifflin in Boston. Recommending it to his colleagues, her friend Ferris Greenslet wrote in his house memo that the novel was distinguished by "excellence of workmanship," "perceptiveness," and "actuality." He also thought there was a "spiritual sense of life that informs it." It is hard to know just what he meant by the last comment, but the company accepted the book immediately, and Cather signed a contract on December first.

If details of the writing are obscure, the materials that went into it are not. Her many months in Boston working on the Christian Science articles, her apartment on Chestnut Street, her visits to Mrs. Fields, and the house at 148 Charles Street gave her much of the American setting. The one scene in New York and the train ride through New England came from her own experience. Her business trips to London, her friendship with William Archer, her attendance at performances of the Abbey Theater, and her sightseeing in the British capital provided the London background. The ocean crossing, though she never had done it in winter, derives from her eight previous trips by ship between the United States and Europe. The narrative technique owes much to Henry James: the dramatic presentation, the invention of a minor-character *ficelle*, the use of a controlling symbol to provide structural unity. James, too, as a pioneer in the international novel, may have influenced the subject matter.

The plot of the novel is based in part on a real event. The collapse of Alexander's bridge over the St. Lawrence at the conclusion of the story parallels closely a similar disaster that occurred near Quebec in 1907. Cather must have used newspaper accounts of this event, for her bridge, like the real one, crumples and drops into the river while workmen are still out on the span. More than eighty men, including the chief engineer, died in the 1907 catastrophe, which took place after warnings of danger reached the builder too late for action. Further, the construction of the real bridge had been hampered by insufficient funds, and the designer had been obliged to skimp on materials. The man in charge of the project was Theodore Cooper, one of the great bridge builders of the day, but he, like Alexander, would not withdraw from the commission because it offered new problems to solve and the promise of fame.

No known engineer sat for the portrait of Bartley Alexander, the bridge builder, but there is a good bit of Cather in the character. The other woman in the novel, however, had a prototype. Edith Lewis remembered that "there was a gifted young actress in the cast" of the *Playboy of the Western World*, whose beauty and engaging personality vividly impressed Cather; "it was from her that she drew the figure of *Hilda Burgoyne*." This actress was no doubt Maire O'Neill, who played the role of Pegeen Mike. Cather saw her on the opening night of the Abbey Theater's London engagement on June 7, 1909, and she could have returned to see her again in one or more of five subsequent performances of the play during her stay in England. The play in which Hilda performs in the novel is housed in the Duke of York's Theater where James M. Barrie's *What Every Woman Knows* then was running. It is likely that the Irish playwright of the story, Hugh MacConnell, is a composite of Synge and Barrie and maybe Yeats too.

The novel tells the story of Bartley Alexander, who at the age of forty-three already is a world-famous engineer. Glowing with strength and cordiality and rugged, blond good looks, he is the bridge builder whose picture the Sunday supplement editors always wanted "because he looked as a tamer of rivers ought to look." He is happily married to a woman who has brought him wealth and social position, but despite the outward appearance of success, he is a restless soul, a man who has found no happiness. When the story opens, he is building a great bridge across the St. Lawrence. On one of his business trips to London he meets Hilda Burgoyne, an actress he once had been in love with in his student days in Paris. They resume their former relationship, and for the next year Bartley lives a double life. After an agonizing struggle he makes the decision to leave his wife for Hilda, but at that moment he is summoned to Quebec by his subordinate in charge of the bridge construction. The bridge has developed alarming evidence of strain, and as Alexander inspects the structure, it falls into the river, killing him and many of the workmen.

Cather explained what she was trying to do in an interview with the *New York Sun*. "This is not the story of a bridge and how it was built, but of a man who built bridges. The bridge builder with whom this story is concerned began life a pagan, a crude force, with little respect for anything but youth and work and power. He married a woman of much more discriminating taste and much more clearly defined standards. He admires and believes in the social order of which she is really a part, though he has been only a participant. Just so long as his ever kindling energy exhibits itself only in his work everything goes well, but he runs the risk of encountering new emotional as well as new intellectual stimuli."

The new stimuli that Bartley meets produce actions that reveal his flawed moral nature. At the beginning of the story Lucius Wilson, his old philosophy professor from a Midwest college, tells him in the course of a visit: "I always used to feel that there was a weak spot where some day strain would tell. . . . The more dazzling the front you presented, the higher your façade rose, the more I expected to see a big crack zigzagging from top to bottom." Wilson, however, at the moment of telling this believes he must have been mistaken. Bartley is at the peak of his career, famous and internationally known. Wilson was right, of course, for Bartley's life comes crashing down at the end, just as his bridge comes tumbling down. He had put too much stress and strain on his life, and he had figured too closely the stresses and strains on his bridge. He had loved his wife, who even at the end "still was, as she had always been, Romance for him, and whenever he was deeply stirred he turned to her." But Winifred with all her charm, taste, and wealth lacked one vital thing, "the energy of youth." This missing *élan vital* he found in

Hilda. The opposing forces of his wife and his mistress ultimately open the fissure that Wilson had foreseen.

As the novel moves towards its denouement, it is Bartley's dalliance with Hilda that delays by a fatal day the telegram warning him of the bridge's danger. He arrives too late to head off disaster, and thus the novel ends by bringing into appropriate conjunction the bridge collapse as symbol of failure and the tragic death of the bridge builder. To give the novel an ironic Jamesian twist at the end, the tragedy that takes place is a lesser one than Bartley can foresee as the train rushes him toward his stricken bridge. In planning to leave his wife for Hilda, he realizes that he will become an outcast doomed to drag out a restless existence "on the Continent—Cannes, Hyères, Algiers, Cairo—among smartly dressed, disabled men of every nationality; forever going on journeys that led nowhere; hurrying to catch trains that he might just as well miss." He perceives the crack in his moral nature before the crack in his bridge hurls him into oblivion. Like John Marcher's in "The Beast in the Jungle," Bartley's self-awareness comes too late. Cather adds further irony in concealing from Winifred her husband's infidelity, for the unmailed letter he had written announcing his decision to leave her goes down with him. But when the body is fished from the river, the writing is illegible, and in after years she holds the torch for his memory. Wilson comments at the end: "She never lets him go. It's the most beautiful and dignified sorrow I've ever known."

Although the world of Bartley Alexander is not the characteristic world of Willa Cather, one should not, as she did, relegate the book to a sort of limbo outside the canon of her works. It fits well into the pattern of her life and her total accomplishment. The character of Bartley foreshadows other characters, and in him the author subconsciously reveals herself. Thematically the novel is linked to the reading of her formative years and to her lifelong preoccupations. In its plot *Alexander's Bridge* uses materials that look both forward and backward.

Bartley is a westerner, a self-made man who has come from somewhere out in Cather country and successfully stormed the eastern citadels. As he reaches forty-three, the spectre of middle age haunts him, and he realizes that he has not got from life all he wants. The crack in his moral nature is caused by his inability to harmonize desire with possibility, and the resultant conflict looks ahead to the similar struggle of Godfrey St. Peter in *The Professor's House*. Alexander's restless dissatisfaction with his Eastern life also anticipates Jim Burden, the narrator in *My Ántonia*. Willa Cather, managing editor of a great national magazine, might have spoken for herself the words she gives Bartley when Wilson comes to visit: "You work like the devil and think you're getting on, and suddenly you discover that you have only been getting yourself tied up. A million details drink you dry. Your life keeps going for things you don't want, and all the while you are being built alive into a social structure you don't care a rap about." Bartley has a divided personality, just as Cather admitted having herself, as she toiled on at *McClure's* and yearned for an escape to a nobler life. Although she managed to harmonize *her* conflicts, characters divided against themselves always fascinated her.

The foreshadowing of *The Professor's House* in this novel is particularly interesting. The creation of the minor character observer Wilson, Bartley's former teacher, looks ahead to Professor St. Peter, whose deep attachment to his brilliant student Tom Outland, informs the later novel. But more important are the parallels between Bartley's vision of himself as a small boy in the Midwest and St. Peter's memory of the boy he had left behind in Kansas. The concept of the second self in *The Professor's House* is more complex than in *Alexander's Bridge*, but the similarity of the two versions suggests perhaps a conscious reworking of the material in the later novel. To reinforce this notion is the appearance in both books of flower-giving scenes in Paris when both protagonists were students. The two passages are almost mirror images of each other. What makes these correspondences especially striking is that *The Professor's House* psychologically is the most autobiographical novel that Cather wrote.

The dominant theme in *Alexander's Bridge*, Bartley's yearning and seeking for something he can't find, runs like a *leitmotif* through Cather's fiction. It is an integral part of her temperament, for she had been searching and questing up to the time she wrote the novel. Bartley's desires are partly her desires, and later the dissatisfied yearning and seeking that motivate Marian Forrester in *A Lost Lady* and destroy Myra Henshawe in *My Mortal Enemy* carry on this preoccupation. Cather universalizes this theme by linking it to classic mythology. So unobtrusive is her use of myth, however, that many readers miss it completely. When Cather has Hilda sing "The Rising of the Moon," she intends to evoke the myth of Diana, the moon goddess, the object of man's desire. Keats's "Endymion," the story of a youth's search for the moon goddess, fed her creative imagination throughout her life. She also used another version of the myth when Bartley refers to the story of Actaeon, who was changed into a stag when he saw Diana naked. Hilda-Diana in this novel represents the lost youth that Bartley seeks, and for Cather nostalgia for youth is a perennial theme. Moon imagery, as Bernice Slote notes, is "one of the most deeply affective and complex symbols in Willa Cather's writing." She already had made use of this symbol in early stories, "Eric Hermannson's

Soul," "The Treasure of Far Island," and "The Enchanted Bluff," and it appears later in *The Song of the Lark*, *A Lost Lady*, and *My Mortal Enemy*.

Cather's use of color to convey meaning is one of the noteworthy aspects of her mature style. Here she uses it effectively to support the Hilda-Diana symbolism. As the full moon rising in the eastern sky is yellow, that color in Cather is associated with love and sexuality. In the novel Bartley first sees Hilda in a yellow gown and slippers, which she wears again the first time he is alone with her in her apartment. Then there are yellow irises in the apartment and a dry, yellow wine for dinner, which Bartley holds up against the yellow light of the candles. Later when Bartley and Hilda go riding in a carriage, it is a glorious sunny afternoon, and as the sun goes down behind them, they drive towards the gold-washed city which is surmounted by golden clouds. Cather had used yellow and gold imagery for the same purpose in "On the Gull's Road" to describe Alexandra Ebbling.

Cather also developed an effective use of contrasts in her fiction, and here she juxtaposes a number of elements. At the start of his career when Alexander is full of creative energy his first bridge is a suspension bridge "delicate as a cobweb hanging in the sky," but the bridge that collapses is "thousands of tons of ironwork" and after the disaster a "great iron carcass." The two women in his life are also opposites: Winifred, a person of distinction, tall, beautiful, proud, a woman who "moved with ease and certainty"; Hilda, vivacious, simple, generous, and giving, but a woman with an Irish temper. The golden moments in the middle of the novel contrast sharply with the cold, wet conclusion. At the last meeting between Bartley and Hilda in New York, Hilda comes into Bartley's apartment on a cold, raw, rainy day dripping wet with water oozing from her boots. She has come to announce her decision to marry, but before she leaves the lovers realize that they cannot part. Then Bartley rushes off to Canada.

The train ride through rural New England gives Cather a chance to insert a remarkable contrast, which gives poignancy to the final chapter. As Bartley looks out the car window, he catches a fleeting glimpse of a group of boys "camped on the edge of a little marsh, crouching under their shelter and looking gravely at their fire." This image takes him back to his boyhood "to a campfire on a sandbar in a Western river, and he wished he could go back and sit down with them." The nostalgia for lost youth juxtaposed against the reality of Bartley's present predicament makes perhaps the most memorable page in the book. Here for a moment Cather has dropped the world of Boston and London, bridges and theater, and is remembering her own past.

The plot of *Alexander's Bridge* is no less a part of the whole design of her fiction than is character and theme. The skeleton of the story is the eternal triangle, a basic plot she already had used with variations in " 'Death in the Desert,' " and "On the Gull's Road" and would use again in "The Bohemian Girl," *O Pioneers!*, and *A Lost Lady*. As one of the oldest plots in literature, the triangular relationship gains universality by being linked to the story of Helen of Troy. Where the myth of Diana reinforces theme, Paris's abduction of Helen underpins plot; but Cather's use of this ancient story is characteristically subtle. One needs to remember that Paris is called Alexander in the *Iliad* and that after the elopement of Paris and Helen (Hilda), the bereft wife Oenone (Winifred) mourns the death of her husband. Bartley's story is also the tale of a person killed by his inability to reconcile the contradictions in his character, and in this respect the novel foreshadows the stories of Myra Henshawe in *My Mortal Enemy*, Claude Wheeler in *One of Ours*, and the heroine in *Lucy Gayheart*. In the last of these three novels Cather reuses death by drowning, not only ending Lucy's life that way but also replicating Bartley's death in the drowning of Clement Sebastian. Finally, Cather's persistent view of romantic love as destructive is nowhere more clearly worked out than in *Alexander's Bridge*.

Cather began disparaging this novel almost as soon as she finished it. Two months after Houghton Mifflin brought it out in book form she wrote Louise Pound not to bother reading it but to wait for "The Bohemian Girl," which would be in *McClure's* for August. That, she thought, was *real*. When she wrote an introduction for a new edition of the book ten years later, she could find nothing to praise in her first novel. She had been a beginner, she wrote, and as a novice had felt that knowledge of life could be gained by going out to look at it, as one would go to a theater. The beginner has to work through "his youthful vanities and gaudy extravagances before he comes to deal with the material that is truly his own." After another nine years passed, she looked back on the book as a "studio picture" that had been the result of meeting some interesting people in London. "Like most young writers, I thought a book should be made out of 'interesting material,' and at that time I found the new more exciting than the familiar. The impressions I tried to communicate on paper were genuine, but they were very shallow."

It would be stretching the truth considerably to call Cather either a young writer or an inexperienced one at this time. She was thirty-eight when the novel appeared and had published at least three dozen stories since leaving college. It is also untrue that she could not tell the difference between stories in her best vein and tales in her Jamesian manner. When she had written Jewett in 1908, she had made a clear distinction between "On the Gull's Road" and "The Enchanted Bluff." She knew then that the western material was the real thing for her. The reason she did not mine her mother lode extensively until after writing *Alexander's Bridge* is probably the obvious one: she was indeed absorbed in her life as managing editor of *McClure's*, and that life was for her then the most interesting subject for fiction. It was only after she made the break from the magazine that she began to devote herself extensively to western settings and characters. She was being disingenuous in her 1922 preface to *Alexander's Bridge* when she quoted the advice she once received from Jewett: "Of course, one day you will write about your own country. In the meantime, get all you can. One must know the world *so well* before one can know the parish."

Cather's feelings about this novel at the time it was published really were ambivalent rather than negative. When she dismissed her novel as unreal in her letter to Pound, she was posing a little before her old friend, who was by then a professor of English literature. When Aunt Franc accused her of allowing a moral flimsiness in the character of Bartley Alexander, she defended the novel vigorously. She admitted the charge but argued that in order to produce work that is taken seriously as literature the writer has to have one of two things: either an unusual knowledge of a character or a peculiar sympathy with him. One cannot write about what one most admires. The writer by some accident must have seen into his character very deeply, and it is this accident of intense realization that gives the writing tone and distinction, lifts it above the commonplace. She went on to say that she had tried to write about several people she admired greatly, but the stories turned out to be utterly commonplace, just like hundreds of other stories. She admitted that she did not know why this was; she wished she knew. She was sure, however, that *O Pioneers!*, which she had just finished, was a much better book, and she was sure her aunt would like the protagonist of it. She must have found the answer to her question very soon when she realized what she had accomplished in her second novel. The answer had been in one of Jewett's letters all the time: "*The thing that teases the mind over and over for years, and at last gets itself put down rightly on paper—whether little or great, it belongs to Literature.*" The material that went into *Alexander's Bridge* or stories about people she admired was too immediate, too recently acquired, to "belong to literature."

Rereading the novel today, one is inclined to agree with Lewis, who discovered after Cather died that the book really is pretty good. The work is contrived and somewhat artificial, but "When it at last moves into its true theme, the moral division in a man's nature, it gathers an intensity and power which come from some deeper level of feeling, and which overflood whatever is 'shallow' or artificial in the story." The novel is in fact a very competent piece of work, tightly written, well organized, very professional. Theme and symbol are carefully worked out, and the focus always remains on the main character. The novel is somewhat bloodless, however, a performance of the head rather than the heart, and it does not take hold of the reader the way Cather's later books do. And it is no doubt true that the novel would be forgotten today if the author had not gone on to write *My Ántonia*, *A Lost Lady*, and *Death Comes for the Archbishop*.

The narrative technique is very well managed for a first novel. The story opens with Professor Wilson arriving in Boston to visit, and the invention of this character gives Cather an observer who can comment on the characters and action. He returns in the middle of the novel and in the epilogue. Throughout the novel the action is presented dramatically as the characters interact with one another. When the narration moves into the mind of the protagonist, his reflections are cogent and sometimes moving. There are some first-rate scenes: Bartley's first view of Hilda on the stage, his first dinner in her apartment, their carriage ride outside London. Especially effective is Bartley's Atlantic crossing in winter when he is torn between his ties to Winifred and his desire for Hilda. Cather places him alone in a deck chair bundled up against the weather, "watching the low, dirty sky and the beating of the heavy rain upon the iron-colored sea." The outer weather mirrors Bartley's inner weather. This method of describing people in terms of natural elements may well have been a lesson learned from *The Country of the Pointed Firs*. Finally, the descriptions of Boston and London convey well Cather's own delight in discovering the charms of Chestnut Street, the Charles River, The Thames Embankment, Westminister Bridge, and the Elgin Marbles in the British Museum.

Despite the novel's competence, the character of Alexander was a little more than she could achieve at this point in her career. He doesn't really come to life, as Professor St. Peter or Archbishop Latour do in the later novels. Susan Rosowski attributes this failure to the novel's basic concept: "*Alexander's Bridge* is an allegory about art in which Cather explored relationships among the creative energy of the artist, the spiritual world, and the physical one. In some respects the major characters *are* these ideas: Alexander is energy, a pagan force with the potential for either order or chaos; Winifred and Hilda are emblems of two worlds of experience, spiritual and physical." Neither woman is comprehensible by human motivation, and the plot is more accurately described by the creative process than by human relationships.

Contemporary reviewers, however, treated the novel kindly. It did not get any major reviews, but only one of the notices, which ran from one hundred to two hundred words, disparaged the work. The others saw much promise in this first novel, and they were in general agreement that the writing was superior. The *New York Times* praised the dramatic situations and the clever conversation; the *Outlook* thought it "brilliant in its reflections of character and life, and admirably restrained and graceful in form and diction." The *Atlantic* welcomed this low-keyed study of passion, which developed its plot and character with "dignity and reticence": "The author's workmanship is deft and skillful, and the swift, clean stroke tells on every page."

Looked after and ministered to by McClung, Cather passed a happy and productive autumn at Cherry Valley. As soon as she finished the revisions of *Alexander's Bridge*, she started work on a long western story. She wrote Cameron Mackenzie on November third that she had sent her manuscript to him in care of Miss Lewis, and two days later wrote McClure that she was at work on another story. She thought it would be about the length of the bridge-builder tale, but it turned out to be her longest story to date rather than a second short novel. She was working on "The Bohemian Girl," her first important use of the immigrant families and the Divide. When she finished this story, she immediately began another, using much the same material. She gave it the tentative title "Alexandra." It remained unfinished until the following year when it became a part of *O Pioneers!*.

The six hard years at *McClure's* took their toll on her health. As a young woman she enjoyed excellent health, but in January, 1912, she was back in the hospital for the third winter out of four. Just what the illness was is not known, but she referred to it in a letter to Mariel Gere as a sharp illness and an exhausting little surgical operation. In February she wrote Zoë Akins from Boston that she had been in a private hospital for several weeks and was then recuperating in Margaret Deland's home. She also was reading proofs for the book version of *Alexander's Bridge* flat on her back. When she was well enough to travel, Elizabeth Sergeant, then visiting her family in Boston, escorted her to New York by Pullman. Cather always hated herself when she was sick, and as the two women left Boston, she was "in this typical down-hearted state of mind." Sergeant remembered: "we watched the flying fields and blue bays, till at last . . . she cast her mood like an old skin, and accepted the world as good again." By later February she was back in New York in her apartment on Washington Place, packing for her trip to Arizona, and feeling very fit.

On 2 March 1912 she attended Howells's seventy-fifth birthday dinner in the ballroom at Sherry's. It was another of Colonel Harvey's gala affairs such as Cather had attended when Mark Twain celebrated his seventieth. This time Harvey invited four hundred guests and managed to get President Taft to come to honor his fellow Ohioan. Besides Taft, other speakers were novelist Winston Churchill, William Allen White, and playwright Augustus Thomas. After the speeches an actor, James Barnes, came in dressed as Silas Lapham and recited verses thanking Howells for his contribution to American literature. Cather still had no enthusiasm for poor, dear, gentle Mr. Howells, but she was rather pleased at the storm of applause and affection displayed for the old dean of American letters.

She had been in a mellow mood the day before the Howells dinner when she wrote Sergeant. Mackenzie had taken her to lunch a few days before and had asked if she didn't have something to show for her sojourn in the country. She told him she had a story too long and too highbrow for *McClure's,* but he guessed he would like to read it. She gave him "The Bohemian Girl" and the next day met him for tea at the Brevoort Hotel. He astonished her by offering seven hundred and fifty dollars. She laughed and replied that *McClure's* never paid such prices for fiction; her story couldn't possibly be worth more than five hundred. He thought she was being silly not to take what he offered, but if she insisted, he would pay her five hundred, provided she agreed to accept the larger figure the next time. Mackenzie was a shrewd editor and recognized quality and knew Cather was becoming a valuable literary property. The magazine also had been getting a good many letters praising *Alexander's Bridge,* which had just begun in the February issue.

Cather was so elated by this success that she indiscreetly told Mackenzie of an idea she had for a novel about an opera singer. He told everyone in the office, and the business department wanted to advertise a forthcoming new serial by Cather in its next prospectus. Under these conditions, she said, she would need the imperturbable nerves of Rex Beach to write the story. The entire episode was giving her a case of stage fright. She did not write an opera singer novel for another three years, if indeed *The Song of the Lark* had its genesis at this time. She learned a lesson from this experience and in the future was very secretive about what she was writing.

Cather left New York on March seventh to begin her pivotal journey to the Southwest. She planned to stop off in Pittsburgh at the McClungs' for a few days before continuing west, but the day after she arrived, Isabelle's mother had a near-fatal stroke. Cather waited and watched with the family and put off continuing her trip until Mrs. McClung had partially recovered. She took advantage of the unexpected delay to revise "The Bohemian Girl" and add a new scene. When she got to Red Cloud on her way to Arizona, she drove out into the Bohemian country and found that she had struck just the right note in her story. When Akins wrote to congratulate her on the tale after it came out in the August *McClure's,* Cather admitted she thought it pretty good. She never reprinted it, however, and in her old age decided it really was a rather immature piece of work.

"The Bohemian Girl" begins with the return of Nils Ericson to his farm home on the Divide, twelve years after leaving as a restless young man to seek his fortune in the old country. His mother and older brothers have stayed on the land, amassing large holdings and prospering materially. His older brother Olaf, stolid, dull, and taciturn, has married Clara Vavrika, the girl Nils was in love with when he left. Clara, the daughter of Joe Vavrika, who keeps a tavern in the Bohemian community, is a handsome, vivacious, unhappy woman. Life with the smug, self-satisfied Olaf is slowly stiffling her natural vitality. None of the Ericsons like Clara, but Olaf, who is in politics, puts up with her in order not to lose the Bohemian vote. Clara finds her only happiness in daily visits to her aging father, whose temperament is like her own. Nils resolves to take Clara away from this deadening environment, and by degrees she succumbs to his urgings. The story ends, except for an epilogue, with the lovers riding off in the night to catch the midnight flyer and escape from Nebraska.

This is as romantic a plot as Cather ever devised. For the moment she had abandoned her belief in the destructive nature of romantic love and left the future of the lovers to the reader's imagination. The story borrows its title, though not its plot, from the romantic nineteenth-century opera by the same name, and Cather also uses its nostalgic aria, "I dreamt that I dwelt in Marble Halls." The story has a fairy-tale quality about it, as though Nils were Prince Charming who awakens the sleeping beauty, or perhaps a better analogue might be a poem by one of Cather's favorites, Keats, "The Eve of St. Agnes," in which young Porphyro steals into the castle and elopes with the fair Madeline under the noses of her kinsmen.

> And they are gone: aye, ages long ago
> These lovers fled away into the storm.

In the epilogue, which probably is the section added to the story in Pittsburgh, she tries to bring the tale back to reality. Eric, Nils' younger brother, who is unhappy on the farm after Nils leaves, attempts to follow him but gets only as far as Iowa before the ties to home and mother prove too strong. Cather might better have left the story a fairy tale, as the final episode is a definite anticlimax.

She was wrestling with a problem, however. She was discovering with affection Nebraska as her flood subject, but neither of her main characters can live there. For Clara life as a member of the Ericson clan is slowly killing her. If she stays, she will become as emotionally starved and dull as any of them.

For Nils the homecoming is a disillusionment. He has returned thinking he would like to settle down on a farm of his own, but the hard, money-grubbing materialism of his brothers repels him. Thus the story ends with Eric returning quietly to the old homestead prepared to resume milking the cows and slopping the hogs for the rest of his life.

When Cather called this story real compared with *Alexander's Bridge*, she wasn't thinking about the plot, obviously, but the Nebraska setting. That part of the story *is* real, and in it Cather had ceased admiring and had begun to remember.

The sights that greet Nils and the feelings he has on his return are Cather's, and she speaks in her own voice in describing them. As Nils steps off the train and starts for the farm: "He gave the town, as he would have said, a wide berth, and cut through a great fenced pasture, emerging, when he rolled under the barbed wire at the farther corner, upon a white dusty road which ran straight up from the river valley to the high prairies, where the ripe wheat stood yellow and the tin roofs and weathercocks were twinkling in the fierce sunlight." Later he is picked up by a farmer who comes along in a wagon, and as they rattle along the farmer talks to him about the people and the land: "Just now he was experiencing something very much like homesickness, and he was wondering what had brought it about. The mention of a name or two, perhaps; the rattle of a wagon along a dusty road; the rank, resinous smell of sunflowers and ironweed, which the night damp brought up from the draws and low places; perhaps, more than all, the dancing lights of the motor that had plunged by." His mother, who owned one of the fourteen cars in the area, has just passed the wagon, but Nils had not wanted to confront her until he reached the old homestead.

There are some highly evocative scenes in the story, and when Cather was remembering the Bohemian community she was particularly good. Joe Vavrika's little garden between his saloon and house is a magical place. It was "enclosed by a high board fence as tight as a partition, and in summer Joe kept beer tables and wooden benches among the gooseberry bushes under his little cherry tree." Nils goes there to see Joe and relive the happy days when he and Clara were young and in love. Joe played the fiddle, Nils the flute, and Clara sang. Clara meets Nils there again on a Sunday afternoon, and Joe brings out from his cellar a rare bottle of Hungarian tokay that he has saved for years, a bottle worth its weight in gold. They drink the heavy yellow wine and once again sing and play. Cather was justified in being pleased with the Bohemian material when she went back to visit after writing the story.

Just as successful is the barn-raising party that Clara and Olaf give for all the neighbors. Again Cather uses yellow imagery of love and sexuality, as

Clara decorates the barn with goldenrod and yellow pumpkins, and as Nils stands in a golden light from the late afternoon sun. What is most memorable in this scene is the description of the old farm women, whom Cather had admired as a child. They were women of all nationalities, Danes, Swedes, Germans, besides the Norwegian Ericsons. They are seen chattering around the stall where Clara's Bohemian aunt is displaying her platters heaped with fried chicken, roasts of beef, boiled tongues, and baked hams "with cloves stuck in the crisp brown fat and garnished with tansy and parsley." Then after the old women have added their provisions to the groaning board, they retire "to the corner behind the pile of watermelons, put on their white aprons, and [fall] to their knitting and fancy work." This scene is vintage Cather.

After this scene of bucolic revelry, which the author herself compares to a Dutch genre painting, the story moves to its romantic climax. We are back into the fairy-tale atmosphere, as moonlight floods the silent land and the reaped fields lie yellow beneath it. Clara, who first appeared in black now comes riding along the dusty road dressed in white. She joins Nils, who is leaning against a straw stack in Olaf's wheat field. After a momentary reluctance, she slides down into his arms, and he kisses her. The scene ends: "There was a start, a thud of hoofs along the moonlit road, two dark shadows going over the hill; and then the great, still land stretched untroubled under the azure night. Two shadows had passed."

There are a number of striking things about this story that foreshadow Cather's later fiction. The Nils-Clara relationship looks ahead to the Emil-Marie subplot in *O Pioneers!*, though the story ends tragically in the latter work. Nils' selfish, materialistic brothers return as Alexandra's brothers, objects of Cather's scorn, as are subsequent characters like Ivy Peters in *A Lost Lady*, Nat Wheeler in *One of Ours*, and others who hold similar values. The one Ericson who comes off untarnished in Nils' indictment of his family is old Mrs. Ericson. Nils tells Clara: "You know, I'm so tickled to see mother . . . I didn't know I was so proud of her." After her preacher-husband's death she has remained on the home place farming her land as successfully as any of her sons farm theirs. In *O Pioneers!* she drops thirty years, her widowhood, and becomes Alexandra Bergson, one of Cather's most memorable heroines. "The Bohemian Girl," it seems in retrospect, was a practice piece for the book she really liked to consider her first novel.

After adding a scene to the story, Cather left for her journey to the Southwest and was gone from April until June. She spent five weeks in Red Cloud, then returned to Pittsburgh where she spent most of the remaining months of 1912. She was well, happy, and full of ideas, but she couldn't escape McClure's problems. He was being forced out of the editorship of the magazine, and he unloaded his troubles on his former managing editor. She couldn't believe the perfidy of his business associates. She couldn't believe there wasn't some way out of the situation. It made her not only sad but fighting Irish mad to have him tormented and bedeviled about money. It was so unjust. He had always been so generous with his employees. She thrashed about for a way to help him and offered her services free to write his autobiography. If she had money or influence, she wrote McClure, it would be his to command. Alas, she did not, but if her wits could help him, she would be pleased to put them at his service. She was not sure she could catch step with him in this enterprise, and she remembered there were some of the Christian Science articles she could not write the way he wanted them, but if as the old song said, "A Willing Heart Goes all the Way," they would do very well, for she was never more willing about a piece of work.

CHAPTER II

O Pioneers!

During the five weeks that Cather spent in Red Cloud in June and July, she again visited the Bohemian country and later watched the wheat harvest for the first time in years. On the edge of a wheat field, she told Sergeant, she had an idea for another story, one that she thought would terrify Mr. Greenslet. She was going to call it "The White Mulberry Tree." Two weeks later she was back in Pittsburgh happily secluded in her sewing-room study at the Mc-Clungs' home and eager to get to work. She began with the new story, the most tragic tale she yet had written, a Nebraska version of the old story from *The Divine Comedy* of Paolo and Francesca, which she had quoted from in " 'A Death in the Desert.' " In the story Frank Shabata, a Bohemian farmer, surprises and kills his wife and her lover Emil Bergson as they lie together in his orchard under a white mulberry tree.

When she finished this tale, she got out the manuscript of "Alexandra" and looked it over. She had read it to Lewis before starting west, but she had not been satisfied with it. It began, Lewis recalled, where *O Pioneers!* starts and continued almost unchanged through Part I ("The Wild Land"), some seventy pages into the novel in its book version. It ended with Alexandra's dream, which now appears in Part III. The story in that form seemed unfinished, but she did not know what to do next. So she put it away and left for Arizona. She knew it was good, however, in her best vein. In Pittsburgh she put "Alexandra" and "The White Mulberry Tree" side by side and suddenly realized that the two stories belonged together. Sergeant asked her later about this moment of illumination: "She said she could only describe this coming together of the two elements . . . as a sudden inner explosion and enlightenment. She had experienced it before only in the conception of a poem. Now she would hope always for similar experience in creating a novel, for the explosion seemed to bring with it the inevitable shape that is not plotted but designs itself." She became a strong believer in organic form, and henceforth let the material dictate the organization and structure of her novels.

She explained this principle in a striking analogy in *The Song of the Lark*. When Thea Kronborg goes to Arizona to rest and find herself, she spends her summer days among the ruins of the ancient cliff dwellings in Panther Canyon. Daily she climbs down to the stream at the bottom of the canyon to bathe. One morning she is struck by the significance of the shards of broken pottery she has been admiring among the ruins. She had wondered why the Indian women lavished such loving care on decorating the ordinary jars used in their daily lives to carry water from the floor of the canyon to their cliff dwellings. As she stands in the stream bathing, it comes to her. The world of the mesa Indians centered on water, the life-giving liquid that she was pouring over herself. "The stream and the broken pottery: what was any art but an effort to make a sheath, a mould in which to imprison for a moment the shining, elusive element which is life itself—life hurrying past us and running away, too strong to stop, too sweet to lose? The Indian women had held it in their jars. In the sculpture she had seen in the Art Institute, it had been caught in a flash of arrested motion. In singing, one made a vessel of one's throat and nostrils and held it on one's breath, caught the stream in a scale of natural intervals." The same principle applied to literature. One made a sheath with words to capture the rushing flow of life. The structural principle of fiction must be organic; form must follow function.

In her 1922 preface to *Alexander's Bridge* she put it another way. When a writer begins to work with his own material, by which she meant for her, Nebraska farmers and their lives, "he has less and less power of choice about the moulding of it. It seems to be there of itself, already moulded. . . . In working with this material he finds that he need have little to do with literary devices; he comes to depend more and more on something else—the thing by which our feet find the road home on a dark night." She added that this is what Henri Bergson, whom she read carefully, "calls the wisdom of intuition as opposed to that of intellect." With this to shape his course "a writer contrives and connives only as regards mechanical details, and questions of effective presentation, always debatable. About the essential matter of his story he cannot argue."

She applied this organic principle when she found her "own material" and wrote *O Pioneers!* The presentation is loosely episodic, and the story paces itself. When she felt like digressing, as she did near the beginning in the chapter introducing old Ivar, she did not hesitate to do so. When she finished sketching in the background of the novel in the first section, "The Wild Land," she did not worry about skipping ten years before resuming the story. After the tragedy in which Frank kills his wife and her lover in the orchard, she wrote another section, all anticlimactic, to finish off the novel. Yet she succeeds brilliantly in creating in about fifty-two thousand words a saga of Nebraska extending from pioneering days to about 1900. Birth, growth, love, death—it is all there.

It took her the next five months, however, to work this out. *McClure's* would not let her alone, and she had to make two trips to New York in late August and September 1912. During her first trip she planned what she thought was going to be her winter's work. She promised two stories to the magazine by December, which she never wrote, and agreed to spend five or six months in the office after the new year. The chief task she performed for *McClure's* that fall was surgery on a serial, *My Little Sister* by Elizabeth Robins, which began in December. She cut it in half and made a better novel out of it, she thought, than the full-length book version that appeared later. She hardly got out of the office during this trip and saw almost no one, though she did spend several evenings with the Arlisses, who were celebrating George's triumph as Disraeli. The magazine agreed to let her stay in Pittsburgh until the end of the year, for which she was grateful. She wrote Sergeant that this extension of her leave was due to the great success of "The Bohemian Girl." The business office had received a lot of mail praising the story, and the magazine finally had realized that she was more valuable as a writer than as an editor. During the second visit she combined magazine and private business, for Lewis had found them a new apartment on Bank Street in the Village. They leased the apartment and Lewis planned to move in right away. Cather would join her after the first of January. This would be her home for the next fifteen years.

Back in Pittsburgh she worked steadily through the rest of the fall. She increased the length of "Alexandra" by fifty percent and made the necessary splices and adjustments to incorporate "The White Mulberry Tree." She wrote Akins at the end of October that the new book would be three times as long as "The Bohemian Girl," and the country itself would be the hero—or heroine. She also thought the people, the Swedes and Bohemians, were rather interesting. She had written a poem about the country, "Prairie Spring," which *McClure's* would publish in December:

> Evening and the flat land,
> Rich and sombre and always silent;

The miles of fresh-plowed soil,
Heavy and black, full of strength and harshness;
The growing wheat, the growing weeds,
The toiling horses, the tired men;
The long empty roads,
Sullen fires of sunset, fading,
The eternal, unresponsive sky.
Against all this, Youth,
Flaming like the wild roses,
Singing like the larks over the plowed fields,
Flashing like a star out of the twilight;
Youth with its insupportable sweetness,
Its fierce necessity,
Its sharp desire,
Singing and singing,
Out of the lips of silence,
Out of the earthy dusk.

This poem became the epigraph for the novel. She had not yet decided to take her title for the book from Whitman's "Pioneers! O Pioneers!," but she anticipated the naming of the novel by trying for the first time some Whitmanesque free verse.

In December she wrote Sergeant that she was on the home stretch. The new story would be better than "The Bohemian Girl," but the writing had been difficult because it was so much more closely knit than anything she had done previously. When she left Pittsburgh to return to New York, she took the completed manuscript. Whether or not she offered the novel to *McClure's* for serialization is not known, but it was not published in any magazine before it appeared in book form. She sent the manuscript to Greenslet at Houghton Mifflin and professed to be very much surprised when he wanted to publish it. When he urged his colleagues to accept the manuscript, he reported that the novel "ought to . . . definitely establish the author as a novelist of the first rank." She signed a contract in late March with more favorable terms than she got for *Alexander's Bridge*, and the book came out at the end of June 1913.

Once back in New York, she plunged again into magazine work and at the same time had to get settled in the new apartment. She had managed, however, to cut her duties at *McClure's* in half in order to have a continuous stretch of free time for writing. She was delighted with the new apartment, which was roomy, quiet and just what she wanted, and never had expected to find a place quite so desirable at a rent she could afford. The same maid, who had been with her for four years, still worked for her, and she never had been so comfortable or happy. She was perfectly well that winter, enough to enjoy everything, work and play alike. Getting the apartment fixed up, however, had been strenuous. During January the place was full of painters, paperers, and furniture dealers. She had had to write an article for *McClure's* while the painters were at work around her.

Number 5 Bank Street was a wide, five-story, brick house converted into apartments. A wide staircase ran up through the middle of the building, dividing it into two apartments on each floor. The one Cather and Lewis rented was on the second floor and had seven big rooms with high ceilings and large windows. The house had thick walls which shut out the cold in the winter and the heat in the summer. There was no central heating, however, and the sitting and dining rooms were heated by coal grates in open fire places. They had to carry coal and build their own fires, but they had so much more space and light than in their cramped quarters on Washington Place that they did not mind a few inconveniences, and they bought small gas stoves to heat the bedrooms. Cather even had a little study off the sitting room. She wrote her aunt that she was now the proud owner of four beautiful Persian rugs. They had very little furniture when they moved in but bought at auction mahogany chests and a dining room table. An Italian carpenter built them low open shelves to house their growing collection of books. Cather hung on the walls copies of Italian Renaissance paintings she had bought in Italy and placed over the mantle a large etching of George Sand by Thomas Couture. Later she added a bust of Keats that she inherited from Mrs. Fields.

Bank Street was a quiet corner of Greenwich Village just off Greenwich Avenue. Number 5 was three houses from the corner on the north side of the street, which gave the sitting room at the front of the house a sunny southern exposure. All the buildings on the street were four or five story brick houses built in the nineteenth century. They were set close to the street, but there were trees planted in the sidewalks. Bank Street was narrow, did not lead anywhere in particular, and traffic was minimal. The area still has escaped most of the change that has overtaken Manhattan through the years, and Cather could recognize Bank Street today. Her own house, however, was torn down about 1930, along with three others beside it to make room for an apartment house, but the rest of the block is intact. The location was convenient. Cather did her shopping at the nearby Jefferson Market. She liked to go out early to buy her meat and produce before starting her morning's work, and found the immigrant vendors of fruits and vegetables more interesting than most of the white collar people she came into contact with. The private

Society Library, to which she belonged and used often, also was close to her apartment, and the Metropolitan Opera House, which Cather and Lewis went to constantly, was only ten minutes by bus up Seventh Avenue. Caruso, Garden, Fremstad, Farrar, Tetrazzini, and many other stars sang regularly, and Toscanini conducted two or three times a week. The area around Washington Square where they formerly lived was becoming very commercial with dance halls, theaters, restaurants, and cabarets, but Bank Street was a quiet backwater with a bit of Old World charm.

From her quiet corner Cather was an observer rather than a participant in the yeasty ferment in Greenwich Village in the years before World War I. The area swarmed with intellectual Bohemians, who published *The Masses* and embraced Marx, Freud, feminism, and worked for woman's suffrage. Cather had no interest in these matters, and there is no evidence that she knew any of the leaders such as Max Eastman, John Sloan, Louis Untermeyer, John Reed, or Margaret Sanger. She did come into contact with Floyd Dell, who wrote an enthusiastic review of *O Pioneers!*, and Carl Van Vechten became a friend. She may have attended Mabel Dodge's famous salon on occasion, as everyone in Greenwich Village seems to have gone there, but her friendship with Dodge came after she married Tony Luhan and was living in New Mexico. About the only thing Cather had in common with these neighbors was her tolerance for a variety of life styles.

The article Cather was writing when her apartment was being painted was one of a series she had promised *McClure's*. She still needed some income from the magazine, because the serial rights to *Alexander's Bridge* and the book royalties, though she said they came to a nice little sum, were not enough to live on for very long. In addition she had agreed to write McClure's autobiography for him, and that would take weeks out of the coming months. Thus it was back to the old grind of journalism, at least part time, for the next nine months. The article she produced first was more drama criticism, "Plays of Real Life," which *McClure's* ran in its March number.

She reviewed half a dozen plays of the 1912–13 season, four of which she thought were first rate: "A dramatic season that presents four pieces so fresh and unhackneyed must be accounted a good one." The good ones that she noticed were *The Mind the Paint Girl*, one of Pinero's witty plays about the theater; *Fanny's First Play*, a vehicle that allowed Shaw plenty of scope for satiric humor at the expense of drama critics; *Hindle Wakes* by Stanley Houghton, a play that upset all the conventions; and *Milestones* by Arnold Bennett and Edward Knoblauch, the most original play of the year. She gave the largest amount of space to the last of these plays because it dealt in a very eloquent way with a theme that interested her very much: youth versus age.

There were no big scenes, no brilliant dialogue; but nevertheless it was intensely dramatic. "All good plays begin with the author's power of creating character. If his people are real enough and interesting enough, anything that happens to them is interesting." One might make the same comment about the novel she had just finished. The major theme of this play was the conflict between youth and age, and Cather agreed with the playwright's view: "Youth is the only really valuable thing in the world . . . because it is force, potency, a physiological fact. . . . The individual possesses this power for only a little while. . . . If he devotes these years to self-sacrifice, to caring for an aged parent or helping to support his brother's children, God may reward him, but Nature will not forgive him. . . . The world *could* get on without the old; without the young it can not." Nostalgia for youth is a perennial theme in Cather's work.

After Cather sent *O Pioneers!* to Houghton Mifflin, she began to have qualms about the book. To get an opinion from someone whose judgment she trusted, she mailed the manuscript to Sergeant, who then was living in Paris, and asked for an honest evaluation. She thought there was some careless writing in it, but on the whole it was either pretty good or an utter fizzle. It was all about crops and cows; yet it seemed interesting to her, and anyway she had done what she intended to do. She let the country be the hero and had taken the little themes that hide in the grass and worked them into the story the best she could, as she thought Dvořák had done in his *New World Symphony* after spending some weeks in pioneer Nebraska in the early eighties. The story was one, she added, that she always wanted to write.

She later said that she wrote the book for herself and "ignored all the situations and accents that were then generally thought to be necessary." The novel of the soil, she remembered, had not yet become fashionable, and she didn't expect people to see anything in such a slow-moving story, especially one set in Nebraska, which was "distinctly déclassé as a literary background." She quoted a critic who had said: "I simply don't care a damn what happens in Nebraska, no matter who writes about it." This pose of fierce independence she adopted later, but in 1913 she was as eager as any new novelist to win recognition. She watched and clipped reviews, sent them to friends and relatives, and often wrote letters of thanks to reviewers who were especially sympathetic. But she was genuinely in doubt when she sent the manuscript to Sergeant.

The story that Sergeant read in Paris opens one January day in 1883 in the little prairie town of Hanover (Red Cloud). Alexandra Bergson, about twenty, and her very little brother Emil have come to town on errands with their German neighbor, Carl Lindstrum. The opening scene also introduces little Marie Tovesky from Omaha, who is visiting her Bohemian uncle. The story then moves to the Bergson farm on the Divide where Alexandra's father, a Swedish immigrant, is dying after eleven years of heroic effort to farm the land, which, as the novel opens, "seemed to overwhelm the little beginnings of human society that struggled in its sombre wastes." He bequeaths to his daughter and sons a full section of unencumbered land, however, and as he dies charges Alexandra, the oldest child, to look after her brothers and mother and farm the land faithfully. John Bergson's death is followed by three fat years and three lean years, after which Lou and Oscar want to quit farming and leave the land. Alexandra says no; now is the time to mortgage their land and buy more. In ten years, she believes, they will be prosperous, independent landowners, and farmers with vision will be rewarded. The wild land is about to be tamed.

Alexandra is right, and when Part II opens a decade later the country is prosperous, Lou and Oscar have their own farms, and Alexandra is the proprietor of "one of the richest farms on the Divide." She lives a lonely life however; Carl, her closest friend, moved away during the hard times; her brothers, now selfish, dull, and mercenary, have grown away from her. She lives for her youngest brother, Emil, now twenty-one; her best friend is young Marie Tovesky, who has married a moody, volatile Bohemian farmer, Frank Shabata. Carl comes back but is driven away by Lou and Oscar, who think he only wants Alexandra's money; Marie and Emil fall in love, and the tragedy takes place under the white mulberry tree. Alexandra, shattered by the event, faces a bleak future, but Carl hears of the tragedy and returns. As the novel ends, Alexandra and Carl plan to marry.

Sergeant read the manuscript with excitement and tried it out on the French family she was living with. "*Très original!*" they thought. "No Frenchwoman for centuries had seen virgin soil. Alexandra's return from the river farms singing a Swedish song, sure of the future of the wheat on the Divide, was poetry and legend." Then Sergeant gave it to an American woman friend who reacted with equal enthusiasm. Though she was a proper Bostonian, she said it made her feel proud of her country to read of the struggle and triumph of the immigrant farmers on the prairie. By the time Cather received these reports in April she was reading proof on the novel and still having doubts about it. She agreed with Sergeant's one criticism that the book had no skeleton but defended it on grounds that the country she was writing about had no skeleton either. There were no rocks or ridges; its black soil ran through one's fingers. It was all soft, and somehow that influenced the mood and the very structure of the novel.

McClung came for a three weeks' visit in April, and at the end of the month Cather went up to Boston to see Mrs. Fields, then seventy-nine. It may have been on this visit that Cather went with Professor George Woodberry of Columbia, another of Mrs. Fields' guests, to call on Amy Lowell. It was an extraordinary experience that Cather couldn't later recount without getting mad. Because Woodberry was much interested in seeing Lowell's Keats manuscripts, Mrs. Fields arranged for Lowell to invite both her guests to her house. Lowell sent her chauffeur and limousine to pick them up and take them to her Victorian mansion in Brookline. When they arrived, Lowell was upstairs in bed dictating to her secretary. They waited and waited and waited; they were served tea and excuses by a houseguest. Finally the high priestess of imagism rushed in on them acting as if nothing were amiss. After a polite interval Woodberry asked to see the Keats materials. Lowell went to her safe, unlocked it, and spread the manuscripts out on the library table. When Woodberry reached to pick up one of the documents, Lowell snatched it up, held it under Woodberry's nose, and said no one but she could touch her precious manuscripts. Cather was outraged. Such discourtesy towards an eminent scholar, Cather wrote in 1942, still made her gorge rise after all those years. Mrs. Fields was greatly distressed, though Cather gave her only an edited version of the visit. One hopes that Cather remembered that three years before, she had turned down a poem Lowell had submitted to *McClure's*. From that time on Cather hated Amy Lowell with a passion, and when Greenslet urged her to write Lowell's biography after she died in 1925, Cather said she would be just as likely to write a history of the Chinese empire. She wouldn't do it for the whole amount of the Lowell estate.

Cather was unable to go west that summer and be on hand in Nebraska when her book came out. She waited eagerly for the reaction from the home folks and was delighted when reviewers from the prairie states were uniformly pleased with the novel. The reviews were so hearty and had such a note of personal enthusiasm about them, she wrote Sergeant. "What has pleased me the most," she told an interviewer, "is that the reviewers in all those Western States say the thing seems to them true to the country and the people." While she was writing the novel, she had told Akins that she wanted to shine a little for the home folks. In her youth she never was able to make much of an impression in Nebraska, because there was not much she could do then that people would admire, except excel in horseback riding. One cannot get a rise out of a cow with a sonnet, she said. She had gotten plenty of rises out of Nebraskans with her drama criticism when she was in college, but it was different now. She had done something she was proud of, as well as the people in Nebraska. She had at last found her subject in the memories of her youth. When she sent a presentation copy of the novel to Carrie Sherwood, she wrote in it: "This was the first time I walked off on my own feet—everything before was half real and half an imitation of writers whom I admired. In this one I hit the home pasture and found that I was Yance Sorgeson and not Henry James." Yance Sorgeson was a prosperous Norwegian farmer who died rich but had refused to give up the old ways and be impressed with his own success.

Nebraska reviewers no doubt were motivated partly by local pride, but also reviewers for eastern papers and national magazines were almost unanimously enthusiastic. Whether there really was a reviewer who didn't give a damn about Nebraska, this attitude does not appear in the notices. The reviewers recognized Cather as a new voice in American literature and her locale as a new country for American fiction. The *Nation* began its notice: "Few American novels of recent years have impressed us so strongly as this," and ended: "The sureness of feeling and touch, the power without strain, . . . lift it far above the ordinary product of contemporary novelists." The *New York Herald* welcomed the subject matter: "With a steady hand this author holds up the mirror of fiction to a people of our land little, if at all, seen therein before: the Scandinavian and Bohemian pioneers . . . we see these Old World pioneers adapting themselves to new conditions, identifying themselves with the prairie soil and becoming a voice in our national life. . . . This is a novel of considerable substance."

Floyd Dell, who would later become an important novelist himself, gave *O Pioneers!* a long review in the *Chicago Evening Post*. "It is touched with genius," he wrote; "it is worthy of being recognized as the most vital, subtle and artistic piece of the year's fiction." Dell despaired of being able to explain in a review why the novel impressed him so strongly. It didn't deal with large ideas; it didn't stun or dazzle. It only told the story of a girl and her younger brothers who live on a Nebraska farm: the story of their struggle with a stubborn land which almost crushed them before it suddenly smiled. And it was "the story, moreover, of such a friendship and love as came, sometimes with wistful autumnal sweetness and again with tragic passion, into their lives. It is not an extraordinary story. Everyone knows a dozen like it."

When Dorothy Canfield Fisher wrote praising the novel, Cather was greatly pleased and remembered the letter eight years later as the most helpful hand-up she had had. Her old friend knew better than anyone else the long way she had to go to get anywhere, and as she was a novelist herself, she knew the difficulties of the road. Cather wrote Fisher while she was working on *One of Ours* that it felt strange to come at last to the point of being able to write with calm enjoyment and certainness after such storms and struggles and shrieking off-key. Now she was able to keep the pitch, but what a lot of life one used up chasing "Bright Medusas."

After three quarters of a century critics have had plenty of time to figure out why this novel makes such a powerful impact. The dedication to Sarah Orne Jewett's memory provides one clue. Cather had followed her friend's precept that the thing which has teased the mind for years is the proper material for serious literature. Once she realized the truth of this she went on to create the best part of *The Song of the Lark*, *My Ántonia*, and *A Lost Lady*, from the flood of memories of her early years. In commenting on this principle, she explained: "The shapes and scenes that have 'teased' the mind for years . . . make a very much higher order of writing, and a much more costly, than the most vivid and vigorous transfer of immediate impressions." *The Country of the Pointed Firs* was a case in point. The sketches in that book were "living things caught in the open, with light and freedom and air-space about them. They melt into the land and the life of the land until they are not stories at all, but life itself." This is what Cather succeeded in doing in *O Pioneers!*

In continuing her discussion of Jewett's work, Cather went on to general-ize on the artist's relation to his work: "If he achieves anything noble, anything enduring, it must be by giving himself absolutely to his material. And this gift of sympathy is his great gift; it is the fine thing in him that alone can make his work fine." The artist fades away into the land and people of his heart only to be born again. These lessons from Jewett could not have been learned quickly or at an early age, and it took Cather twenty years to absorb them. In the light of her attitudes and ideas at the age of forty when *O Pioneers!* came out, it is not surprising that she wanted to consign most of her early writing to oblivion. But in those apprentice years she was learning technique.

No one sensitive to style can fail to be impressed with Cather's ability to use language to create images that linger in the mind. There are myriad passages that leave indelible impressions in this novel. The opening page reveals the little town of Hanover "anchored on a windy Nebraska tableland" and "trying not to be blown away." "A mist of fine snowflakes was curling and eddying about the cluster of low drab buildings huddled on the gray prairie, under a gray sky. The dwelling-houses were set about haphazard on the tough prairie sod; some of them looked as if they had been moved in overnight, and others as if they were straying off by themselves, headed straight for the open plain. None of them had any appearance of permanence, and the howling wind blew under them as well as over them." The first glimpse of little Marie Tovesky is arresting: "She was a dark child, with brown curly hair, like a brunette doll's, a coaxing little red mouth, and round, yellow-brown eyes. Every one noticed her eyes; the brown iris had golden glints that made them look like gold-stone, or, in softer lights, like that Colorado mineral called tiger-eye."

The passage that impressed Sergeant's French family is truly poetry and legend. After the three lean years Alexandra goes to visit the farms along the river. She realizes that her destiny lies on the high land of the Divide, and she turns the wagon and starts for home humming an old Swedish hymn. Her companion, little Emil, "wondered why his sister looked so happy. Her face was so radiant that he felt shy about asking her. For the first time, perhaps, since that land emerged from the waters of geologic ages, a human face was set toward it with love and yearning. It seemed beautiful to her, rich and strong and glorious. Her eyes drank in the breadth of it, until her tears blinded her. Then the Genius of the Divide, the great, free spirit which breathes across it, must have bent lower than it ever bent to a human will before. The history of every country begins in the heart of a man or woman." And at the end of the chapter: "Under the long shaggy ridges, she felt the future stirring." This is superior prose poetry. But equally poetic is Carl's memory of Alexandra as she came out in the morning to do her milking: "He used to feel, when he saw her coming with her free step, her upright head and calm shoulders, that she looked as if she had walked straight out of the morning itself."

Cather's fiction used to be called realistic, but her work is very much different from realism as defined by Howells and other writers of his school. The term realistic could only be applied to the verisimilitude of Cather's settings, the authenticity of her characters, the reality of the events that take place in her stories. She is no more a realist than Homer or Cervantes, though she shares with these writers the kind of reality that Auerbach calls mimesis. His discussion of the two styles in the *Odyssey* also characterizes Cather: "on the one hand fully externalized descriptions, uniform illustration, uninterrupted connection"; on the other hand "certain parts brought into high relief, others left obscure, abruptness, suggestive influence of the unexpressed." Cather is no nineteenth-century positivist; her world view derives, as does Jewett's, from Emerson: "Every natural fact is a symbol of some spiritual fact." And her method, once she reached *O Pioneers!*, is best described in terms of Wordsworth's definition of poetry as the "spontaneous overflow of powerful feelings . . . recollected in tranquility."

This philosophical position is clearly seen in the ending of the novel when Carl returns to Alexandra after the murder of Marie and Emil. Although

Emil has been cut off in the full promise of young manhood, Alexandra and the earth remain. Cather gives her human heroine the promise of a serene, untroubled old age, as she and Carl make plans to marry, but the earth is the ultimate heroine. Cather closes her story: "They went into the house together, leaving the Divide behind them, under the evening star. Fortunate country, that is one day to receive hearts like Alexandra's into its bosom, to give them out again in the yellow wheat, in the rustling corn, in the shining eyes of youth!" Cather belongs in the tradition of American Romanticism, and it is appropriate that her title should have come from Whitman's poem. The echoes of Emersonian transcendentalism in "Song of Myself" reverberate here in the theme of life everlasting:

> What do you think has become of the young and old men?
> And what do you think has become of the women and children?
> They are live and well somewhere,
> The smallest sprout shows there is really no death.

The transcendental theme in *O Pioneers!* is a wistful companion to the elegiac tone that characterizes much of Cather's best fiction. She is a backward-looking author, but the nostalgic note of the Arcadian theme that she struck in *April Twilights* and continued to strike has universal appeal. Everyone longs for the lost innocence of the Garden of Eden, and the older the reader, the greater the appeal. Cather's mourning for the glories of our pioneer past is part of the American mythology of the westward movement. She and Frederick Jackson Turner shared a common view of the poetry of American history. The story of the struggle to tame the wild land captures the imagination.

In contrast to the heroic pioneer days are the years of prosperity that follow. Cather depicts well the difference between the unbroken prairie of Part I and the land ten years later: "a vast checker-board, marked off in squares of wheat and corn; light and dark, dark and light. Telephone wires hum along the white roads, which always run at right angles. From the graveyard gate one can count a dozen gaily painted farmhouses; the gilded weather-vanes on the big red barns wink at each other across the green and brown and yellow fields." On the other hand, this material well-being is juxtaposed with Alexandra's loneliness and the smug, selfish, bigoted men her brothers have become. The new era has brought prosperity and comfort, but something fine has been lost; and in this new age that worships false gods tragedy strikes.

Contrast is an important part of Cather's literary technique. Besides the diversity between the wild land and the settled countryside, the early striving and the later materialism, other differences are sharply delineated. In temperament and personality Alexandra and her brothers are unlike; she is generous, humane, the brothers are mean-spirited, grasping. One sees the three in vivid scenes of confrontation, first over the brothers' desire to commit Ivar to the state insane asylum and second over their fear that Carl will marry Alexandra and get some of her property. The clash between the old values of simple faith, individuality, and integrity and the new gods of money and conformity is sharply focused in these scenes.

Other contrasts occur in events in the novel. Cather reenforces her theme of life everlasting in the death of Amédée, Emil's best friend in the French-Canadian community to the north. Amédée and Angélique, newly married and parents of a baby boy, are deliriously happy, and Amédée works like a devil for his family. He refuses to leave the wheat harvest when he feels sharp pains in his side, and three days later dies of a ruptured appendix. Cather follows this death with the annual confirmation of young communicants in the village. As Amédée is being laid out for burial, the youth are being taken into the church. Death occurs, but life goes on. And soon thereafter occurs the very different death by murder of Emil and Marie. Contrasts in character and within character also occur. The differences between Marie and her dour, excitable husband provide motivation for the tragedy in the orchard, and after Frank kills his wife and her lover, the man we see when Alexandra visits Frank in prison is broken in spirit and body. All of these juxtapositions add drama and tension to the narrative.

There are a number of elements in the novel that derive as much from Cather's own personality and viewpoint as from the logic of the story. Her views on marriage and love are reflected in the lives of various characters. The destructive nature of romantic love is exemplified in the tragic story of Emil and Marie, and her skepticism about marriage kills off Amédée. Alexandra's own plans to marry at the end of the novel illustrate the kind of marriage Cather thought safe. Alexandra says to Carl: "I think we shall be very happy. I haven't any fears. I think when friends marry, they are safe. We don't suffer like—those young ones." This is to be a calm union of middle-aged people after the passions of youth are spent. Cather gives her opera singer Thea Kronborg the same kind of marriage in her next novel. Cather's own suppression or sublimation of sex perhaps is revealed in Alexandra's recurring dream of being carried away by a strong man whose face she could never see. This dream, which sounds like a sexual fantasy, is followed by Alexandra, angry with herself, rushing down to the bathhouse off the kitchen to pour buckets of cold water over her body. The sense of let-down that Alexandra experiences after her struggles are over is also characteristic of Cather. If Alexandra had been a scholar, she might have quoted her creator's favorite line from Michelet: "*Le but n'est rien; le chemin, c'est tout.*" Cather did not know it yet, but Alexandra's feeling anticipates her own depression after she became a Pulitzer Prize winner, rich, and famous.

Because so many of Cather's characters were suggested by real people, one would like to know who, if anyone, sat for the portrait of Alexandra. There are no clues in any of her letters, and she always maintained that her characters were composites. Sergeant, who was more intimately associated with the writing of this novel than anyone else, had no inkling: "How 'close to life' the characters in *O Pioneers!* were I was never to know with exactitude from herself, in spite of our many conversations and talks about the book." Cather was not home frequently or long enough during her *McClure's* years to have had much recent contact with the immigrant women on the Divide; hence it is likely the character is mostly drawn from her imagination. She may have been projecting the image of herself as she might have been in the pioneer days of Nebraska. Alexandra resembles Cather in her energy, determination to succeed, and strong masculine personality. A possible candidate for Alexandra's prototype was Hilda Kron, who emigrated from her native Sweden at the age of sixteen in 1881. Unlike Alexandra, she married and raised a family, but she was a strong, vibrant character and with her husband's help developed one of the richest farms in Webster County.

The creation of a strong female protagonist in *O Pioneers!* has given feminist critics a novel to admire. Rosowski sees Cather as avoiding sexist roles in her pioneer women, for Alexandra combines the attributes of both sexes on the frontier. She has the vision and energy to tame the wild land, a role usually assigned to male pioneers, and the stabilizing, nurturing traits traditionally belonging to pioneer women. To O'Brien, Alexandra is neither the female figure of male fantasy nor a doomed heroine like Chopin's Edna Pontellier or Wharton's Lily Bart in *The House of Mirth,* neither of whom can "achieve self-definition in an oppressive society." Alexandra is the supreme artist. Her selfless passion for the land contrasts sharply with the men's antagonism. Her success in creating order and beauty in the natural world takes place against the failure and defeat of the men. And Alexandra's pale suitor Carl is only half an artist; he can merely copy as an engraver the pictures created by others.

The structure of *O Pioneers!* has troubled a good many readers. Its loose organization, gaps, and digressions have made it seem a flawed work of art. Despite Cather's insistence that the material dictated the form, and the story told itself, art is not nature, and any artist must select and arrange incident and character. Like any other novelist, Cather brings order out of chaos in creating a literary work. She gets away with loose organization, however, because plot is probably the least important part of a novel. Readers want a book to stir their emotions, stimulate their imagination; they want characters who live and breathe; images that linger in the memory after the book is closed. All of these things Cather does well.

Cather has a remarkable ability to create memorable characters, both major and minor. Although Alexandra is bigger than life early in the novel, a monumental figure of myth, by the end she is an ordinary woman who has achieved much, though at the expense of friendships and happiness. Marie, the warm-hearted, vivacious wife of the surly Frank Shabata, is someone people could not help loving, and when she dies in the orchard with her head resting on the shoulder of her slain lover, the tragedy is overwhelming. Her husband, a man of violent passions, always feeling put upon, arouses no sympathy from the reader until Alexandra visits him in prison. Then he is a figure of infinite pity, almost as much a victim of the tragedy as the lovers. Old Ivar functions symbolically as a sort of nature god at the outset and a one-man Greek chorus at the end, but as Alexandra's old-age pensioner, amateur veterinarian, and mender of harness he is also a character of flesh and blood. Emil, the younger brother for whom Alexandra has high hopes, is restless, discontented, and in love with Marie. He is a complex personality who becomes three-dimensional as the reader observes him in his relations with both Marie and Alexandra. Even bit players like Mrs. Lee, Lou Bergson's mother-in-law, spring to life, and Signa, one of the Swedish girls Alexandra imports to help with the housework, is real.

Equally impressive is Cather's skill at creating incident. Scenes remain stamped on the brain long after the book is closed, making concern over weak structure irrelevant. There are many of these: Marie at the age of five entertaining the Bohemian farmers in a Hanover store; Carl climbing a telegraph pole to retrieve Emil's kitten; the visit to old Ivar, the nature god in his cave, like Silenus in Virgil's *Eclogues*; the scene between Marie and Frank in their kitchen when Frank comes in irate because the neighbor's hogs have gotten into his wheat. This last scene epitomizes in two pages the disastrous marital relationship between the two. Other memorable scenes: Carl's meeting Emil and Marie at the duck pond; the fair at the Church of Sainte-Agnès where Emil and Marie exchange a fatal kiss when the lights go out; the young men on horseback escorting the bishop's carriage across the prairie prior to the confirmation service; the confrontations between Alexandra and her brothers; the death in the orchard; the prison scene; Mrs. Lee's visit to Alexandra's where she can escape from Lou's Americanized establishment, hear Swedish spoken, listen to Ivar read the Bible, wear her nightcap, and sleep with the windows closed, and the tea party Alexandra and Mrs. Lee have at Marie's. All these scenes reverberate in the mind and make the novel worth reading more than once.

Cather never worried much about plot. Melding the two stories of Alexandra and the land and the tragic love of Emil and Marie was a bold experiment. David Daiches's study of Cather in 1951 argues that the novel seems to be composed of disparate elements that are never wholly resolved into a unity. If he had known that the novel began as two stories, he might have understood why he came to this conclusion. More recent critics have seen a more unified whole: John Randall notes that the epigraph poem, which describes both the land and youth, announces the two main themes of the novel; David Stouck believes the two stories "stretch back to Genesis. Alexandra's is the story of creation . . . Emil and Marie's is the story of lovers cast from the earth's garden through sin." Bruce Baker argues that the inclusion of the Emil-Marie story is necessary to make a human being out of Alexandra instead of leaving her a totally mythic figure. Rosowski finds unity through analysis of the novel in terms of the two-part pastoral that Cather said it was.

Comparisons with the Bible, myth, the pastoral tradition provide keys to the significance of *O Pioneers!* Cather always wrote with an awareness of her literary predecessors from the Greeks to the major authors of the twentieth century. The reverberations from the past abound in her work and give the experiences of her Nebraska farmers universality. Rosowski has found an astonishing number of parallels with a classic text Cather knew well, the *Eclogues*, which also deal with farmers and poets, the land and love. Stouck in addition to seeing connections with the Bible places the novel in the epic tradition. Alexandra is an idealized epic heroine who is engaged in the creation of public myth. The most likely subject for an American epic is without doubt the conquest of the wild land as it was steadily tamed from Jamestown to the official end of the frontier in 1890. Most sophisticated readers see Alexandra as a mythic figure, but the charm of Cather's mature fiction is the subtlety of her use of myth, symbol, and allusion. The unsophisticated freshman is thrilled by her novels without knowing quite why. Cather's reputation in the academy grew slowly because her novels at first glance seemed so simple and artless that there was little for a teacher to explicate.

More examples of this sort of subtlety exist in *O Pioneers!* than one has time to cite, and a few will have to suffice. At the first meeting between Emil and Marie, Emil is singing the "Jewel" song. There is no further detail, but anyone familiar with Gounod's *Faust* will realize after finishing the book that Cather has introduced it very appropriately. There are similarities between its use as Faust begins his seduction of Marguerite and Emil begins to fall in love with Marie, and both romances have tragic ends. When the murder takes place in the orchard under the white mulberry tree, however, a classicist may remember from Ovid's *Metamorphoses* the story of Pyramus and Thisbe, who die under a white mulberry tree. Again Cather doesn't belabor the connection. At two points in the novel there is a reference to a wild duck that Emil and Alexandra see while on a picnic together. Without any elaboration this symbol from Ibsen's play reinforces meaning and foreshadows the deaths in the orchard. Finally, after the tragedy takes place, Old Ivar, Alexandra's pensioner, sits in the barn mending harness and repeating to himself the one hundred and first psalm. There is no hint of the subject of this psalm, but it begins, "I will sing of mercy and judgment," and is consciously placed at the beginning of the final part of the novel.

Cather's gift of sympathy lifts the novel into that small group of works truly able to engage a reader's emotions. One finishes it touched by his experience. The tragedy in the orchard hits the reader hard, and when old Ivar discovers the bodies under the white mulberry tree and cries out to Alexandra, "Sin and death for the young ones! God have mercy upon us!" no one can fail to be moved. This scene is followed by Alexandra's utter devastation over the deaths of the brother for whom she had hoped so much and her only woman friend. When Ivar finds Alexandra alone in the graveyard drenched from the rain, the most hardened reader suffers with her in her bereavement. Then Carl returns posthaste to join Alexandra in her grief, and one marvels at the author's understanding of humanity, sorrow, and the need for community and closes the book feeling that he has lived through a drama of struggle, achievement, love, death, and anguish against the background of the enduring earth.

By the time *O Pioneers!* was issued Cather was at work on McClure's autobiography. McClure came to her apartment on Bank Street once a week and talked for several hours about his antecedents, his early life in Ireland, his years on an Indiana farm, his struggle for a college education, his career after graduating. Cather, who did not know shorthand, listened carefully. Because she had almost total recall, she had no trouble the next day writing out in longhand McClure's reminiscences. Then she turned over her handwritten manuscript to Sarah Bloom, who did her typing. There are no records of how long this process took, but the *Autobiography* runs to sixty thousand words, more than the total of *O Pioneers!*, and it is reasonable to guess that each of the eight chapters was one week's stint. Thus Cather probably devoted June and July to this project.

She later told Will Owen Jones that she enjoyed writing McClure's auto-biography because he was so honest about it and didn't want to dress up the truth. If he had wanted it ornamented or softened or had wished to put all the emphasis on the pleasant side of farm life in Indiana, the story would have been dull to write and dull to read. He told her the facts exactly as he remembered them and wanted them put down that way. She also said that this work was very severe training for her because she tried hard to give his exact impressions in his most characteristic language and with his nicest feeling. She added that she succeeded so well that Mrs. McClure and Mr. Phillips, his former partner and schoolmate, wrote her that the work seemed to them a perfectly convincing presentation of him as a boy and young man. They thought the sentences themselves had the abruptness and suddenness characteristic of him.

My Autobiography began running in *McClure's* in October. The only hint of Cather's part in producing it was a headnote: "I wish to express my indebted-ness to Miss Willa Sibert Cather for her invaluable assistance in the prepara-tion of these memoirs." The story that readers of the magazine followed for the next eight months recounted McClure's life to approximately the age of forty. Although the final chapter deals with the muckraking movement and the magazine during the first five years of this century, the life concentrates on McClure's early struggles and leaves him when his magazine achieves a great success. The character and personality of the subject come through clearly, and one feels a great deal of empathy for McClure, just as one does for Cather's fictional characters who struggle and succeed. Cather and McClure understood each other very well; both had a sense of destiny. The account of McClure's arrival at Knox College in 1874 with no money but an over-whelming desire for an education is particularly poignant.

One can see Cather's hand in shaping the material when it comes to literary matters. Cather and McClure had similar literary tastes, and the autobiogra-phy stresses the writers they both admired, such as Kipling, Stevenson, Meredith, the first two of whom McClure had discovered for American magazine readers. He also had discovered Booth Tarkington, but Cather never thought much of him and he never is mentioned. Nor does the life ever suggest that McClure had a close association with Hamlin Garland. There also are a number of arresting comments that Cather could have subscribed to: McClure is quoted as saying that Stevenson would let him edit his copy; only inferior writers thought their words couldn't be touched. And at an-other point: "He [Stevenson] often lamented that Balzac did not have some-body to edit and condense his novels for him."

McClure began receiving fan mail as soon as the autobiography appeared.

The Secretary of the Navy, Josephus Daniels, wrote: "Your opening chapter . . . is charming in its simplicity and beauty. I can almost see the route you took to school and hear the voices of the children. The only good history is autobiography, and I am hungry for your next chapter." In writing this book Cather was applying one of her principles, that the essence of art is to simplify. Howells wrote: "I have been reading the very touching and beautiful story of your life. I cannot remember anything of more peculiar interest. As a self-study, temperamental and social, it must stand with the great autobiographies." From Booth Tarkington: "Nothing I have ever read was more touching than these early passages in your memoirs; nor more perfectly and beautifully written. *What* you tell is very wonderful, and the *way* you tell it is just plain noble. . . . It's as simple as a country church—or a Greek statue." Both Mr. and Mrs. McClure were properly grateful to Cather for writing the life, and Hattie McClure wrote her appreciatively in the late fall. Cather, who had become very fond of Mrs. McClure during her years on the magazine, replied that the pleasure she had given Mrs. McClure gave her more satisfaction than anything else connected with the work. People not only seemed to like the autobiography but to love it.

During August Cather had to stay in the city and work on another article she had promised *McClure's*. "Training for the Ballet," which appeared in October with the first installment of McClure's autobiography. It is a competent piece of professional writing occasioned by the prospect of a full American corps de ballet for the first time at the Metropolitan Opera for the next season. Previously the Met had imported its dancers from Europe, but several years before, the Metropolitan School of Ballet Dancing had opened, and at the time of Cather's writing, enough Americans had been trained to supply the Opera. Magazine readers in 1913 knew very little about ballet, and the article presented a very lucid discussion of what it took to become a dancer, the physical equipment required, the rigorous training, the program of study, and all the intricacies of the pirouette, the entrechat, the arabesques. American girls, she learned, made better dancers than European women, because they were stronger, better nourished, had better figures, and were not afraid to make mistakes as they learned.

Since she could not get back to Red Cloud that summer, Cather made a two weeks' trip to her birthplace in Virginia, where she had not been since first going to Pittsburgh. She took McClung with her and went to Winchester in early September. She found the place dull and wrote Sergeant that she no longer cared about the holy and sacred peculiarities of the people she knew when she was little. They were about to start driving through the mountains, however, and that would be better, except for the food. She was sure that even in the provinces of Russia they served better food. She wasn't going to do any visiting because all the people she really loved were dead, but she returned to Back Creek Valley, which had changed its name to Gore in honor of her great aunt, its leading citizen for half a century. The mountains did turn out to be great, and while she stayed at the Valley Home Inn, which her aunt once operated, she walked six miles every day. When she got back to Pittsburgh on the twenty-fifth, she was in high spirits. The trip had been a success despite its sticky beginning. She was full of ideas for her next novel and ready to start writing.

CHAPTER 12

The Song of the Lark

The novel that follows *O Pioneers!* is *The Song of the Lark*, the story of a Swedish immigrant girl who becomes a famous singer. It is what the Germans call a *Künstlerroman*, a novel depicting the growth of an artist. A more apt category for the story of a woman's development, however, might be the "novel of awakening." Cather had wanted to write such a novel before she wrote the story of Alexandra Bergson but had put it aside. Telling Cameron Mackenzie about her idea at the time she sold him "The Bohemian Girl" was a mistake. Apparently the concept was not very clear in her mind, and she did not know quite what she wanted to do with it. But her strong interest in opera and singers and her experience as a music critic were powerful incentives. She wasn't yet fully committed to the use of her Nebraska memories as literary material. While she was reading proof on *O Pioneers!*, she no doubt was pondering the next novel. At that point, however, she had to take time off to fulfill her commitment to *McClure's* for a series of articles. One topic she chose was "Three American Singers," which appeared in the magazine for December 1913. The subjects were Louise Homer from Pittsburgh, Geraldine Farrar from Melrose, Massachusetts, and Olive Fremstad, Swedish-born immigrant, who had grown up in Minnesota. Fremstad then was the reigning Wagnerian soprano at the Metropolitan Opera.

One day in early March Cather made an appointment to interview Fremstad. She went to the singer's apartment on Eighty-sixth Street and found that Fremstad's chauffeur had taken her for a drive. While she waited, she collected from the singer's secretary, Mary Watkins, pertinent biographical and professional data for her article. Fremstad finally arrived, delayed by some mishap that had occurred along the way. She apologized for the delay, but she seemed terribly upset and could hardly speak. Her voice was just a whisper; she was pale and drawn. Cather quickly excused herself and said she would return another day. After she got back from the aborted interview, she told Lewis about the experience. Fremstad looked like an old woman, Cather thought.

That night, March 12, Cather, Edith Lewis, and their houseguest, Isabelle McClung, had tickets for Offenbach's *Tales of Hoffmann* at the Met. Before the curtain went up, William Guard, publicity director of the house, came out to make an announcement. Everyone knew what that meant. There was going to be a change in the cast, and so there was. Mme Duchene, who was to sing the role of Giulietta in the Venetian scene, was indisposed and could not appear. Amid gasps of disappointment Guard went on to say that Mme Fremstad had kindly consented to take over. The audience broke into applause at the prospect of hearing the *prima donna assoluta* instead of Mme Duchene, who wasn't one of the Met's stars. When the curtain went up for the second act, the woman Cather had seen that afternoon looking drawn and haggard was "a vision of dazzling youth and beauty. She sang that night as if she were dreaming the music, not singing it."

"But it's impossible," Cather kept saying, "it's impossible."

The New York *Times* carried a story the next morning headlined "Fremstad Saves an Opera." A few minutes before the opera was to begin the general manager, Giulio Gatti-Casazza, had received a phone call: Mme Duchene had fainted just as she was about to leave her home for the opera house. There was no time to change the opera; people already were entering the theater. They had a little time, however, because Mme Duchene was not due to appear until the second act. Gatti-Casazza called Fremstad and asked if she would sing the part. She had sung Giulietta when *Tales of Hoffmann* opened in January. "Certainly," replied Fremstad, "I'm on my way." She called for her car while her maid packed her costume, and in twenty minutes she was at the opera house. Cather was so impressed by this performance that she used it in her novel much the way it happened.

The interview with Fremstad came off several days later, and the singer in person made a great impact on Cather. She wrote Sergeant a week later that ever since she went to see Fremstad she had been choked up by things unutterable. If one could write all this battered Swede made one know, it would be a project well worthwhile. She was just like the immigrant women on the Divide—with suspicious, defiant, far-seeing pioneer eyes. In fact, she reminded Cather of the fictional Swede she had just created in *O Pioneers!* What was more, Fremstad's apartment was furnished just like Alexandra's house, full of impossible "mission" furniture, gold legs, rocking chairs. The poor woman's ideas of comfort had never had a chance to develop, Cather concluded. She might have been describing Fremstad's apartment when she wrote in *O Pioneers!*: "Alexandra had put herself into the hands of the Hanover furniture dealer, and he had conscientiously done his best to make her dining room look like his display window. . . . she was willing to be governed by the general conviction that the more useless and utterly unusable objects were, the greater their virtue as ornament." What Cather did not know, however, was that the apartment had been furnished by young Mary Watkins, a parson's daughter from Vermont, who had bought the furniture at Wanamakers when Fremstad was ill. Fremstad had better taste, but she was used to living in hotels, was oblivious to her surroundings, and never made any changes.

Several days after the interview Cather attended a Good Friday performance of *Parsifal*, in which Fremstad sang the part of Kundry. After the final curtain Cather ran into Fremstad outside the stage door as she was getting into her car to be driven home. Cather felt like shouting to her something like, "Pretty good for you, Mrs. Ericson!" But she simply bowed to the charming Miss Watkins. Fremstad's eyes were empty glass; she had spent her charge. Cather used this glimpse of her singer drained by a performance in *The Song of the Lark*. After Thea Kronborg sings Elsa in *Lohengrin*, Doctor Archie waits for her in the lobby of her apartment house. "She gave him a piercing, defiant glance through the white scarf that covered her face. Then she lifted her hand and brushed the scarf back from her head. There was still black on her eyebrows and lashes. She was very pale and her face was drawn and deeply lined. She looked, the doctor told himself with a sinking heart, forty years old."

These three glimpses of Fremstad a few days apart had a catalytic effect on Cather's ideas for her new novel. Seeing her pinch-hitting on a moment's notice, talking like Alexandra amidst her tasteless furniture, leaving the theater completely spent after a great performance produced another inner explosion. It was like the moment of illumination that joined the two stories, "Alexandra" and "The White Mulberry Tree," to produce *O Pioneers!* Here was Alexandra Bergson with a voice. Cather always believed that the pioneer women on the Divide possessed many of the traits of the artist—the drive, the perception, the energy, the creative force. They had created a new country out of an idea, just as Fremstad had created the roles of Elsa, Sieglinde, Brunhilde, or Kundry out of her mind and throat. A Swedish immigrant from Minnesota who had fought her way to the pinnacle of artistic success was a character to get excited over. Cather could combine her deep interest in art and artists with her memories of growing up in Nebraska.

Her new novel would be the story of an artist's struggle for recognition and would fuse the careers of both Fremstad and herself. Cather's letters to Sergeant in April are full of Fremstad, and at the end of the month she wrote that finding a new type of human being and getting inside a new skin was the finest sport she knew. She also must have realized that a novel with an opera singer as heroine offered special rewards for a woman writer. In no other field could a woman of genius with obscure origins better achieve international acclaim than she could on the musical stage. It would be surprising, in addition, if she had not remembered that George Sand, whose picture she kept on her mantel, had in her novel *Consuelo* created a fictional portrait of Pauline Garcia, a famous nineteenth-century soprano.

Cather was not able to start working on the novel, however, until fall. Articles for *McClure's* on the three singers and the ballet had to be written, and the trip to Virginia further postponed the writing. Meanwhile, a growing friendship with Fremstad also marked time while the singer spent the summer in Europe. But on her return she invited Cather to visit at her summer place at Bridgton, Maine. Cather found this such a terrifying proposition that she didn't even consider it. She said that in the paths of civilization she was not afraid of Fremstad, but she did not want to risk her uncertain temper in the wilds or to bore her: she was only interested in music. The relationship grew steadily, however, and a year later Cather screwed up her nerve and did go to Maine for a visit. During a four-week period in October and the first half of November 1913, she managed to get down to work and produced twenty-eight thousand words. She was back in her old sewing-room study at the McClungs', the place she most liked to write. She was pleased with her progress, for not only had she written twenty-eight thousand words, but also she had rewritten them. There were interruptions in October, however. The marriage of Edith McClung, Isabelle's sister, was a distraction, and Cather had to make a trip to New York on business—presumably for the magazine.

In mid-November she returned to New York to stay. Although the novel was going well despite everything, she was frustrated by the constant interruptions. She had her phone disconnected, but the only result of that, she wrote Sergeant, was Fremstad's wearing down her two thousand dollar vocal chords trying to get 2036 Chelsea and always getting a brewery. She also said she would like to nail up her front door and have done with it. December too was a month of interruptions, as she had to write her next-to-last *McClure's* article, "New Types of Acting: The Character Actor Displaces the Star," which the magazine ran in February.

The article on acting was really a round-up of five plays currently appearing in New York, but it developed the thesis that the old-style actor who got by on charm and a beautiful voice and little intellection had given way to the character actor. Her chief exhibit was her friend George Arliss, whose impersonation of Disraeli had been captivating New York audiences for four seasons. His performance was "unquestionably the most notable piece of character-acting now before the American public." He had prepared for the part by studying Disraeli's novels and letters and through his intelligence and histrionic skill had created Lord Beaconsfield himself. Then summing up Arliss's entire career and many roles, she repeated perhaps her favorite figure; "We certainly have no other actor who can get into the skins of so many different kinds of people." Although she devoted half of the article to Arliss, she also gave a considerable amount of space to *Potash and Perlmutter*, a play about two New York Jewish businessmen that she thought quite marvelous. After Arliss's play left for the road, this one was the best thing on Broadway, a play with scarcely a plot but one "made by the actors . . . a wonderful pair."

By the time she was at work on this article, "Three American Singers" appeared. She gave Louise Homer, the leading contralto at the Met, only six paragraphs, though she was a very good singer and her performance in a revival of Gluck's *Orfeo* was "a noble rendering" long to be remembered. But Homer was as much devoted to her husband and five children as to her career, and while she never sang badly, she also never swept one away with her art. Cather just couldn't get very excited about her. Geraldine Farrar, on the other hand, was a dedicated artist, beautiful, vivacious, uninhibited, and her performances in Verdi and Puccini roles were thrilling. She and Cather agreed that "conjugal and maternal duties" were not easily compatible with artistic development and that for an artist nothing "can be very real or important except art." Cather predicted even greater things in store for Farrar, who then was only thirty-one, and the two women became friends. Farrar, however, never aspired to climb the frozen heights reached by her teacher, the great Lilli Lehmann.

The article then went on to devote more than half its space to Olive Fremstad, "the singer who is now aspiring and attaining those frozen heights." In the ten years since her debut at the Met she had climbed to the artistic summit to be reached in later generations by her fellow Scandinavians Kirsten Flagstad and Birgit Nilsson. Cather found in her exactly the kind of artist she herself aspired to be. She had learned to work hard as a child, had painstakingly cultivated her natural gifts. She had left Minnesota with no money, gone to New York, supported herself by singing at St. Patrick's Cathedral. After working with a voice teacher in New York for three years, living frugally, she had saved enough to go to Germany for further study. She also studied under Lehmann and then remained in Germany a decade before returning to America. It had taken her a long time to reach the top, as it had taken Cather many years to produce *O Pioneers!* Everything she did came from within herself; her art was a blend of heart, mind, soul, and body.

Fremstad told Cather: "We are born alone, we make our way alone, we die alone." The artist's quest is pursued alone and the greatest rewards are enjoyed alone. "My work is only for serious people. If you ever really find anything in art, it is so subtle and so beautiful that—well, you need never be afraid anyone will take it away from you, for the chances are nobody will ever know you've got it." Cather concluded her profile of Fremstad: "She grew up in a new, crude country where there was neither artistic stimulus nor discriminating taste. She was poor, and always had to earn her own living and pay for her music lessons out of her earnings. She fought her own way toward the intellectual centers of the world. She wrung from fortune the one profit which adversity sometimes leaves with strong natures—the power to conquer." This is a synopsis of *The Song of the Lark*, which melds the lives of Cather and Fremstad. It is no wonder that Fremstad after reading the novel said she couldn't tell where Cather left off and she began.

Although Cather was intimidated by Fremstad at first, the two women were congenial, and the relationship flourished. On Christmas Eve before going to the Met to hear Fremstad sing Isolde, Cather arranged for her florist to deliver a little orange tree with five tiny oranges on it to Fremstad's apartment after the singer left for the opera. Fremstad was so pleased with the gift that she sat down and wrote a note of thanks immediately after she got home from the theater. She had picked up the tree and carried it to her bedroom as soon as she saw it. Cather had thought she would like it, she wrote her sister, while her Isolde mood was still on her. Dwarf orange trees were somehow like the poem that inspired the libretto of *Tristan und Isolde*, a bit magical. All those queens and princesses of northern and stormy countries must have had them, she thought.

Christmas Day 1913, however, was frustrating. Cather had had her books shipped from Pittsburgh, and she and Lewis spent the day unpacking them. They worked all day and by nightfall were exhausted, like soldiers at the end of a losing battle. They put on their oldest clothes, sneaked out to a restaurant in a pouring rain and hoped no one would recognize them. After dinner they gave up the unpacking and went to bed early. For New Year's they went to Boston, Lewis to see her family, Cather to visit Mrs. Fields and Mrs. Deland. She expected Boston to be pleasant but exhausting and was eager to get on with the novel. After she returned, she said, everything had to give way to the book. She wanted the whole world to let her alone for a while. Apparently it did for a month, but there was another sort of interruption awaiting her.

About the middle of February she got a nasty pinprick on the back of her head from a hat pin. She didn't pay much attention to it, and the scratch got infected. The infection led to blood poisoning, an operation on her scalp, three weeks in Roosevelt Hospital, and a bandaged head for five more weeks. Cather, who always hated herself when she was sick, fell into a state of depression. She wrote Sergeant from the hospital that people who have grotesque accidents are clowns, and she felt towards them exactly as the people who used to go from London to Bedlam felt about the sport they meant to behold. At that low moment Fremstad became her therapist, visited her in the hospital, brought baskets of flowers, and after she got back to Bank Street at the beginning of March showed her how to do her hair to cover her partly shaved scalp and bandages. Fremstad, she said, showed so much interest and so little horror of her ugly, shaved head that she lost her own horror of it. After that she snapped out of her depression and her recovery came fast. By the nineteenth McClung had come to visit for a month and the world seemed a good place once more. She was still pretty lethargic and spent a lot of time sitting in the park, but she was beginning to work again. By the end of the month she was out of her bandages and in April spent a few days recuperating in Atlantic City and visiting Mrs. Davidge-Taylor (Clara Davidge) on Staten Island.

In May she got tired of New York and went to Pittsburgh to work again in her sewing-room study. The story had bogged down, and during her last couple of weeks in New York she had spent her time observing singing teachers, singers, Fremstad's performances, and the petty politics of opera singers. The last she found disgusting but interesting because it was something brand new. She had been doing this, she wrote Sergeant, because she had not been able to figure out her next move. She then worked in Pittsburgh but only for a month before accepting the second invitation from Fremstad to visit her in Maine. This was an experience to remember. She spent a week or more, busy every minute. Fremstad fished as though she had no other means of making a living, cleaned her own fish, swam like a walrus, rowed, tramped, cooked, and watered her garden. Cather said she was only an audience for all this activity and felt as though she were living with the wife of the dying gladiator in her prime in deep German forests.

Later that summer she again went west, postponing once more work on the novel, and was in Red Cloud when the "guns of August" announced the start of World War I. She spent two weeks in the French and Bohemian country watching the wheat harvest, visited her Uncle George and Aunt

Franc on their farm, and for the first time as an adult got to know her cousin Grosvenor as they rode the wagons hauling wheat to the grain elevators. The temperature hit one hundred and ten and never dropped below ninety, she wrote Sergeant, but she was seeing old friends and enjoying herself. The heat finally drove her away, and she spent September in the Southwest. She was much upset over the outbreak of war in Europe, and even in the Sangre de Cristo Mountains of New Mexico the alarms of war broke in on things. One couldn't get away from the war, she wrote, as everything one most cared about seemed in danger. By the twenty-fifth she was back in Pittsburgh and ready to work again. She brought her brother Jack with her from Nebraska and put him in Carnegie Tech, and when she wanted a break from writing, she spent her time rubbing the rough edges off her brother and giving him enough English grammar to get by on. Nebraska farm speech, she said, was a slightly inflected grunt.

Except for a two weeks trip back to New York on business she spent the next five and one-half months in Pittsburgh, and finally the novel began to move quickly. By December she wrote Sergeant that the story was writing itself and a few days later told Greenslet that the novel would be done by mid-summer at the latest, perhaps even by April. It would be twice as long as *O Pioneers!* (a huge underestimate), and she had already decided to call it *The Song of the Lark*. She had seen in the Chicago Art Institute Jules Breton's painting of a peasant girl stopping on her way to work to listen to the bird. The title was intended to "suggest a young girl's awakening to something beautiful." When she wrote a preface for the novel in 1932, however, she realized that the title had been a mistake, because readers thought the lark song referred "to the vocal accomplishments of the heroine," who was anything but a sky lark, and she also had to admit that the painting was second rate. By December 21 she was pulling off the novel at a record rate and promised Greenslet it was going to be good. This progress continued, and she stayed in Pittsburgh until early February. By then the manuscript was virtually finished, and she carried it back to New York with her.

By the time she returned to her Bank Street apartment her last article for *McClure's* had appeared, "The Sweated Drama," the writing of which was the business that had taken her to New York in October. She still wasn't earning an adequate income from her book royalties and had to take on outside assignments, but this article completed her commitment to the magazine and except for two later stories *McClure's* bought it was her last appearance there. Her final piece was a lively discussion of seven plays of the 1914–15 season in which she saw a trend towards more originality and more use of contemporary materials on the New York stage. New Yorkers, she wrote, were flocking to dramas about themselves and shunning hackneyed, warmed-over plots that had been their staple diet for many years. She gave Shaw much credit for this development because of his contempt for the old conventions and "the willful eccentricity of his plays." She thought that people had more interest in good plays than in good actors. "No actor, to-day, could repeat Richard Mansfield's successes with plays adapted and translated from hither-and-yon. In New York, at least, there is now such a thing as a play sense."

Drama criticism, however, no longer interested her very much, and it seemed a frivolous activity in view of events taking place in Europe. During those early months of World War I, she wrote her Aunt Franc, she was talking and thinking of little except the war. She had a Belgian friend who had eluded the German occupation of her country and had managed to get to New York. This friend reported that her brothers and sisters in Brussels were starving. Cather also had heard the wife of a Belgian cabinet minister speak in a drive to raise money to feed her countrymen, and she had received a letter from the Belgian Relief Committee in London urging Americans to send food. The United States was the only country the Germans would allow to ship provisions into the occupied country. Cather gave no Christmas presents that year but contributed all she could to Belgian relief. The United States was the only country not suffering, she told her aunt, and she thought history would be ashamed of America if it acted niggardly.

At the end of March 1914 Cather sent Greenslet the greater part of her manuscript. Her cover letter expressed the hope that Houghton Mifflin would push this novel harder than it did *O Pioneers!* She was not dissatisfied with the advertising of the previous novel, but she wanted *The Song of the Lark* to sell at least thirty thousand copies so that she could take her time in writing the next book. She was pleased with her manuscript and told Greenslet he couldn't possibly know how much of the West she had put into it. When she grew old and couldn't run around the desert anymore, she would have the West in her book and she could recapture it merely by lifting the lid.

Greenslet, however, was not entirely enthusiastic about the manuscript. He had a lot of suggestions for revisions. He thought the early parts disproportionately long and found a lack of coherence between the first and last parts. The first parts, he said, were closely documented realism, but toward the end of part three the story became romantic. He wanted cuts in the early books and objected to Dr. Archie's becoming governor while Thea Kronborg is in Germany studying and launching her career. This is what happens to most heroes in novels, he argued. Greenslet went down to New York to talk to her about the book, and Cather agreed to make change in Dr. Archie. She later thanked Greenslet for being stern and strong-minded on this point, but she did not alter the novel or cut it in any significant way. At the end of April when she sent the epilogue, she wrote that she didn't think Greenslet really liked the novel. She felt that he found it eccentric and unsatisfactory, and she offered to take it off his hands. She would do almost anything to please him, she said, except change the story. She had no doubts about it herself.

Later when the book was in press, she wrote Sergeant that the best music critic she knew, Glendinning Keeble of the *Pittsburgh Gazette-Times*, was reading the novel in proof. He told her that she had gotten everything just right. A critic could tell from the account of Thea's early singing lessons just what characteristics her voice would have later; yet nowhere was it described. Cather felt proud of herself. She apparently also had consulted Keeble at an earlier stage of the novel, for there are two extant letters to him about the composition of the book. The first accompanied a revision in the minor character Jessie Darcy that Keeble must have asked for. The second thanked him for his help and comfort and quick return of proofs. He had furnished exactly the information she needed, and until he had given her the names to call things by, she had been unable to state the points she wanted to make in Part V.

Greenslet backpedaled, insisted that she had misinterpreted his criticism, that he *was* enthusiastic about the book. Cather calmed down, and plans for production went ahead. By May she was reading proof on the early parts of the book while still working on the agreed-upon revisions in Dr. Archie in the latter part. By the end of June production was far enough along that she had seen the book dummy and the jacket. The latter pleased her, but she heartily disliked the book's cover and complained that Greenslet never had given her a cover she liked. He listened to her and by September when she received an advance copy of the novel, she was thoroughly satisfied with all the technical details of cover, jacket, typography. The novel was scheduled for publication at the beginning of October.

In the middle of July Cather went to Pittsburgh where she finished her proof-reading and simultaneously made plans for what seems in retrospect a crazy scheme to go to Germany. Sam McClure, who then had become editor of the *New York Evening Mail*, a pro-German paper, was behind this hare-brained notion. His hold on Cather was still strong enough to persuade her to accompany him to wartime Germany for the purpose of interviewing, as he put it grandiosely, the leaders of German thought and makers of German policy. They were to sail to Bergen, Norway, then make their way through Scandinavia to Germany, avoiding the British blockade. The trip was to include Poland, Austria, and Serbia as well as Germany. Because Cather would be traveling with McClure, there obviously had to be a third person in the party. She decided that Isabelle McClung should be the one, especially since the expedition required a person with exquisite social grace, which Cather admitted she did not have. She put the proposition to McClung, who agreed to go, and they began to get ready. Then old Judge McClung woke up in the middle of the night, called Isabelle into his bedroom, and said he considered it a very chancy trip, and he didn't feel strong enough to bear the strain. He enumerated all the things he thought might happen, and the next morning Cather called the trip off. The plan probably did not seem as wild an undertaking in the summer of 1915 as it does now, for the war was less than a year old and anti-German feeling in the United States had not yet reached fever pitch. But Germany already had begun unrestricted submarine warfare, and the *Lusitania* had been sunk in May with a large loss of life, including many Americans.

In explaining this project in great detail to Greenslet, Cather said she did not think the risks were very great, except for the discomforts of wartime travel, and the financial rewards promised to be considerable—far greater than her expectations from *The Song of the Lark*. She also said that she had insisted that she would write nothing pro-German, but then she realized that this might have gotten her into a real impasse with the pro-German owners of McClure's paper, and that would have been disastrous for McClure. All in all, she summed up, the tapping of Judge McClung's cane on the floor in the middle of the night was a fate motif; but she added with a sigh that the trip would have been a tall adventure.

After this trip was aborted, Cather and Lewis made their first trip west together. Apparently Isabelle could not leave her father. Her mother had died two years before, and her father, as it turned out, had only four more months to live. Lewis was able to take a leave of absence from her job as assistant editor of *Every Week* magazine, and the two women headed for Colorado. They took the Burlington Railroad to Denver, then the narrow gauge Denver and Rio Grande over the mountains. They left the Colorado capital at night and by daybreak the little wooden train was crawling over La Veta Pass. All day they spent "swinging back and forth between Colorado and New Mexico, with the Sangre de Cristo and Culebra ranges always in sight." Then they crossed the Continental Divide at Cumbres and began "the wild scurry down the westward slope." They spent most of the day on the open back platform of the little train. This particular part of the route was called the whiplash, Cather wrote, "and most of the way you can signal to the engineer from the rear car." They got to Durango at night and the next morning took another train to Mancos, the nearest town to Mesa Verde National Park, their ultimate destination.

They only expected to stay overnight in Mancos and then go on to the park, but the town charmed them and they remained six days. The town lay at the foot of the La Plata Mountains in a fertile, irrigated valley. The Mancos River, "clear as glass and bordered with poplars [ran] through the middle of the town. The streets [were] lined with trees, the yards [were] a riot of giant sage and Indian paint-brush, shaded with cedars." Then outside of town were golden wheat fields and the whole town was buried in sweet clover. "Not once while I was in Mancos, indoors or out, was there a moment when I could not smell the sweet clover." And from the streets of Mancos "one can always see the green mesa—not green at that distance but a darkish purple, a rather grim mass bulking up in the West."

Cather long had wanted to visit Mesa Verde, which has the largest collection of cliff dwellings in the United States. Her previous visits to Walnut Canyon and other ruins had whetted her appetite for more. Mesa Verde had been a national park since 1906, and the huge Cliff Palace with its 223 rooms had been excavated and opened to visitors a few years before. By the time Cather and Lewis arrived the government had built a road into the park, and they were able to hire a wagon and driver to take them in. There was a comfortable tent camp at Spruce Tree House, and the wife of the forest ranger in charge of the park provided meals. They spent an exciting week climbing about the ruins and an entire day in the Cliff Palace. Cather was storing up impressions which would go into one of her most memorable pieces of short fiction, "Tom Outland's Story," the middle section of *The Professor's House.*

Before they left Mancos, Cather looked up the brother of Richard Wetherill, one of the two cowboys who discovered the ruins at Mesa Verde in 1888. He was still living in the town and told her the story of his brother's riding into the Mesa one December day to chase strayed cattle. He and one of his cowboys forded the Mancos River, entered the mesa by a deep canyon that they followed to its heart. They tied their horses and went on foot up a wide canyon. After a long stretch of hard climbing "Wetherill happened to glance up at the great cliffs above him, and there, through a veil of lightly falling snow, he saw, practically as it stands today, and as it had stood for eight hundred years before, the Cliff Palace . . . It stood as if it had been deserted yesterday; undisturbed and undesecrated, preserved by the dry atmosphere and by its great inaccessibility." This scene, as Wetherill's brother told it, is one of the great moments in "Tom Outland's Story."

On the day before Cather and Lewis were to return to Mancos, they had an adventure that even made the New York *Times* under the headline, "Lost in Colorado Canyon." They had planned to visit an unexcavated cliff dwelling called the Tower House, but their experienced guide was unable to take them and they had to go with a substitute, who thought he knew the way. He got them to the Tower House all right, but they had to descend to the bottom of Soda Canyon by a trail so steep they could not have returned without ropes. Tower House was on the other side of the canyon and a ways beyond. The guide said he would take them back by another trail further down the canyon, but by evening after they had walked a good many miles, the guide had to admit that he was lost. They had come to the junction of Soda Canyon and Cliff Canyon, and the guide thought there was an archeologist's camp about four miles up Cliff Canyon. The two women were exhausted, and Cather said she and Lewis would stay where they were, while the guide hiked up the canyon to see if there really was a camp.

Lewis remembered this scene vividly: "The four or five hours we spent waiting there were, I think, for Willa Cather the most rewarding of our whole trip to Mesa Verde. There was a large flat rock at the mouth of Cliff Canyon, and we settled ourselves comfortably on this rock. . . . We were tired and rather thirsty, but not worried, for we knew we should eventually be found. We did not talk, but watched the long summer twilight come on, and the full moon rise up over the rim of the canyon. The place was very beautiful."

Eventually there were shouts from up the canyon, and men from the camp appeared. Their guide had been so exhausted that he could not come back himself. Cliff Canyon was a mass of broken rocks all the way, and they were pulled and pushed and led by their rescuers for four miles until they came to a place where they could climb out of the canyon by scaling the lopped off branches of a huge pine that had been felled against the cliff like a ladder. They got to the camp of Dr. Walter Fewkes, a Smithsonian archaeologist, at two in the morning. Horses were hitched to a wagon, and they were taken back to park headquarters. When she wrote Sergeant about this adventure, Cather said she still was bruised and sore but happy and ready to go back and be mauled again by the big brutality of Cliff Canyon. She never had learned so much as in the twenty-four hours of that experience. That country, she said, drives one crazy with delight.

After returning to Mancos, Cather and Lewis visited Taos, New Mexico, for the first time. Although there were already a few artists there, it had not yet been discovered as an artist's colony, and the town was remote and hard to get to. They had to travel a long way by horse and wagon over a rough road, and the accommodations they found were primitive. The only place to stay was the Columbian Hotel, an adobe building operated by a Mexican woman on the town plaza. It was furnished with great brass double beds with sagging springs and thin mattresses, huge dark cupboards and wash stands and lighted by coal oil. The price was right, however—a dollar and a half per day including meals. They stayed there a week riding about the country on horseback or hiring a team and wagon, which they drove themselves. It was a glorious week, Cather wrote Sergeant, and she was very happy. Lewis remembered that Cather "was intensely alive to the country— as a musician might be alive to an orchestral composition he was hearing for the first time. She did not talk about it much—but one felt that she was deeply engaged with it always, was continually receiving strong impressions from the things she saw and experienced." She was, of course, storing up the material that eventually would go into *Death Comes for the Archbishop* twelve years later.

Before the middle of September they left New Mexico and started east. Lewis returned to New York, while Cather went to Red Cloud for a visit. She stayed in Nebraska well into October and was there on the publication day, October 2, of *The Song of the Lark*. She had enjoyed her summer travels, but she felt let down after completing the novel. She wrote Sergeant that she missed Thea now that the book was out and she wished she could still feel her character stretching herself inside her skin.

Cather dedicated her novel to Isabelle McClung, under whose loving and watchful eye most of the book was written. It was her second dedication to McClung, and this time she included a verse:

> On uplands,
> At morning,
> The world was young, the winds were free;
> A garden fair,
> In that blue desert air,
> Its guest invited me to be.

The story begins in Moonstone, Colorado, in the 1880s when Thea Kronborg is eleven. In the opening scene the family physician, Howard Archie, attends the child during a serious case of pneumonia, following which a close relationship grows between the doctor and Thea. The doctor, another of Cather's unhappily married characters, becomes the girl's mentor and guardian angel, seeing in her the daughter he never had. Thea has a number of adult friends who play a significant role in helping her grow up:

A. Wunsch, the derelict musician who teaches her to play the piano; Spanish Johnny and Mrs. Tellamantez, residents of the Mexican community of Moonstone; Mr. and Mrs. Kohler, the German tailor and his wife, who live on the outskirts of town; and Ray Kennedy, a brakeman who works on the freight trains between Moonstone and Denver. Part I, "Friends of Childhood," which occupies more than one-third of the novel, comes to a conclusion when Thea at the age of seventeen leaves home to study music in Chicago.

There is no formal plot structure in Part I, as Thea grows from childhood to adolescence, but there are a good many episodes that mark the girl's growth. A. Wunsch discovers Thea's natural musical talent and nurtures it to the best of his ability. By the time he drifts off to another town, Thea is able to take over his piano students. She drops out of high school and becomes self-supporting. She also sings in the church choir and plays the organ for services. She learns about the world beyond Moonstone from the German Kohlers, her music teacher, Spanish Johnny, and Ray Kennedy. When a tramp drowns himself in the town water tank, she discusses life, death, and God with Dr. Archie. She also learns about human nature from her encounters with the mean-spirited Mrs. Archie and the envious Mrs. Livery Johnson, whose untalented protégée Lilly Fisher upstages her in a Christmas talent show. She visits Denver with her mother when Ray Kennedy invites them to ride with him in his caboose. Ray is an honest, simple fellow who loves Thea and watches and waits for her to grow up so that he can ask her to marry him. In the penultimate episode of Part I, however, Ray is killed in a railroad accident; but he leaves a six-hundred-dollar insurance policy to Thea with the stipulation that it be used for her musical education in Chicago.

"The Friends of Childhood" ranks high in the corpus of Cather's work. As the most autobiographical fiction she ever wrote, it draws on early memories of people, places, and incidents of her years between ten and sixteen in Red Cloud. This is material that had teased her mind for years, and it evokes vividly the life of a small town on the prairie in the late nineteenth century. There are scenes that linger in the mind: Dr. Archie ministering to the sick child, Thea with her music teacher, the picnic in the sand hills outside of Moonstone, the trip to Denver in the caboose. There is sentiment without sentimentality: Thea's feelings about Dr. Archie, her distress when Wunsch leaves town, her affection for Ray Kennedy. These aspects of the novel accompany a remarkable characterization of the development of a young girl.

Many of the characters of Part I were suggested by real people. The music teacher had his prototype in Herr Schindelmeisser, Cather's piano teacher. Spanish Johnny was a guitar-playing Mexican who lived in Red Cloud. Cather remembered that she never had heard him when he wasn't either singing or swearing. Dr. Archie was drawn from Dr. McKeeby, the doctor Cather accompanied on his country calls and who looked after her when she was seriously ill with what may have been polio. There was a real, though now unidentifiable Lily Fisher, who performed at an amateur hour Cather attended when she was in college. Ray Kennedy has some of the traits of the brakeman Tooker, whom Cather met in Arizona in 1912, but there was another brakeman, also unidentifiable, whom Cather knew in Red Cloud. She wrote Greenslet when she sent him her manuscript that the death of the noble brakeman was the original germ of the story. The event had happened when she was thirteen. Thea's Aunt Tilly has some of the traits of Cather's cousin Bess Seymour, who lived with the Cathers. Mrs. Kronborg's iron discipline of her seven children, her rawhide whip to enforce it, and her caring about people are characteristics belonging to Jennie Cather. Mrs. Kronborg also looks after the bodies of her children but leaves their minds alone, as Mrs. Cather did hers.

Beyond this use of real people in the novel is the use of real setting and incident. Moonstone, Colorado, is once again Red Cloud, Nebraska, with its railroad depot south of town, the Kronborgs' house, as was the Cathers', located west of the main street, Dr. Archie's home to the north, and the opera house placed where it really was. The railroading ambience is a natural part of a town that was a division point on the Burlington's main line from Chicago to Denver. The room that Thea occupies in the unfinished second story of the Kronborg house still exists as Cather describes it, and Thea's reading of Byron's poems and *Anna Karenina* are Cather's own memories of books she read while growing up. Thea takes care of her younger brother Thor just as Cather entertained her younger siblings.

While Cather's memories of her youth supply character, incident, and setting, Fremstad's childhood in Minnesota also went into the novel. Thea's serious study of the piano, her singing, her playing the organ in church are facts from Fremstad's life, not Cather's. There is nothing of Charles Cather in Thea's father, who is a minister like Fremstad's father. Thea's piano teaching when she is still a young girl also comes from Fremstad's experience. The serious nature of the child, the questions about life, the ability to work hard, the intense desire to make something of herself, however, are traits common to both the author and the opera singer.

Part II, "The Song of the Lark," begins in Chicago. Thea has been escorted to the city by Dr. Archie, who helps her find a piano teacher, a place to live, and a job singing in a church choir. Dr. Archie insists that she go to the best teacher in Chicago, who is Andor Harsanyi, Hungarian-born pianist, the first real artist Thea has known. Wunsch had once been a good musician, but by the time Thea's talent engaged his interest, he had little left to give her. "Harsanyi found in Thea a pupil with sure, strong hands, one who read rapidly and intelligently, who had, he felt, a richly gifted nature. But she had been given no direction, and her ardour was unawakened. She had never heard a symphony orchestra. The literature of the piano was an undiscovered world to her. He wondered how she had been able to work so hard when she knew so little of what she was working toward."

Thea works like a demon, supports herself by singing but never tells Harsanyi about this side of her life until one day she has to change her lesson time because of her church commitments. Harsanyi asks her to sing for him, and he realizes at once that her true vocation is singing. By this time he has become deeply interested in his pupil, but he knows that he must turn her over to a voice teacher. He sends her to Madison Bowers, the best voice coach in Chicago, and when the summer comes and Thea returns to Moonstone, she has begun the long road towards her operatic career. At the end of Part II, however, Thea finds during the summer that one can't go home again. She has grown away from her family, the people in her little prairie town, and from now on she must be on her own.

Cather handles the awakening of her young artist with great skill in this section of the novel. Only a few of the plot details are autobiographical, such as Thea's hearing Dvořák's *New World Symphony* and her discovery of the Chicago Art Institute, but the emotions, perceptions, and aspirations of the young artist are those Cather understood very well. After Thea admits to Harsanyi that she wants more than anything else to be an artist, she realizes that within her there always has been a second self: "It was as if she had an appointment to meet the rest of herself sometime, somewhere." A. Wunsch, Dr. Archie, and Spanish Johnny all had seen this other self within her, and that was why they cared for her. Cather too believed in the two selves in every person, the private self that belongs to family and friends, and the public self. In Alexandra Bergson this public self was developed in the taming of the wild land. In Thea Kronborg, as in Willa Cather, it took the form of an artistic career. For women in the nineteenth century cultural pressures made it hard to cultivate this other self. Society wanted women to be wives and mothers, not writers and opera singers. To achieve her goal, Thea realizes, is as difficult as being born again. Cather, through Harsanyi, describes this process of the emerging second self in a female metaphor when he tells Thea: "Every artist makes himself born." Her mother did not bring her into the world to be a musician, he says; she had to do that for herself. The doing, however, is difficult, and even before Thea knows what her destiny is to be and is being drawn ahead irresistibly, she feels "as if she were being pulled in two, between the desire to go away forever and the desire to stay forever."

One of the great moments in the novel occurs in this part when Thea is given a ticket to the Chicago Symphony. As she listens to Theodore Thomas's musicians play *The New World Symphony*, she undergoes an intense emotional experience, an awakening to life, to art, to vocation. "When the first movement ended, Thea's hands and feet were cold as ice. She was too excited to know anything except that she wanted something desperately." Then as the horns give out the theme of the largo, she loses herself in memories of home: "Here were the sand hills, the grasshoppers and locusts, all the things that wakened and chirped in the early morning; the reaching and reaching of high plains . . . first memories, first mornings long ago; the amazement of a new soul in a new world; a soul new and yet old, that had dreamed something despairing, something glorious, in the dark before it was born; a soul obsessed by what it did not know, under the cloud of a past it could not recall."

In Part III, "Stupid Faces," which is relatively short, Thea returns to Chicago and spends the year studying under Bowers, a competent teacher but a cold, avaricious man. She supports herself by singing in church and playing accompaniments for Bowers' other pupils. Fred Ottenburg, wealthy brewer and amateur musician, enters her life; she sings at a private musicale for an attractive Jewish banker and his wife, the Nathanmeyers; gets sick; and by the end of the year is tired, discouraged, and badly in need of a rest and change of scenery. Fred offers her the use of a ranch his father owns in Arizona. In Part IV, "The Ancient People," Thea goes to Panther Canyon, as we have already seen, and spends the summer resting and pondering her future. Her symbolic rebirth as an artist occurs in that huge fissure in the earth, which one critic has called "the most thoroughly elaborated female landscape in literature." Thea plans to go to Germany to study, but then Fred joins her and she falls in love. Thinking he is going to marry her, she accepts his offer to visit Mexico City with him. He finally has to tell her that he is already married to a woman he detests and who will not give him a divorce.

Part V, "Doctor Archie's Venture," takes place in New York. Because Fred can't marry her, Thea breaks off the relationship, wires Dr. Archie to come to New York and asks him to lend her money to go to Germany. At the end of the section she is about to sail for Europe. The novel then skips ten years, and Part VI, "Kronborg," opens in Denver, where Dr. Archie now lives, with a meeting between Fred and the doctor, who discuss Thea's career in Germany. The scene then moves to New York where Thea has become one of the leading sopranos at the Met. Now the heroine's prototype is Olive Fremstad, no longer Willa Cather. Thea has returned, as Fremstad did, after singing in Germany for a decade.

The novel ends, except for a brief epilogue, with Thea's triumphal performance as Sieglinde in *Die Walküre* with Dr. Archie, Fred Ottenburg, and Andor Harsanyi in the audience. During the second-act intermission a discussion takes place between Thea's admirers about the secret of her success. "What's her secret?" Fred asks Harsanyi. "He rumpled his hair irritably and shrugged his shoulders. 'Her secret? It is every artist's secret'—he waved his hand—'passion. That is all. It is an open secret, and perfectly safe. Like heroism, it is inimitable in cheap materials.'"

The artist who achieves greatly, however, does so at a sacrifice. Alexandra Bergson at the end of *O Pioneers!*, a lonely, middle-aged woman, tries to obtain a balance in her two selves by seeking companionship in marriage to Carl Lindstrum. Thea Kronborg, one finds in the epilogue, has married her old friend Fred Ottenburg, but the artist's life is a lonely one nevertheless. When Dr. Archie visits Thea in New York where she is a prima donna at the Met, he expresses his concern that she does not have enough personal life outside her work. She looks at him and smiles: "My dear doctor, I don't have any. Your work becomes your personal life. You are not much good until it does. It's like being woven into a big web. You can't pull away, because all your little tendrils are woven into the picture. It takes you up, and uses you, and spins you out; and that is your life. Not much else can happen to you."

Cather, as she often does in her fiction, uses myth to reinforce meaning in *The Song of the Lark*. Early in the novel A. Wunsch (whose name means desire) introduces his pupil to Gluck's *Orfeo ed Euridice*, the score of which in German translation is his most prized possession. He plays and sings for Thea the haunting aria, "*Ach, ich habe Sie verloren* [Oh, I have lost you]," which Orfeus sings after the fatal backward look which cost him his beloved. Thea knows the myth of Orfeus, whose beautiful music induced the gods to let him lead his dead wife Euridice back to earth from Hades provided he did not look back, but she does not know there is an opera about it. Thea's introduction to opera with this particular work provides a motif for the novel. As Euridice symbolizes art, man's desire for self-expression, Orfeus stands for the striving artist. Wunsch is a loser and mourns the loss of his Euridice before he drifts away to an alcoholic oblivion somewhere in the depths of Kansas. In the myth Orfeus after losing his Euridice is torn by the Thracian women and thrown into the River Hebrus. Wunsch bequeaths his score of the opera to

Thea, and she carries it with her as she scales the icy heights. Cather ends her novel with her singer at the peak of her career, but the use of the myth haunts the ending. One knows that Thea one day will lose her Euridice and some other singer will replace her, as Thea replaces an ailing Sieglinde at the end of the story.

The Song of the Lark is an impressive study of an artist's growth from childhood to maturity. To anyone interested in music, especially opera, the novel cannot fail to be engrossing. Fremstad herself gave the novel an enthusiastic endorsement. Cather wrote Sergeant that she had met the singer in Lincoln just after she had read the book. She was carrying a dirty, rumpled copy that she said had not been just read but eaten. Cather had been afraid that Fremstad would be furious, but she was glowing with excitement. She especially liked "Friends of Childhood" and the chapters dealing with Panther Canyon. But she also approved of the last part in which she is the protagonist. It had just the right *stimmung* [tone], she said. One might have thought, she told Cather, that the final part was old stuff to her, but she knew what Thea was up against and she wanted her to pull it off. The novel was the only one she ever had read about an artist in which there was something doing in the character. Cather felt as if she had been given a decoration.

She also was much pleased when the people in Red Cloud liked the novel, because, as she explained to Dorothy Canfield Fisher, she had written the book from the Moonstone point of view in Moonstone language. To make this clear, she brings the reader back to Thea's home town in the epilogue, in which the heroine's addlepated Aunt Tilly basks in the triumphant career of her niece. Although Thea has severed all her bonds with the place of her birth, she never denies her origin. Her strength comes from the soil of Moonstone, as she acknowledges when she tells Dr. Archie: "I began the world on six hundred dollars [Ray Kennedy's insurance policy] and it was the price of a man's life. . . . I always measure things by that six hundred dollars, just as I measure high buildings by the Moonstone standpipe. There are standards we can't get away from."

Most reviewers of the novel were enthusiastic. They generally agreed with the *Boston Evening Transcript*, which declared that "Miss Cather has created a flesh and blood woman . . . *The Song of the Lark* is an extremely able piece of writing . . . [and] sorry indeed must be the condition of one in whom Thea Kronborg's struggle would not stir some answering pulse." The authenticity of the characterizations was noted by most of the reviewers, not just the reality of the protagonist, but also of the minor characters: Thea's mother, who realizes early that her daughter is extraordinary and sacrifices a great deal for her; Dr. Archie, Ray Kennedy, and Fred Ottenburg, all of whom contribute selflessly to her success. H. W. Boyton, whose comments on the novel particularly pleased Cather, wrote in the *Nation* that she had succeeded in "that most dangerous of feats—to trace the genesis of genius."

H. L. Mencken, who had been following Cather's career ever since she published *Alexander's Bridge*, welcomed Cather into "the small class of American novelists who are seriously to be reckoned with." Her first novel was full of promise, he wrote; the second showed the beginnings of fulfillment. "In *The Song of the Lark*, she is already happily at ease, a competent journeyman. I have read no late novel, in fact, with a greater sense of intellectual stimulation." Mencken was especially taken with "Friends of Childhood," which was live, full of sharp bits of observation, sly touches of humor, gestures of that gentle pity which is the fruit of understanding. "Miss Cather not only has a desire to write; she also has something to say. . . . From her book comes the notion that she has thought things out, that she is never at a loss, that her mind is plentifully stored."

While *The Song of the Lark* is an enormously interesting and attractive novel, it is not without flaws. Some of the reviewers complained that the novel was overwritten, though they agreed that the excessive detail was far overshadowed by the quality of the characterization. But the novel does go on and on for 490 pages in the original edition, and the total length is about 146,000 words, not much short of three times the length of *O Pioneers!* Cather originally had written two hundred thousand words, a length more like a Dreiser novel than one of hers. She had not yet formulated the principles she proclaims in her later essay, "The Novel Démeublé," in which she says the "higher processes of art are all processes of simplification." She did cut from the manuscript before sending it off a long section which chronicled Thea Kronborg's ten years in Germany, realizing that the tone of that material clashed with the Moonstone point of view of the rest of the novel. But even with these cuts the book still is full of detail that might better have been omitted. On rereading the novel, one is constantly wanting to use the blue pencil to strike out long passages going into great detail about Dr. Archie's wife and his unhappy marriage, the life story of the Rev. Lars Larson of Chicago, Thea's first choir director, Fred Ottenburg's personal history and disastrous marital relationship, and a good bit about reform politics in Colorado. Cather simply enjoyed writing this novel so much that she let herself be carried away. The quality of the novel derives from the intense interest she had in the material, what she called the gift of sympathy, but she failed to exercise proper control over the material.

She began to realize this when her British publisher Heinemann turned down the novel. He had been pleased to bring out *O Pioneers!*, a novel he admired, but he wrote her that she had taken the wrong turn in writing a novel in which she "told everything about everybody." She remembered his letter saying: "I always find the friendly, confidential tone of writing of this sort distressingly familiar, even when the subject matter is very fine." When Cather wrote a preface for the novel in 1932, she found another flaw: "The chief fault of the book is that it describes a descending curve; the life of a successful artist in the full tide of achievement is not so interesting as the life of a talented young girl 'fighting her way,' as we say. Success is never so interesting as struggle—not even to the successful."

She went on to explain: "The interesting and important fact that, in an artist of the type I chose, personal life becomes paler as the imaginative life becomes richer, does not, however, excuse my story for becoming paler. The story set out to tell of an artist's awakening and struggle; her floundering escape from a smug, domestic, self-satisfied provincial world of utter ignorance. It should have been content to do that. I should have disregarded conventional design and stopped where my first conception stopped, telling the latter part of the story by suggestion merely." This statement made long after the fact ignores the fascination that Fremstad had for Cather. She also had convinced herself that Fremstad had had little to do with the characterization of Thea Kronborg. She wrote Greenslet in 1932 not to encourage the rumors that Thea was done from Fremstad. Not one incident had any likeness to the incidents in Fremstad's life, she claimed. Knowing her had some indirect influence, but that was mainly in making her aware of the routine of an opera singer's life. Cather here, as she often did, was rewriting the story of her own life.

When she worked over *The Song of the Lark* for a new edition published in 1932, she cut out about seven thousand words. These were not major cuts, though she trimmed some of the excesses from the latter parts of the novel; but she must have decided on looking over the book more than two decades after writing it that major surgery was inadvisable and it was best to let the novel stand pretty much as it was. Thus she deleted some dated references, some opinions she no longer held, pruned away some indiscretions and lapses of taste, polished up syntax and style here and there, but that was all. She was at work on her last novel by that time and unwilling to revise her early work the way James did his youthful novels for his collected works.

The most negative notice the book received was in an unsigned review in the *New Republic* by Randolph Bourne, who thought *The Song of the Lark* much inferior to *O Pioneers!* His criticism of the title Cather agreed with, but his strictures went a good deal farther. He thought the early parts of the novel, which were written out of the author's own experiences, were excellent, but the story should have ended when Thea goes off to Mexico with Fred Ottenburg. "Cather would perhaps be shocked," he wrote, "to know how sharp were the contrasts between those parts of her book which are built out of her own experience and those which are imagined. Her defects are almost wholly those of unassimilated experience. The musical life of this opera singer who has so fascinated her she has admired, but she has not made it imaginatively her own." This is valid criticism, for Cather was not in the final parts using material that in her own words had "tease[d] the mind over and over for years." She was admiring rather than remembering.

Red Cloud may have been pleased with *The Song of the Lark*, but some of Cather's old friends in Lincoln were not. She wrote Dorothy Canfield Fisher, who by this time had written three novels herself, that Dorothy's public outnumbered hers twenty to one. Dorothy's public was saying insulting things about Willa's public, and vice versa. Dorothy's supporters objected to the immorality in Wilia's novels, the illicit relations of Bartley Alexander, Emil and Marie in *O Pioneers!*, and Thea Kronborg's affair with Fred Ottenburg. The Geres, the Westermanns, and Will Owen Jones all had gone over to Dorothy's camp, while she had five German brewers, Sarah Harris, and Dr. Tyndale. The defection of her old friends, she said, hurt at first, but she was getting used to it.

While she was watching reviews and hearing from friends about the book, she also was taking a great interest in the marketing of the novel. She supplied a biographical sketch and an article on Mesa Verde for a promotional booklet that Houghton Mifflin sent out to reviewers and book stores. When the firm sent her an advance proof of an ad for the book, she rewrote the copy to put some excitement into it. One ounce of enthusiasm, she said, was worth a pound of approbation, and she insisted on seeing the revised copy before the ad was placed. She also wanted the book advertised in the women's colleges because, as she said, girls all wanted that combative, defiant sort of career. It was in the air.

Cather's dissatisfaction with Houghton Mifflin, which eventually led her to switch to Alfred Knopf, began with the publication of *The Song of the Lark*. The book sold about eight thousand copies in its first six months, which she thought very satisfactory, but when Houghton Mifflin sent her a bill of $166.73 for excess corrections in the proof, she complained. It was three times what she expected and fourteen percent of her first royalty check. The same thing happened with her next novel, and she began to be increasingly critical of the company's treatment of her and the promotion of her books. The book only sold another thirteen hundred copies in the second six months, and later she complained to Greenslet that people couldn't get copies of the novel in book stores. If it had not been for her long friendship with Greenslet, she probably would have left Houghton Mifflin long before she did. Her relations with her publisher were no doubt colored by personal problems that were overtaking her in the months following the book's publication. This was the winter of her discontent.

Appropriately enough, this disturbing period was ushered in by the publication in November of the penultimate story she ever wrote for *McClure's*, "Consequences," a somber tale of apparitions and suicide. It is another ghost story that deals with the dark underside of life, things beyond the ken of rational discourse. Readers of the tale have been reminded of Wilde's *The Picture of Dorian Gray*, a novel Cather knew and thought well of, also perhaps Poe's "William Wilson." Both authors create a double whose influence on the principal character is both terrifying and disastrous. Cather in using this idea has divided her notion of the double self into two persons, an attractive young man and a repulsive old one. The story is seen from the perspective of a matter-of-fact New York lawyer whose neighbor is a rich, dissolute young man who lives for pleasure. The young man, as he tells his lawyer friend, is being pursued by a sinister old fellow who appears from time to time dressed in shabby evening clothes and knows intimate details of his life. After a number of these encounters, the young man begins to realize his pursuer is himself projected into the future. The pragmatic lawyer urges his young friend to go West, live on a ranch, work out of doors, and shake off the old fellow following him. But the night before the young man is to leave for Montana, his double visits him, and the next morning the young man is found shot to death by his own hand. This chilling tale is not told baldly, as the summary here suggests, but by inference and indirection. It produces the effect of horror in a manner somewhat reminiscent of Poe. It also reminds readers of Cather that under her calm, well-organized exterior there were doubts and uncertainties.

CHAPTER 13

My Ántonia

While Cather was enjoying the chorus of praise that greeted *The Song of the Lark*, with only an occasional sour note, events in her personal life were soon to strike a discord. She was still in Pittsburgh on November 12, 1915, when old Judge McClung died, the first of three distressing events to come in quick succession. In order to be present for the funeral, she canceled with regret plans to accompany Fremstad to Chicago where she was to sing Isolde, and after the judge was buried she returned to New York. But she soon went back to Pittsburgh to spend her last Christmas there. She wrote her Aunt Franc sadly on Christmas Day that the McClung house, which had been a kind and hospitable home to her for fifteen years, would probably be sold, as Isabelle and her brother Alfred thought it too big and expensive to keep up alone. It was hard to see dear friends and familiar things pass out of her life. She thought she never would feel so safe and happy in any other house. Her own apartment on Bank Street had never seemed like home in the same sense, though she liked it very much. The house was indeed sold early the next year, and Cather's two decades of association with Pittsburgh came to an end.

An even harder blow fell sometime later in the winter when Isabelle McClung announced that she was going to be married to Jan Hambourg, a concert violinist. There is no evidence that Cather had any foreknowledge of this impending event. The *New York Times* reported later that McClung had met Hambourg in London when he was playing there several years before, and Cather must have known that. She also must have heard him play in Pittsburgh in a trio with his brother Mark and her old friend Ethel Litchfield three days after Judge McClung died. But the announcement came as a considerable shock. She wrote Dorothy Canfield Fisher in mid-March that the marriage would bring about an amazing change in her life, and on the best terms she could figure out, it would be a devastating loss. Isabelle expected to be in New York a good deal after her marriage, but things couldn't, of course, be as they were. Cather added ruefully that the pursuit of happiness was not the reality it was supposed to be; the pursuit of pain seemed to be just as irradicable a human instinct. Losses never seemed to come singly; her old friend Mrs. Fields had died in Boston the previous winter, ending another era that had provided her with great happiness and closing another house that she had found great pleasure in visiting.

Elizabeth Sergeant heard of McClung's coming marriage as she and Cather walked together in Central Park one icy day in late winter. As she heard the news, Sergeant remembered, Cather's face was bleak; her eyes were vacant: "All her natural exuberance had drained away." Sergeant's memory probably overdramatizes the impact of the approaching marriage, for Cather's letter to Fisher is restrained. In explaining that the bridegroom was to be Jan Hambourg, she went on to say that Jan was much nicer than his brother. She was glad of this because Isabelle was very happy. The letter continues to talk calmly of plans for the wedding, which was to take place in New York on April 3, to be followed by a small reception at Sherry's. Her friend May Willard was coming on from Pittsburgh to stay with her for the reception. The wedding subsequently took place at the Church of the Messiah with the Reverend John Holmes officiating. Whether Cather found the minister to perform this Protestant-Jewish marriage is not known, but she may well have done so and also arranged for the reception. She admitted that she and Jan were not very congenial, but the letter reveals no hostility. It divides rather equally between regret for the closing of the Pittsburgh chapter of her career and regret over the opening of Isabelle's new life. Both of these events combined to give her a rotten winter, she wrote Greenslet, and to keep her from getting practically any work done. She wrote Fisher that she hadn't been able to start a new novel, though she had an idea in mind. She felt indifferent towards the material, and when her interest was out of commission she had very little wit to work with.

About the same time she received a letter from W. H. Boynton, whom she knew only as an admiring reviewer of her books, asking what she was working on. She replied that nothing much interested her deeply at the moment, only "something rather hard and dry." Perhaps "I'm doing it for the same reasons that violinists play Bach after they have been working hard on very romantic modern things." Her next novel was planned pretty well, she added, but "the winter has been full of changes and troubles, the loss of old friends by death and even by marriage, until I feel [quoting from Poe's "The

Raven"] like the man 'whom merciful disaster followed fast and followed faster.' The milk has been too much disturbed for the cream to rise," but "I am beginning to keep engagements with my desk again, and I hope, if you come into town this spring, that I may have some progress to report to you."

She did manage to write two stories during this stressful period, "The Bookkeeper's Wife," which she sold to the *Century*, and "The Diamond Mine," which her agent placed in *McClure's*, her last appearance in the magazine she once had edited. The former story is a competent piece of professional writing but not a very attractive tale. It must have been the hard and dry thing she referred to in her letter to Boynton. Its chief characters, Percy Bixby and Stella Brown, add another unhappy marriage to the growing list of disastrous romances in Cather's fiction. But neither character is one to arouse a reader's sympathy. Percy is a methodical, meticulous, unimaginative bookkeeper for a New York paper company, and Stella is the beautiful, selfish, much-courted daughter of a very ambitious woman. Percy wants desperately to marry Stella, overstates his salary as he woos this mercenary maiden, and in order to get married embezzles money from his employer by cooking the books. He intends to pay back the money, but, of course, his wife's extravagance makes this impossible. Percy for five years sits on his stool in the accounting office, refusing to take a vacation so that no one else ever will get a look at his books. The crisis comes, however, when the owner of the firm plans a general audit. Percy confesses to the boss, who generously lends him money to reimburse the company, but when Percy has to tell his wife about the embezzlement and the necessity of reducing their standard of living, she spews out all her accumulated resentments against Percy's life style and personality and leaves him to go to work for the other man she was dating when Percy won the prize. Percy is a weak character, a hollow man; Stella is a man-eating monster, and the story is a parable of the corrupting power of money. In this theme it anticipates one of Cather's major preoccupations in her fiction of the twenties.

"The Diamond Mine" is a story of considerably more interest and importance. In the first place, it began her relationship with Paul Reynolds, who acted as her agent in selling her stories and the serial rights to her novels for the next decade. This turned out to be a profitable arrangement for her. She wrote Harry Dwight that she took the greatest satisfaction in Reynolds's conduct of her affairs. She said she never would have tried to sell "The Diamond Mine" to a magazine. Its length (fifteen thousand words), subject matter, method of narration—all were absolutely opposed to magazine requirements. Reynolds got her six hundred dollars for the story when she would have accepted five hundred gladly. She told Greenslet in June that

Reynolds could sell anything and in December that he would make her so rich she could afford to bone down on her long story, *My Ántonia*, which she already had begun to write.

Because the royalties from *The Song of the Lark* were modest, she had to continue writing stories when she much preferred to work on novels. Reynolds worked very effectively to supplement her income in this period, and though he never became a close friend, he and Cather got along well. They lunched together a few times and occasionally went for a walk in Washington Square. Reynolds was the soul of tact, never negotiating with a magazine without consulting her, never presuming too much. Later when Cather moved from Houghton Mifflin to Knopf, she gradually turned over all her business to Knopf's firm and drifted away from Reynolds. But after she won the Pulitzer Prize in 1923, Reynolds began to get many requests for her work from magazines willing to pay a thousand dollars a story, and his correspondence with her, often unanswered, is filled with wistful urging that she write more stories for him to sell. But by that time her book royalties more than supported her, and she almost stopped writing short fiction altogether.

Although "The Diamond Mine" is a fine story, Reynolds had a little trouble selling it. After the *Century* turned it down, he offered it to *The Smart Set*, edited by H. L. Mencken and George Jean Nathan. Mencken was interested but feared the story was potentially libelous. It is based on the life of Lillian Nordica, whose last husband, George Young, is very thinly disguised in the story as the unscrupulous, mercenary character Jerome Brown. Cather answered Mencken's concern by admitting that Nordica was the singer who had inspired the tale; yet she said there was no incident that resembled anything in her life except the shipwreck and the will contest. She added that the will contest in reality had been much nastier than she had made it in the story. She didn't see how George Young could object. He did, however, but he only threatened suit and never followed through. Cather was sure he wouldn't, she wrote Greenslet, but she was probably lucky that she was living in a less litigious age than the present. That the story was a fictionalized life of Nordica was apparent to everyone, and a few days after the October issue of *McClure's* appeared, the *Musical Courier* carried an article commenting on the tale. "[It] reveals the identity of its heroine, with unrelenting frankness, from the very opening paragraph. Her fine, opulent, generous nature and withal showily plate-glass character is drawn with some minuteness."

The story no doubt took shape in Cather's mind as she finished *The Song of the Lark*. It reflects her continuing fascination with opera singers and their bigger-than-life styles. Long before she ever discovered Fremstad, she had been interested in Nordica, having heard her in *Cavalleria Rusticana* in Lincoln and in *Les Huguenots* in Chicago while she was still in college. She even had written one of her "Player Letters" to Nordica and on two other occasions had devoted columns to the singer during her career in journalism. Nordica was indeed an interesting figure. She had been born Lillian Norton in Maine, had grown up in Iowa, and was the granddaughter of a well-known evangelist. She had studied in Europe, attracted the attention of Cosima Wagner, who made her a star at Bayreuth, and returned to America to become one of the workhorses at the Met. She died in 1913 after a shipwreck in the East Indies while on a world tour. She had a great voice, almost no temperament, and several husbands.

Cather's story creates such a singer, Cressida Garnet, who for twenty years has been supporting her accompanist, brothers, sisters, husbands, and son with the hard-earned proceeds of her glorious voice. All of these leeches regard her as a diamond mine, a role she plays without complaining until finally she marries her fourth husband, Jerome Brown, "the most rapacious of the men with whom she had to do." Brown's unsuccessful business ventures almost bankrupt her, but the story ends mercifully when Cressida Garnet goes down with the *Titanic*. The final scene is grim: her accompanist, her oldest brother, and Brown, all sitting in Cressida's sleek limousine anxiously scanning the list of survivors outside the New York office of the steamship company. To end the tale the battle over the will disposing of the singer's greatly reduced wealth is briefly recounted by the narrator.

Cather thought well enough of this story to reprint it in *Youth and the Bright Medusa* four years later. It is an excellent work, narrated by a woman friend of the protagonist, who grew up with the singer in Columbus, Ohio. The use of a female narrator, unusual for Cather, is entirely appropriate here to provide a feminine perspective on the predators, mostly male, who live off Cressida Garnet. The corrupting influence of money is again a dominant theme. Cressida asks Carrie, the narrator: "Why is it? I have never cared about money, except to make people happy with it, and it has been the curse of my life. It has spoiled all my relations with people." Because the story is based on Nordica's life, which was filled with unsuccessful marriages, Cather is again able to make it clear that marriage and art do not mix. The central part of the story is a detailed account of Cressida's middle-aged romance with a Bohemian violinist-composer, her third husband, which ends with the singer returning unexpectedly from a tour and finding her husband in bed with the cook. Ruth St. Denis wrote Cather a fan letter after the story came out and said she knew all about Cressida Garnet's problems; she herself had been a silver mine.

After the McClung-Hambourg wedding Cather immediately began compensating for the loss of Isabelle by stepping up her social activities. She started holding open house at the Bank Street apartment on Friday afternoons for friends to whom she sent formal cards of invitation. There were Alice and Henry Hoyt, his sister Elinor Wylie, Marian and Henry Canby, George Arliss, all of whom were Greenwich Village neighbors; also other New Yorkers like Elizabeth Sergeant, Ida Tarbell, and Viola Roseboro' and out-of-towners such as Zoë Akins, Harry Dwight, Ferris Greenslet, and Dorothy Canfield Fisher came when they were in the city; later there were Blanche and Alfred Knopf, Irita and Carl Van Doren; Pittsburgh friends visiting New York also dropped in. These Fridays went on for a number of years until Cather's growing reputation began attracting more people than she wanted to see.

Lewis remembered: "These Friday afternoons became very popular—so popular, in fact, that eventually she had to give them up; instead of half-a-dozen or so of her friends dropping in for tea, more and more people came, sometimes bringing strangers with them; and it became at last too much of a responsibility. But those informal gatherings around the coal fire in the living-room at 5 Bank Street, with the late winter sunshine slowly changing into dusk, and the melodious sound of the tugboat whistles coming up from the river nearby, were very pleasant while they lasted. Everyone talked as if there was not nearly enough time for all they had to say. Often a small group of Willa Cather's more intimate friends would stay on after the others had drifted away, lingering until eight o'clock or later."

The Friday afternoons, however, went only so far in filling the void, and by mid-June 1916 Cather was fed up with New York and society. She cut away suddenly, taking a train west, and didn't stop until she got to Denver. By early July she was back at the Columbian Hotel in Taos where she had stayed a week the summer before. She wrote Dwight apologizing for leaving so abruptly and reneging on a tentative date she had made to meet some of his friends. There were times, she explained, when she got physically sick of New York—homesick like children at school—so that she couldn't eat or sleep. This year she had been engulfed by such an attack and was just beginning to come to the sunny surface of life again. She loved Taos, which was forty miles from the railroad and up in the Sangre de Cristo Mountains, an adobe town of three thousand without a frame house in it. There were in addition lovely little villages lying about everywhere, and she could visit five or six of them every morning on her daily horseback ride.

She stayed in Taos three weeks, then headed north for Lander, Wyoming, to see her brother Ross. She wrote Sergeant from Wyoming that she'd had a heavenly time in Taos and was having a great visit with her brother and his family. There were two rivers flowing through the backyard, one of which was full of trout, and they were taking long horseback rides into the sand hills to the east and the Wind River Mountains to the west. Isabelle's marriage was still hard to take and always would be, but the rest of the world looked much as it used to and was not overcast. By the end of August she was in Red Cloud where she planned to settle down and write until Thanksgiving. She was in good spirits again and wrote Greenslet she had left the dismal memory of the past winter above timberline in the Rockies. She expected to have another book ready by the next year, probably a story of the Southwest to be called "The Blue Mesa." This apparently was the beginning of "Tom Outland's Story," which she didn't manage to finish for another six years. She was then thinking of it as a novel which would be full of love and hate, as she told Greenslet. She also was thinking of writing a book of nonfiction about the Southwest.

Before settling down to a new novel, however, she had to get opera singers out of her system. She had exorcised Fremstad with *The Song of the Lark* and Nordica with "The Diamond Mine," but she still had two more stories of opera singers to write. While she was stopping briefly in Denver in June, she wrote "Scandal," and after reaching Red Cloud added "The Gold Slipper," both of which are about the same singer, Kitty Ayrshire. Kitty's name and biographical facts suggest Mary Garden, the Scottish-born so-prano for whom Debussy wrote *Pelleas et Melisande*, but her personality is more like Geraldine Ferrar. "Scandal" is an inferior, unpleasant story that Paul Reynolds had a great deal of trouble selling. Fifteen magazines turned it down before he placed it in the *Century*, where it did not appear until August 1919. The story recounts an episode in the career of Kitty Ayrshire in which the unscrupulous millionaire Sigmund Stein perpetrates a fraud at the ex-pense of the singer. He has such a grotesque ambition to be seen with celebrities that he hires Kitty's double (one of his employees) to go about with him in public places to give the impression that he is on intimate terms with her.

Cather must have had doubts about this story because she waited until after Reynolds had sold the second one to *Harper's* before sending "Scandal" to him. "The Gold Slipper" is actually a very good tale, though Cather called it a trifling little story and tried too late to pull it back for revision. She was frank to admit that she needed money and the four hundred and fifty dollars she got for "The Gold Slipper" helped offset the inflation that was accom-panying the war. Her expenses, she explained, were about one-third more in

57. Silas Garber, Captain Forrester of *A Lost Lady*. Courtesy of WCPMC–NSHS

58. Mrs. Silas Garber. Courtesy of WCPMC–NSHS

59. The Garber House. Courtesy of Mrs. Perry D. Weston and WCPMC–NSHS

60. Evangeline King Case, the Miss Knightly of "The Best Years." Courtesy of WCPMC–NSHS

61. G. P. Cather, the model for Claude Wheeler in *One of Ours*. Courtesy of WCPMC–NSHS

62. Olive Fremstad as Isolde. Courtesy of the New York Metropolitan Opera Association Archives

63. Annie Pavelka, protagonist of *My Ántonia.* Courtesy of WCPMC-NSHS

64. Annie Pavelka with her husband and children. Courtesy of WCPMC-NSHS

5. Archbishop Lamy, Father Latour in
Death Comes for the Archbishop.
Courtesy of The Museum of New
Mexico, Santa Fe. Photo by Arthur
Taylor

6. Joseph Machebeuf, the Father
Joseph of the same novel. Courtesy
of the Colorado Historical Society

67. Kit Carson, who appears in *Death
Comes for the Archbishop*. Courtesy of
The Museum of New Mexico

1916 than they had been the year before. It took twenty cents worth of apples to make one pie and beef was thirty-six cents a pound.

"The Gold Slipper" is about Kitty Ayrshire at the peak of her career when she goes to Pittsburgh to give a recital. After the concert she finds herself on the same Pullman car with Marshall McKann, a coal merchant whose wife had dragged him to the performance. Kitty had noticed McKann in the audience, observed his looks of hostility and yawns, and when she gets him alone on the train asks him what he has against artists and singers. His answers are all stereotypes born of prejudice, and Kitty's lively repartee cuts away his pomposity like a scalpel, leaving him exposed as the Philistine he is. Before she goes into her state room, however, she promises to haunt him a little. The next morning when the porter wakes him he finds one of Kitty's gold slippers among his clothes in his berth. "The Gold Slipper" is an entertaining tale that scores some neat points for open-mindedness, risk-taking, and willingness to try things new.

"Scandal," however, besides being a poor story, contains a savage portrait of the Jewish millionaire Stein. He is an ogre, a caricature of the social-climbing, department-store-owning Jewish businessman. Stein is described as "one of the most hideous men in New York" with a "long nose, flattened as if it had been tied down; a scornful chin, long, white teeth; flat cheeks, yellow as a Mongolian's; tiny, black eyes, with puffy lids and no lashes; dingy, dead-looking hair—looks as if it were glued on." This description following hard after a similar one in "The Diamond Mine" of Cressida Garnet's accompanist, Miletus Poppas, comes as something of a shock to Cather readers. Poppas, who has been with Garnet for many years, is thoroughly disagreeable, has a "thin, lupine face," and yellowish green eyes, "always gleaming with something like defeated fury." "He was a vulture of the vulture race, and he had the beak of one," and at the end of the story "he look[s] as old as Jewry" as he waits to read the list of survivors of the *Titanic*.

Characters like Stein and Poppas have led some critics to charge that Cather was anti-Semitic. They cite also other unflattering Jewish figures in her work: the Jewish baby described in one of her earliest newspaper columns, the despicable art dealer in "The Marriage of Phaedra," the villain in "The Affair at Grover Station," who looks Jewish but turns out to be oriental. And in addition Louis Marcellus in *The Professor's House* has been seen as a character created out of an anti-Semitic bias. Marcellus, however, is for most readers a sympathetic figure, despite his brashness and aggressive behavior, and Jews in Cather's fiction represent a miniscule fraction of the totality. There are a good many villians in her works who are white, Anglo-

Saxon protestants: Wick Cutter, Ivy Peters, Jerome Brown, and Buck Scales, to name some; and others, who if not villians, are figures who reap the author's scorn: Alexandra's brothers, Nat Wheeler and his son Bayliss, the bad priests in *Death Comes for the Archbishop*, and so forth. Then there are the good Jews in her fiction such as the Rosens and the Nathanmeyers, the former being modeled after Cather's old friends and neighbors in Red Cloud, the Wieners; and later in her life there was her much beloved Menuhin family—all of them, Yehudi, his sisters, and the parents. She had what one might call a typical Midwestern bias against Jews in the aggregate, the result of growing up in a culture almost devoid of Jews; but to call her anti-Semitic is to exaggerate considerably. She had many loves and many hates, and among each were a few Jews.

It is likely that the creation of Stein and Poppas in the first half of 1916 owes something to Cather's subconscious resentment of Jan Hambourg, who carried off her beloved Isabelle McClung. Both stories in which these unattractive Jewish characters appear were written about the time Hambourg entered Cather's life. It did not take her many months to accept him, and she gradually became fond of him, but at the start she was devastated at the change in her life that his intrusion caused.

Nebraska that summer was blisteringly hot. The amorous lovers of Dante were no more scourged by fire than were the dwellers of the corn country, she wrote Sergeant; but corn took a terrific amount of heat, she added, and they all panted resignedly under the magnificent fire as the crops matured. Sometime in September or October Cather must have driven out into the Bohemian country, as she usually did, to visit her old friend Annie Pavelka. This may have been the trip that Jim Burden takes in the final book of *My Ántonia* when he sees Ántonia, now middle-aged, married, and surrounded by her large brood of children. The idea of her novel had not yet come to her, however, and she spent the fall working on "The Blue Mesa." Two months after getting to Red Cloud she was still making notes for it, but the materials seemed intractable. The experience was too recent for use and needed to remain a few years in the deep well of her unconscious. Her mother also was sick during the three months she spent in Red Cloud, and she had to be cook and housekeeper. On the whole she enjoyed it, she wrote Sergeant, even though there were eight in the family all the time. She had gotten the secret of good pastry at last and thought she never would be intimidated by a kitchen range again. She told another friend that she was now no mean cook. She returned to her Bank Street apartment on Thanksgiving Day with little to show for the first eleven months of 1916 except a few stories.

She arrived in New York, however, with the idea for *My Ántonia*. She wrote R. L. Scaife at Houghton Mifflin the following March that as soon as she had returned from the West, she had put aside "The Blue Mesa" to take up work on a new novel, a western story about the same length as *O Pioneers!* and with a somewhat similar background. In three months she had gotten half way through the first draft, and she thought she might be ready to send the manuscript to Boston by mid-June. She wanted to know the latest date possible to make fall publication, and by April she was already writing about the illustrations for the new novel. But she was too optimistic by far, and it was another fourteen months before she completed the book.

The winter of 1916–17, however, was a happy, productive period. She was riotously well after six months in the West, and the Hambourgs were then living in the city and making a great effort to reconcile her to their marriage. Before Christmas she invited them and S. S. McClure to dinner, and they returned the invitation on Christmas Eve. The next week she lunched at their house with Harold Bauer, the pianist, and his wife and Fritz Kreisler, and she thought Isabelle made a charming hostess for artists and celebrities. Then she went to a concert with the Hambourgs. In between these social occasions she dined with Boston friends and had thirty people in for one of her Friday afternoons. There seems no doubt that she was accepting Isabelle's marriage and beginning to like Jan.

It might have been this winter that Cather went to Elizabeth Sergeant's apartment in the East Sixties for tea. She arrived "flushed and alert from one of her swift wintry walks" in Central Park. While they were having tea, Sergeant remembered: "She then suddenly leaned over . . . and set an old Sicilian apothecary jar of mine, filled with orange-brown flowers of scented stock, in the middle of a bare, round antique table.

" 'I want my new heroine to be like this—like a rare object in the middle of a table, which one may examine from all sides.'

"She moved the lamp so that light streamed brightly down on my Taormina jar, with its glazed orange and blue design.

" 'I want her to stand out—like this—like this—because she is the story.' "

The writing was still going well in April when she interrupted it for a round of musical parties with the Hambourgs. Then in May she went down to Washington to visit her cousin Howard Gore and in June went west to receive her first honorary degree from her alma mater, the first such the University of Nebraska ever had given a woman. She continued on to Red Cloud for a visit, but the heat was unbearable and drove her farther west to Wyoming. When she got back to New York late in the summer, she immediately left for Jaffrey, New Hampshire, to recuperate from the rigors of the Midwest in July and August. She spent three weeks in Jaffrey with the Hambourgs and settled down to finish *My Ántonia*.

Jaffrey was a happy discovery. She rented two rooms on the top floor of the Shattuck Inn and was able to look out over woods and pastures towards Mount Monadnock in the distance. She was so pleased with the accommodations and the setting that she returned to Jaffrey again and again for several weeks in the autumn. She found it a congenial place to work. "The fresh, pine-scented woods and pastures," Edith Lewis remembered, "with their multitudinous wild flowers, the gentle skies, the little enclosed fields, had in them nothing of the disturbing, exalting impelling memories and associations of the past—her own past. Each day there was like an empty canvas, a clean sheet of paper to be filled. She lived with a simple sense of physical well-being, of weather, and of country solitude."

Two of her Pittsburgh friends, who rented a place about a mile from the Shattuck Inn, put up a tent for her in their meadow, and every morning after an early breakfast she crossed the Stony Brook Farm Road and cut through a hedge to the clearing where her tent was pitched. She carried her pens and paper with her but left her ink bottles, table, and camp chair in the tent. At midday she knocked off work, climbed a stone wall, and returned to the inn through the woods. There she wrote Book II ("The Hired Girls"). In the afternoons she took long walks through the countryside and up Mount Mondanock, carrying with her a favorite book, F. Schuyler Matthews's *Field Book of American Wild Flowers*. She stayed at Jaffrey about two months, but when she left the novel still was not finished. She had signed a contract for it already, was pleased with the terms, and hoped she could make Greenslet's deadline for spring publication. She missed by six months.

The problem of money kept nagging her, and she again had to turn to writing short fiction. She sent the editor of the *Century*, by way of Reynolds, a letter proposing a series of stories under the general title "Office Wives." Two of the stories, "Ardessa" and "Little Annie," which later became "Her Boss," accompanied the letter. The magazine liked the first story, which is the one about a magazine editor like McClure and his secretary, but thought the second was too sad to run in wartime. The editor, Douglas Doty, liked the idea of the series and was willing to publish the stories first in the magazine and later in book form. Cather then sent Reynolds a rough draft of another story to be called "Explosives," which never found its way into print, and promised more.

"Her Boss" is indeed a sad story and did not appear until the *Smart Set* published it in October 1919. The protagonist, Paul Wanning, is an elderly lawyer whose doctor has told him he has only a few months to live. His spoiled family, who live expensively in the suburbs, and his law partners show little sympathy. The only person who treats him with understanding is Annie Wooley, a young overworked and underpaid stenographer in his office. He hires her to take from dictation the autobiography he decides to write, and she works late, gives up her weekends to help him carry out this project. She gets only censure from the law partners and staff for this act of kindness, and after the protagonist dies she is fired from her job. Wanning's family refuses to honor a codicil in his will providing compensation for poor little Annie, and no one can believe there wasn't hanky panky going on. The story is a melancholy commentary on what Mark Twain would have called "the damned human race."

Nothing came of "Office Wives," presumably because Cather had to spend all her time and energy finishing *My Ántonia* in order to make fall publication. She began sending copy to Greenslet in driblets in November, but he did not get it all until the twentieth of June. By that time she was reading proof on the early chapters, and had completed complicated negotiations over the Benda illustrations. She was depressed during the winter that she couldn't seem to get the book finished for spring publication. She said she had pushed it along as fast as she could, but writing was a slow business. There was no good reason why *My Ántonia* had taken two winters and she felt rather humble about the matter.

One of the obstacles to finishing the book was an attack of bronchitis that laid her low for two weeks in February. Also her French cook, Josephine Bourda, was ill. Fortunately, at this juncture Fremstad came to the rescue. She had plenty of spare time this winter because she was not singing at the Met, and every night she sent her car and chauffeur to take Cather to her apartment for dinner and music. Wartime shortages also made the winter difficult, for coal was in short supply and Cather was unable to heat her study. Yet there were some pleasant Friday afternoons with interesting people in for tea, and she saw a great deal of the Hambourgs. She wrote Carrie Sherwood in March that she was getting on well with Jan and had really learned to like him.

In late June Cather went to Jaffrey intending to stay three weeks and finish reading proof there. She had to insist that the proofreaders at Houghton Mifflin allow her to use an occasional subjunctive, and she worried a good bit about the placement of the illustrations. She wanted them printed on the book paper and placed within the text as she had indicated, not printed separately and placed at the ends of the gatherings. The stark black-and-white drawings by Benda, who was familiar with the Midwest farm setting, provide a realistic balance for Jim Burden's romantic memoir and contribute to the understanding of the novel. Again Houghton Mifflin gave her what she wanted, and when she received advance copies of the book, she was pleased. Her three weeks in Jaffrey stretched to six weeks, after which she returned to New York to visit the Hambourgs, who had taken a cottage in Scarsdale for the summer.

She spent a week totally immersed in music in Scarsdale. The Hambourgs had musicians visiting and still others were living across the street. They had Beethoven and Mozart quartets every night. The gods on Olympus do not have such music, she wrote Greenslet after an evening of Beethoven's tenth quartet and Schubert's *Death and the Maiden*. Her right to these riches, she explained, resulted from her lending Josephine for the summer. The Hambourgs and their friends were so enamored of Josephine's French cooking and so afraid Cather might take her away, or so she said, that they would even play request programs for her. Josephine, who spoke no English, commented on this orgy of music: "*Les sonates, les quatuors à deux heures le matin, ce n'est pas raisonnable, vous savez, mademoiselle*" ("Sonatas, quartets at two in the morning, it's not tolerable, you know, mademoiselle"). Cather, who was heading for Nebraska after this week in Scarsdale, agreed that the silence of the cornfields would be welcome.

About the middle of August she took the train west and spent a couple of weeks in the Southwest and six weeks in Red Cloud. Again her mother was sick and she took over the cooking. This year she felt so much at home on the range that she wrote Greenslet she wished she were as good a writer as she was a cook. While her mother was convalescing, she visited her Aunt Franc in the country and read the letters of her cousin who had been killed in France in May. She also began thinking about another book and proposed to Greenslet a collection of stories about musicians and singers for the following spring. She would begin with "The Diamond Mine," add "The Gold Slipper" and three or four others not yet written. The volume would be light and breezy. Houghton Mifflin was interested, but by the time she returned to New York at the end of October, traveling by way of Toronto to visit the Hambourgs for ten days, she already was planning a novel inspired by her cousin's letters and had lost interest in the story collection. *My Ántonia* was in the bookstores by this time, and she must have hoped the sales would pay her bills until she could finish another novel.

In one sense Cather had been preparing to write *My Ántonia* for a third of a century. She had known the model for its fictional heroine, Annie Sadilek, later Pavelka, ever since she was a child in Red Cloud, and, as we have seen, the story of Annie's father's suicide was one of the first stories she had heard in Nebraska. As she looked back in her old age, she felt that the character of Ántonia was the embodiment of all her feelings about the early immigrants in the prairie country, and it seemed then that she must have been destined to write this novel if she ever wrote anything. When Margaret Lawrence's *School of Femininity* appeared in 1936 with a perceptive chapter on Cather, she agreed with its thesis: she could only write successfully when she wrote about people or places she loved. The characters she created could be cranky or queer or foolhardy or rash, but they had to have something to them that thrilled her and warmed her heart.

Annie Sadilek Pavelka was such a person. Cather told an interviewer in 1921 that one of the people who had interested her most when she was a child was the Bohemian hired girl who worked for one of their neighbors. "She was one of the truest artists I ever knew in the keenness and sensitiveness of her enjoyment, in her love of people and in her willingness to take pains." After Cather left journalism and began writing novels, she visited the Bohemian country during her summer visits to Red Cloud and saw Annie and her family on their farm. The lives of the Pavelkas and their neighbors seemed to her like stories out of a book that went on and on year after year like *War and Peace*. Whenever she went back to Nebraska, her friends filled her in on the details of the narrative that had taken place in her absence.

Once she decided to make Annie the central figure in her novel, she had to work out the narrative technique to present her. She chose a first-person point of view because she believed that novels of feeling, such as *My Ántonia*, were best narrated by a character in the story. Novels of action, on the other hand, should be told in the third person, using the omniscient author as narrator. But who should the first-person teller of the tale be? She told an interviewer that she rejected Annie's lover as narrator because "my Ántonia deserved something better than the *Saturday Evening Post* sort of stuff." But she wanted a male narrator because, as she explained, most of what she knew about Annie came from talks with young men: "She had a fascination for them, and they used to be with her whenever they could. They had to manage it on the sly because she was only a hired girl." Thus Cather created as narrator Jim Burden, whose age, experience, and personal history closely parallel her own. He tells the story as an adult reminiscence. Of course, Cather had been using male narrators in her short fiction for a long time, and there was no novelty for her in this invention.

She felt obliged, however, to defend her use of a male narrator. When her old friend and editor Will Owen Jones asked her why she had done it, she repeated her explanation that she had gotten her material from young men, then added further rationalization by reminding Jones of her experience in writing McClure's autobiography. She had been so successful in masquerading as McClure then that she felt confident in doing an entire novel from a male perspective. When she first began writing the autobiography, she found it awfully hampering to be McClure all the time, but in the end it became fascinating to work within the limits and color of the personality she knew so well. Even Mrs. McClure and John Phillips, McClure's college classmate and former business partner, found the presentation completely convincing.

Once she had decided on her narrative voice and the first-person method, she further planned to avoid any formal structuring of the novel. Jim Burden's memories, which, of course, were her memories, would shape the narrative. She would avoid the opportunities for melodrama that the materials certainly contained and dwell lightly on the incidents that most novelists would ordinarily emphasize. The story would be made up of little, everyday happenings for the most part, for such events made up the bulk of most people's lives. It would be the other side of the rug, the pattern that is supposed not to count. There would be no love affair, no courtship, no marriage, no broken heart, no struggle for success. "I knew I'd ruin my material if I put it in the usual fictional pattern. I just used it the way I thought absolutely true." The result was the creation of a novel that gives the impression of real autobiography rather than fiction. Since the invented narrator is not a professional writer, the apparent artlessness of his memories seems perfectly logical, and the reader is willing to suspend his belief that he is in the presence of a perfectly controlled art.

The loosely episodic plot in *My Ántonia* follows fairly closely the actual lives of Annie Pavelka and Willa Cather. The novel opens with an introduction in which the author meets Jim Burden on a train going west. Both the author and Jim, who is legal counsel for the railroad, live in New York, and both knew Ántonia when they were growing up in Black Hawk, Nebraska. Jim has been writing down from time to time what he remembers of Ántonia and promises to let her see his manuscript when he finishes it. When he later does so, the narrative begins.

It opens with the arrival of Jim, orphaned at the age of ten, and the hired man Jake in Nebraska about 1883. Jim has come to live with his grandparents, who have a farm on the Divide. Ántonia Shimerda is a neighbor, the daughter of Bohemian immigrants newly arrived in Nebraska. She becomes Jim's playmate and companion, even though she is four years older. The events of Book I take place on the farm and describe the lives of both the Burdens and the Shimerdas, the idyllic autumn in which Jim and Ántonia explore the countryside, and the bitter winter which ends with the suicide of Ántonia's father.

Book II ("The Hired Girls") takes place in town after Jim and his grandparents leave the farm and move into Black Hawk. Ántonia comes to town to work for the Harlings, who live around the block from the Burdens. Cather presents in this section of the novel a full gallery of immigrant women besides Ántonia: Lena Lingard, Tiny Soderball, and Anna Hansen, Norwegians; the Bohemian Marys; the Danish laundry girls; and Selma Kronn, the first Swedish girl to get a job teaching in the high school. All of them have come in from the farm to work. Ántonia is dismissed by the Harlings because she refuses to stop going to dances and goes to work for Wick Cutter, satyr and moneylender, who plans to rape Ántonia but is foiled by Jim. Book II also includes a memorable picnic by the river before Jim goes off to college.

Book III (which takes place in Lincoln) deals with Jim's education and brief romance with Lena, who has come to the state capital to become a dressmaker. Ántonia is absent from this part of the novel, and we next see her in Book IV, in which her story is told to Jim by the Widow Steavens during a summer back home from college. Jim has now transferred to Harvard to finish his education and has lost touch with Ántonia. He learns that Ántonia has been seduced and abandoned by a railroad conductor named Larry Donovan, whom she expected to marry, and has returned to the farm to bear an illegitimate child. The final book of the novel, "Cuzak's Boys," takes place twenty years later when Jim returns from the East and drives out to visit Ántonia. He finds her middle-aged, "battered but not diminished," full of vitality and zest for living, surrounded by her children and married to an easygoing, good-natured Bohemian farmer.

More than most writers, Cather presents readers with the chance to compare biographical data with its transmutation into art. There is a great deal more factual basis in *My Ántonia* than the bare story outline of the title character and the narrator. The town of Black Hawk is again Red Cloud, and the Nebraska farmlands again provide the locale. Ántonia's farm house still stands in the country north of Red Cloud with the fruit cave a few yards from the back door. Jim's grandparents, as we have seen, are drawn from life, the entire Miner family play roles in the story, and Herbert Bates appears as Gaston Cleric, Jim's college teacher. In addition to the main characters and incidents, minor figures and events also are rooted in actuality. The black pianist, Blind d'Arnault, who plays in Black Hawk, was drawn from a real Blind Tom, whom Cather heard in Lincoln, and a Blind Boone, whom she probably heard in Red Cloud. The visitor to the town today can see the home of Wick Cutter, who in actuality was a loan-shark named Bentley and apparently as evil and unsavory as Cather makes him. The hotel-keeping Mrs. Gardener in the novel was a real Mrs. Holland, and the man who fathered Ántonia's first child out of wedlock was James William Murphy.

After the novel appeared, Cather was pestered by literal-minded readers wanting to know where she got this and where she got that. The people in Red Cloud were continually playing guessing games with her characters and incidents. It exasperated her, but she should have expected her drama of memory to provoke this kind of a response. Sometimes she was patient and discussed her sources with friends—sometimes she even answered letters from students—but usually her reaction was annoyance. Often she did not know where she got things, and after *My Ántonia* was published, her father pointed out half a dozen different incidents that were based on things she had done, seen, or heard of with him, all of which she thought she had invented.

One such episode was the story within a story of the two Russians, Pavel and Peter, and the wolves. It illustrates the way Cather's creative imagination worked, as she fashioned her fictional materials from her memories. The wolf story probably came both from herself and from hearing the tale in her father's presence. It is a gruesome account of a wedding party in Russia traveling from one village to another in the dead of winter. Six sledges are attacked by wolves, and one by one they are overturned and the occupants killed by the beasts. Finally the only sledge left is the one carrying Pavel, Peter, and the bride and groom. Just before the sledge reaches the safety of the village, Pavel throws the bride and groom to the wolves. For this inhuman act Pavel and Peter are ostracized and forced to leave Russia for America. This story is a folk tale that folklorists have collected from the oral tradition of Nebraska immigrants in the identical version that Cather uses. She no doubt heard the story from the farm people she knew. At the same time, her idea that she made up the story perhaps comes from having seen a well-known painting by Paul Powis depicting wolves attacking a sledge or from a poem by Browning, "Ivan Ivanovitch," which tells a similar tale. Since Cather took a year-long course in Browning at the University of Nebraska, it seems reasonable to conclude that she remembered the poem.

Cather always insisted that her characters were not drawn from real life but were only suggested by people she knew, or they were composites. You can never get it through people's heads, she wrote Carrie Sherwood, that a story is made out of an emotion or an excitement and is not made out of the legs and arms and faces of one's friends. There was one exception to this, however, in the character of Mrs. Harling. Cather was working on "The

Hired Girls" when she read of Mrs. Miner's death in a Red Cloud newspaper. She made a deliberate effort to remember her tricks of voice and gesture, and she made Mrs. Harling a clear little snapshot of Mrs. Miner as she first knew her. All of the mothers in her fiction, she admitted, had a little of Mrs. Miner in them, but this fictional portrait was unique, and she hoped the Miner daughters would like it. She dedicated the novel to Carrie and Irene "in memory of affections old and true." The older one grows, she added, the clearer one's early impressions somehow become.

Few novels are likely to be read longer than *My Ántonia*. In it character, theme, setting, myth, and incident are combined into a narrative of great emotional power. The prose is limpid, evocative, the product of Cather's nearly three decades of learning to master her instrument. For many readers it is her greatest work. She knew she had done well with this book and told Carrie Sherwood in 1938 that "the best thing I've done is *My Ántonia*. I feel I've made a contribution to American letters with that book." On other occasions she gave this precedence to *Death Comes for the Archbishop*. In 1943 Greenslet wrote her that *My Ántonia* was a novel to cherish. It had sold twenty-five hundred copies in the previous year, and he didn't think there was another novel published a quarter of a century before that had continued to do so well. These were all copies in the regular hardcover edition, and this in the middle of the war. Through the years the novel has always sold steadily and never has been out of print.

Everything went right in this work—a great concept executed with consummate artistry—and it goes well beyond any of her first three novels. While Alexandra Bergson is the strong, intelligent tamer of the wild land, Thea Kronborg with the godlike name the climber of Olympus, Ántonia Shimerda is the mother of races. She is the most heroic figure of all, both the Madonna of the Wheat Fields and the symbol of the American westering myth. Although there are somber tones in her story, it ends on an affirmative note. The suicide of her father, the hard toil on the prairie farm, the desertion by her lover—these things have receded into the past by the final chapter, and what remains at the end is the indelible picture of Ántonia and her children: "It was no wonder that her sons stood tall and straight. She was a rich mine of life, like the founders of early races." Even after several readings one cannot finish this novel without being moved.

Cather managed to avoid the pitfalls inherent in her narrative method. Jim Burden as an unreliable narrator, childless, unhappily married to a promoter of avant garde causes, a man who jots down at random his memories of his youth, could have produced a story excessively sentimental; but he did not. There is the aura of nostalgia frequently found in Cather's fiction, but the sentiment does not become sentimentality. Cather escapes this by her usual juxtaposition of contrasts; in this case good and evil are alternated. Jim Burden's golden memories are constantly being interrupted by the sterner realities. The idyl of Jim's boyhood is punctuated by the rattlesnake episode, the suicide of Ántonia's father, the deviltries of Wick Cutter, the meanness of Ántonia's older brother, the horrible story of Pavel and Peter, and Ántonia's seduction. The cruel and ugly scenes and characters balance nicely the pleasant memories: the wonderful first autumn, the happy Christmas scene, Mrs. Harling's music, the picnic, the exhilarating talk of Gaston Cleric, the final visit to Ántonia's farm.

One of the remarkable aspects of this novel is its appeal to unsophisticated and sophisticated readers alike. The college freshman who has read very little is just as captivated by *My Ántonia* as his English professor who has read everything from Beowulf to Thomas Kennerly Wolfe. The freshman finds a simple, human story dealing with genuine people facing recognizable problems. He can relate to it; he is touched by the real feeling evoked; he can read it without a dictionary or recourse to someone else's notes or annotations. The professor finds in the novel, besides a moving story, a richness of allusion, myth, and symbol presented by one of the great stylists of this century. This wide appeal results from Cather's blending together her native experience and her wide knowledge of European literature and culture. Her memories of Nebraska give her novel color, romance, emotional content; her general culture supplies texture, profundity, intellectual content. Together they make a literary classic.

The reader who plunges into Sinclair Lewis, for example, is likely to hit his head on the bottom, but in Cather there is no danger. He can dive as deep as he wishes and stay down as long as he can. The reader who plunges into the Thomas Wolfe of *Look Homeward, Angel* is swamped by the astonishing vitality of his work but dismayed, as Lionel Trilling puts it, by "the disproportion between the energy of his utterance and his power of mind." It is the intellection coming from European culture that gives one room to swim in Cather's fiction. She did not write intellectual novels, but there is substance in them to nourish the mind, subtly mixed with emotion and feeling. The affective content derives from her prairie youth and what she liked to call "the gift of sympathy." These two kinds of experience are of the body and the mind: friendships with people like Ántonia in post-frontier Nebraska and travel through Europe and books from Homer to Housman. Cather's roots in the soil of Webster County were deep and well-watered; her knowledge and use of Old World culture was substantial and pervading. The warp and woof of her work is native American, but threads of European culture are woven into the fabric.

From the very opening of the novel Jim Burden evokes the land as Cather remembered it when she was a child in Catherton: "As I looked about me I felt that the grass was the country; as the water is the sea. The red of the grass made all the great prairie the colour of wine stains, or of certain seaweeds when they are first washed up. And there was so much motion in it; the whole country seemed, somehow to be running." And later: "I felt motion in the landscape; in the fresh, easy-blowing morning wind, and in the earth itself, as if the shaggy grass were a sort of loose hide, and underneath it herds of wild buffalo were galloping, galloping." When Jim later lies in his grandmother's garden under a warm autumn sun, he listens to the wind, feels the warm earth under him, watches the insects: "I kept as still as I could. Nothing happened. I did not expect anything to happen. I was something that lay under the sun and felt it, like the pumpkins, and I did not want to be anything more. I was entirely happy. Perhaps we feel like that when we die and become a part of something entire, whether it is sun and air, or goodness and knowledge. At any rate, that is happiness; to be dissolved into something complete and great."

Soon Jim and his grandparents drive over to meet the Shimerdas, their new neighbors, who live in a sod house like badgers in a hole. "I saw a door and a window sunk deep in the drawbank. The door stood open, and a woman and a girl of fourteen ran out and looked up at us hopefully." This is Ántonia. Her eyes were "big and warm and full of light, like the sun shining on brown pools in the wood. Her skin was brown, too, and in her cheeks she had a glow of rich, dark colour. Her brown hair was curly and wild-looking." From this first memory comes a lasting relationship that Jim later sums up: "The idea of you is part of my mind; you influence my likes and dislikes, all my tastes, hundreds of times when I don't realize it. You really are a part of me." Then at the end of the novel, for Jim as well as for Cather, the experience of knowing the fictional and the real Ántonia produces the realization that "whatever we had missed, we possessed together the previous, the incommunicable past."

Underlying this affecting story of human friendship is the use of myth and symbol to give the novel universality. This dimension of Cather's art seems more intuitive than deliberate, the result of her assimilation of literary tradition and western culture; but whether it is conscious or instinctive, it adds unobtrusively significance to the narrative. Cather mythologizes American experience in creating Ántonia as an embodiment of the westward movement, the pioneer woman, the symbol of the frontier. Her life is emblematic of the breaking of the sod, the cultivation of the wilderness, the migration of peoples from the Old World to the New. Cather did it earlier in Alexandra's epic struggle to tame the wild land. In *My Ántonia* the symbol comes into sharp focus in the picnic scene. Jim and the hired girls with their picnic baskets meet on the banks of the river outside of Black Hawk. After the meal and a good bit of talk about the girls' immigrant experiences and their families, Jim tells about a Nebraska farmer who found a Spanish stirrup when he was plowing. He tells the girls about Coronado's adventures in the New World and speculates that Coronado must have explored their region in his search for the Seven Golden Cities. Jim concludes his story with the statement from his school textbook that Coronado "died in the wilderness, of a broken heart," a highly colored account of a much more prosaic history. To this tale Ántonia rejoins: "More than him has done that," and the girls murmur assent. This conversation is followed by a remarkable scene:

"Presently we saw a curious thing: There were no clouds, the sun was going down in a limpid, gold-washed sky. Just as the lower edge of the red disk rested on the high fields against the horizon, a great black figure suddenly appeared on the face of the sun. We sprang to our feet, straining our eyes toward it. In a moment we realized what it was. On some upland farm, a plough had been left standing in the field. The sun was sinking just behind it. Magnified across the distance by the horizontal light, it stood out against the sun, was exactly contained within the circle of the disk; the handles, the tongue, the share—black against the molten red. There it was, heroic in size, a picture writing on the sun." As a symbol of the Westward Movement, the plow against the sun appropriately stands for the farming frontier, which had followed the earlier frontiers of the trapper and the miner; and its use here reinforces meaning.

An even more impressive use of myth and symbol occurs in the final book in which Jim Burden returns twenty years later to visit Ántonia. She and her children show Jim their fruit cave, which is a cornucopia of the earth's bounty. They go down into the earth where Jim sees shelf upon shelf of preserved fruit and barrels of pickles. After inspecting the contents of the cave: "We turned to leave the cave; Ántonia and I went up the stairs first, and the children waited. We were standing outside talking, when they all came running up the steps together, big and little, tow heads and gold heads and brown, and flashing little naked legs; a veritable explosion of life out of the dark cave into the sunlight. It made me dizzy for a moment."

The description here has the same effect on the reader, and in this picture of the explosion of life out of the dark womb, myth and symbol again add meaning. This scene climaxes a modern enactment of the ancient Eleusian Mysteries that celebrated the earth's fertility two thousand years before Christ. It is so thoroughly domesticated in the Nebraska landscape, however, that no one need bother about its link to ancient rites, but the image of Ántonia as earth goddess certainly makes a subliminal impact on the reader. In *My Ántonia* Cather has succeeded not only in giving significance to the American westering experience, but she also has tied her story to man's primitive relationship with the earth. This scene resonates in the mind long after one has closed the book. Again the polarity in Cather between primitivism and civilization adds tension to her fiction.

There are two other examples worth noting of general culture and reading that reinforce meaning. In an early scene when Jim and Ántonia are roaming the countryside during their first idyllic autumn, they come to a prairie dog town. Jim kills an enormous rattlesnake that he finds sunning itself amid the burrows. This episode serves nicely as an exciting bit of action and also as a rite of passage for Jim, but it is equally clear from the text that Cather is linking it to myth. Jim's summary reference to himself as a dragon-slayer and the snake as "the ancient, eldest Evil" make a subtle connection between American frontier experience and its cultural antecedents—all the literary examples as well as the visual representations of dragon slayers. Pictures of St. George and the dragon, besides depicting a knight impaling a dragon on his lance, always show an adoring maiden watching the slaying, and in this scene on the Nebraska prairie there are both ingredients. After Jim finishes off the rattler with a spade, Ántonia says in her broken English: "You is just like big mans." When the hero returns to his admiring people in triumph, Cather adds a neat touch of twentieth-century irony. She has Jim reflect that his dragon was old, lazy, well-fed, and an easy mark for a ten-year-old St. George.

The other exhibit is a scene in Lincoln when Jim is squiring Lena about the state capital. He takes her to a performance of *Camille*, a second-rate production by a mediocre road company, but both Jim and Lena are thrilled by the romantic drama as it unfolds accompanied by incidental music from Verdi's version of the same play, *La Traviata*. In this episode literary allusion reinforces events taking place in the novel. The renunciation of love for duty to family, central to the action of the play, is about to be enacted in the parting of Jim and Lena. Gaston Cleric, Jim's professor, plays the same role in the novel as the elder Duval in the play. He calls on Jim to follow his destiny to Harvard and to stop "playing about with this handsome Norwegian." For contemporary readers who had seen Dumas' play on the stage or later generations who remember Greta Garbo's film version or know Verdi's opera, this scene adds significance to the story.

Cather's thorough grounding in Latin also gives depth to her narrative. As Jim studies the classics under Gaston Cleric, he develops a passion for Virgil, whose *Georgics* he is studying one night in his room. His book is open to the passage: "*Optima dies . . . prima fugit*" ("the best days are the first to flee"). Jim reflects on the dying Virgil at Brindisi, who must have remembered his youth in his native Mantua. Jim too has left his native Black Hawk, Ántonia, and his grandparents. His destiny will take him East and turn him into a corporation lawyer. The theme from Virgil supplies a leitmotif for this elegiac narrative. Cather also quotes another line from Virgil: "*Primus ego in patriam mecum . . . deducam Musas*" ["I shall be the first to bring the Muse into my country"], which has a parallel contemporary meaning. Cleric has explained to his class that Virgil meant by *patria* the region along the Mincio River where he had been born, not all of Italy. The reader realizes that what Virgil did for his native place, Cather also was doing for Nebraska—putting it on the literary map.

The strong classical influence on Cather's work affected *My Ántonia* in another significant way. To tell her story, she employed the pastoral mode, a manner of expression that "counters the failures of the present by moving back into the past." Even in her early fiction and poetry she sometimes adopted the pastoral tone of retrospection and elegy in an effort to recapture the past. She was drawn to the classic Arcadian theme of a Golden Age, a grander, more perfect time gone by, and it suited her personality. It also provided a very appropriate method for writing a drama of memory and gave her imagination full scope to fashion a story intensely subjective. The auto-biographical form that she selected was well adapted both to the Arcadian theme and to her own romantic art. It wasn't different from the strategies Wordsworth had used in "Tintern Abbey" and "The Prelude."

The human impulse to remember the past as somehow better than the present, the days of one's youth as happier than the years of adulthood, has a wide appeal. In point of fact, childhood is often unhappy, beset with problems of poverty, broken homes, painful psychological adjustments, but the yearning for the innocence of childhood is undeniably attractive. Cather's youthful nonconformity, sexual ambivalence, and community disapproval kept her own early years from being an unalloyed idyll, but the pastoral ideal always fired her imagination. The tension in the pastoral mode between the desire to return to the past and the knowledge that one cannot go back gives Cather's fiction a dramatic quality, but the conflict can never be resolved. Her life itself had this tension, and *My Ántonia* comes at a point in her career when the past began to seem more attractive than the present. As she was writing this novel during the First World War, her mind began to turn backwards more and more. Personal problems from within and the devastation of Europe from without accentuated her growing nostalgia. She told Sergeant after the war broke out: "Our present is ruined—but we had a beautiful past."

Related to the backward-looking pastoral mode is the yearning for the pre-puberty years of sexual innocence. Cather always regarded the days when she played with her brothers, unconscious of sexual difference, as times of golden memory. Her narrator-persona Jim Burden shares this feeling in his reconstruction of his idyllic months of childhood with Ántonia. His adult life, however, is impoverished by Cather's adult bias against romantic love. Her greatest failing as an artist is her inability to depict heterosexual adult relationships affirmatively. As a celibate writer herself, she gives Jim her own aversion to sex, and when he finishes law school and seeks a wife, she gives him a frigid, unhappy marriage. In compensation, however, he is able to evoke in his memoir a happily married Ántonia, who is one of the memorable characters in American literature.

Jim's aversion to sex is developed early in the novel, first symbolically by the rattlesnake episode and then by the attempted rape scene. When Jim kills the snake, an obvious sex symbol, he is sickened by the experience, but he fights with a fury as he slashes at the reptile with his spade. Later when he is past puberty and getting ready to go to college, Ántonia fears Wick Cutter's lechery and arranges for Jim to sleep in her bed one night while Mrs. Cutter is out of town. Cutter sneaks into the bedroom planning to rape Ántonia, finds Jim, and a furious struggle ensues. Jim runs home through the streets in his night shirt bleeding from the fight and utterly repelled by the experience. As humorous as the reader might find the episode, Jim feels defiled and hates Ántonia for getting him into this predicament.

During the same period in Jim's life his sexual awakening takes place, but Cather allows it to happen only in his mind. He dreams that he is in a harvest field when Lena, now a woman of great physical attraction, comes towards him with a reaping hook in her hand, sits beside him and says: "Now . . . I can kiss you as much as I like." Later in Lincoln Jim carries on an apparently sexless affair with Lena, who is not interested in any permanent emotional attachment to a man. The love-making in that part of the novel takes place on stage when Jim and Lena go to see *Camille*. Jim then goes to Harvard and after he finishes law school remains in the East.

In the final book when Jim returns to visit Ántonia twenty years later, she is a mother figure, and he recaptures his lost youth in his relationship with her children. He finds warmth and happiness in her kitchen, as he once did in his grandmother's; he finds peace in her garden; he sleeps in the barn with the boys. Memories of his childhood friends return in the names Ántonia has given her children. Although he had dreaded going back, fearing that he would find Ántonia aged and broken, he need not have worried. He does not have to abandon his feeling that "some memories are realities, and are better than anything that can ever happen to one again."

Feminist critics are divided in their opinions of *My Ántonia*. Sharon O'Brien regards it as a novel that is consciously "perpetuating and sanctioning limiting male views of women" because Jim is "more the author's mask than a fully imagined male character." Susan Rosowski reads Ántonia's story from a very different perspective: her argument is that Jim Burden's values are all standard male norms but that Ántonia is indeed an autonomous heroine. She goes her own way despite pressure from the male-dominated society she lives in. The moments in the novel when Jim disapproves of Ántonia occur when she refuses to accept male expectations. She is proud of her ability to work in the fields like a man; she refuses to give up going to dances when Mr. Harling issues an ultimatum; she doesn't worry that working for Wick Cutter will tarnish her reputation. She makes no effort to hold Larry Donovan when he deserts her but returns home to have and keep her illegitimate daughter. Her objective in life is to raise children, to be the mother of races, and she carries out this purpose with complete success. Her marriage to Cuzak, whom she cares for like one of her children, is not a love match but a comfortable arrangement for getting offspring into the world. Ántonia is a character a woman can admire.

The novel appeared in late September 1918, when the country was preoccupied with the final days of World War I, which ended with the Armistice on November 11. The book did not become a best seller, though it sold moderately well, passing the five thousand mark by Christmas and reaching about eight thousand by the time it had been out a year. Cather's royalties for the first twelve months amounted to less than two thousand dollars, however; not enough to support her while she wrote another novel. By the end of 1919 it was only selling five hundred copies a year and by late 1920 it was briefly unavailable due to a printers' strike. But the reviewers were nearly unanimous in their praise and recognized the novel as a significant contribution to American letters. Greenslet recorded in his memoirs that when he read the book in manuscript he experienced "the most thrilling shock of recognition of the real thing of any manuscript" he ever received.

H. L. Mencken again led the chorus with two reviews in consecutive issues of the *Smart Set*. *My Ántonia*, he wrote, was merely one more "step upward in the career of a writer who has labored with the utmost patience and industry, and won every foot of the way by hard work." He again praised her earlier novels, but *My Ántonia* was a sudden leap forward, "not only the best [novel] done by Miss Cather herself, but also one of the best that any American has ever done." Then he continued with the utmost enthusiasm: "It is intelligent; it is moving. The means that appear in it are means perfectly adapted to its end. Its people are unquestionably real. Its background is brilliantly vivid. It has form, grace, good literary manners. In a word, it is a capital piece of writing, and it will be heard of long after the baroque balderdash now touted on the 'book pages' is forgotten."

Randolph Bourne, whom Cather thought the best reviewer in the business, was equally pleased: "Miss Cather convinces because she knows her story and carries it along with the surest touch. It has all the artistic simplicity of material that has been patiently shaped until everything irrelevant has been scraped away." He concluded his review with the opinion that Cather "has taken herself out of the rank of provincial writers and given us something we can fairly class with the modern literary art the world over that is earnestly and richly interpreting the spirit of youth." The *New York Sun* carried a long, anonymous notice that particularly pleased Cather because the reviewer really understood what she was doing and made all the right comments. "The most extraordinary thing about *My Ántonia* is the author's surrender of the usual methods of fiction in telling her story." It could have been made into an exciting, dramatic novel, but then it would have been just another piece of fiction. Her method left the reader with the conviction of absolute authenticity. "You picked up *My Ántonia* to read a novel (love story, of course; hope it's a good one) and find yourself enthralled by autobiography."

As time went on, however, Cather reorganized her memory of the novel's reception. Four years later she had convinced herself that it took the critics two years to discover the book. They didn't like it at first because it had no structure. By 1941 she was writing an old friend that the New York reviewers always lament the fact that her new book (whichever it might be) is a marked decline from the previous one. Logically, she said, she should have reached the vanishing point long ago. She had read practically all the reviews of *My Ántonia* and only two of them from coast to coast were favorable. All the others said the book was formless and would be of interest only to the Nebraska State Historical Society.

This hostile stance towards critics is a subject to be explored later, but whether or not there was justification for it, Cather always had many enthusiastic readers. Twelve years after the novel appeared, Greenslet sent Justice Oliver Wendell Holmes a copy. The old jurist, then eighty-nine, wrote

Greenslet that the book "lifts me to all my superlatives. I have not had such a sensation for a long time. To begin with I infinitely respect the author's taking her own environment and not finding it necessary to look for her scenes in Paris or London. I think it a prime mark of a real gift to realize that any piece of the universe may be made poetical if seen by a poet. But to be more concrete, the result seems to me a wonderful success. It has unfailing charm, perhaps not to be defined; a beautiful tenderness, a vivifying imagination that transforms but does not distort or exaggerate—order, proportion." The next year Greenslet sent Holmes *Death Comes for the Archbishop*, and after having his secretary read the novel to him, he wrote Cather directly: "I think you have the gift of the transforming touch. What to another would be prose, under your hand becomes poetry without ceasing to be truth. Among the changes of old age one is that novels are apt to bore me, and I owe you a debt for two exceptions, both of which gave me delight."

CHAPTER 14

One of Ours

As the church bells pealed throughout New York City on November 11, 1918, Cather joined fervently in the general rejoicing over the end of the war. She was in a state of euphoria when she wrote her Aunt Franc, whose son had paid the clear price, as she put it, for what all the world had gained that day through victory over Germany. Think of it, she wrote, for the first time since human society has existed on this planet, the sun rose this morning upon a world in which not one great monarchy or tyranny existed. She quoted Emerson, who had written: one day God would say, "I am tired of kings." She mourned that her cousin had not lived to see the glorious day of victory and to help in the reconstruction that must follow, and she thought of the last act of *Macbeth* when they bring old Siward word that his son has been slain in his first battle. The old man says: "Why then, God's soldier be he!" So was G. P. Cather God's soldier, who had gone from the cornfields of Nebraska to fight in France for an ideal. This intense feeling of elation could not be sustained for long, and Cather, like other writers of her generation, suffered sharp disillusionment when it soon became apparent that the war had neither ended all wars nor saved the world for democracy.

This high level of euphoria, however, was Cather's state of mind when she started *One of Ours*, a novel she had to write, despite the hazards of such an undertaking. She had been at the hairdresser's in New York one day in late June when she read in the paper her cousin's citation for bravery just before he was killed in action at Cantigny on the Western Front on May 23. The *New York Times* reported: "Lt. G. P. Cather (since killed in action)—with splendid courage and coolness he mounted the parapet of a trench and directed a destructive flanking fire from two automatic rifle teams exposed to seven

German machine guns." From that moment on her cousin was constantly in her mind. Then she read his letters to his mother when she was in Nebraska in September, and she could not go on to other things. After writing *Alexander's Bridge*, she had intended not to write another story with a man as the central figure, but she was mixed up by accident of birth with this boy, whom she had known since she was a child on the Divide. She had helped take care of him when they were little, and they were both very much alike and also very much different, she thought. He never could escape the misery of being himself except in action, and whatever he put his hand to turned out either ugly or ridiculous. He resented Willa's escaping from Nebraska prairie life, though he had contempt for her escape through writing and the imagination. They had drifted apart and seldom saw each other after she went to college and later moved east. The United States' entry into the war was a godsend for him: the army offered a chance to get away to a life of action. She was proud of him when he enlisted and was sent off for officer training.

During the summer of 1914 when she had seen him again after the war started in Europe, they had long talks together, and for the first time she began to understand him. His despair over being stuck on the farm and his wistful inquiries about France and the larger world Cather moved in were painful to hear about and to discuss, and she went away trying to forget him. As they talked and she described her life, his lips would twitch and curl, the helplessness that ignorance always feels, she called it. To get away from him and his kind, she wrote Dorothy Canfield Fisher, was why she wrote at all.

Then when he died in action as a member of the American Expeditionary Force in France, she was overwhelmed by the thought that anything so exalted could have happened to someone so disinherited of hope. He had been, in her words, "an inarticulate young man butting his way through the world." That he could lose himself in a cause and die for an idea seemed to her remarkable and exciting. What followed, she said, was three lovely, tormented years of writing the novel. Her cousin was in her blood so long that some of her was buried with him, some of him left alive in her. The war gave him to her and gave him to himself.

She felt a blood identity with her cousin, a Siegmund and Sieglinde sort of thing, and writing about him drained her power to feel things. During the first winter working on the book she never knew when he would come to her—at the symphony, at the tea table—and she got so she had to be alone in case he appeared. It was life at its best, complete possession, but he was an expensive boy to keep, she wrote Fisher. She had to travel with him, cut off every source of income to give him a perfectly undisturbed mind. She thought it had been worth it, for a fortune could not have brought such excitement and pleasure.

This account of the genesis of the novel makes clear that she began her book against formidable obstacles: the necessity of creating a male protagonist, the obligatory use of subject matter she could not know at first hand, and a lack of aesthetic distance between herself and the material. The story cost her an enormous expenditure of time and energy, and she had to devise a new technique to present her character. Because he is a boy who does not see the world pictorially (as, for example, Jim Burden does in *My Ántonia*), she had to cut out all the pictures, which in her previous novels were one of the memorable elements of her success. She told an interviewer that it was hard to stop doing what she did best, but "we all have to pay a price for everything we accomplish and because I was willing to pay so much to write about this boy, I felt that I had a right to do so." She maintained to the end a defensive and protective attitude towards this book, like a parent with a retarded child; but even before it was published, she feared it was doomed. She knew this, she wrote Fisher, when she began to write it. She had tried awfully hard, but good intentions, she added, don't count a damn.

At the outset the novel went well. She wrote Greenslet soon after New Year's that she already had completed the first four chapters, and by the end of July she had written one hundred thousand words, a third more than all of *My Ántonia*. During the winter New York was full of soldiers returning from France, and she spent a lot of time talking to them, especially the men from Nebraska. One of her former high school students, Albert Donovan, who was stationed at an army post in New York, brought groups of enlisted men, four or five at a time, to her Bank Street apartment. She visited the sick ones in the Polyclinic and listened to them recounting their experiences like men in a dream remembering their dead lives. She was greatly moved by these encounters. But the early portions of the novel were easy to write, because they take place in Nebraska, and some of the same materials that she had put her indelible stamp on in *O Pioneers!* and *My Ántonia* went into *One of Ours*. When she got to Book Four, however, and had to send her protagonist to France with his infantry company, the going got much rougher.

In May, Cather took time out to write two articles for the *Red Cross Magazine* as a sort of patriotic contribution to support the work of the Red Cross. Although one of them, "Education You Have to Fight For," has nothing to do with the war, the other, "Roll Call on the Prairies," was an account of the war effort on the plains. The former dealt with one-room schoolhouses on the prairie, early days of the western public universities, and the hunger for education that motivated the pioneer generation. The latter depicted the way farmers, farm wives, and small town people in Nebraska had responded to the war. While New Yorkers grumbled over wartime shortages and inconveniences, Cather wrote, the West reacted with great patriotism. Town men worked to get in crops after business hours, replacing farm boys who had been drafted; the women on farms and in town sewed for refugees and rolled bandages for the troops. Surrounded by plentiful supplies of food from the farms, westerners rationed themselves to send their surpluses to Europe and followed to the letter Herbert Hoover's directives as food administrator for President Wilson. Cather had been greatly impressed by this response to the war when she visited Nebraska in the summers of 1917 and 1918.

While she was writing these articles for the Red Cross, her relations with Houghton Mifflin came to a crisis. Dissatisfaction with her publisher had been building for several years, but when she received a bill for $244 for author's corrections of *My Ántonia*, she exploded. She wrote Greenslet a five-page letter detailing the accumulating grievances and specifically objecting to the charges for corrections. She had been investigating this matter and had found that author's corrections usually cost a publisher about a dollar an hour in printer's time. She figured that if her bill were correct Houghton Mifflin must have had one printer working thirty days to correct her galleys. She could not believe this was possible. She also did not believe it was customary for publishers to charge authors they really had faith in. She had seen some of Dreiser's proofs: his books were practically rewritten after being set in type; yet he never had been charged a cent.

It is apparent from this letter that other publishers were perhaps more aware of Cather's future value as a literary property than Houghton Mifflin. As an old, long-established firm, Houghton Mifflin saw Cather as just another of their many authors and far from their most profitable one. In the same month that she wrote Greenslet three New York publishers made her propositions for her next book, promising her advances and higher royalties than she was receiving from Houghton Mifflin. They also offered to spend more advertising her work. But Cather hated change and business negotiations, and her relations with Greenslet always had been so pleasant that she was very reluctant to think about switching to another publisher. Yet she despaired of her future with Houghton Mifflin. As she put it, the firm didn't believe it could make much money on her; so they were careful not to lose very much either.

One of the publishers wooing her was young Alfred Knopf, who was destined to be one of the canniest men in the business. He had graduated from Columbia in 1912, founded his publishing house in 1915 when he was twenty-three, and already had achieved a good bit of success. In his second year he had brought out a best seller in W. H. Hudson's *Green Mansions*. He had been reading with growing interest Cather's novels as they appeared and quickly realized that she was going to be one of the important writers of the future. His approach to her was very subtle. He explained that his theory of advertising was not to sell just one book but to establish an author's reputation for the future. He also told her that her novels were getting better and better and that she was the kind of author he wanted to invest his time, money, and effort in promoting. This was a very seductive argument, for Cather felt that her reputation among reviewers and the public had outstripped the recognition she was receiving from Houghton Mifflin. She believed that her publisher was making no effort to take advantage of her growing visibility and took account of nothing but sales figures, which in her case, she thought, bore little relationship to the interest her fiction was arousing. She also thought that Houghton Mifflin was not keeping her books in stock.

There was another point of contention: Greenslet did not believe that reviews sold books; both Cather and Knopf did. Cather had been told that the *New Republic*'s review of Joseph Hergesheimer's *Java Head* had sold several thousand copies. She believed this, because she had gone out and bought a copy herself after reading the review. She also understood that the *New Republic* had not even received a review copy of *My Ántonia*, and she reported further that she had had to take her own copy to the *New York Globe* after asking Houghton Mifflin twice to send one. Then, to further the aggravation, one of the reviewers of her novel had remarked that nobody had been afraid to say the book was unique in American fiction except her publisher.

No writer ever thinks his or her books are sufficiently advertised, and Cather was no exception. Publishers really don't know what sells books, and many don't think advertising has much influence on buyers. Houghton Mifflin never budgeted a large amount for Cather's novels, and the ads they did place often did not please Cather. In publicizing *My Ántonia*, she charged, Houghton Mifflin had made no use of the unusual reviews the book had received. In one ad the advertising department even had edited out of a quoted review the words "a new and great writer." On the other hand, Knopf had been pushing *Java Head* with enthusiasm and fire, and she was sure his promotional efforts were selling books. Hergesheimer's novel still was being advertised, while *My Ántonia* had dropped out of Houghton Mifflin ads. To make his blandishments ever more alluring, Knopf had told Cather that he would be willing to lose money on her for the first year or two in order to insure future sales.

Greenslet's efforts at damage control after receiving Cather's grievances were prompt and painstaking. One by one he refuted her charges, beginning with an apology for not having split the correction costs with her. He cut her bill by one hundred dollars but explained patiently that it had taken 181 hours to make her corrections. She had revised extensively in proof and paid no attention to the need to replace cuts and alterations with the same number of words to avoid excessive resetting of type. He said that all publishers charged for excessive changes but that not one author in twenty ever exceeded his allowance. Then he corrected her impression that Houghton Mifflin was not keeping her books in stock and offered her advances on her future novels if she wanted them. He had no idea where she got the notion he didn't think reviews sold books, and it was not true that the *New Republic* did not receive a review copy. He also did not think his firm's advertising copy was timid, and he argued that Houghton Mifflin was doing exactly what Knopf said ads should do: build for the future. As for advertising budgets, ten percent was the usual amount set aside for promotion, but they had spent thirty-eight percent of the proceeds advertising *Alexander's Bridge*, twenty percent on *O Pioneers!*, the same on *The Song of the Lark*, and so far ten percent on *My Ántonia*. By any strict accounting method, he added, this left the company in the hole. Finally, it was not true that they were no longer advertising *My Ántonia*, and he sent her a list of twenty-two papers and magazines that were currently carrying ads. This letter calmed Cather down, but it only papered over her dissatisfactions.

Knopf's next move was very shrewd. Six months later he offered to reissue *The Troll Garden* and made her a very generous proposal. Since *One of Ours* was still many months away from completion and royalties from *My Ántonia* and her earlier novels were modest, she continually needed money. A couple of years before when Doubleday had wanted to get rid of the plates for *The Troll Garden*, Greenslet had advised Cather that there wasn't a market for this book, Houghton Mifflin wasn't interested in reissuing it, and the plates might as well be destroyed. Thus when Knopf offered to reprint the book, Greenslet could only agree lamely that this was a nice break for her. He may have seen the handwriting on the wall at this point, but Cather still planned to let him publish "Claude," which then was the working title of *One of Ours*, and it was not until early in 1921 that she finally made the decision to go over to Knopf.

In the meantime, the writing of *One of Ours* had been moving ahead slowly. Cather spent the months of June and July in Toronto visiting the Hambourgs, but she had to dash back to New York at the beginning of July to find a shelter for her pots and kettles. She had learned that 5 Bank Street was to be torn down to make way for the new subway being built under Greenwich Avenue nearby. This turned out to be a false alarm, and she lived another eight years at Bank Street; but she and Edith Lewis did put their things in storage, only to take them out again a month later. At the beginning of August she went back to the Shattuck Inn at Jaffrey and worked there until mid-October. She kept up her correspondence with Greenslet, urging him not to tell anyone she was writing a war novel, commissioning him to order a new tent for her to pitch in James Robinson's meadow, and asking him to bind the next printing of *O Pioneers!* in something less ugly than its current mud color. There was no trip to Nebraska that summer, but her father came on to New York for a visit after she returned to Bank Street.

While she worked on "Claude," she continued to interest herself in the promotion and distribution of her books. She was pleased when she received the Swedish edition of *O Pioneers!* and later the Czech translation of *My Ántonia* and wrote Greenslet about an article Mary Austin was doing on her in Santa Fe. She also asked him to send her copies of all her novels to forward to William Allen White in Kansas, who wanted to write about them. She was surprised that he had asked for her books, as she and White beheld such different sides of the moon, but she hoped that his interest would attract a large number of low-brow readers. His paper, the *Emporia Gazette*, and his fool poet Walt Mason had previously been rather hostile to her. The books were duly shipped, and White subsequently became one of her admirers.

During the Christmas season of 1919 Cather took a break from her novel and wrote a long story just for fun, an uncharacteristic act but one that turned out well. The story was "Coming, Aphrodite!," an excellent tale that Paul Reynolds sold to the *Smart Set*, which published it in August. This story must have given her the idea for her next book, *Youth and the Bright Medusa*, a collection of tales about artists and musicians, which replaced the proposed reissue of *The Troll Garden*. Knopf certainly was pleased by this change in plans, for he ended up with a new Cather title for his fall list. He did better than he could have expected when he baited his trap with the reprint offer. The new collection would begin with "Coming, Aphrodite!," reprint "The Diamond Mine," "The Gold Slipper," and "Scandal," then include four of the best stories from *The Troll Garden*. Knopf, who was always interested in fine printing and graphic design, would bring out the book in a handsome green-yellow binding with dark blue lettering under his Borzoi imprint. He would order thirty-five hundred copies at the outset, sell them all, and have to reorder another thousand copies before the book was on sale three months. He also would publish a special limited issue of thirty-five copies signed by the author. Cather would make as much money from this minor work in six months as she was making in the entire first year of *My Ántonia*. Knopf's performance on *Youth and the Bright Medusa* was going to insure Cather's complete break with Houghton Mifflin.

After taking time off to write "Coming, Aphrodite!," Cather went back to "Claude," but the novel became increasingly difficult to write. Claude and his unit were now in France, but how was she going to get him across the country, into the trenches, and create the fatal action at Cantigny? She had managed through a lucky break while she was at Jaffrey to describe the convoyed Atlantic crossing by troopship. She was writing in her tent in late September when she came down with the flu and had to call in a local doctor, Frederick Sweeney. She discovered that he had been a medical officer on a troopship during the war and had kept a diary. He obligingly loaned it to her and she mined it for the detail that went into Book Four of her novel, "The Voyage of the *Anchises*." France, however, was another matter. She had been there only once eighteen years before when she and Isabelle McClung went to Europe in the summer of 1902. Her knowledge of the French language and literature was excellent, but she really didn't know the country.

A year and a half after starting "Claude," she decided that she had to revisit France before she could finish the book. Accordingly, she and Lewis, who got a leave of absence from her job, sailed for Cherbourg on the *Royal George* on May 19, 1920, to be gone for six months. By early June they were settled in the Hotel Voltaire on the Quai Voltaire on the left bank across from the Louvre. The weather was good, golden days interspersed with soft gray ones; the Luxembourg Gardens were gold and green, as beautiful as youth itself. The effects of the war, however, were painfully apparent in the gardens where recently crippled veterans were sunning themselves attended by old veterans of 1870. Lewis remembered that Cather said "she wanted to live in the Middle Ages. And we did live in the Middle Ages, so far as was possible. We hardly ever went beyond the Tuileries on the right bank of the Seine, except to get money, and occasionally to hear opera at the *Opéra-Comique*. We spent nearly all our time in the section between the Seine and the Luxembourg Gardens, and on the Île de la Cité and the Île–St. Louis."

A month after arriving in Paris Cather was on hand for a huge Fourth of July celebration honoring American war relief. She was tremendously moved as she watched twenty thousand war orphans march down the Champs Elysées carrying American flags and passing before the American ambassador and the President of France. They were children being supported by American contributions from various states, and many also carried flags of the states that were their sponsors. After the parade Cather talked to some of the children. A little boy pointed to himself and said: "I am Michigan." A little girl told her: "I am Tex-ass." Cather was proud of her country and thought the day the most American Fourth she ever had spent. American flags flew from all the public buildings, and everywhere there was a great outpouring of pro-American sentiment.

One of the first things she wanted to do in France was to see her cousin's grave, but this took some doing. She found travel very difficult, train schedules and routes disrupted, battlegrounds still devastated, no hotels anywhere near Cantigny. She found her cousin's grave registered in Paris and located the specific cemetery in which he was buried, and after the Hambourgs joined her in Paris she made plans to go with Isabelle to visit the grave and photograph it for her aunt. It was not a long trip, but they had to leave at six in the morning, change trains twice to get to Montdidier, from whence they hired a car to take them to the military cemetery at Villers Tournelle, ten miles from Cantigny. They stayed overnight with a French woman who belonged to the Society of French Homes, an organization that assisted Americans hunting for graves of soldiers buried in France.

Her mission accomplished, Cather and the Hambourgs started off in late July on a trip to the south of France. They hoped to get away from the ravages of the war, but provincial France was suffering from postwar shortages and the food was poor. Cather got sick and they had to call off the tour to take her to a quiet place where she could lie in the sun and recuperate. They chose a fishing village, Cavalière, on a stretch of the Mediterranean that had charmed Cather in 1902. She felt that she had spoiled the Hambourgs' trip, but they were very kind about it, and Jan turned out to be a wonderful person to travel with. He was never cross about anything, and she didn't see how any man could be so patient. She got over her illness, and while the Hambourgs swam and sunbathed, she went back to work, once more pitching a tent so that she could write out of doors. The interrupted tour of Provençal cities came off later, but Cather got in six weeks of work in August and September before returning to Paris with Lewis, who had been visiting friends in Italy, and embarking for home about the first of November. The return crossing was rough; for seventeen days high seas buffeted the ship, and Cather arrived back in New York with a sprained ankle. She still was nine months away from completing her novel.

Youth and the Bright Medusa, however, was selling briskly in the bookstores under the talented promotional hand of Alfred Knopf. The reviewers were just as enthusiastic over this book as they had been over *My Ántonia*. They were particularly pleased with the recently written tales, "Coming, Aphrodite!," "The Diamond Mine," and "The Gold Slipper," but even the stories reprinted from *The Troll Garden* made a greater impression than they did in 1905. Under its inspired title they found a unified group of stories dealing with youth's adventures with the many-colored Medusa of art. This theme, wrote Edmund Pearson in the New York *Times* "runs like a golden thread through the entire collection, a thread so dazzling that delight in its gleam swept the reviewer away from sobriety of expression into a mood of molten appreciation." He grabbed a sheet of paper and wrote a friend: "Don't fail to read Willa Cather's latest book if you have to beg the price of it." The anonymous reviewer for the *Nation* raised hackles west of the Missouri River and undoubtedly boosted sales when he called the book "the triumph of mind over Nebraska." He said he wasn't joking: he wanted to emphasize Cather's universality compared with the William Allen Whites and Vachel Lindsays, who were "utterly provincial."

The notices in general agreed that Cather had come into the full maturity of her art. Mencken as usual was among the yea-sayers: "Her grasp upon character is firmer than it was; she writes with much more ease and grace; above all, she has mastered the delicate and difficult art of evoking the feelings." Francis Hackett in the *New Republic* analyzed the beginnings of all eight stories to show how Cather had perfected her technique from the early tales to the later ones. Flo Field in *The Double Dealer*, breathlessly and somewhat incoherently, saw "truth . . . attained with simplicity," "freshness of feeling, the poignant realization of a new unsullied power." And more: "Life flows beneath the eye, unhurried in telling, with every closeness of detail and vision of perspective." Blanche Williams in the *Bookman* believed that "discriminating readers [would] find confirmation of their taste in the recent pronouncement of an English novelist, who place[d] among three American writers highest in achievement the name of Willa Cather." Dorothy Canfield Fisher in the *Yale Review* rejoiced in her friend's "steady upward growth and expansion into tranquil and assured power"; it was a "heartening and inspiring" spectacle.

Nearly all the reviewers singled out "Coming, Aphrodite!," which opened the collection, as the outstanding tale. This story alone, Pearson wrote, would place Cather "beside the greatest creative artists of the day." It was a veritable jewel among the rhinestone and paste baubles of most contemporary literature. The notice in the *Freeman* agreed: "Without a superfluous word or an ounce of sentimentality she tells here the story which has tempted a hundred others, the story of two young artists, in a Washington Square garret, Don Hedger, the painter, and Eden Bower, the singer, who drift together for a passionate interlude, and then drift apart. The thing is told with the utmost skill, and the deftest strokes of descriptive incident. The two contrasted personalities are projected as firmly in a few strokes as if a whole novel had been filled with the details of their careers."

The plot of the story is indeed simple; it is the telling that is everything. The elegant simplicity of style, the economy of language, the ability to make the reader feel and see, the deft creation of minor characters in a few words— all these elements make the story high art. In setting the story, Cather was remembering New York when she first went to work for McClure and lived adjacent to Washington Square. She evokes with marvelous skill the city of about 1906: the dingy apartment house, the life in the public square, the Brevoort Hotel, the scenes on lower Fifth Avenue, Coney Island. In Don Hedger's Boston bull terrier, Caesar III, she creates one of the memorable dogs in literature. In Old Lizzy, the cleaning woman who works for Hedger, she brings to life an old derelict in half a page: She comes in "smelling strong of spirits and wearing several jackets which she had put on one over the other, and a number of skirts, long and short, which made her resemble an animated dish-clout." Molly Welch, Hedger's model who earns extra money by making balloon ascensions on Sundays at Coney Island, is equally vivid as she goes up in the basket in her green tights, waving to the spectators.

The chief characters, of course, are the main attraction, and they are well differentiated: Eden, the girl from Illinois, a talented young opportunist who is on her way to become an opera prima donna; Don, a foundling who has made himself into a successful painter through talent, had work, vision. Eden, who is out for fame and fortune, is in New York taking voice lessons while she waits for her millionaire bachelor friend from Illinois to come to take her to Paris to study. Don, who scorns popular artists who pander to the tastes of rich patrons, lives only for his art and knows that someday his work will command the respect of connoisseurs.

In one of the most remarkable scenes Cather ever wrote Don Hedger one day is cleaning his closet when he discovers a knothole opening on Eden's apartment. He looks through the hole and sees Eden: "Yonder, in a pool of sunlight, stood his new neighbour, wholly unclad, doing exercises of some sort before a long gilt mirror." He watches her entranced: "He had never seen a woman's body so beautiful as this one—positively glorious in action." His fingers curve as if holding a crayon: "Mentally he was doing the whole figure in a single running line, and the charcoal seemed to explode in his hand at the point where the energy of each gesture was discharged into the whirling disc of light, from a foot or shoulder, from the up-thrust chin or the lifted breasts." Cather's insertion of this sensuous scene is very skillful. Because

Hedger is accustomed to painting from nude models, she is able to depict his voyeurism as an aesthetic experience, the vision of the naked goddess as something "out of the remote pagan past." The editor who bought the story would have been startled to have a present-day reader point out to him that the explosive and gesture imagery suggests masturbation.

The physical relationship between Eden and Don begins later after they spend an afternoon at Coney Island. Eden is fascinated by the balloon ascension, surreptitiously trades places with Molly Welch, and makes an ascension herself, Aphrodite rising from the waves, so to speak. Don is furious with her for doing this and at dinner that night tells her the brutal story of a princess—later the Aztec queen—and her forty lovers, the story Cather once heard from Julio, the young Mexican who had fascinated her in Arizona in 1912. Hedger says the story is about rain-making, as the princess is the priestess in charge of producing rain, but sex and fertility are closely related in this primitive tale, which really is about rape, castration, lust, and murder. The princess, whose mother dreamed of being delivered of snakes, is a virgin who "was with difficulty restrained from men." She is given a handsome captive as her slave, whose ardor she so arouses that he rapes her, for which offense he is castrated. The princess then becomes the Aztec queen and takes her eunuch slave with her. As queen and rain-maker her sexual appetite is insatiable, and she begins summoning handsome young men to her quarters where she dallies with these lovers for a while, then has them disposed of in an underground cavern by her eunuch. The story ends when the king one night surprises her in *flagrante delicto*, kills the lover, and has both the queen and the eunuch put to death.

The story foreshadows the shift from the Edenic relationship between the couple to the carnal connection about to begin. That night on the roof of the apartment house Eden and Don fall in love. They open the bolted doors between their rooms and live together for a brief period, but "in time they quarreled, of course," Cather writes. The tiff occurs when Eden tries to help Don by interesting a rich, fashionable artist in his work. She is totally unconscious of his attitude toward money and art, and he is enraged. He goes away for a few days, but when he returns contrite over his part in the quarrel, Eden has gone off to Paris with her rich bachelor. The story has an epilogue that takes place eighteen years later. Eden Bower returns triumphantly to New York, and the electric lights over the Lexington Opera House proclaim "Coming, Aphrodite!" Eden is now a *prima donna assoluta*. As she passes Washington Square in her limousine, she remembers the one uncalculated love affair in her life and goes to an art dealer to find out what has happened to Hedger. She learns that he has become a very influential painter, somewhat puzzling because of his many styles, a sort of Picasso type, though not yet rich and famous.

Despite the high quality of this story, it was turned down more than once before the *Smart Set* took it. The rejections had nothing to do with its intrinsic merit. In March after the *Metropolitan* magazine refused to buy it, Paul Reynolds wrote that he would try another journal. Then he returned the story after Lewis told him it had been sold to the *Century*; but it had not been. The *Century* was afraid to publish it. Tom Smith, the editor, told Mencken that he turned it down because there was too much criminal content in it. "The Comstocks are in violent eruption, and the *Century* has been taking too many chances," he said. In the 1980s this timidity seems strange, but the forces unleashed by Anthony Comstock and his Society for the Suppression of Vice were very active in 1920. Dreiser's publisher, John Lane, who had recently been intimidated by the Society, did not dare issue *The "Genius,"* and Mencken's campaign to fight the censors had been unsuccessful. Cather had signed a petition of protest against this censorship, along with many of the newly emerging literary talents (E. A. Robinson, Robert Frost, Amy Lowell, Ezra Pound, to name some), but the Comstockers charged ahead. Harper's had recently been fined for publishing a vice-crusading article by Judge Ben Lindsay, and another trial was imminent over James Branch Cabell's *Jurgen*.

When Reynolds tried out the story on Nathan at the *Smart Set*, however, he found a buyer, and Cather was delighted to let him have it. She was getting together as much money as she could for her coming trip to Europe, and even though the *Smart Set* didn't pay top rates, she needed to sell the tale. Nathan had two concerns about the story, and his acceptance was tentative: the title "Coming, Aphrodite!" would have to be changed because the character of Eden Bower was too easily associated with a famous singer and the story might be libelous; its sexual descriptions were too explicit not to stir up the censors. The singer suggested by the story was Mary Garden, who had grown up in Illinois after emigrating from Scotland at the age of six, had gone to Paris to study, and had become famous in Europe before returning to America. Further, she had just sung the role of Aphrodite in Erlanger's opera by that title with the Chicago Opera Company at the Lexington Theater. When the story was published in the *Smart Set*, the title was changed to "Coming, Eden Bower!," and the name emblazoned in lights over the theater was altered to "Coming, Clytemnestra," a change that did violence to the mythic overtones of Eden Bower as Venus.

Cather previously had refused to make changes to satisfy the *Century*, and Reynolds was surprised when she was willing to bowdlerize the tale for Nathan. But she never regarded magazine publication as very important; it was the book version of her works that counted, and she needed money. She made changes, sent the manuscript back to Nathan, but a month before she was to leave for France it still was not acceptable. Reynolds arranged a meeting between Cather and Nathan, and at this session further changes were agreed on. Three days later Reynolds sent her a check for four hundred and fifty dollars. When the story came out in the *Smart Set*, the previously naked Eden Bowers did her exercises "clad in a pink chiffon cloud of some sort" and there was no mention of thighs or breasts. The handsome slave "who fell upon the [Aztec] Princess to violate her honour" in the book, merely "embraced" her in the magazine, for which he was "gelded" in the former but merely "maimed" in the latter. Also there were stylistic changes: where Cather had written "smell," Nathan wanted "aroma"; for "sweat" he wanted "perspiration," and for "brutal" story he wanted "fantastic."

On January 12, 1921, Cather made one of the most important decisions of her life: she wrote Greenslet to announce that she was giving "Claude" to Knopf. Since returning from Europe, she had been watching Knopf's ads, comparing them with Houghton Mifflin's, and coming to the conclusion that the young firm pushed its books with much more spirit and effect than her Boston publisher. No longer could she afford to let her old friendship with Greenslet keep her from putting her own financial interests first. She made the decision regretfully, remembering that Greenslet had published her first novel and even before that had encouraged her to try long stories. But Greenslet really didn't understand her very well, and when she was beginning "Claude," he was urging her to write a Pittsburgh or a New York novel. She had not yet announced her decision to Knopf, she told Greenslet, but she planned to see him the next day, if possible.

The next day was Friday the thirteenth, an auspicious day in her career. It began a relationship with Knopf that lasted until she died twenty-six years later and was in every way completely satisfying. For the rest of her life Knopf treated her like a very important person, gave her as much say in the physical format of her books as she wished, allowed her to write jacket copy or advertising blurbs, and made her a wealthy woman. Their fortunes were inextricably linked. As Knopf's superior literary tastes and acumen attracted twenty-six Pulitzer Prizes and sixteen Nobel laureates to his list, Cather's reputation grew under his shrewd management. Not only was Knopf her publisher, but both Alfred and Blanche Knopf, and later their son Pat, became close friends. They had a great many interests in common, liked the same books, enjoyed music together, shared the same values. When she went over to him, he told her: "We haven't much money to spend here . . . but we'll take any amount of pains with a book." That, she thought, was a proper attitude for a publisher.

Edith Lewis summed up: "Next to writing her novels, Willa Cather's choice of Alfred Knopf as a publisher influenced her career, I think, more than any action she ever took. . . . he gave her great encouragement and absolute liberty to write exactly as she chose—protected her in every way he could from outside pressures and interruptions—and made evident, not only to her but to the world in general, his great admiration and belief in her. Life was simply no longer a battle—she no longer had to feel apologetic or on the defensive." Knopf remembered that the relationship "was unique in my experience. From small beginnings it grew into something so close that to the day of her death . . . we never wavered in our respect and affection for each other."

Cather's well-known account of how she came to Knopf is another piece of autobiographical fiction. When the firm of Alfred A. Knopf celebrated its twenty-fifth anniversary in 1940, Cather wrote an essay recalling her relationship with her publisher, and what she chose to remember bears little resemblance to the facts. She said she took the West Side Subway uptown to Knopf's office on West Forty-Second Street one day in the spring of 1920, walked in unannounced, and introduced herself. She said that she never had met him prior to that moment. She remembered that they talked about books and publishing and that she had picked up some blue paper on his desk to examine. He explained to her that he had gone to the Metropolitan Museum of Art to find exactly the right shade of blue from among the Chinese blues because he planned to use the paper to bind a volume of Chinese poems translated by Arthur Waley. As they talked, Cather decided that Knopf was going to do interesting things in his career and she would like to be part of his future. Would he be her publisher? He replied that she should think it over carefully, as changing publishers was very serious business. It was only after their second meeting a few days later, she wrote, that he agreed they might try working together.

Greenslet accepted the inevitable with grace and resignation; "*Pax vobiscum*," he replied, "and best wishes for the prosperity of 'Claude.' As for me, I am planning to spend the evening reading the Book of Job. You have our best wishes for the success of 'Claude' in the clever hands of Mr. Knopf." Cather was relieved that he took it so well and thanked him for his nice letter. She added that she kept telling McClure they never began to be the best possible friends until their business relations were over. She and Greenslet remained friends and corresponded until she died, and Houghton Mifflin continued to publish and market her first four novels. Cather later edited Sarah Orne Jewett's stories for Greenslet, and Houghton Mifflin published her collected works in the thirties.

After Cather signed with Knopf, she still had to finish the novel. She was handicapped by her sprained ankle, which was taped up until after Christmas, but she worked away at the book during the winter and took her recreation in her Friday afternoon teas. When her difficulties with "Claude" persisted, she turned to her old friend Dorothy Canfield Fisher for help. The two women had grown apart over the years (though Cather wrote her twice in 1916), but when Fisher reviewed *Youth and the Bright Medusa*, Cather took the opportunity to reopen the correspondence. She thanked her friend for the review and then began writing frequently. Twenty-four letters went from Bank Street to Arlington, Vermont, in the next twenty months, and for the rest of their lives these old friends remained close, though they seldom saw each other.

When Cather resumed this correspondence in March, she explained her difficulties with the novel and thought Fisher was the only person who could help her, if they only could get together. She needed to talk over her problems, for she despaired of being able to make the French part as good as the Nebraska part. Fisher's knowledge of France and French culture from first-hand experience seemed essential. They did get together in early April, and a few days later Cather wrote a grateful letter, reviewing the entire relationship and hoping that in the future they would see some of the rest of the world together. They had come through storm and stress and she now was a calmer, saner, wiser person. Try me on again, she wrote, and you'll find I'm reasonable now. She wondered how two people who had once had a basic understanding and affection could have drifted apart.

Fisher proved to be a good friend in the ensuing months. She not only served as a sort of technical advisor for "Claude," but she also read the French translation of *My Ántonia* before its publication. Cather didn't think it was much better than she might have done herself and wanted Fisher to tell her if the translation would offend an intelligent French reader. After the new novel was finished and in production, Fisher read proof to check Cather on possible errors in the French scenes. Then later with Knopf's connivance she was able to review the novel in the *New York Times* and give it a good send-off. Her sympathy and interest in the book during its final stages of completion and after publication were an immense help and comfort.

In April Cather went to Toronto to visit the Hambourgs and stayed nearly five months. She and Jan must have been good friends by this time, and Isabelle was still the person she loved the most outside of her family. This protracted visit came on the eve of the Hambourgs' departure for Europe where they planned to live permanently, and Cather knew that she would see Isabelle only rarely and briefly for the rest of her life. She was able to work in Toronto and managed to finish the novel by the end of August, after which she went west for a long sojourn in Nebraska.

There was one distraction, however, early in her stay in Canada. Sinclair Lewis came to lecture and said so many extravagantly appreciative things about her work that three reporters were at the Hambourgs' door the next morning before breakfast. For the first two weeks she was in Toronto it looked as if her life would be wrecked by dinner parties, luncheons, and teas. She finally convinced all the well-intentioned people that they could best show their interest in her work by letting her alone to write, and Isabelle came to her rescue to fend off the lion hunters so that she could get on with the novel. Lewis's lecture began a friendship that continued sporadically, even though Cather really didn't think much of his fiction. Lewis had begun extolling her virtues earlier that month in Omaha where he lectured just before going to Toronto. He had told his Nebraska audience that "Willa Cather is greater than General Pershing; she is incomparably greater than William Jennings Bryan. She is Nebraska's foremost citizen because through her stories she has made the outside world know Nebraska as no one else has done." Cather's father sent her a clipping of these remarks, and she wrote Lewis to thank him. This downright friendly push from his strong hand, she wrote, was something that touched her and pleased her more than she could say. She said she wouldn't be surprised if his vigorous talk had not done more than her novels to get the attention of the homefolks, and she was particularly pleased to have the support of straight-hitting young writers like Lewis.

She was no doubt right in assessing the effect of Lewis's lecture. When she returned to Nebraska for her first visit in three years, she found herself a celebrity. She was beseiged by friends inviting her to parties, reporters wanting to interview her, clubs asking her to speak. She wrote her old friend Dr. Tyndale that she was greatly relieved to have finished her novel and added: "Now I am going to lie in the hammock for a few weeks." She had trouble finding time to do that, however, because all her old friends in Red Cloud wanted to see her and during the two months she was home with her family there was a steady round of socializing. She was interviewed by the *Webster County Argus* and she gave a speech to the Hastings' Women's Club. Three weeks after reaching Red Cloud, she received a telegram from Knopf: "Just finished the book. Congratulations. It is masterly, a perfectly gorgeous novel, far ahead of anything you have ever yet done, and far ahead of anything I have read in a very long while. With it your position should be secure forever. I shall be proud to have my name associated with it." There is a nice retrospective irony in this message from Knopf, but it was to be another year before the critics would have their chance to assail the novel.

Cather gave Knopf's telegram to the *Argus* to publish and after another four weeks at home started back to New York by way of Omaha and Lincoln. She was enjoying being lionized, and for this brief interlude in her life she seemed accessible to everyone. She spent two days in Omaha giving two speeches and three interviews. She talked to the Fine Arts Society one afternoon, attended a dinner given in her honor by the League of Women Voters, and made another speech that night. Then she went on to Lincoln to see old friends and to be interviewed twice more. This burst of public activity stands in astonishing contrast to her great efforts in later years to avoid all publicity. The novelty of being a celebrity soon wore off, however, and she regained her contempt for women's clubs and spoon-fed culture-seekers. Nevertheless, the Fine Arts appearance was a great success. She wrote Greenslet with obvious satisfaction that a thousand people at five dollars a head had come to hear her, the biggest crowd the Society ever had had. She was pleased that Houghton Mifflin had arranged a fine display of her books in the Hotel Fontenelle where the lecture took place.

Though she was chiefly providing entertainment for the Fine Arts Society, she managed to get off some rather sharp criticism of Nebraska. Her subject was "Standardization and Art," a topic that enabled her to attack the "work of overzealous patriots who implant into the foreign minds a distaste for all they have brought from their own country." She went on to say: "The Americanization committee worker who persuades an old Bohemian housewife that it is better for her to feed her family out of tin cans instead of cooking them a steaming goose for dinner is committing a crime against art." Cather certainly was serious about this, but her audience of Omaha club women thought her very funny, and the reporter who wrote up the speech recorded laughter at this point. Then Cather went on to attack the Nebraska law that forbade the teaching of a foreign language in the public schools below the eighth grade. "Will it make a boy or girl any less an American to know one or two other languages?" she asked. "According to that sort of argument, your one hundred percent American would be a deaf mute." She added: "Art can find no place in such an atmosphere as these laws create . . . [it] must have freedom." She was particularly critical of the pressure she saw everywhere towards conformity, machine-made culture. "Everybody is afraid of not being standard . . . art cannot live in an atmosphere of manufactured cheer."

After two days in Omaha Cather went on to Lincoln and then to Chicago where she again spoke, this time to the College Club, and attended a dinner given for her by several of her university classmates. She also was persuaded by Fanny Butcher to visit all the big bookstores in Chicago, an exhausting enterprise, she wrote, but good policy. She arrived back in New York in early November worn out and had to go to bed for a week. Fortunately her French cook Josephine came back to work—but only for half a day because she had gotten married and had her own house to keep. She was cooking dinner every night, however, a delicious French dinner, the kind of food that is so simple, so honest, so truly elegant because it is not over-rich and showy, made chiefly out of human brains and a long and glorious national past. Josephine also was able to cope with the strict diet prescribed for Cather by a stomach specialist.

The strenuous days in the West had been too much for her digestive system. Soon after getting back to New York she had to see a specialist and made an appointment with Dr. William H. Glafke, head of the Stomach Clinic at St. Luke's Hospital. As she sat in his office and began giving him her case history, he asked, "First name, please." When she replied, "Willa," he laid down his pen, leaned back in his chair and said, "Is it really?" When she had made the appointment, he had rather hoped she might be a relative at least. He said he would rather have written *My Ántonia* than any other book ever written in America. In relating this conversation to Irene Weisz, she added that she thought he would try to do his best for her. The only trouble was that he wanted to talk all the time about her job instead of about her misbehaving colon.

Dr. Glafke must have cured her problem, because in early February she reported she was having a gay winter and enjoying her Fridays. Her good health didn't last long, however, and for several weeks she hovered on what her doctors thought was the edge of a mastoid process. Then they decided that her tonsils were causing the infection and she went to the hospital to have them out. She lost a lot of blood during the operation, and as soon as she was able to leave the hospital, her doctor shipped her off to Galen Hall in Wernersville, Pennsylvania, a sanitarium with comfortable appointments but vile food. She paid sixty dollars a week for the use of a ball room, a billiard room, and six sunporches, but she couldn't get one fresh vegetable. She wrote Zoë Akins that she needed good food because she had lost fifteen pounds. She had brought the proof of *One of Ours* with her to read and planned to stay another week if she could stand the food. By May she was back in New York still feeling poorly and ashamed of the weakness of her flesh. She finished reading proof in June and made plans to go to Vermont at the end of the month.

The object of her trip to Vermont was to teach at Bread Loaf in its annual summer session for would-be writers. She had accepted the invitation from

Wilfred Davison, head of the program, in February 1922, when everything was going well. Dorothy Canfield Fisher had been the go-between to recruit her for this first teaching assignment since leaving Allegheny High School in 1906. Her health problems in the spring made her regret her acceptance, but she didn't feel she could renege on her commitment. She had hoped to go to Bread Loaf in June, settle down there for several weeks of writing before she had to give her lectures. She had agreed to give four formal lectures, three on writing and one on the writer and the magazine editor, and hold a fifth session in which she would field questions from her students. Her doctors and her publisher, however, kept her in New York until almost the middle of July, and she didn't get to Vermont until the weekend before classes began.

Cather was housed in a cottage with a view of the mountains where she could write in the mornings, her usual practice, and give her lectures in the afternoons. The four lectures went off very well and the students were much attracted by Cather's lucid discussions delivered with perfect clarity. She was reserved, dignified, and absolutely sincere, wrote one student after the course began. An interviewer wrote about this time that her conversation was staccato and she chopped her spoken sentences out incisively, in short, neat links. She was "alert, alive, quick-witted, vigorous-minded, and assertive." One of the other instructors at Bread Loaf that summer was George Whicher, a young professor of English at Amherst College. She sat in on his classes as critic and after he read a student's story, she would give a critique. Both George and Harriet Whicher subsequently became friends for the rest of her life. At the end of the program on the last night a dinner and sing was scheduled in the piazza facing the sunset. The students wrote and sang a song for Cather:

> O Miss Cather, when we gather
> For your talks so wise and clear
> Now you're going we're all hoping
> You'll come back another year.

But she found her three weeks at Bread Loaf exhausting and never again was tempted, though Davison invited her in successive years to repeat the experience.

The two hundred dollars a lecture she got at Bread Loaf was welcome in the summer of 1922, but she soon began making more money than she could spend and could resist all distracting offers for chores peripheral to her main work. She also never changed her mind about the uselessness of courses in creative writing. She told an interviewer in 1925 that courses in story writing could only teach "those patterns which have proved successful. If one is going to do new business the patterns cannot help." Later she wrote in exasperation to a professor who was working on a textbook and wanted some of her views on writing. She said that twenty-eight other professors were writing similar texts and she had answered all of them but no more. This professor was number twenty-nine and it was too late. Anyway it was sheer nonsense to attempt to teach creative writing to college students. If students were taught to write good sound English sentences, creative writing would take care of itself. At least half of the professors who had written to her, she said, couldn't use *which* and *that* or *should* and *would* correctly.

After leaving Bread Loaf early in August, Cather took a train to New Brunswick via Montreal and for the first time visited Grand Manan Island in the Bay of Fundy. She was immediately charmed by the beauty and isolation of the island and returned again and again for the next twenty years. She later built a cottage, the only house she ever owned, and was able to work there free from civilized distractions. The cool, rainy climate suited her perfectly. During this first summer on Grand Manan she rented a cottage from Sarah Jacobus, who operated a small resort on Whale Cove. She wrote a friend after a month there that she had a quiet cottage with a splendid workroom all to herself and pleasant friends to meet at dinner. Best of all, the mail came only three times a week on a little steamer from the Canadian shore. It was utterly wild country with trails along the wooded cliffs which rose sheer from the sea. She pulled out of her portfolio a long story she thought had gone to pot and finished it promptly. This was probably "Tom Outland's Story," which had begun as "The Blue Mesa" and later became the center section of *The Professor's House*. She was on Grand Manan Island when *One of Ours* came out on September 8.

This novel, which was four years from conception to publication, is an excellent work despite the chorus of hostile criticism that greeted its appearance. It holds up well after two-thirds of a century and after three more wars seems even more significant than it did in 1922. When it reached the bookstores, its working title "Claude" had been replaced by *One of Ours* at the insistence of Alfred Knopf. He argued, no doubt correctly, that Cather's title had no sales appeal, but she was very reluctant to make the change. It wasn't until after she had consulted Fannie Butcher, who agreed with Knopf, that she was willing to switch. "Claude" would have been an appropriate title, however, for the novel focuses squarely on the protagonist, Claude Wheeler, from the time he is nineteen until he dies in France six years later. It is told by an omniscient third-person narrator who continually slips into the protagonist's consciousness. As a result, the reader views the world through Claude's perceptions, which also, to a degree, are Cather's. In the early parts her adopted state comes vividly to life, and in the latter, her second country, France, is effectively evoked.

Claude Wheeler is a Nebraska farm boy whose nature is too sensitive and fine-grained to accept the coarse realities of farm life and the crass prosperity of a materialistic world. His father, Nat Wheeler, who had been one of the pioneers, is a rich, good-natured land-hog, interested chiefly in making money, and completely lacking in any understanding of his son. His older brother Bayliss is mean-spirited, mercenary, "thin and dyspeptic, and a virulent Prohibitionist." His younger brother Ralph is careless, chiefly interested in gadgets and machinery, which he doesn't take care of and discards prodigally. Only Claude's mother and the servant Mahailey have a close and affectionate relationship with him, and life on the farm is stultifying. He tells his best friend, Ernest Havel, a young, energetic, satisfied Bohemian farmer, "It seems like there ought to be something—well, something splendid about life, sometimes."

The first half of the novel carries Claude through his sophomore year at a miserable little church college in Lincoln that his mother insists he attend. Then his father makes him drop out of college in order to take over the farm, while he and Ralph go off further west to run a newly acquired cattle ranch. Claude hates to leave Lincoln where he has made friends with the Erlich family, the opposites in every way from his folks, and has developed a taste for scholarship through a special history course he enrolls in at the state university. After taking over the farm, which he hates, he falls in love with the wrong girl, Enid Royce, a brisk, efficient, frigid woman; a vegetarian who works like a zealot for the anti-saloon league and wants most of all to be a missionary to China like her sister. Everyone but Claude knows that the marriage will be a disaster, and even Enid thinks that perhaps she should not get married. But Claude tells her: "I've never yet done anything that gave me any satisfaction." He thinks that marriage will transform his life: "It would be the beginning of usefulness and content . . . it would restore his soul." But of course he is wrong. On their wedding night, as the Denver Express carries them off for their honeymoon, Enid locks Claude out of their stateroom. This incident, Cather told a friend, actually happened to a young man she knew in Pittsburgh; otherwise she never would have had the courage to use it. "Everything about a man's embrace was distasteful to Enid; something inflicted upon women, like the pain of childbirth." After less than a year of marriage Enid goes off to China to look after her sister, who has fallen ill.

About this time America's entry into the war is imminent, and Claude sees his opportunity to escape from his dreary, lonely life into the army. He enlists before war actually is declared and goes off to camp with other young idealists who believe they are going to fight the war to end all wars. After completing officer candidate school, he is commissioned a second lieutenant in the infantry and sent to France. In this great crusade for democracy Claude finds himself, and en route to Europe, even as many soldiers on the troopship die of influenza, he awakes every morning "with that sense of freedom and going forward, as if the world were growing bigger each day and he were growing with it."

In France Claude discovers a world he previously only dimly had imagined. In spite of the dislocations and deprivations of war, the ancient culture of France lives on. In the weeks before the Argonne Forest offensive in which he is killed he meets a number of French people, who make a profound impression on him. On his twenty-fifth birthday, which he spends on leave with a French family, he begins to feel that he is having his youth in France. "Life had after all turned out well for him and everything had a noble significance. The nervous tension in which he had lived for years now seemed incredible to him . . . he was beginning over again."

Instrumental to his rebirth in France is a fellow officer whom he meets after his company lands in France, David Gerhardt, a concert violinist, an Easterner, city sophisticate, different in every way from the Nebraska farmer. He too has joined the army because of some inner compulsion, not a belief that he is making the world safe for democracy, but from some gut feeling that some good has to come from the sacrifice. He had been unable to go on with his career while Europe was in flames and had rejected a soft job in a regimental band. He too becomes a second lieutenant in Claude's infantry company. With many French friends and a fluent command of the language from having lived in France as a student, David provides Claude with an entrée into French culture, and the two very different individuals become close friends. At the end of the novel both men are killed in action on the same day.

Claude dies during his first major action before he has time to become disillusioned and cynical about the war. The short epilogue that follows Claude's death takes place in Nebraska after the war ends. As his letters keep coming, following the War Department's notification of his death, his mother realizes that "he died believing his own country better than it is, and France better than any country can ever be." Despite her grief she finally is glad that he did not live into the postwar era. "Perhaps it was just as well to see that vision, and then to see no more." His mother would have "dreaded the awakening," and she doubted if "he could have borne at all that last, desolating disappointment."

The novel is not without its faults, but the virtues far outweigh its shortcomings. Particularly effective is the characterization of Claude. Cather was not exaggerating much when she told an interviewer that she knew her character better than herself. Creating character was always her strength, and Claude is no less three dimensional than Alexandra or Ántonia. But he is not an heroic figure; rather, he is a pretty ordinary person, much like other young men who went off to war in 1917 from the Midwest, and he is a hopeless romantic and idealist who believes in the myths of his culture. He is like many a soldier for whom the war was the most thrilling and exciting thing that ever happened to him. In both world wars of this century GI's who didn't have to do much fighting found the camaraderie of the army, the exoticism of foreign lands, and the contact with grateful liberated peoples far more stimulating than the dull jobs they had left behind. Veteran reunions forty years after the wars attest to this memory of war as the high point of many a prosaic life. Claude, unfortunately for Cather, was neither macho nor hard-boiled enough to suit reviewers, who expected "realistic" war novels with he-man heroes. They did not read the novel carefully to see that Cather had no illusions about the war. She thought it had destroyed much of the France she loved without accomplishing a great deal. Many reviewers simply ignored the fact the novel is told mostly from Claude's point of view, and they assumed that Claude's ideas were Cather's. This perhaps was inevitable considering Cather's usual method of incorporating a great deal of auto-biography into her fiction.

Her cousin, of course, suggested the protagonist, as we have seen, but there is a lot of herself in the characterization. Her Uncle George and Aunt Franc sat for the portraits of Nat Wheeler and his wife, Evangeline, and her uncle's farm house, "the tall house with its lighted windows," and his farm are the setting for the rural chapters. Frankfort, where Bayliss sells farm implements, Gladys Farmer, the girl Claude should have married, and Enid Royce live, is again Red Cloud, and the Wheelers' Bohemian and German neighbors replicate the ethnic mixture of the farming community in the previous novels. This time, however, Cather adds a native American neighbor, Leonard Dawson, a contented farmer who also enlists for idealistic reasons about the same time Claude does. The friends that Claude makes in Lincoln, the Erlichs, as we have seen, were suggested by the Westermann family, and the servant Mahailey is an avatar of Marjorie Anderson, the woman who came to Nebraska from Virginia with the Cathers. All of these minor characters are well portrayed, and the Nebraska chapters are vintage Cather.

The rural setting and the incidents of farm life are equally effective. The novel opens with Claude washing the family car in preparation for a day in town at the circus. Later there is a great blizzard, reminiscent of the one in *My Ántonia*, in which the farm is snowed in. During the storm Claude's hogs are buried under the snow when the roof of their shelter collapses. Later the novel describes the great harvest of 1914 when Cather helped transport the grain to market. It shows Claude proudly building the house to which he will take his bride and in which his marriage will founder. In addition, the flora and fauna of Webster County, Nebraska, come vividly to life. In this part of the novel Cather is remembering things that had teased her mind for years.

Cather develops Claude's overly sensitive nature with many revealing details. After washing the car for the circus, Claude doesn't get to drive to town because his father preempts the auto and insists that he haul a load of smelly hides to the butcher in a horse and wagon. He is bitterly disappointed, but even worse, he has to go with Dan and Jerry, his father's dirty, uncouth hired men with whom he hates to associate. He suffers when Jerry mistreats a horse and is humiliated when, through no fault of his own, he loses some of his hogs in the blizzard. He can hardly bear having to give up college, and when he takes over the farm, he worries constantly about the weather and the planting and awakens in the mornings in a panic because he isn't getting on faster. Even his name, which people pronounce "Clod," embarrasses him, a sissy name, he thinks. "Claude had always found life hard to live; he suffered so much over little things." His mother says to him inaudibly, quoting Hamlet's speech to his father's ghost, "Rest, rest perturbed spirit."

Cather shows Claude's romantic nature with the use of myth and allusion. When he takes a special course at the university, he has to write a paper on Joan of Arc, who has been one of his heroines ever since his mother told him her story when he was a little boy. He pictures her surrounded by a luminous cloud with her lilied banner and her soldiers, as he studies the records of her trial. In his paper he acquits her on the evidence, as his professor had expected him to do. On another occasion in Lincoln when Mrs. Erlich's cousin, an opera singer, comes to visit, she finds Claude interesting to talk to and calls him Claude Melnotte, because he reminds her of the protagonist in Bulwer Lytton's romantic novel *Lady of Lyons*. Claude Melnotte goes off to war after a fraudulent marriage, fights in Napoleon's army where he distinguishes himself, and acquires both wealth and a colonelcy in the process. In *One of Ours* when Claude meets on board the troop ship Victor Morse, a young flier from Iowa who has become an ace in the Royal Air Force, he sees him as a story-book hero, and when he later hears of his death over Verdun, he compares him to one of Milton's fallen angels in *Paradise Lost*. Claude is

oblivious of the fact that Victor's London girl friend is a whore who has given
him syphilis, but the reader is aware of the reality behind Claude's roman-
ticizing.

Cather buries in the last book of the novel parallels between Claude and
Parsifal and admitted to a correspondent that she originally had intended to
title this section "The Blameless Fool by Pity Enlightened." Claude is a sort
of Parsifal character seeking the holy grail, but ironically he does not succeed
in healing old Amfortas and dies in his quest. Cather ultimately called this
section "Bidding the Eagles of the West Fly On," a quotation from Vachel
Lindsay's poem on William Jennings Bryan. Critics thought this a jingoistic
caption, but the poem deals with the futile battle of the western populists
against the eastern financial centers and thematically it is consistent with
Claude's futile sacrifice in the Great War. The phrase is jingoistic only if one
misses the author's ironic view of Claude's romantic vision.

Amid the hullabaloo over Cather's presumption in writing a war novel,
critics missed the large amount of satire the book contains. The attacks on
materialism that appear in her short fiction and *O Pioneers!* continue in *One of
Ours.* The novel opens with Claude's reflections on the mismanagement of
the farm by his father, the wastefulness he sees everywhere about him. His
father had been a pioneer but in his later years had adopted all the false values
of a materialistic society. In a revealing episode of Claude's childhood his
mother urges his father to pick the cherries that she can't reach from a tree
loaded with fruit. He gets up and goes out. After he returns, he says: "All
right now, Evangeline . . . Cherries won't give you any trouble. You and
Claude can run along and pick 'em as easy as can be." They go to the orchard
and are appalled to find the tree cut down. Claude "beheld a sight he could
never forget . . . With one scream [he] became a little demon."

Cather continued her criticism of the contemporary world in the character
of Ralph, whose dedication to mechanization goes beyond all reasonable
bounds. He is insensitive to the needs and feelings of his mother and old
Mahailey and extravagantly wasteful. Mahailey, who cherishes old things
and old ways, is grateful to Claude, who put a new haft on her old butcher
knife when everyone else said it had to be thrown away. Bayliss Wheeler is
the character most savagely satirized, a caricature of the self-made businessman. His dessicated body and mind continually infuriate Claude. Not only is
he tight-fisted, but also he has no appreciation of beauty or tradition. He buys
a beautiful old house, a local landmark, but instead of refurbishing it he plans
to tear it down and build something modern. At the end of the novel Claude
thinks: "No battlefield or shattered country he had seen was as ugly as this
world would be if men like his brother Bayliss controlled it altogether."

Religious bigotry and smugness also come under fire in this novel. Claude hates the narrow-minded denominational college he has to attend. The faculty are pious dunces, and their theology full of evasions and sophistries. According to them, the noblest people could be damned while "almost any mean-spirited parasite could be saved by faith." Claude decides that young men went into the ministry "because they were timid or lazy and wanted society to take care of them; because they wanted to be pampered by kind, trusting women like his mother." Claude's mother is fervently pious, the dupe of the sanctimonious Brother Weldon, who comes to visit and stays for long periods, but Cather doesn't satirize her. She is based on her beloved Aunt Franc and treated very sympathetically. It is clear to the reader, nonetheless, that Cather does not subscribe to Claude's mother's view that all of her son's problems would be solved if he could only find his Savior.

This satire of contemporary culture invites comparison with a more famous treatment of a similar theme: Eliot's *The Waste Land*, which appeared in the same year. There is no influence of one work on the other, but both writers on opposite sides of the Atlantic were examining the failures of their societies "transcended by the spiritual visions of another culture." Both works have a five-part structure that follows a similar thematic pattern, beginning with a panorama of society's failures, followed by views of personal failure and a death by water, and ending with a promise of spiritual rebirth. In addition, both works employ the Parsifal motif. It is one of the ironies of literary history that *One of Ours*, which seemed to many sophisticated readers in 1922 to be smugly complacent, really is a document of the "lost generation."

The novel declines in quality when the action moves to France, but even so, there are some moving scenes in the latter parts of the book. These derive from the long-assimilated memories of Cather's first visit to France when she felt like a country cousin in the presence of Dorothy Canfield's fluent French and familiarity with the country. She wrote her friend that the scenes between Claude and David Gerhardt were suggested by her memory of the violinist David Hochstein, whom she had met in New York through the Hambourgs, but only the action—not the emotional quality of the story. That came from her memories of how she felt when they had been together in France in 1902. Claude's envy of David is Cather's envy of Dorothy, but there is also a bit of the feelings G. P. Cather must have had in the presence of his sophisticated, well-traveled cousin. The relationship between Claude and David is created in some memorable scenes. When they first meet, David takes Claude to stay with the French family with whom he is billeted, and later, just before the final action in which both men are killed, he and Claude visit the family of one of David's friends, also a violinist, who had been killed earlier in the war. In a moving scene David is persuaded to play on his dead friend's Amati violin, and as Claude listens, he is "torn between generous admiration, and bitter, bitter envy. What would it mean to be able to do anything as well as that, to have a hand capable of delicacy and precision and power? . . . He felt that a man might have been made of him, but nobody had taken the trouble to do it."

The real David Gerhardt, David Hochstein, had interested Cather a great deal. She gave a long interview to the *New York Herald* after *One of Ours* came out in which she described the impact he had made on her. She had seen him only three times, but she had heard him play the violin part in Schubert's Trout Quintet at Harold Bauer's apartment, she had talked to him twice later, and she had read some letters to his mother that were published after his death. He was much like the fictional character of the novel, and his brief biography gave her confidence in creating the character of Claude. If two such different young men as G. P. Cather of Webster County, Nebraska, and David Hochstein of New York could find common cause in the war effort, surely this was a significant theme for fiction. His life even provided a ready-made symbol: shortly before he went overseas, foreswearing music for the duration, his Stradavarius was smashed in an auto accident.

The theme of youth and idealism sacrificed on the pagan altar of war is surely a universal topic for literature. Critics who objected to a war novel by someone who had had no experience of war did not make the connection between *One of Ours* and authors like Homer, Tolstoy, and Stephen Crane, all of whom managed very good accounts of war without having been soldiers in the conflicts they described. Cather observes war on a broad scale: on the home front in America and on the battlefield in France. The impact of the war in Nebraska is a significant part of the early chapters. Claude and his mother get out a map when the war breaks out in Europe and follow the action through the newspapers. When the Germans are stopped in the Battle of the Marne, Claude is deeply moved by the heroic defense of Paris, "the city which had meant so much through all the centuries." The war to Nat Wheeler, however, means only a rise in wheat prices, and he holds back most of his bumper crop waiting to sell it more advantageously. Later in the story Cather deals with the impact of the war on German-American farmers, who are charged with disloyalty for pro-German sentiments and persecuted as suspected spies. When the novel moves to France, Cather devotes a good deal of attention to the effects of the war on the civilian population.

Much of the hostile criticism must have stemmed from the fact that *One of Ours* was a woman's war novel. Claude Wheeler is given the nurturing qualities conventionally assigned to women. While his father was the tamer of the wild land, Claude wishes to protect the environment. He wants to see the land respected. He hates to see the old cottonwood trees cut down and rejoices when he finds the French have a love for trees lacking in Nebraska farmers. When he finds some rare native quail in the woods near his new house, he does everything he can to keep them hidden from his neighbor who would like to kill them. When the novel creates the all-male society of the army, Claude's nurturing qualities continue very plausibly as he looks after his men. On board the troopship he nurses his fellow soldiers during the flu epidemic; in camp in France he looks out for the welfare of his men, as a mother would her children. He comforts a man suffering from homesickness, and he urges his men to maintain a decorum that will reflect honor on their country. In the final action he sacrifices himself to save the position he is holding in the face of a German attack.

There are also more women in this novel than in most war stories. Besides the vision of Joan of Arc that hovers over the novel, there is Edith Cavell, British nurse executed by the Germans for helping prisoners escape from occupied Belgium. Her death is the reason Leonard Dawson enlists. Victor Morse, the flying ace, shoots down a German flier who turns out to be a woman. All the women Claude meets in France play a significant, humanizing role, especially Mlle de Courcy, who works selflessly for the Red Cross in a ruined village near the front lines. She is a woman of cultivation, a tireless worker in the struggle to restore life in the wake of war. And there also is a moving scene when Claude and his men find and succor a French woman nursing a German baby in the midst of a war zone. These details add depth to Cather's panorama of war and force the reader to realize that the cost of war is heavy in more than lives lost in the front lines.

One cannot ignore the novel's flaws despite its many excellencies. In writing the novel Cather ignored her best method, which required the use of material that had long possessed her. From the troopship crossing worked up from Dr. Sweeney's diary, to the final offensive in the Argonne Forest, she had to work from immediate materials. Her own opinion of fiction written from direct impressions or research was not flattering. She thought it only a kind of higher journalism; but the inner compulsion that made her write the novel in the first place made her carry it to completion. The incidents she could not know first hand no doubt are all authentic accounts told her by the soldiers she talked to, but this second-hand material lacks authenticity. One serious defect lies in the soldier dialogue. Her sergeants, corporals, and privates are given appropriate backgrounds, ideas, and aspirations, but they don't talk like men living in an all-male society. In minor details she goes astray in such things as giving her soldiers a leave after a couple of weeks in the trenches, sending her officers on leave with their rifles, making the battalion an administrative unit, having the troop convoy escorted by battleships. (This last blunder was corrected in the third printing when Greenslet wrote Cather about it.) Cather had the good sense, however, to keep the front-line action to a bare minimum, and the climactic battle in the trenches occupies only twenty pages. Overall the shortcomings are minor, and *One of Ours* may interest readers as a broader view of war long after Dos Passos' *Three Soldiers* is forgotten.

Cather's personal aversion to sex is reflected in Claude's character, as it was in Jim Burden's in *My Ántonia*. His failure in civilian life is sexual as well as social. When he is a student in Lincoln, he recoils from the sexual advances of a coed named Peachy Millmore, and after his marriage, he is not unduly upset by his wife's frigidity, only lonely because she spends her time working for the Anti-Saloon League and not keeping house for him. A critic of war fiction sees *One of Ours* as "a study of erotic war motivation unequaled until John Hersey's *The War Lover* appeared in 1959." The novel is "a case history of a man for whom the idea of death is the only possible aphrodisiac." Claude is more at home in the army, where male comradeship replaces sexual competition, than he was in his life in Nebraska. There is a parallel here in Cather's own preference for female relationships.

Cather, however, is neither prudish nor unaware of sexual needs and nuances in her novel. Her troops in the port of debarkation seek amorous adventure after being cooped up in a troopship for many days. Victor Morse, the flier, brags of his sexual adventures, and Claude's company spends a rest leave in a liberated village where the French girls are only too willing to show their gratitude to the Americans. One of Cather's most subtle touches deals with homosexuality in a scene that many readers perhaps miss. When the company enters the town of Beaufort, which had been in German hands for most of the war, they first mop up enemy soldiers hiding in cellars and send the prisoners to the rear. Suddenly sniper fire from a house on the main street cuts down two villagers. Claude and his men storm the building and kill several Germans, including an officer, immaculately dressed, covered with medals: "His linen and his hands were as white as if he were going to a ball." Around his neck they find a locket with the picture inside of "a young man, pale as snow." Claude studies it wondering, "It looks like a poet, or something. Probably a kid brother." Then Cather writes: "Claude noticed that David looked at him as if he were very much pleased with him." Cather told Fisher that this incident was related to her by an American captain, who had no idea that the young man in the picture was the German officer's lover. She liked the naiveté of the American officer and gave his innocence to Claude. She also makes clear by this scene that the relationship between Claude and David is purely platonic.

Cather was expecting hostile criticism, and she got it, but not by any means in massive doses. The favorable notices outnumbered the unfavorable ones by about two to one. The most influential reviewers, however, were among the nay-sayers, and Cather was particularly upset when some of her admirers, like Sinclair Lewis and Mencken, pronounced *One of Ours* a failure. She had been very pleased when she heard that Lewis was to review the book, and she had tried hard to prepare the way for Mencken to notice it favorably. In a long letter more than six months before the novel appeared, she wrote Mencken explaining in detail what she was trying to do and outlining to him her credentials for doing it. But her effort was futile. Mencken spoke for a good many reviewers who praised the Nebraska parts of the novel as being authentic and in Cather's best vein but dismissed the war chapters as unreal. Her war was "fought out, not in France, but on a Hollywood movie-lot," he wrote.

Mencken set the tone and content for the unfavorable reviews: "What spoils the story is simply that a year or so ago a young soldier named John Dos Passos printed a novel called *Three Soldiers*. Until *Three Soldiers* is forgotten and fancy achieves the inevitable victory over fact, no war story can be written in the United States without challenging comparison with it—and no story that is less meticulously true will stand up to it. At one blast it disposed of oceans of romance and blather." His unkindest cut of all informed readers of the *Smart Set* that the latter part "drops precipitately to the level of a serial in the *Ladies' Home Journal*." Edmund Wilson went farther than Mencken to call the novel "a pretty flat failure." For him neither Claude nor the minor characters came alive, and he wondered if Mencken was simply wrong in calling Cather a great novelist. He admitted, however, that he had not read her earlier novels. Heywood Broun, who had praised *My Ántonia*, was very disappointed. The book to him was just deadly dull: "There are not more than fifty pages out of the four hundred and fifty-nine which established any spell. This is a dogged book, and we read it doggedly." Cather bristled at these unflattering remarks, but she was spared reading Hemingway's devastating comment, which was contained in a letter to Wilson: "Wasn't that last scene in the lines wonderful? Do you know where it came from? The battle scene in *Birth of a Nation*. I identified episode after episode, Catherized. Poor woman, she had to get her war experience somewhere."

It seems in retrospect that no reviewer read the novel with an open mind. It would have been impossible to do so in 1922 when the war was still a hot political issue, and the reviews were more or less shaped by the reviewer's attitude towards the war. Broun was frank enough to admit that his prejudices probably influenced his judgment, and in a subsequent column in the *New York World* he printed a letter from a veteran who said: "I stick with you in your prejudices, but I don't think you gave the book a fair deal." It seems clear that the hostile reviewers wanted a protagonist who experienced boredom and disillusionment in his military service and lived to criticize the society that had sent him to war.

The favorable reviewers included a number of influential people, two of whom were Dorothy Canfield Fisher in the *New York Times* and Burton Rascoe in the *New York Tribune*. Fisher did not deal with the war issue at all but confined herself to praising the novel's honesty and "the glowing portrayal of life on the fertile Western plains." She thought it "an amazingly rich book, rich as no other living American could write, many-peopled, complicated as life itself is complicated, but composed with a harmony and unity which only art can have." Rascoe found *One of Ours* "the best sustained and most powerful novel she has written." He agreed with Cather's own contention that the book really wasn't a war novel: "It [war] is the *deus ex machina* which solves in ironic fashion the perplexities of Claude. It is war which offers him adventure, release for his pent-up energies. The body of the story is concerned with the frustrations of those energies."

Cather didn't take the criticism stoically and imagined the hostility to be far greater than it was. When she wrote to thank Fisher for her friendly notice, she called it the solitary rose in a thorny patch. She was comforted, however, by the large amount of enthusiastic fan mail she received, many of them letters from ex-soldiers who saw themselves in Claude Wheeler, and when she had tea with William Allen White soon after the book appeared, he cheered her up with a quip: "If thy Mencken and thy Nathan desert thee then the Lord will take thee by." But she couldn't let the matter alone and reported sourly to Fisher that the *New Republic* had given her only a paragraph at the end of a review of Kathleen Norris, that the *Dial*, *Freeman*, and *Liberator* all thought she had had a change in her brain tissue and couldn't write any more.

Despite the bruises her ego suffered at the hands of the critics, she could take comfort in the size of her deposit slips. The book became a best seller. Knopf sold sixteen thousand copies in the first month, and it went through seven printings in the first year for a total of more than fifty-four thousand copies. Cather made nineteen thousand dollars in royalties from Knopf in twelve months and for the rest of her life had no money problems. The book stimulated sales of her other titles, and it brought her the Pulitzer Prize in 1923. In many ways it was a turning point in her career.

CHAPTER 15

A Lost Lady

When Cather published her essay collection *Not Under Forty* in 1936, she prefaced the volume with a brief note: "The book will have little interest for people under forty years of age. The world broke in two in 1922 or thereabouts, and the persons and prejudices recalled in these sketches slid back into yesterday's seven thousand years. . . . It is for the backward, and by one of their number, that these sketches were written." Everyone who writes on Cather ponders the meaning and implications of this statement that the world broke in two about 1922. What did she mean? How does one interpret the remark? She had reached the top of her profession. She was a world-class author, affluent, master of her craft. As she approached her fiftieth year, one might have expected her to look forward to a brilliant decade or two of added accomplishment. Indeed, three of her best novels, *A Lost Lady*, *The Professor's House*, and *Death Comes for the Archbishop*, were to appear in the next five years.

Her attitude at this point, however, begins to be increasingly valetudinarian. She felt keenly the truth of the quotation from Michelet that Mr. Rosen in "Old Mrs. Harris" reads to Vicki Templeton as she prepares to leave for college: "The end is nothing, the road is all." The years of struggle for Cather had ended after thirty years of striving, and she felt let down. In addition, there are other explanations of this feeling: the hard knocks from some of the critics over *One of Ours* left scars despite the enthusiasm of the majority. The permanent removal of Isabelle Hambourg to Europe was no doubt a loss felt deeply, though she didn't write about it in any of her extant letters. Certainly mid-life crisis accounts in part for this change, as one sees in *The Professor's House*, which she began writing in 1923. And the wasteland theme that is a strong motif in *One of Ours* underscores her attitude towards American life in the twenties. Disillusionment after World War I, Prohibition, Communist witch hunts, the gaudy extravagances of the Jazz Age—all these extrinsic factors that sent other American writers to self-imposed exile in Europe contributed to Cather's sense of alienation.

Cather's growing disenchantment is clearly discernible in *One of Ours* in Claude's response to Nebraska life at the outset of World War I. The thoughts put into her young protagonist's head are really more appropriate to their middle-aged author: "With prosperity came a kind of callousness; everybody wanted to destroy the old things they used to take pride in." They let their orchards die of neglect because it was easier to run into town to buy fruit than to grow it. In addition, people had changed; Claude can remember "when all the farmers in this community were friendly toward each other; now they were continually having law-suits. Their sons were either stingy and grasping, or extravagant and lazy." This is Claude at the age of twenty-one mourning the good old days of his childhood. Actually he was born about 1895, when conditions were dreadful in Nebraska, when Cather had to go to work in order to put herself through college. Her attitude towards the twenties is further documented in her essay on Sarah Orne Jewett (1925), in which she writes: "There is the new American, whom Mr. Santayana describes as 'the untrained, pushing, cosmopolitan orphan, cocksure in manner but none too sure in his morality, to whom the old Yankee, with his sour integrity, is almost a foreigner.' "

At the end of November 1922, she went west to spend six weeks in Red Cloud with her family, the first time she had been home for Christmas in many years. She had planned to arrive in time for Thanksgiving but was delayed by the proof-reading of a new edition of *April Twilights* that Knopf was indulgently bringing out for her, and she had to eat her turkey on the train. The main purpose of the trip was to attend her parents' golden wedding anniversary on December 5. The pleasure she got from returning to Nebraska at this time was intense, and she wrote she was getting more thrills to the square mile out of the cornfield country than any other place in the world, including New York and Paris, and she doubted if she could live in New York any longer. Red Cloud in winter was a thrilling place: there was blinding sunlight and blue skies all day, crystal moonlight all night. There was lots of snow that winter and the temperatures dropped low enough to freeze over the river. She got out her skates and took up again the sport she had loved as a child. During the days in Red Cloud her father, still vigorous at the age of seventy-five, drove her about the country in his car to visit the Scandinavian and Bohemian settlements. It was a great satisfaction to watch the human stories go on and on among her farm friends, to see how the lives she knew so well were turning out.

The fiftieth wedding celebration was a great success. The entire family, all of Cather's brothers and sisters, gathered for the occasion, and she felt strongly the pull of home and family. Both parents were still in good health and seemed more robust than she. They could drive a hundred miles a day in their car and be ready to go again the next day. Though Cather had to nap after lunch, neither parent did. But she wasn't really tempted to remain in Red Cloud very long after the beginning of 1923, and by the middle of January she was back in her apartment on Bank Street ready to put the finishing touches on *A Lost Lady*.

Another important event took place in Red Cloud, however, before she went back to New York: Cather and her parents joined the Episcopal Church on December 27. The rite of confirmation was performed by the Bishop of Nebraska, George Beecher, a man Cather admired extremely and corresponded with for the rest of her life. Although her family were churchgoers when Cather was growing up a Baptist in Red Cloud, matters of religion and faith never had troubled her very much. Her college classmates remembered that as an undergraduate she professed not to believe in God and expressed great admiration for atheist Robert Ingersoll after he lectured at the University. Some of her early stories reflect contempt for institutionalized religion, and the satiric portrait of Brother Weldon in *One of Ours* gives short shrift to narrow-minded Midwestern Protestantism. But by 1922 when the world was breaking in two, Cather began to feel the need for religion and found it in the Episcopal Church. "Faith is a gift," she once told her old friend Carrie Sherwood. After joining the church she remained a loyal member of the Red Cloud congregation, sent checks regularly to the altar guild, and after her father's death gave the church a stained glass window in his memory.

There is a foreshadowing of Cather's religious seeking in *One of Ours* in the development of Claude's character. In addition to the satire on bigotry, religious discussion is a significant minor component of the novel. Claude's mother is a very devout woman who fervently hopes her son will find his Savior, but Claude, like Cather in her early years, is a freethinker and skeptic throughout the novel. He has outgrown his early religious training and gropes unsuccessfully for a faith that will sustain him. His friend David Gerhardt receives the gift of faith shortly before he is killed. While they are on leave, David confesses to Claude: "I've come to believe in immortality. Do you?" Claude was confused by this quiet question: "I hardly know. I've never been able to make up my mind."

"Oh, don't bother about it! If it comes to you, it comes. You don't have to go after it. I arrived at it in quite the same way I used to get things in art,—knowing them and living on them before I understood them." Cather apparently came to her faith in the same way and by 1922 was ready to believe. In her search for a spiritual mooring she also came to think, as she has Myra Henshawe say in *My Mortal Enemy*, that "*in religion seeking is finding.*"

The winter in New York was not very pleasant. She returned from the West with a cold she had trouble shaking and then had two attacks of appendicitis, but did not have to have an operation. She was thrilled by her royalty statement, however, and did manage to have a dinner at the Knopfs with Myra Hess in late January. Then she came down with the flu and had to go to the hospital, after which she went to a resort at Lakehurst, New Jersey, to recuperate. The winter finally ended, and armed with her new affluence, she sailed alone for Europe in April to spend the next seven months abroad.

The Atlantic crossing restored her spirits, as it usually did, and as soon as she reached France, she went to visit the Hambourgs, who had settled down in a villa at Ville d'Avray outside of Paris. They had fitted up a study for her and hoped she would remain a long time and write there. She had a splendid time visiting with them and meeting their friends, but she was unable to work in France. She told an interviewer: "I hate to leave France or England when I am there, but I cannot produce my kind of work away from the American idiom. It touches the springs of my memory, awaking past experiences and knowledge necessary to my work." She went on to say that she loved the life at Ville d'Avray, but "I was so busy drinking in the beauty of the place that I could not work. I went from there to Paris, hoping to achieve a working state of mind, but again it proved impossible. The Seine absorbed my thoughts. I could look at it for hours as it reflected every mood of the ever-changing skies, and the colorful life surging around me was utterly distracting as well."

She did no writing at all during her stay in France, but the real reason was not the beauties and distractions of the country. She had a persistent case of neuritis in her right arm and shoulder that kept her from working, and for nearly two months in August and September she was in Aix-les-Bains taking baths in the hot mineral springs. She wrote Mencken that she had come to the home of women gastronomically gone wrong, though she was being boiled daily for neuritis, and was leading an utterly indolent sort of life. She planned to be industrious when she returned to New York and had some stories in mind that she hoped to write for his new *American Mercury*. At the moment, however, she was spending her time out of doors and thought that anyone who had not seen Haute Savoie in the autumn didn't know how fine the

8. Cather at Mesa Verde, 1915. Courtesy of Helen Cather Southwick

9. Cather at Jaffrey, New Hampshire, about 1917. Courtesy of Helen Cather Southwick

0. Cather in Jaffrey about a decade later. Courtesy of WCPMC-NSHS

71. Cather in the north woods in the
    twenties. Courtesy of WCPMC-NSHS

72. Cather's cottage on Grand Manan
    Island. Courtesy of Philip South-
    wick

73. Dorothy Canfield Fisher about
1900. Courtesy of the University of
Vermont, Bailey/Howe Library,
Burlington, Vermont

74. Cather and Isabelle McClung Hambourg in France, 1923. Courtesy of Helen Cather Southwick

75. Edith Lewis. Courtesy of Helen Cather Southwick

76. Cather's 1920 passport photo. Courtesy of Nebraska State Historical Society

world could be. The surrounding mountains were magnificent; she was taking wonderful motor trips and soaking up the blue-and-gold weather. In a follow-up letter from Paris in October she sent Mencken a newspaper clipping of some lines going the rounds of cafes in Geneva. They characterized various nationalities, among them the Americans:

> *Un Américain, c'est un buveur;*
> *Deux Américains, deux ivrognes;*
> *Trois Américains, c'est la prohibition.*

> [One American is a drinker
> Two Americans, two drunks
> Three Americans is Prohibition]

She signed her letter, "Prohibitionally yours."

After her cure at Aix-les-Bains Cather had business in Paris with Leon Bakst, the Russian-born painter. The Omaha Public Library wanted to hang her portrait, raised money for it, and asked her to have it painted for them. She picked Bakst, who lived in Paris, and sat for him during October before she sailed for home. Lewis remembered: "She had, I think, as many as twenty sittings with Bakst. His charm and genius, his winning, attractive personality made these sittings a delight, and the two became warm friends." Cather wrote Irene Weisz before the sittings began that the people in Omaha were not going to like the portrait because it would not be a photographic likeness. They did not, nor did her family and friends like it. They all thought it dreadful, but nevertheless it was duly hung in the library in Omaha. Lewis called it, "stiff, dark, heavy, lifeless—everything that Willa Cather was not." Certainly the painting is not flattering, but Bakst's sitter was a middle-aged woman going through a profound physical, emotional, and spiritual crisis. The portrait bares the soul of Professor St. Peter, whose similar problems Cather already had begun to describe.

On October twenty-third Cather boarded the *Berengaria* at Cherbourg for the voyage home. The trip was enlivened by the companionship of Frank ' Swinnerton, the British novelist, who was going to America on a lecture tour. On the apparent theory that writers ought to talk to each other, the dining room steward put her at his table, and he remembered: "A lady joined the table for four at which I had been sitting [he had embarked at Southampton] with two English business men, and took the seat next to mine. She was not a tall lady, but was of middle height, fresh coloured, rather broad-cheeked, and decidedly self-possessed." They had good conversation, and

Cather wrote later that Swinnerton was a warm, human fellow. When she answered a letter from him the next year, she promised to visit him and his wife if she ever came to England.

By the time Cather's ship docked in New York *A Lost Lady* was in the bookstores and selling briskly. It already had been published as a three-part serial in the *Century* in the spring, and the book had appeared in September. She had left the completed manuscript with Knopf before she had departed for Red Cloud for the golden wedding anniversary, and while she was home she had telegraphed her approval of selling the story, provided the magazine paid well. The *Century* offered her two thousand dollars, which she accepted gladly, and after she got back to New York in January, she had only to spend a couple of days making a few verbal changes.

The idea for the novel had come to her nearly two years earlier when she was visiting the Hambourgs in Toronto. One day while she was finishing *One of Ours*, she received a copy of the Red Cloud paper reporting the death of Mrs. Lyra Anderson in Spokane, Washington, on March 21, 1921. Mrs. Anderson had been Mrs. Silas Garber, the wife of the former governor of Nebraska and the leading lady of the town when Cather was growing up. This obituary brought a flood of memories, and after reading the announcement, Cather retired to her room to rest. Up to that moment, she said, she never had thought of writing about Mrs. Garber, but within an hour the story was all worked out in her mind as if she had read it somewhere. This was another epiphany like those that produced both *O Pioneers!* and *The Song of the Lark*.

The new novel, however, had to wait until *One of Ours* was completed before she could work on it. She wrote it during the winter and spring of 1922 between her return from Nebraska and her teaching stint at Bread Loaf in July. One of her students at Bread Loaf remembered hearing her read some of the novel while she was there. Cather had some technical problems in getting the story into the form she wanted, as she told an interviewer after it appeared. "I discarded ever so many drafts, and in the beginning wrote it in the first-person, speaking as the boy [Niel Herbert] himself. The question was, by what medium could I present her [Mrs. Forrester] the most vividly, and that, of course, meant the most truly. There was no fun in it unless I could get her just as I remembered her and produce the effect she had on me and the many others who knew her." She wasn't trying to make a character study, she said, "but just a portrait like a thin miniature painted on ivory. . . . I wasn't interested in her character when I was little, but in her lovely hair and her laugh which made me happy clear down to my toes."

She discarded the first-person narrative in favor of what she called the indirect method, a third-person narration which frequently slips into the mind of Niel, who is the observer of Marian Forrester from childhood to college. "I had to have something for Marian Forrester's charm to work on." Cather maintained that Niel wasn't really a character at all: "he is just a peephole into that world," the world of the "woman I loved very much in my childhood. Now the problem was to get her, not like a standard heroine in fiction, but as she really was, and not to care about anything else in the story except that one character. And there is nothing but that portrait. Everything else is subordinate." She succeeded very well in this plan, and the narrative technique allowed her to enter Niel's consciousness when she wanted but as omniscient author to record the effect Mrs. Forrester has on other characters, to relate events that cannot be revealed through a controlled first-person point of view, and to modify Niel's perceptions with an ironic perspective.

Cather described herself as the type of writer who "has a brain like Limbo, full of ghosts, for which he has always tried to find bodies. *A Lost Lady* was a beautiful ghost in my mind for twenty years before it came together as a possible subject for presentation. All the lovely emotions that one has had some day appear with bodies, and it isn't as if one found ideas suddenly. It is the difference between a remembered face and having that friend one day come in through the door. She is really no more yours than she had been right along in your memory." Marian Forrester, alias Mrs. Silas Garber, walked through the door, so to speak, in her obituary.

In its setting and general outline the story was ready made. Former Governor Garber, one of the pioneer founders of Red Cloud, had married a beautiful, vivacious California woman a generation younger than he and after his term as governor had settled down in a large house on the outskirts of town surrounded by the beautiful cottonwood grove that Cather loved to picnic in when she was a child. Mrs. Garber went to Colorado Springs frequently for her health, and the Garbers entertained graciously, especially the railroad aristocracy whom Cather remembered as the splendor of her youth. The old governor founded the Farmers' and Merchants' Bank in Red Cloud and lost most of his money when the bank failed. Later he had a stroke and spent his last days as a semi-invalid ministered to by his young wife. After his death she went back to California and eventually remarried. All of these details went into the novel with only minor modifications. Cather's addition to the real story was the creation of Frank Ellinger, Marian's lover, and Ivy Peters, the shyster lawyer-cum-businessman, who symbolizes the debased values that follow the demise of the old Captain.

A Lost Lady is a minor masterpiece with scarcely a flaw, and after the exhausting struggle to write *One of Ours* it was a welcome return to the thing

Cather did best. It conjures up a series of indelible pictures from the memories of youth, the sort of writing that made *O Pioneers!*, the first part of *The Song of the Lark*, and *My Ántonia* memorable. The figure of Marian Forrester is authentic, three-dimensional. The town of Sweet Water (Red Cloud again) is as real as Moonstone and Black Hawk in the earlier novels, and the character of the old railroad-builder Daniel Forrester is as solid and believable as his stone bank building that still stands in Red Cloud. The entire story is told with marvelous economy from the opening paragraph to the account of Mrs. Forrester's death some thirty-seven years later.

By the time Cather wrote *A Lost Lady* she had worked out her literary principles and expounded them in an essay published in the *New Republic* in April 1922. This was "The Novel Démeublé," the most significant and best known article she ever wrote. She began by observing that for a long while the novel had been overfurnished. Every writer knows that his powers of observation and his powers of description "form but a low part of his equipment." He must have both, of course, but even the most trivial of writers are often very good observers. She quoted Mérimée in an essay on Gogol: "The art of choosing from among the innumerable elements that nature offers us is, after all, much more difficult than observing them attentively and rendering them accurately." She agreed with this view and in a later essay, "On the Art of Fiction," wrote that almost the entire artistic process was one of simplification, "finding what conventions of form and what detail one can do without and yet preserve the spirit of the whole." She thought that any first-rate novel or story "must have in it the strength of a dozen fairly good stories that have been sacrificed to it. A good workman can't be a cheap workman; he can't be stingy about wasting material, and he cannot compromise."

In "The Novel Démeublé" she goes on to explode the view that realism results from cataloguing a great many material objects, from "explaining mechanical processes, the methods of operating manufactories and trades, and in minutely and unsparingly describing physical sensations." She argued that realism was merely an attitude on the part of the writer towards his material, the "candour with which he accepts, rather than chooses, his theme." Then she asked if the story of a banker who is unfaithful to his wife and ruins himself by speculating to gratify the caprices of his mistresses is "at all reinforced by a masterly exposition of banking, our whole system of credits, the methods of the Stock Exchange." Her answer, of course, was no; in fact, she didn't think the banking system or the stock exchange had any place at all in imaginative art.

"If the novel is a form of imaginative art, it cannot be at the same time a vivid and brilliant form of journalism. Out of the teeming, gleaming stream of the present it must select the eternal material of art." The novelist must learn to write, and then he must unlearn it; just as the modern painter learns to draw, and then learns to utterly disregard his accomplishment, when to subordinate it to a higher and truer effect. "Whatever is felt upon the page without being specifically named there—that, one might say, is created. It is the inexplicable presence of the thing not named, of the overtone divined by the ear but not heard by it, the verbal mood, the emotional aura of the fact or the thing or the deed, that gives high quality to the novel or the drama, as well as to poetry itself." How wonderful, she thought, it would be if we could throw all the furniture out of the window and along with it all the meaningless reiterations concerning physical sensations, all the tiresome old patterns, and leave the room as bare as the stage of a Greek theater. She ended the essay with one of her favorite quotations from the elder Dumas: "to make a drama, a man needed one passion, and four walls."

In writing *A Lost Lady* Cather carried out the principles she laid down in "The Novel Démeublé." The story opens with a brief chapter of exposition setting the stage for a compact narrative of about fifty thousand words. The omniscient narrator begins like the teller of a fairy tale: "Thirty or forty years ago, in one of those grey towns along the Burlington railroad, which are so much greyer today than they were then, there was a house well known from Omaha to Denver for its hospitality and for a certain charm of atmosphere." The novel proceeds in Part One to cover nine years divided into nine chapters, each of which captures a memorable scene in the lives of the characters. Cather makes no effort to supply a continuous narrative but skips seven years between chapters two and three. The second half of the story also is divided into nine chapters, again consisting of unforgettable scenes that complete the history of the dramatis personae. Apparent everywhere is the hand of a consummate artist in the organization, structure, and symmetry of this distinguished novel.

At the outset Marian Forrester is anything but a lost lady. She is the gracious, charming, animated hostess who presides over Captain Forrester's estate outside of Sweet Water. When railroad men traveling over the Burlington route on business stop off to visit, she is always there to greet them. "If she happened to be in the kitchen, helping her Bohemian cook, she came out in her apron, waving a buttery iron spoon, or shook cherry-stained fingers at the new arrival. She never stopped to pin up a lock; she was attractive in dishabille, and she knew it. She had been known to rush to the door in her dressing-gown, brush in hand and her long black hair rippling over her shoulders, to welcome Cyrus Dalzell, president of the Colorado &

Utah; and that great man had never felt more flattered." Even a "narrow-faced Lincoln banker, became animated when he took her hand, tried to meet the gay challenge in her eyes and to reply cleverly to the droll word of greeting on her lips."

Mrs. Forrester also charms the town boys, especially Niel Herbert, who is about the age of Cather when she first encountered Mrs. Garber. In the opening scene after the short introduction the boys ask permission to play in the marsh below the Forrester house and picnic in their grove. It is a beautiful June day at the end of the school year. At noon after they have frolicked all morning in the marsh, Mrs. Forrester appears with a basket of newly baked cookies. The boys see "a white figure coming rapidly down through the grove, under the flickering leaf shadows . . . bareheaded, basket on her arm, her blue-black hair shining in the sun." The boys are all pleased that Mrs. Forrester has come down herself with the cookies, and Niel is "already old enough to see . . . that she was different from the other townswomen."

After Mrs. Forrester leaves, the boys have another visitor, Ivy Peters, a much older boy, who "walked with a rude, arrogant stride" and carried himself "as if he had a steel rod down his back. There was something defiant and suspicious about the way he held his head." Later he is described as having very small eyes "and an absence of eye-lashes [that] gave his pupils the fixed, unblinking hardness of a snake's or a lizard's." And his face "was red, and the flesh looked hard, as if it were swollen from bee-stings." Evil has entered the garden with the appearance of this character, whose symbolic act of cruelty foreshadows later events in the story. Peters shows off to the little boys by stunning a female woodpecker with his slingshot, then slitting its eyes, and turning it loose. The boys are horrified at this act of wanton cruelty, as the bird flies into branches and the tree trunk. Niel climbs the tree to put the bird out of its misery, falls out, and breaks his arm.

He is carried to the Forresters' house, and placed on Marian's bed while someone goes for the doctor. As they await the doctor, Marian ministers to Niel, who lies weak but content: "The room was cool and dusky and quiet. At his house everything was horrid when one was sick. . . . What soft fingers Mrs. Forrester had, and what a lovely lady she was. . . . The little boy was thinking that he would probably never be in so nice a place again. The windows went almost down to the baseboard . . . and the closed green shutters let in streaks of sunlight that quivered on the polished floor and the silver things on the dresser." The scene within the bedroom is paralleled later by a scene outside the bedroom at the moment of Niel's great disillusionment.

From this moment in which Marian symbolizes for Niel ideal womanhood the novel moves inexorably towards disillusionment and beyond to rejection of the ideal. The next chapter takes place seven years later when Niel is nineteen and the Forresters have to stay in Sweet Water all winter. Depression is on and they are too poor to spend the winter in Colorado Springs, as they used to do. Marian hates to be stuck in the prairie town and begins to drink in the afternoons, but for Niel she is the same lovely lady of the preceding chapter. Niel soon is invited to dinner with his uncle, Judge Pomeroy, when the Ogdens, their daughter Constance, and Frank Ellinger from Colorado Springs come to visit. Although Niel is oblivious, the reader soon discovers that Frank is Marian's lover. Niel takes an immediate dislike to him, though he doesn't know why, but the omniscient narrator describes him as a virile, sexually attractive male: "His chin was deeply cleft, his thick curly lips seemed very muscular, very much under his control, and, with his strong white teeth, irregular and curved, gave him the look of a man who could bite an iron bar in two with a snap of his jaws. His whole figure seemed very much alive under his clothes, with a restless, muscular energy that had something of the cruelty of wild animals in it." The dinner party, which lasts two chapters, ends after the guests have left or gone to bed with Marian and Frank alone in the dining room. As they say good-night, "the train of her velvet dress caught the leg of his broadcloth trousers and dragged with a friction that crackled and threw sparks."

The next day Niel is detailed to keep Constance company while Frank and Marian go out by sleigh to cut cedar boughs for Christmas. In this chapter the observer of the action is Adolph Blum, one of the sons of the German tailor. He is out hunting rabbits when he comes upon the empty sleigh parked in the brush beside the woods. He sees Frank and Marian come out of the trees carrying buffalo robes and stand locked in an embrace before getting in the sleigh. As he watches Marian from cover, "he had never seen her before when her mocking eyes and lively manner were not between her and all the world." But with Adolph Blum her secrets were safe. "His mind was feudal; the rich and fortunate were also the privileged. . . . Mrs. Forrester had never been too haughty to smile at him when he came to the back door with his fish. She never haggled about the price. She treated him like a human being."

That winter, writes the omniscient narrator, was for the Forresters "a sort of isthmus between two estates; soon afterward came a change in their fortunes." Niel visits the house frequently, but he still sees Marian through rose-tinted glasses. "Where Mrs. Forrester was, dullness was impossible." Her charm was not so much in what she said "though she was often witty, but in the quick recognition of her eyes, in the living quality of her voice itself. One could talk with her about the most trivial things, and go away with a high sense of elation." Nothing much registers on Niel's consciousness, even when he wades through heavy snowdrifts to bring the mail and smells alcohol on Marian's breath, or when she says to him: "Suppose we should have to stay here all next winter, too. . . . and the next! What will become of me, Niel? There was fear, unmistakable fright in her voice."

It is not until the following summer that Niel's ideal is shattered. The Captain has to go to Denver when a bank he owns stock in fails, and Marian is left alone. Niel finds Frank Ellinger's name on the local hotel register, but he merely thinks it bad taste for him to visit Marian while the Captain is away. He gets up early to go visit Marian before "Ellinger could intrude his unwelcome presence." As he crosses the fields, "there was an almost religious purity about the fresh morning air, the tender sky, the grass and flowers with the sheen of early dew upon them." He comes upon a thicket of wild roses, with flaming buds just beginning to open. "Where they had opened, their petals were stained with that burning rose-colour which is always gone by noon,—a dye made of sunlight and morning and moisture, so intense that it cannot possibly last . . . must fade like ecstasy." Niel cuts some roses, takes them up to the house, a symbolic gesture of love. "He would leave them just outside one of the French windows of her bedroom. When she opened her shutters to let in the light, she would find them." What follows to conclude this chapter is the end of innocence: "As he bent to place the flowers on the sill, he heard from within a woman's soft laughter; impatient, indulgent, teasing, eager. Then another laugh, very different, a man's. And it was fat and lazy,—ended in something like a yawn."

Niel finds himself at the foot of the hill, his face hot, his temples beating, his eyes blind with anger. He throws the roses into a mudhole. "In that instant between stooping to the window-sill and rising, he had lost one of the most beautiful things in his life. Before the dew dried, the morning had been wrecked for him; and all subsequent mornings, he told himself bitterly. This day was the end of that admiration and loyalty that had been like a bloom on his existence. He could never recapture it. It was gone, like the morning freshness of the flowers." This remarkable scene reverberates in the mind long after the novel is closed.

Part One soon ends with the Captain's return from Denver. He has pledged most of his wealth to save the small depositors of his bank from loss and comes back to Sweet Water a poor man. Very soon after this he suffers a stroke and for the rest of the novel until his death is unable to do much besides sit in his rose garden by his sun dial and watch time pass. At the end of the summer Niel goes to Boston to begin prepping for his entrance exams to M.I.T. He leaves with one burning question he would have liked to ask

Marian: "What did she do with all her exquisiteness when she was with a man like Ellinger? Where did she put it away? And having put it away, how could she recover herself, and give one—give even him—the sense of tempered steel, a blade that could fence with anyone and never break?"

Part Two describes the downward curve of Marian's fortunes. Niel returns after two years, but even before reaching Sweet Water he meets Ivy Peters on the train. Peters now is a shyster lawyer who has come up in the world as the Forresters have gone down. He has rented the Forresters' marsh, which the old Captain had loved in its wild state, drained the land, and planted it in wheat. Niel wants to spend his summer vacation reading in the Forresters' grove, but Peters is always hanging around. He can't understand how Marian can stand having him about, but she says: "Remember, we have to get along with Ivy Peters, we simply have to!" Niel also finds that Peters has been investing money for Marian in some crooked scheme by which she hopes to get out of debt. "Ivy Peters is terribly smart, you know. He owns half the town already." And later she tells Niel that rascality in business "succeeds faster than anything else."

Niel is in for further disillusionment later in the summer when he reads in the paper that Frank Ellinger has married Constance Ogden. That night Marian braves flood waters inundating the countryside to come to Judge Pomeroy's office where Niel is working late. She places a call to Ellinger in Colorado Springs, and in the midst of a conversation that is compromising in the extreme, with Mrs. Beasley, the operator and village gossip listening in, Niel cuts the wire. Soon after this episode the Captain has another stroke and becomes completely bedridden. Marian is reduced to being a household drudge, and local busybodies who never had been invited to the Forresters' come in to help, run all over the house, snooping in drawers and closets. Niel can't stand this state of affairs and takes a year off from college to look after the Forresters. After the Captain dies in December, Marian puts all her financial affairs in Peters' hands and tries to make the best of her situation. Niel thinks: "since her husband's death she seemed to have become another woman. . . . without him, she was like a ship without ballast, driven hither and thither by every wind. . . . She seemed to have lost her faculty of discrimination; her power of easily and gracefully keeping everyone in his proper place." She takes up with the young men of the town and tries to civilize them: "I know," she tells Niel when he admonishes her, "they call me the Merry Widow. I rather like it."

In the next-to-last chapter Niel is again invited to a dinner party at the Forrester house. This time the guests are Ivy Peters, his unattractive sister, and several louts from the village. It is a distasteful scene for the fastidious

Niel, but Marian still has charm and during the dinner recounts the romantic story of her first meeting and subsequent marriage to the Captain. "The boys were genuinely moved. While she was answering their questions, Niel thought about the first time he ever heard her tell that story . . . She had, after all not changed so much since then. Niel felt tonight that the right man could save her, even now." But the unscrupulous, reptilian Ivy Peters is not the right man, and at the end of the summer when Niel comes to visit Marian he sees Peters walk up to her in the kitchen "and unconcernedly put both arms around her, his hands meeting over her breast. She did not move, did not look up, but went on rolling out pastry." Niel goes down the hill for the last time. "He had given her a year of his life, and she had thrown it away." Indeed, she is now a lost lady—lost to him and lost to respectability.

The novel ends four pages later with a brief account of Mrs. Forrester's later life. She sells her house to Peters, goes back to California, and Niel loses track of her. It is years before he can think of her without chagrin, but eventually "he came to be very glad that . . . she had had a hand in breaking him in to life." He last hears of her from a childhood friend, Ed Elliott, a mining engineer, who had encountered her in Buenos Aires. She had married a rich Englishman, and lived on a big stock ranch, but since Ed had seen her she had died. Niel's final speech of the book expresses thanks that "she was well cared for, to the very end."

A Lost Lady is rich in thematic material that links it to earlier novels and anticipates later works. Nostalgia for a greater past, already developed in *O Pioneers!* and *My Ántonia*, reechoes in this story evoking the memory of Silas Garber and the pioneering era. Attacks on the materialistic present, strongly accentuated in *One of Ours*, continue here with undiminished vigor. But a new note sounds in *A Lost Lady* in Cather's implicit message that one must learn to live with change, adapt to new conditions, accept the inevitable. And there is the examination of a woman's role in the post-pioneer world of the twentieth century.

The Arcadia theme is assigned to Niel, who learns a great deal about life from Marian Forrester, but he never loses his feeling that the pioneer era was nobler and better than the present. As Niel plans to return to Boston at the end of the novel, he reflects: "He had seen the end of an era, the sunset of the pioneer. He had come upon it when already its glory was nearly spent. . . . This was the very end of the road-making West; the men who had put plains and mountains under the iron harness were old; some were poor, and even the successful ones were hunting for rest and a brief reprieve from death. It was already gone, that age; nothing could ever bring it back. The taste and smell and song of it, the visions those men had seen in the air and followed,—

these he had caught in a kind of afterglow in their own faces,—and this would always be his." Daniel Forrester in his mind was the archetypal pioneer. Niel always had thought that it was Mrs. Forrester who had made the house so different, but "now it was the Captain who seemed the reality."

Cather castigates the new materialism through the character of Ivy Peters. Not only Niel but also the anonymous narrator heap scorn on Peters. Peters had hated the Captain's generous life-style and had drained the marsh to assert "his power over the people who had loved those unproductive meadows for their idleness and silvery beauty. . . . The Old West had been settled by dreamers, great-hearted adventures who were unpractical to the point of magnificence; a courteous brotherhood, strong in attack but weak in defence, who could conquer but could not hold. Now all the vast territory they had won was to be at the mercy of men like Ivy Peters, who had never dared anything, never risked anything." These scavengers who came after the pioneers would drink up the mirage, dispel the morning freshness, root out the great brooding spirit of freedom. This new generation of shrewd young men would destroy and cut things into profitable bits, "as the match factory splinters the pimeval forest." Ivy Peters, who had blinded the female woodpecker, corrupted Marian Forrester, and finally taken over the dead Captain's property, represented for Cather this new type.

Although both Niel and the anonymous narrator deplore the crass, post-pioneer age, the latter adopts a different stance from the point-of-view character. The dominant theme in the novel is the need to reconcile possibility and loss. The old Captain is like a dinosaur unable to cope with change, and as he sits in his garden watching his sundial and time pass, he symbolizes the inability to change. His paralysis is both literal and figurative. Cather describes him in this condition: "His face was fatter and smoother; as if the features were running into each other, as when a wax face melts in the heat." There is a scene of infinite pathos at the end of Part One after the Captain has returned from Denver poor and suffered his first stroke. Niel comes to dinner on the eve of his departure for M.I.T. and the Captain proposes his one, invariable toast: "Happy Days!"

The reconciliation of loss and possibility is most clearly worked out in the character of Marian Forrester. Niel holds it against her that "she was not willing to immolate herself, like the widow of all these great men, and die with the pioneer period to which she belonged." He further resents that she prefers life on any terms. But this is not the narrator's view, for Marian tells Niel: "I feel such a power to live in me. . . . It's grown by being held back." In straitened circumstances after the Captain's loss of wealth, stroke, and death, she refuses to be beaten. She fights back, weathers her adversity, and eventually regains affluence and social position. There is no doubt that Cather admires her strong will and brave spirit, as much as she might have deplored Marian's desire for money, clothes, jewelry, and society.

As a woman's novel dealing with another type of heroine *A Lost Lady* has considerable interest. Alexandra Bergson and Ántonia both were pioneer women with a sense of vocation that gave them strength to compete successfully in a male-dominated world. Thea Kronborg had the "art necessity" that carried her to the pinnacle of artistic success as a singer. Marian Forrester, however, has no vocation, marries young, becomes one of the ornaments of her affluent husband's establishment. Her options in life are strictly limited, and to make matters worse, Captain Forrester at the time the novel opens is no longer sexually active. Marian, on the other hand, has strong sexual needs that find their outlet in the affair with Frank Ellinger. She is a dutiful, attentive wife, however, and takes good care of her husband in his illness. The Captain knows of his wife's extramarital affair but makes no comment on it. Niel reproaches her for her conduct because she has shattered his aesthetic ideal, but "he felt that the Captain knew his wife better even than she knew herself; and that, knowing her, he,—to use one of his own expressions,—valued her." The anonymous narrator, unlike Niel, does not pass judgment on her.

One of the commonplaces of Cather criticism has been the comparison of *A Lost Lady* with *Madame Bovary*, but the parallels are more apparent than real. It is true that Cather admired Flaubert greatly, but there is little resemblance between Emma Bovary and Marian Forrester. While both novels deal with adultery in the provinces, Emma passively reads romantic fiction, wallows in dissatisfaction with her dull husband Charles, and after committing adultery destroys herself. Marian on the other hand is a woman who acts; she's always in motion; she never gives in to despair. She creates her own fate. *A Lost Lady*, however, does derive from the tradition of the nineteenth-century novel of adultery, and two of these, *Anna Karenina* and *The Scarlet Letter*, were among Cather's favorite books. Her disparaging review of Chopin's *The Awakening* in 1899 foreshadows her updating of the novel of adultery. Where the earlier novels of this category dealt with unhappy marriages, Marian's marriage with the Captain is not unhappy. She never blames him for their misfortunes, and they have a satisfactory relationship together. Where Tolstoy and Flaubert were concerned with moral issues and the impact of adultery on family stability, Cather has gone in another direction. Marian has no children to be affected by her affair with Frank Ellinger, nor do matters of religion ever enter the novel. Even to Niel Marian's actions are a matter of aesthetic rather than moral concern. In this novel Cather has chosen "a narrative situation laden with moral implications" but refuses "to address moral questions in traditional ways. . . . In *A Lost Lady* she has, in a sense, 'unfurnished' the nineteenth century adultery novel of its moral purpose."

Critics treated *A Lost Lady* with the greatest respect. Heywood Broun greeted the novel with a sigh of relief after *One of Ours*: "Willa Cather is back from the war safe and sound. She has never done a better novel than *A Lost Lady* nor is she likely to. But then neither is any other writer of our day. This seems to us truly a great book." Edmund Wilson also put his imprimatur on the novel, finding *A Lost Lady* "a charming sketch, performed with exceptional distinction and skill." In fact, he thought Cather was the only writer "who has brought genuine distinction to the description of the West." Joseph Wood Krutch, who was to become one of Cather's admirers, thought the story too short to be a great novel, but it was "that very rare thing in contemporary literature, a nearly perfect one." Cather, he wrote, had succeeded in synthesizing all the qualities that go to make up a novel: "She can evoke by a few characteristic touches and by subtle suggestion a scene and a society without producing merely a 'document'; she can present a character without writing a psychological treatise; she can point a moral without writing a sermon; and hence she is a novelist." Although the favorable reviews outnumbered the unfavorable ones about five to one, a few reviewers were unable to praise a story of adultery in which the guilty lady did not pay for her transgression. But even these critics had to admit that the writing was brilliant. Percy Boynton in the *English Journal*, who thought Cather had lost her bearings altogether in creating Marian Forrester, hoped that she would "find her way back to the elemental people whom she really knows," that is, the Alexandras and the Ántonias.

A Lost Lady not only was admired by reviewers and ordinary readers, but it also had an impact on F. Scott Fitzgerald, who was in the process of writing *The Great Gatsby* when he read Cather's novel. As a fellow artist and Midwesterner, Fitzgerald felt an affinity with Cather, and he described himself as "one of your greatest admirers—an admirer particularly of *My Ántonia*, *A Lost Lady*, 'Paul's Case,' and 'Scandal.' " After he had completed *The Great Gatsby*, he discovered to his horror that he had "plagiarized" (his term) in a paragraph describing Daisy Buchanan a paragraph Cather had written about Marian Forrester. He wrote explaining that the plagiarism was unintentional, unconscious. She replied graciously that she had read and hugely enjoyed his novel before receiving his letter. She had not noticed any similarity between the two passages and thought they both had been trying to express the effect a charming woman had on a young observer. It wasn't only Cather's style that Fitzgerald studied carefully; he may have invented Nick Carraway, his point-of-view character, after reading *A Lost Lady*. The first version of *The Great Gatsby* was narrated by the omniscient author.

Under Knopf's skillful promotion Cather by 1923 had become a popular as well as a critical success. This made her attractive to Hollywood, and Warner Brothers managed to carry off the movie rights to *A Lost Lady* for a reported ten thousand dollars. The film was cast with Irene Rich as Marian Forrester and George Fawcett as the Captain. Douglass Cather, who then lived in southern California, was invited to visit the set during the filming, and the movie was premiered in Red Cloud on January 6, 1925. The local people thought the film very good, and it got favorable reviews in the national press, but Cather didn't like the cinema. She said later that the picture brought her hundreds of fan letters from illiterate and sloppy people, who gave her a low opinion of movie audiences. Then in 1934 when Warner Brothers remade the film with Barbara Stanwyck, Cather was so distressed by the production that she wrote into her will an absolute prohibition against any future dramatization of her works in any form whatsoever. The only ripple that ever appeared on the surface of her long friendship with Zoë Akins occurred over a dramatization of *A Lost Lady*. Some young screen writer whom Akins wanted to help turned the novel into a play script, but when she sent the manuscript to Cather hoping for permission to produce it, she got a furious reply. Cather wrote at great length analyzing the fatuities of the script, which she said either made Marian Forrester talk like a corsetless old Methodist woman or a darling club woman and never like the character she had created, and everything Niel said was the speech of a cotton-mouthed booby.

CHAPTER 16

The Professor's House

While the reviews of *A Lost Lady* were still appearing, Cather plunged into the writing of her next novel, *The Professor's House*. It would come out in the *annus mirabilis* of American literature, 1925, which also saw the publication of *Manhattan Transfer*, *An American Tragedy*, *Arrowsmith*, *Barren Ground*, *The Great Gatsby*, *The Roan Stallion*, the first of Pound's *Cantos*, and *Gentlemen Prefer Blondes*. According to Edith Lewis, she returned from Europe with the idea for the novel in mind. "Tom Outland's Story," which occupies a bit over a quarter of the book, already was in her portfolio ready to use. The winter of 1923–24 was productive, and Cather was able to take time off to plan an edition of Sarah Orne Jewett's best stories for Houghton Mifflin to keep a promise once made. She was having ever-increasing difficulties in preserving her privacy, however, and took to her bed for a week in February, partly because of a stiff neck but also to avoid attending a song recital by one old friend and the opening night of a play by another. Also, invitations to speak at schools and colleges were driving her to distraction. By this time she had hired Sarah Bloom, who previously had typed manuscripts for her, to be her secretary. Bloom worked for her for the next twenty-four years to handle her correspondence, turn down unwanted engagements, and head off people who wanted to take up her time. Bloom remained with her as long as Cather lived.

She was eager to be interrupted, however, when D. H. and Frieda Lawrence and Dorothy Brett arrived in New York in mid-March on their way to Mabel Dodge Luhan's ranch outside of Taos. Cather's painter friend Earl Brewster, who had met the Lawrences in Ceylon in 1922, had urged them to look up Cather when they passed through New York. Cather was captivated by Lawrence, and according to Brett's report of the visit, Lawrence teased Cather about her dedication to art. While she tried to draw him out on his own ideas about art, Lawrence refused to be serious. "I hate literature and literary people," he told her. "People shouldn't fuss so much about art. I hate books and art and the whole business." The more he went on, the more indignant Cather became. Her own version of the visit described the Lawrences as both very unusual, charming, and thrilling people. But she got so tired doing all the things she planned for them that when they left after a week she had to go to a resort in the Pocono Mountains in Pennsylvania to rest up. Lewis remembered that Lawrence was "in his sunniest mood, and his talk was very vivid and amusing. They did not speak at all of books—Lawrence talked chiefly of their life in Ceylon. He had a wonderful faculty for giving one the tastes, the smells, the colours, and the sounds of a place." Cather wrote a friend after Lawrence died that she knew him quite well and liked him. He was unquestionably the most gifted writer of his generation, but he let his hates and his prejudices run away with him. Also his novels were emotionally overfurnished. In "The Novel Démeublé," she had written, "a novel crowded with physical sensations is no less a catalogue than one crowded with furniture. A book like *The Rainbow* by D. H. Lawrence sharply reminds one how vast a distance lies between emotion and mere sensory reactions."

Cather returned from the Poconos in time to attend Robert Frost's fiftieth birthday dinner at the Brevoort Hotel on March 26, 1924. Ever since she had read *A Boy's Will* and *North of Boston* when they were new books, she had admired Frost, who was just about the only contemporary poet she did like. The dinner brought together some forty of Frost's friends including Carl and Irita Van Doren, Mark and Dorothy Van Doren, Elinor Wylie, Sara Teasdale, Jean and Louis Untermeyer, Ridgely Torrence, Dorothy Canfield Fisher, and Elizabeth Sergeant. Frost sat with his family at the head table and allowed himself to be lionized. Sergeant remembered Cather at one of the tables, her "large, impressive head, emerging from some rich low-necked gown with a touch of red that greatly became her. . . . Her neck, if bare, set this head with its springing bronze hair, which never grayed or curled, in just proportion. The hair was always done at the back of her neck in an unfashionable bun. Her lovely oval face brimmed with affection, her blue eyes gazed upon the hero of the evening as if he were a distant prospect, much admired."

When the Lawrences left New York, they urged Cather to visit them in New Mexico during the summer, but she did not go for another sixteen months. She worked steadily in New York through the spring and made plans to visit Nebraska in June. On her way to Red Cloud she stopped off in

Ann Arbor, Michigan, to receive her second honorary degree. Both going and coming she visited Irene Miner Weisz in Chicago, as she often did, and after six weeks in Red Cloud with her parents she headed for New Brunswick and Grand Manan Island. She carried her manuscript with her to work on in the cottage she rented from Sarah Jacobus at Whale Cove.

Grand Manan pleased her more than ever, and after two weeks there she wrote Zoë Akins that she was nearly half finished with the first draft of her novel. She was in high spirits, surrounded by wild woods and wild weather, and wrote her letter on birchbark, kid fashion, she said. She loved the tempests of the Bay of Fundy and after her usual three-hour working stint in the mornings walked along the cliffs overlooking the sea regardless of the weather. She wore her knickerbockers when the weather was really bad. By late September the autumn fogs began to roll in and it was time to pack up and leave. It was probably that summer that she and Lewis decided to build a cottage on the island, but they did nothing about it until 1926. Cather left for the mainland on September 21 on the one and only twice-a-week boat, and after a few days in Boston getting her niece Mary Virginia Auld (her sister Jessica's daughter) started at Dana Hall in Wellesley, she again visited Jaffrey. By the middle of October she was back on Bank Street pushing to finish *The Professor's House*. She took part of the manuscript with her in December when she returned to Red Cloud to spend the Christmas holidays, and as she passed through Chicago, either going or coming, she left the manuscript with Irene Weisz to read. She must have finished the novel after returning to New York in January.

When she got back to New York, the interview she had given to Rose Feld of the *New York Times* before she left was creating a minor furor. She had been asked a lot of big questions about art and culture and had taken the opportunity to air a number of prejudices and convictions, some of which she previously had talked about. Did the large number of books currently being sold mean that Americans were becoming a more cultured or artistic people? Cather was scornful: "Don't confuse reading with culture or art . . . not in this country, at any rate." The prosperous middle class has to have amusement "to fill up commuting boredom every morning" or something to read while "the maid takes care of the apartment housework." Publishers turn out trash to supply this market—the same market that the cinema supplies. Then she went on to extol the virtues of French culture. Americans were good engineers and builders, but they hadn't yet produced anything very important in literature, painting, or sculpture. "We haven't yet acquired the good sense of discrimination possessed by the French." The problem lies in "our prosperity, our judging success in terms of dollars," which makes for comfortable living but not for art. French minds, on the other hand, "have been formed by rubbing up cruelly with the inescapable realities of life . . . The Frenchman doesn't talk nonsense about art, about self-expression; he is too greatly occupied with building the things that make his home."

This blatant display of Francophilia raised some hackles. John Farrar, editor of the *Bookman*, took her to task editorially for overlooking the "beauty of revolt, the beauty of struggle, the beauty of the very rugged unformed state she abhors." And he noted that "the avarice of the French is no prettier a characteristic than our money madness, and the striving of the present generations, Miss Cather, is building up wealth for the leisure of those quietly cultured souls you so miss in this welter of 'cinema' and 'radio' publics."

Cather was particularly annoyed by what she thought were misguided efforts to Americanize the foreign-born. When she was growing up on the Divide, the native Americans respected the alien customs of the immigrants and let them alone. But now "social workers . . . go after them, hound them, pursue them, and devote their days and nights toward the great task of turning them into stupid replicas of smug American citizens." When Cather was criticized for denigrating social workers, she claimed she had been misquoted, and when she had time she was going to make Miss Feld print an interview on her interview. Nothing came of this, however, but in future interviews Cather was more circumspect in what she said and in a few more years stopped giving interviews.

Having finished her novel, which was not scheduled for publication until September, she had leisure to work on other projects. The first was her edition of Jewett's stories. She had selected the tales to go into this two-volume collection the previous spring and had written the first draft of her preface. When she had sent it to Greenslet, she asked for his opinion. Her heart and mind had been full of the subject for years, but when she sat down at her desk it wasn't an easy thing to do. She had to balance her old affection and admiration for Jewett's best work with the realization that her friend had been, after all, a minor writer. When Burton Rascoe interviewed her about this time, she told him that Jewett was too much coddled by her family. "They'd have kept her in cotton wool and smothered her if they'd had entirely their own way about it. She was a very uneven writer. A good portion of her work is not worth preserving. The rest, a small balance—enough to make two volumes—is important." Cather had a further problem with this edition when Sarah's sister Mary wanted to include a feeble story, "Decoration Day." She wrote Greenslet that he would have to persuade her to omit that story. She explained that in her preface she had made high claims for the stories, but no critic could make a claim for that story. If it had to go into the collection, she would withdraw her preface. She did not have to.

Cather's preface paid high tribute to Jewett's best work: "If I were asked to name three American books which have the possibility of a long, long life, I would say at once, *The Scarlet Letter, Huckleberry Finn,* and *The Country of the Pointed Firs.* I can think of no others that confront time and change so serenely." She explained: "The 'Pointed Fir' sketches are living things caught in the open, with light and freedom and air-spaces about them. They melt into the land and the life of the land until they are not stories at all, but life itself." She had to go on to say, however: "To note an artist's limitation is but to define his genius. A reporter can write equally well about everything that is presented to his view, but a creative writer can do his best only with what lies within the range and character of his talent." Jewett wrote of the fisher-folk, seaside villages, juniper pastures, and lonely farms—the people and places she had thoroughly assimilated, and the result was New England itself. When she wrote of the subjects that had teased the mind over and over for years, she was a great artist. Cather would have agreed with James's admonition after Jewett had tried to write an historical novel laid in the eighteenth century: "Go back to the dear Country of the Pointed Firs, *come* back to the palpable present."

Cather was very pleased when the Mayflower Edition of Sarah Orne Jewett appeared in 1925 with her preface and selection of stories, but the editorial work contains a surprise. For a writer so sensitive to the integrity of a work of art, Cather apparently never thought of the 1896 edition of *The Country of the Pointed Firs* as an autonomous entity. The original book contains twenty-one chapters all carefully structured towards a climax, concluding with "A Backward Glance" to end the collection. Cather inserted between chapters twenty and the conclusion three Dunnet Landing stories written later, one of which was unfinished at the time Jewett died. The inserted tales all deal with the same characters, but their inclusion as part of the original *The Country of the Pointed Firs* does violence to the unity of the original work.

Knopf was not to be outdone by Greenslet in getting Cather to edit Jewett, and he persuaded her during this period between novels to write three introductions and an essay for his in-house annual, *The Borzoi.* She introduced an edition of Defoe's *The Fortunate Mistress,* Gertrude Hall's *The Wagnerian Romances,* and *Wounds in the Rain,* one of the volumes in Knopf's edition of Crane's collected works. The essay for *The Borzoi* was a piece on Katherine Mansfield that she later expanded for *Not Under Forty.*

The introduction to *The Fortunate Mistress* is a curious performance. If potential buyers of the book had browsed through it before making their purchase, they might well have left the work in the shop. Cather had a very low opinion of Defoe's ability as an artist, and she warned readers that despite Roxanna's "career of amatory adventure" the most interesting thing about the book is that "with such a warehouse of inflamatory material to draw from, it remains so dull." "Defoe is a writer of ready invention but no imagination. . . . The episodes of Roxanna's narrative never emerge from the level text and become 'scenes.' " She also believed that the book had no atmosphere, and compared Defoe to Bunyan, whose *The Pilgrim's Progress*, written fifty years earlier, is full of "scenes of the most satisfying kind; where little is said but much is felt and communicated." Also the book had no atmosphere. Roxanna's adventures in France "are exactly like those in England . . . all countries and all cities are alike to Roxanna, just as all well-to-do men are alike to her." The theological discussions between Christian and Faithful in *The Pilgrim's Progress* are "more lively and full of feeling than any of Roxanna's dialogues with her lovers."

The introduction to Gertrude Hall's book, however, was another matter. She had discovered this book in a former edition during one of her early trips to the Southwest and had been a great admirer ever since. Hall had the rare gift of "being able to reproduce the emotional effect of the Wagner operas upon the printed page; to suggest the setting, the scenic environment, the dramatic action, the personality of the characters." She was even able to suggest the character of the music itself. "If you wish to know how difficult it is to transfer the feeling of an operatic scene upon a page of narrative, try it!" She added that when she wrote *The Song of the Lark* she had to do this: "I paid Miss Hall the highest compliment one writer can pay another; I stole from her."

Cather's introduction to Crane's *Wounds in the Rain*, his war dispatches from Cuba during the Spanish-American War, renewed interest in a writer she long had admired. She must have been thinking about Crane at this time, for the first good biography recently had appeared, written by Thomas Beer, who was one of her Greenwich Village friends. As we have noted already, she admired Crane's impressionistic style, and she also liked his unassuming and unpretentious character. This side of him, she commented, caused Beer no little trouble. Crane "managed so conspicuously to elude the banquets and bouquets of his own calling that he left a very meager tradition among 'literary people.' Had he been more expansive at coffee-houses and luncheon clubs where his art was intelligently discussed, had he even talked about his own tales among a few friends, or written a few papers about his works for reviews, what a convenience for Thomas Beer!" But he was reticent and unhelpful, just as Cather would be for her biographers.

The essay on Katherine Mansfield, written not long after she died in 1923, is a piece of more than passing interest. Cather had a lot in common with Mansfield, both in style and literary inspiration, and read her stories with delight. Mansfield practiced Cather's own principles laid down in "The Novel Démeublé." "She communicates vastly more than she actually writes," the essay states, and Cather added that one goes back over her text to find out how it is one knows certain things about her characters. But "the text is not there—but something was there, all the same . . . though no typesetter will ever set it. It is the overtone, which is too fine for the printing press and comes through without it, that makes one know that this writer had something of the gift which is one of the rarest things in writing, and quite the most precious." This aspect of Mansfield's style is similar to what Cather called in her essay "the thing not named . . . that gives high quality to the novel."

She also comments on the close relationship between Mansfield and her brother who was killed in action in World War I. Brother and sister had a great affection for. one another, just as Cather and her brothers Douglass and Roscoe did. Mansfield had been living in England for more than a decade when her brother visited her on his way to the war in France. His arrival brought back to her memories of their childhood in New Zealand and in her British exile rekindled her love of home and family. These feelings then infused and made into high art the stories she wrote in her last years. Mansfield's experience was much like Cather's own discovery of Nebraska as a prime source for fiction after she had lived sixteen years in Pittsburgh and New York.

While she was editing Jewett's stories and writing introductions for Knopf, Cather published her first story in five years. This was "Uncle Valentine," a long tale (sixteen thousand words) that belongs among the best of her short fiction. The setting is suburban Pittsburgh as she remembered it from her first years there, and the title character is based on Ethelbert Nevin. This is one of the rare appearances of Pittsburgh in her fiction, and it would be her last use of the city, except for "Double Birthday," a slighter story that she published in 1929. "Uncle Valentine" appeared in two installments of the *Woman's Home Companion* in February and March 1925. There are no references at all in her surviving correspondence to the story's provenance, but she must have written it and placed it in the magazine herself before going to Red Cloud for Christmas.

Although Valentine Ramsay is clearly drawn from Nevin and the setting is suburban Sewickley where the Nevin family estate was located, the factual basis for the tale is slight. The musical neighbor, Charlotte Waterford, who lives next door to the Ramsays, perhaps was suggested by Mrs. John Slack, one of Cather's musician friends, whose house was adjacent to the Nevins. And there was a real choir of little girls, as in the tale, who practiced with Nevin on Sundays. The shopping trip that Charlotte and Valentine take into Pittsburgh recalls the similar expedition that Cather made with Nevin. Also Nevin had just returned to Pennsylvania after years abroad about the time Cather began working in Pittsburgh. The disastrous marriage between Ramsay and socialite Janet Oglethorpe, however, is contrary to fact, but Cather invented it to power the action of the story. Unhappy marriages often provide drama in Cather's fiction, as this one certainly does.

The story opens with a framing device in which Marjorie, the narrator, listens to an aging singer, Louise Ireland, give a lesson to a young American. The singer is the woman Valentine had run off with when he no longer could stand his wife, an act that had shocked and dismayed Pittsburgh society. The narrator then recalls her memories of Valentine when she had met him at the age of sixteen. She was living next door to the Ramsays as the ward of Charlotte Waterford and her husband. He had returned alone to his boyhood home after years abroad. Charlotte, who has been a friend from childhood, is delighted at the prospect but apprehensive about the reception he will receive. All goes well, however, and Valentine recovers his creativity as he settles down with his father and brothers and tramps about the lovely countryside with Charlotte, her daughters, and ward. The narrator is as much attracted to Valentine's engaging personality as Cather was to Nevin's.

There is little plot in the story, but Cather develops in her narrative, with little incidents—afternoon teas, musical evenings, walks through the hills—a warm human relationship between the characters. The story is charged with emotion, but the reader senses that the idyll cannot continue indefinitely. Disharmony intrudes with the appearance of Valentine's ex-wife Janet, who buys a large adjoining estate. It includes Blue Run, Powhattan Creek and goes all the way to the top of Flint Ridge, places which Valentine loves to ramble over in his frequent walks. He had run away before because he could not live near Janet and he does so again, returning to Louise in France. Two years later he is run over by a truck in Paris. He dies young, as Nevin had done in real life.

Although this story belongs among Cather's tales of civilization and sophistication, its dominant theme also runs through her primitivistic fiction of Nebraska pioneers. Valentine's feeling for the woods and fields of his boyhood home is not unlike the attachment of Alexandra or Ántonia for the land. Valentine tramps the hills feeling, like Thoreau, that the land belongs to those who love and draw spiritual nourishment from it. He is shocked when he discovers that his rich ex-wife can buy this property that he always had thought of as belonging to everyone. "The world belongs to what is rich and powerful, not to the imagination and spirit." Valentine describes his former wife as a "common, energetic, close-fisted little tradeswoman, who ought to be keeping a shop and doing people out of their eyeteeth. She thinks, day and night, about common, trivial, worthless things. And what's worse, she talks about them day and night. She bargains in her sleep."

The ending of the story is a kind of *Götterdämmerung* that Cather reinforces with allusions to Wagner's Ring. In the final paragraph the narrator describes the end of the world she had known at sixteen: "The wave of industrial expansion swept down that valley, and roaring mills belch their black smoke up to the heights where those lovely houses used to stand." Earlier in the story when Valentine and his friends are walking in the evening, they suddenly see in the low cut between the hills across the river "a ghostly brightness with mists streaming about it and enfolding it, struggling to quench it. We knew it was the moon, but we could see no form, no solid image; it was a flowing, surging, liquid gleaming; now stronger; now softer." Both Charlotte and Valentine murmur "The Rhinegold" in the same breath. Thus the allusion to the Rhinegold coming in the midst of the idyllic walk in the woods foreshadows their own twilight of the gods. As possession of the ring made from the Rhinegold causes the conflict and downfall in Wagner's Ring Cycle, so does money destroy the happiness of the characters in this story. Cather's use of allusion here is unobtrusive as usual; she never uses a one-for-one correspondence between a myth or allegory and her fiction but introduces her indirect reference briefly and then moves on.

When spring came to Greenwich Village, Cather was ready to begin her annual travels, first going north to Maine in May, then west to Nebraska, Arizona, and New Mexico in June. The trip to Maine was to take part in a centennial celebration of the Bowdoin College Class of 1825, which had included Hawthorne and Longfellow. Nearly two weeks of festivities were arranged for this occasion, for which a galaxy of literary lights was collected, including besides Cather, Carl Sandburg, Edna St. Vincent Millay, Robert Frost, and John Dos Passos. Bliss Perry of Harvard delivered an address on the college's two famous alumni. Cather was asked to talk about the technique of the novel, a subject she never much wanted to speak on because she didn't think technique could be communicated. But she accepted the invitation as a further way of doing homage to Sarah Orne Jewett and thanking the college for once having given her friend an honorary degree. "Longfellow and Hawthorne, whose commencement anniversaries you celebrate, did not bring me here," she told her audience. After all they had the credits to graduate, but Jewett never had been a student and the college didn't have to honor her. "And by conferring the degree Bowdoin College placed itself irrevocably on the side of the highest tradition in American literature. I have come, therefore, to express my gratitude to Bowdoin College."

Before getting down to her announced topic, Cather relieved herself again of a few familiar annoyances: "I sometimes think the modern novel, the cinema, and the radio form an equal menace to human culture. The novel has resolved into a human convenience to be bought and thrown away at the end of a journey. The cinema has had an almost devastating effect on the theater." Then she added that she had tried to buy Longfellow's *Golden Legend* in a Portland bookstore, but the bookseller had told her he couldn't sell such things; all people wanted was Zane Grey. As for writing novels, she continued, "if your friends are like mine every one . . . believes himself a final authority on the novel and quite capable, if he had a minute, to sit down and write one."

Having got these gripes off her chest, Cather then got down to the technique of the novel, but if there were aspiring fiction writers in the audience, they didn't learn much about how to write a novel. Plot she thought unimportant and dismissed the subject. Shakespeare thought so little of plot that he never bothered to make one but borrowed his plots from Plutarch or someone else. Characterization, she explained, is difficult because it is so simple. "The great characters in literature are born out of love, often out of some beautiful experience of the writer." As for atmosphere, it "was invaluable to the novel before it was called that or had a name. Atmosphere should be felt. . . . It is like the sea on your Maine shore—always there." She concluded by observing that the only good novelist was one who wrote, not to please his publisher or the critics, but himself.

Despite these generalities the speech was a great success. The editor of the Lewiston, Maine, *Evening Journal*, who covered the event, reported that people gathered outside Memorial Hall hours before the lecture, and the auditorium was half filled as soon as the janitor unlocked the doors and turned on the lights. Cather charmed the editor, who described her as "a woman of fifty, with a face of exquisite intellectuality and sensitiveness and a suggestion of capability, dignity, force, thought, culture, and all those things that one finds in the faculties of SOME colleges." Cather talked for an hour and twenty-five minutes, and the editor and the audience liked it all.

Mary Jewett was in the hall that night, and after the lecture Cather accompanied her back to South Berwick for a visit. Then she went to Wellesley to see her niece before returning to New York to prepare for her journey west. Edith Lewis accompanied Cather on this trip, and the two women left New York in mid-June for the Grand Canyon. By the end of the month they were settled at the San Gabriel Ranch near Española, New Mexico, and Cather finished reading proof on *The Professor's House*. The serialized version of the novel, which Paul Reynolds had sold to *Collier's* for ten thousand dollars, already was appearing in the magazine. In July they visited Mabel Dodge Luhan at Taos for two weeks, staying in the Pink House where the Lawrences had lived the previous summer.

Mabel Dodge Luhan was a formidible personage. Cather must have met her in New York many years before when she was Mabel Dodge, a rich patron of the arts. She then lived in a mansion on lower Fifth Avenue and kept a salon for the literati of Greenwich Village. She had left New York for New Mexico, bought a ranch near Taos, and built an elaborate house which she surrounded with guest cottages. She was an indefatigable promoter of Taos as an artist's colony, champion of Indian rights, and lion hunter. A procession of artists and intellectuals passed through her establishment before and after Cather: Carl Van Vechten, Georgia O'Keefe, Robinson Jeffers, Ansel Adams, Lincoln Steffens, Leopold Stokowski, Jean Toomer, and, of course, Lawrence. Having discovered New Mexico, Mabel Dodge also discovered Tony Luhan, whom she married after pensioning off his Indian wife.

After a considerable amount of urging, Cather agreed to be Mabel Luhan's guest, provided she could rent one of the guest houses and have privacy. The Pink House where she stayed was across the meadow from the Big House where Mabel and Tony lived, and Mabel left Cather alone, appearing only at meal times when Cather and Lewis crossed the meadow to the Big House to eat. After Cather had agreed to come to Taos, Mabel and Tony drove to Española in their Cadillac and took them back to the ranch. Tony had developed a great affection for cars following his marriage to Mabel, and one of his favorite activities was to act as guide and interpreter for guests who visited her. Lewis remembered: "Willa Cather was very much impressed by Tony Luhan, and felt an instant liking and admiration for him. He was a splendid figure, over six feet tall, with a noble head and dignified carriage; there was great simplicity and kindness in his voice and manner." Mabel sent them off nearly every day in the Cadillac with Tony as driver. "Tony would sit in the driver's seat, in his silver bracelets and purple blanket, often singing softly to himself; while we sat behind. He took us to some of the almost inaccessible Mexican villages hidden in the Cimmeron mountains. . . . Willa

Cather learned many things about the country and the people that she could not have learned otherwise. He talked very little, but what he said was always illuminating and curiously poetic."

How much Cather really knew about Tony is not clear from surviving records. When Tony and Mabel became lovers, Tony began to wear very expensive riding boots and tailored pants, clothing that was not allowed in the pueblo where he had lived with his Indian wife. Elizabeth Sergeant, who also visited Mabel, remembers, as she came through the loggia of the Big House with its great piles of piñon and cedar wood, seeing Tony "detached and hieratical, sitting apart, playing solitaire amidst Mabel's Florentine relics; his two long braids delicately pleated with colored tape; his fine two-colored blanket falling in the proper lines, as the white artists and intellectuals tossed the ball of the higher conversation back and forth." Mabel was never able to interest Cather in the Indian "movement" to help defeat the politicians who were trying to destroy the pueblo lands and ceremonies. "The tribal side of the Indian meant little to her, even though Mabel insisted that one could not know the Pueblo Indian—no, not even Antonio Luhan—until one knew him tribally." Cather also probably never knew of Tony's carnal nature and that he gave Mabel syphilis.

While Cather was visiting the Luhans, she went to call on D. H. Lawrence, who then was living on the ranch Mabel had given him in exchange for the manuscript of *Sons and Lovers*. The ranch was in the mountains about twenty-five miles from Taos. Lawrence and his wife, Frieda, were living a primitive life, baking their own bread in an outdoor oven and milking their own cow. When Cather arrived, Lawrence was out looking for his cow, which had wandered off somewhere in his four-square-mile pasture. Lewis remembered: "His talk, as before, was full of charm and vivacity, sometimes with a satiric edge. . . . Nothing could have been friendlier or more hospitable than their welcome." Cather never saw Lawrence again. Although his tuberculosis was in remission during that summer, he had to leave his beloved ranch in September when his temporary visa expired, and he never returned to America.

After leaving Taos, Cather and Lewis went to Santa Fe where they put up at the La Fonda Hotel and found a large accumulation of mail forwarded from New York. There was an astonishing number of letters from solemn professors and hard-boiled publishers telling her that "Tom Outland's Story" in *Collier's* had, as Cather put it, given them a pulse. While she was in Santa Fe, Cather made the momentous discovery of *The Life of the Right Reverend Joseph P. Machebeuf,* the book that gave her the idea for *Death Comes for the Archbishop*. The story of this find, however, belongs in Chapter Eighteen.

Before returning east the two women took a train to Laguna, then hired a guide to drive them to Ácoma, an Indian village on top of a mesa, some thirty miles away. Three days of cloudbursts and washouts kept them at Laguna in what Lewis recalled as "the roughest and dirtiest [hotel] we had ever stopped in. The poor, overworked woman who kept it never had time to sweep it— there were great clods of earth on the carpets. The windowpanes in our bedroom were broken in jagged holes, and burnt matches and cigarette papers were scattered all over the floor. . . . All the food in the hotel came out of cans, including the milk and butter." The meals were so bad that Cather and Lewis brought crackers and cheese and ate on the ledges behind the pueblo.

Once the weather cleared, however, the drive to Ácoma was a glorious experience. "From the flat red sea of sand rose great rock mesas, Gothic in outline, resembling vast cathedrals. They were not crowded together in disorder, but placed in wide spaces, long vistas between. This plain might once have been an enormous city, all the smaller quarters destroyed by time, only the public buildings left,—piles of architecture that were like mountains." And the sandy soil of the plain had a light sprinkling of junipers and rabbit brush. Further, the plain gave the appearance of great antiquity, one of incompleteness, "with all the materials for world-making assembled," as if "the Creator had desisted, gone away and left everything on the point of being brought together. . . . The country was still waiting to be made into a landscape."

On the way to Ácoma they passed the Enchanted Mesa, "The Enchanted Bluff" of Cather's early story, the place that had excited her imagination when she was a child in Red Cloud. As Bishop Latour and his guide Jacinto pass the Enchanted Mesa en route to Ácoma in *Death Comes for the Archbishop*, the guide tells his companion that on top of this mesa there once had been an Indian village. But the stairway which had been the only access to it was broken off by a great storm many centuries before and its people all had perished up there from hunger. Cather stored up impressions from this trip to use in her later novel.

In August Lewis returned to New York and Cather traveled north to Denver where she rented an apartment and entertained her brother Roscoe and his three daughters from Wyoming, her mother and sister Elsie, who came on from Nebraska. After that she headed east, spent two weeks in Red Cloud, and then continued on to New York, where she stayed only three days before going up to New Hampshire for her usual visit to the Shattuck Inn at Jaffrey. New York was more hideous than ever, and again she said she was soon going to leave the city for good. She was back on Bank Street by the end of October. By this time most of the reviews of her new novel had appeared, and she was surprised at how good they were. *The Professor's House*, she wrote Fisher, was certainly not her favorite among her books. She also had gotten Knopf into something of a bind by switching from her western subjects. She was like an old wild turkey who forsakes the feeding ground as soon as there are signs of people, which in her case meant readers and book buyers.

In this novel Cather left her Nebraska locale for a fictitious university town named Hamilton on the shores of Lake Michigan not far from Chicago. Her protagonist, Godfrey St. Peter, is a professor whose field of specialization is Spanish colonial history. He has recently completed his life's work, a multivolume history, *The Spanish Adventurers in North America*, which has won an important prize and a handsome sum of money. His wife has used the prize money to build a new house and finally move out of the cramped rented place they have lived in for many years. The professor can't bring himself to leave the old house, especially the attic study where he wrote his books and the formal French garden he has created outside. He insists on paying the rent and continuing to use his study.

Book One ("The Family") develops the character of the professor and his relationship with his wife, Lillian, his daughters, Kathleen and Rosamond, and their husbands, Scott McGregor and Louie Marsellus. The reader learns that the professor, who is at the peak of his professional career, is strangely discontented with life and reluctant to face the future. He spends more and more of his time reliving the past. For a long while his marriage has been a loveless union, and his relationship with Rosamond is unhappy. She has been corrupted by the wealth of her husband Louie, a somewhat abrasive Jewish entrepreneur. St. Peter still is close to Kathleen, his younger daughter, but she is married to a dissatisfied newspaperman who is too good for his job. The reader also discovers that the professor mourns the loss of the one truly gifted student he ever had, Tom Outland, who had been killed in World War I.

Book Two ("Tom Outland's Story") is a seventy-page story-within-a-story. It is the record of Tom's life before arriving at the professor's house nearly twenty years earlier. This is the tale inspired by Cather's visit to Mesa Verde ten years before. It is an account of Tom's discovery of the cliff city high up under the rim of the Blue Mesa and his exploration of the ruins with his cowboy companion Roddy Blake. Tom and Roddy work all summer among the cliff dwellings, excavating, collecting, cataloguing; then Tom goes to Washington in the winter to announce the discovery to the director of the Smithsonian Institution. In Washington he meets with monumental indifference, and after six frustrating months returns to New Mexico only to find that his partner has sold the artifacts to a German archeologist. Tom is angry and crushed by this event, quarrels with Roddy, who then disappears. Tom hides himself in the cliff dwellings for the summer, undergoes a spiritual rebirth, begins to educate himself, and then with money from a summer's work on the railroad goes to college.

The novel concludes with a brief final book called "The Professor," which takes place in the late summer and early fall. The professor has stayed home while Louie and Rosamond have taken Mrs. St. Peter to Europe. Louie tried to get his father-in-law to go, but St. Peter begged off. As the fall term begins, the professor has no heart for his lectures. He feels a premonition of death and wants to be alone. His family is about to return from Europe, and he does not see how he can go on living with them. He lies down to take a nap in his attic study, and while he is sleeping, a storm comes up, the window blows shut, and his gas stove goes out. The old sewing woman Augusta, who has come to get the keys to the new house, arrives just in time to save him from asphyxiation. On his couch recovering, he realizes that his temporary unconsciousness has been beneficial: "He had let something go—and it was gone; something very precious, that he could not consciously have relinquished, probably." His family would not realize that he was no longer the same man, but he now could face the future with fortitude. Cather too experienced something like this psychic annihilation in the period before writing the novel. She wrote in the front of a presentation copy to Robert Frost that "This is really a story of 'letting go with the heart.'"

There is no evidence that Cather realized how much autobiography she was putting into the novel. When Fisher joked about her writing a middle-aged story, she admitted she had; doesn't everyone have a middle-aged mood sometimes, she replied. At the same time she called the novel a nasty, grim little tale and wondered why it seemed to be selling better than any of her books so far. She had had one reaction from a friend when she tried out the manuscript on Irene Weisz the previous winter, and she was pleased that Irene got the really fierce feeling that lay behind the rather dry and impersonal manner of the telling. She may have known subconsciously that she was revealing a great deal of herself and for that reason tried to cover her tracks by creating a male protagonist and setting the novel in Michigan. Nothing can hide the spiritual malaise of Professor St. Peter/Willa Cather, however, from anyone in adequate command of her personal history and public statements.

Lillian St. Peter says to her husband midway in the novel: "You are not old enough for the pose you take. . . . Two years ago you were an impetuous young man. Now you save yourself in everything. . . . All at once you begin shutting yourself away from everybody. . . . I can't see any change in your face, though I watch you closely. It's in your mind, in your mood. Something has come over you." The professor replies that he really doesn't know what's wrong with him: "It's the feeling that I've put a great deal behind me, where I can't go back to it again—and I don't really wish to go back. . . . And now I seem to be tremendously tired." He concludes by saying: "I'll get my second wind." One cannot read this passage without remembering Cather's statement made eleven years later (1936) that the world broke in two for her about 1922. The professor does get his second wind after his near death, though life in the future will be a diminished thing. Cather weathered this midlife crisis and continued writing novels, but the resolution of the problem, which for the professor occurs in one dramatic episode at the end of the story, took place undramatically for his creator as a slow process of adjustment extending over several years.

The autobiographical parallels between Cather and St. Peter are striking. The same age as Cather, the professor was born on a farm on the shores of Lake Michigan, which has for him the same emotional pull that the mountains of the Shenandoah Valley had for Cather. He had a strong-willed Protestant mother, a gentle father, and a patriarchial grandfather, all of which Cather had. When he was eight, his parents dragged him out to the wheatlands of Kansas and "St. Peter nearly died of it." As an adult he went back to the region of his childhood for his professional career, just as Cather did. After he had been teaching a number of years, he conceived of his plan for a great historical work and then devoted fifteen years of his life to writing it. "All the while that he was working so fiercely by night, he was earning his living during the day," as Cather earned her living as journalist and teacher while she wrote fiction in her spare time. "St. Peter had managed for years to live two lives. . . . But he had burned his candle at both ends to some purpose—he had got what he wanted." The first three volumes of his history made no stir at all, just as Cather's first three books, *April Twilights*, *The Troll Garden*, and *Alexander's Bridge*, brought her little acclaim. With the professor's fourth volume (for Cather it was *O Pioneers!*) he began to attract attention; with the fifth and sixth (for Cather, *The Song of the Lark* and *My Ántonia*) he began to be well known; and with the last two volumes (for Cather, *One of Ours*, and *A Lost Lady*) he achieved an international reputation. These parallels leave out only *Youth and the Bright Medusa*, which contains all reprinted stories. Then the professor won the Oxford Prize for History, which brought him five thousand pounds. Cather's Pulitzer Prize was a modest sum, but her royalties from Knopf the year before writing *The Professor's House* were close to the equivalent of five thousand pounds.

The autobiographical similarities go much deeper than these rather obvious correspondences. The large preoccupation with houses in the novel has a considerable relevance to one aspect of Cather's life. Leaving a place she had lived and put down roots was for her a painful experience freely acknowledged in her letters and interviews. The removal from Willow Shade, her spacious and comfortable childhood home, had been a wrenching blow. Her departure for college from the cramped little house in Red Cloud was perhaps less traumatic, but she returned to it often in her affections and in her fiction. The loss of the McClung house in Pittsburgh was the most shattering experience of all. That house not only had been her home, but it also had been her refuge even after moving to New York. It was there too that she had worked in a sewing room/study at the top of the house, as the professor does in her novel. When the professor refuses to leave the old house and his study, it is not hard to believe that Cather was giving her fictional character an option that she herself had not enjoyed. The professor's reluctance to move is best explained in terms of Cather's deep feelings, and it also may explain why Cather never left New York, even though she often threatened to.

Besides the biographical significance of houses, their use in the novel structures its disparate parts. What seems to some readers a disjointed work with a long self-contained story inserted in the middle gains unity through houses as subject and symbol. In Book One the new house Mrs. St. Peter has built is no place the professor can feel at home in. Although it is comfortable and modern, it doesn't suit his personality or temperament, and he wants no part of it. He does eat and sleep there but spends much of his time in the old place. Also the house that Rosamond and Louie are building is patterned after a Norwegian manor, which the professor thinks is unsuitable and inappropriate on the shores of Lake Michigan. In contrast to these houses are the cliff dwellings of the Blue Mesa. When Tom Outland discovers the silent city in Book Two he is enraptured by the houses the ancient people have built. Their beauty arises from the harmony of their surroundings; form follows function in their design and construction. Tom's spirits soar as he sits among the ruins high over the canyon, as though suspended in air. The houses of the people who once lived on the mesa symbolize for him a life perfectly adapted to the environment, a stark contrast to the ugly office buildings filled with faceless government workers that he sees when he visits Washington. In the final book of the novel, Cather completes her house symbolism in a dark mood. As the professor lies on his couch in his study almost wishing for death, he has a vision of the grave as one's final house. He quotes from Longfellow's translation of the Anglo-Saxon poem "The Grave":

> For thee a house was built
> Ere thou wast born;
> For thee a mould was made
> Ere thou of woman camest.

Many people apparently asked Cather about the unusual structure of the novel, but she never bothered to reply until Pat Knopf, in whose education she took a great interest, posed the question. She wrote him explaining what she was trying to do, and he showed the letter to Burgess Johnson, his English professor at Union College, who asked and received permission to publish it in the College English Association's newsletter. "When I wrote *The Professor's House*," she said, "I wished to try two experiments in form. The first is the device often used by the early French and Spanish novelists; that of inserting the *Nouvelle* into the *Roman*." This, of course, she already had done to a lesser extent in her earlier novels. The second experiment, which interested her more, was something a little vague, she said, but was "very much akin to the arrangement followed in sonatas in which the academic sonata form was handled somewhat freely." By this musical analogy she seems to have meant only the use of the three-part sonata form with the different parts providing contrast.

There was more to it than this, however, and she went on to explain: "Just before I began the book I had seen, in Paris, an exhibition of old and modern Dutch paintings. In many of them the scene presented was a living-room warmly furnished, or a kitchen full of food and coppers. But in most of the interiors, whether drawing-room or kitchen, there was a square window, open, through which one saw the masts of ships, or a stretch of grey sea." She purposely overfilled the professor's house with stuffy new things, "American proprieties, clothes, furs, petty ambitions, quivering jealousies—until one got rather stifled. Then I wanted to open the square window and let in the fresh air that blew off the Blue Mesa." In this section she presented Tom Outland, who had a fine disregard for all the trivialities that encumbered the lives of the other characters. This interesting explanation may have helped readers in 1940, but today the novel's organization bothers scarcely anyone. Cather told Johnson that she thought the unusual structure was sufficiently bound together in two ways: first, the professor's life with Tom Outland was just as real and vivid to him as his life with his family, and second, Tom was constantly in the professor's house during his student life. Tom and the atmosphere he brought with him really became a part of the old house that the professor could not altogether leave.

Although *The Professor's House* is Cather's most revealing novel for the biographer, there is a great deal more to it than a story that works out personal problems. It is a rich, complex novel, a major accomplishment. There is so much in it to tease the imagination that it generates a steady stream of critical attention. Only *My Ántonia*, *A Lost Lady*, and *Death Comes for the Archbishop* can rival it for exegesis. It may be that a novel with a professor as protagonist has special interest for academics, who write most of the criticism, but the novel is full of ambiguities that invite explication. Cather realized that she had provided plenty of opportunity for critical scrutiny when she wrote Fisher that the reviewers seemed to think her novel a crossword puzzle. E. K. Brown, Cather's first biographer, thought the main theme of the novel was the professor's unconscious preparation for death symbolized through the various houses described in the story. Leon Edel, who completed Brown's biography, made an independent psychoanalytic interpretation of St. Peter. He related the professor's inability to move from the old house to Cather's childhood insecurity and need for maternal protection. Houses symbolized wombs, and the professor's sense of loss revealed Cather's devastation over Isabelle McClung's marriage. Louis Marsellus was a fictional projection of Jan Hambourg. David Stouck read the novel as a powerful piece of social criticism, satire on twentieth-century materialism. Susan Rosowski saw *The Professor's House* as a "book of dreams," also a "watershed book" in Cather's canon. "In redeeming St. Peter's original self by dreams, Cather shifted the terms of identity from individuality developed empirically—through experience—to that which lies beneath experience and which is protected from the vicissitudes of time." To Doris Grumbach it seemed clear that "the professor's problem lies in his late and blinding realization that the life he has been leading, the life of father and husband, is, and always had been, a false one for him, that his existence within these roles is no longer bearable and that death is preferable to living any longer in the stifling, elaborately furnished and *false* (for him) house of women and marriage." All of these readings and others are provocative and insightful, and the novel will continue to receive new analyses.

There are two major themes running through the novel, one personal, the other public. Although there is a great similarity between Cather and her professor, Godfrey St. Peter is also everyman. His problem is the problem of every thinking person: how does one live in a world of change? How does one face the future when the old verities have been blown away, and the world has entered a new era of chaos and uncertainty? No one can evade the issues that this book raises. For Cather it was the world of the twenties, the postwar Jazz Age, but the problem persists in any period: the chaos following World War II or the present uncertainties under the threat of nuclear holocaust. This is the personal equation that St. Peter must try to solve for himself. The public theme of the novel is a strong indictment of materialism. As Cather became richer and richer and America wallowed in prosperity in the years before the stock market crash in 1929, she became increasingly preoccupied with the corrupting power of money. This theme is nothing new in her work, for it appears as early as *O Pioneers!*; but here it is woven into the fabric of the entire novel.

At the outset of the story the professor is confronted with the new house his wife has built with his prize money. After years of struggle in writing his history it has come to this ostentatious display of conspicuous consumption. His wife asks him: "is there something you would rather have done with that money than to have built a house with it?" He says no, but "if with that cheque I could have bought back the fun I had writing my history, you'd never have got your house." As the professor thinks about his daughters, he is even more depressed over the effect money has had on them. Tom Outland, that uncorruptible youth, had left behind him, in the professor's opinion, a disastrous legacy. He had become a scientist and inventor and had willed to his fiancée Rosamond the patent for a revolutionary new aircraft engine. After Tom's death in the war Louis Marsellus had married Rosamond and as a sharp businessman had turned the patent into a fortune. The money has poisoned the relationship between Kathleen and Rosamond. The younger daughter is jealous of her sister's wealth, and the elder has become hard, grasping, mercenary. When Augusta, the sewing woman, loses her life savings in a bad investment, Rosamond refuses to help her, and after St. Peter accompanies Rosamond to Chicago to select furniture for her new house, he returns exhausted by the experience. He tells Lillian: "It turned out to be rather an orgy of acquisition. . . . She was like Napoleon looting the Italian palaces."

The professor sits in his old sewing room study beside the dressmaker's dummies he has refused to let Augusta remove. They remind him of Tom's college days when his daughters were young: "Oh, there had been fine times in this old house then: family festivals and hospitalities, little girls dancing in and out, Augusta coming and going, gay dresses hanging in his study at night. . . . When a man had lovely children in his house, fragrant and happy, full of pretty fancies and generous impulses, why couldn't he keep them? Was there no way but Medea's, he wondered." On another occasion after observing the hostility between his daughters, "two faces at once rose in the shadows outside the yellow circle of his lamp: the handsome face of his older daughter, surrounded by violet-dappled fur, with a cruel upper lip and scornful half-closed eyes, as she had approached her car that afternoon before she saw him; and Kathleen, her square little chin set so fiercely, her white cheeks actually becoming green under her swollen eyes." He goes to the window and looks towards the physics building where Tom had worked in his laboratory: "A sharp pain clutched his heart. Was it for this the light in Outland's laboratory used to burn so far into the night!"

The corrupting power of money extends beyond the professor's family. It also seduces his colleagues, even Robert Crane, St. Peter's staunchest ally over the years in the battle to keep the state legislature and the board of regents from turning the university into a trade school. Crane, a dedicated scientist, had been Tom Outland's teacher and had helped him with his invention. After Louie parlays Tom's invention into a fortune, Crane wants a cut of the wealth. The professor doesn't think this an unreasonable desire, but he is saddened to see his colleague diverted from his passion for science by a greedy wife and her loud-mouthed lawyer brother who want to sue Louie. The professor feels that Louie, if properly approached, would be generous. Everything comes to money in the end, Roddy Blake had told Tom Outland after selling the artifacts to the German archeologist, and St. Peter in his depressed state probably would have agreed. It pained him to admit that even he, whose tastes were simple and unpretentious, had been able to live the life of a scholar amid adequate creature comforts because his wife had a little money of her own.

Godfrey St. Peter, one of Cather's most complex and enigmatic characters, emerges from the novel as a credible, three-dimensional, flawed human being. We see him from all angles—in his relations with his wife, daughters, sons-in-law, colleagues, students, Augusta, the sewing woman, and especially Tom Outland. He has not been a great success as a husband, although he and Lillian live together in harmony after having raised their daughters. Love has gone out of the marriage years before the story opens. Both Tom Outland and the professor's inability to give himself to his family have come between them. Another of Cather's divided personalities, he has for years isolated himself in his study working on his history and living a lonely life of the mind. His students and family have had to make do with only half of him. He is a Hawthornesque character whose mind has developed at the expense of his heart.

But Cather does not overly accentuate his failings. Though he is an elitist who takes refuge in his French garden and his study, he recognizes social obligations. He gets along with his two sons-in-law without approving completely of either; Scott McGregor, who wastes his talents writing good-cheer pieces for his newspaper and Louie Marsellus, who is insensitive and aggressive though good-natured and public-spirited. Nor has he ever short-changed his students, though he thinks most of them dull clods. He loved youth; it kindled him: "If there was one eager eye, one doubting, critical mind, one lively curiosity in a whole lecture-room full of commonplace boys and girls, he was its servant."

We catch a glimpse of the professor in his classroom at the end of one of his lectures. In response to a student question he is thinking out loud about science, art, and religion. "No, Miller, I don't think much of science as a phase of human development. It has given us a lot of ingenious toys; they take our attention away from the real problems, of course, and since the problems are insoluble, I suppose we ought to be grateful for distraction." Science hasn't given us any richer pleasures, as the Renaissance did, nor any new sins. "Indeed, it takes our old ones away. It's the laboratory, not the Lamb of God, that taketh away the sins of the world." In the old days when men and women crowded into the great cathedrals of Europe, each one was a principal "in a gorgeous drama with God, glittering angels on one side and the shadows of evil coming and going on the other." Life was then a rich thing. The professor goes on to say that it makes us happy to surround our creature needs and bodily instincts with as much pomp and circumstance as possible. "Art and religion (they are the same thing in the end, of course) have given man the only happiness he has ever had." St. Peter ends the hour: "You might tell me next week, Miller, what you think science has done for us, besides making us very comfortable."

While the professor goes through his midlife crisis, he lives much in his memories. In one scene he recalls his young days in France when he lived with the Thierault family in Versailles as tutor to their boys, who became closer to him than his own brothers. He remembers those golden days with intense nostalgia. In another scene the professor and his wife attend a performance of *Mignon* in Chicago, an opera he remembers hearing repeatedly in his student days in Paris. He loves the music: it is the expression of youth. When the soprano sings "*Connais-tu-le pays*," it stirs him deeply "like the odours of early spring"; it recalls "the time of sweet, impersonal emotions." He turns to Lillian: "It's been a mistake, our having a family and writing histories and getting middle-aged. We should have been picturesquely ship-wrecked together when we were young." Lillian agrees but quickly adds: "One must go on living, Godfrey."

The final scene of memory occurs late in the novel before the professor's near asphyxiation. In his reverie the boy the professor had left many years before in Kansas returns to him, "the original, unmodified Godfrey St. Peter." It seems now to the professor that "life with this Kansas boy, little as there had been of it, was the realest of his lives." This boy was not a scholar. "He was a primitive. He was only interested in earth and woods and water. Wherever sun sunned and rain rained and snow snowed, wherever life sprouted and decayed, places were alike to him. . . . He seemed to be at the root of the matter; Desire under all desires, Truth under all truths. He seemed to know, among other things, that he was solitary and must always be so." In this important passage the professor strips away the external trappings of his life. What is left is the essential, autonomous human being. He is now ready with the help of the slammed window and blown-out stove to go on with his life, to learn to "live without delight." It is a bleak, unsentimental ending that reflects Cather's mood in 1925.

It is significant at the end of the novel that it is old Augusta who saves the professor. She is solid, real, a woman whose life has been spent serving others, a pious Catholic who asks little of the world. "Augusta, he reflected, had always been a corrective, a remedial influence. . . . Augusta was like the taste of bitter herbs; she was the bloomless side of life that he had always run away from,—yet when he had to face it, he found that it wasn't altogether repugnant." She was unsentimental, practical, and he would rather have her with him at that moment than anyone else. There was "a world full of Augustas with whom one was outward bound."

"Tom Outland's Story," which has been greatly admired by readers and reprinted as a separate tale, is one of the two or three best stories in Cather's canon. It is about the same length as "Coming, Aphrodite!" or "Uncle Valentine," about sixteen thousand words. Cather herself thought it was a good piece of narrative. The title character is particularly engaging—youthful, energetic, full of idealism, talented. Whereas the professor reflects Cather's thoughts and feelings at the age of fifty-three, Tom Outland is her youthful other self. Nowhere does Cather display better her ability to evoke the past and surround it with an aura of romance. The real account of finding the lost civilization of Mesa Verde, the springboard for this tale, is an exciting adventure, but Cather adds a great deal to the story she heard from Dick Wetherell's brother when she visited Mancos in 1915. She makes it a story of youthful idealism and defeat. Not only is Tom frustrated in his efforts to preserve the relics of the cliff dwellings as a national treasure by the indifference of official Washington and Roddy Blake's lack of understanding, but he also goes off, like Claude Wheeler, to fight and die in World War I. But before that final defeat he lives a rich though brief life.

There are wonderful moments in this story that reflect Cather's delight in the Southwest. She answered from Santa Fe a fan letter praising *The Professor's House* while it was still running in *Collier's* by saying that neither years nor miles could ever lessen the pull or the excitement this country had for her. When Tom goes back to the mesa after Roddy Blake has sold the artifacts and departed, he comes to a clear realization of his experience in finding the lost city: "The excitement of my first discovery was a very pale feeling compared to this one. For me the mesa was no longer an adventure, but a religious emotion." Cather must have experienced similar emotions during the hours she and Lewis sat on a rock a thousand feet below the cliff city waiting to be rescued in 1915. The memory of those moments went into Tom's diary, which the professor edits while his wife, daughter, and son-in-law are traveling in Europe: "The grey sage-brush and the blue-grey rock around me were already in shadow, but high above me the canyon walls were dyed flame-colour with the sunset, and the Cliff City lay in a gold haze against its dark cavern. In a few minutes it, too, was grey, and only the rim-rock at the top held the red light. When that was gone, I could still see the copper glow in the piñons along the edge of the top ledges. The arc of sky over the canyon was silvery blue, with its pale yellow moon, and presently stars shivered into it, like crystals dropped into perfectly clear water."

Tom's death, which had occurred a decade before the story opens, was an irreparable blow to the professor. Tom had appeared one day out of nowhere while he was writing his history and had grown closer to him than a younger brother. They were inseparable companions; they traveled together in the Southwest; they had a community of interest and understanding that bound them tightly. So close were they that Lillian was jealous of Tom. "In a lifetime of teaching, I've encountered just one remarkable mind," he tells his daughter. But the memory of Tom lives on, and throughout the novel he is a powerful presence. His legacy, a scientific invention that, like King Midas, turns everything into gold, is the crowning irony.

The reviews of *The Professor's House* are a motley collection ranging from ecstatic praise to complete rejection. The favorable ones far outnumber the unfavorable, but neither those who liked the novel nor those who disliked it could agree on their reasons. James Ford in the *Literary Digest* hailed the book as the best Cather had yet written. He found the professor a great characterization and "Tom Outland's Story" the most thrilling account he ever had read of an extinct civilization. On the other hand the New York *Times* reviewer called the book a catastrophe. The first book of the novel was "ingeniously invented and admirably carried along as far as it goes. It stops in mid-channel. Book the second is an amateurish essay in archeological adventure. It is flat, stale and unprofitable. Book the third finds Miss Cather far beyond her philosophical depth." Henry S. Canby, who was to become one of Cather's friends, reviewed the novel for the newly founded *Saturday Review of Literature*. He was one of the few reviewers who saw beneath the surface the real story of the "slow discovery by Professor St. Peter—of himself." He was more interested in this novel than Cather's others because "the soul, after all, is the greatest subject for art." The experimental structure of the novel bothered many critics even when they thought the performance on the whole superior. The most perceptive critics, however, would have agreed with R. C. Kennedy in the *New Statesman*: "There is no formal shape to the whole; and yet it has the very accent of truth. It would be difficult to convey, without seeming to exaggerate, the ease and precision with which fine inexplicable shades of mood and emotion are rendered."

For Schuyler Ashley in the *Kansas City Star* the professor was "indubitably the most valuable attainment of Willa Cather's new novel. To create such a man, talented, whimsical without eccentricity, and innately attractive; to make him credible and complete is a substantial accomplishment." This reviewer, however, thought Cather was very hard on her own sex, surrounding the professor as she did with a worldly wife, a greedy elder daughter, and a jealous younger one. He quoted St. Peter's comment about Euripides, who went to live in a cave by the sea in his old age: "It seems that houses had become insupportable to him. I wonder whether it was because he had observed women so closely all his life?"

One of the interesting absences from the contemporary criticism is any charge of anti-Semitism. No reviewer saw anything objectionable in the characterization of Louis Marsellus, the professor's Jewish son-in-law. The professor on the whole likes him, though sometimes he thinks there is too much of him, and when Scott blackballs Louis for membership in an exclusive club, St. Peter is overwhelmed by Louie's magnanimous reaction to his brother-in-law's act. It remained for critics of a later generation to suggest that Cather created Louie as a satiric portrait of Jan Hambourg and then to conceal her act dedicated the novel to him: "For Jan, because he likes narrative."

CHAPTER 17

My Mortal Enemy

Cather could not resist two more speaking engagements, and while she still was reading reviews of *The Professor's House*, she went west again to give one of the William Vaughn Moody lectures at the University of Chicago. She visited Irene Weisz once more and asked her old friend to be at the lecture to hold her hand. She was not very happy with the talk, which she gave on November 17, 1925, before a capacity audience in Mandel Hall, but the *Chicago Tribune* reporter who covered it found her remarks full of "pertinent and important things." Her topic was "The Tendency of the Modern Novel." She generalized a good bit from her own practice in matters of length and organization and argued that the novel as an art form, as opposed to the machine-made novel, had changed in this century. For one thing, it could be shorter or longer, as the author wished, and old formulas of plotting now were being ignored. She thought the novel lagged behind painting in its development, and that painters were bolder in their flouting of traditional techniques, but she did not think the new freedom in subject matter that had come in after World War I contributed to a more beautiful art. Reticence, she thought, had an important place in artistic creation. The new novel, however, was becoming more experimental and more concerned with emotional rather than event patterns. And in a remark that anticipated *Death Comes for the Archbishop*, which she was about to begin writing, she noted: "There is such a thing in life as nobility . . . and novels which celebrate it will always be the novels which are finally loved."

Three days later she went on to Cleveland to speak to the Women's City Club on the same subject. She was pleased by this performance and wrote Irene Weisz that she had talked to a large and distinguished audience, mostly young people, very dressy, and one quarter men. She was particularly pleased by the hall, which was done in a deep shade of blue with soft lights, and she thought it was the ambience that made the lecture run along like a rippling stream. She resolved never again to speak in an ugly hall, which only made her stutter and feel wretched. While she was there, a reporter for the *Cleveland Press*, who tracked her down at the Statler Hotel, got a chilly reception. Cather didn't want to talk about her work in progress and bristled when she was asked when her next novel would be out: "Even my publishers don't dare ask me that! I get my books out when I can," and when she was queried about the title, she snapped: "I never give out titles or any information about my books until they are ready." She was, however, willing to talk, as she often did to interviewers, about cooking: "I think the preparation of foods the most important thing in life. And America is too young a nation to realize it." The reporter concluded this interview: "She breezed into Cleveland Friday morning in a bright green and gray fur coat with gold and black toque, and a bright green bag to match." Cather liked bright colors, and interviewers usually commented on the bold combinations she wore. The "green and gray fur coat" was replaced after she returned to New York with a more expensive one. She wrote Irene Weisz in January that the professor had bought her a mink coat, the first valuable thing she ever had owned.

By the time Cather returned to New York from the Midwest, arrangements had been made to publish her next novel, *My Mortal Enemy*, in *McCall's*. For two or three years the magazine, by way of Paul Reynolds, had been trying unsuccessfully to get some stories from her. She must have felt that she had halfway promised something, and when her new story was ready, she let *McCall's* publish it. *My Mortal Enemy* is actually a nouvelle, only about twenty thousand words in length, the shortest of all her works published separately. It appeared in the magazine in March 1926 and Knopf brought it out in book form the following October. It is also the most unfurnished of her novels, a remarkable example of the novel *démeublé*, but it was properly published by itself and not as part of a collection. It is a complete entity and an almost perfect work of art. Cather told her first biographer, E. K. Brown, that she had been glad Knopf was her publisher when the book came out, as Houghton Mifflin surely would have sent it back for revisions. She had had misgivings about her judgment in wanting the book published separately, but Alfred Knopf responded warmly to it and, as he always did, carried out her wishes exactly.

Of all Cather's works *My Mortal Enemy* has the most obscure provenance. Edith Lewis barely mentions it, saying only that it was written in the spring of 1925 at Number Five Bank Street. Where *My Ántonia*, *The Song of the Lark*,

One of Ours, and *A Lost Lady* all have well-known prototypes among Cather's friends and relatives, the prototype for Myra Henshawe in this work has never been identified. Cather wrote in 1940 that she had known Myra's real-life model very well, and the portrait drawn in the story was much as she remembered her. Many of the real Myra's friends and relatives wrote, she said, to tell her they had recognized her immediately. The story, Cather added, was not written until fifteen years after this woman's death. E. K. Brown goes a little farther in identifying Myra as a woman, "older by a full generation, whom Willa Cather had known well through connections in Lincoln," but he was unable to name her. Myra's prototype may have been Myra Tyndale, sister-in-law of Cather's old friend Julius Tyndale, a woman Cather knew in Lincoln during her college years. The daughter of an Irish immigrant, she died of cancer in Seattle in 1903. Cather made a greater effort than usual to cover her tracks in creating this character. She set the story in southern Illinois in a small town that she doesn't describe at all, New York City, and a West Coast city suggestive of San Francisco. It is as though her people were caught in a modern, rootless existence.

It is significant that this short novel was written immediately after the completion of *The Professor's House*. It belongs to the same dark mood that possessed Cather as she and her professor worked themselves through their mid-life crises. It is the most bitter piece of fiction she ever wrote, the most tragic, and it drained the last bit of gall from her system. After *My Mortal Enemy* left her desk, she turned to the rich affirmations of *Death Comes for the Archbishop* and found her happiness in historical recreations. Three of her last four novels are laid in the past before her time: nineteenth-century New Mexico, seventeenth-century Quebec, and Virginia before the Civil War.

My Mortal Enemy is the story of Myra Henshawe, the grandniece of a wealthy Irish Catholic, John Driscoll. As an orphaned child, Myra Driscoll is taken in by her great-uncle and raised in his elegant house, the showplace of the little town of Parthia. She is the intended heiress of Driscoll's wealth, but when she falls in love and elopes with Oswald Henshawe, "the son of a German girl of good family, and an Ulster Protestant whom Driscoll detested," the old uncle cuts off Myra without a cent. She and her husband go to New York to live, and for a time they apparently are happy enough. Myra, however, grows discontented because Oswald never makes enough to support her taste for luxuries, and she discovers that Oswald perhaps is unfaithful to her. Their fortunes and their relations deteriorate slowly; Oswald loses his job; they try to start over on the West Coast. Oswald's new business fails, and he is forced to take a menial job with the street railway company. The Henshawes are reduced to living in relative poverty in a cheap apartment hotel. Myra contracts an incurable disease, and at the end of the story, dies. It is a bleak tale of frustrated hopes and blighted happiness, written with stark economy and not one unnecessary detail.

The story is told from the point of view of Nellie Birdseye, a first-person narrator, who is fifteen when she first meets Myra. One of the romantic stories of Nellie's childhood is the tale of Myra's elopement, which she had heard from her Aunt Lydia, one of Myra's girlhood friends. The first glimpse of Myra comes when she and Oswald return to Parthia for a visit and Nellie is invited to dinner. Nellie sees a woman of about forty-five, short, plump, dressed in black velvet. She had a beautiful voice "bright and gay and carelessly kind" and "her deep-set, flashing grey eyes seemed to be taking me in altogether." She holds her head high, Nellie thinks, "because she was beginning to have a double chin." Nellie is dazzled by Myra but is never sure whether she is making fun of her or the thing talked about. "Her sarcasm was so quick, so fine at the point—it was like being touched by a metal so cold that one doesn't know whether one is burned or chilled."

Nellie and her aunt both are hopeless romantics, and Myra to them is a creature out of a fairy tale. Aunt Lydia never tires of talking about her part in helping Myra elope with Oswald: "I'll never forget the sight of her, coming down that walk and leaving a great fortune behind her." True to his word, Myra's great-uncle disinherited her and gave his money to the Church. The Driscoll property, still the finest place in town, had become a convent, and when Nellie used to walk by the house and grounds after school, she thought of it as "the Sleeping Beauty's palace; it had been in a trance, or lain in its flowers like a beautiful corpse, ever since that winter night when Love went out of the gates and gave the dare to Fate." As Nellie matures, she slowly awakens to reality, and by degrees the romantic illusion of Myra's story is replaced by a knowledge of the true relationship and Myra's real character. This awakening is foreshadowed early in the story when Nellie asks Aunt Lydia if the Henshawes have been happy during the twenty-five years they have been married. "As happy as most people" is the answer, which disheartens Nellie because "the very point of their story was that they should be much happier than other people."

Chapter three takes Nellie and her aunt to New York for a Christmas visit to the Henshawes. Cather told an old friend that the setting of this part of the story was the New York she remembered from about 1904. It is New York in the days when one had to take a ferry from Jersey City to reach Manhattan and a cross-town car from the Twenty-third Street Station to the Fifth Avenue Hotel. The Henshawes live on Madison Square, which was then "at the parting of the ways" with a "double personality, half commercial, half social, with shops to the south and residences to the north." Nellie observes: "It seemed to me so neat, after the raggedness of our Western cities; so protected by good manners and courtesy—like an open-air drawing room." Nellie is enchanted by the city, as Cather had been when she lived in Pittsburgh and made occasional visits to New York. "The trees and shrubbery seemed well-groomed and sociable, like pleasant people. The snow lay in clinging folds on the bushes, and outlined every twig of every tree—a line of white upon a line of black." St. Gaudens' statue of Diana stepped out freely and fearlessly into the grey air. "I lingered long by the intermittent fountain. Its rhythmical splash was like the voice of the place." Nellie still sees the world through her romantic illusions.

Myra and Oswald live comfortably in an apartment on the second floor of an old brownstone house on the north side of the square. It becomes apparent, however, that Myra is both extravagant and discontented. She sends her actress friend Helena Modjeska a holly tree for Christmas, the most expensive item in the florist's shop, much to Oswald's distress, and later she shows her envy of other people's wealth when she and Nellie ride in the park in a hired cab. A private carriage passes from which a wealthy friend leans out and waves. Myra is embarrassed and angry, and Nellie realizes that she "was wishing for a carriage—with stables and a house and servants, and all that went with a carriage!" After they return to Madison Square, Myra tells Nellie: "It's very nasty, being poor!" But there is another side to Myra, her generosity and her kindness towards the people she loves. Nellie says: "My aunt often said that Myra was incorrigibly extravagant; but I saw that her chief extravagance was in caring for so many people and in caring for them so much."

During this visit to New York, which extends over four short chapters and ends Part I, the deteriorating marital relationship of the Henshawes becomes apparent. Before the climactic scene, however, Nellie is present at a New Year's Eve party, at which Modjeska is a guest. Nellie remembers seeing her in Chicago as Mary Stuart and as Katharine in *Henry VIII*, just as Cather had seen her in New York in *Mary Stuart* and had lunched with her in 1898. Modjeska brings with her a Polish soprano who is singing at the Met that winter. When Modjeska looks out on the square, white with moonlight, she turns to her friend and asks her to sing. She obliges by singing "Casta Diva" from Bellini's opera *Norma*, a prayer for peace and one of the most beautiful of *bel canto* arias. After this the party breaks up and the guests go home. A few days later when Nellie goes to the Henshawe's apartment for lunch, she comes in upon a violent quarrel. She overhears Myra catch Oswald in a bald lie over the purpose of a key she has found among his things. Nellie doesn't fully comprehend the meaning of the scene, that Oswald's probable infidelity has been found out, but she is shattered by it: "Everything about me seemed evil. When kindness has left people, even for a few moments, we become afraid of them." Nellie and her aunt soon return to Parthia, and ten years elapse before Part II begins.

Nellie grows up, gets a job teaching in a college in a "sprawling, overgrown Western city which was in the throes of rapid development." This unnamed city "ran about the shore, stumbling all over itself and finally tumbled untidily into the sea." Since Cather did not know San Francisco, she kept her locale purposely vague, but the only setting she really needed was a jerry-built apartment house and a cliff by the sea such as there is at Point Lobos, which overlooks the Golden Gate at the entrance to San Francisco Bay. Nellie finds lodging in an apartment hotel "wretchedly built and already falling to pieces, although it was new." She meets Oswald Henshawe on the stairs. She knew that the Henshawes had fallen on evil days, but she was not prepared for the reality. Myra is now a semi-invalid, but she still has her wit and some of the old charm: "She looked strong and broken, generous and tyrannical, a witty and rather wicked old woman, who hated life for its defeats, and loved it for its absurdities." She despises her poverty, can't stand the "palavery kind of Southerners" who live overhead and tramp up and down all day like cattle, and barely tolerates her husband. Oswald, however, lives in his own world of illusion, patiently taking care of Myra, and looks back on happier days. Myra tells Nellie: "He's a sentimentalist, always was; he can look back on the best of those days when we were young and loved each other, and make himself believe it was all like that. It wasn't. I was always a grasping, worldly woman; I was never satisfied. . . . People can be lovers and enemies at the same time, you know. We were. . . . Perhaps I can't forgive him for the harm I did him." Earlier she had said in Oswald's presence: "We've destroyed each other. I should have stayed with my uncle. It was money I needed. We've thrown our lives away."

One warm April day Nellie and Myra go for a drive along the shore. They come to a bare headland with one twisted tree on it and the sea beneath. "It's like the cliff in *Lear*, Gloucester's cliff," Myra exclaims and then wants to be left alone wrapped in blankets and propped against the tree. Nellie takes a walk, and when she comes back Myra says: "I've had such a beautiful hour . . . Light and silence; they heal all one's wounds—all but one, and that is healed by dark and silence. . . . I'd love to see this place at dawn. . . . That is always such a forgiving time. When that first cold, bright streak comes over the water, it's as if all our sins were pardoned."

Shortly after this Myra's doctors find she has a malignant growth and has barely a month to live. At this point she returns to the faith and discovers that "religion is different from everything else: *because in religion seeking is finding*. . . . Desire was fulfillment, it was the seeking itself that rewarded." But the solace of religion isn't complete, and Nellie overhears her asking herself rhetorically: "Why must I die like this, alone with my mortal enemy?" Oswald, who is sitting on the sofa, doesn't react, but Nellie looks at him in affright: "I felt my hands grow cold and my forehead grow moist with dread. I had never heard a human voice utter such a terrible judgment upon all one hopes for."

The next day Myra asks to be given the Sacrament, and later while no one is with her, she slips out of the apartment, hires a cab to take her to the cliff overlooking the sea. The driver leaves her there, and the next morning she is found: "We found her wrapped in her blankets, leaning against the cedar trunk, facing the sea. Her head had fallen forward, the ebony crucifix was in her hands. She must have died peacefully and painlessly. There was every reason to believe she had lived to see the dawn." After her death Oswald still clings to his belief that they once had been happy and says to Nellie: "Remember her as she was when you were with us on Madison Square, when she was herself, and we were happy." But Nellie is haunted in later life by those dying words: "Why must I die like this, alone with my mortal enemy?" Whenever she watches "the bright beginning of a love story," whenever she sees "a common feeling exalted into beauty by imagination, generosity, and the flaming courage of youth," she hears that terrible question.

Many readers see Myra Henshawe as her own mortal enemy, a reading that the text accommodates easily enough, but Cather did not intend to convey that meaning. At the time the book came out, she wrote her old friend George Seibel: "I had a premonition you would understand [that it was Oswald]—and that most people wouldn't." Fifteen years later in an unusual letter to an aspiring young writer who had asked her about the story, she described in considerable detail what she was trying to do in *My Mortal Enemy*. She was always glad, she wrote, when people told her they liked the nouvelle because it had been rather difficult to write. Her correspondent had wanted to know why two very minor characters, Ewan Grey and Esther Sinclair, did not reenter the story. They had appeared in the Madison Square chapters to illustrate one aspect of Myra's character—her propensity to help young lovers overcome obstacles even though, as she put it, "very likely hell will come of it!" Cather explained patiently that she was painting a portrait of Myra with reflections of her in various looking glasses. It would have been foolish to try to account for any of the people Myra had loved and left behind. It was the extravagance of her devotions that made her in the end feel that

Oswald was her mortal enemy, that he had somehow been the enemy of her soul's peace. Her soul, of course, could never have been at peace. She wasn't that kind of woman.

Cather made other observations on the writing of the story in a letter to a young Englishman who had admired the work. In form she thought the book faulty enough, but she said one had to choose the thing most desired and try for it at the cost of everything else. Nearly all of her books were made out of old experiences that had had time to season. Memory keeps what is essential and lets the rest go. She added that she always was afraid of writing too much, making stories that were like rooms full of things and people with not enough air in them. If writing is easy for one, it's very hard not to overwrite.

The above letter opened a surprising friendship with twenty-one-year-old Stephen Tennant, the youngest son of a British peer. He wrote Anne Douglas Sedgwick, a novelist Cather knew slightly, an admiring note about *My Mortal Enemy*, which Sedgwick forwarded to Cather. She then initiated a correspondence that ripened into a close friendship. That Cather would write the first letter to someone she never had met is totally uncharacteristic, but the open and confidential tone of the letter is perhaps even more surprising. In this relationship, which lasted until Cather's death, there is a considerable amount of evidence to document her elitist leanings. She was quite swept away by this flamboyant scion of a noble lord, this wealthy dilettante who lived a gay life dedicated to world travel, elegant living, and all manner of pleasure. He was noted for his physical beauty and impeccable grooming, and as the youngest son of his aristocratic parents, he did not even have to help manage the family property. But Tennant wasn't just a playboy: he knew Latin and Greek, studied ballet and the piano, painted and wrote esoteric poetry. Cather admired his artistic sensibility, and he in turn found her work perennially exciting. It is another of the dichotomies of her life that she could hold in her affections both Annie Pavelka and Stephen Tennant.

My Mortal Enemy is Cather's most concentrated study of marital relations. She wrote Elizabeth Vermorcken, a former Pittsburgh friend, that Fanny Butcher's review in the *Chicago Tribune* really stated what she was trying to get at in the story. Butcher had written: "Under the flotsam of those lives [Myra's and Oswald's] there is the steady rhythm of the fundamental hatred of the sexes one for the other and their irresistible attraction one for the other." Cather never before had focused exclusively on a marriage. In *Alexander's Bridge*, Bartley dies in mid-career; in *O Pioneers!*, Emil and Marie are killed at the moment they discover they cannot live without each other; in *A Lost Lady*, Marian Forrester is still relatively young when the captain dies and releases her for another life. *The Professor's House* touches lightly on Lillian St. Peter's sorrow over the loss of love in her marriage, but Cather's concern in that novel is with the professor's midlife crisis. *My Mortal Enemy* carries its characters through a lifetime, beginning with the romantic elopement and ending with old age, disillusionment, and death.

The shaping idea behind this novel goes far back into Cather's early career. When she reviewed Chopin's *The Awakening* in 1899, she attacked the protagonist Edna Pontellier as belonging to a class of women "that demands more romance out of life than God put into it." Myra and Oswald's romance was bound to end in unhappiness in Cather's view; in fact, for those who stake all on love, death is the only possible ending. Although Cather was a devoted Romantic, believing in the power of the creative imagination to connect the individual with the world, she regarded romantic love as an over-indulgence in emotion. This excess of emotion degenerates into sentimentalism in the case of Oswald, and with Myra it changes into hate when she realizes that love is not enough. "Oh, if youth but knew," she says to Nellie just before she turns her face to the wall after asking Nellie and Oswald to leave her.

This astringent portrayal of defeat and death marks the end of Cather's own bitter years. Besides being her most searching analysis of the disastrous effects of romantic love, it also is her final comment on the destructive power of money. The attacks on materialism in *One of Ours*, *A Lost Lady*, and *The Professor's House* are mild compared with the devastation caused in this novel by Myra's throwing away her inheritance. Her great-uncle had told her before she eloped: "It's better to be a stray dog in this world than a man without money. . . . A poor man stinks, and God hates him." Myra is wrecked by greed long before cancer kills her.

If there was a great deal of Cather in Godfrey St. Peter, there is more than a trace of her in Myra Henshawe. Myra's ability to hate is a characteristic that Cather also possessed. She believed in creative hate, as she has Thea Kronborg say in *The Song of the Lark*. Both Myra and Cather turn to religion for solace and support in the face of disappointments in life. Cather, in addition, may have seen in the corrosive nay-saying of Myra's character a glimpse of what she could have become, if she had not had art as her salvation. Further, both author and protagonist share a fierce loyalty towards friends and an admirable ability to face life squarely and candidly. It was sometime after this novel came out that Elizabeth Sergeant was surprised to have Cather ask her if she thought psychoanalysis might do her any good. As Cather never had any use for Freud, this probably wasn't a very serious question, and at any event nothing came of the inquiry. *My Mortal Enemy* perhaps provided a final catharsis. By the time she published the book Cather was deep in history and jogging along with the Archbishop and his vicar on their two white mules through their huge diocese in the Territory of New Mexico.

In this novel, as she does in others, Cather reinforces meaning with allusion. It was particularly important to do so in *My Mortal Enemy* because all of Part I is narrated by fifteen-year-old Nellie, who is an unsophisticated observer and cannot be expected to understand all she sees and hears. By the use of allusion Cather is able to convey meaning to the reader that Nellie can't transmit. The introduction of Bellini's opera is an excellent example of her method. The "Casta Diva" aria, which is addressed to the moon goddess, prays for peace between the Romans and the Gauls, and is ironic in view of the sharp quarrel between Myra and Oswald that occurs immediately afterwards. But more than this, the aria comes prior to Norma's discovery that her Roman lover has been unfaithful to her. This situation leads to Norma's tragic end, for she, like Myra, has staked all on love and lost. Also like Myra, who left her Catholic faith to marry a Protestant, Norma broke her vows as a Druid priestess when she fell in love with the Roman proconsul Pollione. Nellie in her innocence only associates the Bellini music with her romantic vision of Myra crouching in the window bathed in moonlight while she listens to the aria. Nellie is unaware of the deeper implications of the music. "For many years I associated Mrs. Henshawe with that music," Nellie says in her narrative.

There are in addition three references to Shakespeare that add significance to the story. The reference to *Lear* in the discovery of Gloucester's cliff prepares the reader for Myra's death. As the blinded Gloucester in the play asks Edgar to lead him to the cliffs of Dover where he intends to kill himself, so Myra, fatally stricken by disease, wants to be taken to the cliff overlooking the Pacific Ocean. Other allusions to Shakespeare are to *Richard II* and *King John*. As Nellie passes Myra's door late in the novel, she hears her murmuring the opening line of *Richard II*: "*Old John of Gaunt, time-honoured Lan-cas-ter,*" a reference to Richard's uncle, who dies after telling Richard that his misrule will bring trouble to England. Myra has just been speaking of her great-uncle, who had warned her against her marriage. By the end of her life she had come to blame her misfortunes on her rejection of her great-uncle's advice. Myra also is like Richard II in her vanity, her extravagance, and her self-pity. The reference to *King John* is only to Myra's fondness for declaiming passages from it. There are no quotations, but King John is in some ways like Myra's Uncle John Driscoll and perhaps reminded her of the happy days when she lived under his roof.

My Mortal Enemy got a much less favorable press than either *A Lost Lady* or

The Professor's House. Fanny Butcher was first among reviewers who praised the book, calling it a "masterpiece of tragedy, a presentation of the great subcurrental rhythms of love and hatred," yet on the surface "a book with the lightest possible touch." It was a book you could read in less than an hour but one that "leaves behind it deep conjecture and pictures which are realer than your own life. It is a really great book." *Time* magazine called it a "very complete, very intense, very subtle" story, and the *New York Sun* added Myra Henshawe to Cather's growing gallery of memorable portraits. The *Saturday Review of Literature* couldn't decide if it was a very short novel or a very long short story, but however many words it had, they were "precisely the right number, placed in the right order by an artist who knows what words are for and what can be done with them and how without seeming effort to do it." Joseph Wood Krutch in the *Nation* admired Cather's technique: "At a time when novelists are seeking above all else 'immediacy' of presentation and are employing not seldom fantastic means to attain it, she has sought no such illusion, has made no effort so to dramatize her narrative as to make it the equivalent of a contemporaneous experience. Events are seen frankly through the haze of distance; the thing immediately present is not these events themselves but the mind in which they are recollected; and the effect is, therefore, not the vividness and the harshness of drama but something almost elegiac in its softness."

On the other hand, many reviewers, perhaps as many as forty per cent, found various faults with the novel. Some thought Myra Henshawe much inferior to Marian Forrester, to whom they compared her; others felt that Cather's unfurnished method had stripped so much detail from her story that *My Mortal Enemy* was underdeveloped. Louis Kronenberger in a long review in the *New York Times* touched on most of the shortcomings that various critics noted. Under the caption, "Willa Cather Fumbles for Another Lost Lady," Kronenberger wrote that "this time . . . Miss Cather has fallen short, rather far short, of her earlier level. Her lost lady [Myra] is not so real, not so moving, not so delightful." Then he also thought that Nellie Birdseye was not nearly as sensitive and significant a narrator as Niel in *A Lost Lady*. "Nellie is a colorless, artistically meaningless character, and her impressions are correspondingly without color or meaning." Kronenberger had severe reservations about the brevity of the novel: "One is forcibly struck by the increasing tendency toward brevity which Miss Cather's novels reveal. . . . Compression and selection grow naturally stronger in most good writers as they master their medium. But in *My Mortal Enemy* they have been carried too far. All bones and no flesh is never a wise method. . . . Significant things are left out, and the reader is left not only unsatisfied, but also puzzled." In his final paragraph he dismissed the novel as "perhaps Miss Cather's least important book."

Kronenberger, however, had read Cather carefully and recognized that *My Mortal Enemy* belonged to the same period as *The Professor's House*: "For with *The Professor's House* Miss Cather began delving into the innermost, fundamental nature of a character, into his mind and soul. One gets the feeling that she was trying to delve so here, and that in part at least, the groping and confusion of her character are responsible for the groping, the confusion, the incompleteness of her method. She seems to be finding life more complex, more elusive, more irreducible than she once did. The simplicity, the openness, the warmth of an Ántonia no longer deeply interest her. She is absorbed by a sophisticated, troubled, neurotic woman here, a woman lost far less circumstantially than Marian Forrester; and she is lost also. Marian Forrester lives. Myra Henshawe does not even begin to live; but Myra is, without question, a 'harder' character to realize."

While Kronenberger read into the novel Cather's personal storm and stress, her family was not aware that she was "finding life more complex, more elusive, more irreducible than she once did." When she went back to Red Cloud to visit, she kept her doubts and uncertainties to herself; and if her parents and brothers and sisters were aware of inner turmoil, there is no record of it. Certainly to her nephews and nieces she was simply the most exciting person in their lives when her annual orbit brought her through Nebraska. Her fierce loyalty to family drew her back to Red Cloud nearly every year in the twenties, usually in the summer, and when she was home she tried to be just Willa Cather, a woman who had grown up in the prairie village. Perennially fond of children, she was particularly interested in watching her nephews and nieces grow up, and because five of them lived in Red Cloud, she had plenty of opportunity. It was a great day in their lives when they heard that Aunt Willie was coming.

The house that Cather visited in this decade was not the old place at Third and Cedar where she had spent her adolescence but a larger house at Sixth and Seward, which Charles Cather had bought after Willa had gone east. It had a two-story porch across the front, which in summer was covered with an awning, and Willa's bedroom opened on to the upper floor of the porch. She liked to have tea there even in a blistering Nebraska July. She said the English always drank hot tea, even in the summer and even in the tropics, and it kept them cool. Her niece Helen, brother James's daughter, then under ten, remembers being allowed to help carry the tea service up to the second story. On other occasions Aunt Willa took Helen and her cousins to the drug store for cherry phosphates, which she liked as well as the children.

Life in Red Cloud during these visits was family oriented, and Cather did her best to avoid social engagements. She went to see old friends, of course, but she didn't want to meet new people or be exhibited as a celebrity. During these stays at home, lunch was always served in the back dining room, and after lunch Cather retired to her room to write letters or nap until tea time. Sometimes they went for drives in the family car, but Cather never felt very comfortable riding with her father at the wheel. She never reconciled herself to the automobile and never considered owning one. In the evenings the family usually listened to Victrola records, which Cather had sent from New York, some of them made by her operatic friends Fremstad and Farrar. Her parents, however, preferred songs of their native South, spirituals, and popular nineteenth-century ballads.

Cather never traveled light when she returned to Red Cloud for a long visit. She always brought a trunk, and one of Helen Cather Southwick's fondest childhood memories is helping Aunt Willa unpack the trunk. It was full of the cotton skirts and middy blouses that she liked to wear in the morning, the clothes she preferred to work in. It also contained elegant city clothes for the afternoon and evening—heavy silk crepe skirts and chiffon and crepe de chine blouses and dresses. Cather liked to dress up and wore the same clothes in Red Cloud that she did in New York. There also was always a box of interesting but inexpensive jewelry to fascinate a child. Lewis said that "she was greatly attracted to beautiful jewels; but she never bought any." She did indulge herself when she bought clothes.

CHAPTER 18

Death Comes for the Archbishop

Cather reached the pinnacle of her success with the publication of *Death Comes for the Archbishop* in 1927. Not only was the book a great critical triumph, but it also brought joy to the publisher's business office and to booksellers everywhere. She knew she had written an important book when she turned the manuscript over to Knopf and asked him for an additional one percent royalty, the only time she ever asked for an increase. She was convinced that the book would have a long and continuing sale and prophesied that years later Knopf's son would be paying royalties to her niece. She was right about the book's longevity and its quality and came to believe before she died that it was her best novel. Whether or not it is superior to *My Ántonia* or *A Lost Lady*, however, is a subject on which Cather's readers are divided.

It seems inevitable in retrospect that some day she would write a novel about the Southwest. It is the culmination of her interest in that region. Long before she made her first trip to Arizona and New Mexico in 1912 her imagination had been kindled by stories of the Spanish conquistadores and the indigenous Indian culture. When she wrote Sarah Orne Jewett in 1908 describing "The Enchanted Bluff," which she had just written, she had explained that in the West there was a Spanish influence, just as in Maine Miss Jewett had grown up with centuries of English tradition behind her. Spanish words had enriched the English language, and even the cowboy saddle was made on the old Spanish model. There was something heady in the wind that blew up from Mexico, she said. Later after she had visited the Southwest, she made effective use of her memories of Walnut Canyon in *The Song of the Lark*, and after her week at Mesa Verde National Park, she created "Tom Outland's

Story." Further evidence of her perennial interest in the Southwest occurs in the picnic scene in *My Ántonia*. There Jim Burden tells his companions of a Spanish stirrup found by a Nebraska farmer and speculates about Coronado's wanderings across the great plains.

If Cather had become a professor of history like Godfrey St. Peter instead of a novelist, it is easy to imagine that her life work might have been St. Peter's project, the Spanish adventurers in North America. Lewis remembered that she "had a great gift for imaginative historical reconstruction. . . . She could make the modern age almost disappear, fade away and become ghostlike, so completely was she able to invoke her vision of the past and recreate its reality." She gives this same ability to Gaston Cleric, Jim Burden's teacher at the University of Nebraska: "How often I have seen him draw his dark brows together, fix his eyes upon some object on the wall or a figure in the carpet, and then flash into the lamplight the very image that was in his brain. He could bring the drama of antique life before one out of the shadows—white figures against blue backgrounds." Cather does equally well in recreating the lives of her archbishop and his vicar general.

She told E. K. Brown six months before she died that she never had intended to write a novel about the Southwest. It was too big and too varied. There were too many individuals involved and all of them too little related to each other. Her trips down there, she wrote, were simply a matter of self-indulgence because she enjoyed the country so much. Then it came to her one day when she was sitting in a gravelly, uncomfortable spot by the Martyr's Cross east of Santa Fe watching the Sangre de Cristo Mountains color with the sunset: the real story of the Southwest was the story of the missionary priests who came from France with cultivated minds, large vision, and a noble purpose.

Exactly when she had this revelation she did not specify, but it must have been a number of years before she began to write the novel. She told Brown that she was seven years getting the material, but actually it was much longer, as she explained in a letter to *Commonweal* published after the book appeared. At that time she remembered meeting in 1912 a Belgian priest, Father Haltermann, "who lived with his sister in the parsonage behind the beautiful old church at Santa Cruz, New Mexico. . . . He was a florid, full-bearded farmer priest, who drove about among his eighteen Indian missions with a spring wagon and a pair of mules. He knew a great deal about the country and the Indians and their traditions." She learned from Father Haltermann, from Father Connolly, who was Douglass Cather's friend, and from others during her many subsequent visits to Arizona and New Mexico. And her trips to

Taos, her daily horseback rides to remote villages, her drives in the cadillac with Tony Luhan added to her knowledge.

She went on to explain to *Commonweal*: "Meanwhile Archbishop Lamy, the first Bishop of New Mexico, had become a sort of invisible personal friend. I had heard a great many interesting stories about him from very old Mexicans and traders who still remembered him, and I never passed the life-size bronze of him which stands before the Cathedral in Santa Fe without wishing that I could learn more about a pioneer churchman who looked so well-bred and distinguished." Her wish was granted one day in 1925 when she was staying at the La Fonda Hotel in Santa Fe after visiting Mabel Dodge Luhan. She came across a rather rare book, *The Life of the Right Reverend Joseph P. Machebeuf*, by a priest named William Howlett, which had been published obscurely in Pueblo, Colorado, in 1908. Father Machebeuf had been Archbishop Lamy's boyhood friend, companion, co-worker, and vicar general in the newly established diocese of New Mexico in the mid-nineteenth century. The biography was full of information about the lives and works of the missionary priests in the Southwest, documented by letters written by Father Machebeuf to his sister in France and by other contemporary accounts, both clerical and secular.

The discovery of Father Howlett's book produced another of those inner explosions, like the ones that had led to the writing of *O Pioneers!*, *The Song of the Lark*, and *A Lost Lady*. Cather stayed up most of the night reading the book, and by morning the design of *Death Comes for the Archbishop* was clearly in her mind. "At last I found out what I wanted to know about how the country and the people of New Mexico seemed to those first missionary priests from France. Without these letters in Father Howlett's book to guide me, I would certainly never have dared to write my book." Cather was eager to get started on the new novel and began to write during her customary visit to Jaffrey in the fall. She was probably sorry that she had accepted invitations to lecture in Chicago and Cleveland, but by December she was back in New York and working like a steam engine and happy, as she wrote Irene Weisz. By Christmas when she took a week off to entertain her niece, who came down from Smith for the holidays, she was well along with the novel. The writing went ahead steadily during the winter and spring, and by the end of April the work was more than half finished.

Before she could complete the book, however, she decided she had to visit the Southwest again. Lewis accompanied her on part of the journey, and on May 15 they left for New Mexico by way of Red Cloud and Denver. The high spot of this trip was riding from Lamy, New Mexico, to Gallup on the same train with Rin-Tin-Tin. Cather wrote Mabel Luhan she had had the pleasure of meeting the canine movie star in Albuquerque, and she was never so excited previously about any celebrity. The two women got off the train at Gallup, a town Cather thought a hell of a place and filled with more low types than she ever had seen before, but they stayed only long enough for the sand storms and rains to abate before going on to visit the Canyon de Chelly, which appears briefly in the last part of the novel.

They hired a driver to take them to the canyon, an important center of Navajo culture, which lies in the midst of the Navajo reservation. Lewis remembered that their driver "lost his way in the midst of a vast plain encircled by great mesas, and was several hours finding it again. Then his car broke down, and for a while it looked as if we might have to spend the night right there in the open." They did not, however, and at the canyon's rim they transferred to horses for a pack trip to the bottom. Cather wrote Blanche Knopf that the visit to the canyon would be a long, hard horseback ride, but she thanked God that motors couldn't get into it. She was feeling very fit, though her eyes were inflamed from the reflection of the blazing sun on the rocks, and the ride into the canyon was a great success. It allowed Cather to see where the Navajos once had made their last stand against government troops intent on moving them off their ancestral lands. When the Archbishop visits the canyon in 1875 to show his French architect some of the country, the Navajos have been allowed to return. He sees "crops growing down at the bottom of the world between the towering sandstone walls; sheep were grazing under the magnificent cottonwoods and drinking at the streams of sweet water; it was like an Indian Garden of Eden."

After the pack trip into the Canyon de Chelly Cather and Lewis retraced their steps to Santa Fe to rest a few days before again visiting Mabel Luhan in Taos and once more renting the pink cottage. For the last part of June they were back at the La Fonda Hotel, and Cather was able to spend her mornings writing. Mary Austin, who was in St. Louis having an operation, had offered the use of her beautiful home for this purpose, and Cather took her up on the invitation. She wrote to her absent hostess that she had gone up to the house to see if she could work there and had not missed a morning since. There was a large, open library with a big window she could look out of, and a cooling breeze blew in while she sat in a little plush chair with her writing pad on her knee. She thanked Austin for the happy, peaceful hours she had spent in her library, and when her book came out she sent an inscribed copy in which she wrote: "For Mary Austin, in whose lovely study I wrote the last chapters of this book. She will be my sternest critic—and she has the right to be."

When Austin exercised this right in her autobiography, *Earth Horizon*, in

1932 she expressed distress that Cather "had given her allegiance to the French blood of the Archbishop; she had sympathized with his desire to build a French cathedral in a Spanish town. It was a calamity to the local culture. We have never got over it." Austin also began showing people the chair Cather had sat in while she wrote her novel. Cather took umbrage at this criticism of her Francophilia and the exaggerated account of the writing she had done in Austin's house. What had been a warm though sporadic correspondence ceased abruptly. Cather wrote Mabel Luhan that she couldn't help it if the Archbishop was French. She also began denying that she had done any writing at all in Austin's house. She told Sergeant that she had left the manuscript of her novel in the bank vault in New York when she went to New Mexico, and while she sometimes had walked up to the house in the afternoon, it was only to write letters. She further told Luhan that she only went to be polite. She definitely did leave the finished portion of the novel in New York, because Paul Reynolds was dickering with magazine editors over the serial rights during her absence, but she still had a significant part of the book to finish after she reached New Mexico.

Cather headed back east about the first of July after six weeks in the Southwest and returned to New York by way of Red Cloud. She stayed in the city only long enough to meet with Reynolds and Henry Leach, editor of the *Forum*, to discuss arrangements for serializing the novel. Then she went to Peterboro, New Hampshire, to the MacDowell Writers' Colony to work on her book. This was the first and only time she ever went to Peterboro. She had a low opinion of communal living and writers' colonies and much preferred her usual quarters at the Shattuck Inn in Jaffrey. Life at the colony consisted of breakfast and dinner in common with lunch delivered at the writer's studio in a basket to permit a long, uninterrupted day of work. For most of the resident artists this was an ideal arrangement, but Cather never wrote for more than three hours, and always in the mornings, and she liked a hearty, hot lunch. Sergeant was told that at noon "she stole away to an inn . . . taking young, red-haired witty Mary Colum along to enliven and prick her mind. The Colony lunch was saved for tea that was equally essential to her."

Dinner was early and the evenings were long and full of social activity, poetry, music, and croquet. Mrs. MacDowell remembered Cather as always evading pursuit. Her bedroom was at The Eaves, an old red farm house, with the other women. Some she liked and some she didn't, but few of them were willing to let her alone. Thornton Wilder, who was at the beginning of his career in 1926, also was there that summer. He remembered that she sat at what the younger colonists thought of as the head table because that was where E. A. Robinson always sat. She was handsome, serene, and reserved, and the only time anyone saw her was at the morning and evening meals. She never stayed around after dinner for games or talk. Wilder valued the occasions when he was able to sit beside her, but the acquaintance did not grow into a friendship. Cather, however, came to admire Wilder's talent, and twelve years later when *Our Town* appeared on Broadway, she wrote him a fan letter, praising the play as the loveliest thing produced in this country in a long time. It was absolutely true to everything she had seen and felt in the many years she had been visiting New Hampshire.

After a few weeks at the MacDowell Colony, Cather made a short visit to Grand Manan Island, then returned to Jaffrey where she again occupied her usual room in the Shattuck Inn on the top floor under the eaves. There she found perfect quiet. She was surrounded by storerooms, the other guests were all below her, and there was no noise overhead except the rain. She could work well in that room, just as she had been able to work in the third-floor sewing room at the McClungs' house in Pittsburgh or in her own attic room under the roof of her old home in Red Cloud. She was almost finished with the novel when she left Jaffrey at the end of October, and she put the final touches on the manuscript in her Bank Street apartment the following month. The *Forum* received the final installments just before Christmas, and serialization began in January 1927.

Cather was almost sorry to end the novel, because the writing of it, she told Ida Tarbell, was the most unalloyed pleasure of her life. Working on her Archbishop was almost like working with him, and she missed him after the manuscript left her desk. Her mood was happy and serene during the months she was writing the book. It was an altogether new kind of thing she had done, and she was pleased with the result. She thought she had taken some risks, however, in writing this story and wrote Fanny Butcher: "I think I succeed[ed] fairly well, but a story with no woman in it but the Virgin Mary [not literally true, of course] has very definite limitations. It's a very special kind of thing, and you like it or you don't." To Carl Van Vechten, who wrote praising the novel, she said his letter gave her a fine glow of satisfaction. As a sophisticated city dweller, he was a test case. She had wondered if the book would seem at all true to people who knew the world well and the Southwest only a little.

Several months before completing the novel, Cather described her story to Reynolds so that he could negotiate with editors for serialization. She said it was concerned with the picturesque conditions of life in the Southwest just at the time that New Mexico was taken over from Old Mexico, and with the experiences of two Catholic missionaries who were sent there to bring order out of the mixture of Indian and Mexican superstitions. The hero of the story was Father Latour (his real name was Lamy), the young Frenchman who was made Bishop of New Mexico at the age of thirty-seven, a man of old and noble family in Puy de Dôme in Auvergne, a man of wide culture, an idealist, and from his youth hungry for the world's frontiers. He was finally made an archbishop and died in 1888. In other words, she added, he went there in the days of the buffalo and Indian massacres, and he lived to see the Santa Fe Railroad cross New Mexico.

The novel follows a rough chronological order, beginning with a prologue set in Rome in 1848 in which a missionary bishop from America appears before a group of cardinals urging the appointment of Jean Latour as bishop of the new diocese of New Mexico. He wins his point when the Spanish cardinal, spokesman for the group, concedes that the French make the best missionaries. "Our Spanish fathers made good martyrs, but the French Jesuits accomplish more. They are the great organizers." After the prologue the first of the nine books of the novel opens with Bishop Latour making a lonely journey of three thousand miles roundtrip through a trackless wilderness of mountains and desert to Durango, Mexico, to obtain his credentials which had not been forwarded. When he arrived at Santa Fe the Mexican priests in his new diocese had refused to recognize his authority, thus necessitating the long trek to Old Mexico. The opening chapters set the mood for the novel: the cheerful acceptance of the physical hardships and the joyful conduct of the missionary labors. This mood is uniformly sustained through the narrative.

In subsequent books the novel proceeds to recount the lives and works of Father Latour and his vicar general Father Joseph Vaillant. The two priests complement each other nicely, Father Latour being scholarly, intellectual, aloof, a man of vision and wisdom, and Father Joseph being a man of great faith and energy, force of will, and practical know-how. Bishop Lamy had said to Father Machebeuf when he urged him to go to New Mexico with him: "They wish that I should be a Vicar Apostolic, and I wish you to be my Vicar General, and from these two vicars we shall try to make one good Pastor." What plot there is concerns itself with the gradual organization of the vast diocese and the bringing under central authority after many decades of neglect all the parishes scattered over hundreds of miles of the new territory. The book is loosely episodic in a way reminiscent of earlier Cather novels, and it contains, also characteristically, stories-within-stories. Most of the novel deals with the missionary work of the two priests between their arrival in Santa Fe in 1851 and the building of the cathedral about ten years later; but the prologue takes place three years before, and Book Nine begins at the time of the Archbishop's death a generation later. The chapters within the various books have a thematic arrangement, and the progression follows generally the real life on which it is based. Early in the novel Cather relates the story of the Virgin of Guadaloupe, and towards the end tells one of the legends that grew up about the life of Father Junipero Serra in the California missions. These inserts are digressions but reinforce the tone of faith and religious dedication. The book has also a great deal of variety and contrast. In Book Two ("Missionary Journeys"), for example, the sequence of chapters opens with an amusing account of how Father Joseph talks a rich rancher, Manuel Lujon, out of his prized white mules, Angelica and Contento, who then carry the missionaries through the rest of the novel. Immediately after this chapter follows the story of the degenerate Yankee murderer, Buck Scales, and his abused Mexican wife, Magdalena, whom the priests meet on "The Lonely Road to Mora." Next, Book Three ("The Mass at Ácoma") juxtaposes an evocative description of Bishop Latour's visit to the mesa-top village of Acoma with the legend of Friar Baltazar, a glutton and tyrant whose Indian parishioners one day happily tossed him over the cliff. Book Four ("Snake Root") is the chilling account of a night the bishop and his Indian guide Jacinto spend in a cave used by the Indians to practice secretly their ancestral rites of snake worship. It precedes the duel between the bishop and old Father Martinez of Taos in Book Five. In this climactic battle the well-entrenched old reprobate Martinez is excommunicated and his parish, the last holdout under the old dispensation, is brought under the bishop's control. Then comes the death of the miserly Father Lucero, whose lust for money was as great as Martinez' lust for women. This is followed by the very funny story of the rich widow Doña Isabella, who, like Cather, refused to admit her age. The Bishop persuades her in court to tell her real age in order to prevent her dead husband's brothers from breaking his will.

The novel also provides rich contrasts in character in a large gallery of Indians, Mexicans, rich and poor, and even Yankees. There are Jacinto, the young guide, and Eusabio, the old Navajo; Sada, an old Mexican woman, who is the slave of a hostile Protestant American family, and the coy Doña Isabella. The pious, good priests, Padre Jesus de Baca and Padre Herrera, contrast sharply with the high-living Father Gallegos of Albuquerque, who has to be removed from his parish, and the profligate Martinez. And opposed to Buck Scales, who is hanged for his crimes, is Kit Carson, the old scout who lives quietly in Taos with his Mexican wife and appears several times as friend, admirer, and supporter of the Bishop.

Death Comes for the Archbishop is the most innovative of all Cather's experiments with the novel form. Whether or not it was a novel bothered contemporary reviewers, and Cather herself preferred to call it a narrative. She wrote Norman Foerster, who wanted to reprint part of it, that the book could easily be anthologized because it was scarcely a novel. She thought of the work as a narrative that moved along in a straight line on the two white mules that did not hurry themselves very much. Her theories of organic form, which took shape when she wrote *O Pioneers!*, are carried out once more in this novel. Her unconventional selection of detail, which in *My Ántonia* she compared to using the design on the other side of the carpet, continues here.

In addition, she had another idea that she wanted to try in telling Father Latour's story. In her letter to *Commonweal* she recalled seeing the frescoes by Puvis de Chavannes of the life of Ste. Geneviève "in my student days," (actually in the Pantheon in Paris in 1902 during her first visit to France). These frescoes of the patron saint of the French capital apparently left a lasting impression, and she had wanted since then, she said, to do something in the style of legend. Such a narration, she explained, would be the absolute reverse of dramatic treatment. Her notion was to try "something a little like that in prose, something without accent, with none of the artificial elements of composition."

These frescoes, which consist of a series of panels, each depicting an episode in the life of the saint, provide an instructive analogy with Cather's novel, for the paintings are monumental, static, and stylized. Their movement is from one tableau to the next, each giving the viewer a feeling of intense calm and stillness. The central figure of Ste. Geneviève sets the tone for the whole series, all of which are rendered with flat tones, few contrasts, and no vivid colors. The overall effect is that of figures and objects suspended outside of time. Insofar as one can speak of a visual art in terms of literature, the main characteristics of the frescoes are analogous in general terms to the novel. There may be more contrast and color in the book, but certainly it is a story without accent, monumental, timeless. To carry out the pictorial parallel, Cather used titles that name the dominant image in individual chapters. In Book One, for example, the opening episode is called "The Cruciform Tree," and it is followed by "Hidden Water" and "The Bishop *Chez Lui*." In the second book one finds "The White Mules" and "The Lonely Road to Mora," and so on throughout the novel until finally Book Nine, which is not divided into chapters, but has only the book's graphic image from the title, "Death Comes for the Archbishop," as its caption.

Cather's *Commonweal* letter used, in addition, a second analogy for her story: the Medieval manual of ecclesiastical lore known as *The Golden Legend*. She pointed out that the lives of the saints recounted in this source are told in a manner similar to the visual representation in the murals. The martyrdoms of the saints are "no more dwelt upon than are the trivial incidents of their lives; it is as though all human experience, measured against one supreme spiritual adventure, were of about the same importance. The essence of such writing is not to hold the note, not to use an incident for all there is in it—but to touch and pass on." Cather does this with considerable success in *Death Comes for the Archbishop*.

To illustrate how she carried out this design one may look at the chapter describing the journey to Mora. This is a scene rich in melodramatic possibilities, but Cather foregoes the chance to extract maximum drama from the episode. Fathers Latour and Vaillant are on their way to Mora, following a tortuous, lonely trail on their white mules. They cannot complete their journey in one day and seek shelter for the night in an isolated cabin occupied by the degenerate Buck Scales and his battered wife. When Scales leaves the cabin and orders his terrified wife to follow, she turns back momentarily and signals to the two priests that their lives are in danger. On Scales's return Father Latour pulls out his pistol and covers Scales, while Father Joseph brings the mules from the barn. The two travelers then continue their journey. The capture, trial, and execution of Buck Scales for having murdered four previous travelers is not rendered dramatically at all. The third-person narrator simply tells the reader what happened in a few sentences, and what would have been an exciting chapter in any western from Zane Gray to Louis L'Amour is left unwritten. Cather concludes the chapter with the rehabilitation of the abused Mexican wife Magdalena after Scales's death. She is ministered to by the Bishop and then taken into the household of Kit Carson at Taos. In the concluding paragraph, Magdalena, some time later, becomes the housekeeper for the newly established Sisters of Loretto, and "after the blight of her horrible youth was over, she seemed to bloom again in the household of God."

Cather's primary source material for the novel, as she acknowledged in her *Commonweal* letter, was Howlett's biography of Father Machebeuf, "though I used many of my own experiences, and some of my father's." She told Reynolds that she described some of the episodes almost literally as they happened, one such being the chapter called "The White Mules." She later wrote Carrie Sherwood that these mules had been owned by Mexicans she knew. But the mules also appear in Howlett, though there the color is bay; thus the animals that she put into her book actually had two antecedents. Howlett's biography was only a partial source, however, because it is mostly about Father Joseph, who was sent to Colorado as Bishop of Denver to organize a new diocese just nine years after arriving in Santa Fe as Bishop

Lamy's vicar general. Only about one hundred pages deal with Father Joseph's work in New Mexico, but this was enough to fire Cather's imagination, and what she didn't know about Lamy she made up. The ousting of Gallegos and Martinez is based on Howlett, but most of the novel came from Cather's invention.

She did not change any of the major facts of history, but she rewrote Archbishop Lamy's life when it suited her artistic purpose, sometimes rearranging detail and altering circumstances. When the two priests arrived in Santa Fe, for example, Howlett says they were met joyfully by thousands of people, but in the novel they arrive alone. Both Howlett and Cather agree, however, that they were resented by the local priesthood. In both the biography and the novel Father Latour has to make his long journey to Durango, but in the former he travels with a knowledgable companion, while in the latter he is a solitary horseman following a trail he has never seen. Cather also speeded up the construction of the new cathedral so that it was finished before the Archbishop retired, while in fact he did not live to see the church's completion. The biggest change Cather made in the biographical facts was in having Father Joseph die first, when in reality he outlived the Archbishop. It would have been anticlimactic to have Father Joseph attend the Archbishop's funeral and then live on instead of the other way around. The emphasis throughout the novel is on Jean Latour and not his vicar general.

There are other departures from historicity in the characters in the novel. Jean Latour is quite a different person from Archbishop Lamy in his attitudes towards the social and economic development of his diocese. Lamy, who was one of the prime movers in getting the railroad to come to New Mexico, viewed it, as did most of the settlers in the West before the railroad, as a blessing. It would bring New Mexico closer to the East, carry supplies more cheaply and abundantly than the wagon trains that crawled over the old Santa Fe Trail, and it would draw new settlers to fill in the empty spaces and help pacify the marauding Navajos and Comanches. Lamy supported the government's treatment of the Indians and held a typically optimistic nineteenth-century view of progress and civilization. Cather's Archbishop deplores the changes that are overtaking Santa Fe and opposes Federal efforts to relocate the Navajos. Similarly, the views of Father Latour's Navajo friend Eusabio are the author's, not the Indian's. It is pure Cather when Eusabio comes by train to visit the old Archbishop before he dies and comments: "Men travel faster now, but I do not know if they go to better things."

Cather's alterations of history are intrinsically unimportant, but they give one an exceptionally clear view of the creative mind at work. They serve the purpose of art by enhancing the unity and maintaining the tone of the novel.

From her shaping of the inert facts came a large work of the imagination built upon vivid characterizations, enobling themes, and remarkable evocations of place. History comes alive in this narrative, as it does in the best of historical fiction. Cather succeeded in doing what Hawthorne accomplished in *The Scarlet Letter* (one of her three greatest American novels), and both authors achieve their effects by simplifying the narrative and eliminating the minutiae of history. Cather commented specifically on the uncluttered text when she reviewed Mary Johnston's *To Have and to Hold* in 1900. She liked the novel, because if the author worked up her historical sources, she had "the grace not to show it."

Perhaps even more important for Cather than Hawthorne's model of historical narration was his critical statement about his novels. Cather might have made the same distinction he did in calling his long fictions romances rather than novels (by which he meant realistic novels) in order to avoid being held accountable for strict probability. Cather also wanted the larger latitude of romance. In addition, she would have seconded Hawthorne's notion that the romance "sins unpardonably so far as it may swerve aside from the truth of the human heart." *Death Comes for the Archbishop* does not depart from this truth despite the liberties Cather took. Her view of Bishop Lamy's ministry is perhaps more idealized than the reality. His work certainly did not proceed as smoothly, and contained more hardships than Father Latour's. The tone of the novel also comes more from Howlett than from history, for Howlett was a co-worker with Machebeuf and viewed the labors of the two French priests as the inevitable working out of God's plan for New Mexico. Yet viewed from the perspective of more than a century, one has to agree that the abiding faith and missionary zeal of Archbishop Lamy and his vicar general left a permanent imprint on the history of the Southwest. In her novel Cather remains faithful to the grand design of her material.

There was another pictorial source for the novel besides the paintings she saw in Paris. While Puvis de Chavannes's frescoes suggested a pattern for the nine books of the narrative, another French painter inspired the prologue. This is a surprising source, for the artist was Jehan Georges Vibert, an academic painter whose work was the antithesis of the impressionists and post-impressionists Cather admired. She told an interviewer, however, that Vibert's painting called "The Missionary's Story" had given her the idea for the prologue. The painting is a large canvas showing several prelates sitting on sofas and arm chairs after dinner in a richly furnished salon. The prelates are dressed in white, violet, purple, and scarlet. Opposite them in somber black is the missionary priest, who is earnestly recounting his experiences somewhere on the bright edges of the world. Cather's prologue, however, is set outside so that she can have Rome and her Spanish cardinal's garden for her background. By moving outdoors she turned Vibert's forgotten salon painting, rendered with photographic realism, into an impressionistic landscape with figures. St. Peter's dome looms in the background "bluish grey like the flattened top of a great balloon," and the setting sun bores into the ilex trees, "illuminating their mahogany trunks and blurring their dark foliage; it warmed the bright green of the orange trees and the rose of the oleander blooms to gold." In the foreground of Cather's prologue are the cardinals, the Spanish host and his companions, one French, the other Italian, dressed in black cassocks with red pipings and crimson buttons, while the missionary priest wears a long black coat over a violet vest. Cather here and elsewhere in her fiction is a verbal colorist. Perhaps she learned this use of color when she read Crane as a college student.

A third visual source supplies the title for the novel. The *Commonweal* letter explained that she had found her title in Holbein's *Dance of Death*, a series of woodcuts executed by Hans Holbein the Younger in the early part of the sixteenth century. In this work a host of skeletons summon various mortals to their posthumous rewards. In one of the woodcuts a skeleton comes for an archbishop, and in another for a priest. The entire series provides another visual analogy for the novel because of the wide variety of individuals depicted. In the course of the story death comes for a great many more people than the Archbishop and Father Joseph: Buck Scales, Friar Baltazar, Padre Martinez, Padre Lucero, Don Antonio Olivares, and many anonymous Indians and Spaniards, to name some of them. One critic has counted ninety-six specific deaths in the novel. "The passing of these people varies ingeniously: humor, irony, horror, and acquiescence, for example, are all represented as they are in Holbein's woodcuts." Finally, one might note that in woodcutting, as in Cather's *démeublé* style, excess material must be cut away, leaving only clean, simple lines.

A great deal more could be said about the materials that went into *Death Comes for the Archbishop*, because Cather supplemented her reading of Howlett, her personal experiences, and her talks with people of all sorts, with a great deal of reading in historical sources. Michael Williams in reviewing the novel for *Commonweal* wrote: "In order to write this book, she has read a great deal in other books." This was literally true, as Edith Lewis confirmed, for in addition to Howlett she read at least eight or ten other volumes on the Southwest. These included, among others, the works of Charles Loomis, Ralph Twitchell, and J. B. Salpointe's *Soldiers of the Cross*. She also mined the *Catholic Encyclopedia*. She may have read of the massacre of the Spanish in 1680 in H. H. Bancroft's *History of New Mexico and Arizona*, and she certainly got her account of Manuel Chavez, the American-hater who appears at Doña Isabella's party in Book Six, from Loomis's *A New Mexico David*. The account of the Archbishop's death, not treated at all in Howlett, comes from *Soldiers of the Cross*. A great deal of Southwestern history is worked unobtrusively into the novel, though the focus always remains on the title character.

Cather's turn to historical fiction in *Death Comes for the Archbishop* was both a retreat into the past from an uncongenial present and a continuation of preoccupations long manifested. After her day of anger in which she wrote *The Professor's House* and *My Mortal Enemy*, it was a relief for her to stumble on Howlett's book and find a way to recreate an historical epoch. When she reread her book in 1945—the first time she had done so since it was published, or so she said—she was able to recapture the intense pleasure she had experienced in her years of visiting the Southwest, and her feeling of loss when she finished the book was an emotion expressed several times in her letters. At the same time, the novel is in another sense a continuation of her interest in pioneer times. The frontier was long gone in Nebraska, and she had celebrated its passing in her earlier novels, but in *Death Comes for the Archbishop* she was able to recreate pioneer times in New Mexico. Of course, Santa Fe was an old town when Fathers Lamy and Machebeuf arrived, but the country had changed little since the Spanish first appeared, and the two French priests were movers and shakers in the modern development of New Mexico after it became a part of the United States. When the Archbishop of the novel reflects late in his life about the changes that have come over the land as the agricultural frontier moved west, he thinks: "Parts of Texas and Kansas that he had first known as open range had since been made into rich farming districts, and the air had quite lost that lightness, that dry aromatic odour . . . . One could breathe that only on the bright edges of the world, on the great plains or the sage-brush desert." From the moment that Cather discovered pioneer Nebraska as her flood subject, it was the bright edges of the world that fired her imagination.

Among the many interesting aspects of this important novel, none is more impressive than the fully realized characterizations of the two French priests. Cather's success in creating character, which began with Bartley Alexander and Alexandra Bergson, reaches its apogee in this novel. Drawing contemporary characters that come alive on the pages of a novel is hard enough, but to breathe life into historical figures is infinitely more difficult. And to make the task even harder, Cather selected as her protagonist and his co-worker men few of her readers could possibly identify with. The emotions one feels in reading about the lives of Bishop Latour and Father Joseph are of a higher order than personal identity. These lives increase one's awareness of the values of saintliness, and one closes the book feeling morally uplifted. It is not at all necessary to be religious to appreciate the nobility and dedication to spiritual matters that motivate these characters. Their lives renew faith in human possibilities, much like the lives of Socrates, Jesus, St. Francis of Assisi, or Gandhi.

Although her two priests are alike in their dedication to God's work and the propagation of the faith, Cather does a careful job of differentiating their characters. On a superficial level the Bishop is fastidious, aristocratic, urbane, slow to make friends, while his vicar-general is rough and ready, a promoter, and an organizer; but Cather goes much farther. In their approach to their faith the differences are sharply drawn. When Father Herrera tells the story of the Virgin of Guadaloupe after his pilgrimage to her shrine in Old Mexico, Father Joseph declares: "Doctrine is well enough for the wise, Jean; but the miracle is something we can hold in our hands and love." To this Bishop Latour replies: "Where there is great love there are always miracles. . . . One might almost say that an apparition is human vision corrected by divine love. I do not see you as you really are, Joseph; I see you through my affection for you. The Miracles of the Church seem to me to rest not so much upon faces or voices or healing power coming suddenly near to us from afar off, but upon our perceptions being made finer, so that for a moment our eyes can see and our ears can hear what is there about us always."

Another facet of the novel, one very characteristic of Cather, is the affection displayed for French culture—from French cuisine to French architecture. When the two priests sit down to their first Christmas dinner in Santa Fe, the handy one, Father Joseph, is the cook. He serves his friend a dark onion soup with croutons. Father Latour tastes it, leans back with satisfaction and remarks: "A soup like this is not the work of one man. It is the result of a constantly refined tradition. There are nearly a thousand years of history in this soup." To this the practical Father Joseph replies: "*C'est ça, c'est vrai,* . . . but how . . . can a man make a proper soup without leeks, that king of vegetables?" Later in the novel the Bishop takes Father Joseph out of Santa Fe to a ridge high over the Rio Grande Valley. When they come upon a face of yellow rock, the Bishop informs his friend that here is his cathedral. He is immensely excited about having found a stone that is the color of the old Palace of the Popes at Avignon. The Bishop has the worldly ambition to build for his diocese a cathedral, as his ancestors had built the cathedral in his native Clermont. Cather's enthusiasm for this project of constructing a French church in a Spanish town, which dismayed Mary Austin, is very clear. She agreed with her bishop that Midi Romanesque was the right thing for New

Mexico. The pragmatic Father Joseph, however, couldn't care less. "Whether it was Midi Romanesque or Ohio German in style, seemed to him of little consequence."

Death Comes for the Archbishop has been the subject of more critical exegesis than any of Cather's other novels. A close reading of the text reveals intricate patterns beneath a disarmingly simple surface. As with other Cather novels, the unsophisticated can read it with pleasure for its stories and characters, its wonderful use of setting, and its elevating themes. Below its smooth face, however, the novel resonates with allegory, symbol, and allusion. Form still follows function in the organization, but the structure required this time to write a modern saint's life was far more complex than the structures she had used before. Previously causal relationships connected events in her novels, but here she made no effort to explain how or why things happened. Events are narrated without being related to causes or linked to results, and things have importance in proportion to their religious significance. This is Cather's most elaborately contrived fiction and invites comparison with the allusiveness and technical virtuosity of other major twentieth-century modernist works. One critic writes: "Behind its plain face she built, as it were, a complicated cathedral into which busy critics of her time and ours [1966] seldom glance. That this novel has become standard high school fare is a joke almost as preposterous as the comparable fate of *Gulliver's Travels*."

According to a contemporary cultural anthropologist, Robert Armstrong, human consciousness creates two kinds of art, that which is organic and that which is accumulative. The first type he calls *synthetic*, an art that develops through one thing growing out of another in a linear fashion; the second he terms *syndetic*, an art that is constructed of discrete parts, each juxtaposed to the other without having any necessary relationship. Most novels from *Robinson Crusoe* to the latest best seller are organized synthetically, but the Book of Proverbs, *The Golden Legend*, Puvis's frescoes, Holbein's woodcuts, and the African dances of the Yoruba people (Armstrong's particular interest) are organized syndetically. So are many works of modern art, such as the experimental writing of Gertrude Stein, a good bit of modern music, collages, the endless Campbell soup cans of Andy Warhol, and the novel published loose-leaf that can be shuffled and read in any order. What is remarkable about *Death Comes for the Archbishop*, however, is that Cather's novel is boldly experimental, a prime example of twentieth-century modernism; yet it is a work of wide appeal and intelligible to anyone.

"My book was a conjunction of the general and the particular," Cather told the readers of *Commonweal*. "Particular" applies to the fictional life of Bishop Lamy, which is the burden of the novel; "general" applies to the allegory and symbol that link the narrative to world literature. Although it takes place in New Mexico in the nineteenth century, it tells the story of the Gospels, the *Divine Comedy*, *Pilgrim's Progress*, and the quest motif is as old as narrative itself. That there is more than one level of meaning is clear from the opening book, which recounts the Bishop's journey from Santa Fe to Durango. The novel begins in a manner familiar to any reader of westerns: "One afternoon in the autumn of 1851 a solitary horseman, followed by a pack-mule, was pushing through an arid stretch of country somewhere in central New Mexico." But immediately the reader plunges into an allegorical landscape of "conical red hills . . . exactly like one another," a "geometrical nightmare," and "every conical hill was spotted with smaller cones of juniper." These fantastic cones crowd upon the weary traveler's retina hundreds of times as he looks about him in the burning heat. He is lost in the desert and has been without water for a day. Suddenly he comes upon a juniper in the shape of a cross. He takes it for a sign, kneels to pray, loses himself in the contemplation of Christ's passion. He remembers "that cry, wrung from his Saviour on the Cross, '*J'ai soif!*' [I thirst]." After his prayers the Bishop remounts and his horse plods on. An hour later the horse scents water, quickens its steps, and presently the Bishop arrives at a fertile, well-watered valley in the midst of the desert, appropriately named "Agua Secreta." To any reader of Medieval saints' lives the Bishop has been saved by a miracle; to a reader of westerns it is horse sense and luck. The biblical allusion, however, signals to the experienced reader that the Bishop has embarked on a Christ-like ministry, a journey through life toward the ultimate goal of salvation, as Dante traveled through the Inferno to Purgatory and finally to Paradise, or as John Bunyan's Christian toiled with his load of sins through the Valley of the Shadow of Death towards his heavenly destination. The Biblical parallel is further reinforced by the necessity of the Bishop's journey: he, like Christ, has been rejected by those he came to save.

Symbolism to reinforce spiritual values abounds in *Death Comes for the Archbishop*. Cather's minor characters, while often clearly drawn and particularized, usually serve to exemplify some moral trait. All the seven deadly sins are represented in her gallery of figures: pride in Doña Isabella, covetousness and envy in the miserly Padre Lucero, lust in Padre Martinez, gluttony in Trinidad Lucero; anger and gluttony in Friar Baltazar, and sloth in the degenerate Buck Scales. These symbolic characters often are shown in the Medieval manner in which appearance reflects moral nature: Buck Scales is "tall, gaunt and ill-formed, with a snake-like neck, terminating in a small bony head," and as Padre Lucero lies on his death bed, "his cheeks were sunken, his hooked nose was clay-coloured and waxy, his eyes were wild with fever . . . great, black, glittering, distrustful eyes." On the other hand the good guys are similarly characterized. Cather's idealized description of Kit Carson, seen through the eyes of Bishop Latour, reflects an admirable moral nature: "His face was both thoughtful and alert . . . Under his blond mustache his mouth had a singular refinement. . . . [It] suggested a capacity for tenderness."

In addition to the effective opening chapter under the cruciform tree, some of the most moving scenes in the novel are also the most symbolic. One is the chapter in which Bishop Latour and Jacinto take refuge in the cave to escape an oncoming blizzard. They enter through a rock formation that suggests stone lips and find themselves in a lofty cavern shaped something like a Gothic chapel. The Bishop feels an instinctive distaste for the place, the presence of evil. He is in the secret chamber used by the Pecos Indians for their ancient pagan rituals. After his Indian guide seals up a mysterious hole in the wall of the cave and builds a fire, the Bishop senses a vibration in the rock. Jacinto takes him to a fissure in the floor where he can put his ear to the roar of an underground river, "a flood moving in utter blackness under ribs of antediluvian rock." "It is terrible," he said at last as he rose. This is a frightening scene, superbly managed, and for those fond of seeking Christian motifs in the novel, the Bishop, who suffered as Christ on the Cross in Chapter One, now has descended into hell after the crucifixion.

Another poignant scene of symbolic import takes place later in the novel on a cold December night. The Bishop is going through a crisis of faith, a dark night of the soul. He gets out of bed, goes to the church to pray. In the doorway of the sacristy he finds the old enslaved Mexican woman Sada weeping bitterly. She has crept out of the house of her masters and dared to visit the church. She wears no stockings and her clothes are rags. The Bishop takes her into the church and they pray together. Despite her miserable condition the old woman never has lost her faith. After the Bishop hears her confession, he takes the fur-lined cloak from his shoulders and gives it to Sada. Outside of the church the moon shines on a silent, snowy landscape, and the Bishop looks up at the night: "The peace without seemed all one with the peace in his own soul."

Cather's idea, expressed by Professor St. Peter, that in the end art and religion come to the same thing is well exemplified in *Death Comes for the Archbishop*. In the "December Night" chapter just cited the Bishop gives old Sada a silver medal with a figure of the Virgin embossed on it. The medal will be a "treasure to hide and guard, to adore while her watchers slept. Ah, he thought, for one who cannot read—or think—the Image, the physical form of Love!" Here the small work of art and religion are joined. The large work of art and religion merge in the Bishop's cathedral, which is the capstone of his career and his legacy to his diocese. It is both a creative act to build the cathedral, motivated by worldly ambition, but at the same time it is a religious act of piety growing out of faith.

Cather commented specifically in her *Commonweal* letter on the relationship between art and religion. She described the art she had seen adorning the mission churches scattered about New Mexico. They were decorated with "utterly unconventional frescoes," "countless fanciful figures of the saints, no two of them alike." They seemed "a direct expression of some very real and lively human feeling. . . . Almost every one of those many remote little adobe churches in the mountains or in the desert had something lovely that was its own." And she went on to say that in somber villages in the mountains "the martyrdoms [were] bloodier, the grief of the Virgin more agonized, the figure of Death more terrifying," while in "warm, gentle valleys everything about the churches was milder."

Garden imagery and symbolism, which appear in most of Cather's works, is used here effectively to give meaning to the Bishop's ministry. His entire life has been spent cultivating his parishes and nurturing souls. The vegetable and flower garden and the orchard he has planted symbolize his civilizing of the wilderness. The fruit trees he has planted, like his imported religion, have been brought in bare root in wagons over the Santa Fe Trail. Father Joseph comments that people in the new territory who have never seen a priest are "like seeds, full of germination but with no moisture. A mere contact is enough to make them a living part of the Church." The human flowering under the Bishop's hand is strikingly epitomized by the appearance of the rehabilitated Magdalena as the two priests walk in the garden. She comes each day to feed the doves, and "at one moment the whole flock of doves caught the light in such a way that they all became invisible at once, dissolved in light and disappeared as salt dissolves in water." It would be hard to find another literary passage more eloquently objectifying the concept of the Holy Spirit. At the end of his life the old Archbishop in retirement spends his days working in his garden where he has "such fruit as was hardly to be found even in the old orchards of California" and masses of flowers that he has domesticated and developed from the native plants. Finally, as he nears death, he likes to quote to the seminary students he teaches "that passage from their fellow Auvergnat, Pascal: that Man was lost and saved in a garden."

When the Archbishop reached magazine and newspaper reviewers, he was buried under an avalanche of superlatives. The novel was greeted with phrases like "a story of absorbing interest," "one of the most superb pieces of literary endeavor this reviewer has ever read," "the fruition of her literary artistry," "one of the finest she has written," and "a book which will remain an American classic." Her perfection of style, her ability to evoke, not just describe, the landscape of New Mexico, her recreation of living history—all of these aspects of the novel impressed the contemporary critics. Only about one reviewer out of ten found the book a disappointment, but even the naÿ-sayers had to praise the quality of the writing.

Robert Morss Lovett, who greeted the book as an American classic, wrote one of the most perceptive reviews. Despite the fact Cather had only been a visitor to New Mexico, he noted that "she has entered fully into her back-ground. She had lived into her New Mexican environment until the desert land, scarred by canyons and arroyos and swelling into mesas, with its people, Mexican, Navajo, Hopi, are substantial to her as they became to the Archbishop." As for the narrative, she "tells her story not with the directness of a chronicle, but with an interlacing of theme, a shifting of material, which breaks the flat surface of the narrative into facets from which the light is variously reflected." Lovett concluded with a paragraph that pleased Cather so much she sent part of it to Knopf to use in advertising her book: "Miss Cather has recaptured for America an aspect of its history, in this story of the Church, venerable and rich in tradition, becoming primitive amid pioneer conditions, among childlike people, in the piety of its missionary saints. It is not a tragic or a pathetic tale, but one full of happiness and triumph; and yet it moves one to tears, by the picture of such goodness and beauty seen through the medium of a faultless art."

Michael Williams felt it his duty to call attention to the book so that "all readers competent to appreciate a great work of literary art may have their opportunity to enjoy it." He went on to add that it was not just a book for highbrows: "For readers who delight in . . . 'style,' to whom the rhythms and the verbal coloring of 'fine writing' are delight-giving . . . there are indeed many wonderful pages in this book." But he noted that "the simplest and most humble of readers may and surely will find this book accept-able . . . I know few books so deep, even so profound, in subject matter, which are expressed in so simple a vocabulary." Williams also observed that "Miss Cather is not a Catholic, yet certainly no Catholic American writer that I know of has ever written so many pages so steeped in spiritual knowledge and understanding of Catholic motives and so sympathetically illustrative of the wonder and beauty of Catholic mysteries, as she has done in this book."

It was unfortunate for Cather that all Catholics did not read *Commonweal*, where Williams' review appeared. A complication was added to her life when Vernon Loggins in *I Hear America* stated as fact that Cather had become a

Catholic. She began receiving letters from Catholics asking about her conversion. One in particular was a student at Mount St. Mary's College in Maryland, who was writing a senior thesis and wanted to know how her conversion influenced her writing. After he had written her twice, Cather sent an exasperated letter to the head of his English Department asking him to call off this persistent young man. He seemed to find it incredible, she complained, that anyone should admire and reverence the Roman Church as a great organization and spiritual power without being a Catholic.

She repeated in her letter that she was an Episcopalian and that church was home to her, as indeed it remained for the rest of her life. She maintained strong ties with the Episcopal Church in Red Cloud and a friendship with George Beecher, the Episcopal bishop of Nebraska, a man she admired greatly. One knowledgeable Cather scholar believes that Cather's success in creating an American saint in Jean Marie Latour partly lay in her affectionate relationship with Beecher. At the time Bishop Beecher celebrated the twenty-fifth anniversary of his consecration as bishop, Cather wrote Carrie Sherwood that she had met many bishops in her day but that none of them looked the part or was the part as much as her own Bishop Beecher. She also wrote a public letter to the committee in charge of the anniversary celebration: "He has the power of making one feel that the present service, the present moment, is rich and precious; that life is full of splendid realizations which have nothing to do with material gains or losses. I have never spent an hour in his company without feeling the happier for it, and these meetings, sometimes years apart, have left such vivid pictures in my memory that I often turn to them." Cather was lucky she had a strong faith to sustain her, for by the time *Death Comes for the Archbishop* appeared in book form, she had suffered one calamity and was soon to sustain another.

CHAPTER 19

Shadows on the Rock

The first six months of 1927 were a quiet period before the storm. While *Death Comes for the Archbishop* was running in *Forum*, Cather was happily reading proof for Knopf's edition of her book. It was like having a gorgeous party all over again, she said, but the pleasure of this moment could not last. By summer she had to give up the apartment she had lived in for fifteen years. It was a wrenching blow to leave the place she had loved and worked so well in for so long. Godfrey St. Peter's reluctance to give up his old house was reenacted in real life, but this time there was scarcely any choice. Number Five Bank Street was to be pulled down soon to make way for an apartment building, but even if the house had remained, life in this backwater of Greenwich Village would have become increasingly difficult. For a year or more the new Independent Subway had been burrowing its way under Greenwich Avenue three doors from Cather's apartment, and the noise, dirt, and confusion of the excavations had become intolerable.

Cather wrote her friends that she was having to leave Bank Street because a new subway station was being built under her house. This was not at all true, though it may have seemed that way; but since her building and the two adjoining ones were scheduled for demolition, she would have to get out sooner or later. To escape the turmoil, she made plans early in June to go west to visit Roscoe and his family in Wyoming and then sail for Europe in the summer. The trip to Wyoming came off on schedule, but not the trip to Europe. While she was in Red Cloud on her way back from Wyoming, her father had a mild heart attack and she canceled her steamship reservations. She stayed in Nebraska until her father seemed well recovered, then returned to New York to put her goods into storage and quit Bank Street forever.

After the trauma of breaking up housekeeping, she went to Jaffrey for two months. She wrote Akins from the Shattuck Inn that she and Lewis had come to New Hampshire to rest up from the rigors of moving. Going into storage was a good bit like having a funeral, and she was going to spend the next few weeks walking in the woods and lying about among the junipers before making any further plans. She had neither the idea nor the inclination to do any writing. She wrote Mary Austin, who had complained about her life being messed up, that she wasn't the only one. There were only occasional intervals, Cather said, when she could make things run smoothly and snatch a piece of work out of the temporary calm.

By November she was back in New York living at the Grosvenor Hotel, which she expected to be only a temporary solution to the housing problem. Located on lower Fifth Avenue not far from Washington Square, the Grosvenor was a convenient and familiar address; but when she moved in there, she would have been appalled if she had known the Grosvenor would be her home in the city for the next five years. This half decade was to be the most stressful and discouraging period of her entire life. At the peak of her career, a famous author, enjoying universal acclaim for her latest novel, she was a ship without moorings. Initially, however, she stayed at the Grosvenor only until the first of December, after which she returned to Red Cloud to spend Christmas with her parents. It was a truly happy time, she wrote Fisher, surrounded by her large family, parents, brothers and sisters, nephews and nieces. She remained until late February, took charge of having repairs made on the old house (aided by weak local talent, she reported), then returned to New York once more in late February.

On March 3 one week after she left Nebraska, her father had a fatal heart attack. Cather took the first train west and arrived back in Red Cloud at three in the morning the day after her father died. Friends met her at the Burlington depot and took her home. Recalling this moment thirteen years later, she told Akins that she had gone to her father's room without waking anyone in the house. He was lying on a couch in the bay window. She spent several unforgettable hours with him before anyone else got up. When the red dawn broke, it flushed his face with the rosy color he always had and he looked entirely himself and happy. Later as the body was lying in Grace Church before the funeral, her calm apparently vanished, and friends remembered her pacing frantically back and forth between the house and the church, wringing her hands, overcome with grief. Burial took place in the family plot on the edge of town, and she remained in Red Cloud for more than a month, not wanting to tear herself away from the place her father had lived for many years. When Douglass took their mother back to California with him, she stayed on alone in the house. She told Fisher a month later that the silence in the old place and in her father's room had done a great deal for her. She felt rested and strong as if her father himself had restored her soul. His death was a heavy blow, for Charles Cather and his oldest child always had been very close. All the kind, gentle fathers in Cather's fiction have her father in them.

The year 1928 was a totally discouraging and almost unproductive time. She spent many of her days in Red Cloud getting the house ready for her mother's expected return from California. She put up new curtains, had the house papered, the furniture polished and painted, planted new shrubs and flowers in the yard. Then she started back towards New York by way of Rochester, Minnesota, stopping off at the Mayo Clinic for some sort of examination. She had what she described as a bothering hurt, but it turned out to be a slight matter and after two weeks at the Clinic, she returned to New York at the end of April. She arrived back in the city, however, feeling for the first time in her life absolutely tired. She had done no writing for the last six months and said she was not going to do any for at least another six. She hardly had reached New York before she caught a virulent form of the flu from a chambermaid at the Grosvenor and spent the next two weeks in bed, with two nurses in attendance and a persistent temperature. In early June she barely managed to summon strength to get to Morningside Heights to accept another honorary degree from Columbia.

Later that month she planned to go to Grand Manan Island to recuperate in the cool climate of the Bay of Fundy. She wanted to travel by way of Boston and visit Mary Jewett, who had been sick, but did not feel up to a side trip to South Berwick, Maine. Life does beat us up sometimes, she wrote Jewett, and we must take our drubbing. To get to the Island as easily as possible, she decided to take the fast night train to Montreal and rest there a few days before continuing on. She planned to break the trip again in Quebec, to visit a city she never had seen, then continue on to St. John, New Brunswick, where she could catch the ferry for Grand Manan. The stopover in Quebec turned out to have far-reaching consequences.

Cather was feeling pretty fit by the time she reached Quebec, but Edith Lewis, who was traveling with her, came down with the flu, and they had to stay ten days. Cather never had thought of writing a book about French Canada, but she was immediately attracted to it. Lewis remembered: "From the first moment that she looked down from the windows of the [Chateau] Frontenac [Hotel] on the pointed roofs and Norman outlines of the town of Quebec, Willa Cather was not merely stirred and charmed—she was over-whelmed by the flood of memory, recognition, surmise it called up; by the sense of its extraordinarily French character, isolated and kept intact through hundreds of years, as if by a miracle, on this great un-French continent." Once again she found a subject for a novel, and during the days Lewis was ill in the hotel, Cather tramped about the city visiting all the historic spots, and she read Canadian history in the hotel's library. It was not until the end of 1930, however, that she was able to finish *Shadows on the Rock*.

Inspiration for a new novel alone would have revived her spirits at this juncture, but Grand Manan provided added therapy. She had awaiting her a new summer cottage, built in her absence, the first and only piece of real estate she ever would own. She had made a hurried trip to the island in September 1926 to buy some land, finally having decided to put down roots somewhere. She was tired of making new arrangements every time she wanted to return to Grand Manan. During her brief visit she staked out the location of her house and hired two local carpenters from North Head, the nearby village, to construct a Cape Cod cottage. It was ready when she arrived about the end of July.

The building site was located about a quarter of a mile through the woods from Sarah Jacobus's establishment at Whale Cove. "The cabin modestly squatted on a tiny clearing between a tall spruce wood and the sea, —sat about fifty yards back from the edge of the red sandstone cliff which dropped . . . to a narrow beach—so narrow that it was covered at high tide. The cliffs rose sheer on this side of the island, were undercut in places, and faced the east." Offshore were the weirs of the local fishermen, and along the top of the cliffs ran a secluded trail. The cottage had two bedrooms, a kitchen, a washroom, and a large living room with fireplace. Overhead was a floored attic running the length of the building. This loft with exposed rafters and only the shingles and sheathing shutting out the sky is reminiscent of Cather's old attic bedroom in Red Cloud. It became her workroom for the many subsequent summers she spent on the island.

Life in this cottage on Grand Manan in the 1920s was primitive. There was no indoor plumbing in the cottage, and electricity had not yet come to the island, but Cather did not mind the inconveniences. Also there was no telephone, a convenience she was happy to do without. If people wanted to get in touch, they probably could reach her in a week by mail from New York, or if they were in a hurry, they could telegraph. She took great satisfaction in having her own hut, as she called it, and five acres of woodland. This rock island, she wrote Akins, is as green as Ireland and as cool as England. The weather was just right for leather coats and sweaters in the middle of the summer. It suited her more than any place in the world, she thought, but she admitted it was rough living. Nothing was so hard to get in this world as silence, a piece of seashore that is wild and empty of humans, and wild forest. To have these she could do without a bathtub and eat rough food.

The rough food was what she consumed daily at Sarah Jacobus's resort where she took her meals with the summer boarders, perhaps as many as twenty. Lewis recalled: "We often rebelled against the rather austere provision of the only little boardinghouse within reach; so that it was necessary to have a constant stream of supplies winging their way from distant points: garlic and olive oil from New York, bread from Montreal, wild strawberry jam from Quebec; and shipments every week from an excellent grocer in St. John." As they were in Canada and out of the reach of Prohibition, they were also able to get vintage French wines. One of the many services that Blanche Knopf performed for Cather was having Charles, her New York grocer, send Italian tomato paste, wild rice, and caviar. Lewis added: "With these we were able to break the monotony of our fare with splendid banquets, cooked on a little wood-burning range."

Though the food paled in comparison with the culinary efforts of her own French cook, Cather was not a difficult boarder. Kathleen Buckley, who waited tables for Jacobus during the thirties, remembers her as an uncomplaining guest. She had her own coffee and had it brewed specially, but that was because she drank it decaffeinated. She did insist on having it very hot. What she did not want to do was fraternize with the other summer boarders. She never suffered fools gladly. If she didn't mingle with the summer people, she also wanted to be left alone by the permanent residents. The only Grand Manan islander she made friends with was Doctor Macaulay, a cultivated graduate of McGill Medical School, surgeon, and physician of more than ordinary skill.

Most of the time Cather kept to herself, worked in the morning at a table in the attic, and walked for miles in the afternoons along the cliffs where she could be completely alone. Occasionally, however, she invited her nieces to visit her, and then the daily routine changed. Margaret and Elizabeth, her brother Roscoe's twin daughters, spent two summers there when they were in college. They slept in the loft of the barn on Jacobus's property and every morning met their aunt for breakfast at the Main House. After breakfast they went for a long walk along the cliff trail. As Margaret remembers: "Aunt Willa knew every turn and tree—many of the places she and Miss Lewis had named, often using names or phrases from *Alice in Wonderland*. At noon, we would be back at the Main House for lunch. Then Aunt Willa and Miss Lewis retired to their cottage . . . for three or four hours. We would see them again around four o'clock when Elizabeth and I walked to the cottage for tea. Those were the best times. There would be a fire in the fireplace . . . and we would have tea or sherry, and a special bread from St. John. It was a grand time of conversation and reading aloud from their favorite books." Then they all would walk to the dining room and after dinner go back to the cottage. At the end of the evening the two girls retraced their steps through the woods by flashlight to their quarters in the barn loft. Cather greatly enjoyed having her nieces from Wyoming visit her, she wrote Akins, and added that the girls, who never before had seen the sea, were dizzy with delight.

After two restful months in her new cottage, Cather returned to the Grosvenor Hotel refreshed and ready to begin work again, but she barely had started the new novel before another misfortune overtook her. In December, 1928, her mother, still visiting Douglass in Long Beach, had a stroke that left her paralyzed on one side and almost unable to speak, but with mind unimpaired. This distressing event blighted the Christmas season, and Cather made plans to go to California in early March. The only bright spot of this winter was the appearance in the *Forum* of her first publication in seventeen months, "Double Birthday," a substantial short story probably written the previous summer at Grand Manan.

One of her few Pittsburgh tales, "Double Birthday" is an excellent piece of short fiction even though Cather never wanted to reprint it. It is fashioned from materials that had teased her mind for many years: her old Lincoln friends, Dr. Tyndale and the Westermann boys; Judge McClung and Isabelle, her many visits to the Seibels in their southside apartment, memories of life in Pittsburgh, and her old interest in singers. Following the death of her father, which was the first loss of someone very close to her, she had been brooding on themes later put in this story: the need to cherish old friendships, to rise above unimportant differences, to face the future squarely. As she did in *Death Comes for the Archbishop*, she again strikes a note of affirmation.

The story opens with a chance meeting between Judge Hammersley and Albert Englehardt on the steps of the Pittsburgh court house. The judge, a man of stern rectitude, imbued with the Protestant work ethic, disapproves of Albert, fifty-five years old with nothing to show for it. He was one of the five charming Englehardt boys who had squandered in pleasures a large estate left them by their hardworking German immigrant father. Albert now has a minor job in the county clerk's office and lives with his eighty-year-old uncle, also Albert, in a working-class flat in South Pittsburgh. Both Alberts are bachelors. He is not at all ashamed of his life. He makes enough money to get by, doesn't worry or feel sorry for himself. He plays the piano beautifully and would not trade his memories of a gorgeous youth. When he walks past the wealthy homes on Squirrel Hill, he doesn't want to change places with any of his former friends who live there, whose lives are encumbered with middle-class responsibilities. "Money? oh yes, he would like to have some, but not what went with it." The judge had remarked to a colleague: "If it weren't for his father's old friends seeing that he got something [a job], that fellow wouldn't be able to make a living." Next to a charge of dishonesty, the judge thought this was the worst that could be said of anyone.

Albert tells the judge that his old uncle is about to have a birthday, and the judge, who still respects the uncle, offers a gift of champagne from his cellar. When Albert goes to get the champagne, he meets the judge's daughter, Marjorie Parmenter, an old friend he hadn't seen for many years, who lives with her father. She is a childless widow, a wealthy woman of forty, very social and gracious. She suddenly realizes that she has missed a lot by not keeping up her old friendships and plans to salute old Albert Englehardt on his birthday. The reader learns it is to be a double celebration, because young Albert was born on his uncle's twenty-fifth birthday.

Before the special dinner young Albert had planned, the narrative flashes back to recount the great sorrow of the old man's life. He had been a physician, a throat specialist, who was particularly interested in the problems of singers and in his practice had treated many of them. One day he had discovered in a Pittsburgh high school girl a glorious, untrained voice, and his greatest ambition had been to nurture this voice and to present to the public a world-class prima donna. But just as his discovery was beginning her career, she developed an inoperable cancer and died at the age of twenty-six. The doctor, shattered by this loss, soon retired and moved in with his namesake.

The final scene is a moving dramatization of the birthday dinner. Marjorie sweeps in with an armload of flowers and more champagne and joins the two Alberts in a splendid meal prepared by the German housewife who lives below. During the meal they renew their old friendship, exchange memories of the past, and at the conclusion each offers a toast. The old doctor drinks "to a memory; to the lost Lenore." Young Albert drinks "to my youth, to my beautiful youth!" When Marjorie's turn comes, she says: "And I . . . will drink to the future; to our renewed friendship, and many dinners together. I like you two better than anyone I know." As she grew older and older, Cather clung tenaciously to old friendships, and as members of her family and friends dropped off one by one, she died a little each time.

The entire story is an evocative remembrance of things past. Judge Hammersley bears a strong resemblance to Judge McClung in his judicial probity and aristocratic attitudes, and his daughter Marjorie is much as Isabelle Hambourg might have been if she had returned to Pittsburgh as a widow in the twenties. When Albert meets her after many years, he thinks that "she had all her father's authority, with much more sweep and freedom. She was impulsive and careless, where he was strong and shrinking . . . She had proved more than once that if you aren't afraid of gossip, it is harmless. She did as she pleased." The modest house in South Pittsburgh where the two Alberts live obscurely is modeled closely on the apartment where Cather went to read French and to spend her Christmases. When George and Helen Seibel read the story, they experienced a shock of recognition. There was the place they had lived at the turn of the century, the little two story brick house on a dingy street, the upstairs apartment reached by going down a paved alley and climbing an outside flight of wooden stairs at the back.

The most impressive character in the story is the old doctor Englehardt, a man of strong opinions, who boasts of his former success with women, and is knowledgeable about wines and music. He is drawn very much from life, from Dr. Julius Tyndale, who was then eighty-five. By 1929 Cather was more circumspect about making fictional characters out of her friends and wrote Dr. Tyndale before "Double Birthday" came out hoping he would not be displeased by the story. He replied: "As to your story, how did you ever get it into your head that I could or would take offense at anything you might borrow of my characteristics, etc. The fact is that I am vain enough to feel flattered by any mention of my person." Dr. Tyndale died four months after Cather's story appeared. There is no evidence that the Westermann brothers saw themselves in the story, but if one compares the Erlich boys in *One of Ours* with the Englehardts, the resemblance is unmistakable. Marjorie remembers them "lying about in tennis clothes, making mint juleps before lunch, having coffee under the sycamore trees after dinner. The Englehardt boys were different, like people in a book or play. [Compared with the boys in her set] she had felt that the Englehardt boys admired her without in the least wanting to grab her, that they enjoyed her aesthetically, so to speak, and it pleased her to be liked in that way."

When Cather reached California in March, she relieved her brother of some of the burden of looking after their mother. She found her mother's situation infinitely sad. A month later she wrote that she had no time for anything but the struggle with the grave material difficulties of helping to care for a helpless and very sick person stricken away from home. She grieved that the stroke had not occurred in her mother's home in Red Cloud among family and old friends. Cather was living in a hotel and going back and forth every day by taxi to see her mother. She thought Long Beach was the most hideous and vulgar place in the world and hated southern California. She wrote Mary Jewett in April that she would give a lot for a breath of a real New England spring. In Long Beach she was living in an artificial climate; it was like living on the stage. Nothing was real; there was no soul; it was full of homeless, drifting people. Hollywood was the complete expression of California life. She escaped from Long Beach at the end of May and went to New Haven to receive another honorary degree. The Yale faculty gave a dinner in her honor, and after commencement she returned to Grand Manan by way of Quebec for a long summer on the island.

By the end of the summer she was well into *Shadows on the Rock*, but the writing went slowly. This time she had to work up the material, an uncongenial method she had steered clear of since *One of Ours*. The feeling she had for the Southwest through long possession gave authenticity to the Archbishop's story, but her interest in Quebec was newly acquired. She left Grand Manan in September, spent a month in Jaffrey, two weeks in New York, then went back to Quebec in November for another firsthand look at the locale of *Shadows on the Rock*. This was not enough and she returned to spend New Year's there to experience the city in the dead of winter. Early in 1930 she interrupted her writing to return to California for another long visit with her mother.

Cather felt in this period that life was treating her badly. Having to make her home when in New York at the Grosvenor, she wrote Fisher, was a dreary way of living, but she had to stay there because of her long trips to see her mother. She had been feeling rested after returning from New Brunswick and was beginning to like life once more, but New York made her feel all used up again. When Zona Gale invited her to make a long visit to Portage, Wisconsin, she wished she could, but she had to go to California. Things had been hitting her pretty hard, she said, and quoted from *Lear* Kent's line as he sits in the stocks: "Fortune turn thy wheel." Her second trip to California, however, was pleasanter than the first, because her mother's condition had stabilized and she had been moved to a sanitarium in Pasadena (which Cather was paying for). Her mother had an English nurse, who had been with her for a year, the food was good, and Cather herself had a private cottage on the grounds. Also her old friend Zoë Akins lived in Los Angeles and they were able to visit with each other.

Although Cather told friends she was practically living on transcontinental trains and had spent four months with her mother, she actually stayed only six weeks, a much shorter stay than her first visit. By the beginning of May, she was back in New York packing to sail on the *Berengaria* May 14 for five months in Europe. She went immediately to Paris so that she could visit the Hambourgs, who had an apartment on the left bank in Paris. She had not seen Isabelle for seven years. Again she was traveling with Lewis, and they visited friends near Marseilles in July. In August Cather returned to Aix-les-Bains, which she had liked enormously in 1923.

She put up at the Grand Hotel and was pleased to find that Aix had not changed. The town was a lovely, quiet place, she wrote Akins, as worldly as a capital and as simple as a village. The food was so good that she put on four pounds in the first couple of weeks. The hotel was an old one built years before, but it had large rooms and a very comfortable atmosphere, and she liked it much better than the smart new ones on the hills above the town. The Grand Hotel opened on a sloping little square that exhibited a bronze head of Queen Victoria, commemorating a visit she once had made to the spa. The casino and opera house were just across the gardens.

While she was staying at the Grand Hotel, she had an amazing adventure. Night after night she noticed in the dining room a distinguished old French woman, well over eighty, who usually sat alone. "The thing one especially noticed was her fine head, so well set upon her shoulders and beautiful in shape, recalling some of the portrait busts of Roman ladies." In the mornings Cather also saw the old lady come out of the hotel, get into her car, and drive off with her chauffeur towards the mountains. She carried paints and canvas and a camp stool with her, even though Aix was having one of its hottest Augusts in many years. Cather, while she read French fluently, had little oral command of the language and hesitated to speak to the old woman. One day, however, the Frenchwoman spoke to her in excellent English, and from this beginning an acquaintanceship quickly developed.

Cather later described this meeting vividly in "A Chance Meeting," one of the essays in *Not Under Forty* collected in 1936. It was a memorable experience. At first she had no idea who the woman was, but when they began discussing writers and Turgenev's name was mentioned, the French woman remarked: "I knew him well at one time."

"I looked at her in astonishment. Yes, of course, it was possible. She was very old."

The woman went on to say: "My mother died at my birth, and I was brought up in my uncle's house. He was more than father to me. My uncle also was a man of letters, Gustave Flaubert, you may perhaps know."

Cather knew immediately that her new acquaintance was the "Caro" of Flaubert's *Lettres à sa nièce Caroline*. "The room was absolutely quiet, but there was nothing to say to this disclosure. It was like being suddenly brought up against a mountain of memories." The old lady, Mme Franklin Grout, was astonished in her turn to meet someone who not only knew her uncle's works but knew them intimately and was passionately fond of them. At their subsequent meetings they discussed at length various books of the master, particularly *L'Education sentimentale* and Cather's favorite, the romantic *Salammbô* laid in ancient Carthage. Mme Grout eventually discovered that her new friend also was a distinguished novelist and invited her to visit at Antibes. Cather said she had to return home because of her mother's illness, but she hoped to come back to Europe the following year. The visit never occurred, however, because Mme Grout died the following February at the age of eighty-four.

The meeting of Mme Grout was a marvelous coincidence, but another meeting of far greater significance also took place during this trip to Europe. Through the Hambourgs in Paris Cather met Yehudi Menuhin and his family. This relationship grew stronger and stronger as the years went on until Yehudi and his sisters were as close to Cather as her own nephews and nieces. This friendship with the Menuhins, however, is a subject that properly belongs in the story of Cather's later years.

In late September Cather embarked on *The Empress of France* to return to America. This time she took the northern route up the St. Lawrence River to Quebec where she again stopped off to study the setting for *Shadows on the Rock*, her fifth visit to the old city. Then she spent a month at Jaffrey working on the book before going back to New York. She finished the novel the day after Christmas at the Grosvenor Hotel. While she was completing the book, she was awarded the Howells Medal by the American Academy of Arts and Letters for *Death Comes for the Archbishop*. The death of her father and two years of anxiety over her mother's condition had taken their toll. Hamlin Garland wrote in his diary after the ceremony: "Willa Cather was on the platform and I did not recognize her, so changed was she. She is a plain, short, ungraceful, elderly woman. . . . I had remembered her in quite different guise. She spoke without force or grace, with awkward gestures, but she did a noble book." Edith Lewis remembered that the long illness of her mother had a profound effect on Cather. "She had to watch her continually growing weaker, more ailing, yet unable to die. It was one of those experiences that make a lasting change in the climate of one's mind."

During January and February 1931, Cather remained in New York awaiting proofs of her novel. She read Mabel Luhan's *Lorenzo in Taos* and wrote her friend a long letter praising the book. She thought Luhan was perhaps a little hard on Frieda and Brett, but she had done Tony magnificently and the book was amazingly spontaneous and true. It was the best portrait of Lawrence there ever would be, and the rendering of the country around Taos was a delight. She also read *Toward Standards* by her old pupil Norman Foerster and wrote him a long letter discussing critics. She agreed with him in the main but thought he took contemporary New York critics too seriously. Randolph Bourne, who died in 1918, and to a lesser extent Henry Canby, then editor of the *Saturday Review of Literature*, were the only critics she thought much of. They had an instantaneous perception of and an absolute conviction about quality. It was like having an ear for music: you could tell when a singer flats or you couldn't. It was instinctive; you couldn't learn it. She cited Stuart Sherman (who had been generous to her) as someone absolutely lacking in that quality. But then she really didn't think much of professional critics. James and Pater—also Mérimée—were the critics she liked best. Cather also took time that winter to answer some of her fan mail, something she did rarely and then only when she received a letter that aroused her interest. She wrote a correspondent who must have commented on the problems of women writers that it was a very distinct disadvantage to be a lady author and anyone who said otherwise was just foolish. Virginia Woolf, she observed, had made a pretty fair statement of the disadvantages.

Early in March Cather boarded a westbound train once more for her third and last visit to her mother in California. As usual, she stopped off briefly in Chicago to see Irene Weisz, then continued her journey. While she was crossing Kansas on the Santa Fe, she wrote her old friend in a reminiscent mood, reviewing her life and relationships. She thought that she never had been a very thoughtful daughter. Her heart and mind always were full of her all-absorbing passion, and she had taken her parents for granted. Irene was the only one of her friends who reached back to her very beginnings, who had kept on being a part of her life. With her she could speak both her languages, as Irene knew the people dear to Cather's childhood and also the names of those who had grown into her life.

When she reached Pasadena, she found her mother weaker but little changed. By then she had been paralyzed nearly two and a half years. This condition was the cruelest thing that could happen to a person, Cather wrote Sara Teasdale from the sanitarium. But not only was her mother's situation too sad for words, living among sick people was for Cather extremely depressing. Fortunately she had Zoë Akins, who lived just an hour away, to comfort her. While she was staying at the sanitarium, she finished reading the proof she had begun in New York. She wrote Fisher that *Shadows on the Rock* had been her only refuge for the past three years.

While she was in California, she took one break when she went to Berkeley to receive an honorary degree. She enjoyed the ceremony and wrote Blanche Knopf that it was a gorgeous spectacle—blue sky and golden sunlight over the Greek Theater against a background of dark cypress trees. She stayed a couple of nights with President and Mrs. Sproul, then moved to the

Fairmont Hotel in San Francisco for a few days before returning to Pasadena. In June she crossed the country again, stopping at Princeton to collect still another honorary degree, this time the first such honor ever given a woman. She had a wonderful time on this occasion, the high spot of her many academic laurels. She received the most applause of any recipient, more than Charles Lindbergh; Newton D. Baker, Wilson's Secretary of War; or Frank Kellogg, former Secretary of State, all of whom also received degrees, and at the president's house the night before Commencement, Lindbergh took her in to dinner and sat on her right. The next day she had lunch with both Charles and Anne Morrow Lindbergh and liked them tremendously. She wrote Akins after the festivities that Princeton had gone off with a bang. Following this excitement Cather went up to Grand Manan in July, opened her cottage for the first time in two years, and waited for August first, publication day for *Shadows on the Rock*.

Cather's new novel was a story laid in Quebec during the last decade of the seventeenth century. Its chief characters are Euclide Auclair, a middle-aged widower and apothecary, and his twelve-year-old daughter Cécile, who keeps house for him. Two important minor figures are Bishop Laval and Count Frontenac, both drawn from the history of the old city. The novel, which has no real plot, is structured by the changing of the seasons, and it tells the story of one year in the lives of the people of Quebec. There are six books, four dealing with characters and two with events. The story opens in the autumn when the annual convoy of supply ships from France sets out for home, leaving the two thousand inhabitants of the town isolated on their rock in the St. Lawrence River until the ships return the following summer.

The focus of the novel is on the shop and home of Auclair and Cécile. Book One, "The Apothecary," sets the stage, recounts the circumstances that have brought Count Frontenac and his medical advisor, the apothecary, from France to the New World, and depicts the domestic arrangements of the Auclairs. The subsequent books relate a series of small events in the lives of the characters: Cécile obtains shoes for her little friend Jacques; Cécile and Jacques go coasting in December; Cécile, her father, Jacques, and a neighbor unpack the crèche sent in last summer's ships from France; Cécile gets sick and is ministered to by her father; Pierre Charron, their *coureur de bois* friend, comes to visit; Pierre takes Cécile to visit a family on the Ile d'Orléans; the ships return; the old count dies. The novel ends with a brief epilogue fifteen years later after Cécile has grown up, married Pierre, and produced four sons, the Canadians of the future. In France the Age of Louis XIV is about to end, and in Canada a new era is beginning.

When Governor Wilbur Cross of Connecticut, ex-professor of English at

Yale, wrote a review of *Shadows on the Rock* that particularly pleased Cather, she wrote him a letter of appreciation. "You seem to have seen what a different kind of method I tried to use from that which I used in the *Archbishop*. I tried, as you say, to state the mood and the viewpoint in the title. To me the rock of Quebec is not only a stronghold on which many strange figures have for a little time cast a shadow in the sun; it is the curious endurance of a kind of culture, narrow but definite. There another age persists." She tried to tell her story in a "prose composition not too conclusive, not too definite: a series of pictures remembered rather than experienced." She organized it around "an orderly little French household that went on trying to live decently, just as ants begin to rebuild when you kick their house down." The domestic life of the Auclaires interested her "more than Indian raids or the wild life in the forests" and, she told Cross, "as you seem to recognize, once having adopted a tone so definite, once having taken your seat in the close air by the apothecary's fire, you can't explode into military glory, any more than you can pour champagne into a salad dressing . . . and really, a new society begins with the salad dressing more than with the destruction of Indian villages. Those people brought a kind of French culture there and somehow kept it alive on that rock."

Although Cather struck out boldly in her letter to Governor Cross, she was somewhat apologetic about the novel in letters to friends. She admitted that the book had no fire at all and almost no energy. One simply had to like the book's quietness. It was all of a piece; she knew the tone was good, but she feared that to some it would seem goody-goody. The problem had been to keep the feeling of Quebec life all the year around. To Akins she made the same point stressed in the Cross letter: in music one could have a stormy and passionate movement next to a reflective one, but one could not mix such things in writing. This generalization, of course, is not true, and Cather's fiction is filled with sharply contrasting scenes. Even *Shadows on the Rock* introduces scenes of violence and strenuous physical activity which stand out sharply against the domestic tranquility of the Auclair household. The contrasting elements in this novel, however, all are inserted stories told at the apothecary's hearth. By this strategy Cather was able to maintain the quiet mood.

An historical novel laid in Quebec in the seventeenth century seems an unlikely product from the pen of Willa Cather. How does one reconcile this subject with the declaration that her heart never got across the Missouri River and that she could only write successfully about people or places she long had loved? Or her quotation from Jewett that the "thing that teases the mind over and over for years . . . belongs to literature"? Or her statement that she had gotten all her material before she was fifteen? The answer perhaps lies in Emerson's view that "a foolish consistency is the hobgoblin of little minds" or in another of Jewett's observations: "If [a writer] achieves anything noble, anything enduring, it must be by giving himself absolutely to his material. And this gift of sympathy is his great gift." Cather had this gift of sympathy; it is the secret ingredient in her fiction. In her essay on Mansfield she wrote: "The qualities of a second-rate writer can easily be defined, but a first-rate writer can only be experienced. It is just the thing in him which escapes analysis that makes him first-rate." Thus Cather tried another experiment and wrote a novel unlike anything she had done previously. As she said of her experiment in the letter to Cross: "I made an honest try, and I got a good deal of pleasure out of it, if nobody else does! And surely you'll agree with me that our writers experiment too little, and produce their own special brand too readily." The question for readers of Cather in 1931 was not, would she produce a good novel, but how good would it be. Critical opinion after more than half a century ranks *Shadows on the Rock* considerably below her best works. Yet it is a successful novel well worth reading and inferior only if placed beside a masterpiece like *Death Comes for the Archbishop*.

The material in the novel, however, is not quite so alien to Cather's experience as it might appear at first glance. Even though she had only visited Quebec five times, never spending more than ten days, a number of elements in the book had been long assimilated. Her deep feeling for French culture had begun before she ever visited France. She had written as early as 1895 that "most things come from France, chefs and salads, gowns and bonnets, dolls and music boxes, plays and players, scientists and inventors, sculptors and painters, novelists and poets. . . . If it were to take a landslide into the channel some day there would not be much creative power of any sort left in the world." Her interest in the establishment of the Catholic Church in the New World went back to her earliest visits to the Southwest, and her preoccupation with Pioneer experience is reflected in this story of the early days of New France. Her familiarity with French housekeeping, which is crucial to *Shadows on the Rock*, had been absorbed from her French cook over many years. She wrote Akins after the book came out that her knowledge of French pots and pans all came from Josephine, but she never had realized while she was working on the book why she found herself able to write about French household economics with care and conviction. Finally, her acute rendering of the forests and rocky seascapes of Quebec owed a lot to the five summers she spent on Grand Manan, and the loving father she created in Auclair was in a sense a fictional portrait of Charles Cather. He was much on her mind three months after his death when she conceived of the plan for her novel.

Shadows on the Rock contains a number of familiar Cather themes: the New World versus the Old, stability versus mutability, the virtues of friendship, and the perpetuation of tradition. The New World is a refuge from the abuses of class society, the necessity to truckle to those in authority, the unjust operation of the law. Old Blinker, who works for the baker next door to the Auclairs, emigrated to escape the trade he had been born into as one of the King's torturers. He is a pitiful, guilt-ridden creature who is befriended and comforted by Cécile and her father. One of the inserted stories told by the apothecary's fireside recounts an outrage that occurred before Auclair left France. It is the tale of poor old Bichet, a man hanged in Paris for petty theft on the evidence of a half-witted informer. Every year Auclair has a Mass said for the soul of Bichet. The iniquities of the Old World affect the great as well as the humble, for Count Frontenac, the governor of Quebec and one of the great figures in French colonial history, also suffers. He never receives his due from Louis XIV and dies relatively poor because he is too forthright and insufficiently obsequious. In the end the King even refuses his request to return to France to die.

The theme of stability versus mutability is carried out by the central image of the novel, the rock. It symbolizes safety, refuge, durability, faith. Cather used this symbol earlier in *Death Comes for the Archbishop* in "The Mass at Ácoma." When the Bishop sees the Enchanted Mesa, he reflects on the ancient village that once had existed on top of the rock. The Acoma Indians had built on the rock for safety from marauding Navajos and Apaches, and he thinks: "The rock, when one came to think of it, was the utmost expression of human need; even mere feeling yearned for it; it was the highest comparison of loyalty in love and friendship. Christ himself had used that comparison for the disciple to whom He gave the keys of His Church." When Cather saw Quebec perched on its rock, she must have been reminded of the Southwest, and this memory may well have inspired *Shadows on the Rock*. In both novels the secular and religious meanings of the symbol converge. In "The Long Winter" section of *Shadows* Cather writes: "Quebec seemed shrunk to a mere group of shivering spires; the whole rock looked like one great white church"; and after the ships return from France Cécile wonders how they could ever find this refuge, "this rock in the St. Lawrence . . . a goal so tiny, out of an approach so vast." Yet return they do, like birds coming back to nest on the barren islands in the river. The rock endures, unchanging, timeless. At the end of the novel when the new bishop, now an old man, returns from fifteen years of captivity in England and exile in France, he says to Auclair: "You have done well to remain here where nothing changes. Here with you I find everything the same." And the old apothecary thinks that he was "indeed fortunate to spend his old age here where nothing changed; to watch his grandsons grow up in a country where the death of the King, the probable evils of a long regency, would never touch them."

While this outpost of civilization clings to the safety of the rock, all about it is the menacing wilderness. Cather symbolizes the forest as a dark, evil, threatening unknown, much as it appears in seventeenth-century Puritan typology. It is full of howling savages and lurking danger. The third-person narrator writes: "The forest was suffocation, annihilation; there European man was quickly swallowed up in silence, distance, mould, black mud, and the stinging swarms of insect life that bred in it." And later one learns: "Blinker . . . had such a horror of the forest that he would not even go into the near-by woods to help fell trees for firewood." Among the inserted stories reported to the Auclair fireside are tales of the perils and evils of the woods: the fatal accident in the forest of Michael Proulx, Antoine Frichette's rupture that ends his active life, the cannibalism forced on Noël Chabanel by the Hurons.

The symbolic use of the wilderness, however, is overshadowed by a more important symbol—fire—used here in a benign sense. It represents home, continuity, warmth, domesticity. As Cather wrote Wilbur Cross, the French settlers on their rock sheltered and tended their culture "as if it really were a sacred fire." Scene after scene takes place around the fire where outcasts like old Blinker, little Jacques, son of a prostitute, the missionary priest Father Hector, Pierre Charron, and various neighbors gather, and like the fire, the warmth of Auclair and Cécile radiates outward. In the kitchen Cécile's fire transmutes the raw materials of woods, field, and stream into the glories of French cuisine. Everyone who comes to the apothecary shop is warmed by the view into the sitting room beyond the dispensary where the fire burns. To those born in France the Auclairs's fireside reminds them of home. When Cécile is sick she lies by the fire as her father gets dinner, listening to the drip of the rain, watching the "grey daylight fade away in the salon, and the firelight grow redder and redder on the old chairs and the sofa."

The theme of loyalty, which Cather found the most characteristic trait of the Quebecois, is closely woven into the texture of the novel. All the characters are held in interlocking relationships of loyalty. Auclair is loyal to his patron, the count, who in turn is devoted to his faithful apothecary. Auclair solaces old Blinker and is faithful to the memory of Bichet. Cécile's great friend is little Jacques, for whom she is both mother and playmate, and he is devoted to father and daughter. Pierre Charron is both son and elder brother, and after the count dies becomes the protector of the Auclairs. Old Bishop Laval's love for his flock is unstinting, and everyone in Quebec, except the vain young bishop, adores their old spiritual leader. And finally, binding the entire community together is the everlasting love of God, given and returned. Loyalty was also one of Cather's strongest traits, and she said later in her life that nothing really matters but the people one loves. She had to admit, however, that if people realized this fact when young and spent their time loving one another, the beds would not get made and little of the world's work would get done.

The perpetuation of tradition, like friendship, became more and more important to Cather as she grew older. In this novel French culture endures like the rock on which the city is built. The Auclairs replicate the life they left in France. The apothecary shop in Quebec is a carbon copy of the one they left on the Quai des Célestins in Paris. Their house is furnished with the same pieces brought from the Old World, and their arrangement never changes. Cécile conducts the ménage in exactly the same way her mother had before her. When she was dying, Mme Auclair had admonished her daughter: "At home in France, we have learned to do all these things in the best way, and we are conscientious, and that is why we are called the most civilized people in Europe and other nations envy us."

One of the key factors in perpetuating tradition is the Catholic Church. Its role in Cather's Canadian novel is similar to its role in her story of the Southwest. Many of the minor figures besides the two bishops are priests and nuns, and the life on the rock centers on the churches and religious observances. Cather writes: "When an adventurer carries his gods with him into a remote and savage country, the colony he founds will, from the beginning, have graces, traditions, riches of the mind and spirit. Its history will shine with bright incidents, slight, perhaps, but precious, as in life itself, where the great matters are often as worthless as astronomical distances, and the trifles dear as the heart's blood."

As a stylist and impressionist in words, Cather never wrote anything better than *Shadows on the Rock*. Her ability to render landscape is again superb, and her visits to Quebec at different times of the year resulted in some marvelous evocations of place. The novel opens with the apothecary standing on the top of Cap Diamant gazing at the empty river after the supply ships have left on a day late in October. He looks down at the "scattered spires and slated roofs flashing in the rich, autumnal sunlight" and beyond to the great river "rolling north toward the purple line of the Laurentian Mountains" and across the river to the black pine forest that comes down to the water's edge.

Later Quebec under the deep snows of winter is sketched memorably, especially when Cécile and Jacques go coasting on a December day. They slide down the hill from the cathedral still bathed in sunlight "through constantly changing colour; deeper and deeper into violet, blue, purple, until at the bottom it was almost black." As they climb up again, they watch the "last flames of orange light burn off the high points of the rock." The slender spire of the Recollet Chapel, up by the Chateau, holds the "gleam longest of all." Winter gives way to spring reluctantly in that northern latitude, but finally the snows melt, the first swallow returns, and life begins to stir again. Summer brings the supply ships, and on the day the ships are due the entire town turns out in holiday spirit. The great excitement of this event, the gaiety and carnival atmosphere, are vividly created, and the reader shares the emotional response of the people, who are for eight months of the year completely cut off from France.

Though no particular visual art inspired *Shadows on the Rock*, as Puvis de Chavannes and Holbein had suggested the method for *Death Comes for the Archbishop*, this novel is intensely pictorial. Reading the book is like walking through a gallery of impressionist paintings. There is no progression of plot from one tableau to another, and color dominates line, as in impressionist art. One is reminded of Monet painting Rouen Cathedral over and over at different times of day and in different light. Similarly Cather catches Quebec at different hours and at different seasons. How Monet painted was more important than what he painted, and in Cather's novel the way she sees the material is more important than the story she tells. Wilbur Cross in his review, seeing the analogy with visual art, noted that the sketches "are slight and delicate like the pastels of Latour [*sic*] or Watteau." Neither painter was an impressionist, but Watteau's portrait sketches, like Cather's are drawn with a light touch, idealized, and highly selective in detail. In addition, Watteau painted at the time the novel takes place.

The pictorial analogy may explain in part why characterization is the least satisfactory aspect of *Shadows on the Rock*. Like figures on a canvas, the dramatis personae of the novel tend to be flat, two-dimensional. Auclair, even though he is tinctured with Cather's feelings about her father, never quite comes to life and reminds one of a Theophrastean character exemplifying the loyal friend and loving father. Cécile has no reality at all. She is insufferably pious in town, and when she visits the Harnois family in the country, she is an intolerable prig. Her friendship with little Jacques is touching, but the child, who actually was suggested by Cather's young nephew, is unbelievable. Although he is the offspring of a woman of the town, who neglects and mistreats him, he is as devout as a saint and a contradiction of all the probabilities of genetics and environment. The most real characters are the two historical figures, Count Frontenac and Bishop Laval. They spring to life whenever they appear. The images of the old bishop ringing the bell for Mass in the dark hours of the early morning and the old count on his deathbed linger in the mind.

It must be said, however, that Cather was not trying to make Cécile and Jacques realistic characters. She was writing a symbolic novel. Certainly no child of twelve was ever as good, obedient, selfless as Cécile, and no boy of seven like Jacques ever existed. Susan Rosowski explains these characterizations: "Cather makes no pretense at presenting childhood as it is lived in the real world; instead in *Shadows on the Rock* she wrote a saint's life to tell of the apotheosis of a French girl into a Canadian Holy Mother." The general pattern of Cécile's life parallels the Virgin Mary's in its purity, sinlessness, and virginity, and when Cécile is seen tenderly ministering to little Jacques, one thinks of visual representations of the madonna and child from Cimabue to Raphael. To make her intention clear, Cather introduces a flashback to the time when Jacques was four and the old Bishop found him wandering about on the streets alone at night. He takes Jacques back to his own quarters, bathes, feeds, clothes, and identifies him with "his Infant Saviour." "As the Virgin Mother is a mediator for all living, Cécile is a mediator for the boy: she intercedes for him with her father and Bishop Laval, introduces him to the saints and Jesus, prepares a fête of the crèche especially for him."

In preparing to write *Shadows on the Rock* Cather had to do a great deal of reading. While she was visiting Quebec for the first time, she reread Francis Parkman's *Count Frontenac and New France under Louis XIV*, which she already knew, and other books she found in the hotel library. One of them was the biography of Bishop Laval by Abbé Henri Scott, vicar of Ste. Foy, a village near Quebec. This book interested her so much that she arranged to go see the old priest. He turned out to be a very helpful authority on the ecclesiastical history of Canada. At the Grosvenor Hotel while she was writing her novel, she read in the *Jesuit Relations*, Lahontan's *Voyages*, and the memoirs of Saint-Simon. She also went through Juchereau's history of the Hotel Dieu at Quebec, the letters of Mother Marie de l'Incarnation, from which came the epigraph of the novel, and various volumes of the "Makers of Canada," which she bought. She made good use of her sources and tucked a considerable amount of history into her book, as she had done with southwestern history in *Death Comes for the Archbishop*. She adopted Parkman's admiring estimate of Count Frontenac, but his anti-clerical bias sent her to Abbé Scott for the character of Laval. When the novel was in proof and she began to doubt her knowledge of Church practice, she asked a Catholic friend to check her manuscript.

Other research involved trips to the private Society Library where she consulted old herbals, old maps, and histories of Paris. And when she visited France in 1930 before the novel was completed, she spent several mornings at the Musée Carnavalet, the former home of the Marquise de Sévigné, looking at seventeenth-century artifacts. She followed the trail of Count Frontenac in Paris and walked along the Quai des Célestins. She visited the Church of St. Paul, mentioned in the book, and Saint Nicolas-des-Champs, where the count's heart is buried. With Jan and Isabelle Hambourg she went to St. Malo to see the home port of Captain Pondaven, a minor character late in the novel.

Among the various facets of the novel that hold a reader's attention are the many *things* it contains. Cather told a friend while she was working on the book that it was not going to have a trace of movement or suspense, but it would have people and things; and it does. These things give it what form it has: Cécile's silver cup, which is a marvelous object to Jacques; the parsley that Cécile cultivates through the winter; the glass fruit that Count Frontenac gives to Cécile; the cooking utensils and other housekeeping paraphenalia; Jacques' wooden beaver carved for him by a friendly sailor; the five battered ships from France; Captain Pondaven's parrot; the stuffed baby alligator Auclair brought from Paris. All of these objects make pictures on the brain.

The wooden beaver, which is especially memorable, is the focus of a poignant scene. It is Jacques' one possession, his treasure, and when the animals and figures for the crèche are unpacked, he offers it to place beside the Christ child. Cécile is perplexed, because no crèche ever before had a beaver in it, but Mme Pommier, the cobbler's mother, who is on hand, says it is appropriate: "Our Lord died for Canada as well as for the world over there, and the beaver is our very special animal." Cather created this scene from the memory of her young nephew Charles, who had made a similar offer for a crèche in Red Cloud the Christmas she was home before her father's death. As for the household equipment, Cather writes of Cécile's feeling about it: "These coppers, big and little, these brooms and clouts and brushes, were tools; and with them one made, not shoes or cabinetwork, but life itself."

Reaction to the novel from reviewers and friends was mixed. When Cather wrote Elizabeth Vermorcken thanking her for liking the book, she said that some of her friends detested it, as if they had ordered a highball and she had given them chicken broth. The reviewers all treated the appearance of a new Cather novel as an important event, and the book received many notices, many of them extended essays by well-known critics. By 1931

Cather was generally regarded as one of the major American novelists, and no book review editor ignored her. Simultaneously with the book's publication the *New Yorker* ran a profile of her by Louise Bogan, and *Time* put her on its cover. The selection of the novel by the Book of the Month Club insured wide distribution and large sales, and it became the most popular book in the United States during the next year. Two years later it was awarded the *Prix Femina Américain*. Knopf shipped 167,679 copies from ten printings before the end of 1931, and in subsequent years it was reprinted ten more times from the same plates.

Even though *Shadows on the Rock* received a good many unfavorable reviews, perhaps three-quarters praised the book, though some did so with reservations. Even the dissenters had to concede Cather's consummate artistry. Carl Van Doren in the *New York Herald Tribune Books*, writing a generally favorable notice, found the novel pictorially rich but dramatically weak, while Dorothy Van Doren in the *Nation* believed that "no American writer writes more beautifully than Miss Cather," but she hoped her next novel would have "more edge to it." Newton Arvin in the *New Republic* was flat out hostile: the novel was born dead; it had no center, no forward drive. Fanny Butcher, however, was enchanted by the book, finding it superior to *Death Comes for the Archbishop* and "one of the most excitingly exquisite bits of prose in the English language." The *Atlantic Monthly* regarded the novel as "one of her more beautifully constructed works marked by a trait without which no novelist . . . reaches greatness—compassion." To Granville Hicks, always a *bête noire* to Cather, the book betrayed "a failure of will."

Michael Williams in *Commonweal* found the book so rich and full of life he hardly knew where to begin writing about it: "It has a quality similar to that of the best folk-lore, in which a story that is almost naive is yet so deeply rooted in the ultimate mystery of human life, and the simple incidents are yet so suggestive of inner meanings as to become mystical in the best sense of the word, full of haunting understanding and overtones of spiritual values, like a parable in Scripture." On the other hand, the *Des Moines Register* described the novel as a trifle dull, and Louis Kronenberger in the *Bookman* gave Cather another cudgeling for writing a book without life: "There is no blood in it, no muscle, no bodily emotion . . . it is commonplace flavored with lavender, domesticity without domestic strife, old Quebec swept clean and fresh by human hands, but unpeopled by human beings."

Because contemporary critics often review the book they would have preferred to read rather than the one actually written, most of the unflattering notices seem wrong-headed at this late date. The novel, however, is definitely the work of an aging author, even though Cather had not yet reached sixty. It is preoccupied with time and eternity. Youthful striving is far behind her, and the emphasis is constantly on order, decorum, and resistance to change. The central symbol, the rock, which stands for stability and permanence, also could represent petrification and intransigence. Mme Auclair once told her daughter: "Without order our lives would be disgusting, like those of the poor savages," and Cécile will grow to be a woman like her mother with the unattractive traits of the bourgeoisie as well as the virtues. She too will adhere blindly to tradition. Auclair also resists change. Cather stacks the deck so that when he says, "I think the methods of the last century better than those of the present time," the statement in context seems right. But he is talking to the young bishop who wants him to treat the old bishop with a medical procedure that anyone in the twentieth century would know to be ridiculous.

In the final analysis *Shadows on the Rock* was a novel to which no one remained indifferent, and for its author it was the rock to which she clung during four years of personal upheaval. Cather wrote rather plaintively to Fanny Butcher: "Doesn't one have a perfect right to love a small Georgian pitcher better than the Empire State Building? . . . I did the book to keep me going and I'm well satisfied if a few old friends, like yourself, get a little happiness out of it." Another old friend, Ferris Greenslet wrote in his autobiography: "I read *Shadows on the Rock* oftener and with keener relish than any other, even *Ántonia*." One of his readings took place in Quebec. "No other book that I had ever read so completely recaptured the spirit of a place."

CHAPTER 20

Obscure Destinies

One month after *Shadows on the Rock* came out, while Cather was at Grand Manan, her mother died in California. It was a relief to have the long ordeal over, but the pain of parting was nonetheless agonizing. With both parents gone Cather now was a member of the generation next to death. With neither husband nor children to cling to, the loss of parents was a heavier blow to Cather than to most people. She had come to appreciate her mother more and more as she grew older, and the sharp clash of personalities that once had struck sparks had long since given way to mutual love and respect. Jennie Cather, however, had remained an imperious, demanding mother to the end, and during the many months that she lay paralyzed in Pasadena, her daughter dared not revisit Red Cloud for fear of arousing her jealousy. Cather did not try to return to California for the funeral, nor did she go back to Nebraska when the body was brought to Red Cloud for burial.

She stayed on Grand Manan until the beginning of October, taking her daily walks along the solitary cliffs and adjusting to her new condition of life. She wrote Blanche Knopf three weeks after her mother's death that she was trying to get used to the strange feeling of having nobody behind her, nobody to report to. Helpless as her mother was, she expected an account of her children's activities, and Cather was glad her mind had not dimmed, as it would have in time. The next few months would be hard, Cather thought, and she didn't know just what she would do after leaving New Brunswick. She probably would go to Jaffrey, but then she might visit Virginia, where she had not been for nearly two decades. At any event, she was back in New York at the Grosvenor by the end of October 1931. She sent a note to Mrs. Canby on the thirtieth saying she wanted to see her as soon as she pulled herself together, but at that moment she felt unanchored, purposeless, and didn't know where to turn. The following year Cather wrote Zoë Akins that after forty-five it simply rains death and after fifty the storms grow fiercer. It seemed that she never opened a newspaper any more without reading of the death of someone she used to know. When she first knew Akins in her *McClure* days, she added, people didn't use to die at all.

During November she was sufficiently collected to make plans and decided to organize a family reunion in Red Cloud. At the end of the month she took a train west for her last visit to Nebraska. As soon as she reached Red Cloud, she plunged into the task of opening and cleaning her parents' house, which had been closed since her father died nearly four years before. She also had the roof reshingled and arranged for her mother's former maid, Lizzie Huffmann, to come from Colorado to keep house during the reunion. The family gathering was a great success, and Cather had a strong feeling of her mother's presence during the holiday season. With both parents gone her old ties of affection for her brothers must have seemed doubly precious. Her love for her brothers never had wavered since childhood, and she thought brother-sister relationships "the strongest and most satisfactory relation of human life." In an essay she wrote in 1897, commenting on the love of Tom and Maggie Tulliver for each other in *The Mill on the Floss*, she had observed that the world didn't realize how strong this love can be that "sometimes exists between a brother and sister, a boy and girl who have laughed and sorrowed and learned the world together . . . who have entered into each other's lives and minds more completely than ever man or woman can again."

The family reunion was good therapy. When Cather wrote Blanche Knopf to thank her for the gift of a gorgeous dressing gown, she reported having a wonderful Christmas season. She had been flying about in the car with her family seeing old friends, and the little town decked out with candles and Christmas trees was a beautiful sight under a full winter moon. They were having glorious weather, and she was feeling great affection for her *patria*, which to most people seemed so unattractive. Her parents' home was full of greens from New England and California and flowers from everywhere. She was planning a children's party on Holy Innocents' Day and had engaged the Grace Church choir boys to sing carols. She also had a lovely crèche with thirty figures that Isabelle Hambourg had sent her from France. This was her first real Christmas since her father's last Christmas in 1928.

Cather was almost totally unproductive in 1932. The only thing she wrote was her essay "A Chance Meeting," which she published in the *Atlantic Monthly* early the next year. She returned from Red Cloud in January and in February went to bed with the flu. During the spring she read proof on her next book, *Obscure Destinies*, a collection of three stories she had written while at work on *Shadows on the Rock*, but apparently the next novel had not yet been conceived. The deepening Depression troubled her, though she was getting rich from her royalties. She had lost money on gilt-edged bonds; her old farm friends in Nebraska were in real trouble; and some of her friends and relatives had lost their jobs. When Mary Austin asked her to donate to a favorite charity, she declined on grounds that she already was helping keep half a dozen families and had loaned money to others who were in such dire straits she was sure they never could repay her. She continued her private benefactions throughout the Depression, and when her old friends on the farm were burned out during the terrible droughts of the thirties, she helped them survive. She even paid some of the taxes for the Pavelkas so that they would not lose their farm. She wrote Greenslet that she was willing to sell the movie rights to *The Song of the Lark* provided he could get a good price. Nothing came of this, however, but she did serialize her next novel, something she hated to do, in order to raise more money to assist people she loved.

The bright spot in her life at this time was the growing friendship with Yehudi Menuhin and his family. The meeting in Paris in 1930 quickly developed into a close relationship. Yehudi, who was fifteen in 1931, made a West Coast concert tour when she was visiting her mother in Pasadena, and she was able to attend his performances and spend some time with him. She was so taken with the Menuhin children, Yehudi and his sisters Yaltah and Hephzibah, that she wanted to dedicate *Shadows on the Rock* to them. She was talked out of this by a friend of the family, who thought the Menuhin parents were overly sensitive to the lionizing of their children and would have taken offense. In New York after the Red Cloud reunion Cather saw Yehudi several times. She recovered from the flu in time to have dinner with him and attend one of his concerts, and the day before he sailed for Europe they had breakfast together and then spent the entire morning in the park. She wrote Carrie Sherwood that his whole nature was as beautiful as his face and his talent. According to his nephew, Cather was one of the few outsiders who penetrated the defenses the elder Menuhins placed around their prodigies. When she decided people were worth her affection, she had a talent for friendship, and neither the Menuhin parents nor their children could resist her.

Lewis remembered: "She loved the Menuhin family as a whole, and each separate member of it individually." Yehudi, of course, was the star, but she admired the mother and "found the two little girls—Yaltah was about seven, and Hephzibah a year or two older—endlessly captivating, amusing, and endearing." "They were not only the most gifted children Willa Cather had ever known . . . they were also extremely lovable, affectionate, and unspoiled; in some ways funnily naive, in others sensitive and discerning far beyond their years. They had an immense capacity for admiration and hero-worship, and Willa Cather became, I think, their greatest hero." Lewis called this friendship a "rare, devoted, and unclouded" relationship "that lighted all the years that followed."

Obscure Destinies was published by Knopf in August 1932, even before all three of the stories in the collection had been serialized. The first of the trio, "Neighbour Rosicky," had appeared in the *Woman's Home Companion* in April and May 1930, and the third tale, "Two Friends," ran in the same magazine the month before book publication. "Old Mrs. Harris," however, did not come out in the *Ladies' Home Journal* until September, October, and November 1932. All three stories return to Nebraska and old memories, and for some of Cather's public her abandonment of historical fiction came as a relief. Her father's death and her mother's long illness turned her mind to family and friends of her youth. The months she spent in Red Cloud both before and after her father died rekindled her enthusiasm for her adopted state. She wrote "Neighbour Rosicky" in New York before the end of 1928, "Two Friends" in Pasadena during her last visit to her mother, and "Old Mrs. Harris" at Grand Manan about the time her mother died.

"Neighbor Rosicky" is one of Cather's best known and most admired stories; best known because she allowed Whit Burnett to anthologize it in *This Is My Best* (1942), and Knopf subsequently let it be reprinted ten times in the two decades after her death; most admired because it ranks with "Coming, Aphrodite!" "Uncle Valentine," "Old Mrs. Harris," and "Tom Outland's Story" as the cream of her short fiction. The story is in a sense a sequel to *My Ántonia*, for Annie Pavelka's husband sat for the portrait of the Bohemian farmer Rosicky; but the emotional power of the tale derives from Cather's feelings about her father, and the title character's death by heart failure parallels the death of Charles Cather. She infused her memories of her father into Anton Rosicky much more successfully than she did into the apothecary Auclair in *Shadows on the Rock*. This story rarely fails to move even the most blasé reader.

At the outset of the tale one recognizes Ántonia's family some ten years after Jim Burden left them prospering on their farm. The children that Jim saw running up the stairs of the fruit cave, "a veritable explosion of life out of the dark cave into sunlight," now are between twelve and twenty. Ántonia here is called Mary, an even more appropriate name for the Madonna of the Wheat Fields. The relationship between father and sons, husband and wife, is devoted and sympathetic, and the human equation in the Rosicky family always takes precedence over the economic one. Mary would rather put roses in her children's cheeks than sell her cream in town, and Rosicky, like Cuzak in *My Ántonia*, is an easygoing, good-natured husband. Rosicky is much less affluent than some of his neighbors, who are reminiscent of Nat Wheeler in *One of Ours*, but he owns his own land unencumbered and enjoys life.

The tone of "Neighbour Rosicky" is retrospective and elegiac and the story in Cather's usual fashion has little plot. It begins with Rosicky learning from his doctor that he has a bad heart and must take it easy for the rest of his life. This presents no problem because his five sons are old enough and willing to take over management of the farm. The conflict, which supplies what plot there is, concerns Rosicky's efforts to keep his oldest son from leaving the farm to work in the city. As an immigrant who had come to America from the slums of Europe, Rosicky has a horror of city life. Owning the land he has cultivated lovingly is for him the *summum bonum*. His son Rudolph, however, has married a town girl of native stock who is dissatisfied with farm life. Through a series of small incidents Cather draws Rosicky and his daughter-in-law Polly together, and at the conclusion when the old farmer dies he knows that Polly has become an integral part of his family. She is carrying his first grandchild, who will carry on the tradition, and he ends his life happy and fulfilled.

Rosicky is one of Cather's memorable characters. At the beginning and end he is observed through the eyes of Dr. Burleigh, and at key intervals in the narrative Cather inserts flashbacks to account for his life and attitudes up to the point at which the story begins. He also is seen in dramatic situations with the doctor, town merchants, Mary, and his children. On occasion the third-person narrative slips into Rosicky's consciousness to convey his ideas, and Cather's physical descriptions of the old man are highly evocative. All of these narrative strategies serve to create a fully developed, three-dimensional character. To accomplish this in a piece of short fiction requires the greatest artistry.

In the first of the small incidents that move the story along Rosicky asks his four boys who still live at home if they would be willing to forego driving into town Saturday night. He wants to take the Ford over to Rudolph and Polly so that they can go to the movies alone. The boys are disappointed, but Rosicky explains: "Polly ain't lookin' so good. I don't like to see nobody lookin' so sad. It comes hard fur a town girl to be a farmer's wife. I don't want no trouble to start in Rudolph's family. When it starts, it ain't so easy to stop. An American girl don't git used to our ways all at once." He takes the car to Rudolph's nearby farm, insists that Polly leave washing the dishes to him while she gets fixed up for town. Polly is rather aloof at this point, still calls her father-in-law "Mr. Rosicky."

Later Rudolph, Polly, and the rest of the family are together at Christmas. They discuss the outlook for crops the next summer. The last year was dry, and it looks as if the next one will be equally dry. The prospect is dismal, and Rudolph talks about getting a job in the city. At that point Mary tells about hard times when the children were little. It was one blistering day in July when a hot wind burned up the crops completely. Rosicky came in from the fields and announced that he was knocking off for the day. They were going to have a picnic in the orchard. He killed two chickens to fry and Mary prepared their supper. While they were eating, he announced that the crops had been ruined that day. There would be no corn at all that year. "That's why we're havin' a picnic. We might as well enjoy what we got." Mary tells the children: "An' that's how your father behaved, when all the neighbours was so discouraged they couldn't look you in the face. An' we enjoyed ourselves that year, poor as we was, an' our neighbours wasn't a bit better off for bein' miserable."

Following Mary's story, Rosicky tells of hard times when he was a young man. He had drifted from his native Bohemia to London where he apprenticed himself to a poor tailor. He boarded with his employer and his family, and none of them ever had enough to eat. One Christmas Eve the tailor's wife, who had been saving so she could have a goose for Christmas dinner, hid the roast goose in the cubby hole where Rosicky slept. He came in to bed late, smelled the goose, and was so hungry he ate half of it before he could stop. Later he was rescued from poverty in London by affluent Czechs, who helped him get to New York, where he made good wages as a journeyman tailor and for some years enjoyed a carefree bachelor life. Eventually he realized that city life was a dead end, went west to Nebraska, and became a farmer. After hearing this affecting story, Polly decides to invite all the Rosickys to her house for New Year's Eve.

The weather continues dry, but nonetheless Rudolph's alfalfa field comes up beautifully green in the spring. Rosicky worries that the Russian thistles blown in during the winter will take root and ruin the alfalfa, symbolically important because the field lies between parent and child. Because Rudolph is too busy to rake out the thistles, Rosicky does it without telling anyone. The work is too strenuous for him, and he has a heart attack. Polly finds him leaning against the windmill, gets him into the house, ministers to him, and the attack passes. She tells him before anyone else that she is pregnant, and as Polly sits beside him, she thinks: "Nobody in the world, not her mother, not Rudolph, or anyone really loved her as much as old Rosicky did. It perplexed her. She sat frowning and trying to puzzle it out. It was as if Rosicky had a special gift for loving people, something that was like an ear for music or an eye for colour. It was quiet, unobtrusive; it was merely there. You saw it in his eyes."

Shortly thereafter Rosicky has his fatal attack. The doctor is out of town when Rosicky dies, but several weeks later when his practice takes him into the country, he passes the graveyard adjacent to the Rosicky farm. He realizes that the old Bohemian farmer is no longer over on the hill where he sees red lamp light but here in the moonlight. He stops his car and sits there for a while. It strikes him that the graveyard is a beautiful place, unlike urban cemeteries, which are cities of the dead. "This was open and free, this little square of long grass which the wind for ever stirred. Nothing but the sky overhead, and the many-coloured fields running on until they met the sky." Rosicky's mowing machine stands nearby where one of his boys was cutting hay that afternoon; neighbors pass by the graveyard on their way to town, and in the cornfield over yonder Rosicky's own cattle will be eating fodder in the winter. "Nothing could be more undeathlike than this place; nothing could be more right for a man who had helped do the work of great cities and had always longed for the open country and had got it at last. Rosicky's life seemed to him complete and beautiful."

"Old Mrs. Harris" is a major accomplishment, perhaps the best story Cather ever wrote. It actually is longer than *My Mortal Enemy* and could have been published separately, but it fits in well with the other two stories in *Obscure Destinies*. All of them deal with humble individuals, "their homely joys and destiny obscure," as Gray puts it in his famous "Elegy." Anton Rosicky, Grandma Harris, and the two friends of the third story exist "Far from the madding crowd's ignoble strife" in Webster County, Nebraska. Old Mrs. Harris, who was inspired by Cather's grandmother Boak, is the most unforgettable character of all—as memorable as Ántonia Shimerda or Marian Forrester. When Cather sent the manuscript of "Old Mrs. Harris" and "Two Friends" to her publisher at the end of the summer of 1931, Blanche Knopf wrote that the former seemed to her one of the great stories of all time. "I have never before read anything that got right inside me as that did." She said she would never cease to wonder at Cather's ability to depict both atmosphere and people "in such a way that they become a good deal more real than the landscape outside the window or the person sitting across the table." Cather herself thought she had done well in "Old Mrs. Harris." When Akins wrote praising the story, she replied that the right things had come together in the right combination. It was the best story of the three.

"Old Mrs. Harris" appeared in the *Ladies' Home Journal* as "Three Women," a title that the editors perhaps thought more appealing to the magazine's audience. Nevertheless, its focus is on Grandma Harris, although it also deals with two other generations: young Vickie Templeton, fifteen, and her mother Victoria, who is about to have her sixth child. The story's auto-biographical elements, which already have been discussed, give the tale the antique, nostalgic flavor of Cather's best Nebraska fiction. The setting is Skyline, Colorado, which in actuality is Red Cloud once more. There also is a fourth important woman character in Mrs. Rosen, the neighbor modeled after Mrs. Wiener in real life, and the servant Mandy, one recalls, is another fictional portrait of Marjorie Anderson.

The story begins when Mrs. Rosen, carrying a pot of coffee and a coffee cake, crosses her lawn to the Templeton house to see Grandma Harris. She waits until she sees Victoria leave dressed for town because she wants to visit with the old woman alone. She admires Mrs. Harris a great deal and feels that her daughter and grandchildren take her too much for granted. A fine dramatic scene follows in which a great deal is revealed about the Templeton family and the grandmother. The setting for this tête-à-tête is the little Cather home in Red Cloud where Charles and Jennie Cather lived with their seven children, Grandmother Boak, and Marjorie Anderson. Grandma Harris occupies a queer little room, more like a hall than a bedroom, furnished with a sewing machine, a rocking horse, a wash stand, a curtained-off area for a closet, and a wooden lounge where Grandma Harris sleeps. The old woman is ill at ease having a caller who comes while her daughter is out and insists on her leaving before Victoria returns.

The next scene, also dramatically rendered, takes place that night and introduces Vickie, the other children, and Mandy, "the bound girl they had brought with them from the South." Old Mrs. Harris is feeling poorly, her breath comes short, and her feet and legs are swollen. While Vickie reads to the smaller children, her grandmother darns stockings for the boys. Before she goes to bed, Mandy offers to rub her feet and legs and performs, as the third-person narrator says, "one of the oldest rites of compassion." Then Grandma Harris retires to her lounge, which has no springs and "only a thin cotton mattress between her and the wooden slats."

The following episode belongs to Vickie, who goes to the Rosens to borrow a book from their well-stocked library. Vickie, who is in her last year of high school, is a bright, attractive, self-centered youngster, eager for knowledge. Mrs. Rosen doesn't wholly approve of her, but the two carry on a conversation about books. Vickie opens an illustrated German edition of *Faust* and wishes she could read it. Soon she runs across the text of *Dies Irae*, which she can read, and translates the Latin haltingly. Mrs. Rosen says that she will try to get an English translation of *Faust* for Vickie the next time she goes to Chicago, but Vickie replies: "What I want is to pick up any of these books and just read them, like you and Mr. Rosen do." This pleases Mrs. Rosen: "Vickie never paid compliments, absolutely never; but if she really admired anyone, something in her voice betrayed it so convincingly that one felt flattered."

From this relationship between Vickie and the Rosens follows one strand of the slight plot. Vickie desperately wants to go to college, but her parents can't afford to send her. Encouraged by the Rosens, she studies hard and wins a special scholarship to the University of Michigan. But the award is not enough to pay all her expenses, and she is bitterly disappointed. As far as the Templetons are concerned, this is the end of the matter. Vickie's parents have no particular respect for education and expect their daughter to hang around Skyline until she finds a husband. Grandma Harris, however, knows what an education means to Vickie and surreptitiously asks the Rosens to lend her enough so that she can accept the scholarship. They do so, and Vickie prepares to leave for Ann Arbor.

Much of the story is seen through the eyes of Mrs. Rosen, who keeps the next-door Templetons under steady surveillance. Her central European Jewish background gives her a perspective from which to view her neighbors. She doesn't condone their easygoing Southern ways, but she likes to go to their house: "There was something easy, cordial, and carefree in the parlour that never smelled of being shut up, and the ugly furniture looked hospitable. One felt a pleasantness in the human relationships." The Templetons don't know there is such a thing as exactness or competition in the world, and they are always glad to see people. When Mrs. Rosen first met Victoria, they had struggled home together in a blizzard from a card party in the north end of town. Victoria had invited her in to get warm and dry. As she sat with her feet on the base of the stove, Victoria disappeared into her bedroom, changed into a negligee, and brought out the baby. While they visited, she nursed the child. Mrs. Rosen, who never had been able to have children, was charmed by the scene of domestic intimacy, Victoria's warmth, and the baby's beauty.

The story develops through a succession of small incidents. The Rosens attend a Methodist lawn party in June where they observe the generous side of Victoria's character. They are pleased at her conduct towards the poor children of their laundress, who hang longingly over the fence. She invites them to the party, gives each a dime, and instructs Vickie to see that they get plenty of ice cream and cake. The next scene concerns Blue Boy, the children's pet cat, who gets distemper. The children are upset, but they go unthinkingly about their daily routine while Grandma Harris nurses the cat. She knows the cat will die; she's seen it all happen before. When Albert wants to know why Blue Boy has to suffer so much, she replies: "Everything that's alive has got to suffer." Yet she who "had seen so much misery" wondered "why it hurt so to see her tom-cat die." After the death of Blue Boy, the children have a backyard circus, Vickie wins the scholarship, and Victoria discovers she is pregnant once more. This is traumatic for her, and she takes to her bed while her husband conveniently leaves town to inspect a farm he owns. With five children already and a daughter ready for college, she can't bear the thought of another baby. She feels abused and put upon. "Why must she be for ever shut up in a little cluttered house with children and fresh babies and an old woman and a stupid bound girl and a husband who wasn't very successful? Life hadn't brought her what she expected."

The second strand of plot ends with the death of old Mrs. Harris as Vickie is getting ready to leave for college. One morning Mandy finds the old woman unconscious on her lounge. "Then there was a great stir and bustle; Victoria, and even Vickie, were startled out of their intense self-absorption. Mrs. Harris was hastily carried out of the play-room and laid in Victoria's bed, put into one of Victoria's best nightgowns." But grandmother was out of it all and never knew "she was the object of so much attention and excitement," which in life she never had had. The self-effacing grandmother dies as she has lived, quietly and unobtrusively. The third-person narrator summarizes in the final paragraph: "Thus Mrs. Harris slipped out of the Templeton's story; but Victoria and Vickie had still to go on, to follow the long road that leads through things unguessed at and unforeseeable. When they are old, they will come closer and closer to Grandma Harris. They will think a great deal about her, and remember things they never noticed; and their lot will be more or less like hers. They will regret that they heeded her so little; but they, too, will look into the eager unseeing eyes of young people and feel themselves alone. They will say to themselves: 'I was heartless, because I was young and strong and wanted things so much. But now I know.'"

This was Cather's mood as her mother was dying and she looked back over her life in her fifty-eighth year. She had been thoughtless and self-absorbed in her youth, as she wrote to Irene Weisz, and in this story she was laying out some of the wisdom she had acquired. Although both "Neighbour Rosicky" and "Old Mrs. Harris" end in the deaths of the title characters, they affirm life. Cather wrote Akins at this time that biologically speaking, life was rather a failure, but something rather nice happens in the mind as one grows older. A kind of golden light comes as a compensation for many losses. With this attitude Cather faced the fifteen years she had left to live, and while her physical strength steadily diminished and she gradually contracted the world she moved in, her spirit remained resolute.

The final story in *Obscure Destinies*, "Two Friends," is the slightest of the three as well as the shortest. It is a small drama of memory built out of the effect two Red Cloud businessmen had had on Cather when she was between ten and thirteen. The Mr. Dillon of the story is based on the father of the Miner sisters, and Mr. Trueman on William N. Richardson, Red Cloud live-stock dealer. The two friends used to sit on the boardwalk outside Dillon's store on pleasant evenings and carry on long conversations. The first-person narrator, an adolescent girl, loves to eavesdrop on the two friends: "I liked to listen to those two because theirs was the only 'conversation' one could hear about the streets. The older men talked of nothing but politics and their business, and the very young men's talk was entirely what they called 'josh'; very personal, supposed to be funny, and really not funny at all. It was scarcely speech, but noises, snorts, giggles, yawns, sneezes, with a few abbreviated words and slang expressions which stood for a hundred things." Dillon and Trueman, however, talked about everything: weather, planting, cattle, farmers, plays they had seen in the city. They had wide interests and their talks opened a window on the world for the young narrator. She found many pretexts for lingering near them and they never seemed to mind having her about. "I was very quiet. I often sat on the edge of the sidewalk with my feet hanging down and played jacks by the hour when there was moonlight. On dark nights I sometimes perched on top of one of the big goods-boxes."

The denouement of the story comes after Mr. Dillon goes to Chicago on a buying trip for his store and happens to be there at the time of the Democratic National Convention of 1896. This was the occasion when Bryan delivered his electrifying "Cross of Gold" speech. Dillon, a lifelong Democrat, is on hand for the speech, is thrilled by it, and returns home full of Bryan. "We've found a great leader in this country, and a great orator," he tells Mr. Trueman, who is a life-long Republican. "Great windbag!" mutters Trueman, and from this exchange ensues a heated political discussion that the narrator listens to with breathless interest. The debate, however, grows into a bitter quarrel, and the two friends part for good. Several years later Mr. Dillon dies and Mr. Trueman goes west to settle in San Francisco. This story is the unique exhibit in the canon of Cather's fiction in which politics provides plot.

After the story came out, Cather wrote Carrie Sherwood, Mr. Dillon's daughter, hoping that she and her sister Mary, who also lived in Red Cloud, liked the tale, or at least saw nothing in it that struck a false note. It was not meant to be a portrait of the two men, she said, but a picture of something that they suggested to a child. In a later letter she explained further that it was not really made out of the two friends at all but was just a memory. A story is made out of an emotion or an excitement and not out of the legs and arms and faces of one's friends, she added. This story, like the others in *Obscure Destinies*, has the nostalgic, retrospective mood of her best work, but Cather did not like to be told this. Several years later when Carl Van Vechten threw the word "nostalgic" at her, intending to be complimentary, she bridled. Everyone uses that term, she said, so don't you. Moreover, they used it about every book she wrote, and, my God, she wasn't always homesick. But she had to admit that one got sentimental when writing about old delights.

Cather's return to Nebraska in *Obscure Destinies* pleased the reviewers enormously. The critical reaction was similar to the sighs of relief that greeted *A Lost Lady* after *One of Ours* had been savaged in some of its notices. Again the chorus of praise was nearly unanimous. Michael Williams in *Commonweal* was typical of the enthusiastic reception. He was convinced that Cather possessed in a degree unique "among all contemporary American writers two supremely important qualities of the creative writer: sympathetic imagination, and mastery of language." And he went on to rhapsodize: "How marvelously Willa Cather has restored the virtue of words to serve in the conveyance of an artist's sense of the wonder, and pity, and beauty, and mystery of human life is amply demonstrated in her latest book." Even though all the characters die at the ends of their stories, Williams thought they would continue to live in this book "as long as authentic literature possesses any power in America. For there can be no stinting of one's statement concerning Willa Cather's work. She is permanently great."

When the notices began appearing, Cather was again hidden away in her cottage on Grand Manan. She went to Canada in June and remained until September. She continued to delight in her island retreat and took pleasure that summer in having her niece Mary Virginia Auld visit her, but she was between literary projects and perhaps somewhat at loose ends. Even though she was beginning to slow down, work was her habit of a lifetime. She returned to New York after a short stay at Jaffrey, and by October was once again at the Grosvenor. She still professed to hate New York and to say that it was becoming ever less attractive as a place to live, but she couldn't bring herself to leave. She had written Akins earlier in the year, after her old friend had gotten married in middle age, that she envied Akins's willingness to take chances and her natural power of enjoying life. She was taking a chance on matrimony, but if anyone could make it go, she could. She had come to New York at the right time, left at the right time, and bought a house at the right time. Cather wrote that if she had enough courage she would leave New York for San Francisco. But this was only talk. It was, however, time to end her five-year bivouac at the Grosvenor Hotel.

She spent November house-hunting and by the end of the month had found an apartment she was willing to lease. It was on Park Avenue, number 570, at Sixty-third Street in a building with a uniformed doorman, a rather ritzy address for a person with Cather's distaste for ostentation. She had been persuaded by someone, perhaps Blanche Knopf, that this would be the right place for her, and after she moved in, she was pleased with her new quarters and the convenience of the location. After five years at the Grosvenor Hotel with all her own things in storage, she was happy to be surrounded once more by the books and furnishings she formerly had on Bank Street. She and Lewis moved into the new apartment before Christmas and spent the next few weeks getting settled. She wrote Irene Weisz in January that she now had a home, a somewhat glorified Bank Street, and best of all Josephine was back. She was the old original Josephine, somewhat subdued by misfortune, but with all her bubbling southern nature still in force. She was an even better cook than before, and oh what good meals they were having!

Sergeant went to see Cather soon after she moved into 570 Park Avenue and found the new apartment depressing. She then lived in a shabby part of New York and wrote potboilers to stay alive in the Depression. She rather resented the snobbish elegance of Park Avenue. As she entered the lobby of the apartment building, she couldn't help remembering all of Cather's previous comments about the hostility of comfortable, self-satisfied people to any serious efforts of the artist. She felt that the uniformed personnel guarding the building were there chiefly to keep out undesirable characters and wondered if Neighbour Rosicky or Grandma Harris would even have been allowed into the building. When she reached Cather's apartment, however, her old friend opened the door herself "and met me in the eager, warm, unchanged way with which she greeted old friends."

She led Sergeant down a long hall to her bedroom at the back to dispose of her coat. That room seemed bright and attractive. Cather's bed was covered with a calico patchwork counterpane that must have been made in Red Cloud. Sergeant thought Cather might be able to work in that room, but she didn't see how she could work in the "luxurious sheltered cave of connecting rooms—spacious but not spatial. Noiseless but with no view of the sun." All the windows of the apartment faced the blank north wall of the Colony Club. Cather, however, liked the quiet and had taken the apartment because there were no distractions. The walls and floor were thick, the windows far from the roar of Park Avenue; there was no one tramping about in high heels overhead, no radios to be heard. Cather told Marion King, librarian of the Society Library, that she had sat for hours in the apartment to test its quiet before signing the lease.

In the drawing room there was a fireplace, but it was not a hearth one could draw up chairs to, and the new furniture that supplemented the Bank Street pieces were more formal than the old things. There were many familiar objects, however: the orange tree, the freesias, the George Sand engraving, the bust of Keats. Something new Sergeant saw was "a melting, angelic photograph of young Yehudi Menuhin." Cather went into the dining room, brought back glasses and served her guest sherry. They drank it in the drawing room, which was large enough for a party of thirty, and talked over *Obscure Destinies*, which Sergeant greatly admired. This reunion of old friends turned out to be a very satisfactory meeting, but they had to stay away from politics, because Sergeant was an ardent New Dealer and Cather disapproved of both Eleanor and Franklin Roosevelt.

Once settled in, Cather's creative energy began to return, and she was ready to start working again, but the new apartment was something of a cocoon. It sheltered her from the horrendous events taking place in the nation and in the world. Her letters reflect no preoccupation with the rise of Hitler to power in January, 1933, the closing of the banks in the United States, or even the end of Prohibition. She was much worried over the economic distress of friends and relatives, but she was, as always, apolitical, and it was not until the signs of World War II became unmistakable that her correspondence expressed larger concerns. She withdrew into a small circle of friends and found her recreation in music. In January the Menuhin family returned to New York, and Myra Hess, whom she knew through the Knopfs, also arrived from England for a concert tour. The Knopfs gave her a Capehart phonograph, then the Rolls Royce of sound reproduction, which afforded her many hours of enjoyment, and Yehudi presented her with recordings he had made. Her old Pittsburgh friend, Ethel Litchfield, whose husband had died, moved to New York to be close to her, and through her Cather met pianist Joseph Lhevinne, whose concerts she hardly ever missed. Lewis believed that "it was in part the happiness of living again in an atmosphere of music—she heard scarcely any music during the Grosvenor period—that gave Willa Cather the theme of *Lucy Gayheart*," her next novel.

CHAPTER 21

Lucy Gayheart

Lucy Gayheart, however, is not a cheerful novel produced by a mind moored serenely in a snug harbor. It is instead a story of death and blasted hopes, a tale that explores the dark Gothic underside of life, a novel revealing its author's darkening vision. It is also distinctly the work of an aging novelist who began her seventh decade of life during its composition. In a very general sense it returns to the materials of *The Song of the Lark*, beginning and ending in a fictional Red Cloud and taking its heroine to Chicago to study in preparation for a musical career. The idea for the novel came from the memory of a Red Cloud girl Cather had known in her youth, Sadie Becker, who used to skate on the old rink in a red jersey. She had golden-brown eyes, Cather recalled, and she could hear her contralto laugh as clearly in her old age as she did in 1885. Perhaps Cather remembered this girl during her last visit to Red Cloud in the winter of 1931–32, for the winter landscape and the skating scenes on the river impress themselves vividly on the reader of this novel. In addition, Sadie Becker was a musician, the accompanist of a local singer; a girl whose lover married someone else, and who left Red Cloud to continue her music studies. All of these details have parallels in the plot of *Lucy Gayheart*.

The heroine's symbolic name and her general characteristics also have their foreground in another real person and an early story. The vivacious young schoolteacher Cather had met and instantly liked when she was visiting Red Cloud in the summer of 1896, one recalls, was named Gayhardt, and "The Joy of Nellie Dean," published in 1911, created a character full of *joie de vivre* and perpetually in motion, as is Lucy of this novel. Nellie's blasted hopes of going to Chicago, taking singing lessons, attending operas, her disappointment in love, and her premature death all foreshadow *Lucy*

Gayheart. Its general outline suggests that Cather had asked herself what might have happened to Nellie if she had managed to escape from her small Midwestern town, gone to Chicago to study music, and there had fallen in love with a famous singer. The result of her speculations then, written from the perspective of an older woman, might have been the story of Lucy Gayheart.

Lewis recalled that Cather began work on the novel in the spring of 1933, but she did not attack it with any great vigor or enthusiasm. She had not recovered from the strain of the previous half decade, and she often wrote "very tired" or "deadly tired" in the line-a-day diary she began keeping about this time. The story, however, had been in her mind for several years, Lewis remembered, and she originally was going to call it "Blue Eyes on the Platte." She asked her old friend McClure at the end of May to wish her luck with the new book because she needed it: the project seemed to her at that point rather stupid. Three months later when the novel was well under way, she wrote Akins that her heroine was a silly young girl and she was losing patience with her. Perhaps she was too old for this sort of a book, she thought, and added that the work was not putting her in a holiday mood, as some of her previous books had done. With these liabilities it is a wonder that the novel turned out as well as it did, but by this time Cather was an old hand at creating character and situation, and the well-honed style never deserted her.

Two events in the spring of 1933 intruded on her concentration in getting the new book started. First, she was persuaded to make an after-dinner speech at a Princeton banquet in the Plaza Hotel in New York. The speech on May fourth was carried nationally on the NBC radio network, and Cather, despite her usual pretense about shunning publicity, looked forward to the experience. She wrote Carrie Sherwood a week before the dinner to tune in that night to hear her talk. The other event was the appearance later in May of an article on her career by her old friend Dorothy Canfield Fisher for the New York *Herald-Tribune*. She fretted and agonized over that essay while it was in preparation, but after it came out in print she was not displeased.

The radio speech, which was only about seven hundred and fifty words in length, summed up Cather's view of the history of the novel. It pulled together better than she had done before ideas she often had expressed in previous speeches, letters, and interviews. The novel, she said, was a new arrival among the arts, and she thought its most interesting developments were still to come. She was impressed by the astonishing variety in the long gallery of great books that we must call novels for want of a better term and cited, to illustrate her point, *Anna Karenina*, *Robinson Crusoe*, *The Pilgrim's Progress*, and *Don Quixote*, as examples of this wide range. Because the novel is the most modern of literary forms, she added, its gets nearer the people than any other genre.

Despite the novel's rich variety of subject matter during its short history, Cather argued, the American novel was only beginning to break out of old molds. Until very lately American novelists had confined themselves to two themes: how the young man got his girl or how he succeeded in business. She thought that editors and writers in this country until recently both believed love and success were the only major motives in literature. She went on to credit the great Russian novelists of the nineteenth century with showing American novelists how to struggle out of the love-success straightjacket. The Russians had had no benumbing literary traditions behind them, and their work caught the attention of every sensitive imagination the world over. The old icebergs began melting; the old forms began to break up. Conrad wrote *The Nigger of the Narcissus* without a woman in it, and American writers began to wake up. They began to look about and see a few things in God's world and stop making books like barrel-organ tunes grinding out the same old stuff. She concluded:

"We have begun to look about us, but we have a long way to go. We cling to our old formulae; for the moment we stress the bad-girl instead of the good, the rowdy who is kicked out of his great corporation instead of the smoothly polished young man who becomes its president. We won't face the fact that it's the formula itself which is pernicious, the frame-up.

"When we learn to give our purpose the form that exactly clothes it and no more; when we make a form for every story instead of trying to crowd it into one of the stock moulds on the shelf, then we shall be on the right road, at last. We all start with something true, and then in the effort to make it bigger than it really is, we try to weld something false onto it; something delightful, usually, but that was not in the original impulse. Electrical engineers haven't yet produced a device that will do that kind of welding.

"The novel is the child of Democracy and of the coming years. There is a Latin inscription on the wall of the Luxembourg art gallery in Paris which expresses a sane and rational attitude toward art. It reads something like this: 'Because of the past, we have hope for the future.' And we may say that for this latest and, not loveliest, child of the arts, from the past, from the Russian and the French and the English past, we may hope for the future."

When the *New York Herald-Tribune* asked Fisher to write a retrospective article on her friend, she wrote Cather to explain what she was up to. Cather replied that she would rather have Dorothy write the piece than anyone else. She particularly wanted to put to rest the legend that she had sacrificed herself to art. She was sick of hearing this said of her. She saw herself as always avoiding what was less agreeable and actually leading a life of indulgence. She asked her old friend not to make her either noble or pathetic. She acknowledged the struggles of youth, but that was what youth was for. She never had shut herself off from people she cared for, only from the crowd. That she was apprehensive about the article is clear from the letters she wrote Fisher at this time. She read the article before it went to the newspaper, and apparently fired off a telegram asking that the project be dropped. Then she changed her mind and apologized for the wire. She said that after reading the piece she had awakened the next morning feeling that life was over, there was no use in going on, she might as well lay her ashes besides those of the real pioneers. She felt aged and decrepit.

When the article appeared in print, she liked it well enough to send a copy to the Hambourgs, but she said that articles about her made her self-conscious. As soon as she began thinking of herself as a human being in the past—Red Cloud, Colorado, New Mexico—the scenes were spoiled for her. She had been a jumble of sensations and enthusiasms, not a person. She had been running from herself all her life and was happiest when she was running the fastest. But she had to agree with Fisher's notion that there was a common theme to her work, though she never had thought of a consistent strain running through her novels. Each book at the time had seemed totally new to her.

She summed up the common theme as "escape" and admitted that she had often had the feeling of escape while she was traveling by train through miles of empty country surrounded by sky and wind. This had been her happiest feeling, one she had had since childhood, and she still felt homesick for the untainted air of the West. If she had stopped to take inventory, she would have discovered that her novels and stories are full of scenes laid on trains or, in the case of Bishop Latour and his vicar, on muleback moving across the open terrain. In 1933, however, her trips back to Red Cloud and her visits to New Mexico were all behind her, and as she sat comfortably aging in her Park Avenue cocoon, the experiences were now only memories. It must have shocked her to have all this summarized in Fisher's article and caused the feeling of terror that made her at first want the essay killed.

What Fisher wrote was indeed perceptive: "I offer you a hypothesis about Willa Cather's work: that the only real subject of all her books is the effect a new country—our new country—has on people transplanted to it from the old traditions of a stable, complex civilization. Such a hypothesis, if true, would show her as the only American author who has concentrated on the only unique quality of our national life, on the one element which is present more or less in every American life and unknown and unguessable to Europeans or European colonials. . . . Americans have no choice but to accept the definite break with the past. They are like people who have married against their parents' wishes and know they must make the best of their bargain. Is there one of Miss Cather's novels which is not centered around the situation of a human being whose inherited traits come from centuries of European or English forebears, but who is set down in a new country to live a new life which is not European or English, whatever else it may be?" Then Fisher reviewed Cather's life, her move from Virginia to Nebraska, her college days in Lincoln, her career in journalism in Pittsburgh and New York, and finally her launching out as a free lance novelist. All this must have seemed something like reading her own obituary.

When summer came Cather made her annual trek to her summer cottage in New Brunswick. She took her manuscript with her, but for the first two weeks or more she spent her days walking along the deserted cliffs, usually alone, watching the wild flowers come out. She wrote Blanche Knopf that nothing was happening on Grand Manan except weather. She was feeling too lazy to do any work and was ashamed to write Alfred because she hadn't yet been able to get to her desk. She would write him as soon as she had put in an honest week's work. Her niece, Mary Virginia, again visited her that summer, and, as usual Edith Lewis was her constant companion. The outside world intruded only once, in August, when Mussolini's air force returned from a goodwill visit to the United States and flew over Grand Manan in midafternoon waking Cather from her nap. She wasn't at all thrilled by this flight and wrote Pat Knopf that the planes were ugly beasts and she had shaken her fist at them.

But the normal tranquility of the island was conducive to work, and the writing went along well. By the time she left Grand Manan to go to Jaffrey for her annual visit in October, she had nearly finished the first draft of the novel, and she completed it while she was staying at the Shattuck Inn. She wrote the Knopfs that she wasn't yet out of the jungle, but she now knew there was a trail through. She still had a lot to do before the manuscript would be ready to publish. It would take a hard winter of revising in New York and the help of the Knopfs to keep the dogs off of her. She hadn't yet learned to work very well in her Park Avenue apartment. In the meantime the weather at Jaffrey was glorious, and she was taking four mile walks. There were wild, low clouds, as in France; Mount Monadnock had been a dark purple all the day before, the top of it powdered with snow; and the sky was rolling masses of silver and purple and black from morning to night.

When Cather returned to New York from her idyllic retreats at Grand Manan and Jaffrey, the deepening Depression brought her face to face with economic reality. At the end of November she received a letter from Ida Tarbell reporting that McClure was entirely without funds, all the members of his family from whom he could rightly expect assistance being unemployed or barely able to support themselves, and John Phillips was raising money from McClure's old friends. Would Cather like to help? Of course, she would. She sent off a check immediately and later followed up with additional contributions. McClure had been one of her first dinner guests in the new apartment in March, but she never had suspected that her old boss was even then being supported by his friends.

The terrible economic plight of family and old friends, especially old farm friends in Nebraska, continued to intrude on her Park Avenue comfort, but there were compensations. Her growing relationship with the Menuhin family, especially Yehudi, provided a constant source of pleasure. It was the bright spot of the winter as she struggled to revise *Lucy Gayheart*. The Menuhins lived across Central Park from Cather's apartment at Sixty-third Street and Park Avenue, and in mid-February she wrote Carrie Sherwood that she had spent the morning coasting in the park with Yehudi, who kept his sled in her building. After coasting they had lunched together in the Menuhin's apartment to celebrate his eighteenth birthday. The Menuhin children were the chief treasure of her life, she added. Twice a week all three of them joined her to read Shakespeare. Lewis remembered: "They began with *Richard II* and went on to *Macbeth* and *Henry IV*. Willa Cather hunted through the bookstores of New York to get each of the children a copy of these plays in the original Temple Edition, the only one she herself cared to read." Yehudi Menuhin in his autobiography recalls that she took "us by the hand through Shakespeare's plays. In our apartment there was a little room, nobody's property in particular, small enough to be cozy, and furnished with a table around which Aunt Willa, Hephzibah, Yaltah, myself and often Aunt Willa's companion, Edith Lewis, gathered for Shakespearean reading, each taking several parts, and Aunt Willa commenting on the language and situations in such a way as to draw us into her own pleasure and excitement."

Cather was an important influence on Menuhin in his formative years: "She was a rock of strength and sweetness. Ever since coming east she had reserved time during the week for walking in Central Park, which was to her native Nebraska as a nosegay to an interminable prairie. Her favorite walk was around the reservoir in the park, where contact with the earth renewed her sense of belonging in a metropolis in which so much conspired to alienation. Park veterans ourselves, my sisters and I often joined her, taking turns at the honor of walking by her side. . . . At one period I had particular cause to lean on her: in the unhappiness of my first marriage Aunt Willa was someone to be utterly trusted. One could tell her everything in one's heart: it would never be misused, never turned against one, never cause her to alter her regard. In those days she and I took many a walk around the reservoir. Her strength had a patience and evenness which did not preclude a certain severity. There were abuses and vulgarities she refused to tolerate, such as exposure in newspapers or on radio. She had a contempt for anything too much owned or determined by mobs, reserving admiration for high individual endeavor, withdrawing more and more from society even as she drew closer to us. . . . "

"She adored what she felt had not been her birthright—the old, the European, the multilayered, and above all music. But her reverence did not cause her to stray into the self-doubt which some Americans used to show when confronting Europe. Early in 1936, on the point of returning to California, I must have expressed some uncertainties about the future, for in reply I received these words (words which, it must be said, have been overtaken by time): 'Yes, my dear boy, you *are* confronting a problem. But it is the problem which every American artist confronts. If we remain always in our own land we miss the companionship of seasoned and disciplined minds. Here there are no standards of taste, and no responses to art *except emotional* ones.' "

" 'On the other hand, if we adopt Europe altogether, we lose that sense of *belonging* which is so important, and we lose part of our reality. I know a few very talented young writers who at the age of twenty-one or two decided that they would be French. They went abroad to live, and have never amounted to anything since. They can't *really* be French, you see, so they are just unconscious imposters. The things his own country makes him feel (the earth, the sky, the slang in the streets) are about the best capital a writer has to draw upon. A musician is much less restricted. The very nature of your work means "pack your kit." You, Yehudi, will simply have to do both things and live two lives. But I think you must spend your vacations in your own country when possible.' "

At the beginning of March while she was still laboring over *Lucy Gayheart*, misfortune overtook her. She sprained the big tendon in her left wrist, didn't go to the doctor, and ended up with a serious inflammation. She had to carry her wrist and hand in splints for six weeks. This accident made her overwork her right hand so much that she had to stop writing altogether. She reported to Akins in September, with characteristic exaggeration, that she had had her hand strapped to a board for three months and was unable to work for the entire time. While she was laid up, however, the Menuhins were in town and did their best to help her pass the time pleasantly. But she fretted over the inactivity, and when she did get back to work in April, the delay forced her to stay in town well into July to finish the revisions of her novel. She turned the manuscript over to Knopf before leaving for Grand Manan, but the book was still more than a year from publication. She was going to disregard her usual reluctance to serialize her books and give *Lucy* to the *Woman's Home Companion*. She wanted to make as much money as she honorably could from the novel in order to help friends in the West and to recover from her own bad investments. She was not in a happy mood when she started north.

She felt guilty being off in the Bay of Fundy where the temperature seldom rose over eighty degrees, while her friends in the Midwest were suffering from a terrible heat wave. She wrote Akins that Nebraska had endured forty-two days of temperatures over one hundred that summer. Her left wrist, however, had recovered from the painful inflammation of the spring, and she was enjoying her leisure after the hard sprint to finish her novel. By the beginning of September she was feeling very fit and wrote Blanche Knopf that she had passed a perfect summer. She felt as if she had had a new coat of paint.

There is no evidence that Cather did any writing during the summer and fall of 1934. She stayed quietly on Grand Manan until September, then returned to Jaffrey for her annual visit. Back in New York in November for the winter, she resumed her social activities, saw the Menuhins often, attended Yehudi's concerts, dined with the Knopfs, heard the Philharmonic play a Brahms cycle, entertained Bishop Beecher from Nebraska, and awaited the serialization of her novel, which began in March and ran through July. The winter passed without any further creative effort, and when spring came she was totally preoccupied with other matters.

In mid-March and again in April she had attacks of appendicitis and feared she would have to have an operation. She was relieved when her doctor concluded that surgery was unnecessary, but there was further anxiety when her niece Mary Virginia, who lived in New York and was often with her, had to have an operation removing part of her jawbone. Next her French cook Josephine decided to return to France to spend her old age. Cather wrote Akins that this departure would destroy her life, but Josephine was a fine creature and deserved to get back to her native village in the Pyrenees. The most distressing event of all the spring was the arrival at the end of March of a very sick Isabelle Hambourg. She had come to consult American doctors and in mid-April was taken to the Lennox Hill Hospital. The kidney stones that were found responded to treatment, but the doctors also discovered that she was suffering from an incurable kidney ailment. Cather was plunged into despair over this dark, discouraging turn of events.

In the meantime Jan Hambourg was off on a concert tour to make some money, even though he had not played professionally for many years. The Depression had savaged Isabelle's inherited wealth, and the Hambourgs were hard up. The care of her beloved friend was left in Cather's hands. She devoted all of her time to Isabelle during the spring and early summer. She went to the hospital every day, and in June when Jan returned to New York, she accompanied them to Chicago. Jan had committed himself to giving master classes at the Bush Music School, and Cather made the trip because Isabelle couldn't stay alone in the hotel while her husband was teaching. In July Cather went back to New York and made plans to sail for Europe. The Hambourgs would follow her, and she would rejoin them in Paris after visiting Italy.

She was tired physically and drained emotionally when she boarded the *Rex* for Italy. She wrote Carrie Sherwood that she hoped a couple of months abroad would make a new creature out of her. She was pretty limp at the moment and wanted to be alone among the lakes of northern Italy. Solitude, she thought, was the best way to recover one's soul after having lost it for a while. After a few days at sea she wrote that she was beginning to feel like herself again. For the first day out she had stayed in bed twenty-four hours and had eaten her meals in her stateroom, the only time in all her Atlantic crossings she ever had done that. By the time the ship reached Gibraltar, however, she was eagerly anticipating her return to Italy for the first time since 1908. But instead of going to the Italian lakes, she settled down in Cortina in the Dolomites and rested there for several weeks before going down to Venice, which she found to be the fairest of the cities of men. Although she stayed about three weeks, there is no record of what she did. Apparently she did not feel much like writing letters, and most of her correspondents had to be content with postcards.

By the end of September she was in Paris for a six week visit with the Hambourgs. This was both a sad and a happy time. Isabelle was well enough to go out for drives several times a week, and each time they stopped for tea in some attractive place. But Isabelle's condition, Cather wrote sorrowfully, would never improve, and when Cather left Paris in November, she must have known that she would never see her beloved friend again. The return passage was rough, but there was nothing Cather liked better than stormy weather at sea, and she arrived back in New York refreshed and ready to find out how the critics were treating *Lucy Gayheart*, which had come out in book form on August first.

Readers of Cather's new novel found on the surface a rather conventional love story with a tragic ending, though the treatment of the material is anything but conventional. The story opens in the small prairie town of Haverford, which is Red Cloud once more, despite its location on the Platte River instead of the Republican. An anonymous narrator, speaking retrospectively, recalls the image of Lucy, "a slight figure always in motion; dancing or skating, or walking swiftly with intense direction, like a bird flying home." There was also "something direct and unhesitating and joyous" in her movements, and her eyes "flashed with gold sparks like that Colorado stone we call the tiger-eye," a description that reminds one of Marie Tovesky in *O Pioneers!* It was Lucy's gaiety and grace that the people of Haverford loved, and life in her seemed to lie very near the surface. She is another of Cather's many orphaned characters and lives with her German father, an easygoing watchmaker by profession and an amateur musician by avocation, and her sister Pauline, a hardworking, practical housekeeper, the direct opposite of Lucy.

After the opening chapter, the story flashes back to 1901, Lucy's third winter after going to Chicago to study music. She is home for the Christmas holidays, and we see her skating on the river with other Haverford youth. Harry Gordon, the handsome, athletic young banker, who is strongly attracted to the vivacious Lucy, joins the group and skates off arm in arm with Lucy. Cather, who loved to skate herself, evokes memorably this scene: "The sun was dropping low in the south, and all the flat snow-covered country, as far as the eye could see, was beginning to glow with a rose-coloured light, which presently would deepen to orange and flame. The black tangle of willows on the island made a thicket like a thorn hedge, and the knotty, twisted, slow-growing scrub-oaks with flat tops took on a bronze glimmer in that intense oblique light which seemed to be setting them on fire." After Harry and Lucy sit down to rest, the sun as it drops to the horizon sends quivering fans of red and gold over the wide country. "For a moment Lucy and Harry Gordon were sitting in a stream of blinding light; it burned on their skates and on the flask and the metal cup. Their faces became so brilliant that they looked at each other and laughed. In an instant the light was gone; the frozen stream and the snow-masked prairie land became violet, under the blue-green sky. Wherever one looked there was nothing but flat country and low hills, all violet and grey." This image of the light going out foreshadows the action of the story.

After the memorable skating scene the story moves to Chicago, where Lucy returns to her room over a German bakery and her piano lessons from Paul Auerbach. The narrative flashes back to the previous October when her teacher had persuaded her to go hear his old friend, the famous baritone Clement Sebastian, who was in Chicago that winter giving recitals. She did so and had been overwhelmed by the experience. When he sang an old setting of Byron's poem "When We Two Parted," Lucy went home "tired and frightened, with a feeling that some protecting barrier was gone," and as she sat in her room, she whispered over and over the words of the song. The song prefigures coming events, for Lucy soon gets a job accompanying Sebastian while his regular accompanist rests up for an operation, falls in love with the singer, and thereby seals her fate.

Sebastian, who is nearly fifty and world-weary, is charmed by Lucy's youth and vitality. He is another of Cather's unhappily married husbands. His wife prefers to remain in Europe while he fulfills his concert engagements in the United States. He is much preoccupied with thoughts of aging and death and regrets the loss of youth. When Lucy reads in the paper that one of Sebastian's old friends, a French singer, has died in Chicago, she slips into the church to attend the funeral service. As the pallbearers carry the coffin up the aisle, Lucy watches Sebastian: "Sebastian's eyes never left it; turning his head slowly, he followed it with a look that struck a chill to Lucy's heart. It was a terrible look; anguish and despair, and something like entreaty." In Lucy Sebastian finds renewal and hope and clings to her as if he were trying to recapture his lost youth. "Nothing had ever made Sebastian admit to himself that his youth was forever and irrevocably gone." His view of life, however, is valetudinarian, and when Lucy admires an opulent display of flowers in Sebastian's apartment, he picks up the vase and says: "Yes, they're nice, aren't they? Very suggestive: youth, love, hope—all the things that pass."

Later Sebastian tells Lucy that he loves her, that she has made a great difference in his life. "When you knocked, it was like springtime coming in at the door. I went to work with more spirit because things were new and wonderful to you." Lucy is deliriously happy at this point, but almost immediately, in comes James Mockford, the regular accompanist and Sebastian's longtime associate. He is Lucy's rival for Sebastian's affections, and he enters the room like the mocking figure his name suggests. He appears at various intervals in this role, and in the end wins the duel with Lucy for Sebastian. But there is still a long way to go before the denouement.

Harry Gordon comes to Chicago in the spring to replenish his wardrobe and to spend a week with Lucy going to the opera. He has decided to marry for love, though he doesn't really approve of Lucy's lifestyle, and at the end of his visit asks Lucy if it isn't time for her to stop playing around at being a musician and come back to Haverford with him. Lucy, of course, is infatuated with Sebastian and when Harry offers her all the things any Haverford girl ought to want, a fine house, plenty of money, social position, she feels trapped. She tells him she is in love with another man, and when Harry wants to know how far her affair has gone, she says: "All the way!" He interprets this sexually, gets up abruptly from the restaurant table where they are dining and leaves her.

Sebastian and Mockford then go to Europe for the summer, but before he leaves, Sebastian persuades Lucy to use his apartment while he is gone. She doesn't want to live there but agrees to do her practicing on his piano. She then passes a quiet summer playing and dreaming in her lover's cool, spacious quarters. Professor Auerbach tells her she ought to go back to her home town, that in the musical world there are many disappointments: "A nice house and garden in a little town, with money enough not to worry, a family—that's the best life." Lucy replies that family life in a little town is pretty deadly: "It's being planted in the earth, like one of your carrots there. I'd rather be pulled up and thrown away." She asks if there isn't some other way of living. "Not for a girl like you, Lucy; you are too kind." Lucy's tragedy is that she has the desire but not the will or talent for an artistic career. She is made for love.

Lucy's hopes are shattered when a cable comes from Italy reporting that Sebastian and Mockford have been drowned when their boat capsized during a storm on Lake Como. Mockford, who could not swim, dragged Sebastian down, just as the anonymous workman caused the death of Bartley Alexander in Cather's first novel. With her world in collapse Lucy returns to Haverford and for several months lives a life of quiet desperation. Harry Gordon in the meantime has married and hardened his heart toward Lucy. She desperately wants to be friends with him again, but her efforts to pierce his armor are of no avail. After several months of languishing, however, Lucy comes to the realization that life must go on. Old Mrs. Ramsay, who observes the village life from her sitting room, tells Lucy: "Life is short; gather roses while you may. . . . Nothing really matters but living. Get all you can out of it." On Christmas Eve something flashes into Lucy's mind: "What if—what if Life itself were the sweetheart? It was like a love waiting for her in distant cities—across the sea; drawing her, enticing her, weaving a spell over her." She decides to go back to Chicago and resume her study and teaching.

After the desire to live returns, she walks out towards the river to go skating once more before leaving Haverford. It's a long walk, however, and the day is bitterly cold, almost too cold for skating. She decides to call off the outing and beg a ride back to town from the first person who comes along. This person happens to be Harry Gordon, who passes her in his sleigh. She stops him, asks for a lift, and he refuses. Lucy then goes on to skate, doesn't know that the river has changed course since she was last home, skates out into the main channel where the ice is thin, breaks through, and is drowned. "When Harry Gordon and his singing sleighbells came over the hills from Harlem that night, he overtook a train of lanterns and wagons crawling along the frozen land. In one of those wagons they were taking Lucy Gayheart home."

The novel ends with an epilogue (Book III) that takes place twenty-five years later. Harry Gordon has had to live with the memory of that day when he "refused Lucy Gayheart a courtesy he wouldn't have refused the most worthless old loafer in town." His marriage already had turned out badly when Lucy returned to Haverford, and he had wanted to make contact with Lucy, but his pride had prevented him. He finds a lifetime sentence in living with his remorse. After Pauline and old Jacob Gayheart die, Harry buys their old home and turns it over to his retired cashier. In the final scene he shows the cashier three footprints in the sidewalk outside the house. When Lucy was thirteen, Harry had come down the street on his bicycle and had seen her dart across the wet cement of the newly laid sidewalk. "After all these years the three footprints were still there in the sidewalk; the straight, slender foot of a girl of thirteen, delicately and clearly stamped in the grey-white composition." The wheel has come full circle; Lucy in death, as in life, is in motion.

This is an extremely interesting novel without being a superior piece of fiction. Cather wrote Carrie Sherwood that it wasn't one of her best and told her first biographer, E. K. Brown, that she didn't think much of *Lucy Gayheart*. But she also reported, with obvious satisfaction, that Myra Hess, the Hambourgs, and other musicians disagreed with her on the quality of the book. She did think she had got the ending right; yet to many readers Harry Gordon's bittersweet memories in the epilogue come as a somewhat saccharine anticlimax. Cather's impatience with her heroine while she was writing the novel is pretty well concealed, but Lucy Gayheart was not a character Cather loved, as she did Ántonia or Marian Forrester, and Lucy suffers from this lack of sympathy. Cather also had no patience with failures, especially sentimental artistic failures. Twenty years earlier she would have heaped contempt on an artist manqué like Lucy, but in 1935, mellowed by age, she felt compassion for the small-town girl caught in a love affair that she was emotionally not equipped to handle. She told Elizabeth Vermorcken that she was trying to show youth's tendency to hero-worship, which somehow "seems a little ridiculous, . . . though it is a natural feeling in all ardent young people." The novel moves along swiftly, as Lucy herself moved through life and was intended, as Cather explained to Akins, to be read at a gallop. It has enough emotional power to move most readers and perhaps it has been unduly neglected by the critics.

David Daiches is fairly representative of the critics who are disappointed in the novel when they come to it after reading Cather's great works of the twenties: "*Lucy Gayheart* is certainly the work of an accomplished and experienced writer, and we read it with interest and pleasure—but not with real conviction, and not with the excitement that a novel by Willa Cather in the fullness of her powers might be expected to produce." The strength that one finds in Cather's best work, such as *Death Comes for the Archbishop*, is missing here. Cather's physical powers were diminishing, and one has to conclude that the creative fires were burning lower. Individual scenes are memorable: the skating party, the funeral of Sebastian's friend, the breakup with Harry, Lucy's appeal to Pauline not to cut down the old orchard (reminiscent of *The Cherry Orchard*), Lucy's struggle to escape drowning, her final trip to Haverford in a farmer's wagon. There also are a good many well-drawn minor characters: Jacob Gayheart; Pauline; old Mrs. Ramsay; Giuseppe, Sebastian's valet; the sinister homosexual, Mockford; the vulgar little flirt, Fairy Blair; the bank cashier, Milton Chase.

The difference in energy level between this novel and Cather's earlier work may be seen in comparing *Lucy Gayheart* with *The Song of the Lark*, which is partly made out of similar materials. Cather's creation of her own young self striking out for Chicago and a musical career is powerfully evoked, and the scenes in Chicago (when Thea's piano teacher discovers she has a voice or when she sings for the Nathanmeyers, for example) strike sparks. In contrast, Lucy's experiences in her musical education in Chicago seem like a reworking of old material with far less emotional charge. One has to note in fairness, of course, that Cather wasn't creating a genuine artist in Lucy, only a country girl with a moderate talent—and youthful charm—and the focus of the story is entirely different.

Despite the fact that there are three deaths by drowning and the only surviving major character lives on consumed by remorse, Cather classified her novel as a romance. A more precise designation, however, might be Gothic romance, for the story contains the classic elements of the Gothic tale as it has appeared in literature from *The Castle of Otranto* to the present. One needs to remember that Poe was one of the formative influences on Cather, that she tried her hand at Gothic tales early in her career, and that Gothic elements abound in her novels. The most interesting reading of *Lucy Gayheart* that has yet appeared is Susan Rosowski's discussion of Cather's novel as a Gothic romance. The soul-weary Sebastian is a descendant of the Gothic Byronic hero, "a lonely figure beneath whose sophisticated manner lies a secret renunciation of life." He turns to Lucy, feeds on her, in an effort to regain his lost youth and vitality. It's a sinister relationship, a trap into which the innocent Lucy walks unsuspectingly, a trap which springs when Lucy attends Sebastian's recital and literally loses consciousness as she listens to him singing. From this point on, Rosowski writes: "Cather's story resembles nothing so much as Bram Stoker's 1897 tale of dark possession and threatening sexuality, *Dracula*." Even the characters in both novels are named Lucy.

In Stoker's *Dracula*, however, Lucy is both victim and villain, for after she is violated by the count, she then preys on other men. "In her Stoker suggests awakened female sexuality as monstrous, all the more terrifying because hidden beneath an appearance of virginal innocence." *Dracula* is a story of terrifying female sexuality told from a male point of view; *Lucy Gayheart* retells Stoker's story from a woman's perspective. Cather's Lucy is victim alone. "As Sebastian embraces Lucy Gayheart, he grows stronger, fresher, younger, while she becomes increasingly passive and dependent." The result for Lucy is loss of self, as her lover draws the life from her. Rosowski concludes: "In *Lucy Gayheart* Cather takes her place in the long line of woman writers who have explored the terrors that accompany female sexuality." As Cather approached the last decade of her life, she became more and more preoccupied with the irreconcilable dualities of life and had to acknowledge "the triumph of paradox and ambiguity—the impossibility of ultimate synthesis."

In another provocative reading of *Lucy Gayheart*, David Stouck finds the novel Cather's most complex and philosophical work, containing some of the author's most profound reflections on art and human relationships— "above all, on the human condition as defined by mortality." Through Sebastian, her aging singer, Cather reflected on the meaning of life and death. If Sebastian seems the most fully realized character in the novel, as he does to many readers, it is the result of Cather's identification with him. His thoughts as an aging artist must in a sense have been her thoughts. His singing of Schubert's "Der Doppelgänger" "is filled with the tragic conviction that all human effort is doomed to oblivion, that all desire must eventually return in death to a nonhuman void. The vision underlying Sebastian's song might popularly be called nihilism or perhaps existentialism." When he sings "When We Two Parted," he laments the fragility and inevitable dissolution of human relationships. Later he sings Schubert's *Die Winterreise*, which "presents a rejected lover psychically resurrected in winter" only to feel again his loss. Sebastian is, as Cather was, a human being coming to grips with the fact that one must someday die. To heighten the grimness of this vision, which Stouck calls a dance of death, Cather created the ubiquitous accompanist Mockford, who is a sort of personification of Death, a young man with the ghostly pallor of death and a limp to emphasize human mortality.

Even though Cather knew *Lucy Gayheart* was not one of her best novels, she was as much concerned as ever with the book's presentation to the public. When Knopf sent her a sample of the type he proposed to use for the novel, she telegraphed him from Grand Manan that she didn't like it. It was too large and monotonous for a romantic story, she said. She wanted the same type they had used for *A Lost Lady*. The Knopfs, as usual, gave her what she wanted and sent a wire immediately: "Book will be set exactly as you want it." How good they were to consider her preferences, Cather replied appreciatively, and added that she had drunk her tea that afternoon with a light heart. The Knopfs and Cather by this time had become intimate friends, and Cather really felt that they were more interested in her welfare than in making money on her. Be that as it may, they took great pains to keep her happy, which was, of course, good business. Her usual correspondent with the Knopfs was Blanche, who always answered Cather's letters promptly, and while her epistles were excessively effusive, there was genuine affection behind them.

The appearance of a new novel by Cather was again an important publishing event, especially since it was her first long fiction in four years. The public bought the book in large numbers, despite the appalling business conditions in the depths of the Depression. The American News Company ordered ten thousand copies before publication, an unusual order, and the book headed the best-seller list for eight weeks. Knopf printed fifty-two thousand, five hundred copies before publication day and another ten thousand during the month the book was issued. But the novel reached only half the sales of *Shadows on the Rock* in its first five months. Cather's royalties from the book sales were about seventeen thousand dollars in the first year, which was a large amount of money in 1935, when it cost only a nickel to ride the subway and a good restaurant meal could be bought for fifty cents.

The reviewers for the most part praised *Lucy Gayheart*. About two out of three wrote very positive appraisals, but there were also a few fence straddlers. Cather had no reason to be disappointed in the notices, though she wouldn't have been pleased even if all the reviews had been affirmative: some would have been favorable for the wrong reasons. She was by 1935 America's foremost woman novelist, as Joseph Henry Jackson noted in his column in the *San Francisco Chronicle*. Nebraska reviewers again took pride in the local girl who had made good and were especially pleased that she had placed most of the story in their state. This compensated for her failure to come back to Nebraska any more. Over and over the reviewers commented on Cather's perfection of style with such observations as: "She is incapable of writing a false or blundering sentence," or "She knows how to use words better than nine out of ten novelists writing today."

The majority of reviewers greeted *Lucy Gayheart* with more enthusiasm than the later academic critics have mustered. Fanny Butcher in the *Chicago Tribune*, who always led the cheers in the Midwest, found the story of Lucy and Sebastian one of the few real idylls in modern literature and the novel's form boldly experimental. Cather had told her when she was in Chicago with the Hambourgs in June that "I see no reason why one cannot write a novel as a composer writes a symphony," and that, Butcher thought, was the form the novel took. In its symphony-like structure Book I recounted Lucy's relationship with Sebastian, Book II detailed Lucy's life back in Haverford, and Book III was the coda depicting Harry Gordon's life sentence of regret. Paul Jordan-Smith in the *Los Angeles Times* was delighted with the novel and did not expect any of Cather's growing circle of fans to find evidence in it of waning powers. J. Donald Adams told *New York Times Book Review* readers that *Lucy Gayheart* had not the scope of major fiction, "but within the confines she has set for it her story achieves a rounded quality, a substance, that only disciplined art could give."

With this novel there began to creep into Cather's reviews a certain amount of polemic. Some critics took her severely to task for not concerning herself in her fiction with social and economic issues, while others rejoiced just as loudly that she did not write fictional tracts for the times. Howard Mumford Jones in the *Saturday Review of Literature* wrote that "the American novel is in danger of becoming a prose pamphlet. . . . Seduced by the plausible simplicities of what they regard as Marxian doctrine, a younger group is striving to transform the novel into a sociological treatise with fictional attachments." Jones was grateful that Cather "has held to the simple and perdurable principle that the primary business of the novelist is to create a work of art, which arising out of human experience, returns through the long arc of the writer's shaping power, to enrich human experience. *Lucy Gayheart* is such a book." On the other hand, one of the most negative reviewers, Robert Cantwell in the *New Republic*, placed Cather in a group of once-acclaimed writers whose latest novels "have revealed their inability to deal with the emotional and practical problems of the contemporary world in even the most elementary form." He judged *Lucy Gayheart* "simply a maudlin book, peopled with stock characters who move through stock situations and who die, unexpectedly and accidentally, to bring the story to a ramshackle conclusion." He then went on to cudgel critics like Jones for trying to "bolster up such fatigued writers" as Cather, calling their efforts a "debauching of critical standards."

CHAPTER 22

Sapphira and the Slave Girl

The winter of 1935–36 passed with no untoward incident as Cather rested on her oars. There was more music, more Menuhins, more seclusion. The Knopfs invited her to their annual party for the Koussevitskys when the Boston Symphony came to New York, and she continued her walks around the reservoir in Central Park. She finally sat for photographs by Carl Van Vechten, who had been importuning her for years. She had put him off so many times that she finally felt ashamed to meet him, and when she saw him at the Knopfs' Christmas party, she agreed to a date. She liked Van Vechten and they had a lot in common, but she hated to have her picture taken. She began visiting the private Society Library, which she had belonged to for years, when it moved uptown to East Seventy-ninth Street in 1936. She would go to the library, look over the stacks, and sigh. "It's easy enough to see what you don't want to read," she told Marion King, the assistant librarian. Once when King gave her *Miss Hench*, a novel by Henry Sydnor Harrison, and later asked if she liked it, she replied: "I did indeed. I bought that story for *McClure's*." The high spot of the winter was the arrival of her young English friend Stephen Tennant for a visit to the United States.

Cather got a great deal of satisfaction out of Tennant's company. She had been corresponding with him for a decade, and according to Lewis, "kept all his letters—the only ones she kept like this, except Miss Jewett's." She had long talks with him in her Park Avenue living room about literature, music, art, found him congenial, knowledgable, charming, and to the manor born. He was a handsome fellow of great talent, she wrote Greenslet, but his health was frail. She sent him to New Hampshire to spend the winter at the Shattuck Inn in Jaffrey where he gained thirty pounds and had, she reported, a thrilling time. In March she went up to Jaffrey herself, the only time she ever was there in the spring.

Tennant, however, caused her some embarrassment two years later when he sent her a book of his drawings and asked her to find an American publisher for them. She wrote Greenslet that she had promised to do this, but when she saw the drawings were ribald she knew no American publisher would touch them. She asked Greenslet to write her a letter she could send Tennant explaining why he couldn't publish the drawings. She found it hard to explain why Americans were indecent in some things and drew the line at others. She thought that Americans wanted Hemingway and the four-letter words but without any perfume. Alfred Knopf already had obliged her by writing a letter to forward to Tennant, and she hoped for similar help from Houghton Mifflin.

During this period when she was lying fallow, Cather took time to argue against the teaching of contemporary literature in the schools. When Chilson Leonard, an English teacher at Phillips Exeter Academy, wanted to know where she got her material for *My Ántonia*, she replied patiently and rather uncharacteristically, then went on to say what really was on her mind. The present fashion of assigning contemporary writers in English courses, she thought, was very unfortunate. A thorough knowledge of the great English authors and, when possible, the great Latin writers, was necessary to the formation of a discriminating literary taste. That taste could not be developed by reading contemporary writers. She thought the present era was a particularly low point in English writing. Later she expanded on this theme when she wrote Pat Knopf's English professor, Burgess Johnson, at Union College. The classics she wanted undergraduates to read were Shakespeare, Milton, Fielding, Austen, Thackeray, George Eliot, Meredith, and Hardy. She didn't really think that works like *Henry Esmond* or *Macbeth* could be taught (in the sense that Latin can be taught), but youngsters should be exposed to them. If the germ took hold, it would give students a great deal of pleasure in later life. Those who did not catch the infection wouldn't be harmed. She concluded by saying that no book should be called a classic until it was one hundred years old.

By spring when Cather was ready to work again, she began revising her novels and stories for a collected edition of her works to be published by Houghton Mifflin, a task that occupied her off and on for the better part of the next two years. In her letters to friends during this period she often complained about the task that had been put upon her, and said that Knopf had told her she had to do it. But the first mention of the project comes in a letter Cather wrote Ferris Greenslet in March 1936, asking if Houghton Mifflin was still interested in bringing out her complete works. The answer was a prompt "yes," and she set about getting her books ready for the edition. In none of her letters to Greenslet in the ensuing months is there any hint of impatience or annoyance over the enterprise, and when the books came from the press she wrote her publisher to express her pleasure.

Lewis recalled that as early as 1932 Maxwell Perkins of Scribner's had written to Knopf proposing that his firm publish a complete limited edition of Cather's works. "Certainly," Perkins wrote, "if there is any distinction in this form of publication, she of all Americans is entitled to it." Alfred Knopf did not publish sets like this and hence was not in a position to give Cather such an edition. Houghton Mifflin, however, refused to release the rights to Cather's first four novels and wanted to bring out the collected works themselves. Knopf then negotiated with the Boston firm to do the work. Houghton Mifflin engaged Bruce Rogers to design the books and took great pains to issue a handsome edition, which began appearing at the end of 1937. Cather went over her works very carefully, made many substantive changes, though she did not rewrite her early works as Henry James did for the New York Edition of his novels and stories. Cather's greatest changes, the cuts in *The Song of the Lark* and the shortened introduction to *My Ántonia* already had been made for earlier editions. The *Autograph Edition* appeared in twelve elegant volumes, and when *Sapphira and the Slave Girl* came out in 1940, a thirteenth volume was added. Also in that year, a cheaper *Library Edition* was printed from the same plates.

When the *Autograph Edition* was about to appear, Cather sent a prospectus to Carrie Sherwood to explain what she had been up to lately. She said she hated revising her books but Rogers had been so interested in the work that she felt she couldn't seem indifferent, and, of course, such an edition was considered a great compliment by the general publishing world. She wasn't letting Houghton Mifflin send announcements to her friends, however, as she thought the price of the set, one hundred and twenty-four dollars, a ridiculous figure. But as merchandise, she said, the volumes were worth the cost, because the rag paper had been imported from England and the beautiful typography and bindings ran into a great deal of money. She didn't want any of her friends to think she was a book agent.

While she was tooling up for the edition of her collected works, she was invited by the editor of the conservative *Commonweal* to comment on a hot contemporary topic: art as an escape. This gave her a chance to answer the hostile critics who had begun assigning her works to oblivion because she never had leaped on the barricades to fight for the reformation of society. As the thirties went on, the left and the right battled furiously in the special interest journals. Bright young critics in the *Nation*, the *New Republic*, the *New Masses*, and the *Partisan Review*, some of them Marxists, found in Cather a convenient target. They also attacked Thornton Wilder, Elizabeth Maddox Roberts, Ellen Glasgow, and others; but Cather's position as perhaps the preeminent novelist by 1931 made her the largest target on the horizon.

One of her most formidable enemies was Granville Hicks, whose 1933 essay, "The Case Against Willa Cather," in the *English Journal*, a publication Cather respected, rankled deeply. He wrote that Cather had "fallen into supine romanticism because of a refusal to examine life." He thought it easy "to understand why many writers turn from our industrial civilization. On the one hand, they cannot accept the cruelty and rapacity that are so integral a part of it and its inevitable destruction of institutions and ways of life they cherish. On the other hand, they are so much bound up in it that they cannot throw themselves, as the revolutionary writers have done, into the movement to destroy and rebuild it. Flight is the only alternative. But flight is and always has been destructive of the artistic virtues, which are rooted in integrity."

To accuse Cather of lacking integrity makes these polemics of the thirties seem, half a century later, as quaint as fossils chipped from Pleistocene rock; but in those years of controversy they were taken very seriously by many young intellectuals. The right also had its vociferous spokesmen, but it must be said that for the vast bulk of novel readers the waves of argument dashed against them with little effect. The *Atlantic Monthly* and the *Saturday Review of Literature* stayed out of the fray, and newspaper reviewers of Cather's novels remained enthusiastic about her work and didn't care that she was not writing fictional tracts for the times. It is a testimony to the fury of the debate that Cather herself was drawn into it, contrary to all her instincts, but her letter to the *Commonweal*, which grew into a substantial essay, was her only entry into the lists.

"What has art ever been but escape?" Cather began. "To be sure, this definition is for the moment used in a derogatory sense, implying an evasion of duty. . . . When the world is in a bad way, we are told, it is the business of the composer and the poet to devote himself to propaganda and fan the flames of indignation." But the world has a habit of being in a bad way from time to time and art has never contributed anything to help matters—except escape. Then she went back to the origins of art. Primitive man, she argued, did not create art as a means of "increasing the game supply or promoting tribal security." His impulse came from "an unaccountable predilection of the one unaccountable thing in man"—the desire to create. The cry of the thirties, she went on, is the same cry which went up during the French Revolution, but she didn't think the artists and poets of that day had accomplished very much with their brushes and pens.

"Citizen Shelley stepped into line and drove his pen—but he was not very useful to the reforms which fired his imagination. He was 'useful,' if you like that word, only as all true poets are, because they refresh and recharge the spirit of those who can read their language." Nor did she think that if Tolstoy and Goethe, Descartes and Newton were brought together and induced to work with a will that their efforts would "materially help Mayor La Guardia to better living conditions in New York City." She concluded her long letter to the editor by saying: "The condition every art requires is, not so much freedom from restriction, as freedom from adulteration and from the intrusion of foreign matter." In the great age of Gothic architecture, the sculptors and stonecutters left their art on the façades of cathedrals and churches all over Europe. "How many clumsy experiments in government, futile revolutions and reforms those buildings have looked down upon without losing a shadow of their dignity and power. . . . Economics and art are strangers."

Five years later, after the polemics of the thirties had died down and the world had been plunged into war once more, Cather reflected further on the relationship between art and social action. In reply to a thoughtful letter from an unknown correspondent, she said she never tried to write propaganda, that is, rules for life or theories about the betterment of human society. She by no means despised that kind of writing. At its best it could be noble and useful, but she thought it lost its strength disguised as fiction. She disputed her correspondent, who apparently had cited Dickens (never one of her favorites) as a social propagandist. Important reforms resulted from his novels, she admitted, but she didn't think he wrote in the reformer's spirit. He wrote because his heart was touched or his indignation aroused by certain abuses. In other words, he wrote about life itself, as it moved him. She concluded by saying that too many books on social betterment were written out of ill feeling or class hatred or by young writers who were vain and conceited and thought they knew a lot more about the history of the world than they did. These new writers thought they could manage the age-old tragedies of life very neatly.

With the advent of summer Cather turned down another honorary degree, this time from Brown, and made her usual trek to Grand Manan Island. She took along her books to revise at her summer cottage and by fall had three of them ready to send to Greenslet. She also was working on a collection of her essays that Knopf would bring out in November. Her nieces from Wyoming visited her, and she greatly enjoyed their company and their excitement. While she was enjoying the bracing climate of New Brunswick, however, farms in the Midwest were burning up during the terrible years of drought that accompanied the Great Depression. So many sad and bitter things were happening to her old farm friends in Nebraska, she wrote Akins. She could send them canned fruit and vegetables and checks, but she couldn't bring their dead trees and ruined pastures back to life. Five years of drought and frightful heat had destroyed the farms and the health of the people she loved. Farm women she had known all her life could raise no garden vegetables, and some had had to kill their chickens because they could not even buy feed for them. Their husbands could raise no grain or animals. It seemed wicked to be at Grand Manan on a leafy, flowery island with the fireplace going and wearing sweaters. She hadn't been very well that summer, but she thought it was probably the worry about her old friends that had taken all the energy out of her. When Mabel Luhan asked her at Christmas to donate to a hospital, she said all her spare cash was going to Nebraska where dozens of old friends were absolutely on the edge of want. She already had sent off two great boxes of blankets and warm clothing and was cutting out Christmas gifts for everyone except those destitute farm people.

At the end of the summer Cather made her usual stopover at the Shattuck Inn in Jaffrey and continued to work on the revision of her books. She was sleeping well, the air was bracing, and she was ashamed of her appetite. On the evening of October 5 she wrote her longtime companion and first-mate Edith Lewis, who had gone directly from New Brunswick back to New York, the only letter that has survived between the two. She described minute by minute the unparalleled sight of Jupiter and Venus, almost in conjunction, shining in the golden rosy western sky midway between the horizon and the zenith. For an hour she watched the superb splendor of the sky deepening in color every minute in the still daylight evening, guiltless of other stars. The moon was not yet up, and the sun had already dropped behind the mountain. She gazed from her window in ecstasy as the silvery planet slipped down the sky following the sun, while Jupiter hung alone in the night sky. The spectacle, she said, reminded her of Dante's eternal wheels. She ended this rhetorical flourish to her "darling Edith" with the practical news that everything Edith had packed for her had carried wonderfully well and without a wrinkle. By early November, Cather was back in New York and on hand for the publication of her essay collection, *Not Under Forty*.

All of the pieces in this collection had appeared previously between 1922 and the previous spring. The volume led off with "A Chance Meeting," the fortuitous encounter with Flaubert's niece at Aix-les-Bains; followed with "The Novel Démeublé"; "148 Charles Street," the reminiscence of Mrs. Fields; "Miss Jewett," which she had used to introduce Sarah Orne Jewett's stories; the piece on Katherine Mansfield, written for *The Borzoi* in 1925; and "*Joseph and His Brothers,*" an appreciation of Thomas Mann's work, which she had published in the *Saturday Review of Literature* only the previous June. Cather had not been an admirer of Mann until he wrote *The Tales of Jacob* (1934) and *The Young Joseph* (1935), the first parts of what became a tetralogy written during Mann's exile from Nazi Germany. She had not liked *The Magic Mountain*, but his biblical fiction thrilled her. She read the first two volumes of this work three times, and after the third reading she decided to write an essay about him. Her friend Henry Canby, editor of the *Saturday Review*, was delighted to print it.

Fanny Butcher remembered that in *Joseph and His Brothers* Cather "found a new book that carried her into a new world . . . the oldest world of all." As a writer of historical fiction herself, Cather was much interested in Mann's imaginative recreation of Biblical times. There were two ways to "approach a theme set in the distant past," she explained: the way Flaubert did it in *Salammbô*, in which he stood in the present and looked back, or as Mann did it. He "gets behind the epoch of his story and looks forward." She thought the prologue, which prepares the reader for the story to come, was a "marvel of imaginative power." Then the tale opens, bringing to life characters and stories that most adult readers have known from childhood. "We emerge from Mann's Prologue to find ourselves not only in a familiar land, but among people we have always known. . . . The Book of Genesis lies like a faded tapestry deep in the consciousness of almost every individual who is more than forty years of age." Despite the title, *Joseph and His Brothers*, Cather thought "the creation of Jacob, in the flesh and in the spirit, is the great achievement of his work," but the interplay between Joseph and his father impressed her almost as strongly. In addition, she concluded, the "story of Joseph and his brothers is not only forever repeated in literature, it forever repeats itself in life. The natural antagonism between the sane and commonplace, and the exceptional and inventive, is never so bitter as when it occurs in a family." She eagerly awaited the next volume of the series, but she was glad she knew how it would turn out. "This is one of the advantages of making a new story out of an old one. . . . The course of destiny is already known." "What we most love," she added, "is not bizarre invention, but to have the old story brought home to us closer than ever before. . . . Shakespeare knew this fact very well, and the Greek dramatists long before him."

Reviewers of *Not Under Forty* in general found the essays interesting and significant. Written with Cather's usual charm and polish, they reflected a remarkable sensibility and good judgment. As she seldom wrote criticism, it was a significant contribution to American letters to have these fugitive pieces gathered into a single volume. Most of the notices rejected and protested her prefatory statement that the essays were written for people over forty: "It is for the backward, and by one of their number, that these sketches were written." Canby thought the preface too pessimistic, that young readers would be greatly interested in this collection of criticism "which insists so much upon discipline, upon fineness of perception, upon the strength which comes from real knowledge." He added that it would be well "for any one to read this little book if only to see the importance of taste in criticism."

Cather led with her chin, however, in publishing that prefatory statement, and Alfred Knopf might have served her interests better if he had persuaded her to omit it. She also laid herself open to hostile criticism by reprinting the Jewett essay, which defended Jewett's fiction and also exposed her own literary credo to the rude gaze of Freudian, Marxist, and social-activist critics. She had misgivings about reviving that piece, and when she wrote Greenslet about using it, she had said it might be better not to call forth Miss Jewett's shade into the present world, which would be so objectionable to her. The language in which she was such an artist had almost ceased to exist. The brassy young Jews and Greeks from New York University, she wrote, had made the only language then heard in New York. But she went ahead and reprinted the essay, expanded it to more than twice its original length, and made it a profile of Jewett as well as a critical essay. She stated rather defensively in the new material that a taste for Jewett would always be limited to readers who had a sympathetic relation to the subject matter and a sensitive ear. It wasn't, however, so much Cather's analysis of the quality of Jewett's fiction as her gratuitous comments on contemporary readers that raised the hackles of her detractors. She added this to the original essay: "Imagine a young man, or woman, born in New York City, educated at a New York university, violently inoculated with Freud, hurried into journalism, knowing no more about New England country people (or country folk anywhere) than he has caught from motor trips or observed from summer hotels: what is there for him in *The Country of the Pointed Firs?*"

Louis Kronenberger in the *Nation* was representative of the unfriendly critics. Beginning with an attack on the prefatory note, especially Cather's statement that the world for her had broken in two about 1922, he detected throughout the book "smugness springing from uncertainty, of an odd feeling of guilt, of a deep feeling of regret for the past and a self-righteous loyalty in going to the past's defense." Then he blasted her recent fiction in which she had run "out on the present to hide in the past," and had rejected "even such portions of the past as had the poor judgment to be unsavory or ungovernable." Even in "The Novel Démeublé," in which he admitted she had said something important, he found her sniffing and pursing her lips "as though the fate of literature lay with her alone." In conclusion, Kronenberger lumped Cather with T. S. Eliot, who by the thirties had left the wasteland for the Anglican Church: "Each had mistaken a hothouse for a garden; each had forfeited much power, much understanding, in exchange for the consolation of a measured formal attitude toward life."

Reviews like this raised Cather's blood pressure, but she had enough good sense not to write angry letters to the editors. She wrote Akins the next year that she hoped her friend would not bring out a new play, as she was a Romantic and Romanticism was not in fashion. She couldn't get a fair hearing from the reviewers. Akins, she added, had grown in wisdom in every way except in the matter of self-protection. She played into the hands of the critics by writing to the papers to explain herself. Cather went on to say that she had her haters who went for her every chance they had, John Chamberlain, Lionel Trilling, and Kronenberger being three of them, among others. If she ever replied to them, she said, Knopf probably would want to hand her over to another publisher. She regretted that she had reprinted the Jewett essay, for it had shown her how unwise it was to make public one's articles of faith. They ought to be one's most protected secrets. Her comment on young men inoculated with Freud had been an ill-considered outburst, because she had been so incensed by recent articles by some of those horrid N.Y.U. graduates with foreign names and foreign manners who had been publishing articles on sex-starvation among New England writers. It was a silly performance on her part, she admitted, and she had learned that if she was consistently silent about herself, she had to be silent also when her friends were attacked. Friends reflect one's point of view, and to speak for them is in a manner to speak for oneself. She also learned that it would be prudent to drop the preface and change the title of her essay collection for her collected works. When volume twelve of the *Autograph Edition* came out, it contained *Obscure Destinies and Literary Encounters*. The introductory note had been scrubbed.

For a book of reprinted essays *Not Under Forty* sold very well, going through four printings totalling nearly fourteen thousand copies before the end of 1936. Cather, however, was not in a holiday mood the day before her sixty-third birthday when she wrote Mary Creighton. She had been in high spirits, she said, when she returned to New York from Grand Manan and New Hampshire, but getting out a new book always entailed a lot of useless work, floods of letters and telegrams, nervy requests, and demands to answer. It was all a waste of time, and she regretted that she had not been in Europe when the book came out, as she was at the time *Lucy Gayheart* had appeared. She also found it was taking more and more out of her fighting the constant battle to keep her works out of "omnibuses," off the radio, and off the stage. Usually Knopf acted as the buffer between her and the anthologists, Hollywood, and all manner of people she thought were bent on exploiting her. On one occasion when a man from the Frigidaire Corporation wanted to talk about her over the radio, she had Knopf tell him she "never would give him permission to use her name." Her desire for privacy amounted to almost an obsession. As this year ended, she was feeling out of sorts with life. She thought the world used to be a great deal happier for everyone, young and old, and she was glad her gentle father had not lived into the hard times of the thirties. This attitude, which came with the aging process, crept into her letters more and more frequently as she moved into her declining years.

During this winter of discontent Cather sustained a severe blow to her ego and morale. For the first time since she was an apprentice writer she had a story rejected. She didn't receive an impersonal printed rejection slip, such as unknown authors get from overworked editors, but she was rebuffed nonetheless. During the fall of 1936, presumably after she had sent off copy to Knopf for *Not Under Forty*, she had managed to write a long story, her first since "Old Mrs. Harris" in 1931. It was "The Old Beauty," a tale laid in Aix-les-Bains and perhaps suggested to her at the time she had visited the French spa in 1930. She liked the story, thought it successful, and sent it off to her old friend Gertrude Lane at the *Woman's Home Companion*. To her obvious surprise and dismay Lane didn't like the tale, thought it below her usual standard. Lewis's version of this incident: "Miss Lane said at once that she would publish the story, but that she could not feel the enthusiasm for it she felt for Miss Cather's other work. So Willa Cather asked her to return it. She put it aside for inclusion in a book of short stories, if she should publish one later. She herself thought highly of 'The Old Beauty.' She had found it interesting to write, and she felt that she had carried through her idea successfully." Cather, however, never published the story, and it seems more than likely that she accepted Lane's evaluation of it. In any event, the tale remained in manuscript among her papers until she died in 1947. It was Lewis and Knopf who brought it out in 1948 in *The Old Beauty and Others*, a volume containing this story and two others Cather wrote in her very last years.

The story Cather sent Lane takes place in 1922, the year the world broke in two. Most of it is seen through the eyes of Henry Seabury, a fifty-five-year-old American who has returned from a business career in China. He is visiting Aix-les-Bains when he encounters Mme de Coucy, the former Gabrielle Longstreet, whom he had known briefly in the 1890s. She had been a dazzling beauty in her day, the toast of London and New York, but now she is old and plain. When Seabury sees her, he hardly recognizes the old beauty. "Plain women, he reflected, when they grow old are—simply plain women. Often they improve. But a beautiful woman may become a ruin." Such is the case with this old beauty, whose physical ruin is symbolic of the world she once had inhabited. Gabrielle's history is sketched in through a series of flashbacks. She had been discovered on the Island of Martinique at the age of nineteen by the rich, young, yachting Lord Longstreet, who had married her and carried her off to London. She had overshown him so much that he eventually divorced her, but she had lived on with a brilliant circle of friends, mostly male, until World War I came along and destroyed everything. After a second marriage to a Frenchman, who was killed in action, and a serious illness, she turns up spending the summer in Aix with an aging ex-music hall comedienne, Cherry Beamish, who out of compassion for the old woman has become her companion.

In the course of the story Seabury spends his days with Gabrielle and Cherry. They talk over old times and travel about the country in a hired car. Gabrielle hates the present, lives with her memories, and travels with the pictures of her old friends, all of whom are dead. In the climactic episode they visit the famous old monastery, La Grande Chartreuse, and on the return trip have an accident caused by the reckless driving of two brash American women. Seabury and his two companions are badly shaken up, though not seriously hurt, but that night after returning to the hotel Gabrielle dies in her sleep.

The story, which is definitely below Cather's usual mark, had none of the old power of her best fiction to grapple the emotions. Compared with "Old Mrs. Harris" or "Neighbour Rosicky," for example, it pales greatly. Gabrielle Longstreet is a character no one can care much about. She is drawn with Cather's usual skill, but when she dies both the reader and the author are relieved. The point-of-view character Seabury also arouses no sympathy, for he is a lot like Gabrielle, a person who lives in the past and deplores the vanished world of his youth.

There is an ambivalence in Cather's attitude towards Gabrielle, which detracts from the effectiveness of the story. On the one hand, the character's distaste for everything in the postwar modern world reflects Cather's own feeling. She had deplored Prohibition, the Jazz Age, the flapper, the relaxation of moral standards, the deterioration of taste, the scramble for money; she didn't like cubism, couldn't take Gertrude Stein or Ezra Pound seriously, wouldn't go to see an O'Neill play, and probably could not have been dragged to hear Schönberg. Her anonymous third-person narrator describes the women who cause the accident as Gabrielle would have: "They were

Americans; bobbed, hatless, clad in dirty white knickers and sweaters. They addressed each other as 'Marge' and 'Jim.'" On the other hand, Gabrielle's blanket condemnation of everything new goes far beyond Cather's. She is depicted as a literal ruin, as much out of date as the archeological remains of a departed civilization. She also has a nasty mind. When she and Seabury, after dining at the Maison des Fleurs, remain to watch the young people dance, she finds the spectacle disgusting: "They look to me like lizards dancing—or reptiles coupling." The one sympathetic character in the story is Cherry Beamish, appropriately named, who is in her fifties but still young and bubbly in spirit. She, like Cather, has a flock of nephews and nieces whom she adores and who keep her young. She finds the postwar world absorbing and watches the pageant of youth with intense interest. She is a reincarnation of the vivacious, sensible Jimmy Broadwood in the early story "Flavia and Her Artists." It seems clear enough that Cather is more in sympathy with Cherry's lifestyle than with Gabrielle's.

About the time Cather was getting her story back from the *Woman's Home Companion*, she found herself unable to refrain from writing to an editor. The letter had nothing to do with her own work but followed an exchange between Edmund Wilson and Bernard De Voto, then editor of the *Saturday Review of Literature*. Wilson had asked De Voto what principles he followed in editing the magazine, what theory of the world, what metaphysics, what structure of abstraction. Cather was so pleased with his answer that she sent him a letter of thanks. She prefaced her comments with the admonition that her letter was not for publication; then she went on to say that after several weeks of thinking about his reply to Wilson, she wanted him to know how clearly he had stated what she believed. De Voto had written that he followed no theories or philosophy in editing the magazine. He profoundly disbelieved in such systems and had come to think that absolutes were a mirage. He opposed people who were out of touch with known facts and common experience, who preferred logical conclusions to the testimony of their senses. He was a pluralist, relativist, and empiricist. Wilson, he charged, was something of a Marxist. De Voto declared that he was primarily interested in human emotions and experiences that had only a secondary connection with social movements. The human tragedy did not seem to him an economic tragedy.

In her letter Cather elaborated on the idea that our lives are very little made up of economic conditions. They affect us on the outside, she said, but they certainly are not what life means to you or me or the taxi driver or the elevator operator. Theories of economic reform and social reconstruction, she thought, really seemed to interest nobody very much except the men who wrote about them, those who had made it a profession to be interested in them. Then she quoted Tolstoy, who decided after spending most of his career pondering how to make life better for men of both high and low estate that the European desire to organize society more efficiently was a mistake. He concluded that "the state of a man's mind has always been more important to him than the conditions of his life." Of course, she added, Tolstoy tried to be a Marxist and failed, but no one ever took the puzzle of human life more to heart or puzzled over it more agonizingly than he—not even the *New Republic*.

Nearly three years after sending *Lucy Gayheart* off to her publisher, Cather began work on her last novel, *Sapphira and the Slave Girl*. She started writing in the spring of 1937 and did not finish for three and a half years. Much to her annoyance, she had to stop writing from time to time to work on the collected edition. She again spent the summer at Grand Manan, invited her nieces to visit her a second time, and by fall when she returned to New York she was well into the new book. Being continually interrupted in order to fuss with the *Autograph Edition*, however, exasperated her. She wrote Akins in November that she was once more working on a new book, which was a great pleasure for her, but God and man seemed agreed that she shouldn't get ahead with it. She complained loudly that the collected edition was breaking into her time. Nothing disturbed her more than to have to work with Houghton Mifflin, and she had fallen into their net again. The entire project had given her a hell of a spring and summer, and now it was breaking into her winter as well. She didn't want anything but quiet and a pleasant place to write, but could she get it? And what was even more infuriating, the Goddam movies were after *My Ántonia*; she was living in terror that Houghton Mifflin would sell her out. In her more innocent days she had let the dramatic rights go with the novel, and Houghton Mifflin could have done this to her. She begged Greenslet not to, and he respected her wishes.

The next twelve months were to be the hardest year in Cather's life. This period began, however, on a very happy note, when her brother Douglass, the member of her remaining family she loved the most, spent two weeks in New York with her, arriving in time for her birthday on December 7. She stuffed a turkey for him because her cook couldn't do it the way Grandma Boak did, and that was the way Douglass liked it. When he left, it never crossed her mind she would not see him again. She made good progress on her novel that winter, though she had to go to bed with the flu in February. In April 1938, she felt the need to revisit the locale of her novel-in-progress and went down to Virginia with Edith Lewis. She greatly enjoyed going back to the scenes of her childhood for the first time in a quarter of a century. She found again the wild azaleas growing on the gravelly banks of the road up Timber Ridge, and the dogwood was in bloom in the almost leafless woods of early spring. The countryside was much changed, of course, but Lewis recalled that Cather seemed to look through modern Virginia to see the country she had lived in for her first nine-plus years. Her old home Willow Shade, which then was owned by a man who had cut down all the willow trees, was a great disappointment. The place looked so forlorn and nude that she didn't want to go in, but just stood and looked at it from a distance.

The visit to Virginia was the last pleasant thing that happened that year. In May someone accidentally smashed her hand when she was in the drugstore, but this was a trifle compared to the blows to come. In June Douglass died suddenly of a heart attack in San Diego at the age of fifty-eight. This was such a devastating loss that Cather did not have the strength to go to the funeral. The only close member of her family left was Roscoe. There was still more bad news to come. In October her beloved Isabelle died in Sorrento of kidney failure. Although her death had been anticipated, when it came, Cather was shattered by the event. She wrote Irene Weisz four days later that she didn't know how she could go on living after losing both Douglass and Isabelle, the two people in the world dearest to her. Her brother, she felt, was almost like a twin, and Isabelle, who had grown more beautiful every year in person and spirit, was the one for whom all her books had been written. There is a three month blank in the record of Cather's life between the deaths of Douglass and Isabelle. She wrote an old friend at the end of the year that she had been sick a good while after her brother died. If she wrote any letters in this period, none has survived. She apparently did not go to Grand Manan as usual that summer but stayed in New York. In November, however, she went up to Jaffrey where she found the devastation caused by the great hurricane of 1938 had left the external world as ravaged as her internal one. She had come to New Hampshire in a comatose state, she wrote Akins from the Shattuck Inn; the power to feel anything was utterly gone. The only bright spot left in her life at this point was Yehudi Menuhin.

Bereft and growing old in a world moving inexorably towards war; such was Cather's predicament in those dark months of 1938. She had written Sinclair Lewis at the beginning of the year that Americans were the most gullible and easily taken in of all peoples because they could not think evil of anyone. We think that Stalin must have his good points, and we know how comfortable Mussolini has made Italy for tourists. She didn't believe that we would wake up until the knife was at our throat. Then she watched Hitler invade Austria and Neville Chamberlain go to Munich and sign the agreement that was to preserve peace in our time. When England and France agreed to let Hitler dismember Czechoslovakia, she was profoundly depressed, as Czechoslovakia was a country for which she had an emotional attachment through her Bohemian immigrant friends in Nebraska and a personal relationship with Jan Masaryk. The following January, Republican though she was, she applauded Herbert Lehman's inaugural address, as governor of New York, assailing dictators and intolerance. He was the one real idealist she knew.

It is no wonder that for a long while in this period Cather was unable to work on her novel. She wrote Akins in May 1939, that she had been in disgrace with herself all winter and there had been no spring. She caught the flu in February and didn't throw it off until April. Then she went down to Atlantic City for a month to recuperate, and it rained all the time she was there. She felt she just could not pull herself up after the deaths of Douglass and Isabelle. She did so eventually, however, and by summer was back at work after a year's delay. She went to Jaffrey for a month in June, then returned to New York in July. Lewis remembered this period in the book's composition: "She worked at *Sapphira* with a resoluteness, a sort of fixed determination which I think was different from her ordinary working mood; as if she were bringing all her powers into play to save this, whatever else was lost. She often worked far beyond her strength." At the beginning of August she went up to Grand Manan for her next-to-last visit to the island. There she continued plugging away at the book, but it still wasn't finished when she returned to New York in the fall. It took another winter, spring, and summer to complete the novel.

In the meantime World War II began. Hitler invaded Poland, and for the second time in her life the lights began to go out all over Europe. The book became her refuge from the horrendous events taking place abroad. She wrote to Greenslet on the day France fell that none of the personal sorrows she had recently lived through had shaken her days and nights as the doom that had been gathering for the last few months over almost everything that had made the world worth living in or for. Lewis reported that she wrote in her line-a-day diary when the French army surrendered: "There seems to be no future at all for people of my generation." Knopf must have had most of the manuscript of *Sapphira* in hand when Cather went to Grand Manan in the summer of 1940 for the last time. She stayed in New York until the end of July because her beloved niece Mary Virginia (now married to an orthopedic surgeon, Richard Mellen) was in the hospital with a serious illness. At Grand Manan in August she put the finishing touches on the novel and the next month began reading proof. Knopf published the book on her birthday, December 7.

Cather wrote Alexander Woollcott that in this novel her end was her beginning. She was referring to the epilogue describing the return to Back Creek Valley of Nancy Till, the scene she had witnessed as a child, but her end was quite literally her beginning, her last novel finally in her old age evoking her earliest memories of Virginia. The idea for a Virginia novel must have been in her mind for a number of years because there is a reference to it in a letter Blanche Knopf wrote Cather in 1931. Cather had sent Mrs. Knopf a copy of her poem "Poor Marty," written after the death of Marjorie Anderson, and Mrs. Knopf after reading it with delight replied that she hoped Cather was now "seriously thinking about doing the Virginia book." Six years later when she did begin the novel, memories of Virginia came flooding back. She sent Viola Roseboro' an advance copy and wrote that she hoped her old friend would like the novel despite the fact that she had said in her last letter that she didn't much care for fiction any more. Maybe this book will get by, Cather said, because not very much of it was actually fiction. It was made so largely of old family and neighborhood stories that she scarcely knew where her contribution began. So much of Virginia came back to her that she wrote a great deal more than she used. Lewis recalled: "She could have written two or three *Sapphiras* out of her material; and in fact she did write, in her first draft, twice as much as she used." Cather told Bruce Rogers when he was preparing to add the novel to the *Autograph Edition*, that she had been so afraid of being diffuse that she had cut the manuscript severely. In the first draft she even had written an entire chapter on the mill, but she had made the cuts because, after all, she was not writing a history of Virginia manners and customs before the Civil War. The parts she omitted, she claimed, weighed exactly six pounds. The book finally came out at approximately sixty thousand words, a rather average length for a Cather novel.

Sapphira and the Slave Girl, except for the epilogue, takes place in Back Creek Valley, Virginia, in 1856 during the final years of slavery. Sapphira Dodderidge Colbert is an imperious old woman, semi-invalid, who originally came from Loudoun County, Virginia, on the Potomac River farther east. She had inexplicably married Henry Colbert, a miller, and taken her husband and twenty slaves to live in the Shenandoah Valley on property that she had inherited. Her widowed daughter Rachel Blake lives in the village with her children, and the story opens with a breakfast table scene between Sapphira and the miller. Their marriage has been one mainly of convenience, with Sapphira managing the farm and Henry running the mill. He lives at the mill but takes his meals at the mill house, and the two pretty much go their own way. At the breakfast table Sapphira proposes to sell her housemaid Nancy, a bright, attractive mulatto girl who is the by-blow of an itinerant portrait painter and Till, the housekeeper. Henry will not hear of the sale. He is very fond of Nancy, who besides being Sapphira's lady's maid also acts as his housekeeper at the mill. Sapphira, as a patrician Southerner, can't stand the affectionate relationship that exists between the slave and her husband, and perhaps she is jealous of Nancy's youth. Sexual relations between the master and a slave probably wouldn't bother her, but Henry's treating Nancy like an equal human being is unendurable. Yet she can't sell Nancy without her husband's signature on the deed and thus must find other means of getting rid of the girl.

From this sharp dramatic conflict follows the action of the novel. Sapphira invites her husband's profligate nephew Martin to come for a protracted visit. She plans to give him every opportunity to rape Nancy. Martin is very willing to be used in this manner, but he is circumvented one way or another by the other slaves and Rachel Blake until finally the situation becomes intolerable to Rachel and her father. Rachel plans a midnight escape and takes the girl to free soil where she is passed along through the underground railroad to Canada. The one thing Sapphira never had counted on was that her own daughter, even though she had Yankee ideas about slavery, would steal her property with the connivance of her own husband. Henry's part in the escape, however, is passive, for he is too much a Southerner to aid his daughter openly. He puts money in his coat and hangs it by an open window on the night the escape is planned.

There is a final section of the novel that takes place after Nancy has been spirited away to Canada. Sapphira breaks with her daughter, forbids her to visit the mill house any more. After a fine autumn, winter comes and with it the usual diphtheria epidemic. Sapphira's little granddaughters contract the disease, and when one of them dies Rachel and her mother are reconciled. Sapphira invites Rachel and her surviving daughter to come live at the mill house, and the story ends on a note of harmony, as Sapphira tells her husband: "We would all do better if we had our lives to live over again." The reader learns in the epilogue that Sapphira's health rapidly declined and she died a few months later.

As we have seen, the basic plot and most of the characters in *Sapphira and the Slave Girl* were ready made. Rachel Blake is a fictional portrait of Grandma Boak; the miller and Sapphira were suggested by Cather's maternal great-grandparents, Jacob and Ruhamah Seibert; and Nancy and Till were drawn from real blacks and put into the novel without even a name change. Mrs. Ringer's prototype was Marjorie Anderson's mother, and the postmistress had her source in Cather's Great-Aunt Sidney Gore. Even little Mary, the child who survives the diphtheria epidemic, is the author's mother as a child.

The family history, however, has little to say about the Seiberts, both of whom died before Cather was born, and it is more than likely that these characters and their relationship to each other were largely an invention. The record also is silent regarding Martin Colbert, the wastrel nephew, who is probably entirely a product of the imagination. Cather had vivid memories of Mrs. Anderson, who worked for the Cathers on occasion; old Till, who was virtually a member of the family; and, of course, Nancy, whose return was the strongest recollection of her childhood. The setting of the novel is the present village of Gore, Virginia, the woods, and the surrounding countryside. The old mill no longer exists except as a ruinous pile of lumber; but the mill house, a small-scale Mount Vernon, is still well preserved and occupied today. It stands south of Highway 50 and forms a triangle with Willow Shade and Grandmother Boak's house in the village where Cather was born.

Readers familiar only with Cather's Nebraska fiction find *Sapphira* a great surprise. The Romantic affirmations of the earlier novels are completely missing here: there is no heroine to empathize with; the subject matter is dark and sinister. How does one reconcile Cather's own statement to Carrie Sherwood written as she put the finishing touches on this novel: that she could only write successfully when she wrote about people or places which she greatly admired or actually loved? Sapphira is one of Cather's great creations in a large gallery of memorable characters, but she is a person without a moral sense, a figure of ambiguity, someone no reader could love. In *Lucy Gayheart* Cather created a heroine she grew weary of, and the result was not a complete success; in *Sapphira* she invented an overbearing, unattractive protagonist with remarkable success. It is a triumphant achievement at the end of a long and distinguished career.

Critics who have charged Cather with retreating into the past in her historical fiction need to reexamine *Sapphira and the Slave Girl*. The story is one hundred and eighty degrees removed from being a nostalgic return to the memories of a happy Virginia childhood. It is another Gothic tale, more sinister than *Lucy Gayheart*, more deeply probing into the nature of evil and the dark, irrational forces that are always threatening us. It is tempting to read this novel as a commentary on events then taking place in the external world, first the malignant spread of Nazism into Austria and Czechoslovakia, then the outbreak of war in September 1939. It seemed the end of the world she had loved, the final debasement of values she held dear, the destruction of all tradition and culture. The novel is deeply pessimistic.

As a Gothic tale, it fits the classic pattern: a tyrant, who is law unto himself, living in a gloomy castle deep in the forest, lures an innocent young woman to her intended violation; the victim is saved at the eleventh hour by a rescuer, who snatches her out of the villain's clutches. The Gothicism is complete—even to the creaking staircase and the footsteps of the ravisher, as the victim lies helpless at night on a pallet before her mistress's doorway. In its bald outline the story is pure melodrama. What Cather does with this plot, however, is to turn it into a searching examination of the contradictions of character, the springs of human motivation, the vulnerability of hope. Her setting in the antebellum South was an appropriate background for exploring these issues. When O'Neill wanted to write an American version of a Greek tragedy, he put the story of the House of Atreus into a post-Civil War frame in *Mourning Becomes Electra*. Cather used Virginia in the waning days of the slave system to provide the milieu for her contest between good and evil. The iniquities of slavery served well as a vehicle for her darkening vision.

Although attempted rape is the central plot element, the novel does not seem at all sensational. Cather's ability to create vivid minor characters and communicate a sense of place muffle the melodrama. In these aspects of the novel Cather was as successful in *Sapphira* as she was when she wrote about Nebraska prairies and immigrant farmers, French priests in New Mexico, or early settlers in Quebec. When she sat down to write the novel, she was able to recall clearly conversations she had heard between old Till and her grand-mother. She also remembered the speech of the blacks. It was like hearing a phonograph record, she said, and it all came back to her, even the differentia-tion between the way the blacks spoke to each other and the language they used for their masters. She explained to Fisher that all well-trained blacks spoke two languages: one for the house and one for the cabin, and when they got excited they always reverted to the latter idiom.

Cather evokes the Virginia landscape in this novel as memorably as she had called up the Nebraska prairie. When Mrs. Blake goes about her rounds as amateur nurse, Cather takes her up the "Double S" road to Timber Ridge where she can "look down over hills and valleys, as if she were at the top of the world." She sits down to rest above a deep ravine where "a mountain stream . . . coffee brown, throwing up chrystal rainbows . . . gurgled over rock ledges. On the steep hillside across the creek the tall forest trees were still bare,—the oak leaves no bigger than a squirrel's ear. From out the naked grey wood the dogwood thrust its crooked forks starred with white blossoms." Mrs. Blake is on her way to see old Mrs. Ringer, who has dropped a flatiron on her foot. The old mill that stood on the west bank of Back Creek also is indelibly described with its big water wheel hanging over the stream, the dam lying in the green meadow beyond; and the mill house is particularized with its steep-pitched roof, dormer windows, and front porch supported by square frame posts that ran the length of the house. Behind the house, ten yards from the back door, is the separate kitchen, and still farther away are the slave cabins, the laundry, and the smoke house draped with Virginia creeper, trumpet vine, Dutchman's pipe, and morning glories.

Cather makes no effort to write a polemic against slavery; it would have been out of character and inappropriate in 1940. The evils of the system, however, are implicit in the story. Her purpose was to construct a narrative against the background of Virginia life as she could remember it from the 1870s and from the stories she had heard. Most of the fiction she had read about antebellum days was strongly partisan, either for or against the South's peculiar institution. She felt that slavery had been neither a torture prison nor a benevolent training school. It had had its pleasant domestic surfaces, she wrote Greenslet in response to a letter praising the novel. She did not remember Till, who was Aunt Till to the Cather family, as a person to be pitied, even though she had been a slave most of her life. If Cather's family had been antislavery people from tidewater Virginia or from South Carolina or Louisiana, she might have grown up with much stronger feelings about slavery. But there never had been many slaves in Back Creek Valley.

In this leisurely paced novel, Cather takes time to create scenes of village life and farm operations. She also inserts anecdotes into her narrative in her customary fashion, and the result is a rich panorama of life in the Shenandoah Valley before the Civil War. Many images linger in the mind: Sapphira out riding in her fine carriage, not so much to see the countryside, as to be seen elegantly dressed in her aristocratic equippage; fat Lizzie, the cook, and her slovenly daughter Bluebell singing in the black loft of the village church; Tansy Dave, the half-witted slave falling in love and rolling in the herb bed to make himself smell sweet; the miller and the slaves mowing hay on a hot summer morning; the diphtheria epidemic, and, of course, the return of Nancy twenty-five years later. The most notable digression is the story of old Jezebel, whose history gets an entire section of the novel. She is a venerable old slave, the matriarch of the black community, a woman who had been born in Africa and brought to America from Guinea by slave traders in the 1780s. When she dies at the age of ninety-five, Sapphira gives her a magnificent funeral. The whole history of slavery and the patriarchal social structure of the old South is encapsulated in the story of Jezebel's life.

The narrative method of *Sapphira and the Slave Girl* is third-person, author omniscient, the manner of telling Cather thought proper for a novel of action. The backgrounds of characters are supplied by inserts that flashback to fill in the reader. The early history of Sapphira and her husband, Nancy's parentage, old Till's early life, Rachel Blake's marriage and widowhood, and

Jezebel's life are supplied this way. In structure the novel is conventional and moves along chronologically with time out for digressions and background. Cather was no longer interested in experiments, as she had been in *The Professor's House* or *Death Comes for the Archbishop*. Her preoccupation in this novel was with character and theme.

Sapphira is a complex figure, patrician, amoral, steel-willed. She is in addition a grotesque, as befits the protagonist of a Gothic novel. Cather has varied the old formula for the Gothic tale both by making the villain a woman and by making her an enigmatic figure. "Sapphira . . . usually acted upon motives which she disclosed to no one." She spends her days in a wheel chair because she suffers from dropsy, and her legs are so swollen that she can't walk. She had been a very active woman in her youth and hates her present condition. This grotesquerie symbolizes the misshapen end product of a deformed social structure, a society that tolerates slavery. When Sapphira sets about to get rid of Nancy by having her raped by her husband's nephew, she acts with no scruples at all. In fact, she enjoys the drama she has set in motion, and on one of the rare occasions when the narrative slips into her mind, she thinks of herself as taking part in a play.

Yet Sapphira is not all bad. She is perfectly capable of planning Nancy's rape, but she also runs the farm efficiently and has a strong sense of *noblesse oblige* towards the slaves. She treats Tansy Dave indulgently when he runs away after being disappointed in love and has a genuine attachment to Old Jezebel. She takes part in celebrations and likes to see her people happy. "On Christmas morning she sat in the long hall and had all the men on the place come in to get their presents and their Christmas drink. She served each man a strong toddy in one of the big glass tumblers that had been her father's. When Tap, the mill boy, smacked his lips and said: 'Miss Sapphy, if my mammy's titty had a-tasted like that, I never would a-got weaned,' she laughed as if she had never heard the old joke before."

At the end of the novel, after this allegory of the battle between good and evil, after Rachel Blake, the angel of mercy, has foiled Satan, Sapphira changes. She is softened by the loss of her granddaughter and her approaching death, and the novel ends on a note of peace and harmony. It is as though Cather did not want to end her career with a novel totally bleak in its outlook. But one is left, nonetheless, with the strong impression that the evil of this world is very real and always lurks below the surface. Though the iniquities of slavery provide the dominant evil, other evils emerge throughout the novel. When Mrs. Blake, for example, goes to visit Mrs. Ringer on her mountaintop farm, the setting is idyllic, but while she is there, she witnesses an ugly scene: redneck Buck Keyser and his loutish brothers torturing Casper

Flight, who is stripped and tied to a stake in the nearby woods. Later in Jezebel's story we see the brutal conditions under which blacks were transported to America and auctioned off in the slave markets, and we learn that old Till as a child had seen her mother burned to death. Finally, after Rachel rescues Nancy, taking her away from the tomblike mill house in a hearse (another Gothic touch), the diphtheria epidemic breaks out distributing death at random among the innocents of the village. As Henry Adams put it: "Chaos is the law of nature; order the dream of man."

The miller is a carefully drawn and sympathetic character, but he is overshadowed by Sapphira. He is weak where Sapphira is strong, full of doubts where she is resolute, moral where she is amoral. He hates the slave system but unlike his daughter is too much a part of it to aid in Nancy's escape and forces Rachel to "steal" his money to finance the fugitive slave's journey. He also is never sure of his own nature, and because the Colbert men, like his nephew Martin, have a reputation as lechers, he worries that he may have the family taint. He is the only Colbert with a conscience, and Sapphira sometimes wishes he hadn't quite so much. That Cather was thinking in terms of allegory in writing this novel is suggested by her use of Bunyan and his works. The miller identifies Nancy with Mercy, Christiana's sweet companion in *The Pilgrim's Progress*, the book Cather had read many times; and later when he is agonizing over Nancy's danger, he turns to Bunyan's *Holy War* and reads the account of the capture of the town of Mansoul by the Son of God, who drives out Diabolus and his followers. This reading comforts him in his anxiety.

Cather was pleased when Roseboro' read the novel and pronounced it a success. It had been a comfort to her, she wrote, to turn back to early memories of Virginia and away from the sorrows of the present. When she had taken up the story after the long hiatus in its composition, there had been a kind of religious comfort in remembering and in trying to treat the material humbly and truthfully and not to overcolor it. She felt proud and honored that the novel rang true to Roseboro', another exiled Southerner, and she remembered that her old friend had been brave enough in the *McClure's* days to tell her that she was going wrong when she tried to write about things of which she had only a superficial knowledge. Another personal reaction that would have pleased Cather, if she had known of it, was Wallace Stevens's comment in a letter to a friend: "You may not like the book," he wrote; "moreover, you may think she is more or less formless. Nevertheless, we have nothing better than she is. She takes so much pains to conceal her sophistication that it is easy to miss her quality."

Sapphira and the Slave Girl was a great commercial success. Two mor' before publication day Knopf advertised in *Publisher's Weekly* that he was ordering an advance printing of twenty-five thousand copies, and the next month he announced that so many orders had come in that he was doubling the press run. Then the Book of the Month Club adopted the novel for distribution in January and bought more than two hundred thousand copies. When the reviews began to appear, there was hardly a dissenting note. A few notices fell into the "yes-but" category, but no one damned the book. There was a lively interest in trying to assess the quality of the novel in relation to Cather's other works. Even Cather thought the novel had a better press than any of her previous books. Morton Zabel in the *Nation*, the journal that usually panned her, ranked *Sapphira* as one of her five best novels.

Henry Canby in the *Saturday Review of Literature* wrote a notice she liked so much that she sent copies to friends. For one who long had followed American fiction, noted Canby, it was a pleasure to come across a novel "where all that is needed is included, and all that is needless is left out." He praised Cather for being able to do in three hundred pages what it took most novelists nine hundred to accomplish. He also observed accurately that she was not "writing a melodrama of slavery and seduction, but recreating, with subtle selection of incident, a society and a culture and a sociology in which a conflict of morals and of philosophies produces an inner, ever more tightly coiled spring."

Other reviewers were equally enthusiastic. The notice in the *San Francisco Chronicle* ranked Sapphira with Marian Forrester and Ántonia Shimerda as one of Cather's most memorable characters, despite the fact "she lacks their warmth of human appeal and possesses a most unlovely capacity for malice." *The New York Herald-Tribune* reviewer thought the novel particularly distinguished for its credible black men and women, something new in Cather's fiction. It is true that Jezebel, Till, Nancy, Bluebell, Lizzy, Sampson (the mill foreman) are all individuals. There is not a stereotype in the lot, and the accomplishment is a marvel of memory and observation. Cather from her tenth year on grew up in a culture almost devoid of blacks, and her only experience with blacks as an adult was with maids and cooks. The only recorded instance in which she ever sat down socially with a black was once at the Menuhins' apartment when she was invited to meet Paul Robeson.

Perhaps the most problematic aspect of the novel was the epilogue, in which Cather, speaking in her own voice, enters the story and becomes a character. She had some doubts about the propriety of this, but the memory of Nancy's return was so strong she couldn't resist using it as she remembered. When Woollcott wrote that he liked the epilogue, she was very glad and explained to him that a little thrill went through her whenever she thought about that scene. She remembered that she had sat in the kitchen at Willow Shade as Nancy, Till, and her grandmother discussed everything that had happened since the flight to Canada. Those were the happiest hours Cather could remember. The epilogue was a favorite device, as we have seen, throughout her long career. From *Alexander's Bridge* to *Sapphira and the Slave Girl*, she ended eight of her novels with epilogues of one sort or another.

CHAPTER 23

Last Years

Near the end of her career in 1940 Cather must have seemed to many of her admirers something like a national monument. For thirty-five years she had been engaged in building an *oeuvre* that had eventually challenged the accomplishments of the greatest of Americans. The tone of her last interviewers, Stephen and Rosemary Benét in the *New York Herald-Tribune*, is awed and reverential. In summing up her life and work a week after *Sapphira* appeared, the Benéts began with an assumption: this is a genuine artist: "Like fine silver or porcelain, her product is unmistakable. We do not have to turn the piece to find the hallmark or the crown and crossed swords imprint. We know by the look and the shape and the weight in hand." They could not decide in their analysis just what made the artist, from whence came the creative gift, but they knew that with Cather they were looking at the real thing. As a person and artist, they concluded, "she is very civilized and very American."

Cather's pleasure in the enthusiastic response to her novel was tempered by physical problems and the ever-grimmer news coming out of Europe. Knopf, who had the habit of bringing out special printings of his books for collectors, sent Cather five hundred sheets to sign for the first issue of the first edition. This chore, which she had to do in three days, proved a disaster, for it inflamed the tendon of her right thumb, and again she had to have her hand in splints and her arm in a sling, as she had six years before. The problem was more serious this time, however, as it was her right hand. She spent the Christmas season in the French Hospital undergoing treatment for this problem, and later an orthopedic surgeon from Boston made her a special brace that she had to wear off and on for the rest of her life. Yehudi Menuhin went to the hospital to comfort her, and the French Hospital turned out to be the pleasantest place she ever had been laid up in. She stayed several weeks. The rooms had glorious light and sun, no ugly furniture, and she could hear French spoken all day. It was the only hospital she ever was in where she could eat the food. But by the end of February she still was in splints and unable to write. At times she could not even sign her name, and her dictated letters were signed by Sarah Bloom, her secretary.

Cather hated not being able to write her friends in longhand, but she was even more depressed over the outlook for her career. She had no trouble dictating letters (she'd been doing that ever since the *Home Monthly* days), but she simply could not write stories or novels that way. Composing by dictation, she wrote, was like playing solitaire with one's back to the card table. She had to see the words before her eyes; then the thing she was creating took shape on the paper like a picture. This inability had serious implications, and she began wondering if she ever would be able to write again. She couldn't do it much of the time and only managed to write two more stories before she died. She worked on another novel from time to time during her last six years, but she never was able to finish it.

Cather's despair over the fall of France in June had been followed by the horrendous Battle of Britain, which began in the summer and continued while she was awaiting the appearance of her book. She followed the news from England with intense interest, and as the British defended themselves against the nonstop German bombing of London and other cities, she was awed by the magnificence of their resistance. She wrote Greenslet that the splendor of British behavior under the Nazi attacks was so wonderful a thing that she could hardly speak of it without losing self-control. Churchill became her hero, as he led his countrymen through their darkest hours. When Franklin D. Roosevelt was returned to office for his third term in November, despite the fact she almost certainly voted for Wendell Willkie, she said she was satisfied with the outcome of the election. Roosevelt, she thought, would do more for Britain than anyone else, and that was all she cared about.

To physical disability and the war was added that spring the death of May Willard, Cather's oldest friend in Pittsburgh. May dated back at least two years before Isabelle McClung and was the most vital and vivid part of her early years in Pennsylvania. May, Ethel Litchfield, Isabelle, and Cather formed a group that had just melted together. Those were beautiful days to remember, Cather wrote May's sister Marie. When she called Ethel to break the news of May's death, Ethel had simply hung up, unable to talk. When she later called back, she begged Cather not to quit this world before she did. She couldn't go through another death, she said, and Cather added that this was exactly her own feeling. Meantime, Roscoe Cather was very ill in California with a heart condition. He had moved west from Wyoming and gone into the savings and loan business in Colusa, a hot town in the Central Valley. Cather was haunted by the fear she would never see her brother again and decided to visit him in the summer. But the trip promised to be difficult; she was wearing the brace on her right hand and couldn't dress herself. Fortunately, Lewis was able to accompany her on the trip, and the two women left New York in June.

They took a train to Chicago, then transferred to the Santa Fe for the journey to the West Coast. As the train passed through New Mexico and Arizona, she saw for the first time in fifteen years the country she had written about so movingly. "The country never had been more beautiful," Lewis recalled. "The rose acacias were in bloom for miles along the railroad tracks after we left Trinidad. In all the little Mexican villages, one saw the tamarisk, with its long drifts of blossom—the tree Willa Cather had so celebrated in the *Archbishop*. There had been plentiful rains, and everything was fresh and green. She saw it all with tears. She knew it was for the last time." When they reached California, they made their headquarters at the Fairmont Hotel in San Francisco, and Roscoe and his wife came in from Colusa on weekends to visit. Roscoe thought his sister looked very frail, but the reunion between the two was a happy occasion. Cather stayed six weeks.

From San Francisco she and her companion went north to British Columbia. Cather long had wished to visit Victoria on Vancouver Island, but when she got there she did not feel up to sight-seeing and spent most of her time in the gardens of the Empress Hotel. "She would sit under a hawthorne tree among the flowering rosebushes, and read; or not even read; the shortest walk tired her." Canada was at war in 1941 and the trip back to the East Coast via the Canadian Pacific Railroad was uncomfortable. The best accommodations they could get were on an ancient Pullman car called back from twenty years of retirement. They stopped en route at Lake Louise and Montreal, but after they returned to New York, Cather went to the French Hospital for a week to rest.

The journey may have exhausted her, but she returned to Park Avenue with the idea for a new novel. Lewis remembered that for years she had wanted to write a story laid in Avignon, the city of all French cities she loved the most. With much of France occupied by the German army and Marshal Pétain's feeble regime installed at Vichy, her mind turned back to France of the Middle Ages, the period of the Babylonian captivity when the Church of Rome was ruled from Avignon. Cather had been moved by her first visit to the city in 1902, and the Papal Palace built in the fourteenth century by Benedict XII "stirred her as no building in the world ever had done." She must have revisited Avignon in 1920 when she toured Provence with the Hambourgs, and she stopped there again when she was on her way from Venice to Paris in 1935. Lewis, who was present on the last occasion, recalled: "One day, as we wandered through the great chambers of white, almost translucent stone, alone except for a guide, this young fellow suddenly stopped still in one of the rooms and began to sing, with a beautiful voice. It echoed down the corridors and under the arched ceilings like a great bell sounding—but sounding from some remote past; its vibrations seemed laden, weighted down with the passions of another age—cruelties, splendours, lost and unimaginable to us in our time." Cather was entranced by this performance, and she may have conceived of her Avignon story then. During her weeks in San Francisco in the summer of 1941 she had plenty of spare time and filled her days reading very closely a copy of Thomas Okey's *The Story of Avignon* in the roof garden of the Fairmont Hotel. When she was able to remove the brace from her right hand after wearing it for eight months, she must have done the underlining, marking of passages, and annotating that were in the volume when she died.

She worked fitfully at the Avignon novel during her last years, but her right hand kept bothering her, and there were periods when she couldn't write at all. The story was still unfinished at the time she died, though she had managed to complete a good part of it. At Cather's request Lewis destroyed the manuscript, much to the disservice of literature, but she has left an account of the novel. It was to have been called "Hard Punishments" and was set in Avignon during the reign of Benedict XII. It concerned the friendship of two boys, Pierre and André, both of whom had been victims of Medieval justice. Pierre, was a simple-minded peasant lad who had been strung up by the thumbs for petty theft and left maimed for life; the other was the son of a high official in the papal palace, but he too had been mutilated for blasphemy by having his tongue torn out. Just what Cather intended to do with this relationship is not known, but Lewis remembered that there was a moving scene between André and his confessor as the boy lay tossing on his cot after his punishment. The priest talked to the boy, soothed him, and finally absolved him. "This was perhaps the central scene in the story." Despite Lewis's destruction of the manuscript, four pages of it miraculously survived and turned up in a dealer's catalogue many years later. It is clear from this fragment that Cather had not lost her stylistic grace and evocative power. These pages describe Father Ambrose, the confessor, as he listens to a midnight Christmas Mass with both André and Pierre. It is a scene that calls to mind the remarkable "December Night" chapter from *Death Comes for the Archbishop*.

Although Cather's health was beginning to break down in this period, there were pleasant occasions. Even as the United States entered the war following the Japanese attack on Pearl Harbor, Lewis remembered lively parties at 570 Park Avenue during the early months of 1942. There were also happy hours with Yehudi Menuhin and his wife before their separation and with a new friend, Sigrid Undset, who had escaped with her son from occupied Norway. They had reached New York by way of Siberia, Japan, and San Francisco, and soon after reaching the city Undset wanted to meet Cather, whose work she greatly admired. Alfred Knopf, who was Undset's American publisher, promptly arranged a meeting, and the two writers became very good friends.

The arrival of Undset, however, was offset by a loss that Cather felt deeply. It was not a death but the departure of Mary Virginia and her doctor husband for a hospital position in Chattanooga. After the couple left New York in February, Cather wrote Irene Weisz that she didn't know how she could get along without her niece. During the thirties they had grown very close, and Cather had come more and more to depend on her for many services, both physical and spiritual. She admired her niece's character, her spirit, her good nature. When Mary Virginia had graduated from Smith in 1930, she had come quietly to New York, gotten a job selling at Lord and Taylor before letting her aunt know that she was in the city. During the years that followed, whenever Cather felt tired and blue, she invited Mary Virginia to tea or supper, and she always felt better afterwards. In addition to being a tonic for sagging spirits, Mary Virginia also did her aunt's packing whenever she went away for the summer, and she would go to dress sales and phone her aunt whenever she found something she knew Cather would like.

Cather kept to her normal routines and concealed from all but old friends and family her personal problems and anguish over the state of the world. She continued going to the Society Library, and to people who saw her there browsing among the stacks, she seemed a commanding presence. One of these observers was young Truman Capote, recently out of high school and a very junior member of the *New Yorker* staff. A quarter of a century later he had vivid memories of meeting her there. He was in the habit of going to the library to do research and "three or four times I noticed this absolutely marvelous-looking woman. She had a wonderful open, extraordinary face, and hair combed back in a bun. Her suits were soft, but rather severe—very distinguished-looking—and her eyes . . . were the most amazing pale, pale blue. Like pieces of sky floating in her face."

"One day about five-thirty, I came out of the library, and there she was, standing under the canopy. It was snowing hard, and she was looking this way and that, as if she couldn't decide whether to walk or wait for a taxi. I stood there, too, and she said she didn't think there were any taxis. I said no, I guess there was no point trying to get back to the office, I guessed I'd just go home. Suddenly she said, 'Would you like a hot chocolate? There's a Longchamps restaurant just around the corner, and we could walk there.' Well, we walked there, and she said she'd noticed me in the library several times. I told her I was from the South, was working on a magazine, and that I wanted to be a writer. She said, 'Oh, really? What writers do you like?' We talked about Turgenev and Flaubert. Then she asked what *American* writers I liked. I told her that my favorite was Willa Cather. Which of her works did I like best? Well, I said, *My Mortal Enemy* and *A Lost Lady* were both perfect works of art. 'That's very interesting,' she said. 'Why?' So I told her why, and we talked for a while. 'Well,' she said finally, 'I'm Willa Cather.' It was one of the great *frissons* of my life! I knew it was true the minute she said it. Of *course* she was Willa Cather."

In April, 1942, Cather went to see her doctor to have a sore throat painted with argyrol. When the doctor took her temperature, he found she was running a high fever and conducted her personally to the hospital without even letting her go home for a toothbrush. The doctors at the hospital found she had an inflamed gall bladder and wanted to operate, but Cather wouldn't have it and went home when her temperature dropped to normal. The respite from surgery, however, was only temporary, and in the summer she had to have the gall bladder removed. The operation went very well, but her recovery was slow and painful, and her stay at the Presbyterian Hospital was miserable. She couldn't eat the food at all, and after a while the nurses stopped trying to make her. It all came up again and spoiled their lovely blankets, she wrote Irene Weisz. The faithful Lewis came to the rescue and had all of Cather's meals except breakfast prepared on Park Avenue and she took them herself to the hospital by taxi.

The operation kept Cather in New York that summer, but in the fall she and Lewis went up to Williamstown, Massachusetts, to stay for several weeks at the Williams Inn, which had been recommended by a friend. She would have preferred Jaffrey, but it was too hard to get there by rail in wartime, and there was a special train for Williams College students that ran once a week directly from New York to Williamstown. The weather wasn't very good while she was there. It rained much of the time, and she had little chance to be outdoors. Having lost fifteen pounds in the hospital, she was down to one hundred and ten and needed to build herself up. She now had the most fashionable type of figure, she wrote Viola Roseboro'. She enjoyed the Williams students very much, but her attempt to travel incognito wasn't a great success. She got bawled out by the college librarian and was followed about by a professor who had come from near Winchester, Virginia, and recognized her by her accent.

As the war went on, Cather found life increasingly difficult and the systematic destruction of Europe infinitely depressing. Perhaps intuitively anticipating the ravages of aerial bombardment and armored divisions, she had written Fisher five weeks after hostilities began that she wished gasoline had continued to slumber in the depths of the earth where it belonged along with other prehistoric things. Later as she slowly came back to life after her operation, she wondered what point there was in recovering. The world she loved so much was being destroyed along with beloved friends. She wouldn't live to see the emergence of the new world people were talking about and she really didn't want to live in it. The war had taken the joy out of life for everyone but the young, who had no beautiful past to remember. Life in New York in wartime for two aging women living alone involved the problem of keeping house with inadequate help. Cather and Lewis got their own breakfasts, then wandered about the godforsaken city looking for good places to eat dinner. The food was shocking, Cather wrote Akins, even at the Hotel Pierre, where her old friend usually stayed.

To get away from the war and New York, Cather and Lewis went to Maine for the summer. Returning to Grand Manan was out of the question for the duration, but at Mt. Desert Island near Northeast Harbor, Maine, they found the Asticou Inn, a quiet, secluded place well off the beaten track. They rented quarters from the proprietor in a cottage which had a large fireplace in the living room and comfortable bedrooms and took their meals at the inn. Their host was Charles Savage, a cultivated innkeeper with a taste for books and a well-stocked library. As Mt. Desert was less than seventy miles from the Bay of Fundy, the new summer retreat was very similar in climate and flora to Whale Cove and proved a satisfactory substitute. Cather wrote a friend at the end of the second summer there that she had gotten as far away from civilization as possible on Mt. Desert, which was served only occasionally by boats from the coast of Maine. She had left no forwarding address in New York and had been completely cut off from all the unreasonable, pompous, and obtrusive requests that usually followed her by post. All told, she spent her last four summers at the Asticou Inn and never returned to her cottage at Grand Manan.

One of her pleasures during her summers at Mt. Desert was the hotel library, which contained all the standard classics. Cather returned from dinner one evening with an armload of volumes from an old Houghton Mifflin edition of Scott and began reading and rereading the Waverley novels. They had been her mother's favorites before the family had left Virginia, and Cather had enjoyed at least some of them in her youth and early adulthood, along with other British romancers like Stanley Weyman and Anthony Hope. But she wearied of Scott, Lewis reported, after having to teach *Ivanhoe* to class after class of Pittsburgh high school students. When she discovered him again in her old age, however, she found his novels "a revelation of delight. She talked of them, lived in them. In the succeeding summers we spent at the Asticou Inn, she always reread them; and in New York she bought herself copies of the ones she liked best."

During 1943 and into 1944 Cather's despair over the death of the world was a consuming preoccupation. Why should the beautiful cities that were a thousand years in the making tumble down on our heads now, she wrote Roseboro', as the allied air forces pounded the Continent in preparation for D-Day. She and her old friend had lived through one great war, and there was sorrow aplenty then. Now countries were being sponged off the map, just as kids used to do when they had drawn them on the blackboard at school. She quoted from a lecture she once had heard Sir James Jeans deliver in which he had said: "Next to man's longing for personal immortality, he longs to feel that his world is immortal and will go on indefinitely as he has known it." She recognized the truth of that statement in her anguish.

Cather saw a great deal more of her nephews and nieces during the war than she had before, but their going and coming on military duties taxed her waning strength. She wrote Fisher the month before the Normandy landings that she was living a sort of communal life, as in her childhood when she lived in the little house in Red Cloud with all her siblings. She had three nieces and one nephew within short commuting distance of New York and more were coming. They were delightful and absorbing but exhausting. There also was worry over other members of her family and friends who were scattered about the world. Mary Virginia and her husband were then at Camp Carson, Colorado, her brother Tom was in Arizona, and another niece's husband was somewhere in the Pacific on an aircraft carrier. Two young Amherst professors she liked had written her from the mud of Guadalcanal, and many of the boys from Red Cloud also were fighting on those terrible Pacific islands.

She felt keenly the waste of war, the uprooting of youth from their former lives and families. None of the young people were doing what they wanted to do or had prepared themselves for or were already accomplishing with great happiness.

Pleasure and pain came in alternate doses during the war. Shortly before she wrote Fisher, she was awarded the gold medal for fiction by the National Institute of Arts and Letters at its New York headquarters in a well-publicized ceremony. This award, given once a decade for an author's total accomplishment, previously had gone to Howells, Wharton, and Tarkington. Cather had been a member of the Institute since 1929 and the more prestigious American Academy since 1938. She had received a medal from the Academy for *Death Comes for the Archbishop*, but the gold medal was perhaps the next best thing to the Nobel Prize. She appeared on the platform to receive her accolade along with Robeson and Dreiser, who received lesser awards, and her old friend and former employer McClure, who was given the Institute's "Order of Merit" for his contribution to journalism.

Witnesses of the ceremony saw a moving scene when Cather recognized McClure at the other end of the platform. She got up from her chair, walked across the stage, and flung her arms about him. He was then eighty-seven, and she had not seen him for years. Her uncharacteristic gesture, born of old affection, was entirely spontaneous. Soon after, she wrote McClure a note asking if she could come down to see him, and before she went away for the summer, she had tea with him at the Union League Club where he lived. She wrote a mutual friend afterwards that he was rather frail, but she seldom had seen anyone grow old so beautifully. He had become very handsome and was so gentle and dignified. As she sat and talked with him, she thought she never had heard a voice that had so many shades of compassion and kindliness, a kind of forgiveness for all the wrong things in the world. Whatever faults he once had came from his enthusiasms and nervous excitability. Now he was as calm as a harvest moon when it shone over the wheat fields after reaping was over.

After the presentation of the gold medal she went back to Mt. Desert for the second time. During this summer of 1944 she was able to write a story, but the effort was costly, and after she returned to New York she had to put on her brace again. The story was "Before Breakfast," her only tale laid on Grand Manan. It is good Cather, though a chilly piece that reflects the old-age preoccupations of its author. Yet it ends on a note of affirmation that is quite different from the pessimistic tone of her letters to old friends at this time. "Before Breakfast" concerns an aging businessman, Henry Grenfell, senior

77. Cather by photographer Edward Steichen in the twenties. Courtesy of Helen Cather Southwick

78. Cather at Grand Manan in the thirties. Courtesy of Helen Cather Southwick

79. Cather at Grand Manan in the thirties also. Courtesy of Helen Cather Southwick

80. Cather by photographer Nicholas
    Muray. Courtesy of WCPMC-NSHS

81. Cather's portrait by Leon Bakst,
    Paris, 1923, which now hangs in the
    Omaha Public Library. Courtesy of
    the Omaha Public Library

82. Cather's portrait by Nikolai Fechin,
    which hung in Cather's apartment.
    Courtesy of Helen Cather South-
    wick

83. Honorary degree recipients at Princeton, June, 1931. From left to right: Charles Lindbergh, Frank Kellogg, President Hibben, Willa Cather, and Newton D. Baker. Courtesy of Princeton University

84. 570 Park Avenue, with doorman Gilbert Rutledge. Courtesy of Lucia Woods, photographer

85. Cather at Grant Manan in 1931.
Courtesy of Helen Cather Southwick

6. Cather on her sixty-third birthday. Courtesy of WCPMC-NSHS

7. Cather and Yehudi Menuhin, Pasadena, 1931.

8. Alfred Knopf, 1947. Courtesy of Fabian Bachrach

89. Cather's grave at Jaffrey, New
    Hampshire. Courtesy of Helen
    Cather Southwick

90. Mount Monadnock viewed from
    the cemetery. Courtesy of WCPMC-
    NSHS

partner in a brokerage house, who reflects on life and death in his cabin on the island and during an early morning walk along the cliffs. His cottage, like Cather's summer home, lies in a clearing between a spruce wood and the sea about fifty yards back from a red sandstone cliff overlooking the water. Grenfell is out of sorts with the world. He comes to the island each summer to get away from his family and his business. His wife is a terribly efficient person, his sons have turned out well, one being a distinguished physicist, but they are cold as ice. The father is the only humanist of the lot, despite the fact he has fought his way up in business, and has brought with him a copy of *Henry IV, Part I*. Normally he loved getting back to the rocky, wooded island, but the night before he had ridden across the Bay of Fundy with a geologist who had annoyed him greatly by expounding the geologic history of the island. The scientist had taken all the romance out of his hideaway and put him in a foul mood.

Science long had been for Cather a *bête noire*, even though she had begun life wanting to be a doctor. Her attitude in this story reminds one of Professor St. Peter's lecture in which he had wanted to know what science ever had done for man except make him more comfortable. Or it recalls the recent letter to Roseboro' bemoaning the death of the world, which ended with the observation that the outrageous fate overtaking civilization in World War II had been brought on us by our smart scientists. Grenfell gets up early, the morning after arriving on his island, and is about to put in his eye drops, but he does not squeeze the bulb. He looks out toward the eastern horizon as dawn is beginning to break. There is a red streak on the water, a fleecy rose cloud in the sky, and Venus shining in the brightening air. "Merciless perfection, ageless sovereignty. . . . Poor Grenfell and his eye-drops!" He is overwhelmed by human frailty in the face of nature. "Why patch up? What was the use . . . of anything?"

When he goes for his walk before breakfast, he sees someone down on the shingle beach. It is a girl, the daughter of the geologist he had met. She is preparing for a morning dip. He is appalled at the thought of anyone trying to swim in that cold water, but he is powerless to stop her. She opens her robe, shivers, closes it, and then steps out of it. He sees she is wearing a pink bathing suit. "If a clam stood upright and graciously opened its shell, it would look like that," Grenfell thinks. She plunges in, struggles to a rock offshore, rests a moment there, and then weaves her way back. He thinks she is crazy to pull such a stunt. It is surely foolhardy, but her triumphant emergence from the sea somehow changes his mood. He returns to his cabin hungry and ready to face the world. Life will go on. That girl on the beach, like the first creatures that crawled out of the primeval seas, will endure. Grenfell thinks, as he walks back to his cabin: "Plucky youth is more bracing than enduring age."

Back in New York during the fall and winter of 1944–45, Cather's life went on quietly. She was in bed with the flu for two weeks in January, but the doctor let her take off her brace for two hours a day, and she was able to write in the mornings. She told Greenslet that she was working on a story that interested her very much, probably the Avignon novel, but she had to spend a lot of her energy answering letters from homesick soldiers in fox holes around the world. She had allowed some of her novels to be put into the special Armed Forces Editions, and this had let her in for a flood of mail. The only contribution she could make to the war effort, it seemed, was to respond to her fan mail from the far-flung battlefields. She could dictate these letters, of course, but they were an emotional strain.

Soon after the war ended in Europe, Cather went back to Mt. Desert Island for the third time. She was able to write a little each day and spent the summer working on her last story, "The Best Years," a tale that returns to Nebraska and family memories. She planned it as a gift for Roscoe, a reminder of their life together when they were children in Red Cloud. It is an excellent story, vintage Cather, and shows that the old artistry was still there, even at the age of seventy-one. The story takes place on the Divide and in Red Cloud, which is called MacAlpin in this avatar. The protagonist is Lesley Ferguesson, a sixteen-year-old girl who has taken a job teaching country school to help her large family make ends meet. Roscoe Cather also had done that while Willa was a student at the University of Nebraska.

The tale opens in the country when Evangeline Knightly, county superintendent of public instruction (a character modeled from Cather's memory of her favorite teacher, Evangeline King), is visiting rural schools. She goes to Lesley's one-room school house, listens to the children recite, alters her itinerary so that she can take the homesick Lesley back to MacAlpin for a weekend with her family. She is very fond of the girl and had given her a school the year before even though she was under the legal age for employment. This part of the story calls up vividly the Nebraska countryside that Cather remembered from her visits home after first going to Pittsburgh. The time is 1899 as Miss Knightly drives in her buggy along the dusty, sunflower-bordered roads. The season is autumn, Cather's favorite part of the year, the sky is blue and cloudless, and the land lies level as far as the eye can see. "The horizon was like a perfect circle, a great embrace, and within it lay the cornfields, still green, and the yellow wheat stubble, miles and miles of it, and the pasture lands where the white-faced cattle led lives of utter content."

The scene then moves into town as Miss Knightly deposits Lesley on her family's doorstep. Lesley is overjoyed to be home, especially with her four brothers, all of whom she adores and misses dreadfully when she is boarding out in the country during the school term. She is especially close to her oldest brother Hector, who is in action a practical, executive type but in mind something of a dreamer. This characterization is a pretty good likeness of Roscoe Cather, and the relationship between Lesley, and her mother and brothers is particularly well created. There is a good bit of Mrs. Cather in Mrs. Ferguesson, who has a strong, forceful personality, but the father is unlike Charles Cather. He is a very unconventional, not very successful farmer who lives in town and commutes to his farm and also a populist politician, the butt of many jokes. The house the Ferguessons live in, as already noted, is a replica of the story-and-a-half frame house the Cathers lived in on Cedar Street. Cather was remembering her pleasure in getting back home when her third-person narrator describes Lesley's return: "She gave herself up to the feeling of being at home. It went all through her, that feeling, like getting into a warm bath when one is tired. She was safe from everything, was where she wanted to be. . . . A plant that has been washed out by a rain storm feels like that, when a kind gardner puts it gently back into its own earth."

After Lesley returns to her school, there is a very short episode that takes place on Christmas Eve in which Hector is shown on his rounds as a telegraph messenger boy. Then the story continues from Miss Knightly's point of view. She goes to a convention of school superintendents in Lincoln and is stranded there when a great blizzard paralyzes the country. When the trains begin running again after a week, she returns to MacAlpin and learns that Lesley caught pneumonia and died when she was trapped in her schoolhouse by the storm. In an epilogue twenty years after, Miss Knightly goes back to the town for a visit and finds that the Ferguesson boys, all of whom turned out well, cherish the memory of their sister. "The Best Years" is a beautiful story with the genuine Cather tone of elegy and exquisite regret.

The death of Lesley Ferguesson in the story presaged the death of Roscoe in California. Cather had finished the tale and was getting ready to send it to her brother when she received a telegram announcing a fatal heart attack. She wrote Irene Weisz in the fall that Roscoe's death broke the last spring in her. Now she didn't care about writing any more books. She had brought home from Mt. Desert Island the unfinished novel, but she hadn't the energy or heart to put it in shape for Knopf to publish. When Douglass had died in 1938, she had thought that he was the member of her family she had been closest to, but after Roscoe died, she believed he was the one. She and Douglass, she wrote, had twice quarreled, but there never had been the slightest ruffle on the surface of her relationship with Roscoe. Also it seemed that the most real and interesting parts of her life were the times she had spent with Roscoe in Wyoming. In all the time they lived apart, she added, a fortnight seldom went by without an exchange of letters. The death of Roscoe severed the last close link between Cather and her family. Five months later she wrote Akins that she had been ill and lifeless and seemed to be only half herself.

From the death of Roscoe until Cather's own death "the rest is silence," to quote one of her favorite lines from *Hamlet*. She was only seventy-two, but her health was steadily deteriorating. She did no more writing and did not revise the unfinished Avignon novel. During the last twenty months of her life she was calmly waiting for the end. There was nothing in her medical history to suggest that her death was imminent, no heart attacks such as killed her father and brothers, but the machinery was running down. Although she spent 1946 pretty much in seclusion, she was never bedridden; nor did she act like an invalid, and with old friends her conversation remained animated.

Lewis recalled this final period: "In the last year, it was the little things one lived in; the pleasure of flowers; of a letter from an old friend in Red Cloud, the flying visit of a young niece; of playing, perhaps, Yehudi's recording with Enesco of the Mozart Concerto in D major, made when he was a young boy; immortal youth, singing its lovely song; and one great thing, beyond and above all the rest—the glory of great poetry, filling all the days. She turned almost entirely to Shakespeare and Chaucer that last winter; as if in their company she found her greatest content, best preferred to confront the future."

She also summed up her career in letters to old friends. She wrote Irene Weisz that she had managed to capture a good many pleasures of the past in one book or another, and told Akins that she had got a good deal of what she wanted out of life. Above all she had pretty well escaped the things she violently did not want, some of which were too much money, noisy publicity, and the bother of meeting lots of people. She also had achieved recognition from many writers she most admired. It had been a pleasure when James Barrie wanted autographed copies of her books; she was deeply touched to have Stephen Tennant relay to her Thomas Hardy's high opinion of her work; she enjoyed Undset's admiration. She was satisfied with her career, and her last letters do not suggest in any way that she felt unfulfilled. She had worked hard, and she knew that her accomplishments were significant.

At the same time, she thought that she had had to pay a high price for her success and became increasingly paranoid about her real and supposed enemies. She imagined more hostile critics than there were and often complained about them. More than once Granville Hicks appeared in her letters as a person who almost had made a career out of explaining to people what a second-rate writer she was. One of her last letters, written to Carrie Sherwood, stated flatly that she had bitter enemies in Red Cloud, and she cautioned her old friend not to talk to people about her books. She was constantly worrying about "the town cats," but she wanted at least one person in her home town to know how her books were really written. Carrie, more than anyone else, knew what went into some of her novels, but those things were private and did not belong to the gossips.

During her last spring, 1947, Cather began to pull herself up a bit. She attended a concert in which Menuhin and his sister played together, but that was the last time she went out. In late March the Menuhins came to visit her for the last time, Yehudi and his two children, Hephzibah, her husband, and two little boys. It was like old times (except for the addition of the children) as they sat around her living room. She was reminded of the many times they had gathered to read Shakespeare together. They were all relaxed, the children quiet. Concert-trained people, Cather explained to E. K. Brown, have perfect relaxation. They never think about what they are going to do in the next hour until the present one is entirely spent. At eleven-thirty in the morning the Menuhins stood up, got the children into their wraps, and without any fuss, dropped in the elevator to the street floor where cabs were waiting to take them to the North River docks. They were to sail for Europe on the *Queen Elizabeth* at one o'clock. Their luggage had all gone aboard the day before. They knew they never would see Aunt Willa again.

Cather in summing up her relationship with Yehudi and his sisters said that for sixteen years they had been one of the chief interests and joys of her life. There was an inherent beauty in their natures that went far beyond any "giftedness"—and yet natural beauty of mind and heart was a very great part of "giftedness." She would rather have had almost any part of her life left out than the Menuhin chapter. She was filled with the wonderful morning she had spent with those dear children, as they still were to her, and their children. The next day, March thirtieth, her rooms still seemed full of their presence and their faithful, loving friendship.

As April began Cather started making plans for the summer, even talking about another trip west. She also was thinking about doing some writing, and on the seventeenth wrote Fisher wanting to know what she remembered about their visit to Housman in 1902. She was going to write an article correcting all the misinformation that had gotten about regarding that episode in her life. A week later, April 24, Cather stayed in bed all morning and had her lunch brought to her. "She was never more herself than on the last morning," Lewis wrote. "Her spirit was as high, her grasp of reality as firm as always. And she had kept that warmth of heart, that youthful, fiery generosity which life so often burns out." After lunch she went to sleep and awoke in midafternoon complaining of a headache. Sarah Bloom was with her at four-thirty p.m. when she suffered a massive cerebral hemorrhage.

After Cather died, a private funeral was held at 570 Park Avenue attended by a few friends and relatives. Edith Lewis then arranged for burial in the old cemetery at Jaffrey Center. The body was taken by train and automobile from New York to New Hampshire by her brothers James and John and several other relatives, and at the burial ground on April 27 a service was conducted by the Reverend A. G. Lund, Junior, of the Church of the Good Shepherd of Wareham, Massachusetts. Cather's remains lie at the lower edge of the graveyard beside those of the pioneers of Jaffrey. Off to the immediate west rises the great bulk of Mt. Monadnock. The cemetery, fringed by large old trees, is peaceful and quiet, for Jaffrey Center long since has ceased to be the focus of life in that community and lies several miles west of the present town. Only the old meeting house and a cluster of homes remain there. Although the cemetery was full in 1947, a place was found for Cather, who loved Jaffrey, had finished *My Ántonia*, begun and ended *Death Comes for the Archbishop*, and had written much of *Shadows on the Rock* there. Cather's grave is marked by a simple white headstone, on which is carved lines from *My Ántonia*: "That is happiness; to be dissolved into something complete and great." Later, in November, 1947, a memorial service was held in Red Cloud conducted by Cather's old friend Bishop Beecher.

Under terms of Cather's will, executed in 1943, Edith Lewis became executor and trustee of the estate. She inherited her friend's physical property, one third of her estate, and royalties from her Knopf titles; she lived on in the Park Avenue apartment until her death in 1972 and was buried at the foot of her friend's grave with a plain flat stone marking the spot. The rest of the estate went to a nephew and nieces. With the help of Alfred Knopf, Lewis carried out zealously Cather's wishes in regard to keeping her works away from the movies, off the air, and out of anthologies and cheap reprints. She also did her best to destroy letters and prevent their publication, as Cather had stipulated in her will. To keep Houghton Mifflin from selling movie rights to the novels they controlled, she allowed the firm to bring out paperback editions, and later when the cost of hardcover books began to price Cather's novels out of the reach of a large readership, Knopf persuaded her to permit paperback editions of all the novels.

Meanwhile, in Red Cloud the Willa Cather Pioneer Memorial Foundation was created to preserve the childhood home and other buildings associated with her life and fiction. Over the years this organization has flourished and has aided significantly in perpetuating Cather's memory. Its annual conferences draw people from all over the country, and its tours of Cather country have made Red Cloud a center for literary pilgrimage. In 1973, the centennial year of Cather's birth, the University of Nebraska held an international conference that brought scholars together from all over the world, and in the same year the Menuhins played a memorial concert in Lincoln. In more recent years there have been many Cather conferences and special programs devoted to her work. Her literary reputation as one of the major American authors of the twentieth century today is alive and growing.

ACRONYMS, SOURCES,

AND ABBREVIATIONS

Cather's Writings

AB	*Alexander's Bridge* (1912)
ALL	*A Lost Lady* (1923)
AT	*April Twilights* (1903)
ATO	*April Twilights and Other Poems* (1923)
CSF	*Willa Cather's Collected Short Fiction, 1892–1912*, ed. Virginia Faulkner, intro. Mildred Bennett (1965)
CY	*Writings from Willa Cather's Campus Years*, ed. James Shively (1950)
DCA	*Death Comes for the Archbishop* (1927)
KA	*The Kingdom of Art: Willa Cather's First Principles and Critical Statements*, ed. Bernice Slote (1967)
LG	*Lucy Gayheart* (1935)
MA	*My Ántonia* (1918)
MME	*My Mortal Enemy* (1926)
NUF	*Not Under Forty* (1936)
OBO	*The Old Beauty and Others* (1948)
OD	*Obscure Destinies* (1932)

OO	*One of Ours* (1922)
OP	*O Pioneers!* (1913)
OW	*Willa Cather on Writing* (1949)
PH	*The Professor's House* (1925)
SOL	*The Song of the Lark* (1915)
SOR	*Shadows on the Rock* (1931)
SSG	*Sapphira and the Slave Girl* (1940)
TG	*The Troll Garden* (1905)
UVO	*Uncle Valentine and Other Stories: Willa Cather's Uncollected Short Fiction, 1915–1929*, ed. Bernice Slote (1972)
W&P	*The World and the Parish: Willa Cather's Articles and Reviews, 1893–1902*, ed. William M. Curtin (1970)
YBM	*Youth and the Bright Medusa* (1920)

Because there is not yet a definitive edition of the novels and stories Cather published under the Houghton Mifflin and Knopf imprints, I have quoted from the most accessible texts. These are the currently in-print titles available from both commercial publishers. Quotations from *Alexander's Bridge*, however, come from the Univ. of Neb. Press ed. of 1977. For *April Twilights* and *The Troll Garden* there are definitive editions, from which I have quoted, the former edited by Bernice Slote in 1968 and the latter by myself in 1983. Other quotations from Cather's writings are from the edited texts listed above.

Journals Cited

AL	*American Literature*
GPQ	*Great Plains Quarterly*
SLR	*Saturday Review of Literature*
WCPMN	*Willa Cather Pioneer Memorial Newsletter*
WS	*Women's Studies*

Secondary Works

Art of WC	*The Art of Willa Cather*, ed. Bernice Slote and Virginia Faulkner (1973)
Bennett	Mildred Bennett, *The World of Willa Cather* (1951; repr. 1961)
Brown	E. K. Brown, *Willa Cather: A Critical Biography* (1953; repr. 1987)
Crane	Joan Crane, *Willa Cather: A Bibliography* (1982)
Lewis	Edith Lewis, *Willa Cather Living* (1953; repr. 1976)
Rosowski	Susan Rosowski, *The Voyage Perilous: Willa Cather's Romanticism* (1986)
Sergeant	Elizabeth Shepley Sergeant, *Willa Cather: A Memoir* (1953; repr. 1963)
Stouck	David Stouck, *Willa Cather's Imagination* (1975)

Other standard works for the study of Cather, some of which I have cited in my notes, are as follows:

BIBLIOGRAPHICAL ESSAYS

Bernice Slote, in *Sixteen Modern American Authors*, ed. Jackson R. Bryer (1973); updated by James Woodress in a second edition (1987)

American Literary Scholarship: An Annual

COLLECTIONS OF CRITICISM

Critical Essays on Willa Cather, ed. John Murphy (1983)

Willa Cather and Her Critics, ed. James Schroeter (1967)

WORKS ABOUT CATHER

Marilyn Arnold, *Willa Cather's Short Fiction* (1984)

Edward A. and Lillian D. Bloom, *Willa Cather's Gift of Sympathy*

(1962)

Kathleen D. Byrne and Richard C. Snyder, *Chrysalis: Willa Cather in Pittsburgh, 1896–1906* (1980)

David Daiches, *Willa Cather: A Critical Introduction* (1951)

Philip L. Gerber, *Willa Cather* (1975)

Richard Giannone, *Music in Willa Cather's Fiction* (1968)

Dorothy Van Ghent, *Willa Cather* (1964)

John H. Randall III, *The Landscape and the Looking Glass: Willa Cather's Search for Value* (1960)

Names of Individuals

AF	Frances Cather (Aunt Franc)
AK	Alfred Knopf
BK	Blanche Knopf
CMS	Carrie Miner Sherwood
DCF	Dorothy Canfield Fisher
EL	Edith Lewis
ES	Elizabeth Sergeant
FG	Ferris Greenslet
IMW	Irene Miner Weisz
LP	Louise Pound
MDL	Mabel Dodge Luhan
MG	Mariel Gere
PR	Paul Reynolds
SOJ	Sarah Orne Jewett
SSM	S. S. McClure
WC	Willa Cather
WOJ	Will Owen Jones
ZA	Zoë Akins

Sources of Cather Correspondence and Method of Citation

In citing letters I have used the following form: WC to ZA, 29 Mar. 1929, for a letter from Cather to Zoë Akins written on the given day. When the letter is part of a significant amount of correspondence to or from the same recipient, housed in a single collection, I have not given the location in the citation, but I have listed the main collections below. Thus the citation WC to ZA, 29 Mar. 1929, is to a letter at the Huntington Library (HEH), but a citation such as WC to ZA, 19 Feb. 1924 (Va.) is to a letter at the University of Virginia. The principal correspondents and the location of letter collections are listed as follows; the location is followed by the acronym, abbreviation, or key word I have used to identify it:

Correspondent Collection

AK and/or BK
> Harry Ransom Humanities Research Center, University of Texas Library, Austin (Tex.)

CMS Willa Cather Historical Center, Red Cloud (WCHC)

DCF University of Vermont Library (Vt.)

ES Morgan Library, New York (Morgan); there are also copies of these letters at the University of Virginia Library

FG and Houghton Mifflin correspondence
> Houghton Library, Harvard University (Harvard)

IMW The Newberry Library, Chicago (Newberry)

MDL The Beinecke Rare Book and Manuscript Library, Yale University (Yale)

MG and other members of the Gere family
> Nebraska State Historical Society, Lincoln (NSHS)

PR Columbia University Library (Columbia)

SOJ Houghton Library, Harvard University (Harvard)

SSM and Mrs. McClure
> Lilly Library at Indiana University (Lilly)

ZA Henry E. Huntington Library, San Marino (HEH)

NOTES

For the benefit of scholars and students I have documented extensively the sources I used in writing this biography. The following notes are keyed to the text by page number and the first few words of a quotation or by page number and a key phrase of the text or a paraphrased source.

When several quotations lying close together in my text all come from the same page of a source, I have given the source only once, keyed to the first quotation. Thus, it may be assumed that when a citation such as w&p, p. 274, is followed by two or three quotations not documented in the notes, the source for all is identical.

PREFACE

xiii   "No American novelist": *New York Times Book Review*, 11 May 1947, p. 2. "No American writer": *The Literature of the American People*, ed. Arthur Hobson Quinn (1951), p. 911.
xiv   "Anyone who abhors": *Art of* wc, p. 215.
xvi   wc wrote an old friend: wc to imw, 6 June 1945.
xvii   "If I were asked": ow, p. 58.

PROLOGUE

Many people who knew wc have described her physical appearance. There is general agreement on her build, features, complexion, and manner. Her eyes have been variously described as gray-blue, dark blue, and sailor blue; her hair as light brown, chestnut brown, dark brown, and even black. She called it a strong brown. Her weight and height she has reported herself in letters. Sources here are the memoirs of Lewis, Sergeant, and Elizabeth Moorhead (Vermorcken), *These Two Were Here: Louise Homer and Willa Cather* (1950); Profile by Louise Bogan in the *New Yorker* (8 Aug. 1931); reminiscences by Mary Ellen Chase in *Mass. Rev.* (Spring 1962) and Marion King in *Books and People: Five Decades of New York's Oldest Library* (1954); interviews by Burton Rascoe in *Arts and Decoration* (Apr. 1924) and Latrobe Carroll in *The Bookman* (May 1921); see also WC to Mr. Robbins, 21 May 1924 (Michigan), and WC to CMS, 9 Sept. 1942.

A great deal in this prologue comes from letters from WC to ES, but see in particular 20 and 26 Apr., 21 May, 15 June, 14 Aug. 1912; also see letters describing trip to SSM, 22 Apr., 9 and 12 June 1912.

5   For Arizona history, see Odie B. Faulk, *Arizona: A Short History* (1970).

6   Father T. Connolly is identified in WC to "Dear Sister," 23 Nov. 1940 (Loyola Univ., New Orleans); see also Lewis, p. 82.

7   "How could she help it?": Sergeant, p. 206. "Coming, Aphrodite!" is reprinted in YBM. "The Mexican dance": SOL, p. 289.

9   "Like a thousand others": SOL, p. 369. "From there on to": SOL, p. 370.

10   "Out of the stream": SOL, p. 373. "The personality of": SOL, p. 368. "She had been hurrying": SOL, p. 372.

CHAPTER I: VIRGINIA

Sources for Cather family history are Bennett, Brown, and Lewis; Garland R. Quarles, *Some Old Homes in Frederick County, Virginia* (1971); letter from W. W. Glass, archivist of Frederick County is in CY. Also see Bennett's two-part article in WCPMN, no. 4 (1979), pp. 1–4; nos. 2–3 (1981), pp. 5–9. I have added to and sometimes corrected these sources with material from the Frederick County Historical Society archives, Cather family letters in the NSHS, WC's reminiscences contained in letters to friends, and other works, as noted below. Information on the Cather coat of arms comes from the Slote Papers (Univ. of Nebraska) and Sir John Bernard Burke, *General Armory of England, Scotland, Ireland, and Wales* (1884).

13   "So rapidly did it change": James Howard Gore, *My Mother's Story* (1923), p. 91.

14   "Above the average farmer": T. K. Cartmell, *Shenandoah Pioneers and Their Descendants: A History of Frederick County, Virginia, from Its Foundation in 1738*

to 1909 (1909), p. 475. "Talk had a flavour": SSG, p. 135. "With all my devotion": Douglas Southall Freeman, *R. E. Lee: A Biography* (1945), 1:443. "My grandfather said": MA, pp. 11–12.

15   "A spare, tall woman": MA, pp. 10–11. Memories of the kitchen: SSG, pp. 286–87.

16   Sidney Gore's diary is in Howard Gore, *My Mother's Story.*

17   "I staid to-night": *Specimen Days,* entry entitled "Two Brothers, One South, One North." "The Rebel soldiers": SSG, pp. 276–77.

18   "Somewhere there among the stones": AT, p. 25; "The Namesake" is reprinted in CSF.

19   "Of those unprofessional nurses": W&P, p. 320. "Short, stalwart woman": SSG, p. 11. "There was a kind": OD, p. 81. "His boyish, eager-to-please": OD, pp. 112–13. Bennett, whose informant was Elsie Cather, reports that Charles Cather studied law at a Quaker college in Baltimore, while EL, whose informant must have been WC, reports that he read law in a Washington law office.

20   Charles Cather's success as a farmer was noted by the *Red Cloud Chief* when it reported on 3 October 1884: "At the stock sale of Chas. F. Cather near Catherton the other day, the property sold high, returning something over $9,000. A little over eighteen months ago Mr. Cather went into the ranch business with $4,000 cash, and in that time has made $5,000 over his investment." WC remembered in old age: WC to Helen Cather Southwick, 24 Oct. 1946 (copy at Yale). "Victoria had a good heart": OD, pp. 97–98. "I went up to see her": Caroline Cather to Jennie Ayre, 17 Apr. 1873 (NSHS).

21   She was named Wilella: WC's parents did not give her a middle name, but as a child she called herself Willa Love Cather for the doctor who delivered her. When she was in college, she Latinzied Love to Lova. After going to Pittsburgh she adopted Sibert as her middle name, but in February 1918, she wrote Houghton Mifflin twice asking to have the middle name left off the title page of MA, then in press. She thought the "Sibert" looked too businesslike. The book appeared, however, with Sibert on the title page. It was not until Alfred Knopf published YBM (1920) that her name appeared simply as WC. She continued to use the S in the monogram on her stationery, and the full name Sibert appears in her will. She never liked the name Willa. When she wrote Bishop Beecher, 25 Feb. 1941 (NSHS), asking him to call her Willa, she said she didn't like feminized forms of masculine names. She added that if she had known when she began writing that she would be rather extensively published, she would have used her mother's name. On another occasion she wrote R. L. Scaife at Houghton Mifflin (21 Feb. 1920) complaining that book salesmen habitually mispronounced her name. Most

salesmen, she said, called her "Kay-thur." One had better be named Jones. Also salesmen kept correcting her pronunciation of her name. A Mr. Sell had written a paragraph saying the name rhymed with "rather," but that did not convince salesmen. Just as Ralph Waldo Emerson had dropped the Ralph he disliked and Walter Whitman, Jr., had become Walt Whitman when he began publishing *The Leaves of Grass*, so Wilella Cather became Willa Sibert Cather. "Every artist makes himself born," Harsanyi tells Thea Kronborg in SOL. "We have just been treated": Charles Cather to George Cather, 22 Jan. 1874, WCPMN, no. 4 (1979), p. 1. This letter and WC's birth certificate on file in Richmond establish her birth date as 7 December 1873. Older reference sources usually list 1876. WC cut two years off her age when she was on *McClure's Magazine*, and *Who's Who* from 1909 to 1919 gives her birth date as 1875. After 1920 she dropped another year, and *Who's Who* listed the date as 1876. To perpetuate the confusion EL had the date 1876 carved on WC's tombstone at Jaffrey, N.H.

22   "The Swedish Mother" is reprinted in ATO (1923). The Snowden Anderson incident: WC to Mrs. Ackroyd, 27 Dec. 1942 (Va.).

23   "My cradle is all": Lewis, p. 9. It is interesting to note that Fred Ottenberg's first two names in SOL are Philip Frederick. "*Cato thou art*": Lewis, p. 10. "Scenes of the most": OW, p. 79. "Was born interested": SSG, p. 119; memories of Mary Ann Anderson: WC to Mrs. Ackroyd, 16 May 1941 (Va.)

24   "She had never been sent": OO, p. 22. "Little had she here to leave": ATO, pp. 69–70.

25   "I stood on the bridge": Brown, p. 21; these are the opening lines of Longfellow's "The Bridge." "Period of life which most influences": "Daughter of the Frontier," *NY Herald-Tribune*, 28 May 1933, sec. 11, p. 7. "Till had already risen": SSG, p. 283.

26   Memory of Nancy's dress: WC to Miss Masterson, 15 Mar. 1943 (WCHC). Story of half-witted boy: Lewis, p. 10.

27   Quotations from the five stories are from CSF, pp. 521, 125, 40, 144, and 45; also from OO, p. 447; SOR, p. 152; SSG, p. 89. The Avignon novel is discussed by George N. Kates in "WC's Unfinished Avignon Story," *Five Stories by* WC (1956). The trouble with WC's hands is referred to in many letters, particularly after 1940; see notes for Chapters 21 and 23, below.

28   "I'se a dang'ous nigger": Lewis, p. 13. "Even as a little girl": Lewis, p. 13. Attitudes towards South: WC to ES, 12 Sept. 1913; WC to J. S. Wilson, 3 Mar. 1931 (Va.); WC to IMW, 27 Feb. 1942; WC to ZA, 22 Dec. 1932; WC to Viola Roseboro', 18 Dec. 1942 (Amherst); Lewis, p. 182.

29   "It was the kind of": KA, p. 438. "A Night at Greenway Court" and "The Sentimentality of William Tavener" are reprinted in CSF.

30   "It was a stiff": CSF, pp. 145–46.

31   The story of old Vic comes from Brown, p. 22.

CHAPTER 2: ON THE DIVIDE

32   For an account of the westering fever in Frederick County, Virginia, see an
         unpublished MS by Miles B. Dean (Duke).

33   There are a number of letters from AF to her sister-in-law Jennie Ayre,
         written between 1873 and 1876, describing life in Nebraska (NSHS). Family
         history is treated in Bennett. Catherton: Details of the post office are from
         Wesley Cowley, "Catherton Post Office," Nebr. Hist. (Winter 1973).

34   My description of Nebraska comes from WC's essay "Nebraska: The End of
         the First Cycle," Nation, 5 Sept. 1923; data on Webster County comes from a
         brochure published by Webster County, Historic Webster County: Then and
         Now; data on Red Cloud is from a booklet, One Hundred Years in Red Cloud,
         published in Red Cloud in 1971.

35   "An old and conservative": WC: A Biographical Sketch, an English Opinion, and
         an Abridged Bibliography (1926). The biographical sketch in this brochure,
         published by Knopf for promotional purposes, is written in the third person
         and unsigned, but Cather scholars are agreed that WC wrote it herself.

36   "We drove out": KA, p. 448. This interview originally appeared in the Phila-
         delphia Record under the dateline 9 August 1913. "I was little": Omaha Bee, 29
         Oct. 1921, p. 2. "Cautiously I slipped": MA, pp. 7–8.

37   "Huddled together": MA, pp. 5–6. "Getting acquainted with": WC: A Bio-
         graphical Sketch.

38   Demographic figures come from WC's Nation essay; also her comments on
         foreign languages and attitudes towards immigrants. "We had very few":
         KA, p. 448.

39   They loved her, she added: WC to DCF, 20 Dec. 1929. "They were a fine
         company": CSF, p. 29. A friend once had told her: WC is quoting WOJ in an
         interview in the Lincoln Sunday Star, 24 Oct. 1915, repr. KA, p. 452. "When I
         sit down": interview by Latrobe Carroll, The Bookman (May 1921); this
         interview also reports her saying a writer's basic material is acquired before
         the age of 15.

40   "Life began for me": Sergeant, p. 107. The scene in the Miners' store:
         Bennett, p. 1. Description of grandfather's house and farm: MA, pp. 9, 13–
         14. "lay the black pond": TG, p. 101.

41   WC is indulging: Cowley's memoir ("Catherton Post Office") makes clear
         that from the beginning the settlers brought in lumber by wagon from the

railroad to the north to build houses. By 1879 Red Cloud was linked to the railroad. "Peter" is reprinted in CSF. "All the years that have passed": MA, p. 28. "Sometimes I went south": MA, p. 29.

42 One of the memorable episodes: Although Jim Burden kills the snake in MA, Leo Pavelka, Annie Pavelka's son, writes in an unpublished memoir that it was his mother who killed the snake. This may well be true—if, indeed, anyone killed a huge rattler—as Annie was 14 and Willa 10. Pavelka's memoir, however, is of doubtful accuracy, and some of the "facts" in it come from the novel, such as his saying that the Cathers and the Sadileks both arrived on the same train in 1883, an event demonstrably untrue. "Willa Cather did not go to school": WC: A Biographical Sketch; that WC was enrolled in school in 1883–84 is documented by Bennett: "The Childhood Worlds of WC," GPQ, Fall 1982, p. 206. "After I began": MA, p. 127; details of the schoolhouse-cum-church are from Cowley, "Catherton Post Office." "All the while": WC: A Biographical Sketch. She wrote Witter Bynner: 5 June 1905 (Harvard).

43 The incident of the fire: Bennett, p. 19. The public sale was advertised in the Red Cloud press.

CHAPTER 3: RED CLOUD

44 Data on Red Cloud history comes from One Hundred Years in Red Cloud and from Bennett.

45 To work well she had to be carefree: WC to CMS, 12 Feb. 1934?. The Garber house: ALL, pp. 10–11.

46 Description of Moonstone: SOL, pp. 38–39.

47 "They turned into": SOL, p. 7. "Where there were no": OBO, p. 107. "Snugly lined": SOL, p. 71.

48 "The dog is a very": Bennett, p. 196. "A stalwart young woman": WC to E. J. Overing, Jr., Red Cloud Chief, 27 May 1909, partly reprinted in Bennett, pp. 256–57. "Miss Knightly was": OBO, pp. 75–76.

49 She wrote Mrs. Goudy: WC to Alice Goudy, 3 May 1908 (WCHC). "Both the Goudys became": Lewis, p. 20; this is the best account of Goudys' relationship with WC. I don't know what EL meant by "great gaps in her knowledge." WC had a mind like a sponge, and I don't take this statement seriously. It seems more of a rhetorical flourish than anything else. Even the statement about WC's spelling is not accurate, as her letters contain few misspelled words. WC liked to say she couldn't spell, but she did as well as most teachers whose spelling has been corrupted by years of grading semi-literate student

themes. Data on the Wieners: Bennett, p. 119. "She wasn't pretty": OD, pp. 102–3.

50   The family bookcase: KA, pp. 38–39. "Ray Kennedy on his way": SOL, pp. 73–74.

51   Memory of discovering Tolstoy: WC to H. L. Mencken, 6 Feb. 1922 (Enoch Pratt Lib., Baltimore). She wanted to read about life: WC to Alexander Woollcott, 5 Dec. 1942 (Morgan). Details of WC's private library: KA, pp. 39–40. She later told EL: Lewis, p. 14. Reading *Huck Finn* for twentieth time: WC to Cyril Clemens, 21 Nov. 1934 (WCHC). "That dear old book": W&P, pp. 335–37. "Will Mr. Howard Pyle accept": Frederick B. Adams, Jr., "WC, Early Years: Trial and Error," *The Colophon*, no. 3 (1939), p. 90.

52   Data on Drs. McKeeby and Damerell: Bennett, pp. 110–14. Bennett conjectures that WC had polio on the basis of Carrie Sherwood's memory of hearing the doctor say WC would never walk again. "How I loved": interview in *Omaha Daily News*, 29 Oct. 1921, p. 2.

53   Identification of Dillon and Trueman: WC to CMS, 27 Jan. 1934? Account of Ducker: Lewis, pp. 21–23. Data on Mrs. Miner: Bennett, pp. 59–66. "Mrs. Harling was short": MA, p. 148.

54   "Mrs. Harling had studied": MA, p. 158. WC's letter of condolence: WC to CMS, 29 Oct. 1917 (Va.). The Miner daughters: Bennett, pp. 178–79. Schindelmeisser: Bennett, pp. 152–54.

55   "Wunsch was short": SOL, p. 32. Cutting hair short: Bennett, pp. 178–79. The album entries are reproduced in Bennett, pp. 112–13. For a discussion of WC as adolescent, see Sharon O'Brien, "Tomboying and Adolescent Conflict: Three Nineteenth-Century Case Studies," in *Woman's Being, Woman's Place: Female Identity and Vocation in American History*, ed. Mary Kelly (1979), pp. 351–72. Since these notes were written O'Brien's biography of WC's early years, WC: *The Emerging Voice* (New York, 1986), has appeared. It deals extensively with WC's sexual orientation and psychological development through adolescence and young womanhood.

56   "Positive carriage and freedom": MA, pp. 198–99. "She was just one of them": CSF, p. 474. "We have been playing": CSF, p. 479. The political skirmish: Bennett, pp. 24–26.

57   The play town "Sandy Point": Bennett, pp. 172–73; "The Way of the World" is reprinted in CSF. WC in amateur theatricals: Bennett, pp. 173–76.

58   "Half a dozen times": written for the *Omaha World-Herald*, 27 Oct. 1929, reprinted by Bennett in *Nebr. Hist.* (Winter 1968).

59   "Personal affairs in the": interview in *Red Cloud Argus*, 29 Sept. 1921, reprinted in *Resources for Amer. Lit. Study* (Spring 1979). "Far Island is an oval": CSF, p. 265. "It was still dark": CSF, p. 76.

60   "The three who lay": AT, p. 3. "A man should blow": Bennett, p. 178. "It stated with fervor": MA, p. 229. The text of the oration is from a transcript made by Bernice Slote from the *Red Cloud Argus* for 15 June 1890. A few apparent errors due to careless typesetting or defective copy have been corrected, and punctuation has occasionally been supplied for clarity.

63   Charles Cather's borrowing is reported by Bennett, p. 233. "On a sheet of purple paper": OD, p. 158.

CHAPTER 4: UNIVERSITY DAYS

A major source for this chapter is KA, especially the opening chapter, "Writer in Nebraska," pp. 2–29, which is a pioneering account of WC at the Univ. of Neb. Occasionally I have used details from Bennett, Lewis, and Brown. For background on Lincoln I have used KA; Andrew J. Sawyer, *Lincoln, the Capital City, and Lancaster County, Nebraska*, vol. 1 (1916); and Neale Copple, *Tower on the Plains* (1959). The exact population of Lincoln in 1890 is not known. The 1890 census reports 55,154, but this figure was grossly exaggerated, as was the population of Omaha, apparently for the purpose of getting more congressmen for Nebraska. Edgar Z. Palmer in "The Correctness of the 1890 Census of Population for Nebraska Cities," *Nebr. Hist.*, Dec. 1951, estimates the correct population at 34,440 plus or minus 6% for error.

65   "Were the pioneers": KA, p. 7.
66   "There before me": Alvin Johnson, *Pioneer's Progress: An Autobiography* (1952), p. 76. "In those days": MA, p. 258. "Chief mission of": Johnson, *Pioneer's Progress*, p. 82.
67   "The University of Nebraska": KA, p. 9. "If youth did not": SOL, pp. 198–99.
68   Memory of poverty in college: WC to Atcheson Hench, 16 May 1940 (Va.). "There were no college dormitories": MA, p. 258.
69   "I worked at": MA, p. 259. Memories of WC's classmates: CY. Louise Pound's memory: LP to Clarence Gohdes, 14 Oct. 1957 (Duke). WC's memory of Mrs. Gere: WC to MG, 24 Apr. 1912. Westermann's memory: Brown, pp. 49–50.
70   "Touching because of": Lewis, p. 39. The only letter to Mrs. Goudy to survive is one dated 3 May 1908 (WCHC). Apparently WC's letters to Mrs. Goudy were retrieved after her death and were available to EL when she wrote her memoir. She must have destroyed them later, as she did with others. She told Abbott: WC to Ned Abbott, 25 Oct. 1921? (NSHS). "Gad! how we like": WC to MG, 25 Apr. 1897.
71   "It was his pupil's power": SOL, p. 37. "If Willa Cather had been": Lewis, p.

30. "Life is one damn grind": WC to MG, 2 May 1896. She wrote Mrs. Goudy: Lewis, p. 29. Letter about dissecting frogs: WC to MG, 16 July 1891; this is earliest extant WC letter. The transcript of WC's college program is available from the Univ. of Neb. registrar's office, but no grades are recorded.

72   Passed exams on inspiration: Lewis, p. 34. "Like the lone survivor": KA, pp. 424–25; the entire essay is reprinted in KA, pp. 421–25, from which all quotations are taken. "A young girl sixteen": *Neb. State Journal*, 1 Mar. 1891.

73   "Up to that time": WC to WOJ, 22 Mar. 1927 (Va.); this letter was published in the *Neb. State Journal*, 24 July 1927, p. 6F.

74   "I never knew anyone": Fanny Butcher, *Many Lives—One Love* (1972), p. 354. No god but one god: WC to MG, 4 Aug. 1896. The Shakespeare essay is reprinted in KA, pp. 426–36, from which my quotations are taken.

75   "One felt that he": W&P, p. 56. "Art and religion": PH, p. 69. "The truth is": Brown, p. 57. "In plain, unornamented": KA, p. 11.

76   "I had to produce": quoted in Sergeant, p. 10.

77   "He took Antone's shotgun": CSF, p. 543. The 1892 and 1900 versions of "Peter" are reprinted together in *Early Stories of* WC, ed. Mildred Bennett (1957), pp. 1–8. WC's Latin version of the Lord's Prayer must be her own translation, as it is not the text of the Roman Catholic Missal, which is "*Pater noster, qui es in caelis.*"

78   "His bill of fare": CSF, pp. 535–36.

79   She wrote him a testy letter: WC to Edward Wagenknecht, 31 Dec. 1938 (Morgan). "A Son of the Celestial" and "A Tale of the White Pyramid" are reprinted in CSF. "The Clemency of the Court" also is in CSF. Tree's address: W&P, p. 198.

80   "I knew that I": MA, p. 262. "She amazed": Fisher, "Daughter of the Frontier", p. 9. "Came down to mere": KA, p. 18. "I am dying": KA, p. 19.

81   Defense of *Trilby*: W&P, pp. 132–34. "What did the noble matron": Brown, p. 55. "They never feel": KA, p. 429. "In the classical courses": Brown, p. 52. "I have sometimes thought": MA, pp. 260–61.

82   "Julius turned in": OO, p. 39. "Seemed to him very young": OO, p. 40. "Depiction of the dinners": CY, p. 134.

83   "Regarded him not only": Johnson, *Pioneer's Progress*, p. 81. " 'The Fear that Walks by Noonday' " is reprinted in CSF. "At a football game": Ida Washington, DCF: *A Biography* (1982), p. 21. "Yet because it": Rosowski, pp. 208–9.

84   "I was paid one dollar": WC to WOJ, 22 Mar. 1927 (Va.). "A severe iconoclast": Lewis, p. 38. "A dreary waste of": KA, p. 14. "That was the last straw": *Lincoln Star*, 29 June 1924, p. 6.

85   WC fell in love: My discussion of WC's relationship with LP is based on WC to

LP, 15 June 1892 and 29 June 1893 (Duke); WC to MG, 1 Aug. 1893. For another discussion of WC's relationship with LP, see Sharon O'Brien, " 'The Thing Not Named': WC as a Lesbian Writer," *Signs* (Summer 1984), pp. 576–99. Also see O'Brien's WC: *The Emerging Voice*. She confessed to DCF: WC to DCF, 8 Apr. 1923.

86   "Around the halls": W&P, p. 122.

87   It is pure speculation: *Willa: The Life of* WC (1983), pp. 59–61. My source for Roscoe Pound is David Widger, *Roscoe Pound: Philosopher of Law* (1974). "The breach of ettiquette": *Omaha World-Herald*, 19 May 1937. Angry response from a minister: see Mildred Bennett, "How WC Chose Her Names," *Names* (1962), pp. 31–32.

88   Based on a real person: see notes for p. 380. Mariel had been a bracer: WC to MG, 2 May 1896. WC was writing her from Pittsburgh: WC to LP, 18 Oct. 1897 (Duke).

CHAPTER 5: TURNING PROFESSIONAL

89   She probably turned out more copy: Crane identifies 561 articles, reviews, and essays written between 1893 and 1902, but there certainly are others yet to be discovered, either signed with a pseudonym still unrecognized or published anonymously. Much pioneering work has been done in locating this fugitive material. John Hinz, Phyllis Hutchinson, James Shively, William Curtin, Mildred Bennett, and especially Bernice Slote contributed to this enterprise. Much, but by no means all, of this journalism has been reprinted in KA and W&P.

90   "The church was crowded": W&P, p. 5. "In a bare, barn-like": W&P, p. 6. "By what is man ever": W&P, p. 7.

91   "The one great drama": W&P, p. 223. "To commend, even to speak": W&P, pp. 43–44. "Drama on one man's": W&P, p. 28. "Someone ought to have": W&P, p. 29. "Mr. Downing is": W&P, p. 27.

92   "The best theatrical critics": KA, pp. 14–15. "Lincoln newspapers are": W&P, p. 226 (WC's interview with Frohman). "Many an actor": KA, p. 17. "It is a score of years": W&P, p. 46.

93   "The Society claim": W&P, p. 50. "The artist, poor fellow": W&P, p. 52. "Julia Marlow has come": W&P, p. 36. "The most finished performance": W&P, pp. 54–55.

94   "Mademoiselle Celeste is": KA, p. 139. "They dug Shakespeare's grave": W&P, p. 62. "Mr. Warde has no talent": W&P, p. 63. "No critic enjoys": W&P, pp. 93–94. "This is for 'Billy' ": KA, p. 22. "No worse than those": *Omaha World-Herald*, 1 Feb. 1920, Feature Sec., p. 1.

95   "A critic's first instincts": W&P, p. 70. "One never realizes": W&P, p. 177. "The general sentiment": W&P, p. 176.

96   "Sylvan wanderings": Bernice Slote, "WC Reports Chautauqua, 1894," *Prairie Schooner* (Spring 1969), p. 119.

97   "Literally strewn": ibid., p. 126. "It is almost unheard of": W&P, p. 103. "A Resurrection" is reprinted in CSF, "When the government thermometer": W&P, p. 778.

98   "Was fascinated by": Lewis, p. 37. "When I Knew Stephen Crane" is reprinted in W&P, pp. 772–78, from which my quotations are taken.

99   "Crane's western journey": John Berryman, *Stephen Crane* (1950), pp. 97–98. "Poe found short story": W&P, p. 158; the Poe essay appears on pp. 157–63.

100 "with large, universal": W&P, p. 705. "When you examine": OW, pp. 69–70; see also Slote, "Stephen Crane and WC," *The Serif* (Dec. 1969). "He died young": NUF, p. 91. "The Personal Side of William Jennings Bryan" is in W&P, pp. 782–89, from which my quotations are taken.

102 For the trip to Chicago, see Bennett, p. 156; KA, p. 20; W&P, p. 178. The review of *Falstaff* is in W&P, pp. 178–82. Serious illness: Charles Cather to Sidney Gore, 27 Apr. 1895, *Neb. Hist.* (Winter 1973), pp. 590–91.

103 WC's roast of Hugh Walker: KA, p. 21. WC's activities after graduation are covered in KA, pp. 22–28. "Miss Willa Cather": KA, p. 23.

104 "A young woman with": KA, pp. 26–27. "A young woman who is": KA, p. 27.

105 She wrote Mariel's father: WC to Charles Gere, 14 Mar. 1896.

106 "Near Rattlesnake Creek": CSF, p. 493. "So it was that Canute": CSF, p. 501. "The immigrant's spiritual confrontation": Rosowski, p. 18.

107 "She said her professor had touched it up: WC to Wagenknecht, 31 Dec. 1938 (Morgan). "It was a veritable Dance": CSF, p. 494. "We are growing too": W&P, p. 269–70. "Doesn't Mr. Howells know": W&P, p. 259–60.

108 "I suppose the curse": W&P, p. 262. "To every man": W&P, p. 264. "The chaos and": W&P, p. 265. "I picked up": W&P, p. 274. "Volume of verse worth": W&P, p. 290. "In all the literature": W&P, p. 274. "Sins unpardonably": opening paragraph of preface to *The House of the Seven Gables*.

109 "May find out": W&P, p. 275. "We work in the dark": partially quoted, W&P, p. 271. "One could read him"; W&P, p. 275. "The greatest living master": W&P, p. 297. "The entire Ruskin essay is reprinted in W&P, pp. 297–301, from which all of my quotations are taken. "Dirty old man": W&P, pp. 282–83.

110 "Compared to the greatness": W&P, p. 284. "Sometimes I wonder": W&P, p. 275. "Adjectives and sentimentality": W&P, p. 276. "It is a very grave question": W&P, p. 146.

111 "There is one woman poet": W&P, p. 147. For speculation on how WC got her

Pittsburgh job, see KA, p. 29; also see Lewis, p. 40. EL thought Axtell and Gere were friends, but she also believed that WC met Axtell when he visited Lincoln in the spring of 1896. This visit probably did not take place, for when he met WC at the station in Pittsburgh in July, she did not recognize him (see WC to MG, 3? July 1896).

CHAPTER 6: EARLY DAYS IN PITTSBURGH

Byrne and Snyder's *Chrysalis* is the most exhaustive account of WC's Pittsburgh years. See Crane for a listing of WC's identified writings of this period.

112   The Doré exhibit: WC to MG, 3? July 1896. Meeting with Axtell: ibid. The Axtell family: WC to "Neddius" [Ellen Gere], undated 1896.

113   The row over Anna Held: W&P, pp. 505–6.

114   The Carnegie Library: WC to "Neddius," undated 1896. She had taken the veil: WC to MG, 10 Aug. 1896. Racing the electric cars: WC to Mrs. Gere, 13 July 1896. "These pages will be": reprinted in Byrne and Snyder, *Chrysalis*, p. 4.

115   The magazine was the worst trash: WC to MG, 27 Apr. 1897. DCF remembered that WC made $100 per month ("Blue and Gold Pittsburgh," *Chicago Tribune Mag. of Books*, 21 Dec. 1947, p. 12), but she probably was paid in addition for the articles and stories she wrote for the magazine. Other compensations: WC to MG, 4 Aug. 1896.

116   "Dirty, prosaic Pittsburgh": W&P, p. 393. Trip to Homestead: WC to MG, 7 Mar. 1898. "He was born a Presbyterian": YBM, pp. 131–32.

117   "He felt a sudden zest": TG, p. 105. WC's involvement in social life: WC to MG, 10 Aug. 1896.

118   Mrs. Canfield's visit" WC to MG, 10 Jan. 1898 (misdated as 1897). DCF's visit: WC to MG, 25 Apr. 1897. Feelings about DCF: WC to DCF, 8 Apr. 1921. "My occasional brief stopovers": DCF, "Blue and Gold Pittsburgh."

119   Relations with May Willard: WC to Mary Willard, 6 May 1941 (Va.). "Stand listening to": Lewis, p. 49. Seibel's memories are in his "Miss WC from Nebraska," *New Colophon* (1949), pp. 195–208.

120   If DCF's memory of hearing Seibel recite Heine (DCF, "Blue and Gold Pittsburgh") is correct, it took place Christmas 1897, when she visited Pittsburgh. However, Cather's translation of the poem appeared in the *Home Monthly* (Dec., 1896). Since the December issue of the magazine appeared before Christmas, WC's translation must have been made before

she ever had spent a Christmas in Pittsburgh. Seibel's article does not mention this translation. WC's statement that she did not remember translating the poem appears in WC to DCF, 3 Jan. n.y. The lines quoted are the last stanza of "Die heil'gen drei Könige aus Morganland."

121   "It's all very fine": CSF, pp. 475–76.

122   Published pseudonymously: This story was signed Elizabeth L. Seymour. "Is a crucial story": Sharon O'Brien, "Mothers, Daughters, and the 'Art Necessity': WC and the Creative Process," in *American Novelists Revisited: Essays in Feminist Criticism*, ed. Fritz Fleishmann (1982), p. 275. "Willie, Willie!": CSF, p. 562. "He has returned": O'Brien, "Mothers, Daughters," p. 275. See also WC: *The Emerging Voice.*

123   Writing Mrs. Gere about Mrs. Bryan: WC to Mrs. Gere, 13 July 1896. "Greatest of all": W&P, p. 359. "Was one of the boys' ": W&P, p. 339. "I know of no one": W&P, p. 365. "Who Mr. Housman may be": W&P, p. 358.

124   "I never feel": W&P, pp. 343–44. "Letter to MG after DCF's visit: WC to MG, 25 Apr. 1897. He was Charles Moore: After I published WC: *Her Life and Art* (1970), I received a letter from Charles Moore's niece, Mrs. Lois Adele Dailey, who said that in 1929 she had visited her aunt and uncle in Nebraska and had asked Uncle Charlie about his friendship with WC. He unlocked his rolltop desk and took out of a locked cubbyhole a packet of letters "about 5 inches thick." He would not let his niece examine them and returned the packet to his desk. After both aunt and uncle died, the letters were never found. The ring that Cather wore is now worn by her niece, Helen Cather Southwick. The proposal of marriage: WC to MG, 27 Apr. 1897.

125   Preston Farrar: WC to MG, 10 Jan. 1898. "If an artist does": KA, pp. 434–35.

126   Comments on Mary Anderson: W&P, pp. 201–2. "Where thou goest": W&P, p. 176. "If they are actresses": W&P, p. 193. "He travels the swiftest": W&P, p. 194. "Her own house": "Three American Singers," *McClure's* (Dec. 1913), p. 34. "art instinct": KA, p. 158. "I have not a great deal": W&P, p. 362. Letter to Mary Miner Creighton: WC to Mrs. Creighton, Aug. ? 1934 (Va.).

127   WC's desire to preserve the inviolability of the self is discussed perceptively in Blanche Gelfant, "The Forgotten Reaping-Hook: Sex in *My Ántonia*," AL (Mar., 1971).

128   "*Rip Van Winkle* has been": W&P, pp. 422–23. "The matronly Fanny": W&P, p. 424. "Her Juliet is": W&P, p. 427. "Such a rambling": W&P, pp. 430–31. "Just as nearly no play": W&P, p. 437. "As an actor he": W&P, p. 439. "It comes nearer": W&P, pp. 469–70. "Very common little men": KA, p. 407.

129   "Comes in long": W&P, p. 377. "She bursts upon you": W&P, pp. 397–98. "Which beset every singer": W&P, p. 404.

130   "So beautiful": W&P, pp. 407–8. Selling of *Home Monthly*: WC to Helen

Seibel, 23 July 1897 (WCHC). "After spending the summer": WC to class secretary, 7 June 1898, published in brochure by Class of 1895 (1900). She wrote WOJ: WC to WOJ, 7 Sept. 1897 (NSHS). She wrote LP: WC to LP, 13 Oct. 1897 (Duke).

131   Grilling in the heat: WC to Frances Gere, 23 June 1898 (NSHS).

132   "Temperamentally Mr. Nevin": "The Man Who Wrote 'Narcissis,'" *Ladies' Home Journal* (Nov. 1900), p. 11. She wrote MG twice: WC to MG, Dec. ? 1897, 10 Jan. 1898. "Uncle Valentine" and "'A Death in the Desert'" appear in UVO and TG respectively. Possible rivalry between WC and Anne Nevin: Byrne and Snyder, *Chrysalis*, pp. 27–36.

133   "I am dependent on": Vance Thompson, *Life of Ethelbert Nevin* (1913), p. 203. "Sleep, Minstrel, Sleep": AT, p. 14. WC wrote the editor: WC to William V. Alexander, 29 Feb. 1901 (Va.). "Was inclined to think": W&P, p. 388. "Flawless perfection": W&P, p. 416.

134   "Few really great plays": W&P, p. 447. "The naked truth": W&P, p. 448. "By its biting satire": W&P, p. 489. "That will always echo": W&P, p. 518. "He went because": W&P, p. 523.

135   Thanksgiving in Columbus: WC to MG, Dec.? 1897. "Trip to New York: WC to MG, 7 Mar. 1898. "Beautifully graceful": W&P, p. 458. Job offer on *Sun*: WC to Fred Otte, 15 Aug. 1898 (WCHC). Visit to Washington: WC to Frances Gere, 23 June 1898 (NSHS). No one ever has identified WC's account of the polar expedition.

136   Summer activities: WC to Fred Otte, 15 Aug. 1898; WC to Winifred Richardson, 15 Aug. 1898 (WCHC); WC to Helen Seibel, 20 Aug. 1898 (WCHC).

CHAPTER 7: ISABELLE MCCLUNG AND A NEW CAREER

137   "She is a very different": DCF to MG, Oct. 1898 (NSHS).

138   A series of open letters: generally called "The Player Letters," they are discussed in Frederick B. Adams, Jr., "WC, Early Years: Trial and Error," *The Colophon*, (no. 3, 1939), p. 92. "Stedman did nothing": WC to Van Noppen, Jan. 1900, ibid. "At any rate we like you": W&P, p. 464.

139   "When she arrived at": W&P, p. 548. Then she nursed her: Lewis, p. 45; "I never come out of": W&P, p. 443. There is a good bit of material on the McClung family and their house in *Chrysalis*, pp. 37–53. Helen Cather Southwick in "WC's Early Career: Origins of a Legend," *West. Penn. Hist. Mag.* (Apr., 1982), pp. 85–98, demonstrates that the account of WC and Isabelle McClung by Elizabeth Moorhead (Vermorcken), *These Two Were*

Here, is quite inaccurate. My article, "WC and Her Friends," in *Critical Essays on WC*, also contains errors, as do previous biographies of Brown, Gerber, Robinson, and myself, all of which made unwary use of Moorhead.

140 "Apparently had no difficulty": Lewis, p. 53; some insubstantial evidence of discord over WC's living at the McClungs is reported in Byrne and Snyder, *Chrysalis*, pp. 41–42; there is extant a collection of letters, extending over a period of years, from WC to Edith McClung in the possession of the McClung family. Although I have been unable to see these, their existence suggests a cordial relationship. "There was a good deal of": Brown, p. 96.

141 Except for three letters: published in Marion Marsh Brown and Ruth Crone, *Only One Point of the Compass: WC in the Northeast* (1980), pp. 66–69, 79–84. Internal evidence of these undated letters suggests they were written between 1926 and 1930. The definition of lesbianism adopted by some feminists: Lillian Faderman, *Surpassing the Love of Men: Romantic Friendship and Love between Women from the Renaissance to the Present* (1981), pp. 17–18. For discussions of WC as lesbian, see O'Brien, *WC: The Emerging Voice*, and "'The Thing Not Named': WC as a Lesbian Writer," *Signs* (Summer 1984), pp. 576–99; Jane Rule, *Lesbian Images* (1975); Deborah Lambert, "The Defeat of a Hero: Autonomy and Sexuality in *My Ántonia*," AL (Jan., 1982), pp. 676–90. "WC was a lesbian": Lambert, p. 676. "She bore a burden": Rule, p. 76.

142 "remarkable story": W&P, p. 553. "Happiest years of": W&P, p. 598. "Either Mr. Crane": W&P, pp. 700–701. "A new and great book": W&P, pp. 605–6. "Exquisite and sensitive": W&P, p. 697. "More romance out of": W&P, p. 698.

143 "Greatest mind in": W&P, p. 724. "As good as anything": W&P, p. 711. "Penetrating intellect": W&P, p. 659. "Interesting and artistic": W&P, p. 677. "Something long to be": W&P, p. 619. Trip home for summer: WC to MG, 2 Aug. 1899; WC's parents lived in Lincoln off and on in the late nineties when Charles Cather was working there. "The Westbound Train" is reprinted in CSF.

144 Letter to DCF: WC to DCF, 12 Oct. 1899.

145 "Sobered by toil": CSF, p. 360. "Probably the first good music": CSF, p. 366. "Which seemed to reach": CSF, p. 376.

146 The sentimental ending: In 1912 when WC wrote "The Bohemian Girl," she did use the boy-gets-girl plot. All the stories that appeared in the *Library* are reprinted in CSF. "It's a grewsome tale": CSF, p. 340.

147 Writing WOJ from Pittsburgh: WC to WOJ, 29 Sept. 1900 (Va.). Found a job translating: There is no proof of this, but it is family tradition that came from Elsie Cather. That she worked for the Commission to the Paris Exposition is

my inference based on the fact she wrote on the Commission's letterhead during this period. "How it did use to": PH, pp. 232, 234.

148   "Came in like a lamb": W&P, p. 796. "The street corners were": W&P, p. 801. "During the W.C.T.U.": W&P, p. 802. "One of the most intelligent": W&P, p. 799. "A complete analysis": W&P, p. 814.

149   "Once heard cannot": W&P, p. 817. "One of the quaint": W&P, p. 830. "Jack-a-Boy" and "Kansas: A Recessional" are reprinted in CSF.

150   *Chrysalis*, pp. 54–67, contains a great deal of material on WC's teaching career, particularly memories of former students. There also is material in Southwick, "WC's Early Career," and in an unpublished memoir by Fred Otte, Jr., that I found in the Slote Papers at the Univ. of Neb. The *High School Journal*, quoted by Southwick, p. 91, gives the first clear evidence that WC taught algebra. About losing 20 pounds: WC to Helen Seibel, 17 July 1901 (WCHC). "Asking for champagne": W&P, p. 842.

151   "There are thousands": W&P, p. 843. "A remarkable new book": W&P, p. 846. "Could write of the": W&P, p. 848. "They tell the story": W&P, p. 853. "The whisky drunk in Homestead": W&P, p. 858.

152   "The bosses and draughtsmen": W&P, p. 857. She could have stuck it out: WC to Fred Otte, Jr., 28 Nov. 1940 (WCHC). "A fortress set upon": CSF, p. 286. "Often, when some lad": W&P, p. 287.

153   "Her voice was deeper": Brown, p. 93. "One of the very few": *Chrysalis*, p. 55. "Beautiful, even white teeth": Phyllis Martin Hutchinson, "Reminiscences of WC as a Teacher," *Bul. of N. Y. Pub. Lib.* (June, 1956), p. 264; "She set us to writing": ibid. "That drudge": OW, p. 41. "Designed to teach us": Hutchinson, "Reminiscences".

154   "If you don't hand in": related in letter to me from Thomas H. Foster, 31 Mar. 1971. "there is many a youth": Hutchinson, "Reminiscences," p. 265. "Devotion to the brilliant": *Chrysalis*, p. 62.

155   She liked her work: WC to MG, 30 Sept. 1905. "A city high school": CSF, p. 285. "Like the ruin of": CSF, p. 289. "Died wretchedly": CSF, p. 290.

156   "The Treasure of Far Island" is reprinted in CSF. WC wrote FG (26 Nov. 1945) that she taught from nine to four, then spent two hours every night working on stories.

157   "I have been in England": W&P, pp. 890–91. "Hearing only English": W&P, p. 891. "One can understand": W&P, p. 895.

158   "Had been born in": W&P, p. 904. Housman's bond slave: WC to Viola Roseboro', 14 June 1903 (Harvard). "Which is nowhere more": W&P, p. 897. "High green hills": W&P, p. 898. She wrote a friend the following year: Roseboro', 14 June 1903.

159   As we went out together": DCF to WC, Apr. 1947, published in Bennett, p.

126. There is another undated letter (Harvard) written in 1903 or 1904 describing this visit. WC wrote DCF asking for her memories of the visit on 17 Apr. 1947. So far as I know, this is the last extant letter WC wrote. The person who discovered that WC invented the account of seeing Housman's poems in the local newspaper files was William White in "A Note on Scholarship: WC on A. E. Housman," *Victorian Newsletter* (No. 13, 1958). See also WC's letters about Housman to Cyril Clemens (WCHC) and to Carl Weber (Colby College). Ford's story is in *Return to Yesterday* (1932), pp. 330–32. WC's possession of a Housman MS was reported to a Mr. Hooker in a letter dated only 27 June (Texas). "He was courteous": Bennett, p. 127.

160   "Almost under the dome": W&P, p. 907. "Her voice is harder": W&P, p. 909. "Whose resemblance to Shakespeare": W&P, p. 919. "Above the roar": W&P, p. 921.

161   "When he reached the choir": OO, p. 342.

162   "To complete the resemblance": W&P, p. 931. "Probably from some young": W&P, p. 926. "Lives in every street": W&P, p. 928. "Are all very well": W&P, p. 934. "Looked very much like": W&P, p. 935.

163   "Each better than the last": W&P, p. 936. "The sunlight played": W&P, p. 939. "Blue lightning and": W&P, p. 941. "Still and motionless": W&P, p. 942. "Oppressive splendor": W&P, p. 946. "The sea was too blue": W&P, p. 947.

CHAPTER 8: *APRIL TWILIGHTS* AND *THE TROLL GARDEN*

164   "The dwarfed children": AT, p. 61. "I do not take myself": quoted in Alice H. Bartless, "The Dynamics of American Poetry," *Poetry Rev.* (1925), p. 408.

165   "The befriender of the": AT, p. xxii. She wrote WOJ: WC to WOJ, 2 Jan. 1903 (Va.). Concerning ES's copy of AT; WC to ES, 2 June 1912.

166   "Achievement of excellence": W&P, p. 883. "In AT," writes Bernice Slote: AT, pp. xxiv-xxv.

167   All the poems quoted here are from the 1903 version. Revisions made in later printings are recorded in Slote's textual apparatus.

168   She wrote ES disparaging her poems: WC to ES, 2 June 1912.

170   "A book of genuine poetry": AT, pp. xxi-xxiii; other reviews are also quoted from this source. "This is a book": *Poetry*, (July, 1923), pp. 221–22.

171   She wrote Jones afterwards: WC to WOJ, 7 May 1903 (Va.). "I sat and held": quoted in Harold Wilson, *McClure's Magazine and the Muckrakers* (1970), p. 119n.

172   "The world is weary": W&P, p. 847.

173   "Never has the purchase": W&P, p. 145; for a feminist reading of "The Goblin

Market" see Sandra Gilbert and Susan Gubar, *The Madwoman in the Attic* (1979), pp. 564–71. "Hotel, habited by freaks". TG, p. 22. The estrangement between WC and DCF is inferred from an undated letter from WC to Mrs. Canfield (Vt.) written about the time TG was published; WC refers to something too painful to discuss that has caused DCF pain.

174   "Temple to the gods": TG, p. 10. Concerning the origin of "Paul's Case": WC to John Phillipson, 15 Mar. 1943 (WCHC).

175   Another ingredient that she never mentioned: *Bookman* (July, 1905), pp. 456–57. Foerster's memory: Norman Foerster to Clarence Gohdes, 23 Mar. 1971 (privately owned). She did concede that: WC to Mr. and Mrs. Partington, 23 June 1921 (Newberry). "A blinding stretch": TG, p. 66.

176   "This is my tragedy": TG, p. 72. "To beat no more": TG, p. 68. Account of Reinhart funeral: W&P, pp. 510–12. "What Harve needed": TG, p. 41.

177   "Ill-fitting false teeth": TG, p. 96. "Stretched and twisted": TG, p. 99. "The stranger to this state": *Journal*, 27 Feb. 1904; reprinted in Bennett, p. 254. WC's defense: WC to WOJ, 6 Mar. 1904 (Va.).

178   WC wrote a friend: WC to Viola Roseboro', Feb.? 1904 (copy at WCHC). Manna in the wilderness: WC to MG, 1 Aug. 1893. "Caroline had served": TG, p. 49. "It was not enough": TG, p. 55.

179   The invention of the valet was discovered by John March (see Bennett, p. 249). "Collection of freak stories": *Bookman* (Aug., 1905), pp. 612–14. Other reviews are quoted in TG, p. xxiv.

180   Bynner's efforts to interest James are reported in Sergeant, pp. 68–69, which reprints the James letter. WC's response to James's letter: WC to Bynner, 24 Feb. 1906 (Harvard). "Joy and critical estimate": Sergeant, p. 67. "That they now hardly seemed": WC to ES, 27 June 1911; ES's paraphrase. When WC was chiding: WC to Wagenknecht, 15 Oct. 1936 (Morgan).

181   "Smooth away crudeness": "Some Books of Short Stories," *Yale Rev.* (1921), p. 671. Account of summer of 1905: WC to MG, 30 Sept. 1905.

182   "In an entirely different vein": Bernice Slote, "WC as a Regional Writer," *Kans. Quart.* (Spring, 1970), p. 13. Not bad enough to throw away: WC to Bynner, 24 Feb. 1906? (Harvard). Twain dinner: *N. Y. Times*, 6 Dec. 1905, p. 1. Opinion of *Huck Finn*: OW, p. 58.

183   "When we return": Southwick, "WC's Early Career," p. 94. "Dear Boys and Girls": reprinted in *Chrysalis*, p. 63.

CHAPTER 9: *MC CLURE'S MAGAZINE*

The general sources for this chapter are Harold Wilson, *McClure's Magazine and the Muckrakers* (1970); Peter Lyon, *Success Story: The Life and Times of S. S. McClure*

(1963); James Woodress, "The Preeminent Magazine Genius: S. S. McClure," in *Essays Mostly on Periodical Publishing in America* (1973), pp. 171–92.

184   "Was the pre-eminent": Mark Sullivan, *The Education of an American* (1938), p. 193. "More pages of": *McClure's* (Feb., 1896), p. 364.

185   "Was the most exciting": Lyon, *Success Story*, p. 113. Baker's memory: *American Chronicle* (1945), pp. 93–94. "I spent the greater part": *All in the Day's Work* (1939), p. 258.

186   "Kings who have come": *Success Story*, p. 291. "Bynner, are you leaving?": ibid., p. 294.

187   "Was the precise reversal": *The Happy Profession* (1948), p. 142. "Sam had three hundred": *Autobiography* (1946), p. 386. "Some of his ideas": Lewis, p. 60. "They leave me": ssm to Robert Mather, 14 Apr. 1906 (Lilly).

188   "It amused him": uvo, p. 102. "O'Mally went in for": uvo, p. 104. "I can't do anything": uvo, p. 113. "Economics and art": ow, p. 27. She suggested changes: wc to Dwight, 3 July 1906 (Amherst).

189   She must have been blunt: wc to Dwight, 20 July 1906 (Amherst). A letter after he had gone back: wc to Dwight, 12 Jan. 1907 (Amherst). A feeling could be a story: wc to Dwight, 9 Oct. 1906 (Amherst). The city was big and raw: wc to Dwight, 12 Jan. 1907 (Amherst).

190   "Throwing up a mist": ybm, p. 7.

191   Bynner's memory of "The Profile" being suggested by a friend's disfigurement comes from his "Autobiography in the Shape of a Book Review" in *Prose Pieces,* ed. James Craft (1979). I use this memory because the incident is characteristic of wc's practice, but Bynner's old-age memories are unreliable, and he remembered things that are demonstrably untrue. For example, he remembered that McClure asked him to cut hundreds of words from "The Sculptor's Funeral" and when wc saw the proofs she blew up. wc was not yet on McClure's staff when the story was printed, and between the magazine version of the story and the tg version there is no difference in length. "The Profile" is reprinted in csf; also "The Willing Muse."

192   "Eleanor's House" is reprinted in csf. So tepid and bloodless: wc to Pattee, 2 Dec. 1926 (Penn. State). The story of wc and the Eddy biography is fashioned from the following: L. Brent Bohlke, "wc and *The Life of Mary Baker G. Eddy*," al (May, 1982), pp. 288–94; Bohlke found the letter to Anderson, 24 Nov. 1922 (N. Y. Pub. Lib.); Mark Sullivan, *Education of an American*, p. 202; *Success Story*, pp. 299–302; wc to Charles Cather, 17 Dec. 1906 (copy at Va.); wc to Harrison Dwight, 12 Jan. 1907 (Amherst).

194   "The novelist must learn": ow, p. 40. "The most costly church": *McClure's* (Dec., 1906), p. 211.

195   *Times* editorial: *McClure's* (Feb., 1907), p. 452.

196   "Frail, diminished in force": "148 Charles Street" in NUF, p. 57. "It was at tea-time": NUF, pp. 62–63. WC insisted her letters be destroyed: WC to DeWolfe Howe, 11 Dec. 1931 (Harvard). The line from Donne is from "The Relique". "That's very nice": NUF, p. 65.

197   "Virtue is concerned": NUF, p. 72. "Who looked very like": NUF, p. 54. "I wish that I could": *Letters of* SOJ. ed. Annie Fields (1911), p. 235. "I was sorry to miss": ibid., p. 245.

198   Not the least interested in SOJ: WC to Alexander Woollcott, 5 Dec. 1942 (Morgan). Account of 1908 trip to Europe: WC to Alice Goudy, 3 May 1908 (WCHC); Megaris now is known as Castel dell'Ovo.

199   Visit to Ravello: WC to SOJ, 10 May 1908.

200   "Clearly the two of them": Sergeant, p. 39. "As a curb on genius": Will Irwin, *The Making of a Reporter* (1942), p. 137. "A captain, as Will White": Sergeant, p. 202.

201   WC had doubts about this story: WC to SOJ, 24 Oct. 1908. "Deep happiness": SOJ to WC, 27 Dec. 1980 (*Letters of* SOJ, pp. 246–47).

202   "I threw my cigar away": CSF, p. 90. "I returned to the deck": CSF, p. 83. "I cannot help saying": SOJ to WC, 13 Dec. 1908 (*Letters of* SOJ, pp. 247–50).

203   She responded with an eight-page reply: WC to SOJ, 19 Dec. 1908.

205   The couplet, quoted a little inaccurately, is from "The Deserted Village." WC refers to being in the hospital: WC to DCF, 15 Apr. 1909. "I am anxious": SSM to WC, 16 Mar. 1909 (Wilson, *McClure's Mag. and the Muckrakers*, p. 192). "The best magazine executive": *Success Story*, p. 390.

206   "We had our swim before sundown": CSF, p. 69. "I have been greatly pleased": SSM to WC, 18 June 1909. "I am awfully proud": SSM to WC, 19 June 1909. "How can I learn?": *Autobiography of Lincoln Steffens* (1958), p. 364. Meredith's funeral and Yeats's box: WC to FG, 19 Oct. 1939; also see Lewis, p. 68.

207   About the *Rising of the Moon*: WC to E. K. Brown, 24 Jan. 1947 (Yale). Two letters about the death of SOJ: WC to Mrs. Fields, 27 June, 13 July 1909 (Harvard); these two letters somehow survived the destruction of the correspondence: McClure made 149 Atlantic crossings in his career, which means he spent something like four years of his life on ocean liners. WC's life at end of 1909: WC to AF, 5 Jan. 1910 (privately owned).

208   The negotiations with Munsterberg are documented by eight letters at the Boston Pub. Lib. According to figures in the McClure Papers at the Lilly Library, the magazine reached a circulation of 400,000 by Oct., 1898, 470,000 by the following March; in Oct., 1909, it was 485,000; in Oct., 1910, it was 565,000 and in Oct., 1911, 660,000. But the magazine was always short of cash in those years. The head of the London office wrote on

20 Mar. 1908 (Lilly) that they had only 12 £ in the bank and owed authors 1,500 £. These circulation figures were no doubt exaggerated, as H. W. Ayers's *Newspaper Annual and Directory* gives *McClure's* an average circulation for 1910 of 425,000 and for 1912 450,000.

209   "Tell me . . . why": Sergeant, p. 35.

210   WC's memory of Twain: WC to William Lyon Phelps, 17 Feb. 1936 (Yale); see also WC to Allen Nevins, 18 Mar. 1939 (Columbia). "Here is a fine poem, a great poem, I think," Twain said to A. B. Paine, handing him a copy of WC's poem that he had cut from the N. Y. *Times* book section that had reprinted it from *McClure's*. Paine reported this conversation and reprinted three stanzas in his *Mark Twain: A Biography* (1912), pp. 1501–02. She wrote her former pupil: WC to Norman Foerster, 20 July 1910 (Univ. of Neb.). Christmas, 1910: WC to AF, 22 Feb. 1911 (privately owned).

211   She woke up with an earache: Lewis, pp. 75–76. Visit to Mrs. Fields: WC to Louise Guiney, 25 May 1911 (Holy Cross College). Visit to Mary Jewett: WC to ES, 27 June 1911. Turning down poem: WC to Dwight, 24 Aug. 1911 (Amherst).

212   "What was going to happen": *Success Story*, p. 335.

CHAPTER 10: *ALEXANDER'S BRIDGE*

213   For Cherry Valley sojourn, see WC to SSM, 21 Oct., 5, 17 Nov. 1911. "You must dismiss": SSM to WC, 14 Oct. 1911.

214   "Prettiest girl": CSF, p. 56.

215   "He had the flush": CSF, p. 68. Wanting to change title: WC to Robert U. Johnson, 30 Aug. 1910 (N. Y. Pub. Lib.). A story she thought "yellow": WC to Johnson, 22 Oct. 1911 (N. Y. Pub. Lib.).

216   "Like iron dust": CSF, p. 53. "Over the city and harbor": CSF, p. 46. Revising AB: WC to C. Mackenzie, 3 Nov. 1911 (Lilly). For the statement that she wrote novel in 1911, see "Preface" to 1922 ed. The best study of AB is Slote's introduction to the 1977 Univ. of Neb. Press ed. of the novel. Slote quotes a story from the *Journal* (her introduction, p. vi) saying that WC, wanting to test the quality of her work, sent the MS to *McClure's* from St. Louis under the pseudonym of Fannie Cadwallader, and didn't reveal her identity until the novel had been accepted. I have run across no other reference to this act and have concluded that the story is apocryphal. WC had been buying fiction for years and certainly knew a publishable story when she read one. In addition, I find it hard to believe that Viola Roseboro' and other staff

members of the magazine would not have known that she was writing a novel. FG's house memo: Brown, p. 159.

217   For more detail on the St. Lawrence bridge disaster, see John P. Hinz, "The Real Alexander's Bridge," AL (Jan. 1950), pp. 473–76, and Brown, pp. 157–59. "There was a gifted": Lewis, p. 68.

218   "Because he looked as a": AB, p. 9. "This is not the story": Slote, AB, p. x. Slote's source is an undated clipping in a Cather family scrapbook (NSHS). "I always used to feel": AB, p. 12. "Still was, as she had": AB, p. 115.

219   "On the Continent": AB, pp. 113–14. "She never lets him go": AB, p. 136. "You work like the devil": AB, pp. 12–13.

220   "One of the most deeply": KA, p. 97; KA, pp. 97–103, are particularly good on WC's use of the moon myth in her fiction.

221   "Delicate as a cobweb": AB, pp. 17–18. "Thousands of tons": AB, p. 125. "A great iron carcass," AB, p. 127. "Moved with ease": AB, p. 3. "Camped on the edge": AB, p. 116.

222   Wait for "The Bohemian Girl": WC to LP, 28 June 1912 (Va.). "His youthful vanities": preface to 1922 ed., p. vii. "Like most young writers": OW, p. 91.

223   "Of course, one day": preface, to 1922 ed., p. vii. She admitted the charge: WC to AF, 23 Feb. 1913 (privately owned). "The thing that teases": NUF, p. 76; also OW, p. 47. "When it at last moves": Lewis, p. 78.

224   "Watching the low, dirty": AB, p. 73: "AB is an allegory": Rosowski, p. 35. Reviews: N. Y. Times Book Review, 12 May 1912, p. 295; Outlook, 8 June 1912, p. 317; Atlantic (Nov., 1912), p. 683.

225   Illness in 1912: WC to MG, 24 Apr. 1912; WC to ZA, 6 Feb. 1912. "In this typical": Sergeant, p. 90. The Howells dinner: N. Y. Times, 3 Mar. 1912, pp. 1, 8.

226   If she didn't have something to show: WC to ES, 1 Mar. 1912. An idea for a novel: ibid. Mrs. McClung's stroke: WC to SSM, 13 Mar. 1912. Revising "The Bohemian Girl": WC to ES, 20 Apr. 1912. She thought it pretty good: WC to ZA, 31 Oct. 1912.

227   Old age view of story: WC to Wagenknecht, 15 Oct. 1936 (Morgan).

228   "He gave the town": CSF, p. 4. "Just now he was": CSF, p. 6.

229   "With cloves stuck": CSF, pp. 28–29. "There was a start": CSF, p. 38. "You know, I'm": CSF, p. 18. Problems of SSM: WC to SSM, 9, 12 June 1912.

CHAPTER 11: *O PIONEERS!*

231   Idea for another story: WC to ES, 5 July 1913. She had read it to EL: Lewis, p. 83. "She said she could only": Sergeant, p. 116.

232   "The stream and the broken pottery": SOL, p. 378. "He has less and less":

preface to AB (1922), pp. viii-ix. "Calls the wisdom": This is WC's only reference to Bergson in her writings, but she must have known his work well. She wrote ES (12 Sept. 1912) that she was reading Bergson's *Creative Evolution*. Loretta Wasserman in "The Music of Time: Henri Bergson and WC," AL (May 1985) argues persuasively that WC was much influenced by Bergson's ideas on unconscious memory and his two notions of time: chronological time and lived time. She sees these ideas as important in understanding MA and PH.

233   "Trips to New York: WC to ES, 12 Sept., 6 Oct. 1912. Surgery on a serial: WC to PR, 25 Sept. 1916. New book three times as long: WC to ZA, 31 Oct. 1912 (Va.).

234   On the home stretch: WC to ES, 7 Dec. 1912. "Ought to . . . definitely establish": Brown, p. 179. She signed a contract: Crane, p. 30.

235   The Bank St. apartment: WC to AF, 23 Feb. 1913 (privately owned); Lewis, pp. 86–90; Sergeant, pp. 88–89, 116, 202–3.

236   For a good account of Greenwich Village in this era, see Leslie Fishbein, *Rebels in Bohemia: The Radicals of "The Masses," 1911–1917* (1982). "A dramatic season": "Plays of Real Life," *McClure's* (Mar., 1913), p. 63.

237   "All good plays": ibid., p. 72. All about crops and cows: WC to ES, undated. "Ignored all the situations": OW, p. 93. "Distinctly déclassé": OW, p. 94.

238   "Seemed to overwhelm": OP, p. 15. "One of the richest": OP, p. 83. "*Très original*": Sergeant, p. 93. Doubts about the novel: WC to ES, 22 Apr. 1913.

239   The visit to Amy Lowell: Sergeant, pp. 168–69; WC to FG, 5 Nov. 1942. When FG urged her: WC to Mary Austin, 9 May 1928 (HEH). The reviews were so hearty: WC to ES, Aug. 1913. "What has pleased me": KA, p. 449. She wanted to shine: WC to ZA, 31 Oct. 1912 (Va.).

240   "This was the first time": reproduced in facsimile, Bennett, between pp. 222–23. Reviews: *Nation*, 4 Sept. 1913, pp. 210–11; *N. Y. Herald*, 18 July 1913, p. 8; *Chicago Eve. Post*, 25 July 1913; the last was reprinted in *Dictionary of Literary Biography, Documentary Series*, Vol. 1 (1982), pp. 67–68. WC remembered eight years later: WC to DCF, 21 Mar. 1921.

241   "The shapes and scenes": OW, p. 48. "Living things caught": OW, p. 49. "If he achieves any thing": OW, p. 51. "Anchored on a windy": OP, p. 3.

242   "She was a dark child": OP, p. 11. "wondered why his sister": OP, p. 65. "Under the long, shaggy": OP, p. 71. "He used to feel": OP, p. 126. "On the one hand": Eric Auerbach, *Mimesis: The Representation of Reality in Western Literature* (1953), p. 23. "Every natural fact": *Nature*, part IV. "Spontaneous overflow": preface to 2nd ed., *Lyrical Ballads* (1800), p. 2.

243   "They went into": OP, p. 309. "What do you think": "Song of Myself," lines 123–26, in *Leaves of Grass*. "A vast checker-board": OP, p. 75.

244   "I think we shall be": OP, p. 308.

245   "How 'close to life' ": Sergeant, p. 90. WC avoiding sexist roles: "WC's Pioneer
Women: A Feminist Interpretation," *Where the West Begins: Essays on Middle
Border and Siouxland Writing in Honor of Herbert Kraus*, ed. Arthur R. Huseboe
and William Geyer (1978), pp. 135–42. "Achieve self-definition": "Mothers,
Daughters, and the 'Art Necessity,' " *American Novelists Revisited*, p. 279.

247   Composed of disparate elements: Daiches, WC: *A Critical Introduction* (1951),
p. 29. Randall notes: *The Landscape and the Looking Glass* (1960), pp. 64–65.
"Stretch back to Genesis": Stouck, p. 31. Baker's argument: "OP, the Problem
of Structure," GPQ (Fall, 1982). Novel as two-part pastoral: Rosowski, p. 45;
parallels with Virgil: ibid., pp. 46–49; OP as epic: Stouck, pp. 21–34.

248   "Sin and death": OP, p. 271. The account of writing SSM's autobiography:
Sarah Bloom to Edward Wagenknecht, undated (Morgan); WC to WOJ, 29
May 1914, 20 May 1919 (Va.).

249   *My Autobiography* was published in book form by Frederick A. Stokes
(1914); reprinted by Frederick Ungar with introduction by Louis Filler
(1963). "He often lamented": *My Autobiography* (1963), p. 197.

250   "Your opening chapter": Lyon, *Success Story*, p. 346. "I have been reading":
ibid., p. 346–47. "Nothing I have ever read": ibid., p. 347. More satisfaction
than anything else: WC to Mrs. McClure, 10 Dec. 1913. "Training for the
Ballet," *McClure's* (Oct., 1913), pp. 85–95. Trip to Virginia: WC to ES, 12, 22
Sept. 1913.

CHAPTER 12: *THE SONG OF THE LARK*

252   See Rosowski, "The Novel of Awakening," *Genre* (Fall, 1979), pp. 313–32.
Fremstad, Swedish-born: Fremstad's mother was Swedish and her father
Norwegian; she was born in Stockholm but lived in Christiana (Olso)
during her childhood; Norway also was ruled by Sweden until 1905. There
are two accounts of WC's aborted interview: Lewis, p. 91, and Mary Watkins
Cushing, *The Rainbow Bridge* (1954), p. 243, the latter being a biography of
Fremstad. Both were written many years after the fact and vary in some
details. I have put them together as best I could.

253   The account of Fremstad replacing Mme. Duchene: Lewis, pp. 91–92;
Cushing, p. 219; *N. Y. Times*, 13 Mar. 1913; the discrepancies I have resolved
in favor of the *Times* account. "A vision of": Lewis, p. 92. "Certainly, I'm on
my way": *Times* report. The interview: WC to ES, 22 Mar. 1913.

254   "Alexandra had put": OP, p. 97. The Good Friday *Parsifal*: WC to ES, 22 Mar.
1913. "Pretty good for you": ibid. "She gave him a piercing": SOL, p. 503;

my quotations from SOL are from the 1932 text, which is the same as the 1937 Autograph Edition; this is the one still in print.

255   Fremstad is talked of in WC to ES, 14, 28 Apr., 22 Sept. 1913. Early progress on the novel: WC to ES, 19 Nov. 1913.

256   "Unquestionably the most": *McClure's* (Feb., 1914), p. 41. "We certainly have no other": ibid., p. 44. "Made by the actors": ibid., p. 46. "A noble rendering": *McClure's* (Dec., 1913), p. 36. "The singer who now is": ibid., p. 42.

257   "She grew up in a new": ibid., p. 48. Couldn't tell where WC left off: Lewis, p. 93. Sending Fremstad orange tree: WC to Elsie Cather, 30 Dec. 1913 (privately owned). Unpacking books: ibid.

258   Blood-poisoning episode: WC to ES, 14, 24 Feb., 2, 14, 19 Mar. 1914. Went to Pittsburgh: WC to ES, 30 Apr. 1914. Visit to Fremstad: WC to ES, 23 June 1914. Cushing's account, written 40 years later (p. 244) is different: the cook quit, the plumbing broke down, and "Madam's mood was joyless and grim". Summer travels: WC to ES, 10 Aug., 28 Sept. 1914.

259   Rubbing off rough edges: WC to ES, 13 Nov. 1914. Story writing itself: WC to ES, 5 Dec. 1914. Progress on novel: WC to FG, 13 Dec. 1914. "Suggest a young girl's": preface to 1932 ed. of SOL, p. v.

260   "The willful eccentricity": *McClure's* (Jan., 1915), p. 28. "No actor today": ibid., p. 18. Thinking of little except the war: WC to AF, 17 Dec. 1914 (NSHS). Details about the MS, negotiations, revisions: WC to FG, 15 Mar., 6, 8, 22, 28 Apr., 5, 10 May 1915; see also FG to WC, 5 Apr. 1915.

261   About critic Keeble: WC to ES, 27 June 1915; see also WC to Keeble, 19 and undated July 1915 (Carnegie-Mellon Univ.). Satisfied with the technical details: WC to FG, 13 Sept. 1915. Plans to go to Germany: WC to FG, 24 July 1915.

262   The trip west: Lewis, pp. 93–99. "Swinging back and forth": *Denver Times*, 31 Jan. 1916; reprinted in Rosowski and Slote, "WC's 1916 Mesa Verde Essay: The Genesis of PH," *Prairie Schooner* (Winter, 1984), pp. 81–92; partially reprinted in *Book News Monthly* (Jan., 1916), p. 214.

263   "Clear as glass": "WC's Mesa Verde Essay," p. 83. "Wetherill happened to glance": ibid., p. 84.

264   "Lost in Colorado Canyon": 26 Aug. 1915, p. 20. "The four or five hours": Lewis, p. 97. Sore but happy: WC to ES, 21 Sept. 1915. Visit to Taos: Lewis, pp. 99–100; EL's memory is faulty when she says they stayed a month.

265   Description of the Columbian Hotel: Mabel Dodge Luhan, *Edge of Taos Desert: An Escape from Reality*, vol. 4 of *Intimate Memoirs* (1937), p. 38. "Was intensely alive": Lewis, p. 101. Stretching herself inside her skin: WC to ES, 7 Dec. 1915.

267   Spanish Johnny was: WC to SSM, 1 Feb. 1915. For Lily Fisher, Dr. McKeeby,

and Schindelmeisser, see Bennett, pp. 32, 110, 152–53. The death of the noble brakeman: WC to FG, 28 Mar. 1915. Details of Fremstad's life are from WC's *McClure's* article: also see Cushing, *Rainbow Bridge*.

268   "Harsanyi found in Thea": SOL, p. 220. "It was as if she had": SOL, p. 272. For an illuminating discussion of the second-self idea: Rosowski, "WC's Women," *Studies in Amer. Fiction* (Autumn, 1981), pp. 261–75. "Every artist makes himself": SOL, p. 221.

269   "As if she were being": SOL, p. 177. "When the first movement": SOL, p. 251. "The most thoroughly elaborated": Ellen Moers, *Literary Women* (1976), p. 258.

270   "What's her secret?": SOL, pp. 570–71. "My dear doctor": SOL, p. 546. For a discussion of WC's use of the Orpheus myth, see Giannone's *Music in WC's Fiction*, pp. 88–90.

271   Fremstad's reaction: WC to ES, 7 Dec. 1915. Cushing's memory nearly 40 years later was that Fremstad said to WC: "My poor Willa . . . it wasn't really much like that. But after all, what can you know about me? Nothing!" (*Rainbow Bridge*, p. 244). Red Cloud reaction: WC to DCF, 15 Mar. 1916. "I began the world": SOL, p. 548. Reviews: *Boston Eve. Transcript*, 13 Oct. 1915, p. 22; *Nation*, 14 Oct. 1915, pp. 461–62; Mencken in *Smart Set* (Jan., 1916), pp. 306–8.

272   Original length 200,000 words: WC to ZA, 1 Feb. 1915.

273   "Told everything about everybody": OW, p. 96. "The chief fault": p. v. "The interesting and important": p. vi. Revisions of SOL in 1932: see Robin Hayeck and James Woodress, "WC's Cuts and Revisions in SOL," *Mod. Fiction Studies* (Winter, 1979–80), pp. 651–58.

274   "WC would perhaps be shocked": 11 Dec. 1915, p. 154. There is no proof that Bourne wrote this review, but he was a regular reviewer for the *New Republic*, and WC thought he wrote it (see OW, p. 96). She would have learned this from ES, who was a friend and correspondent of Bourne. I originally eliminated Bourne because the reviewer says he grew up in North Dakota, whereas Bourne grew up in the East. More recently I found that Bourne was in love with a farm girl from N.D. who was a student at Barnard and previously had sent her a copy of WC's poem "Prairie Spring," which he greatly liked. It apparently suited his purpose to voice his criticism from the point of view of someone who had grown up on the plains. He says in a letter to ES (9 Nov. 1915) that he has just finished both Dreiser and WC and hopes that his negative comments will not cause misunderstanding. He admired both writers. The *New Republic* did carry his review of The "*Genius*" signed, but the review of SOL was unsigned. Reaction in Lincoln: WC to DCF, 2 Sept. 1916. Marketing the novel: WC to R. L. Scaife, 27, 30 Oct. 1915. Data on

royalties and correction charges: WC to FG, 18 Apr. 1916, and FG to WC, 1
Apr., 4 Oct. 1916. People couldn't get copies: WC to FG, 21 Jan. 1917.
275   "Consequences" is reprinted in UVO.

CHAPTER 13: *MY ÁNTONIA*

276   WC's reactions and movements at end of 1915: WC to FG, 17 Nov., 19 Dec.
1915; 18 Apr. 1916. The last Christmas in Pittsburgh: WC to AF, 25 Dec. 1915
(privately owned). The *Times* reported later: 5 Apr. 1916, p. 24. About
Isabelle's marriage: WC to DCF, 15 Mar. 1916.

277   "All her natural exhuberance": Sergeant, p. 140. A rotten winter: WC to FG,
undated 1916. Unable to start a new novel: WC to DCF, 15 Mar. 1916.
"Something rather hard and dry": WC to W. H. Boynton, 7 Mar. 1916 (pub. in
Cat. no. 43, Spring, 1985, Serendipity Books, Berkeley, Ca.).

278   "The Bookkeeper's Wife" is reprinted in UVO. WC's relationship with PR is
documented by 16 letters to him and carbons of many more from him at
Columbia; also WC to Dwight, 16 July 1916 (Amherst); WC to FG, 30 June, 16
Dec. 1916.

279   Mencken's rejection of "The Diamond Mine": WC to HLM, 12 May 1916
(N. Y. Pub. Lib.). "It reveals the identity": "Nordica in Fiction," 28 Sept.
1916, p. 22.

280   Previous writing on Nordica: W&P, pp. 381–82, 642–46, 758–59. "The
most rapacious of the men": YBM, p. 116. "Why is it?": YBM, pp. 116–17.
About St. Denis: WC to FG, 10 Oct. 1916.

281   Friday teas on Bank St.: there are various references to these scattered
through WC's letters; the earliest is WC to Dwight, 4 Apr. 1916 (Amherst); it
also includes a formal card of invitation. "These Friday afternoons": Lewis,
p. 134. She cut away suddenly: WC to Dwight, 16 July 1916 (Amherst).
Summer travels: WC to ES, 3 Aug. 1916; WC to FG, 22 Aug. 1916.

282   For list of magazines that turned down "Scandal," see PR to WC, 19 Oct.
1917. Selling "The Gold Slipper" and inflation: WC to Elsie Cather, 30 Dec.
1916 (privately owned); this story is reprinted in YBM.

283   "One of the most hideous men": YBM, p. 166. "Thin, lupin face": YBM, pp. 70,
75, 118. For discussions of anti-Semitism in WC, see Robinson, *Willa*, pp.
48–49, 205–7, and WC *and Her Critics*, pp. 363–81.

284   The hot summer: WC to ES, 13 Nov. 1916. Working on "The Blue Mesa": WC
to FG, 23 Oct. 1916. Now no mean cook: WC to Mary Jewett, 29 Dec. 1916.

285   She put aside "The Blue Mesa": WC to R. L. Scaife, 8 Mar. 1917. Writing
about illustrations: there are many letters on this topic, but see WC to FG, 24

Nov. 1917, Feb.?, 9 Mar. 1918; WC to Scaife, 7 Apr., 1, 9 Dec. 1917, 7 Mar. 1918. Christmas activities: WC to Elsie Cather, 30 Dec. 1916 (privately owned). "Flushed and alert": Sergeant, p. 139. Honorary degree and summer travel: WC to FG, 25 June 1917; WC to ES, 23 June 1917; WC to AF, 14 July, 9 Sept. 1917 (privately owned).

286   "The fresh, pine-scented woods": Lewis, p. 105. Writing in tent: Lewis, p. 104; WC to AF, 9 Sept. 1917 (privately owned); WC to Harrison Blaine, 20 Dec. 1940 (WCHC). "Office Wives": WC to FG, 18, 20 Oct. 1917; WC to PR, 14, 19 Sept. 1917. "Her Boss" is reprinted in UVO; the MS of "Explosives" has not survived.

287   Depression over not finishing book: WC to FG, 28 Feb. 1918. Fremstad to the rescue and seeing the Hambourgs: WC to CMS: 13 Mar. 1918. Proofreading MA: WC to FG, 2, 9, 11, 28 July, 3 Aug. 1918. For an excellent article on the significance of the Benda drawings, see Jean Schwind, "The Benda Illustrations to MA: WC's 'Silent' Supplement to Jim Burden's Narrative," PMLA (Jan., 1985), pp. 51–67.

288   Visit to Scarsdale: WC to FG, Aug. 1918. Western trip: WC to FG, 6 Sept. 1918. Proposed story collection: WC to FG, 6 Sept. 1918. Loss of interest in it: WC to FG, 2 Dec. 1918; MA was published on Sept. 21.

289   The embodiment of all her feelings: WC to CMS, 27 Jan. 1934. Comment on *School of Feminity*: WC to CMS, 28 June 1939. "She was one of the truest": Eleanor Hinman in *Lincoln Sunday Star*, 6 Nov. 1921. Stories like *War and Peace*: WC to ES, 10 Aug. 1914. Novels of feeling vs. novels of action: WC to Mr. Miller, 24 Oct. 1924 (Newberry). "My Ántonia deserved": Hinman, *Lincoln Sunday Star*. Defense of male narrator: WC to WOJ, 20 May 1919 (Va.).

290   Avoiding melodrama: Hinman, *Lincoln Sunday Star*. "I knew I'd ruin": Flora Merrill in N. Y. *World*, 19 Apr. 1925.

291   "Battered but not diminished": MA, p. 332. Bennett is good on relating fact to fiction in MA. About Blind d'Arnault: WC to Miss Vouilles, undated (Newberry), says she has no memory of Blind Tom but that she based her character on Blind Boone, who played in the Midwest and whom she could have heard in Red Cloud. However, she reviewed a performance of Blind Tom in Lincoln, 18 May 1894 (W&P, pp. 166–67); for a biog. sketch of Blind Tom, see Ella May Thornton, "The Mystery of Blind Tom," *Ga. Rev.* (Winter, 1961), pp. 395–400.

292   Bentley actually did kill his wife and commit suicide. "Drama of memory" is part of the title of an excellent article on MA by Terence Martin (PMLA, Mar., 1969). She didn't know where she got things: WC to IMW, 6 Jan. 1945. The wolf story: See Paul Schach, "Russian Wolves in Folktales and Litera-

ture of the Plains," GPQ (Spring, 1983), pp. 67–78. Characters not drawn from life: WC to CMS, 27 Jan. 1934. Mrs. Harling drawn from life: WC to CMS, 29 Oct. 1917.

293   "The best thing I've done": Bennett, p. 203; quoted from conversation with CMS. A novel to cherish: FG to WC, 5 May 1944. "It was no wonder that": MA, p. 353.

294   "The disproportion between": *The Liberal Imagination* (1950), pp. 295–96.

295   "As I looked about": MA, p. 15. "I felt motion": MA, p. 16; "I kept as still": MA, p. 18. "I saw a door": MA, p. 22. "Big and warm": MA, p. 23. "The idea of you": MA, p. 321. "Whatever we had missed": MA, p. 372.

296   "Died in the wilderness": MA, p. 244. "Presently we saw": MA, p. 245. "We turned to leave": MA, pp. 338–39.

297   "The ancient, eldest Evil": MA, p. 47. "You is just": MA, p. 46. "Playing about with": MA, p. 289.

298   "*Optima dies*": MA, p. 264. "Counters the failures of the present": Stouck, p. 35; Stouck is good on WC's use of the pastoral mode.

299   "Our present is ruined": Sergeant, p. 121. "Now I can kiss you": MA, p. 226.

300   "Some memories are realities": MA, p. 328. O'Brien: "Mothers, Daughters," pp. 286–87. Rosowski: "WC's Women," *Studies in Amer. Fiction* (Autumn, 1981), pp. 265–68. Sales figures on MA: FG to WC, 3 Dec., 1918, 4 Mar., 20 Oct. 1919, 28 Oct. 1920. "the most thrilling shock: *Under the Bridge* (1943), p. 119; however, FG did not get the MS all at once but piecemeal.

301   Reviews: *Smart Set* (Mar., 1919), pp. 140–41: Bourne in *Dial*, 14 Dec. 1918, p. 557; reprinted in *Crit. Essays on* WC, pp. 145–46; *Sun*: 6 Oct. 1918, Sec. 5, p. 1. WC's memory of reception: WC to Lorna Birtwell, 27 Nov. 1922 (Columbia); WC to Roseboro', 20 Jan. 1941 (Va.).

302   "Lifts me to all": Sergeant, p. 244. "I think you have": ibid., p. 245.

CHAPTER 14: *ONE OF OURS*

303   In a state of euphoria: WC to Aunt Franc, 11 Nov. 1918 (privately owned). "Why then, God's soldier": Act. V, Sc. 7, l. 76. She had been at the hairdresser's: WC to DCF: 8 Mar. 1922. "Lt. G. P. Cather (since killed": 25 June 1918, p. 4.

304   To get away from him and his kind: WC to DCF, late Mar. 1922. "An inarticulate young man": N. Y. *World*, 11 Apr. 1925, sec 3, p. 6. Three lovely, tormented years: WC to DCF, 12 Mar. 1922. She felt a blood identity: WC to DCF, 7 Apr. 1922.

305   She had to devise a new technique: WC to DCF, 8 Mar. 1922. "We all have to

pay": Eva Mahoney in the *Omaha Sunday World-Herald*, 27 Nov. 1921, mag. sec., p. 1. Good intentions don't count: WC to DCF, 18 Mar. 1922. Completed first four chapters: WC to FG, 29 July 1919. Talking to soldiers: WC to DCF, late Mar. 1922. Memory of Donovan: Lewis, p. 118. Two articles in *Red Cross Mag.*: Oct., 1919, pp. 54–55; July, 1919, pp. 27–30.

306   Relations with Houghton Mifflin: WC to FG, 19 May 1919.

308   FG's efforts at damage control: FG to WC, 23 May 1919. Knopf's offer to reprint TG: WC to FG, 28 Dec. 1919.

309   Wants no one to know she's writing a war novel: WC to FG, 29 July 1919. Ugly binding of OP: WC to FG, 18 Oct. 1919. Father's visit to N. Y.: WC to FG, 2 Nov. 1919. Swedish ed. of OP: WC to FG, 17 Nov. 1919. Czech translation: WC to FG, 8 Dec. 1919. Copies for White: WC to FG, 26 Nov. 1919. She wrote a long story for fun: WC to FG, 7 Jan. 1920. Publishing data for YBM: Crane, pp. 79–83.

310   Dr. Sweeney's diary: Lewis, p. 118. Golden days interspersed: WC to Roseboro', 5 June 1920 (Va.). "She wanted to live in": Lewis, p. 119. Fourth of July in Paris: WC to AF, 4 July 1920 (privately owned).

311   Finding and visiting grave: WC to father, 7 July 1920 (privately owned). Trip with Hambourgs: WC to mother, 12 Aug. 1920 (privately owned). Writing in a tent: WC to Mrs. Charlotte Stanfield, June 1921 (Va.). Return trip: WC to ES, 1 Nov. 1920. Reviews of YBM: *Times*, 3 Oct. 1920, p. 24: *Nation*, 25 Sept. 1920, p. 352; Mencken in the *Smart Set* (Dec., 1920), pp. 139–40; *New Republic*, 19 Jan. 1920, pp. 233–34; *Double Dealer* (Feb., 1921), pp. 73–74; *Bookman* (Oct., 1920), pp. 169–70; *Yale Rev.* (1921), p. 671; *Freeman*, 1 Dec. 1920, p. 286.

313   "smelling strong of spirits": YBM, p. 19. "Yonder, in a pool": YBM, pp. 17–18.

314   "was with difficulty": YBM, p. 43. "In time they quarrelled": YBM, p. 51.

315   Selling the story: PR to WC, 5, 15 Mar. 1920. "The Comstocks are": H. L. Mencken to Fielding H. Garrison, 11 Feb. 1921 (*Letters of H. L. Mencken* [1961], p. 218). WC had signed a petition: F. O. Matthiessen, *Theodore Dreiser* (1951), p. 169. Negotiations with *Smart Set*: PR to WC, 2 Apr. 1920; WC to PR, 2 Apr. 1920; see also PR to WC, 8, 9, 16, 22 Apr. 1920. For identification of Eden Bower as Mary Garden, see Slote's introduction to UVO, pp. xxi–xxii.

316   The *Smart Set* and YBM versions of the story are collated in the appendix to UVO. Urging her to write a Pittsburgh novel: FG to WC, 3 Dec. 1918. "We haven't much money": WC's "Portrait of the Publisher as a Young Man," in *Alfred A. Knopf Quarter Century* (1940), p. 11; the entire essay is reprinted in Lewis, pp. 108–15.

317   "Next to writing her novels": Lewis, pp. 115–16. "Was unique in my experience": *The Art of* WC, p. 206. "*Pax vobiscum*": FG to WC, 14 Jan. 1921.

318   She turned to her old friend: WC to DCF, 21 Mar. 1921. If they could get together: WC to DCF, 8 Apr. 1921. About French trans. of MA: WC to DCF, 10 Apr. 1921. Reading proof: WC to DCF, 6 Feb., 13, 21 Mar. 1922. DCF's review: WC to DCF, 7 Apr., 8, 22 May 1922.

319   Lewis's lecture: WC to Mrs. Stanfield, 11 June 1921 (Va.); "WC is greater than": *Omaha World-Herald*, 9 Apr. 1921. This friendly push: WC to Lewis, 14 Apr. 1921 (Yale). "Now I am going to lie": *Journal*, 24 Sept. 1921. The *Argus* interview (29 Sept. 1921) published Knopf's telegram.

320   Account of Fine Arts speech: WC to FG, 10 Nov. 1921. "Work of overzealous patriots": *Omaha World-Herald*, 30 Oct. 1921. "Will it make a boy or girl": *Lincoln Eve. State Journal*, 31 Oct. 1921. "Everybody is afraid": *Omaha Bee*, 30 Oct. 1921.

321   Visit to Chicago: WC to IMW, 10 Nov. 1921. French cooking and Dr. Glafke: WC to IMW, 10 Dec. 1921. Having a gay winter: WC to IMW, 4 Feb. 1922. Tonsilectomy: WC to Mrs. Stanfield, 10 June 1922 (Va.). About the sanitarium: WC to ZA, 20 Apr. 1922.

322   Correspondence concerning Bread Loaf: WC to DCF, 6, 18 Feb. 1922; WC to Davison, 15 Feb., 2 July 1922 (Middlebury). WC at Bread Loaf: *Bookman* (Sept., 1922), p. 127. There is a student's account of WC at Bread Loaf in the Slote Papers. "Alert, alive, quick-witted": Burton Rascoe, "Contemporary Reminiscences," *Arts and Decorations* (Apr., 1924), p. 28. The song is from the student paper. WC as Whicher's critic: Lorna Birtwell, "Remembering WC," *The Woman's Press* (Nov., 1948), pp. 8–9. "Those patterns which have proved": Flora Merrill, *N. Y. World*, 19 Apr. 1925.

323   She wrote in exasperation: WC to Egbert Oliver, 13 Dec. 1934 (Morgan). First visit to Grand Manan: WC to DCF, 1 Sept. 1922. She had a quiet cottage: WC to Mrs. Stanfield, 4 Sept. 1922 (Va.). Change of title for OO: Knopf, *Art of WC*, p. 206.

324   "Thin and dyspeptic": OO, p. 8; "it seems like": OO, p. 52. "I've never yet": OO, p. 143. "It would be the beginning": OO, p. 146. The incident actually happened: WC to DCF, 13 Apr. 1922. "Everything about a man's": OO, p. 210.

325   "With that sense of": OO, p. 311. "Life had after all": OO, p. 411. "He died believing": OO, p. 458.

326   She knew her character better than herself: Eva Mahoney, *Omaha World-Herald*, 21 Nov. 1921. "The tall house": OO, p. 46.

327   "Claude had always found": OO, p. 68. "Rest, rest": OO, p. 69.

328   The Parsifal theme: WC to Mr. Johns, 17 Nov. 1922 (Va.). "All right now": OO, p. 27. "No battlefield or": OO, p. 419.

329   "Almost any mean-spirited": OO, p. 50. Comparison with Eliot: Stouck, pp. 88–89. WC's feelings about DCF in France: WC to DCF, late Mar. 1922.

330   "Torn between generous": OO, p. 418. She gave a long interview: 24 Dec.
       1922; reprinted in Sergeant, pp. 174–80. "The city which had meant so
       much": OO, p. 173.

332   "A study of erotic": Stanley Cooperman, *World War I and the American Novel*
       (1967), p. 129; the chap. on OO is reprinted in *Critical Essays on* WC, pp. 169–
       78; a good article on OO is Frederick Griffiths, "WC and OO," WS (No. 3,
       1984), pp. 261–85. "His linen and his hands": OO, p. 430. "It looks like a
       poet": OO, p. 431. "Claude noticed": OO, p. 432. Incident related to her" WC
       to DCF, late Mar. 1922.

333   I have read 23 reviews: 13 favorable, 6 unfavorable, 4 ambivalent. What she
       was trying to do: WC to Mencken, 6 Feb. 1922 (Enoch Pratt Lib.). Reviews:
       Mencken, *Smart Set* (Oct., 1922), pp. 140–42; Wilson, *Vanity Fair* (Oct.,
       1922), pp. 26–27; Broun, *N. Y. World*, 13 Sept. 1922, p. 13. Hemingway's
       comment: quoted by Wilson in his *Shores of Light* (1952), p. 118.

334   "I stick with you": *N. Y. World*, 20 Sept. 1922. DCF's review: *N. Y. Times Book
       Rev.*, 10 Sept. 1922; Rascoe's: *N. Y. Tribune*, 10 Sept. 1922, p. 6. The solitary
       rose: WC to DCF, 29 Sept. 1922. "If thy Mencken": Sergeant, p. 171. Con-
       cerning other reviews, WC to DCF, 10 Oct. 1922. Publication data: Crane, pp.
       89–95. Royalties: Lewis, p. 115.

CHAPTER 15: *A LOST LADY*

335   "The book will have": NUF, p. v. "The end is nothing": OD, p. 158.

336   "With prosperity came": OO, pp. 101–2; "There is the new American": NUF,
       p. 94. Plans for trip west: WC to Lorna Birtwell, 27 Nov. 1922 (Columbia).
       The golden wedding: WC to BK, 4 Dec. 1922. More thrills to the square mile:
       WC to ZA, 4 Dec. 1922. Skating: WC to ZA, undated (Va.).

337   Back in N. Y.: WC to IMW, 13 Jan. 1923. Joining church: Bennett, p. 137.
       "Faith is a gift": ibid. "I've come to believe": OO, p. 410.

338   "*In religion seeking*": MME, p. 94. Health problems: WC to BK, 15 Jan. 1923.
       Dinner at Knopfs: WC to IMW, 24 Jan. 1923. Flu and recuperation: WC to Pitts
       Sanborn, 2 Mar. 1923 (Va.); WC to Birtwell, 12 Mar. 1923 (Columbia). They
       had fitted up a study: Lewis, p. 131. "I hate to leave France": Walter Tittle,
       Century (Aug. 1925), p. 312. Persistent case of neuritis: WC to Mencken,
       Sept. 1923 (Enoch Pratt Lib.).

339   Wonderful motor trips: WC to ZA, 14 Sept. 1923 (Va.); she sent a clipping: WC
       to Mencken, Oct. 1923 (Enoch Pratt Lib.). "She had, I think": Lewis, pp.
       131–32; Omaha not going to like portrait: WC to IMW, 11 Aug. 1923. "A lady

joined the table": Frank A. Swinnerton, *Autobiography* (1936), pp. 317–18. Return trip: WC to DCF, 29 Nov. 1923.

340   Sale to *Century*: telegrams—BK to WC, 15, 28 Dec. 1922. WC to BK, 28 Dec. 1922; Idea for novel: WC to IMW, 6 Jan. 1945. One of her students at Bread Loaf remembered: the student was Reginald Cook, and the information comes from the Slote Papers. "I discarded": Flora Merrill, *N. Y. World*, 19 Apr. 1925.

341   Memory of the railroad aristocracy: WC to BK, 10 Sept. 1934.

342   "Form but a low part": OW, p. 36. "The art of choosing": OW, p. 37. WC quotes this passage in French. "Finding what conventions": OW, p. 102. "Must have in it": OW, p. 103. "Explaining mechanical processes": OW, p. 37. "If the novel": OW, p. 40.

343   "Whatever is felt": OW, p. 41–42. "To make a drama": OW, p. 43. "Thirty or forty years ago": ALL, p. 9. "If she happened to be": ALL, p. 12.

344   "a white figure": ALL, p. 17. "Already old enough": ALL, p. 19. "Walks with a rude": ALL, p. 20. "And an absence": ALL, pp. 21–22. "The room was cool": ALL, p. 28.

345   "His chin was": ALL, p. 46. "The train of her velvet dress": ALL, p. 60. "He had never seen her": ALL, p. 68. "A sort of isthmus": ALL, p. 69. "Where Mrs. Forrester was": ALL, p. 70.

346   "Suppose we should have to": ALL, p. 77. "Ellinger could intrude": ALL, p. 84. "There was an almost": ALL, p. 84. "Where they had opened": ALL, p. 85. "As he bent to place": ALL, p. 86.

347   "What did she do with": ALL, p. 100. "Remember, we have to": ALL, p. 123. "Succeeds faster": ALL, p. 124. "Since her husband's death": ALL, p. 152. "I know . . . they call me": ALL, p. 156.

348   "The boys were genuinely": ALL, p. 166. "And unconcernedly put": ALL, pp. 169–70. "He had given her": ALL, p. 170. "He came to be very glad": ALL, p. 171. "She was well cared for": ALL, p. 174. "He had seen the end": ALL, pp. 168–69.

349   "Now it was the Captain": ALL, p. 170. "His power over the people": ALL, p. 106. "His face was fatter": ALL, p. 109. "She was not willing to": ALL, p. 169. "I feel such a power": ALL, p. 125.

350   "He felt that the Captain": ALL, p. 143.

351   "A narrative situation": Nancy Morrow, "WC's ALL and the Nineteenth-Century Novel of Adultery," WS (No. 3, 1984), p. 301. Reviews: Broun, *N. Y. World*, 28 Sept. 1923, p. 9; Wilson, *The Dial* (Jan., 1924), p. 79; Krutch, *Nation*, 28 Nov. 1923, p. 610; Boynton, *Eng. Journal* (June, 1924), p. 380. ALL and Fitzgerald: see Tom Quirk, "Fitzgerald and WC: *The Great Gatsby*," AL (Dec., 1982); Matthew J. Bruccoli, " 'An Instance of Apparent Plagiarism':

F. Scott Fitzgerald, WC, and the First Gatsby Manuscript," *Princeton Univ. Lib. Chronicle* (1978). "One of your greatest admirers": ibid., p. 171. She replied graciously: WC to Fitzgerald, 28 Apr. 1925 (Princeton).

352   Data on movie versions: Bennett, pp. 75–76; WCPMN (No. 2, 1977), pp. 2–3. Hundreds of fan letters: WC to FG, 13 Mar. 1932. For a review, see Olivia Taylor, *Liberty*, 14 Feb. 1925. There is a copy of WC's will at NSHS. Analysis of play script: WC to ZA, 19 Apr. 1937.

CHAPTER 16: *THE PROFESSOR'S HOUSE*

353   Returned from Europe with the idea: Lewis, p. 133. Edition of SOJ's best stories: WC to FG, 17 Feb. 1924; WC to DCF, 27 Feb. 1924. Lawrence's visit: Dorothy Brett, *Lawrence and Brett* (1933), p. 39; Lewis, p. 139.

354   "I hate literature": Brett, p. 39. WC's version of the visit: WC to Eliz. Vermorcken, 23 Mar. 1924 (Morgan). "In his sunniest mood": Lewis, p. 139. WC wrote a friend: WC to CMS, 4 Aug. 1932. "A novel crowded with": OW, p. 42. Frost's birthday dinner: Sergeant, p. 210.

355   Grand Manan pleased her: WC to ZA, 2, 7 Sept. 1924; WC to Frank Swinnerton, 18 Sept. 1924 (Univ. of Ark.) Getting her niece started: WC to FG, 8 Oct. 1924. Left the MS with Irene: WC to IMW, 17 Feb. 1925. Feld interview: *N. Y. Times Book Rev.*, 21 Dec. 1924, p. 11.

356   "Beauty of revolt": *Bookman* (Mar., 1925), pp. 4–5; I assume that the editor wrote this, though the piece is unsigned. SOJ edition: WC to FG, 17 Feb., 15 Apr., 10 May, 1924. "They'd have kept her": Barton Rascoe, *Arts and Decorations* (Apr., 1928), p. 28. About "Decoration Day": WC to FG, 10 May 1924.

357   "If I were asked": OW, p. 58. "To note an artist's": OW, p. 54. "Go back to the dear country": Firman Bishop, "Henry James Criticizes *The Tory Lover*, AL (May 1958), p. 264.

358   "Career of amatory adventure": OW, p. 77. "With such a warehouse": OW, p. 78. "Scenes of the most": OW, p. 79. "Are exactly like those": OW, p. 80. "More lively and full": OW, p. 82. "Being able to reproduce": OW, p. 61. "If you wish to know": OW, p. 64. "I paid Miss Hall": OW, p. 65. "Managed so conspicuously": OW, pp. 73–74.

359   "She communicates vastly": OW, pp. 110–11. This essay appeared in an expanded version in NUF from the original *Borzoi* printing. The NUF version begins with a long reminiscence of meeting on shipboard a man who knew Mansfield as a child. The man is unidentified, and the story may be apocryphal. WC says she met the man when she sailed from Italy to the U.S., but

the only time she ever did that was in 1908. She did make Atlantic crossings in 1920 and 1923. The background for "Uncle Valentine" is discussed by Slote in her introduction to uvo.

361   "The world belongs": Slote, uvo, p. xxiv. "A common, energetic": uvo, p. 13. "The wave of industrial expansion": uvo, p. 38. "A ghostly brightness": uvo, p. 25.

362   "Longfellow and Hawthorne": *Christian Science Monitor*, 14 May 1925; a ms of this speech is at wchc. "A woman of fifty": Arthur G. Staples, "wc— Novelist" in *An Institute of Modern Literature at Bowdoin College from May 5 to May 16, 1925, in Commemoration of the Centennial of the Graduation of the Class of 1825* (1926), p. 89.

363   Visit to Mary Jewett: wc to za, 9 May 1925 (Va.). The trip west: wc to Mable Dodge Luhan, 23 May 1925 (Yale). Other data on trip and the Luhans: wc to mdl, 12, 26 June 1925. Data on Tony and Mabel: Lois P. Rudnick, mdl: *New Woman, New World* (1984). "wc was much impressed": Lewis, p. 142.

364   "Detached and hieratical": Sergeant, p. 206. "The tribal side": ibid., p. 207. "His talk, as before": Lewis, p. 143. After leaving Taos: wc to mdl, July 1925.

365   Trip to Laguna and Acoma: wc to mdl, 7 Aug. 1925. "The roughest and dirtiest": Lewis, p. 144. "From the flat red sea": dca, p. 95. wc traveled north to Denver: wc to dcf, 22 Oct. 1925.

366   Like an old wild turkey: wc to dcf, 27 Feb. 1925.

367   "He had let something go": ph, p. 282. "This is really a story": Sergeant, p. 215. A middle-aged story: wc to dcf, 22 Oct. 1925. Pleased with Irene's reaction: wc to imw, 17 Feb. 1925. "You are not old enough": ph, pp. 162–63.

368   "It's the feeling that": ph, pp. 163–64. "St. Peter near died": ph, p. 30. "All the while that": ph, pp. 28–29.

370   "For thee a house was built": ph, p. 272, wc, as she often did, quoted a little incorrectly from memory. The correct text, "For thee was a house built / Ere thou wast born, / For thee was a mould meant / Ere thou of mother camest." "When I wrote ph": ow, p. 30. "Very much akin": ow, p. 31. The unusual structure was sufficiently bound": wc to Johnson, 12 Jan. 1939 (Amherst).

371   The novel a cross-word puzzle: wc to dcf, 22 Oct. 1925. Preparation for death: Brown, pp. 237–47. Psychoanalytic interpretation: *Literary Biography* (1959), pp. 91–122; revised in *The Stuff of Dreams* (1982), pp. 219–40, where Edel writes: "wc could not admit to herself that she felt deceived and cast aside; and we may conjecture that it was difficult for her to accept the

triangular relationship Isabelle had in mind when she prepared a study for the writer in her French home. Moreover, WC was in no position to state openly her feeling that Jan Hambourg was a usurper who had taken her place in the life of her dearest friend. She expressed it by creating the unpleasant Louie Marsellus and then glossed the portrait with an implicit semblance of affection in the dedication. If we wanted to pursue the psychological speculation, we might find that, to a woman as driving and masculine and as bold as WC, the loss of Isabelle McClung brought to the surface older defeats and awakened hurts received in her younger days" (p. 238). Powerful piece of social criticism: Stouck, pp. 96–106. "Book of dreams": Rosowski, p. 130. "Watershed book": ibid., p. 142. "The professor's problem lies in his late and blinding realization": "A Study of the Small Room in PH," WS (No. 3, 1984), p. 337.

372   "Is there something you would": PH, p. 33. "It turned out to be": PH, p. 154. "Oh, there had been fine times": PH, pp. 125–26.

373   "Two faces at once": PH, pp. 89–90.

374   "If there was one eager": PH, p. 28. "No, Miller, I don't think": PH, pp. 67–68. "Art and religion": PH, p. 69. "*Connais-tu-le pays*": PH, p. 93. "It's been a mistake": PH, p. 94.

375   "The original, unmodified": PH, p. 263. "Life with this": PH, p. 264. "He was a primitive": PH, p. 265. "Live without delight": PH, p. 282. "Augusta, he reflected": PH, p. 280. "A world of Augustas": PH, p. 281.

376   She answered a fan letter: WC to Mr. Graff, 19 July 1925 (WCHC). "The excitement of my first": PH, p. 251. "The grey sage-brush": PH, p. 250. "In a lifetime of teaching": PH, p. 62. Reviews: Ford, *Lit. Digest International Book Rev.* (Nov., 1925), p. 775; *N. Y. Times Book Rev.*, 6 Sept. 1925, p. 8; Canby, SRL, 26 Sept. 1925, p. 151; Kennedy, *New Statesman*, 19 Dec. 1925, p. 306; Ashley, *Kansas City Star*, 3 Oct. 1925.

377   "It seems that houses": PH, p. 156.

CHAPTER 17: *MY MORTAL ENEMY*

378   Chicago lecture: WC to IMW, 4, 10 Nov. 1925. "Pertinent and important things": *Chicago Tribune*, 21 Nov. 1925. Cleveland lecture: WC to IMW, 21 Nov. 1925.

379   "Even my publishers": *Cleveland Press*, 20 Nov. 1925. Her mink coat: WC to IMW, 11 Jan. 1926. WC's relations with *McCall's* is documented in the PR correspondence at Columbia. WC told her first biographer: WC to Brown, 7 Oct. 1946 (Yale). EL barely mentions it: Lewis, p. 138.

380   She had known Myra's real-life model: WC to Pendleton Hogan, 5 Feb. 1940
      (Va.). "Older by a full": Brown, p. 248. Myra's possible prototype: This
      information comes from a letter written by Mrs. Walter Trent, granddaugh-
      ter of the Lincoln Westermanns to John March, 10 May 1960: WCPMN (No. 3,
      1986), p. 19. "The son of a German girl": MME, p. 13.

381   "Bright and gay": MME, p. 6. "Her sarcasm was so quick": MME, p. 7; "I'll
      never forget": MME, p. 16. "The sleeping Beauty's palace": MME, p. 17. The
      New York she remembered: WC to Mrs. Stanfield, 16 Oct. 1926 (Va.). "At a
      parting of the": MME, p. 24.

382   "The trees and shrubbery": MME, p. 25. "Was wishing for a carriage": MME, p.
      41. "My aunt often said": MME, p. 43.

383   "Everything about me": MME, p. 51. "Sprawling, overgrown": MME, p. 57.
      "Wretchedly built": MME, p. 58. "She looked strong and broken": MME, p. 65.
      "The palavery kind of Southerners": MME, p. 67. "He's a sentimentalist":
      MME, p. 88. "We've destroyed each other": MME, p. 75. "It's like the cliff":
      MME, p. 72. "I've had such a": MME, p. 73.

384   "Religion is different": MME, p. 94. "Why must I die": MME, p. 95. "We found
      her wrapped": MME, p. 101. "Remember her as she was": MME, p. 104. "I had
      a premonition": WC to Seibel, undated 1926, quoted in "Miss WC from
      Nebraska," New Colophon (1949), p. 207. An unusual letter: WC to Hogan, 5
      Feb. 1940 (Va.). "Very likely hell": MME, p. 31.

385   A letter to a young Englishman: WC to Stephen Tennant, 25 Mar. 1927
      (privately owned). The authority on Tennant's relationship to WC is Patricia
      Yongue, from whose article I have drawn my facts: "WC's Aristocrats (Part
      I), "Southern Humanities Rev. (Winter, 1980), pp. 43–56. Yongue points out
      in this essay that EL's version of the beginning of this relationship is incorrect.
      EL says (pp. 177–78) that Tennant first wrote WC praising ALL and then WC
      replied. Yongue suggests that EL deliberately misrepresented the facts be-
      cause it appeared to her unseemly that WC should have initiated the corre-
      spondence to an unknown person. Butcher's review: WC to Eliz. Ver-
      morcken, 27 Oct. 1926 (Morgan). "Under the flotsam": Chicago Tribune, 23
      Oct. 1926, p. 15.

386   "That demands more romance": W&P, p. 698. "Oh, if youth but knew": MME,
      p. 75. "It's better to be a stray": MME, p. 15. ES was surprised: Sergeant, p.
      238.

387   For a discussion of allusions in MME, see Harry B. Eichorn, "A Falling Out
      with Love: MME," Colby Lib. Quart. (Sept., 1973); reprinted in Crit. Essays on
      WC. "For many years I associated": MME, p. 48. "Old John of Gaunt,": MME, p.
      83.

388   Reviews: Butcher, Chicago Tribune, 23 Oct. 1926, p. 15; Time, 18 Oct. 1926,

pp. 38–39; *Sun*, 22 Oct. 1926; SRL, 23 Oct. 1926, p. 234; *Nation*, 10 Nov. 1926, p. 484; *N. Y. Times Book Rev.*, 24 Oct. 1926, p. 2.

389   WC's visits to Red Cloud in the summer: this material is drawn from Helen Cather Southwick's memoir: WCPMN (No. 3, 1985), pp. 11–13.

390   "She was greatly attracted to": Lewis, p. 149.

CHAPTER 18: *DEATH COMES FOR THE ARCHBISHOP*

391   Asking for increase and prophecy: AK in *Art of* WC, p. 210. Her best novel: WC to Brown, 26 Oct. 1946 (Yale).

392   "Had a great gift for": Lewis, pp. 119–20. "How often I have seen": MA, pp. 260–61. She never had intended to write: WC to Brown, 26 Oct. 1946. "Who lived with his sister": OW, p. 4.

393   "Meanwhile Archbishop Lamy": OW, p. 7. "At last I found out": OW, p. 8. Stayed up most of the night: Sergeant, p. 223. Working like a steam engine: WC to IMW, 1 Dec. 1925. The 1926 visit to the Southwest: Lewis, p. 140–41.

394   Gallup and Rin-Tin-Tin: WC to MDL, 26 May 1926 (Yale). In a letter to Mary Virginia Auld (19 Feb. 1927—Slote Papers) WC reported that she had been to the movies to see her crush, Rin-Tin-Tin. "Lost his way in the midst": Lewis, p. 141. The visit to the canyon: WC to BK, 28 May 1926. Trip a success: WC to MDL, June 1926 (Yale). "Crops growing down at the bottom": DCA, pp. 300–301. WC took her up on the invitation: WC to Mary Austin, 26 June 1926 (HEH). "For Mary Austin, in whose": *Literary America, 1903–1934: The Mary Austin Letters*, ed. T. M. Pearce (1979), p. 205.

395   "Had given her allegiance": p. 359. She couldn't help it if: WC to MDL, 22 Nov. 1932 (Yale). She had left the MS in the bank: Sergeant, p. 226. Negotiations over serial rights: 10 letters from PR to WC, written between 10 July 1926 and 21 Mar. 1927. WC received $500 for each of the six installments. WC at the MacDowell Colony: Sergeant, pp. 224–25. Wilder's memory: this appears at the bottom of a letter from Ted Jones to Isabelle Wilder, 8 Mar. 1968 (Yale).

396   Praise for *Our Town*: WC to Wilder, 9 Oct. 1938 (Yale). Visit to Grand Manan: there is no proof I have found that WC actually went to the island in Sept., 1926, but the land for her cottage was bought then. The deed is registered in EL's name, and it is possible that EL went to Grand Manan alone. However, she says in her memoir (p. 130), though she remembered the year incorrectly as 1925, that one or the other of them staked out the location of the cottage, then hired a builder to build the cottage in their absence. See p. 415, this text. Description of her room at Shattuck Inn: WC to Wilder, 15 July

1940 (Yale). Finishing touches at Bank St.: WC to Brown, 26 Oct. 1946. The most unalloyed pleasure: WC to Tarbell, Sept.? 1927 (Allegheny College). "I think I succeeded fairly well": Butcher, *Many Lives*, p. 358. A fine glow of satisfaction: WC to Van Vechten, 16 Sept. 1927 (Univ. of Richmond). WC's description of novel: WC to PR, 26 Apr.? 1926.

397   "Our Spanish fathers made": DCA, p. 7. "They wish that I should be": *The Life of . . . Machebeuf*, p. 154.

399   The book could easily be anthologized: WC to Foerster, 22 May 1933 (Univ. of Neb.). "In my student days": OW, p. 9. For a discussion of DCA and the frescos, see Clinton Keeler, "Narrative without Accent: WC and Puvis de Chavannes," *Crit. Essays on* WC.

400   "No more dwelt upon": OW, p. 9. "After the blight of": DCA, p. 79. "Though I used many": OW, p. 12. The white mules: WC to PR, 26 Apr. 1926; WC to CMS, 29 Apr. 1945. She rewrote Lamy's life: see Paul Horgan's excellent biography, *Lamy of Santa Fe: His Life and Times* (1975), which covers exhaustively the career of Lamy, who left his native Auvergne in 1838 to become a missionary in America. Horgan's biography reveals dozens of differences between Lamy and Latour. Met joyfully by thousands: Horgan confirms Howlett. All of my statements about the historical Lamy come from Horgan.

401   "Men travel faster now": DCA, p. 294.

402   "The grace not to show it": W&P, p. 742. "Sins unpardonably": intro. to *House of the Seven Gables*. Another French painter: see James Woodress, "The Genesis of the Prologue of DCA," AL (Nov., 1978), pp. 473–78. She told an interviewer: Harold Small in the *San Francisco Chronicle*, 23 Mar. 1931, p. 19.

403   "Bluish grey like": DCA, p. 2. Source of title: OW, p. 11. "The passing of these": D. H. Stewart, "WC's Mortal Comedy," *Queen's Quart.* (Summer, 1966), p. 247. Stewart is the critic who counted 96 deaths. "In order to write this book": 28 Sept. 1927, p. 490. My source for WC's background reading is chiefly an excellent chapter, "On the Composition of a Novel," in Edward and Lillian Bloom, WC's *Gift of Sympathy* (1962), pp. 197–236. "Parts of Texas and Kansas": DCA, p. 276.

405   Awareness of the values of saintliness: this is a paraphrase of Stouck, p. 135, whose chap. on DCA has influenced me considerably. "Doctrine is well enough": DCA, pp. 50–51. "A soup like this": DCA, p. 38.

406   "Whether it was Midi Romanesque": DCA, p. 245. "Behind its plain face": Stewart, "WC's Mortal Comedy," p. 244. For Armstrong's ideas, see his *The Powers of Presence* (1981). For this paragraph I am indebted to David Robertson, "The Book of Proverbs," *Hudson Rev.* (Winter, 1985–1986), pp. 570–78. In an article of considerable significance Phyllis Rose studies Cather

from the standpoint of modernism in "Modernism: the Case of Willa Cather" in *Modernism Reconsidered*, eds., Robert Kiely and John Hildebidle (Cambridge, Mass., 1983). Rose writes: "In modernist critical writings, including Cather's, certain themes recur: an urge to shake loose of clutter, a refusal to accept the mimetic function of art as previously defined, a feeling that certain 'spirit' was escaping the older forms, an urge toward anonymity. The vessel is emphasized rather than the content; art is imagined as a fragile container for the ineffable substance of life." "My book was a conjunction": ow, p. 9.

407   "One afternoon in the autumn": DCA, p. 14. "Conical red hills": DCA, p. 15. "That cry, wrung": DCA, p. 17. "Tall, gaunt and ill-formed": DCA, p. 67. "His cheeks were sunken": DCA, p. 169.

408   "His face was both thoughtful": DCA, p. 76. "A flood moving": DCA, p. 132. "The peace without seemed": DCA, p. 220.

409   "Utterly unconventional frescoes": ow, p. 5. "Like seeds, full of": DCA, p. 206. "At one moment": DCA, p. 210. "Such fruit as": DCA, p. 267. "That passage from their": DCA, p. 268. The phrases from reviews are in this order: *Catholic World* (Nov., 1927), p. 275. *Boston Eve. Transcript*, 10 Sept. 1927, p. 2; *Independent*, 17 Sept. 1927, p. 283; *Neb. Alumnus* (Nov., 1927), p. 452; *New Republic*, 26 Oct. 1927, p. 266. Lovett, *New Republic*. Williams, *Commonweal*, 28 Sept. 1927, pp. 490–92.

411   The business of her "conversion": three letters at Va.—two from John J. Walsh to wc and one from wc to head of Eng. Dept., 7 Feb. 1940. One knowledgeable wc scholar: L. Brent Bohlke, "wc's Nebraska Priests and DCA," GPQ (Fall, 1984). Bohlke also thought that the rector of Grace Church in Red Cloud, John Mallory Bates, may have contributed to the characterization. At the time of the 25th anniversary: wc to CMS, 25 Nov. 1935. "He has the power of making": wc to the Committee and Dean of St. Marks Pro-Cathedral, Hastings, Neb., 24 Nov. 1935 (NSHS).

CHAPTER 19: *SHADOWS ON THE ROCK*

412   Having a gorgeous party: wc to M. V. Auld, 19 Feb. 1927 (copy in Slote Papers). Leaving Bank St.: a number of letters tell of the move: wc to FG, 8 Oct. 1927; wc to MDL, 17 Sept, 1927; wc to William Allen White, 17 Sept. 1927 (Lib. of Congress); wc to Zona Gale, 17 Sept. 1927 (Wisc. State Hist. Soc.); wc to Mary Austin, 9 Nov. 1927 (HEH). Summer plans: wc to M. V. Auld, 8 June 1927 (copy in Slote Papers).

413   resting up from moving: wc to ZA, 13 Sept. 1927. Life being messed up: wc

to Mary Austin, 9 Nov. 1927. Living at the Grosvenor: Lewis, p. 152. Christmas in Red Cloud: WC to DCF, 18 Jan. 1928. Having repairs made: WC to PR, 23 Jan. 1928. Arrived back in Red Cloud: WC to ZA, 7 June 1941. Friends remembered her pacing: Bennett, p. 28. (information from CMS).

414　She felt rested and strong: WC to DCF, 3 Apr. 1928. Refurbishing house: WC to mother, 9 Apr. and undated 1928 (privately owned). Vist to Mayo Clinic: WC to Austin, 9 May 1928 (HEH). A virulent form of the flu: WC to Mary Jewett, 30 May 1928 (Harvard). "From the first moment": Lewis, pp. 153–54.

415　Cottage on Grand Manan: see note for p. 396. The cottage was built by Charles Green and Oscar Locke (see L. K. Ingersoll, On This Rock: An Island Anthology (Grand Manan, N. B., 1963), p. 60. For a description of the cottage: Lewis, pp. 130–31. "The cabin modestly squatted": OBO, p. 142. The cabin, restored, still stands. Having her own hut: WC to ZA, July 1935.

416　"We often rebelled against": Lewis, p. 193. One of the many services: WC to BK, 10 July 1931; Kathleen Buckley's memory: interview at Grand Manan, Sept., 1985. Dr. Macaulay: Lewis, p. 194; Ingersoll, On This Rock, p. 56. Visit of nieces: memoir by Margaret Cather Shannon in typescript at WCHC.

417　The twins were dizzy with delight: WC to ZA, July 1935. Mother's stroke: WC to George and Harriet Whicher, 1 Jan. 1929 (Morgan). WC to Mary Jewett, 7 Apr. 1929.

418　"Money, oh yes": UVO, p. 55. "If it weren't": UVO, p. 43. "To a memory": UVO, p. 62. "She had all her father's": UVO, p. 55.

419　A shock of recognition: Helen Seibel told this to Bernice Slote; see introduction to UVO, p. xxviii. He is drawn from Dr. Tyndale: the similarities are quite clear, but his reply, "As to your story . . . " is quoted by Slote, pp. xxviii-xxix. "Lying about in tennis": UVO, p. 57. She grieved that the stroke: WC to Mary Jewett, 7 Apr. 1929 (Harvard). Long Beach was hideous: WC to DCF, undated 1929.

420　Her Yale degree: WC to Will Auld, 25 July 1929 (copy in Slote Papers). WC to ES, 14 May 1929. Movements in summer and fall, 1929: WC to ZA, 8 July, 31 Dec. 1929; WC to ES, 2 Oct. 1929; WC to CMS, 27 Oct. 1929; WC to FG, 11 Nov. 1929. Plans to return to California: WC to Zona Gale, 29 Nov. 1929 (Wisc. State Hist. Soc.); WC to CMS, 18 Jan. 1930. A dreary way of living: WC to DCF, 20 Dec. 1929. "Fortune turn thy wheel": WC to Zona Gale, 29 Nov. 1929. Second trip to California: WC to DCF, 10 Mar. 1930. Trip to Europe: Lewis, pp. 158–60; WC to FG, 5 May 1930; WC to Helen McNeny (card), 15 June 1930 (WCHC); WC to MDL, 1 July 1930; WC to CMS, 17 July 1930; WC to ZA, 22 Aug. 1930; WC to the Whichers, 23 Aug. 1930 (Morgan); WC to DCF, 30 Sept. 1930.

421　"The thing one especially noticed": A Chance Meeting," NUF, p. 4. "I knew him well": NUF, p. 14. "My mother died": NUF, p. 15. "The room was absolutely quiet": NUF, p. 16.

422   Meeting the Menuhins: Lewis, p. 168. Quebec and Jaffrey: WC to FG, 20 Oct. 1930; WC to the Whichers, Oct., Nov. 1930. Finished novel: WC to ZA, 15 Jan. 1931. Howells Medal: WC to DCF, 18 Nov. 1930. "WC was on the platform": *Hamlin Garland's Diaries*, ed. Donald Pizer (1968), p. 117. "She had to watch": Lewis, p. 157. The best portrait of Lawrence: WC to MDL, 17 Jan. 1931. She read *Towards Standards*: WC to Foerster, 14 Jan. 1931 (Univ. of Neb.).

423   A disadvantage to be a lady author: WC to Mr. Bain, 14 Jan. 1931 (Univ. of Mich.). Though she doesn't say so, she was no doubt referring to *A Room of One's Own*. While she was crossing Kansas: WC to IMW, 12 Mar. 1931. Third trip to California: WC to Sara Teasdale, 10 May 1931 (Wellesley). Finished proof: WC to DCF, 1 May 1931. Degree from Berkeley: WC to ZA, 21 Apr. 1931; WC to BK, undated 1931.

424   Princeton degree: WC to CMS, June 1931; WC to ZA, 21 June 1931.

425   Cross's review: SRL, 22 Aug. 1931, pp. 67–68. "You seem to have seen": OW, p. 14. "An orderly little French": OW, p. 16. She made the same point: WC to ZA, 18 Dec. 1931. Her heart never got across: WC to CMS, 1 Sept. 1922. She could only write successfully: WC to CMS, 28 June 1939. "The thing that teases": OW, p. 47.

426   She had gotten all her material: Carroll interview, *Bookman* (May, 1921). "A foolish consistency": "Self-Reliance". "If a writer achieves": OW, p. 51. "The qualities of a second-rate": OW, p. 107. "I made an honest try": OW, p. 17. "Most things come from France": W&P, p. 223.

427   "The rock when one came": DCA, p. 98. "Quebec seemed shrunk": SOR, p. 136. "This rock in the": SOR, p. 208.

428   "You have done well": SOR, p. 277. "Indeed fortunate": SOR, p. 280; "The forest was suffocation": SOR, p. 7; "Blinker had such a horror": SOR, p. 16; "Grey daylight fade": SOR, p. 157.

429   She had to admit, however: WC to IMW, 22 Oct. 1945. "At home in France": SOR, pp. 24–25. "When an adventurer carries": SOR, p. 98. "Scattered spires and slated roofs": SOR, p. 4. "Rolling north toward": SOR, p. 6.

430   "Through constantly changing colour": SOR, pp. 99–100. "Are slight and delicate": Cross, SRL, 22 Aug. 1931, p. 68.

431   "WC makes no pretense": Rosowski, p, 184. WC's reading for SOR: Brown, pp. 270–78; Lewis, pp. 154, 158. She read in the *Jesuit Relations*: EL says she read this work, but her statement is no doubt a great exaggeration, as *The Jesuit Relations and Allied Documents: Travels and Explorations of the Jesuit Missionaries in New France, 1610–1791*, ed. Reuben Gold Thwaites (1896–1901),

which was the standard edition of this work, runs to 73 volumes. EL also says WC "re-read" the memoirs of St. Simon, but the complete text of the *Mémoires* of Louis de Rouvroy, Duc de Saint-Simon, runs to 43 vols. Juchereau's history: Saint-Ignace, *mère* (Jean-Françoise Juchereau), *Histoire de l'Hotel Dieu de Québec* (1751).

432   Other research: see King, *Books and People*, p. 209. It would have people and things: Mary Ellen Chase, *Mass. Rev.* (Spring, 1962). "Our Lord died for Canada": SOR, p. 111. WC created this scene from the memory: WC to DCF, June 1931. "These coppers": SOR, p. 198. Some of her friends detested it: WC to Eliz. Vermorcken, 24 Aug. 1931 (Morgan).

433   *New Yorker* profile: 8 Aug. Publication day was 1 Aug. Publication data: Crane, pp. 152–66. The *Prix Femina Américain*: *N. Y. Times*, 3 Feb. 1933, reported that SOR was the most popular novel of 1932. The same article, describing the awarding of the prize, said the ceremony took place at the home of Mr. and Mrs. Henry Goddard Leach on E. 64th St. Mrs. Dwight Morrow gave a speech, and Edna St. Vincent Millary made the presentation; WC in responding said: "French literature has always been one of the chief pleasures of my life." The *Times* said on 4 Feb. (p. 14): "WC is our finest novelist." In awarding the *Prix* an American committee selected three works for French translation, and a French committee then picked one of them. This was the first such award. Reviews: C. Van Doren: 1 Aug. 1931, p. 1; D. Van Doren: 12 Aug. 1931, p. 160; Arvin: 12 Aug. 1931, pp. 345–46; Butcher: Chicago *Tribune*, 15 Aug. 1931, p. 10; Ethel Wallace Hawkins, "Atlantic Bookshelf," Aug.-Sept. 1931; Hicks: *Forum* (Sept., 1921), pp. vi-vii; Williams: 30 Sept. 1931, p. 528. *Des Moines Register*, 27 Sept. 1931; Kronenberger: Oct. 1931, pp. 134–40. The *Bookman* (Mar., 1932, pp. 634–40) carried a long rebuttal of Kronenberger written by Archer Winsten.

434   "Without order our lives": SOR, p. 24. "I think the methods": SOR, p. 119. "Doesn't one have a perfect right": Butcher, *Many Lives*, p. 361. "I read SOR oftener": Greenslet, *Under the Bridge*, p. 119.

CHAPTER 20: *OBSCURE DESTINIES*

435   Having nobody behind her: WC to BK, 20 Sept. 1931. She also wrote ZA about mother's death: 18 Dec. 1931. As soon as she pulled herself together: WC to Mrs. Canby, 30 Oct. 1931 (Yale).

436   It simply rains death: WC to ZA, 21 Nov. 1932. Plans for the reunion: WC to DCF, 2 Oct. 1931. Opening house: WC to BK, 16 Dec. 1931. "The strongest and most satisfactory": W&P, p. 363. To thank her for the gift: WC to BK, 26 Dec. 1931. Flu in February: WC to CMS, 19 Feb. 1932.

437   Lost money on bonds: WC to ZA, 2 Jan. 1934. Asked to donate to charity: WC
to Mary Austin, 22 Oct. 1931 (HEH). Movie rights to SOL: WC to FG, 13 Mar.
1932. The Menuhin relationship is documented by many references in letters
written after 1930. Lewis, pp. 168–72, treats it extensively; also see the
following: Yehudi Menuhin, *Unfinished Journey* (1976); Robert Magidoff,
Yehudi Menuhin (1956); Lionel Menuhin Rolfe, *The Menuhins: A Family
Odyssey* (1978). Spent the morning in the park: WC to CMS, 2 May 1932. "She
loved the Menuhin family": Lewis, pp. 168–69. "They were not only the":
Lewis, p. 170.

438   "A veritable explosion": MA, p. 339.

439   "Polly ain't looking so good": OD, p. 34.

440   "That's why we're having'": OD, p. 49. "Nobody in the world": OD, p. 66.

441   "This was open and free": OD, p. 71. "I have never before read": BK to WC, 10
Sept. 1931. The right things had come together": WC to ZA, 16 Sept. 1932.

442   "The bound girl they had brought": OD, p. 88. "One of the oldest rites": OD,
p. 93. "Only a thin cotton": OD, p. 94. "What I want is to": OD, p. 108.

443   "There was something easy": OD, p. 111. "Everything that's alive": OD, p.
141.

444   "Why must she be forever": OD, p. 178. "Then there was a great stir": OD, p.
189. "Thus Mrs. Harris slipped out": OD, p. 190. Life was rather a failure: WC
to ZA, 21 Nov. 1932.

445   "I liked to listen": OD, pp. 207–8. "We've found a great leader": OD, p. 220.
Not meant to be a portrait: WC to CMS, 4 July 1932. Not made out of the two
friends: WC to CMS, 27 Jan. 1934.

446   Threw the word "nostalgic": WC to Van Vechten, 30 Jan. 1937 (Morgan).
"Among all contemporary": 31 Aug. 1932, pp. 433–34. Summer at Grand
Manan: WC to CMS, 4 Aug. 1932. She envied Akins's willingness: WC to ZA,
20 Mar. 1932.

447   The Park Ave. apartment: WC to MDL, 22 Nov. 1932; WC to IMW, 19 Jan.
1933; Lewis, p. 167. "And met me in the eager": Sergeant, p. 251. She had sat
for hours: King, *Books and People*, p. 209.

448   "A melting, angelic": Sergeant, p. 253. "It was in part the happiness": Lewis,
p. 173.

CHAPTER 21: *LUCY GAYHEART*

449   The idea for the novel: WC to CMS, 28 June 1939. On Sadie Becker: Bennett,
p. 42.

450   She began the novel in the spring of 1933: Lewis, pp. 173–74. She asked SSM

to wish her luck: WC to SSM, 26 May 1933. A silly young girl: WC to ZA, 26 Aug. 1933. Speech over NBC: MS of speech is at Princeton. She wrote Carrie to tune in: WC to CMS, 26 Apr. 1933.

451   "We have begun to look about us": the three paragraphs quoted here were published in *Princeton Alumni Weekly*, 12 May 1933, p. 692. WC wrote DCF four times about the article: 22 June 1933 and three undated.

452   "I offer you a hypothesis": *N. Y. Herald-Tribune*, 28 May 1933, sec. 11, pp. 7, 9.

453   Nothing was happening on Grand Manan: WC to BK, 20 July 1933. The account of Mussolini's air force: WC to Pat Knopf, 15 Aug. 1933 (Wellesley). She wasn't out of the jungle: WC to BK and AK, 26 Oct. 1933.

454   She received a letter from Tarbell: 28 Nov. 1933 (Allegheny College). Her reply: WC to Trabell, 13 Dec. 1933 (Allegheny); two subsequent notes enclosing checks are undated. She spent the morning with Yehudi: WC to CMS, 12 Feb. 1934. "They began with *Richard II*": Lewis, p. 171. *The Temple Shakespeare*, with preface and glossary by Israel Gollancz (London: Dent, 1894–1926) in 40 vols., is a beautifully printed edition in small format with a separate volume devoted to each play. "Us by the hand": Yehudi Menuhin, *Unfinished Journey*, p. 130. "She was a rock of strength": ibid., pp. 129–30.

455   "Yes, my dear boy": ibid. She sprained the big tendon: WC to ZA, 9 Sept. 1934; WC to Mary Creighton, 29 Mar. 1934 (Newberry). Lewis says it was the right wrist, but I have followed WC's own account.

456   Forced to stay in town: WC to CMS, 3 July 1934. Reason for serializing: WC to ZA, 9 Sept. 1934. 42 days over 100: ibid. As if she had a new coat of paint: WC to BK, 10 Sept. 1934. Attack of appendicitis: WC to ZA, 19 Apr. 1935. Josephine's return to France: ibid. The Hambourgs's visit: WC to FG, 11 Apr., 29 June 1935; WC to ZA, 19 Apr., 10 May 1935.

457   Plans for Europe: WC to FG, 29 June 1935. She was tired physically: WC to CMS, 26 July 1935. Beginning to feel like herself: WC to Mary Creighton, 8 Aug. 1935 (Newberry). Visit to Hambourgs in Paris: WC to FG, 20 Nov. 1935. The return passage: WC to CMS, 25 Nov. 1935.

458   "A slight figure always in motion": LG, p. 3. "Something direct and un-hesitating": LG, p. 4. "The sun was dropping low": LG, p. 9. "For a moment Lucy and Harry": LG, p. 10.

459   "Tired and frightened": LG, p. 32. "Sebastian's eyes never left it": LG, p. 54. "Nothing had ever made": LG, p. 77. "Yes, they're nice": LG, p. 69. "When you knocked": LG, p. 88.

460   "All the way!": LG, p. 11. "A nice house and garden": LG, p. 134. "Life is short": LG, p. 165. "What if—what if": LG, p. 184.

461   "When Harry Gordon": LG, p. 201. "Refused Lucy Gayheart": LG, p. 220.

"After all these years": LG, p. 226. It wasn't one of her best: WC to CMS, 9 Dec. 1935. She didn't think much of LG: WC to Brown, 7 Oct. 1946 (Yale). "Seems a little ridiculous": Eliz. Moorhead (Vermorcken), *These Two Were Here*, p. 59. To be read at a gallop: WC to ZA, 19 Apr. 1935.

462   "LG is certainly": Daiches, WC: *Critical Introduction*, p. 131. "Classified novel as romance": telegram to AK, 25 July 1934. "A lonely figure beneath": Rosowski, p. 222.

463   "Cather's story resembles": ibid., p. 223. "In her Stoker": ibid., p. 224. "As Sebastian embraces": ibid., p. 225. "In *Lucy Gayheart*": ibid., p. 229. "The triumph of paradox": G. Richard Thompson, "Gothic Fiction of the Romantic Age: Context and Mode," in *Romantic Gothic Tales, 1790–1840* (1979), p. 9. "Above all, on the human": Stouck, p. 214. "Is filled with": ibid., p. 216. "Presents a rejected": ibid., p. 217.

464   "Book will be set": BK to WC, 26 July 1934. WC replied appreciatively: WC to BK, 26 July 1934. Print order and sales: Crane, pp. 175–78. WC to CMS, 9 Dec. 1935. Reviews: Jackson, 4 Aug. 1935, p. 4D; ("She is incapable") H. M. Jones, SRL, 3 Aug. 1935, p. 7 ("She knows how to use"): Jackson, 4 Aug. 1935.

465   Butcher, 3 Aug. 1935, p. 11. "I see no reason": ibid. Other reviews: Jordan-Smith, 4 Aug. 1935; Adams, 4 Aug. 1935, p. 1; Cantwell, 11 Dec. 1935, pp. 149–50.

CHAPTER 22: *SAPPHIRA AND THE SLAVE GIRL*

466   Koussevitsky party: BK to WC, 17 Dec. 1935. Photos by Van Vechten: WC to Pat Knopf, 19 Jan. 1936 (Va.); WC to Van Vechten, 3, 8 Apr. 1936 (Morgan). "It's easy enough": King, *Books and People*, p. 208. Tennant's visit: WC to Pat Knopf, 19 Jan. 1936. WC to FG, 24 Jan. 1938; Lewis, pp. 177–78.

467   Tennant's book of drawings: WC to FG, 24 Jan. 1938. Teaching contemporary literature: WC to Leonard, 19 Mar. 1936 (Phillips Exeter). She expanded on theme: WC to Johnson, undated 1939 (Yale); this letter was published in the College English Assn.'s *Newsletter* (Dec., 1939), p. 2. Asking if Houghton Mifflin was interested: WC to FG, 8 Mar. 1936.

468   "Certainly," Perkins wrote: Lewis, pp. 180–81; for AK's version, see *Art of WC*, p. 215. WC sent a prospectus: WC to CMS, 20 Oct. 1937.

469   "Fallen into supine romanticism": Nov., 1937, pp. 703–10; reprinted in WC *and Her Critics*. "What has art ever been": OW, p. 18. "Increasing the game supply": OW, p. 19.

470   "Citizen Shelley": OW, p. 20. "Materially help Mayor": OW, p. 21. "The condition every art": OW, p. 26. "How many clumsy": OW, p. 27. In reply to

a thoughtful letter": wc to Mr. Watson, 12 Feb. 1941 (Erie Co. Pub. Lib., Buffalo). Turned down another degree: wc to Pres. of Brown, 23 May 1936 (Brown). Enjoyed her nieces: wc to Mary Creighton, 6 Dec. 1936 (Newberry).

471   So many sad and bitter things: wc to za, Aug. 1936?. Asked for hospital donation: wc to mdl, 15 Dec. 1936. The single surviving letter from wc to el is at wchc.

472   Had not liked *The Magic Mountain*: Butcher, *Many Lives*, p. 361. "Found a new book": ibid. "Approach a theme set": nuf, p. 97. "Gets behind the epoch": nuf, p. 98. "We emerge from Mann's": nuf, p. 102. "The creation of Jacob": nuf, p. 108. "The story of Joseph": nuf, p. 114. "This is one of the": nuf, p. 119.

473   "It is for the backward": nuf, p. v. "Which insists so much": srl, 28 Nov. 1936, p. 7. She had misgivings: wc to fg, 8 Mar. 1936. "Imagine a young man": nuf, pp. 92–93. "Smugness springing from": 19 Dec. 1936, p. 738.

474   She hoped her friend would not: wc to za, 28 Oct. 1937. Not in a holiday mood: wc to Mary Creighton, 6 Dec. 1936 (Newberry).

475   To keep her works out of "omnibuses": wc to za, 18 Jan. 1936. "Never would give": ak in *Art of* wc, p. 214. In a letter in 1935 to cms she described this incident as an occasion in which she had to bring an action against the individual involved—a great exaggeration. The world used to be happier: wc to Mary Creighton, 6 Dec. 1936. "Miss Lane said at once": Lewis, p. 180.

476   "Plain women, he reflected": obo, pp. 24–25. "They were Americans": obo, p. 66.

477   "They look to me like": obo, p. 58. DeVoto's answer to Wilson: srl, 13 Feb. 1937, pp. 8, 20. wc elaborated on the idea: wc to DeVoto, 10 Mar. 1937 (Stanford).

478   Started writing in the spring: wc to za, 16 Mar. 1937. Once more working on new book: wc to za, 8 Nov. 1937; Douglass's visit: wc to cms, 28 June 1939. The flu in Feb.: wc to fg, 2 Mar. 1938; Visit to Va.: Lewis, pp. 182–83.

479   Smashed her hand: wc to za, 4 June 1938. Death of brother: wc to za, 13 Nov. 1938. Death of Isabelle: wc to imw, 14 Oct. 1938; other comments on Douglass and Isabelle: wc to dcf, summer 1939; wc to fg, 12 Oct. 1938. Isabelle for whom all her books were written: wc to za, 2 May 1939. She had been sick a good while: wc to Lydia Lambrecht, Dec. 1941 (wchc). Devastation by hurricane: Lewis, p. 184. In a comatose state: wc to za, 13 Nov. 1938. Americans were the most gullible: wc to Lewis, 14 Jan. 1938 (Yale).

480   Czechoslovakia was a country: wc to Dayton Kohler, 16 Mar. 1939 (Va. Polytech). She applauded Lehman's: wc to Elsie Cather, 5 Jan. 1935 (N. Y.

Pub. Lib.). In disgrace with herself: WC to ZA, 20 May 1939. "She worked at *Sapphira*": Lewis, p. 184. On the day France fell: WC to FG, 10 June 1940. "There seems to be no future": Lewis, p. 184. Stayed in N. Y. until end of July: WC to IMW, 27 Feb. 1942. Finishing touches on novel: WC to ZA, Sept. 1940 (Va.).

481   Her end was her beginning: WC to Woollcott, 5 Dec. 1942 (Morgan). "Seriously thinking about": BK to WC, 4 May 1931. Sending an advance copy: WC to Roseboro', 9 Nov. 1940 (Va.). "She could have written": Lewis, p. 183. So afraid of being diffuse: WC to Rogers, 25 Jan. 1941 (Newberry).

482   "We would all do better": SSG, p. 269.

483   Till virtually a member of the family: WC to FG, Dec. 1940. She could only write successfully: WC to CMS, 28 June 1939; It is another Gothic tale: see Rosowski, "WC's American Gothic: SSG," GPQ (Fall, 1984), pp. 220–30.

484   Remembering black speech: WC to DCF, 14 Oct. 1940; WC to FG, Dec. 1940. "Look down over hills": SSG, p. 117. "A mountain stream": SSG, p. 115.

485   It had its pleasant surfaces: WC to FG, Dec. 1940.

486   "Sapphira . . . usually acted": SSG, p. 22. "On Christmas morning": SSG, p. 220.

487   It had been a comfort to her: WC to Roseboro', 28 Nov. 1940 (Va.). "You may not like the book": *Letters of Wallace Stevens*, ed. Holly Stevens (1966), p. 381.

488   Publication data: Crane, pp. 185–91. Reviews: Zabel, 7 Dec. 1940, pp. 574–76; Canby, 14 Dec. 1940, p. 5; *Chronicle*, 15 Dec. 1940, p. 14; *Herald-Tribune Books*, 8 Dec. 1940, p. 1. He liked the epilogue: WC to Woollcott, 5 Dec. 1942 (Morgan).

CHAPTER 23: *LAST YEARS*

490   "Like fine silver or porcelain": 15 Dec. 1940, p. 6. Signing 500 sheets: WC to Laura Hills, 9 Dec. 1940 (Morgan). Other letters about hand: WC to CMS, 6 Dec. 1940, 22 Mar., 16 May 1941; WC to Roseboro', 13 Dec. 1940, 20 Feb. 1941 (Va.). The surgeon was Dr. F. R. Ober (see Sergeant, p. 274); Menuhin comforting her: WC to CMS, undated Christmas card 1940. Account of French Hospital: WC to Woollcott, 17 Mar. 1940 (Harvard).

491   The splendor of British behavior: WC to FG, 21 Sept. 1940. Roosevelt's reelection: WC to FG, 9 Nov. 1940. WC never discussed politics in her letters, but I would assume she voted. There is at least one reference in her letters to getting an absentee ballot so that she could vote when she was out of the city. The death of May Willard: WC to Mary Willard, 6 May 1941 (Amherst); WC always called Mary Willard "Marie".

492   The trip west: WC to FG, 20 Oct. 1941; WC to CMS, 16 May 1941; WC to ZA, 17 Sept. 1941. "The country never had been": Lewis, pp. 188–91. The Avignon novel: the fullest account of this is George Kates's "WC's Unfinished Avignon Story" in *Five Stories* (1956), pp. 177–214.

493   "Stirred her as no building": Lewis, p. 190. EL summarized the story for Kates, also let him use the annotated edition of *The Story of Avignon*. "This was perhaps": Lewis's summary, quoted by Kates, p. 202; the fragment is at Va.

494   Meeting with Undset: AK in *Art of* WC, p. 218. The departure of Mary Virginia: WC to IMW, 27 Feb. 1942. Capote's memory of WC: quoted in interview with Gloria Steinem, *McCall's* (Nov. 1967), p. 151.

495   Went to see her doctor: WC to IMW, 18 Apr. 1942. The operation: Lewis, p. 191; WC to CMS, 9 Sept. 1942; WC to ZA, 4 Dec. 1943; WC to IMW, 26 Dec. 1942.

496   Vist to Williamstown: WC to Roseboro', 18 Dec. 1942 (Amherst). The most fashionable type of figure: WC to Roseboro', 29 Aug. 1942 (Va.). She wished gasoline had continued: WC to DCF, 8 Nov. 1939. Comments on war: WC to Laura Hills, 23 Sept. 1943 (Morgan); WC to DCF, 31 Mar. 1943; life in wartime: WC to ZA, 2 Nov. n.y.; WC to IMW, 26 Dec. 1942; WC to FG, 15 Nov. 1942. Summers in Maine: Lewis, pp. 194, 196; WC wrote a friend at end of second summer: WC to Mrs. Belloc-Lowndes, 4 Oct. 1944 (Tex.). There is a lot about the Asticou Inn in Brown and Crone, *One Point of the Compass*, pp. 101–14, but this source must be used with extreme caution, as much of it is fiction.

497   Reading Scott at Asticou Inn: Lewis, pp. 194–95. EL is wrong in saying WC never liked Scott; she recommended *Ivanhoe* highly to readers of the *Home Monthly* in 1897 (W&P, p. 338), but at that time she had not yet had to teach the novel to Pittsburgh high school students. Despair over the death of the world: WC to Roseboro', 12 Feb. 1944 (Va.). Living a sort of communal life: WC to DCF, 26 May 1944. Other comments on family and friends in war: WC to Harriet Whicher, 24 Jan. 1944 (Morgan); WC to Roseboro', 12 Feb. 1944 (Va.).

498   The gold medal for fiction: *N. Y. Times*, 20 May 1944, p. 28; also Sergeant, p. 275. Asking to see SSM: WC to SSM, 26 May 1944. Description of visit: WC to Belloc-Lowndes, 4 Oct. 1944.

499   "Merciless perfection": OBO, p. 144. "Why patch up?": OBO, p. 148. "If a clam stood upright": OBO, p. 164.

500   "Plucky youth": OBO, p. 166. A story that interested her very much: WC to FG, 24 Jan. 1945. Another comment on Armed Forces Editions: WC to Harriet Whicher, 31 Jan. 1945 (Morgan). "The horizon was like": OBO, p. 78.

501   "She gave herself up": OBO, p. 96. The death of Roscoe: WC to ZA, 3 Jan. 1946; WC to IMW, 22 Oct. 1945; WC to Harriet Whicher, 3 Jan. 1946; WC to ES, 21 Nov. 1945; Lewis, p. 196.

502   "In the last year": Lewis, p. 196. She summed up her career: WC to IMW, 6 Jan. 1945; WC to ZA, 5 Jan. 1945; autographed copies for Barrie: WC to Marie Melony, 26 Aug., 6 Oct. 1934 (Columbia).

503   WC's paranoia: WC to CMS, 28 June 1939, 26 Jan. 1947. Comment on Hicks: WC to IMW, 5 Jan. 1945. The Menuhins' last visit: WC to Brown, 30 Mar. 1947 (Yale); also Lewis, pp. 171–72. Asked DCF about Housman visit: WC to DCF, 17 Apr. 1947.

504   Account of death: Lewis, p. 197; also obituary in *N. Y. Times*, 25 Apr. 1947, p. 21.

EPILOGUE

505   Sources for funeral and burial: *N. Y. Times*, 30 Apr. 1947; *Art of WC*, p. 221; Sergeant, pp. 280–83. The epitaph: MA, p. 18. There is a copy of the will at NSHS. Concerning burial at Jaffrey: There is no extant document stating WC's wish to be buried at Jaffrey, but Elsie Cather wrote E. K. Brown, 25 Sept. 1949 (MS at Yale) that WC had made this known to her brother Roscoe at the time Douglass Cather died in 1938. The family had been making plans to return Douglass' body to Red Cloud for burial when Willa called Roscoe to say that Douglass had told her he wanted to be buried in California. In the same conversation, which was relayed to Elsie by Roscoe, WC said that "she had no intention of being brought home herself—that she wanted to be buried on the mountain in New Hampshire near the inn where she and Edith used to spend their summers."

506   For details of EL and Knopf's efforts to carry out WC's will, see *Art of WC*, "postscript," pp. 222–24.

INDEX

Cather, Willa

LIFE: ancestry, 13–18; grandparents, 14; birth, 21; name, 21, 515; infancy, 21; Virginia childhood, 15, 22–27; early education, 23, 42; life at Willow Shade, 25; move to Nebraska, 31; life on the Divide, 34–43; move to Red Cloud, 43; earliest writing, 48; education in Red Cloud, 48; Red Cloud friends, 52–54; adolescent reading, 49–51; early interest in classics, 53; early interest in music, 54–55; early interest in theater, 57–58; graduates from high school, 60; goes to Lincoln, 67; preps for university, 70; college program, 71–72; Carlyle essay published, 72; extracurricular activities, 75–76; publishes first story, 77; college friends, 82; relationship with Louise Pound and family, 84–87; begins writing for the *Journal*, 89; writes first play notice, 91; acquires reputation as tough critic, 92; begins reviewing music, 95; writes first long feature story, 97; meets Crane, 98; meets Bryan, 101; attends opera in Chicago, 102; graduates from college, 103; begins writing for the *Courier*, 103; postgraduate year, 104; gets job in Pittsburgh, 1896, 111, 523; reacts to Presbyterian Pittsburgh, 113; edits *Home Monthly*, 114–15; begins to write for the *Leader*, 117; social life in Pittsburgh, 117–18; Pittsburgh friends, 119; continues French studies, 119; discovers Housman, 123; received marriage proposals, 124; gets full-time job on *Leader*, 130; meets Nevin, 131–32; makes first visit to Washington, 135; meets Isabelle McClung, 139; leaves *Leader*, 146; visits Washington, 147; begins teaching at Central High School, 150; moves to Allegheny High School, 155; makes first trip to Europe, 156; visits Housman, 159;

publishes *April Twilights,* 165; meets S. S. McClure, 171; publishes *The Troll Garden,* 172; tries to write novel, 181; hired by McClure, 182; begins working for *McClure's,* 186; works on life of Mary Baker G. Eddy, 192–93; denies authorship of Mrs. Eddy's life, 194; meets Mrs. Fields, 195; meets Sarah Orne Jewett, 197; visits Italy, 198; becomes managing editor of *McClure's,* 199; begins living with Edith Lewis, 200; gets advice from Jewett, 202; takes stock of self at thirty-five, 203; meets Elizabeth Sergeant, 208; meets Zoë Akins, 209; resigns as managing editor, 212; goes to Cherry Valley, 213; publishes *Alexander's Bridge,* 217; publishes "The Bohemian Girl," 227; visits the Southwest, 4–11; moves to Bank Street apartment, 234; publishes *O Pioneers!,* 239; writes McClure's autobiography, 248; revisits Virginia, 250–51; gets to know Fremstad, 255, 257, 258; reacts to World War I, 259–60; aborts trip to Germany, 261–62; visits Mesa Verde, 263; makes first visit to Taos, 264; publishes *The Song of the Lark,* 265; ends Pittsburgh visits, 276; Isabelle McClung is married, 277; begins Friday open houses, 281; makes second visit to Taos, 281; discovers Jaffrey, N. H., 286; publishes *My Ántonia,* 288; becomes increasingly dissatisfied with Houghton Mifflin, 306; is approached by Knopf, 307; revisits France, 310; publishes *Youth and the Bright Medusa,* 311; goes over to Knopf, 316; resumes correspondence with Fisher, 318; spends five months in Toronto, 318; lectures and is lionized in Nebraska, 319; teaches at Bread Loaf, 322; makes first visit to Grand Manan, 323; publishes *One of Ours,* 323; joins Episcopal Church,

MAY

NO
OCT

APR 2 1

Brodart Co.   Printed in USA